An Ed-Tech Tragedy?

Educational Technologies and School Closures in the Time of COVID-19

NEW YORK AND LONDON

UNESCO – a global leader in education

Education is UNESCO's top priority because it is a basic human right and the foundation for peace and sustainable development. UNESCO is the United Nations' specialized agency for education, providing global and regional leadership to drive progress, strengthening the resilience and capacity of national systems to serve all learners. UNESCO also leads efforts to respond to contemporary global challenges through transformative learning, with special focus on gender equality and Africa across all actions.

The Global Education 2030 Agenda

UNESCO, as the United Nations' specialized agency for education, is entrusted to lead and coordinate the Education 2030 Agenda, which is part of a global movement to eradicate poverty through 17 Sustainable Development Goals by 2030. Education, essential to achieve all of these goals, has its own dedicated Goal 4, which aims to *"ensure inclusive and equitable quality education and promote lifelong learning opportunities for all."* The Education 2030 Framework for Action provides guidance for the implementation of this ambitious goal and commitments.

Published by the United Nations Educational, Scientific and Cultural Organization (UNESCO), 7, place de Fontenoy, 75352 Paris 07 SP, France, and Routledge, Taylor & Francis Group, 605 Third Avenue, New York, NY 10158, United States of America

© UNESCO 2025

ISBN: 9781041123675 (hardback)
ISBN: 9781041123668 (paperback)
ISBN: 9781003664406 (ebook)

DOI (Routledge): 10.4324/9781003664406

Originally published 2023 by UNESCO under open access (CC-BY-SA 3.0 IGO) as
ISBN: 9789231006111
DOI: https://doi.org/10.54675/LYGF2153

This publication is available in Open Access at www.unesco.org and www.taylorfrancis.com under the Attribution-NonCommercial-NoDerivs 3.0 IGO (CC-BY-NC-ND 3.0 IGO) license (http://creativecommons.org/licenses/by-ncnd/3.0/igo/). By using the content of this publication, the users accept to be bound by the terms of use of the UNESCO Open Access Repository (https://www.unesco.org/en/open-access/cc-nc-nd).

Any third party material in this book is not included in the OA Creative Commons license, unless indicated otherwise in a credit line to the material. Please direct any permissions enquiries to the original rightsholder.

The designations employed and the presentation of material throughout this publication do not imply the expression of any opinion whatsoever on the part of UNESCO concerning the legal status of any country, territory, city or area or of its authorities, or concerning the delimitation of its frontiers or boundaries.

The ideas and opinions expressed in this publication are those of the authors; they are not necessarily those of UNESCO and do not commit the Organization.

Author: Mark West
Editors: Kate Davison and Rebecca Yaghmour
Graphic designer: Huieun Kim
Cover and inside illustrations: © UNESCO / Eleni Debo and Rob Dobi

SHORT SUMMARY

Looking back to see ahead: Crisis, technology and the future of education

An Ed-Tech Tragedy? is a detailed analysis of what happened when education became largely reliant on connected technology during school closures stemming from the COVID-19 pandemic, the largest global disruption to education in history.

Many claim that the hurried embrace of technology-dependent remote learning facilitated innovations and transformations that have propelled education into desirable digital futures. Others assert that the turn to ed-tech was the best and perhaps only viable solution to confront the educational challenges imposed by the pandemic. A popular view holds that both groups are correct: technology-centric approaches to education saved the day in an emergency by preserving the continuity of formal learning and normalized practices that have improved and modernized education.

The global evidence, however, reveals a more sombre picture. It exposes the ways unprecedented educational dependence on technology often resulted in unchecked exclusion, staggering inequality, inadvertent harm and the elevation of learning models that put machines and profit before people.

Revisiting the promises and realities of ed-tech during the COVID-19 disruption to education

Using tragedy as a metaphor and borrowing the organization of a three-act theatrical play, this publication shows how technology-first modes of learning introduced novel health and safety risks, handed significant control of public education to for-profit companies, expanded invasive digital surveillance and carried detrimental environmental repercussions, in addition to adversely impacting educational access, equity, quality and outcomes in most contexts. Dedicated sections consider alternative and less technology-reliant educational responses to COVID-19 disruptions that had the potential to be more inclusive and equitable. The analysis further explains how pandemic models of learning are rippling beyond school closures and influencing the future of education.

Holistically, the work invites readers to reconsider a turbulent chapter in education history and reexamine the purposes and roles of technology in education. It extracts lessons and recommendations to chart new and more humanistic courses for the development, integration and use of technology in education.

"Since wars begin in the minds of men and women, it is in the minds of men and women that the defences of peace must be constructed"

Evgeny Morozov
Author of *The Net Delusion* and *To Save Everything, Click Here*

 An Ed-Tech Tragedy? is timely, urgent, and important. To date, it represents the most detailed analysis of how the rhetoric of 'technological solutionism' comes to shape both policy debates and specific action on the ground. The copious references that the book makes to the real-world experiences of students offer incontrovertible evidence of just how consequential – but also painful – this new digital turn has been. To call it a tragedy is no exaggeration at all. This should be required reading for policy-makers in the field of education and learning.

Diane Ravitch
Historian and author of *Slaying Goliath, The Death and Life of the Great American School System* and *Reign of Error*

 This is a wonderful and important publication. It sounds a warning that we ignore at our peril. What we learned from the pandemic is that educational technology is an ineffective substitute for human teachers, for teachers who listen to and care for each student. Yet now the ed-tech industry seeks to monetize its failure by expanding its control of students and classrooms around the world. We cannot allow failure to triumph.

Arjun Appadurai
Social-cultural anthropologist and author of *Modernity at Large* and *Fear of Small Numbers*

 Boldly resisting the temptation to forget the lessons of the COVID years, this landmark work gives us a sober guide to where the new educational technologies can help us, and how they could lead us significantly astray. It is a must-read for citizens and policy-makers worldwide.

Adam Alter
Professor of marketing and psychology, New York University, and author of *Drunk Tank Pink, Irresistible* and *Anatomy of a Breakthrough*

 An Ed-Tech Tragedy? is an important and timely examination of whether and how the COVID-19 pandemic influenced the welfare of school students who were forced to grapple with online learning environments. The book is thorough, methodical and well-researched, and the result is a nuanced assessment of the promises of ed-tech and where those promises fall short.

Farida Shaheed
United Nations Special Rapporteur on the right to education

 This landmark report brings strong evidence of the detrimental impact of the digitalization of education on the right to education, especially but not only for the most marginalized. Its forceful voice amplifies the chorus of voices opposing the digitalization of education as a replacement to on-site schooling with teachers. We must carefully examine digital solutions for their quality, relevance and consequences for the right to education and refuse technology-centric approaches that encourage adopting a path that deviates from what the right to education really means. Too often, easy solutions based on digital technologies to address educational challenges worldwide are just siren songs, hiding the profit-driven agenda of digital technology lobbyists and companies.

Ben Williamson
Professor of education, University of Edinburgh, and author of *Big Data in Education*

 An Ed-Tech Tragedy? is a forensic examination of the global 'ed-tech experiment' that took shape the moment COVID-19 struck schools in 2020. Based on painstaking global research, it shows how the pivot to ed-tech during school closures was driven by far more than emergency necessity. Powerful organizations, from big tech corporations and financial investors to ed-tech consultancies and international bodies, exploited school closures to try to reform the social institution of schooling into a digital-first or even digital-only ecosystem. While the publication is critical, its final message is a hopeful one: now that the limits, constraints and failures of ed-tech have become clear, it's time to think more creatively, imaginatively and ambitiously about the aims and future of education as a public good and a human right. This work is an immense achievement, and a hugely important critical intervention into debates about the future role of digital technologies in education.

Bede Sheppard
Deputy director of children's rights at Human Rights Watch and author of *Years Don't Wait for Them*

 The COVID-19 pandemic wrought disastrous consequences on an unparalleled scale for children's right to education globally. It's vital that we learn from what went wrong. The analysis and recommendations detailed in *An Ed-Tech Tragedy?* provide policy-makers an opportunity to consider how to use technology within education to strengthen and enable – rather than endanger – the wide spectrum of children's rights.

Payal Arora
Digital anthropologist, Erasmus University Rotterdam, and author of *The Next Billion Users*

 This groundbreaking and timely book succeeds in re-pivoting our attention to one of the most important social inventions of any time – the school. It provides a crucial moral and intellectual compass to direct us away from the ed-tech solutionism that is causing unparalleled exclusion and is in process of untethering the right to education from that of schooling. This is an essential read for policy makers, governments, parents, educators, aid agencies and anyone who is a conscientious and concerned citizen invested in the future of our learning and is looking for ethical and mindful guidance on how to optimize tech innovations while being intrinsically human-centred.

Beeban Kidron
Member of the UK House of Lords, Oxford University Fellow, Broadband Commissioner and founder and chair of 5Rights Foundation

 An Ed-Tech Tragedy? debunks the widely held assumption that ed-tech saved the day for children during the pandemic. Page by page, the analysis of tragedy unfolds, in which governments and school leaders unwittingly collude with the tech sector to transform education from a public good into private gain. In the process, teacher-led education was undermined and troubling new norms emerged: unfettered pupil surveillance, an amplification of existing inequalities and algorithmic injustice at an unprecedented scale. Not for a moment tech-phobic, the book challenges us to make child development, curiosity and the collective good the primary goals of education and to demand greater transparency and evidence from ed-tech. Thoughtful, fair and frightening, this is a book that exposes the folly of outsourcing education provision on the shiny – and unsupported – promises of new technology rather than investing in the long-term health of buildings, teachers and families. It deserves attention from all.

Dan Wagner
Professor of education, University of Pennsylvania, UNESCO Chair in Learning and Literacy and author of *Learning as Development* and *Learning at the Bottom of the Pyramid*

 Like the best histories, *An Ed-Tech Tragedy?* shows us how we have arrived at our present moment, and how we can learn lessons from our past to achieve more equitable and inclusive futures. This impressive contribution from UNESCO invites us to reassess and reimagine the most profound disruption to education in generations.

Shafika Isaacs
Professor of practice, University of Johannesburg, and founding executive director of SchoolNet Africa

> *An Ed-Tech Tragedy?* offers a sobering, incisive critical analysis of the global remote and digital learning response to the COVID-19 historical moment. It is courageous in its challenge of dominant commercialised ed-tech saviour narratives, signalling a post-digital turn in mainstream education discourse. It invites renewed educational leadership towards a reflexive critical imagination that prioritises humane, community-centred, contextually relevant, rights-based, socially and environmentally just alternatives – an invitation that needs to be heeded with urgency.

Justin Reich
Professor of digital media, Massachusetts Institute of Technology, and author of *Failure to Disrupt*

> *An Ed-Tech Tragedy?* offers an important argument that educational technology was a force multiplier for inequality during the pandemic, accelerating broader forces that protected the educational experiences of affluent students while severely curtailing opportunities for their less well off peers. These dynamics operated differently in different political and cultural contexts, and UNESCO shows this complexity, citing and analyzing research studies around the world. It will take many years to reckon with the consequences of the pandemic, and this work will be essential in this endeavor. Today schools are at ever-greater risk of interruption from the accumulating effects of the global climate emergency, and understanding choices, successes and missteps during the COVID-19 pandemic will help us navigate the challenges that lie ahead.

Sonia Livingstone
Professor of social psychology, London School of Economics, and leader of the Digital Futures Commission

> How could society's high hopes for educational technology go so wrong? It is indeed a tragedy that, in the face of a global emergency, big tech chose to prioritise profit over children's best interests, and that governments failed to make good on their commitment to human rights. This timely book sets out a clear path to avoid such problems in the future. We must all hope its insights will be properly digested.

Audrey Watters
Author of *Teaching Machines* and creator of Hack Education

 Technologists tend to ignore history and instead eagerly talk about some shiny future, where all the robots and gadgets and algorithms have solved every imaginable problem. But it's a fantasy – and as the title of this important publication suggests – a tragedy. What we see in these pages are the ways in which the pandemic and the embrace of digital education exacerbated many of the problems and inequalities that schools were already suffering from – historical problems and historical inequalities. It's crucial that we examine what happened during the pandemic in schools rather than, in our rush to 'return to normal', ignore and bury this history. We cannot build a future in which our educational institutions are more human-centred if we ignore the toll that new technologies have taken.

Neil Selwyn
Professor of education, Monash University, and author of *Is Technology Good for Education?* and *Distrusting Educational Technology*

 An Ed-Tech Tragedy? is destined to become a key piece of the evidence base around digital technology and education. It demonstrates how the pandemic foregrounded many long-standing fault lines and tensions that had previously been glossed over in the hype around digital education. Above all, the book makes a persuasive case that while much of what happened during the pandemic was wholly unprecedented, it was also utterly predictable. It exposes the hubris of the ed-tech industry and points to alternate ways that technologies might be used in more humane, inclusive and empowering ways. This unflinching analysis should be read by policy-makers, IT executives and developers, school leaders, teachers, parents and anyone else in a position to ensure that we do not find ourselves enduring the same mistakes again.

Kishore Singh
Former United Nations Special Rapporteur on the right to education

 An Ed-Tech Tragedy? provides groundbreaking analysis of technology-centric approaches to education. It exposes the way ed-tech crippled access to education, aggravated inequities, fortified private sector control over education, and uprooted education to virtual worlds devoid of human touch during the COVID-19 pandemic. Yet, it does not despair. With refreshing exactness, it shows us how to chart a new course for education in the digital age, safeguarding it as a human right and public good.

Michael Trucano
Visiting fellow, Brookings Institution, and global lead for technology and innovation in education, World Bank

 An Ed-Tech Tragedy? examines the results, and lack of results, from history's largest ever global educational experiment: the mass use of technology to support remote learning during the COVID-19 pandemic. It is a cautionary tale, recounting what happened when many education systems, reflexively or because they didn't have any other options at hand, turned to technological fixes when schools were closed for months and, in some cases, years. As the book demonstrates, remote learning worked best, and with the greatest impacts, in communities that already enjoyed the most advantages, for students who were already the best performing. 'Pro-poor' approaches to utilizing educational technologies are possible, but they don't happen automatically. While technologies new and old certainly have important roles to play in supporting teaching and learning, *An Ed-Tech Tragedy?* reminds us that education remains a fundamentally human endeavour.

Rebecca Stromeyer
Founder and CEO of eLearning Africa and co-founder of Online Educa Berlin

 In *An Ed-Tech Tragedy?* UNESCO crafts a poignant narrative, unravelling the complexities of ed-tech's seemingly promising allure during the COVID-19 pandemic. This book masterfully underscores that while technology holds considerable potential, its hasty application during the crisis often led to more harm than good. It doesn't merely bemoan the challenges but encourages a deeper introspection, emphasising the human-centred core of education over blind tech adoption. With profound insights, the narrative brings to light the multifaceted role schools play beyond mere academics and pushes for a recalibration of our tech-in-education ethos. What is here is a history, but it's also much more than that: it is a roadmap for the future of digital learning.

Halla B. Holmarsdottir
Professor of education, Oslo Metropolitan University, and editor-in-chief of the *Nordic Journal of Comparative and International Education*

 This publication is an important milestone. It provides alternatives and adds needed nuance and caution to the technology-first discourses that tend to dominate conversations about the future of education. In doing so, it points us towards more equitable and desirable paths ahead for digital learning.

Foreword

―――

Since the very beginning of the COVID-19 pandemic, UNESCO has worked to help countries and its many other partners understand and navigate the educational ramifications of this unprecedented period.

Our global monitoring gave specificity to the daunting scale of school closures and their varied durations. We convened education ministers to facilitate cross-border knowledge and resource sharing. We forged alliances to provide guidance about how to safely reopen schools and launched the Global Education Coalition which helped bring distance learning opportunities to students through no-tech, low-tech and high-tech channels and continues to support education. And throughout the crisis, we stressed the importance of prioritizing inclusion and equity in response to the immense challenges of the disruption to education.

We were all operating in a deeply uncertain environment and under time pressures. It was a moment that demanded decision-making with limited information.

The global health emergency is now over, and schools have conclusively reopened. We now have the luxury to consider – with greater remove, more experience and more data – the impact of school closures and attempts to conduct teaching and learning remotely through digital and online portals.

The seismic events that gripped us for the better part of 2020 to 2023, demand introspection. We must learn from what occurred – both from the actions we took as well as those we might have taken and may wish to consider in the future. *An Ed-Tech Tragedy?* captures this learning. Act by act, chapter by chapter, it marshals evidence from around the world to document and analyse the effects of moving education from schools to ed-tech. It also scrutinizes why technology was so uniformly elevated as the centrepiece of solutions to preserve the continuity of learning.

Our critical treatment of this turbulent history is infused with concern for the future. We observe that educational relationships with technology have, in concerning ways, shifted out of balance. In coming to terms with the realities of ed-tech modes of teaching and learning during the pandemic, we propose clear ideas to redesign and reorient this relationship and ensure that education, our most humanistic endeavour, remains in human hands and centres human actors.

Tellingly perhaps, this publication's release coincides with a surge in excitement about the educational potentials of newly powerful AI applications. We would be wise to study the analysis offered here as we consider this new class of technology. It reveals the many limitations of ed-tech and cautions us away from the temptation to habitually elevate technology as a quick solution to challenges that stem from social causes rather than technical ones. It clarifies that education is not automatable – nor can it be principally driven by amoral machines. Technologies that excel at pattern recognition and prediction are useful tools no doubt, but they are insufficient foundations for learning that helps people develop autonomy, cooperate with others, live freely and ethically, and nurture creativity. For this we require schools, professional human teachers and collaborative and social academic communities.

Ultimately, we should heed this publication's recommendation to exercise greater humility and caution when considering the educational promises of the latest technological marvels. The pandemic experience has much to teach us about the future of digital learning. It shows us how we can successfully recalibrate – as we must – the ways that technology is used in education, by whom, towards what ends, and on whose terms.

This work advances UNESCO's long tradition in serving as a laboratory of ideas about education. A disruption of the magnitude of COVID-19 deserves a volume of this breadth and scope. We hope that you find inspiration in it.

Stefania Giannini
Assistant Director-General for Education
UNESCO

Acknowledgements

This publication was conceived and prepared by the Future of Learning and Innovation Team at UNESCO.

The research and writing was led by Mark West, UNESCO Programme Specialist, with guidance from Sobhi Tawil, UNESCO Director of Future of Learning and Innovation.

The following UNESCO colleagues contributed to the research, review and editing of the manuscript: Aida Alhabshi, Evan Chuu, Huhua Fan, Edelmira Ferri, Shereen Joseph, Alina Kirillina, Kiyeon Lee, Nina Meyzen, Fengchun Miao, Michela Pagano, Rachel Pollack, Sam Pairavi, Nathalie Popa, Maya Prince, Clare Sharkey, Noah W. Sobe, Mary de Sousa, Elena Toukan, Thu Truong and John YoHan Jin.

The Future of Learning and Innovation Team is grateful to the many experts who peer-reviewed early drafts of this publication, in particular: Karim Abdelghani, Payal Arora, Nathan Castillo, Halla Holmarsdottir, Shafika Isaacs, Evgeny Morozov, Jacqueline Strecker, Michael Trucano, Steven Vosloo and Charley Wright.

Contents

Foreword	09
Acknowledgements	11
Epigraph	17
Summary	18
Organization	20
Genesis and research methods	23

INTRODUCTION — 27

Defining ed-tech	28
The origins and rise of ed-tech	29
Ed-tech and technology solutionism	32
Why tragedy?	34
Situating the disruption	37
A Netflix moment for commercial ed-tech	39

Act 1: THE HOPE OF TECH SALVATION — 41

Reformatting schools with technology — 43
- The Proteus of machines and a new edifice for education — 44
- All it takes is a hole in the wall — 48
- The stage is set for ed-tech — 53

Cut the red tape and catapult education to a better future — 57

Act 2: FROM PROMISES TO REALITY — 61

Most learners were left behind — 63
- Ed-tech? What ed-tech? — 64
- Technology barriers mirrored and widened existing divides — 69
- Heightened demand for connectivity and devices put a strain on poor families — 71
- A dearth of digital skills prevented teaching and learning — 79
- Teachers were unprepared to support remote learning — 82

Inequalities were supercharged	**85**
Learning by radio versus real-time, teacher-led video	87
Digital aspirations and investments favoured the privileged	88
Efforts to leapfrog progress skipped over disadvantaged learners	89
Variable connectivity quality and new forms of digital exclusion	93
Efforts to provide digital skills training left low-level users behind	100
Technology privileged families with time to support education at home	102
Wealthy families found alternative solutions	104
Sociocultural differences put poor families at a disadvantage	107
School-based inequities were amplified in the transition to remote learning	110
No room for anywhere learning and fixed times for anytime education	114
Video classes made inequity jarringly visible	120
Hardship and heightened exclusion for students with disabilities	129
An amplification of digital gender divides	134
A step backwards for the labour participation of mothers	139
School closures contributed to increases in child labour	142
Learners engaged less, achieved less and left state-provisioned education	**144**
Time dedicated to education declined dramatically	145
Lower and slower learning gains with online learning	148
Disengagement and dropout followed the shift to ed-tech	154
A flight from public education to home-schooling	163
Education was narrowed and impoverished	**165**
Engines of socialization and acculturation slowed	167
Student well-being and protection was neglected in digital spaces	169
A void of support to navigate bereavement	174
Technology stifled pedagogical possibilities and the agency of teachers	175
Corporate aesthetics and linguistic hegemony replaced the vibrancy of the classroom	179
Automation, standardization and homogenization of the learning process	183
Immersion in technology was unhealthy	**186**
Negative impacts of increased screen time	189
Pains, weight gain and malnutrition	192
Physical education online and in isolation	194
Touchless worlds	195
A retreat into games and proto-metaverses	198
A subversion of learning to live together	204
Zoom dysmorphia and digital excarnation	209
Isolation, invisibility and alienation in school-less schooldays	213
A parallel mental health pandemic among young people	218
A digital conveyor belt of personalized learning and the normalization of learning alone	221
Frustration and stress mark the transition into unfamiliar modes of digital learning	225
The hidden dangers of rushed online immersion	229
A curtailing of conversation	231
Digital addiction and being alone together	234
Ed-tech is poorly suited for young children	238

Environmental tolls multiplied with the ed-tech boom	**248**
New material and energy needs	250
The mounting scourge of e-waste	254
Ed-tech for some, mines and landfills for others	257
The private sector tightened its grip on public education	**260**
Unprecedented growth and lucrative IPOs for commercial ed-tech providers	263
Corporate dependencies and reduced government oversight	281
Cultivating consumer behaviour in students, families and teachers	289
Surveillance, control and machine processes marked the move to ed-tech	**302**
New data gold and the many eyes of ed-tech surveillance	306
Forced consent and new levers of control	314
Privacy and personal data slip away in the digital environments of education	321
Datafication of learning and humans	325
Emotion-recognition technologies gain a toehold despite flimsy science	333
Self-censorship and classroom control	338
Technology aimed at individuals tilts educational research away from groups	345
Automation and machine processes weaken teacher authority	346
Fallible algorithms	349
Remote proctoring, suspicion scores and software sedimentation	355
Complexity, poor transparency and limited capacity make algorithmic audits rare	372
Contesting spurious machine judgements and privacy overreach	374
End of Act 2	**380**

Inter-Act: LOOKING BACK TO SEE AHEAD — 383

LOOKING BACK — 385

School closures, the shift to remote learning and public health	**387**
Did technology-mediated remote learning contribute to the prolongation of school closures?	**394**
If not ed-tech, then what?	**398**
Alternative A: Keeping schools open or reopening them quickly	399
Alternative B: Pause formal education until the resumption of in-person schooling	404
Alternative C: Focus on supporting caregivers and prioritizing non-technological learning resources	411
Was COVID-19 an education crisis?	**417**

LOOKING AHEAD — 424

Ed-tech finds a new rationale – resilience	**425**
Is technology a pillar of educational resilience?	**430**
If ed-tech is the answer, what is the question?	**439**

Act 3: NEW DIRECTIONS FOR ED-TECH — 443

Prioritize the best interests of students and teachers — 447
- Redesign online environments to centre students' needs — 448
- Give teachers agency in ed-tech pedagogies — 452
- Design codes, regulation and legislation to put students first — 455

Reaffirm the primacy of in-person learning — 459
- Buttress schools as essential social institutions — 460
- Guard against the homogenization of education — 462
- Question the logic of technology solutionism — 465

Strengthen digital connectivity, capacities and content — 468
- Centre the most marginalized in ed-tech planning and deployment — 470
- Champion school-first and public connectivity as a step towards ed-tech inclusion — 474
- Support the development of free, high-quality digital content and platforms — 476
- Build digital capacities and foster pedagogical innovation — 479

Protect the right to education from shrinking ground — 483
- Anchor the right to education in standards and definitions that prioritize in-person learning — 485
- Ensure children's safety and well-being in physical and digital learning spaces — 489
- Reconstruct ed-tech to support holistic education and accommodate educational diversity — 491

CONCLUSION — 495
Remembering the ed-tech experiences of the pandemic — 497
The arc of tragedy — 498
Reorienting and steering the digital transformation of education — 500

WORKS CITED — 503
Narrative text — 504
Voices from the ground — 577
Figures — 588

BIBLIOGRAPHY — 591

The protagonist of a tragedy should be neither eminently virtuous or just, nor yet involved in misfortune by deliberate vice or villainy, but by some error of human frailty.

—Aristotle, *Poetics*, 335 BCE

We are all [technology] solutionists now. When our lives are at stake, abstract promises of political emancipation are less reassuring than the promise of an app that tells you when it's safe to leave your house. The real question is whether we will still be solutionists tomorrow.

—Evgeny Morozov, *The Guardian*, 15 April 2020

We must go into emergency mode to put humanity at the centre of technology. … Our choices are taken away from us without us even knowing it.

—António Guterres, *Secretary-General's address to the United Nations General Assembly*, 21 January 2022

Summary

―――

An Ed-Tech Tragedy? documents how widespread school closures and the hard pivot to remote learning with connected technology during the COVID-19 pandemic resulted in numerous unintended and undesirable consequences.

Although connected technology supported the continuation of education for many learners, many more were left behind. Exclusion soared and inequities widened. Achievement levels fell, even for those with access to distance learning. Educational experiences narrowed. Physical and mental health declined. Privatization accelerated, threatening education's unique standing as a public good and human right. Invasive surveillance endangered the free and open exchange of ideas and undermined trust. Automation replaced human interactions with machine-mediated experiences. And technology production and disposal placed new strains on the environment.

Visions that technology could form the backbone of education and supplant school-based learning – in wide circulation at the outset of the health crisis – had promised better outcomes. Ed-tech proponents held that the immense challenges of school closures could be met with technology and that deeper technology integration would transform education for the better. But these high hopes and expectations unravelled when ed-tech was hurriedly deployed to maintain formal education as COVID-19 tore across countries.

An Ed-Tech Tragedy? recounts this tumultuous period, documenting the actions and decisions taken by governments, schools and technology companies. The publication contrasts the promises of ed-tech with the realities of what ed-tech delivered as a response to school closures that impacted over 1.6 billion learners and stretched intermittently from the beginning of 2020 to early 2023. The evidence and analysis highlight trends observed across countries and zoom in on the specificities of local experiences, creating a global mosaic of what students, teachers and families experienced when connected technology was elevated as a singular portal to teaching and learning.

Aimed at general and specialist audiences alike, this book shows how the abrupt and deep changes brought about by the recourse to remote digital learning during the pandemic continue to ripple through the education sector even as schools have fully reopened. It questions whether more and faster integration of technology is desirable for learners and if ed-tech is, as it is often billed, a key ingredient of educational resilience.

An Ed-Tech Tragedy? posits that new principles are needed to forge more humanistic directions for ed-tech development and use. In-person schooling and teaching should be guaranteed even as technologies improve and connectivity becomes more ubiquitous. Governments need to anchor this guarantee in the legal architecture upholding the right to education, especially for young learners. Moreover, future applications of ed-tech must show greater concern for holistic student well-being. While academic learning is central to education, it is not the only component. Ed-tech needs to support the multiple individual and collective purposes of education, from socio-emotional and personal development, to learning to live together, with the planet, as well as with technology.

Mirroring the organization of a theatrical tragedy and broken across three 'acts', this book endeavors to explain why ed-tech was widely elevated as a singular solution to the challenges of pandemic school closures, what happened when ed-tech was deployed to uphold formal education in diverse contexts around the world and, perhaps most importantly, what can be learned from this unprecedented experience. Recommendations clarify how the education community can move beyond merely reacting to technological change and instead move more assertively to steer this change, guided by educational needs and reflecting educational ambitions to establish more inclusive, just and sustainable societies.

The future of education needs to be a humanistic one. The lessons extracted from what is premised here as an ed-tech tragedy illuminate the ways technology can better facilitate education that teaches and revitalizes human values, strengthens human relationships and upholds human rights.

Organization

An Ed-Tech Tragedy? borrows the structure of a theatrical play to document and analyse the impacts and repercussions of the pivot from school-based education to remote distance learning with ed-tech during the COVID-19 pandemic.

The publication explains the hopes and promises ascribed to ed-tech prior to the emergence of COVID-19, documents the realities and ripple effects of large-scale technology deployments in response to massive school closures, and extracts salient lessons from this experience to steer future digital transformations of education in more human-centred directions.

The **Introduction** defines the publication's use of the terms 'ed-tech' and 'technology solutionism' and explains the framing concept of 'tragedy' as used in the analysis. It also presents and contextualizes the scale and severity of the educational disruption stemming from the pandemic.

Act 1, *The Hope of Tech Salvation*, examines why countries almost uniformly turned to digital technology as a primary response to school closures. It traces the rise and dissemination of ideas that internet-connected technologies could – and even should – replace schools as the primary nexus of formal education. Visions of technology-reliant and technology-guided education rested on assumptions that mainstream schooling models were outdated and no longer fit for a digital age of instant information and the possibility of ubiquitous learning. Technology, it was thought, would better facilitate the types of learning and skills development demanded in a connected world awash in data and digital content. When governments mandated widespread school closures to stem the transmission of COVID-19, expectations were high that ed-tech would not only ensure continued learning during a global health emergency but also improve it and lay foundations for educational transformations centred around digital hardware and software.

> Act 1 details the ambition that often marked the initial transition from schools to ed-tech as the pandemic took hold.

Act 2, *From Promises to Reality*, contrasts the promises of ed-tech against the realities of what it delivered and did not deliver in the challenging contexts of the pandemic. It draws on a wide range of sources available at community, national and regional levels to illuminate global trends. The evidence shows how the uprooting of education from the physical and social sites of schools to technology-reliant remote learning left most learners behind and supercharged inequalities. It reveals that even when connected technology was available, technology-centric modes of learning tended to result in low student engagement and poor achievement. Looking beyond learning, the analysis explains the many ways young people's immersion into technology for education and other purposes was unhealthy. Finally, dedicated subsections outline how the centrality of ed-tech has empowered and enriched powerful private sector actors, enabled new and invasive forms of surveillance and control, and ushered in often overlooked environmental impacts, among other harms.

> *Act 2 explains the many ways the promises of ed-tech collapsed when technology was deployed globally as a primary solution to maintain education during widespread and prolonged school closures. It reveals the harm, hardships and unintended consequences that resulted from the endeavour to transition from in-person and school-based education to technology-reliant distance learning.*

The **Inter-Act,** *Looking Back to See Ahead*, probes difficult questions about technology-first responses to the education challenges of the pandemic by looking beyond the reality of what happened to the more contested space of possible alternatives.

Some questions look to the past: Did school closures and the shift to remote learning protect public health and save lives? Did remote learning alternatives to in-person education contribute to the prolongation of school closures? Were there options beyond connected technology to maintain education when schools were shuttered? And was COVID-19 an education crisis in addition to a health crisis?

Other questions look ahead: To what extent do ed-tech investments strengthen the resilience of education systems? Is the education sector a 'digital laggard', as many voices claim? Should governments allocate a greater proportion of education budgets towards digital hardware and software?

> *The Inter-Act questions dominant narratives to emerge from the technology-centric experiences of the pandemic period.*

Act 3, *New Directions for Ed-Tech*, proposes ideas to better ensure that technology complements and enriches the deeply human enterprise of education, reflecting lessons learned during the pandemic. It advises moderating expectations for ed-tech and applying technology in ways that advance the best interests of students and teachers without recourse to full-fledged privatization. It further recommends elevating a concern for equity in future ed-tech deployments in order to break the cycle of technology exacerbating educational and opportunity divides. Subsections clarify that physical schools should remain principal hubs for teaching and learning, especially for children, even as technology offers options to extend education and enrich the vital work that happens in classrooms.

> *Act 3 puts forward recommendations to guide future efforts to leverage technology for education while keeping schools and humans at the centre of teaching and learning.*

The **Conclusion** calls for continued dialogue to both remember and extract lessons from the ed-tech experiences of the pandemic. These recollections and lessons will help societies negotiate and perhaps reimagine the places and roles for technology in education. Going forward, technology must better support the humanistic aims of education and more reliably improve the learning and well-being of students, teachers, families and communities.

Genesis and research methods

―

The foundations for this publication were laid in February 2020, a few weeks before the World Health Organization (WHO) declared the spread of COVID-19 a global pandemic. At that time, countries ordering school closures, first largely in Asia, were quickly and quite uniformly turning to ed-tech to provision distance education and assure the continuity of formal learning. Observing this trend, UNESCO wrote:

> *Pundits have often said nationwide digital learning is inevitable, but few predicted it would be triggered by a health emergency. We are about to witness what works and does not work in terms of bringing education to students remotely at a pace and scale that has never before been seriously contemplated, let alone attempted in practice. … Those of us in the international education community (and the edu-tech community, in particular) would do well to pay close attention. … The varied approaches attempted in [different countries] will reveal what happens when formal education moves abruptly from brick- and-mortar buildings to the cloud. … Keep your notebooks handy. This is an edu-tech experiment of unprecedented size.*[1]

This foresight prompted a three-year-long endeavour to monitor and synthesize the consequences of the large-scale shift to technology-dependent remote learning that swept the world. The aim was to understand, recount and explain the significance of what happened when education was uprooted from schools and moved to remote learning technologies. At the heart of this inquiry was the ed-tech – the technologies and also the approaches and ideologies – that supported the transition to distance learning during periods of school closure.

Because the shift to ed-tech occurred in the context of other seismic social disruptions, it was challenging to tease out which impacts were attributable to new, technology-dependent modes of teaching and learning and which were attributable to other factors such as wider restrictions on movement and socialization. Pandemic or no pandemic, learning almost never occurs in a vacuum where it is possible to attribute with full confidence a particular intervention or condition to an observed change or result.

Yet, trying to understand the causes and effects of changes to education remains vital. Indeed, few educational changes have ever, certainly at the global level, been as profound as the pivot from in-person and school-based education to instruction delivered remotely and almost exclusively through technology. It is necessary, despite the methodological challenges involved, to better understand the effects of this monumental shift, and this publication is the culmination of efforts to do so.

In addition to centring ed-tech, the analysis offered here considers some of the far-reaching and perhaps underappreciated implications of school closures. While concerns about disease transmission triggered school closures in 2020, 2021, 2022 and early 2023, technology itself can enable approaches to education that are not reliant on schools, regardless of whether there is a pandemic or another external justification to shutter brick-and-mortar learning institutions. Some people understand these digital-only approaches to be desirable and believe they will result in substantial cost savings and other efficiencies. A popular maxim holds that 'everything that can be digitalized will be digitalized'. The experiences of school closures during COVID-19 offered a preview of what the world might look like if the digital transformation of education is carried to extremes. Sections of this publication should therefore be understood as offering an early warning about the foreseeable repercussions of future decisions to close schools and elevate technology as the primary connective tissue and infrastructure of education, outside the context of a pandemic or another emergency that might necessitate some form of temporary remote learning.

The analysis reviews relevant English language literature from early 2020 to early 2023, including news articles, government reports and publications from international organizations. Scholarly research published before and during the pandemic was also considered.

> This publication offers an early warning about the foreseeable repercussions of future decisions to close schools and elevate technology as the primary connective tissue and infrastructure of education outside the context of a pandemic.

Writing about experiences of school closures across the globe and attempts to transition to technology-mediated remote learning invariably entails making generalizations that do not apply neatly to every context. Nigeria is a very different place than Norway, as is Guam from Guatemala. For this reason, the analysis tours the world at high and low orbits. It takes stock of trends that cut across countries and regions, but it also regularly zooms in just above the ground to describe and explain the specificity of practices, actions and outcomes in particular communities, districts, schools or universities.

This alternating focus – far and near, local and global – helps to provide readers a more complete picture of the diversity of ed-tech experiences and, at the same time, show how they interlock to form a wider mosaic.

A concerted effort has been made to ensure the publication gives due attention to the realities of fully remote learning during the pandemic in every region. Despite this, substantively more research and testimonies surfaced from high- and middle-income countries than from low-income countries. Much of the analysis explores how education and educational relationships changed when internet-connected digital ed-tech was available and worked as intended. Less attention is paid to experiences with low-tech solutions like television and radio, mainly because these were harder to capture and the research about the deployment and uptake of these technologies as a response to school closures was significantly thinner. The technology and connectivity to power digital learning was out of reach in large swathes of the global South and many pockets of the global North. The experience in these areas was all too commonly one of educational exclusion. The sections that examine digital learning consequently tend to focus on high- and middle-income contexts. This also reflects the availability of reliable research, which tended to concentrate in countries and communities where many families had access to technologies that enabled remote digital learning. A significant share of data and examples relate to the United States of America (USA) where evidence and studies about ed-tech experiences were especially plentiful. This country is also home to a considerable number of influential ed-tech companies that had international reach before and during the pandemic.

Qualitative observations, drawn from various media sources, are interwoven throughout the publication to call attention to the lived experiences of individuals participating in fully remote learning with ed-tech. The pandemic, the ensuing school closures and the switch to technology-reliant learning unfolded with such velocity that quality media reports were initially among the best sources of information. While surveys and analyses on the influence and impacts of remote learning became increasingly available as of late 2020, media reports, often carrying interviews with students, teachers, parents and school leaders, remained valuable sources of information. These close-up views and testimonials, unique to particular people and contexts, are peppered throughout the publication and give granularity to its treatment of global, regional and national evidence. While anecdotal, they help readers see pandemic ed-tech experiences from the perspectives of those closest to education.

Drafting for this publication started in late 2020. The work was regularly expanded, updated and amended as more data and evidence came to light. The way the analysis is organized changed numerous times to adequately capture and explain the many branches and sub-branches of ed-tech realities during the pandemic. The final work is organized to contrast the promises of ed-tech with the realities of what ed-tech delivered during periods of school closure.

The use of tragedy as a framing concept and narrative arc emerged only after careful analysis of the available evidence. Research and testimonials that became available in 2021 and throughout 2022 and early 2023 increasingly revealed that harm and unintended consequences were stemming from heavy and extended reliance on connected technology for education during periods of school closure. Tragedy provided a helpful metaphor to centre this evidence.

This publication helps fulfil UNESCO's mandate to function as a laboratory of ideas about the future of education. It marshals extensive evidence to prompt reflection about the wisdom of a global turn to ed-tech as a response to school closures during the pandemic. It also aims to question the extent to which deepened educational reliance on technology – largely guided by technology solutionist thinking – is as inevitable and desirable as it is often portrayed.

Ultimately, this publication invites an overdue critical examination of the technology-first responses to the educational disruptions of the pandemic. In doing so, it hopes to spark more vigorous debate about the uses and misuses of technology in education going forward.

INTRODUCTION

This publication critically reviews the impacts of efforts, observed in different countries, to leverage technology-enabled remote learning as a primary or singular response to school closures during the COVID-19 pandemic. It identifies the many ways in which these efforts fell short of their objectives and extracts forward-looking lessons.

The introduction lays foundations for the publication by defining the term 'ed-tech' and tracing its expansion from the financial sector to the education community. Ed-tech is also linked to the concept of 'technology solutionism', an ideology that positions technology as an optimal, default and complete solution to complex societal problems. The introduction further explains the publication's use of tragedy as a metaphor and clarifies both the enormity of COVID-19 disruptions to education and the explosive growth of private and for-profit ed-tech solutions during the pandemic. These definitions and explanations frame the analysis presented in the main 'acts' of the book.

DEFINING ED-TECH

Ed-tech, short for educational technology, refers to digital and other connected technologies used to conduct or support education.

This publication examines ed-tech within the parameters of technology-mediated or technology-dependent systems of distance learning deployed in response to COVID-19 school closures. It considers modes of teaching and learning with technology that were unhooked from the physical and social sites of schools, the primary nexus of education prior to 2020. While ed-tech is often used inside classroom and school settings, this work does not closely consider this application, but stays within the narrower bands of fully remote modes of education.

Ed-tech should be understood as covering a wide range of technologies – digital and analogue, interactive and broadcast, synchronous and asynchronous – that were deployed in attempts to maintain educational continuity through an unprecedented disruption. While radio and television are important forms of ed-tech, the publication looks most closely at high-tech internet-connected technologies such as laptops, tablets and mobile phones.

> As a conceptual term, 'ed-tech' has meanings that ripple beyond specific hardware and software products.

In addition to the physical devices that are habitually considered 'educational technology', ed-tech also includes software, systems, content, platforms, connections, networks and online apps that render hardware useful for educational purposes. Ed-tech further encompasses the services, organizational arrangements, ecosystems, policy regimes, assumptions and logics that undergird the educational application of technology. As such, the term enfolds not only devices but processes and services. This publication gives ample treatment to these extended meanings of ed-tech.

"'Edtech' has become an increasingly capacious category. It designates a huge variety of actors (human and nonhuman), organizations (public, private or multisector), material and technical forms (hardware, software, supporting documents), modes of practice (of teachers, designers, promoters), and framing discourses, as well as being a highly varied field of research, development and critical inquiry."

– Ben Williamson, education scholar[1]

THE ORIGINS AND RISE OF ED-TECH

The term 'ed-tech' came into popular use first as a corporate and financial marketing term. It was a label preferred by investors and entrepreneurs to classify technologies and technology-centric solutions that could be bought and sold in the education sector. Use of this label spread from the business world where it originated to governments and schools and, eventually, into the lexicon of scholarly education journals.

"Predicted to triple in value to USD 350 billion by 2025, the EdTech sector has been rapidly gaining ground in countries like India and Kenya where efforts to improve failing education systems have led to a proliferation of online learning solutions."

– Kinda Chebib, research manager, GSMA[1]

Despite the widening use of 'ed-tech', the term continues to be aimed primarily at business and financial audiences. Indeed, a number of ed-tech organizations and outlets have sprung up to broker connections between education, technology, business and investor communities, including EdSurge, eSchool News and HolonIQ, among others. A prominent example in this genre is *EdTech*, a magazine that purports to "[explore] technology and education issues that IT leaders and educators face when they're evaluating and implementing a solution".[2] Through its articles, the magazine advances the idea that technology can improve education under headings such as "New Adobe product simplifies digital design"[3] and "Educators are leaving the profession at alarming rates, but experts say upgrading their technology can contribute to job satisfaction".[4] All the articles are tagged with one- or two-word labels, such as 'cloud', 'data analytics', 'digital workspace', 'management', 'networking', 'security' or 'software', that provide a sense of ed-tech's many branches. Like many sources of ed-tech news, *EdTech*'s parent company is a larger technology corporation – in this case, CDW. A Fortune 500 company with annual net sales in 2021 of USD 21 billion, CDW offers, according to its website, a "broad array of products and services [ranging] from hardware and software to integrated IT solutions such as security, cloud, hybrid infrastructure and digital experience".[5] It counts Intel, Dell, Adobe and other large technology companies as network partners. Apart from *EdTech* magazine, CDW's research arm also publishes *HealthTech*, *BizTech*, *StateTech* and *FedTech*, showing that education is hardly unique among sectors in having the term 'tech' appended to it.

In addition to being featured in the title of various magazines, newsletters and websites, 'ed-tech' is attached to the name of numerous investment funds.

> One of the most comprehensive formal definitions of 'ed-tech' does not come from education literature but rather from a nearly 1,000-word-long entry on Investopedia, a popular source of investment information.

The website of one of these funds, the EdTech Fund, states: "Technology is finally disrupting education", "Schools are adopting digital products en masse" and "There is a massive open market share for the taking".[6] More recently, 'ed-tech' has formed the basis for exchange-traded funds (ETFs). Launched for the first time in 2020, these financial products are effectively baskets of shares held in publicly traded ed-tech companies.[7] This is a significant development because ETFs allow investors to move money in and out of ed-tech as a stand-alone subsector of financial markets without having to buy shares in individual companies. While there have long been specific ETFs for sectors such as technology, health and energy, there had never previously been ed-tech funds. This development further linked conceptualizations of ed-tech to markets and market logics. Tellingly, one of the most comprehensive formal definitions of 'ed-tech' does not come from education literature but rather from a nearly 1,000-word-long entry on Investopedia,[8] a popular source of investment information. Ed-tech's connections to finance and business continue to colour its meaning even as the term moves into wider circulation.

> The term 'ed-tech' carries close associations with entrepreneurship, start-ups, fundraising, venture capital and privatization.

Also, while ed-tech might, at first glance, appear to be neutral on issues of educational efficacy, it tends to be linked with ideas that technology can *successfully* provision education. So, while the term is a contraction of 'educational technology', it has implications that are distinct from the definition of the spelled-out version. Just as 'fin-tech' does not carry quite the same meaning as 'financial technology', 'ed-tech' has a semantic resonance unique from 'educational technology'. Ed-tech's starting point is not usually a question of *whether* a particular technological approach might be useful for education. The term instead assumes educational utility from the outset. It also carries close associations with entrepreneurship, start-ups, fundraising, venture capital and privatization.

"Edtech roars with over USD 3.2 billion invested in first half of 2021."
– Tony Wan, head of investor content, Reach Capital[8]

The balance of the two constituent parts of ed-tech – education and technology – is also significant and helps reveal its utility as a corporate and financial marketing term. The 'tech' portion, as an abbreviation of 'technology', is longer and more complete or – in the words of Martin Weller, a professor of educational technology at the Open University – "walks taller"[9] than the 'ed' portion, a highly compressed abbreviation of 'education'. This stands in contrast to previous terminology such as 'e-learning' and 'e-education' that attempted to conjoin technology and education but kept the primary emphasis on education or learning. With 'ed-tech', the central focus is on technology – 'education' is the modifier, while 'technology' is the noun.

Interestingly, the closer one moves to education-focused discourses, the more likely 'education', in the formulation 'educational technology', will be written out in full, while the nearer one moves to technology- and business-focused discourses, the more likely the term will be abbreviated as 'ed-tech'. Most education journals about educational technology present the words in full – for example, *Educational Technology and Society*, *Educational Technology Research and Development* and the *British Journal of Educational Technology*.[10] Other education-focused journals affix the word 'learning' to 'technology', as in *Learning, Media and Technology*, but a shorthand connecting the two words, such 'learn-tech', is virtually non-existent. Some of the most widely cited journals about education and technology do not use the word 'technology' at all, but rather words that refer to a particular technology such as 'computer', as exemplified by the journal *Computers and Education*.[11]

Yet the popularity of 'ed-tech' as a term to neatly contain varied ideas about education and technology has been building since at least 2015. In 2019, a few months before the emergence of COVID-19, the UK government and the World Bank, along with a long roster of partner and supporting organizations including the Overseas Development Institute, the University of Cambridge, Results for Development, the Bill and Melinda Gates Foundation and UNICEF, launched EdTech Hub[12] with an initial budget of USD 25 million to be spent over eight years.[13] Half of the money has been allocated to research on ed-tech in low-income countries, 35 per cent towards direct support for ed-tech deployments in partnership with governments and 15 per cent on ed-tech innovation.[14] The project's website lists eight directors and a team of 50 professionals.[15] The creation of EdTech Hub was noteworthy because its size and budget make it something of a de facto international organization dedicated exclusively to ed-tech research and implementation. Previously, large educational organizations had treated technology as a branch of work but never as the main trunk.

In 2020, as the shock of the pandemic gripped the world and schools closed, the term 'ed-tech' became inescapable. It quickly eclipsed, superseded or enveloped terms as varied as 'information and communication technology (ICT) in education', 'distance learning', 'mobile learning' and 'virtual learning'. It was on the tongues of heads of state, ministers, school and university leaders, writers, thinkers and the general public. There were calls to have countries establish federal departments of ed-tech that would be lateral to ministries of education.[16] Ministries of education, perhaps hoping to maintain control of the mounting and sometimes singular focus on technology, largely embraced the term. Ministries established ed-tech departments and offices,[17] developed ed-tech plans[18] and hosted ed-tech summits.[19] Among international organizations, the World Bank, UNICEF, the Global Partnership for Education and UNESCO have teams dedicated to educational technology, even if some, such as UNESCO, eschew overt use of the term 'ed-tech'. In March 2022, UNICEF announced the launch of the UNICEF EdTech Award to "identify and showcase bold entrepreneurs demonstrating the greatest potential to become 'Blue Unicorns' – ventures that impact at least 100 million children's learning experiences".[20] UNICEF's use of the word 'unicorn' in reference to '100 million children' riffs on ed-tech's links to start-ups and venture capital. In financial circles, a 'unicorn' is a start-up company that exceeds a valuation of USD 100 million. There are so many ed-tech conferences and events that it is possible to attend one or more somewhere in the world nearly every day of the year.

> The English formulation 'ed-tech' is used across languages, much like other technology words such as 'cryptocurrency'.

The English formulation 'ed-tech' was added to dictionaries and style manuals in non-English languages letter for letter and without translation, further entrenching it as a global concept. Whereas a phrase like 'educational technology' would likely be translated when it moved to a different language and carry slightly different meanings and associations from the English formulation, 'ed-tech' did not change – it is used across languages, much like other technology words such as 'cryptocurrency'.[21] The pandemic played a major role in cementing 'ed-tech' as a household term, one highly recognizable in various corners of the globe.

The analysis presented here is an effort to help better see and understand ed-tech and the ideas associated with it within the context of the pandemic and with critical distance. It acknowledges but also pushes back against the term's commercial and financial associations. It strives to reveal ed-tech as a concept and phenomenon that demands greater scrutiny.

The choice to style 'ed-tech' with a hyphen and lower-case letters is intentional and aligned with the objective to cleave the term of its marketing hype. The hyphen preserves some separation between education and technology that 'edtech', without the hyphen, wipes away. The lower-case characters, in contrast to 'EdTech' written with capital letters, ensures that the term is not infused with special or revered status.

ED-TECH AND TECHNOLOGY SOLUTIONISM

The review and analysis presented in this book help explain how fully remote online education was quickly presented as the preferred or ideal solution to the educational disruptions of COVID-19. This kind of technology solutionism – the belief that problems can be readily solved through the application of technology, especially internet technologies – is not unique to education, even as it has taken deep roots in the sector.

INTRODUCTION | 33

"'Solutionism' … is indeed the name of the game: issues are interpreted as puzzles to which there is a solution, rather than problems to which there may be a response."

– Gilles Paquet, economist and academic[iv]

Evgeny Morozov, the writer who coined the term 'technological solutionism' and carefully critiqued the assumptions that support it, explains that what characterizes this worldview is the way it reaches for specific answers and tools before questions have been fully asked or adequately contemplated. In his 2013 book *To Save Everything, Click Here*, he observes that the flaw of technological solutionism is not necessarily that a particular technology fix cannot or will not solve a problem, "but that in solving the 'problem', solutionists twist it in such an ugly and unfamiliar way that, by the time it is 'solved', the problem becomes something else entirely".[22] This twisting has been apparent in a variety of sectors, from health care to politics, as Morozov's book memorably elaborates. The concepts of technology solutionism and 'internet centrism', another of Morozov's terms, help explain how the rapid elevation of an untested technology to accomplish sweeping goals can open a floodgate for new challenges and recast some of the problems the original implementation of technology sought to assuage.

"Silicon Valley's promise of eternal amelioration has blunted our ability to question the adequacy and appropriateness of its tools and interventions."

– Evgeny Morozov, author of *To Save Everything, Click Here*[v]

An Ed-Tech Tragedy? examines the many ways that the hurried embrace of technology solutionism steered responses to a global education challenge directly towards ed-tech. Along the way, the logic of technology solutionism changed understandings of educational problems to be solved. The analysis

The problem that ed-tech initially set out to solve morphed from assuring the continuity of learning to remedying lost learning.

presented in this publication helps reveal, for example, how technological solutions deployed during school closures took a narrow view of education and focused almost exclusively on furthering the academic progress of students in pared-down curricular subjects. This meant that little attention was paid to other education goals, such as fostering curiosity and inquiry and supporting physical health, mental well-being and social and emotional learning. The analysis also shows how ed-tech, originally cast as a solution to maintain learning continuity in the face of widespread disruptions to schooling, has more recently been positioned as a tool to help reverse learning loss. This 'loss', however, grew out of the deficiencies of technology-dependent remote learning to preserve the pace of academic learning that would have been typical without school closures stemming from the pandemic. The problem that ed-tech initially set out to solve morphed from assuring the continuity of learning to remedying lost learning. The way the problem was reframed while maintaining connected technology as the centrepiece of the solution is an example of technology solutionism at work.

"Embedded in every tool is an ideological bias, a predisposition to construct the world as one thing rather than another, to value one thing over another, to amplify one sense or skill or attitude more loudly than another."

– Neil Postman, educator, media theorist and cultural critic [vi]

Much of the analysis here critiques the technology solutionism that elevated ed-tech to first- and often only-resort modes of education when schools were closed. Technology solutionism is a concept and outlook deeply intertwined with the notion of ed-tech.

"We shape our tools and thereafter they shape us."

– John M. Culkin, professor of communications [vii]

WHY TRAGEDY?

Running through this publication is a contention that the unintended consequences of ed-tech responses to the pandemic can be likened to a tragedy, in the classical sense. This framing – with its connotations of misfortune and undesired outcomes – is useful for two main reasons.

Firstly, the term 'tragedy' calls attention to the many failures of ed-tech deployments to facilitate equitable and inclusive access to educational opportunities, despite enormous efforts and investments to ensure this

> 'Tragedy' signals the educational loss that occurred despite concerted efforts to prevent it – a reversal of intent.

access and enable academic learning. Although the labour and ingenuity of different education stakeholders may very well have prevented worse outcomes given the stark realities of the pandemic, they nevertheless fell far short of meeting the needs of most students. 'Tragedy' in this sense signals the educational loss that occurred despite concerted efforts to prevent it – a reversal of intent. The narrative that technology 'saved the day' and provided teachers, parents, policy-makers and learners with the tools needed to successfully assure the continuity of fair and high-quality education is inconsistent with the available evidence.

Secondly, recognizing the chaotic pivot from in-school learning to technology-facilitated distance learning as having a tragic arc provides a forceful rebuttal to a growing consensus that the education sector somehow 'advanced', 'leapfrogged', 'catapulted' or 'disrupted' itself to a better future when it deployed technology on a massive scale as an interim measure to confront a crisis. The evidence overwhelmingly points in the opposite direction: education became less accessible, less effective and less engaging when it pivoted away from physical schools and teachers and towards technology exclusively. 'Tragedy' in this sense signals regression – a denigration of the status quo, rather than a desired evolution. The narrative that ed-tech should be or must be a central component of 'building education back better' warrants new scrutiny after a careful examination of the experiences during the pandemic.

> Investments to protect education wrongly shifted away from people and towards machines.

The invocation of tragedy also facilitates awareness that connected technologies, despite their growing reach, power and potential, remain tools in a repertoire of many others to construct stronger, more agile and more flexible education systems that can respond and adapt to disruption. Other tools include strengthened teacher training and support; enhanced school leadership and pedagogical management of schools; curricular renewal; smaller class sizes; and improved physical resources and infrastructure for schools and classrooms. Crises that necessitate the prolonged closure of schools and demand heavy or total reliance on technology have been exceedingly rare historically. Future crises may present entirely different challenges. The trauma of the pandemic has, in many circles, functioned to elevate technology as an almost singular solution to assure educational resilience by providing flexibility in times of disruption. Investments to protect education wrongly shifted away from people and towards machines, digital connections and platforms. This elevation of the technical over the human is contradictory to education's aim to further human development and cultivate humanistic values. It is human capacity, rather than technological capacity, that is central to ensuring greater resilience of education systems to withstand shocks and manage crises.

> The sudden shift to ed-tech accelerated a concerning transfer of authority away from teachers, schools and communities and towards private, for-profit interests.

Overall, the pandemic is a case study in how technology in its current iterations is not yet a suitable foundation for actualizing the diverse goals that communities assign to education. Expectations that technology may, in time, help further increase the reach, improve the quality and strengthen the agility of education are valid. For now, though, the experiences since early 2020 have shown it to be an alarmingly brittle solution – one incapable of effectively responding to widespread and extended school shutdowns. For far too many students, it was a solution that either never started in earnest or quickly broke down. The sudden shift to ed-tech also accelerated a concerning transfer of authority away from teachers, schools and communities and towards private, for-profit interests. Additionally, the censorship, data extraction, advertising, top-down control, intimidation and surveillance that so often characterize current models of digital transformation have made education less free and, arguably, less capable of facilitating critiques of and positive changes to the status quo.

Countries made massive investments to digitalize education through much of the COVID-19 pandemic. But it remains far from clear whether these investments will improve education over the longer term and make it an engine of just, inclusive and sustainable development, especially when compared with conventional school-based and teacher-facilitated education. The digital transformation of education may yet be a force for beneficial change. But the logic of technological solutionism and its associated business models currently steering this transformation, led largely by the commercial technology entities that are remaking so many aspects of society, tend to treat education and knowledge as private commodities and not as global public goods that provide collective as well as individual benefits.

> Examining the unintended negative consequences of ed-tech responses during the COVID-19 pandemic inverts the triumphalist narratives that often accompanied the switch to technology.

It is hoped that this analysis and its use of tragedy as a metaphor might moderate the discourse and popular view that the pandemic has 'unshackled' education systems and 'launched' them into desirable futures characterized by greater technology use. Documenting the severity and scope of the many negative consequences of ed-tech responses during the health crisis inverts the triumphalist narratives that accompany many descriptions of technology deployments to address the educational disruption caused by school closures. A critical examination of the assumptions of technology solutionism and a review of the existing evidence provide a corrective and a counterargument to notions that more, deeper and accelerated use of technology is uniformly positive for education.

SITUATING THE DISRUPTION

The impact of COVID-19 on formal education, as in so many other areas of society, was extremely disruptive. At the peak of global school closures in April 2020, formal learning either stopped completely or was severely interrupted for approximately 90 per cent of the world's students – 1.6 billion students in over 190 countries.[23] Educational institutions closed for prolonged periods of time, ranging from a few weeks to upwards of two years.

One year into the disruption, in March 2021, approximately half of the world's student population was still affected by full or partial school closures.[24] By September 2021, 86 million children in just one region, Latin America and the Caribbean, remained unable to learn in school classrooms.[25] In late 2021 and early 2022, amid new concerns of virus outbreaks and surges, many schools that had opened, sometimes months before, were once again shutting their doors in an attempt to mitigate the spread of disease, although not with the uniformity and extended durations that marked the experiences of 2020 and early 2021. Decisions about whether to close schools because of concerns about COVID-19 and for how long were deeply fraught – among the most factious of the pandemic – and resulted in abrupt policy shifts, with students sometimes returning to school only to be sent home again.

When the pandemic passed its two-year mark in March 2022, hundreds of millions of children, youth and adults continued to face significant and ongoing interruptions to their education. Full or partial school closures remained a reality in some communities deep into 2022 and, on rare occasion, stretched into early 2023.

As the pandemic passed the three-year mark in March 2023, widespread school closures were, at last, fully in the rear-view mirror. In May 2023, the WHO declared that COVID-19 was no longer a global health emergency.[26] While future school closures due to the pandemic appear unlikely in the short term, this does not change the fact that for learners and teachers in countries around the world reliance on ed-tech for participation in formal education had been a day-to-day reality for significant stretches from early 2020 to early 2023.

The total tally of in-person schooldays lost to the COVID-19 pandemic is without precedent. At the end of 2021, UNESCO estimated that, globally, over 50 per cent of school instructional time had been lost since the beginning of the pandemic.[27] At the end of February 2022 (the cut-off date of global tracking), UNESCO estimated that students had missed a global average of slightly over 20 weeks of school-based education due to full school closures and a similar amount of time because of partial school closures. A typical student experienced major disruptions to schooling, whether intermittent or continuous, for ten months cumulatively between the onset of the crisis and early 2022.

> The COVID-19 disruption to schooling and the failure or insufficiencies of ed-tech to provide alternatives translated into some students missing a sixth or more of their lifetime education.

During the pandemic, students made dramatically less academic progress than would have been expected without school closures. This 'lost' education – along with the wider socio-emotional tolls of the pandemic – carried individual, familial, social and economic consequences, especially in contexts where the average years of school completion are already low. In countries where learners typically complete only a few years of formal education, the COVID-19 disruption to schooling and the failure or insufficiencies of ed-tech to provide alternatives translated into some students missing a sixth or more of their lifetime education.[28] This missed schooling is expected to reverberate for years, both personally for individuals and at the level of countries. In late 2021, the World Bank projected the global financial cost in decreased lifetime earnings due to learning loss for the COVID-19 lockdown generation to be as high as USD 17 trillion, or 14 per cent of global gross domestic product (GDP).[29] This figure was revised upwards to USD 21 trillion or 17 per cent of global GDP in June 2022 as the severity of the pandemic disruptions to education and the insufficiencies of ed-tech to fill the gap became more apparent.[30] While these financial projections should be treated with caution, they help to highlight the scale of the educational chasms that cracked open during the pandemic.

While 2023 brought a definitive end to COVID-19 school closures and intensive or singular reliance on ed-tech to provision formal education remotely, a prolonged respite from a pandemic is not guaranteed. The emergence of dangerous new viruses, including ones that might present unique dangers to children and youth, remain a risk. In July 2022, the WHO declared the Monkeypox virus (later designated Mpox) a "public health emergency of international concern".[31] It joined only two other diseases, COVID-19 and polio, to receive this alarming designation, reminding the world anew that novel diseases are likely to continue plaguing humanity into the future. Future global shocks and disruptions to education, while historically very rare, cannot be discounted.

A NETFLIX MOMENT FOR COMMERCIAL ED-TECH

With a speed that few had anticipated, technology, rather than schools, became the primary interface for education.

The massive uptake of educational technologies that could be used outside of schools was anchored in a hard truth about disease transmission: strictly speaking, people are biohazards and technology used in isolation is not. So while schools were forced to close because they put large numbers of children and adults in close physical proximity, learners were asked to use technology because it accommodated social distancing and stay-at-home directives. As technology-mediated education replaced face-to-face learning in schools as the locus of formal education, technology use was widely mandated by governments in line with commitments to make education compulsory. Even families that had no previous experience with ed-tech or saw it as purely peripheral to school-based education commonly operated under the assumption that they needed to secure and use technology for educational purposes. With a speed that few had anticipated, technology, rather than schools, became the primary interface for education.

Unsurprisingly, these changes resulted in an enormous uptake of ed-tech – and an overnight boom for the ed-tech industry, a constellation of mostly private companies. In March and April 2020, international business newspapers, including the *Wall Street Journal* and the *Financial Times*, were awash with headlines such as "Ed-tech start-ups and investors shift into overdrive amid coronavirus crisis",[32] "Education is having its 'Netflix' moment as a result of the coronavirus pandemic"[33] and "Coronavirus proves a bonanza for ed-tech start-ups".[34] The mobile data and analytics company App Annie observed that compared with the weekly averages in the fourth quarter of 2019, global downloads of education-related mobile apps grew by nearly 100 per cent in March 2020 – the same month the WHO declared the COVID-19 outbreak a pandemic.[35] Many online and distance learning utilities, a large number of them offered by for-profit companies, saw their user bases double, triple, quadruple, quintuple and even sextuple in the early weeks and months of the pandemic.[36] Google, for example, reported in February 2021 that the number of people using Google Classroom, an online platform to support teaching and learning, had grown from 40 million to 150 million in the previous year.[37] Whereas it had taken Google Classroom over five years (between mid-2014 and early 2020) to achieve a user base of 40 million, this user base swelled over threefold in the first 12 months of the pandemic. This growth continued into the second and third year of the pandemic. Newspaper articles with titles such as "Ed tech use continues beyond the peak of the pandemic" cropped up frequently in late 2021 and into 2022.[38] The unprecedented nature of these spikes led leaders of commercial businesses providing online education services to marvel at the good fortune of vertical growth.[39]

"The Coronavirus pandemic ... planted the seeds of a new type of learning model for coming decades – one that will be very different from that which has been operating largely unchanged for thousands of years."

– James Gifford and Kirill Pyshkin, senior fund managers, Credit Suisse[viii]

The rush to distance and remote learning with ed-tech accelerated the privatization of education.

Throughout the review that follows, considerable evidence illustrates how the rush to distance and remote learning with ed-tech accelerated the privatization of education. While some countries and localities managed a shift to digital learning with limited privatization of the educational experience, a defining characteristic of the technology-centric responses to the pandemic tended to be the elevation of for-profit, private ed-tech companies. In addition to considering the ways reliance on ed-tech impacted educational inclusion, equity and quality, this publication also explores the complex and often symbiotic links between ed-tech and private sector companies.

Act 1

THE HOPE OF

TECH SALVATION

In response to the cascade of school closures ordered to mitigate the transmission of COVID-19 starting in early 2020, many governments elevated technology, particularly high-tech solutions reliant on internet-connected devices, as the primary – and, in some contexts, only – channel to maintain the continuity of formal education. While this was done to provide a substitute for established school-based education, the shift was also driven by deeper and older currents of technology solutionism.

Prior to the pandemic, a number of influential groups and thinkers, many from outside education, argued that connected technologies could provide superior foundations for education than schools. This view was contested, and vigorous debates played out about the appropriate role of technology in teaching and learning. But as connected technology became more powerful and ubiquitous, its promise seemed to grow ever brighter. By the late 2010s, views that the moment was right for a full-fledged educational transformation with digital technologies at the core had become widespread and carried a sense of inevitability. For many, it was less a matter of *whether* technology would deeply disrupt education and perhaps make schools obsolete, than of *when* this would occur.

With these ideas in wide circulation at the outset of the COVID-19 pandemic, resources were rapidly directed towards efforts to establish computers and online spaces as the principal hubs of learning, rather than brick-and-mortar classrooms. Ed-tech became the de facto replacement for schools with dizzying speed. Consultation and debate were largely bypassed in the context of the health emergency. In countries where digital networks and hardware were largely unavailable, lower-tech solutions using television and radio broadcasts often accompanied the ever-present high-tech strategies. At the peak of the pandemic, well over 1 billion students were expected to rely on technology solutions to continue their education.[40]

Many tragedies, in the literary sense, begin with presumption, grand ambition and even hubris, and these elements were abundant during the initial phase of the transition to ed-tech and fully remote learning. People had high expectations for the educational possibilities of technology when news of a novel coronavirus reached the world.

Reformatting schools with technology

"It is possible to teach every branch of human knowledge with the motion picture. Our school system will be completely changed inside of ten years [from 1913 to 1923]."

– Thomas Edison, inventor[ix]

The idea that technology might, could, should or invariably would replace schools as the primary interface for education has deep roots. In the modern era, education historians have traced predictions of the end of school-based teaching and learning as far back as the widespread availability of radios.[41] As Audrey Watters traces in her book *Teaching Machines*, a long list of technological breakthroughs, whether televisions, various iterations of computers or, more recently, the mobile internet, artificial intelligence (AI) and metaverses, have been held up as final and exultant forms for education.[42] As far back as 1913, Thomas Edison stated that his new motion picture machine would make books and schools "obsolete". He insisted that "scholars will soon be instructed through the eye" and maintained these predictions throughout his life even as they consistently failed to come true.[43]

The advent of personal computers followed by the internet and inexpensive mobile devices made visions of school-free education particularly palpable – as did technological transformations in business and other fields, including those long-dependent on physical locations and associated with education, such as libraries and bookstores. As Watters explains, the idea that affordable and connected computers would usher in an educational utopia of personalized learning guided by intelligent machines and unbound by schools carried considerable cultural and political sway prior to 2020. Parents and policy-makers alike tended to see digital classrooms as "imminent" and computational futures for teaching and learning as "inescapable", if not desirable.[44]

Upon close inspection, the uniformity of the global pivot to ed-tech as a response to the educational disruption of the pandemic can be traced to ideas that had been in the popular imagination for at least a century. They gathered considerable speed and momentum in the digital age.

"There is a certain inevitability to the way in which education technology is pitched and packaged. One has no choice but to accept that schooling – and society at large – will become more technological, more 'data-fied,' more computerized, more automated. Resistance to this fate has kept education chained to its moribund methods, so we're told."

– Audrey Watters, author of *Teaching Machines*[k]

THE PROTEUS OF MACHINES AND A NEW EDIFICE FOR EDUCATION

Computers, the thinking went, would finally and fully unchain learning from schools, which were assumed to be oppressive.

As demonstrated by Morgan Ames in her book *The Charisma Machine*, by the early 1980s computers were starting to move from businesses into family homes in wealthy countries, prompting reflection on what these powerful tools might mean for – and do to – education.[45] Thinkers such as Seymour Papert, a professor who went on to help establish the MIT Media Lab, trumpeted the ascent of "a new kind of learning environment", one that "demands free contact between children and computers".[46] Papert, and many after him, argued that computers were fundamentally different from technologies that had come before. For Papert, computers were the "Proteus of machines", a reference to a sea god from Greek mythology who possessed prodigious strength, flexibility and adaptability and who could predict the future. These superhuman devices, Papert argued, would finally and fully unchain learning from schools that were, in his view, oppressive. With the rapidly expanding diffusion of personal computers, Papert said, it was "inconceivable" that traditional schools would continue as locations where young people of similar ages learn with professional teachers in classes segregated by age and academic subject.[47]

This strand of thought has, in fits and starts, continued largely unabated. It has also won over legions of believers – people convinced that education must be remade in a world more and more awash in powerful and connected technology. The idea gave rise to One Laptop per Child (OLPC) in the early 2000s, perhaps the best-known multi-country initiative that aimed to disrupt traditional learning models with computer technology, including in developing countries. OLPC was rooted in the idea that computers would enhance education and help unhinge it from schooling models that were understood to be constraining for students and of low quality. The OLPC initiative was launched by Nicolas Negroponte, who had studied under Papert.

"Schools and universities today would be recognised by our forebears in the year 1600. This will be swept away by an AI education revolution. Barely a single facet of this education model will remain unchanged."

– Anthony Seldon and Oladimeji Abidoye, authors of *The Fourth Education Revolution*[xi]

OLPC and similar efforts to elevate computers as a favoured medium for education exchange were fuelled by best-selling books. One example in this genre was *Disrupting Class: How Disruptive Innovation Will Change the Way the World Learns*. Published in 2008, it announced that by 2019 half of primary and secondary school classes would be displaced by online options that "will be one-third of today's costs, and the courses will be much better".[48] The *New York Times* declared 2012 "the year of the MOOC" (massive open online course), calling attention to claims that "free [online] courses can bring the best education in the world to the most remote corners of the planet, help people in their careers and expand intellectual and personal networks".[49] These ideas continued to gain currency – and in the case of Rwanda, were literally printed on currency. The Rwandan 500 franc note, worth about USD 0.50 and among the most widely used paper bills for day-to-day cash transactions, pictures three young students in school uniforms working individually on laptops. The laptops appear to be XO devices, distinctly shaped machines developed specifically for the OLPC initiative and a staple of early OLPC hardware deployments in Rwanda and other countries. As education historians Larry Cuban and David Tyack observed in the late 1990s, education leaders "impatient with the glacial pace of incremental reform, free of institutional memories of past shooting-star reforms and sometimes hoping for quick profits as well as a quick fix" will reliably look to technology as the best route to fix or reinvent education.[50] The pull of technology solutionism was strong indeed. Media, governments, celebrities, salespeople and even money itself carried a message that connected computers could solve long-standing educational problems and unleash a learning revolution.

Figure 1:

Rwanda's 500 franc note shows schoolchildren learning with laptop computers

Source: CoinsWeekly, 2019

Beyond fuelling expectations of massive educational transformations, technology has also long been offered as a remedy for crises – educational or otherwise.

Beyond fuelling expectations of massive educational transformations, technology has also long been offered as a remedy for crises – educational or otherwise. Thomas Mullaney in *Your Computer Is on Fire* (2021) highlighted how "a chorus of techno-utopian voices" will predictably announce that there is always a way to "code" people out of dilemmas with minimal inconvenience.[51] Education regularly, even if perhaps more cautiously than other sectors, embraced this outlook. For at least the past two decades, educational responses to calamities, whether natural disasters or human conflict, have often been accompanied by – or in some instances, shaped by – a flurry of technology initiatives to keep learners connected to education through screens. Initiatives to assure education for refugees, for instance, are often heavily reliant on technology, and some of UNESCO's own work has highlighted the ways connected digital devices can support displaced and vulnerable learners.[52]

Closely linked to these technology-centric views is a belief, popular well before the pandemic, that schools are deeply flawed institutions, relics of an earlier era that stubbornly resist modernity. Ames's research, for instance, reveals the power and pervasiveness of the social imagery that schools are outdated and dehumanizing factories, a theme regularly evoked in popular culture and academic literature alike. The school as a factory metaphor can be traced all the way back to the early stages of the industrial revolution, which saw the rise of philanthropic schools provided by factory owners.[53] More recent associations, especially since the 1990s, often draw a straight line between technology and reforms to educational organization and

> Tinkering and iterative improvement would not suffice. The right path to change was to uproot flawed learning paradigms and grow them anew around internet-connected and AI-enabled technologies.

curricula, resting on beliefs that technology should transform education in bold and disruptive ways.[54] The overall thinking holds that tinkering and iterative improvement do not suffice. The right path to change, according to this view, is to uproot flawed learning paradigms and grow them anew, less around buildings, classrooms and teachers – the old edifice – and more around efficient and powerful internet-connected and, more recently, AI-enabled technologies – the new edifice.

"We believe nothing if not that history is moving us toward some preordained paradise and that technology is the force behind that movement."

– Neil Postman, educator, media theorist and cultural critic[xii]

By the early 2000s, this new edifice was often positioned as having special relevance in underprivileged communities, whether in the global North or the global South. Various groups, intrigued by Papert's ideas of emancipation and Negroponte's vision of large-scale transformation with OLPC, started to view technology as offering a superior backbone for formal learning, not necessarily in places where school-based education was healthy, but rather in places where traditional schooling models were assumed to be broken beyond repair or had never functioned properly. Although UNESCO and other organizations insisted that technology should complement, enrich and extend school-based education rather than seek to replace it, many remained convinced that ed-tech, even in isolation, could dramatically enhance educational opportunities and outcomes. This had the added benefit of sidestepping expensive and time-consuming investments in teacher training; improvements to the physical infrastructure of schools; and difficult-to-implement changes to the organization, processes and culture of traditional education systems. Technology offered the promise of fast, here-and-now fixes to vexing problems that plagued many schools and school systems.

While the wisdom and value of parachuting ed-tech to learners to bypass school 'failure' was hotly debated, it had many advocates, particularly in the technology sector, which was growing rapidly and exercising considerable economic, cultural and political power. By the 2010s, connected technology was widely perceived as a 'commonsense' tool to provide good-quality learning opportunities in places where schools struggled to do so. It was not unusual for development organizations to bring connected technology to far-flung and extremely under-resourced areas where educational and other social needs were immense. Various advances made it possible to bring internet connectivity and devices, such as smartphones or tablets, to almost any location, no matter how remote and regardless of the condition or even the existence of physical schools. Sometimes projects went ahead even in areas where electricity was scarce. This work was predicated on assumptions that teachers and students would use fuel-powered generators, solar panels or other means to charge devices. The condition of health and transportation services did not factor into the mix, nor did the state of playgrounds, toilets, desks, chalkboards, laboratories, libraries and other physical infrastructure found in schools. Technology, it was thought, was the best investment to provide underprivileged learners with a fair shot at education – and in a hurry.

ALL IT TAKES IS A HOLE IN THE WALL

Sugata Mitra's famous 1999 'hole-in-the-wall' experiment was one of many that lent an air of scientific legitimacy to ideas that young people, including very disadvantaged learners, could make remarkable educational progress with nothing more than a computer. The experiment – and the powerful imagery and hope it evoked – helped normalize ideas that computers might provide a backbone for education superior to traditional teacher-led schools.

For the experiment, Mitra, an Indian academic with training in physics, put a freely accessible personal computer with a Microsoft Windows operating system in the niche of a wall separating his university in New Delhi from an adjoining slum. His team observed how children from the slum, presumably with no prior computer experience, used the technology. A short time later, Mitra announced breathless results: with minimal intervention from adults, children were using the computer to teach themselves languages, improve

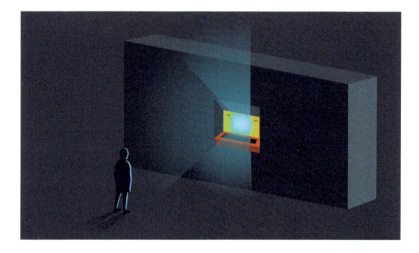

Mitra announced breathless results: with minimal intervention from adults, children were using the computer to teach themselves languages, improve their knowledge of mathematics and science, form independent opinions, and develop strong digital skills.

their knowledge of mathematics and science, form independent opinions and develop strong digital skills, among other achievements.[55] "In nine months, a group of children left alone with a computer in any language will reach the same standard as an office secretary in the West", he declared.[56] Mitra coined his hole-in-the-wall approach a "minimally invasive approach to learning". The unsubtle reference to surgery was likely intentional. In medical terms, 'minimally invasive' refers to a surgical operation performed through very small incisions to lessen damage to the body.[57] Applied to education, the term suggested that the heavier formal structures of learning – schools, teachers, regimented schedules, disciplinary boundaries and so forth – were the 'invasive' approach to learning, an apparatus that could get in the way and could do harm. The computer, by contrast, allowed students to learn freely, uninhibited and 'uninvaded'.

Encouraged by Mitra's claims, a cooperative venture with backing from the World Bank began setting up unsupervised 'learning stations' in underprivileged sections of New Delhi and other communities.[58] Mitra quickly built a personal brand as well as a company, Hole-in-the-Wall Education Ltd, around the promise of frictionless learning with technology. In short order, hole-in-the-wall-style learning stations began popping up around the world, in Cambodia, Uganda and beyond.[59] Notably, Mitra and Negroponte (of OLPC fame) were ideological allies, and Negroponte wrote the foreword to one of Mitra's early books about the potential of computers to "power self-organized learning" that would "make kids smarter and more creative".[60]

"This idea [minimally invasive education] has captured the world's imagination and triggered a romance which tells of learning free from the restrictions of formal schooling and children liberated through self-learning."

– Payal Arora, professor of technology and media, Erasmus University Rotterdam[xiii]

The hole-in-the-wall experiment contained compelling narratives about innovation, the ingenuity and curiosity of children and the human ability to heal long-standing inequities with simple technological solutions.

As news spread of the hole-in-the-wall experiment, it was greeted with praise and excitement: it contained compelling narratives about innovation, the ingenuity and curiosity of children and the human ability to heal long-standing inequities with simple technological solutions. Vikas Swarup, the author of the book that became the basis for the Academy Award-winning film *Slumdog Millionaire*, said descriptions of Mitra's research helped inspire his rags-to-riches novel and reminded him that there is "an innate ability in everyone to do something extraordinary, provided they are given an opportunity".[61] *The Guardian* newspaper later labelled Mitra the "Slumdog professor" – the man who brought computers to the poorest communities in the world with an unwavering faith that they could – and indeed would – nurture the learning of young people, without the heavy-handed and curiosity-depleting practices of formal schooling.[62]

With the growing availability of the internet, Mitra's claims grew steadily bolder: kids from anywhere and any background could figure out complex subjects such as DNA sequencing, trigonometry and avionics without curriculum, professional teachers, schools or other traditional components of school-based education.[63] All that was needed was a connected computer and occasional encouragement from adults. Without irony, Mitra advocated recruiting "Grans" – a shorthand for 'grandmothers' or retired teachers – for this unspecialized work of encouragement: "If there's a child in trouble, we beam in a Gran … she sorts things out."[64] A 2009 paper he published titled "Remote presence: Technologies for 'beaming' teachers where they cannot go" describes, with considerable specificity, how a synchronous distance learning platform could work, foreshadowing practices that would be taken up, with slight modifications, over a decade later on a global scale during the COVID-19 pandemic.[65]

In addition to computers and 'Grans', Mitra's vision of education was dependent on the advantages of student communication and peer teaching. Unlike many of his contemporary ed-tech proponents, Mitra held that children should learn with connected technology in groups rather than individually. His initial experiment saw multiple children using a single device. Despite problems noted by other researchers, such as the tendency of boys and older children to crowd out peers and dominate control of scarce technology without adult guidance and intervention, he considered the child-to-child collaboration with technology essential to the success of his 'minimally invasive' learning model. But as the prices of connected technology dropped during the 2010s, learning approaches reliant on groups of children collaborating with technology were largely pushed aside in favour of one-student-to-one-device paradigms, which were promoted and normalized by Negroponte's OLPC work and other initiatives. It was easy for people to skim over Mitra's descriptions of student communication and peer teaching and focus instead on his enthusiasm for technology. The 'hole in the wall' was occupied by a computer after all, not other learners.

"It's quite fashionable to say that the education system's broken. It's not broken. It's wonderfully constructed. It's just that we don't need it anymore. It's outdated."
– Sugata Mitra, education researcher[xiv]

In 2010, Mitra delivered a presentation entitled "The child-driven education" at a TED (Technology, Entertainment, Design) conference.[66] The talk was uploaded to the TED Talks website, a then three-year-old media platform that promised to share "ideas worth spreading" in the form of short, video-recorded talks of 18 minutes or less. The platform was quickly rising to global prominence thanks to a carefully curated library of talks from TED conferences. The exposure brought global attention to Mitra and his ideas about the emancipatory educational potential of technology – ideas that had previously circulated in relatively obscure conference papers and specialized academic journals. Many of the videos that helped fuel the popularity of TED Talks were about education and delivered by speakers from technology backgrounds who were enthusiastic about ed-tech and critical of traditional schools. The most watched TED Talk ever given is titled "Do schools kill creativity?"[67] Delivered in 2006 by Ken Robinson, a British author with leadership positions in arts education, it had been viewed over 74 million times by the end of 2022.[68] While Robinson's video contained reasoned critiques of school-based education, its title – and those of his later TED Talks, including "How to escape education's death valley", delivered as part of the 2013 TED Talks Education series – evoked messages of school failure and drove ideas that schools were oppressive and conformist institutions in need of "revolution".[69] Like Robinson, Negroponte was also regularly featured by TED Talks and used the platform to provide reassuring updates on his OLPC programme.

Mitra's various TED Talk videos had been viewed over 9 million times by the end of 2022, giving them a reach that far exceeds the readership of popular writing about education and makes the subscriber bases of the best-known education journals look minuscule.[70] Mitra also features prominently on the TED platform. When a TED user searches the word 'education', the first of 3,845 results is a playlist of Sugata Mitra's five favourite education talks, which includes Robinson's megahit "Do schools kill creativity?" along with other talks advocating for child-driven learning approaches, often with a technology tilt, such as "Kids take charge" and "My wish: Find the next Einstein in Africa".[71]

> Schools, the thinking went, subverted learning by imposing rigid and constraining hierarchies; they suffocated rather than facilitated education. The key was to take the school away and replace it with a connected computer that could power self-organized and self-motivated learning.

In 2013, Mitra delivered his third TED Talk, entitled "Build a school in the cloud". It opened with a punchier premise than his earlier TED Talks: a takedown of schools. "Schools as we know them now, they're obsolete," he said. A holder of a Ph.D. and a long-time university educator, he waved off primary and secondary schools as factories producing "identical people" who could become cogs in the "bureaucratic administrative machine" that powers the modern state. He advocated instead for "Self-Organized Learning Environments ... basically broadband, collaboration and encouragement put together". In Mitra's view, learning emerges when the educational process is self-organized. Schools, he held, subvert learning by imposing organization through rigid and constraining hierarchies; they suffocate rather than facilitate education. The key, in his mind, was to take the school away and replace it with a connected computer that could power self-organized and self-motivated learning. The teacher or grandma facilitator – the role was interchangeable – needed only to pose good questions, provide encouragement and then "stand back in awe and watch" as children progressed.[72]

Mitra won a TED award of USD 1 million for his "Build a school in the cloud" talk. The award propelled Mitra and his ideas to greater fame, often with a boost from TED itself. The young organization awarded a grant of USD 125,000 to British film-maker Jerry Rothwell to make a documentary about Mitra and his ideas.[73] The trailer for the finished film, released in 2018, features Mitra's voice playing over images of overcrowded classrooms and bored students: "What is the future of learning? Could it be that we don't need to go to school at all?" He answers these questions with another question: "Could it be that the point in time when you need to know something, you can find out in two minutes?" With music rising to a crescendo, the trailer shows people carrying computer equipment to remote villages in India and enthusiastic children crowded around screens, conducting internet searches and – the viewer is led to assume – learning. As the trailer reaches its climatic moment, Mitra's voice-over says, "If children are allowed to wonder in a chaotic fashion, they will crystalize around big ideas. And at the edge of chaos, everything happens." The video shows rapid clips of internet searches: "What is electricity?", "Why do birds sing?", "Who invented the internet?"[74] The unambiguous message is that spontaneous, messy and "chaotic" learning with connected technology is the richest and deepest type of learning, and one that avoids the oppressive controls of formal schooling. In addition to a film, Mitra's "Build a school in the cloud" TED Talk became the basis for a book of the same title, which argues that "children in groups – when given access to the internet – can learn anything by themselves". Published just a few months before the pandemic, it promised to help readers "glimpse the emerging future of learning with technology".[75] The book's cover features a pencil represented by futuristic and interconnected nodes, evoking connected technology.

"Factories weren't designed to support personalization. Neither were schools. . . . It's time to unhinge ourselves from many of the assumptions that undergird how we deliver instruction and begin to design new models that are better able to leverage talent, time and technology to best meet the unique needs of each student."

– Joel Rose, technology and education entrepreneur[iv]

THE STAGE IS SET FOR ED-TECH

Even the contemporary language of school reform, with its calls to 'update', 'recode', 'rewire' and 'reformat' traditional educational processes, had adopted the lexicon of technology and computing.

With these ideas in mainstream circulation by 2020, the stage was set for ed-tech. Pandemic or no pandemic, people inside and outside the education field viewed technology as uniquely ready to improve and transform education. It was understood as the go-to engine to drag schools out of the conveyor belt logic of industrialization and into the newer, networked logics of the 'information age', the 'knowledge economy' and the 'Fourth Industrial Revolution'. Even the contemporary language of school reform, with its calls to 'update', 'recode', 'rewire' and 'reformat' traditional educational processes, had adopted the lexicon of technology and computing. Finally – and crucially – technology was widely perceived as a first-option solution to education crises.

Not everyone in the education community enthusiastically adhered to this optimistic view of the revolutionary power of technology for learning. Work by scholars pointed out how the metaphor of school as a factory can be "misleading or hyperbolic or superannuated"[76] and how it is often used in calculated ways in emergency contexts to advance commercial technology interests. However, these warnings were generally ignored, as were more specific attempts to question whether ed-tech was really achieving the strong educational results its boosters claimed. Anthropologist Payal Arora, for example, visited two sites in India where hole-in-the-wall learning kiosks had been set up and used by children. She discovered that despite significant investments of resources, the kiosks had "ground to a halt" and seemed to have "barely touched the community". Only two years after the project's implementation, she was surprised to discover that there was almost no "community memory of it". Arora also flagged "the absence of independent empirical research" to confirm claims that hole-in-the-wall kiosks were leading to measurable educational gains, a condition that was not uncommon among ed-tech field projects.[77] The few education researchers who visited active hole-in-the-wall kiosks were unimpressed and found little to suggest that they were facilitating meaningful and sustained learning. After observing children using the kiosks in New Delhi and speaking to parents in the community, education scholar Mark Warschauer concluded that a more accurate term for Mitra's technology-centric model of 'minimally invasive education' was, in practice, "minimally effective education".[78] He strongly criticized the hole-in-the-wall project and others like it for disregarding the human and social systems where technology was deployed.

"In India, as elsewhere, scarcely a day goes by without another story in a newspaper or journal about a successful IT project that is bringing benefits to ordinary people. No state in the Indian union is without a plan for bringing ICT to the masses; every major NGO has its IT projects. … But unfortunately, the hopes so widely expressed are built almost entirely on an empirical vacuum."

- Kenneth Keniston, professor of human development, Massachusetts Institute of Technology[xvi]

Perhaps the most rigorous investigation of the hole-in-the-wall project was undertaken by Frank van Cappelle in 2003 and 2005. He spent six months in India conducting field research in the villages where some of the kiosks were located – observing the use of kiosk computers; speaking to children, parents and teachers; and studying screenshots taken at 10-minute intervals, among other modes of research. His central finding was that the kiosks, which were almost always set up in unsupervised public spaces, replicated existing inequalities in the community across dividing lines of caste, gender, socio-economic status and age. The kiosks he studied most closely were dominated by social networks from privileged in-groups and were largely off-limits to networks of children from out-groups. The main users of the computers were generally older (12 years old and above), wealthier, digitally literate and male. Some of them had alternative access to computer technology and thus pre-existing digital skills. Less advantaged children did occasionally use the kiosks, but because they were infrequent users, they never developed the same level of skills. For them the computers were more of a toy than a tool. Van Cappelle further noticed that when the hole-in-the-wall computers were connected to the internet, they were used almost exclusively for entertainment. The children who used the kiosks to access the pre-installed educational games and content did so only when there was no alternative content.[79]

According to van Cappelle, regular users of the kiosks did pick up some basic digital literacy skills, such as navigating an operating system with a mouse, dragging and dropping digital objects, using Google to perform internet searches, drawing in simple programs like Microsoft Paint, and typing their names (an activity that was particularly popular). The children who spent the most time at the kiosks also appeared to develop confidence in their use of computers. Additionally, when children spent time at the kiosks in groups, as they often did, they interacted, communicated and collaborated, as they did in other settings.[80] But these flashes of positive findings did not at all corroborate the impressive educational gains touted by Mitra. Van Cappelle observed little to suggest that users of the kiosks were making meaningful or sustained gains in literacy and numeracy or other areas of education – even if they did sometimes acquire or strengthen rudimentary digital skills. His main takeaway was that the kiosks mirrored – and indeed could inflame – existing social inequalities, a finding that formed the basis for the title of the research: "The darker side of the digital divide". He concluded that it is "very possible and even likely" that hole-in-the-wall kiosks and similar ICT initiatives seeking to narrow digital and educational divides would "inadvertently widen them" without careful planning, implementation and oversight.[81]

> Number one in the list of 'worst practices' for ed-tech was dumping hardware in schools and hoping for magic to happen.

The educational limitations of projects to parachute technology to disadvantaged communities extended to initiatives like OLPC that placed ed-tech in disadvantaged schools, usually in developing countries. Concrete evidence of improved learning achievement after large, expensive and logistically complex OLPC laptop deployments were frustratingly elusive. A rare independent evaluation of an OLPC implementation in Peru, for example, found no evidence of increased learning in mathematics or language.[82] But rigorous evaluations of OLPC rollouts in other countries were hard to find,[83] suggesting to some that the implementations only had weak indicators of improved learning results or perhaps none. Michael Trucano, the lead ICT and education specialist for the World Bank, suggested that the dearth of conclusive impact assessments of ed-tech initiatives was connected to a reality that has "frustrated many people in the educational technology community for a long time": namely, that "long term, sustained positive change (in the education sector, if not more broadly), whether as a result of an explicit reform process or slower, evolutionary changes in behaviour, typically does not happen as the result of a single discrete intervention," such as the addition of technology.[84] In other words, simply layering technology on education was unlikely to meaningfully improve it. Trucano found it necessary to repeat this message frequently. In 2010, he rated as number one on his list of worst ed-tech practices, "Dump hardware in schools, hope for magic to happen",[85] a position this 'worst practice' retained throughout the decade. Larry Cuban, a Stanford University historian of education and a long-time sceptic of technology fixes for education, lamented, like Trucano, that there seemed to be "no end to magical thinking when it comes to high-tech schooling".[86]

Yet despite these cautionary voices, many people – mesmerized by the growing power and ubiquity of connected technology – rested firm in their conviction that transformational educational changes were just around the corner. They often pointed to the inside-out technology disruptions observed in other sectors (e.g. media, commerce and finance) as evidence. Warnings that education was unique and not easily compared to the business models of newspapers, retail businesses or banks were easily overrun by the hope that new technology might be able to catalyse learning with greater ease, lower cost and fewer school and teacher interventions, while at the same time facilitating more educational freedom and superior academic achievement. By the time a novel virus began spreading around the world in early 2020, ed-tech was broadly accepted – even if not necessarily by people closest to education – as a commonsense tool to transform education for the better. It was *the* tool at hand, and people believed in it fervently.

"There is just one problem with the 'disruptive innovation' theory: It doesn't work. … Time and again, strategies that depend on disruption have failed our students."
– David Kirp, Marjorie Wechsler, Madelyn Gardner and Titilayo Tinubu Ali, authors of *Disrupting Disruption*[xvii]

Cut the red tape and catapult education to a better future

Given the long history of technology solutionism in education, it is unsurprising that the onset of the pandemic was met with optimism about ed-tech and the possibility of swift digital transformations in education. Many in the education community saw the shift to technology-mediated distance learning as a forced acceleration of existing plans to reimagine the how, what and where – and sometimes even the why – of learning, drawing on lessons from past experiments with ed-tech. In this way, the recourse to technology was seen less as a short-term mitigation strategy than as the beginnings of a tectonic educational shift that would position technology more squarely at the centre of the education experience rather than schools. UNESCO, as a global leader in promoting education for all, also noted the importance of connected technology playing a supportive role in the educational response to the pandemic, but it kept as a first imperative the reopening of physical schools and regularly affirmed the importance of keeping teachers and the human dimensions of learning at the centre of education, even when conducted remotely.[87]

> Many felt the time was right to implement bolder changes than would have been possible or permissible absent the emergency context and usher in a more modern era of education.

Early in the crisis, many organizations and individuals, including prominent education thinkers, declared the embrace of technology as a "great moment" for learning and predicted that technological solutions would finally be deployed at scales that had been persistently difficult to achieve.[88] 'Necessity is the mother of invention' and 'never waste a crisis' were common refrains. There was a sense that long-awaited tech-powered transformations such as personalized learning would finally come to pass. The pandemic provided a "unique opportunity" for teachers and educators to catch the "digital wave".[89] Many felt the time was right to implement bolder changes than would have been possible or permissible were it not for the emergency context, with a goal to usher in a more modern era of education. Organizations and individuals routinely expressed a belief that the pandemic had finally pushed the tech genie out of the bottle and that learning would be disentangled from the often inconvenient strictures and head-spinning inefficiencies of traditional schooling. There were countless affirmations that post-pandemic 'normal' would not be pre-pandemic 'normal'. Some education ministers mirrored this sentiment during UNESCO-organized meetings in March and April 2020, stating that their countries were quickly learning how to scale up and ensure lasting impact with ed-tech. These education leaders claimed that they would not look back to pre-pandemic models of education when the crisis abated but rather forge ahead with disruptive digital transformations. Google announced that education was indeed, as it had declared as early as 2018, "evolving at a faster pace than any other period in recent history"[90] thanks to the unreserved embrace of technology.

"Only a crisis – actual or perceived – produces real change. When that crisis occurs, the actions that are taken depend on the ideas that are lying around."

– Milton Friedman, economist[xviii]

Much of the media latched onto this theme of digital renewal. Headlines such as "Like it or not, K-12 schools are doing a digital leapfrog during COVID-19"[91] and "Remote learning shows the power of the cloud to transform education"[92] were typical in 2020 and continued to appear in 2021, 2022 and 2023. Some surveys suggested that these refrains were, at least initially, being echoed by the public as well. A Harris Poll survey commissioned by Pearson and completed by over 7,000 respondents from various countries in June 2020 inferred, for example, that "COVID-19 is the catalyst for modernizing education", based on affirmative answers respondents gave to questions such as "Thinking about the future state of primary and secondary/higher education, to what extent do you agree that [education] will fundamentally change because of the COVID-19 pandemic?"[93] However, this survey and others like it were completed voluntarily by people via an online platform, introducing a selection bias that likely skewed results to show a stronger positive reception to technology-first educational transformations than a random-sample telephone or door-to-door survey would have done. The way questions were phrased also tended to nudge respondents to provide answers that signalled enthusiasm for ed-tech. Commonly, the questions rather than the respondents themselves introduced concepts, such as a coming digital transformation of education, that reflected a tilt towards technology.

While different technologies were quickly deployed to facilitate distance learning during school closures, ranging from simple radios to high-tech laptops and tablet computers, governments tended to focus most of their efforts on connected digital technologies. The perceived benefits of internet-based strategies vis-à-vis radio and television alternatives were assumed to be considerable, as connected digital technologies allowed for the possibility of real-time communication, gamified learning, personalized education pathways and teacher feedback, among other advantages. Embracing digital technology was also seen as forward-looking, whereas reliance on older, if more widely owned, technologies like televisions was often interpreted as backward looking. Many governments – often encouraged by international organizations – chose to invest heavily in rising, future-oriented internet technologies. Countries and schools sometimes announced bleeding-edge AI, blockchain and virtual reality solutions to improve distance learning during the pandemic. They also outlined strategies to leapfrog over less advanced technologies to the most sophisticated (and expensive) forms of ed-tech – even if these technologies were very rarely used by more than a handful of teachers and students. Internationally, there was a desire to be perceived as standing at the vanguard of ed-tech, to be hitching education systems to the power and dynamism of Papert's "Proteus of machines".

Act 2
FROM PROMISES TO REALITY

The high expectations for ed-tech, pervasive at the outset of the pandemic, clouded as evidence mounted that the move from schools and classrooms to technology-mediated remote education was excluding huge numbers of learners. The assumed readiness of connected technology to carry and support education unravelled with alarming speed. Promises that ed-tech would 'save the day' and indelibly transform education collided into the challenges of implementation at scales and paces that had never been attempted in the past, let alone in the midst of a health crisis. Although many individuals, organizations, companies and educational institutions endeavoured to rise to the challenge of assuring educational continuity with new tools and from a distance, the obstacles were relentless and many of them unforeseen. Assumptions about the strengths of technology as a primary platform for education began to splinter and crack.

As the health crisis and school closures stretched on, it became increasingly apparent that technology-dependent remote learning in response to school closures was disrupting family dynamics, amplifying existing educational disparities, causing emotional and physical distress, lowering academic achievement, narrowing aims and possibilities for education, and damaging the environment. Distance learning with connected technology also began to threaten hard-won understandings of education as a human right, a public service and a common good. Models of technology-centric education further enabled new forms of surveillance and control on top of facilitating and accelerating private sector capture of public education.

Act 2 of this publication examines the adverse effects of actions and efforts to elevate connected technologies as a largely singular solution to the sweeping disruptions COVID-19 brought to education. It does this by contrasting the optimistic visions held for ed-tech against the realities of what it delivered on the ground and in practice. Borrowing the metaphor of 'tragedy', Act 2 is the drama – the evidence-based history of the technology-first responses to the immense educational challenges imposed by the pandemic. This Act further considers the far-reaching repercussions of mobilizations to make technology the main interface for teaching and learning.

Most learners were left behind

Many people believed that digital ed-tech was uniquely capable of facilitating more inclusive access to learning for all. When millions of schools around the world shut down early in the pandemic, ed-tech appeared to offer a lifeline to formal education – a solution to ensure that learning would not stop. It was the means to mitigate and prevent interruption. Ed-tech had long been positioned as a powerful set of tools to expand the reach of education, such that it might finally become universally available. Affordable connectivity and hardware in the form of smartphones, tablets and cheap laptops heralded a promise to bring high-quality education to all, to reach the unreached, and to make formal and informal learning opportunities for children and adults alike a global reality, anytime, anywhere. Many assumed ed-tech was up to the task of finally transforming teaching and learning, turning scarce and expensive educational opportunities into plentiful ones such that no one would be left behind. Where schools, universities and other location-dependent forms of education had excluded many, the new digital spaces of education would accommodate everyone. And once technology, prompted by the disruption of the pandemic, had stood in for schools at a global scale, it would prove capable of bypassing the often exclusionary gates and tolls of schools. There would be no looking back.

With education moved to interlinked digital clouds, it would float above all, always on and available for seamless access with a simple click or swipe of the finger. The future had arrived via a shock to the educational status quo.

Seen through a wide-angle lens, ed-tech's defining characteristic at the moment it was being hailed as a tool of educational resilience was less its effectiveness or lack of effectiveness, but rather its absence.

But these vivid promises of improved inclusion did not come to pass. Due to gaps in technology access, affordability and skills, efforts to actualize a shift to ed-tech to sustain education during the pandemic fell far short of what was needed to maintain the continuity of learning. This was true for hundreds of millions of students who had been attending schools. Despite attempts to pivot learning to technology, the closure of schools marked an abrupt halt to formal education for most students. Ed-tech solutions, especially in the form of internet-connected digital technologies, failed for many reasons. The most common of these, by a wide margin, traced to insurmountable barriers to access. For learners, teachers and families around the world, technology solutions for education during school closures never really started. Seen through this wide-angle lens, ed-tech's defining characteristic at the moment it was being hailed as a tool of educational resilience and transformation was less its effectiveness or lack of effectiveness, but rather its absence.

ED-TECH? WHAT ED-TECH?

In many parts of the world, accessing education via a technology portal was so uncommon and so unrealistic that many families did not even know that the option existed.

UNESCO data show that the shift to technology-dependent distance learning failed to maintain links to formal learning for a majority of students globally. This was primarily due to learners' inability to access education provisioned through the internet but also through older technologies, including television and radio. It is estimated that at least half of all students expected to access remote learning systems to continue their education were unable to do so due to technology gaps.[94] Similar divides existed for teachers. Much like students, they were also largely locked out of education when it moved over wires and waves. In many parts of the world, accessing education via a technology portal was so uncommon and so unrealistic that many families did not even know that the option existed when schools closed. A 2021 survey in Pakistan, for instance, found that only 30 per cent of households were aware of remote learning opportunities, and from this group, fewer than half had the technology needed to take advantage of these opportunities.[95] For huge numbers of people, education either continued to be school based, albeit with interruptions, or came to a complete standstill when schools closed. In countless communities and families, there was no such thing as a pivot to ed-tech-reliant learning.

"The COVID-19 crisis has underlined the connectivity chasm – the digital divide between those who are connected and those who are not."

– Lilia Burunciuc, World Bank Regional Director[xiv]

This should not have come as a particular surprise. The International Telecommunication Union (ITU), the specialized agency of the United Nations for ICT, estimated that approximately 3.7 billion people – roughly half of the world's population – lacked a functional internet connection in 2020.[96] UNICEF and ITU data show that these divides often grow larger still when children and youth are considered. Two-thirds of the world's population under the age of 25 did not have wired internet access at home as COVID-19 swept the globe.[97] Despite efforts of governments and other stakeholders, the United Nations estimated that nearly 500 million learners from pre-primary to upper secondary school had no access to remote learning, of which three-quarters belonged to the poorest households and/or lived in rural areas.[98] These connectivity deficits translated into severed educational opportunities during the pandemic.

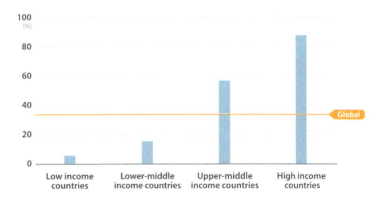

Figure 2:

Percentage of school-aged children with internet access at home, by country income group

Source: Adapted from UNICEF and ITU, 2020

Only 4 per cent of school-age children in Africa were using any form of ed-tech at the height of the pandemic.

Data from Africa helped clarify how absent ed-tech could be on the ground and in practice. The Center for Global Development (CGD) analysed the most comprehensive database of ed-tech products and initiatives serving African learners and concluded that only 19 million of 450 million school-age children on the continent (approximately 4 per cent) were using any form of ed-tech at the height of the pandemic.[99] Within this 4 per cent sliver, the vast majority of learners were linking to education not through internet-connected devices but rather through more widely available television or radio technologies. Although the total number of African students that benefited from ed-tech during the pandemic was staggeringly low, it was, nevertheless, much higher than it had been prior to the pandemic. According to CGD analysis, twice as many students were using ed-tech in the early months of 2020 when schools first closed en masse than before the pandemic. But because the initial starting point was so low, the peak number of users represented only a small fraction of the continent's large student population. While the CGD research relied on imperfect data sources, as did most regional and global estimations of ed-tech use during the crisis, its unambiguous conclusion was that ed-tech failed to reach huge numbers of learners, regardless of modality.

"I have been practically unemployed for the past four months and barely manage to pay the essential bills and for food … How can I pay for a computer, an internet bill, and a school bill while my income is zero? I have discontinued my daughter's education."

– Mother, Pakistan[xx]

This broad finding was corroborated by more methodologically rigorous telephone surveys. An NGO in Kenya, the Usawa Agenda, for instance, surveyed 3,700 heads of households in 42 of the 47 counties in the country and estimated that around 80 per cent of school-age children were not using ed-tech of any type. When accounting for children attending public schools, the percentage dropped even lower: just 10 per cent of these students were using ed-tech. Across Kenya, as in so many other developing countries, laptop, mobile phone, television and radio learning solutions never reached more than a slim minority of school-age children and youth. Practically speaking, this translated into a complete cessation of formal education for millions of learners who had been attending in-person schools prior to the pandemic. These results led the authors of the Usawa Agenda study to conclude: "We have been found unprepared. The reality check on how little our efforts to integrate ICT in education have achieved is painfully sobering."[100] It is significant that this study was limited to Kenya, which is widely considered to be among the most technology-ready countries in East Africa and has a digital infrastructure that surpasses many of its neighbours in terms of reach, quality and affordability.[101] The ed-tech access gaps were almost certainly more severe in less developed neighbouring countries, including Somalia, South Sudan and Uganda, where technology infrastructure is considerably less advanced.

Similar severe gaps were also observed in West Africa and Central Africa. A survey of over 1,000 households in Senegal, for example, found that only 11 per cent of young people were making use of ed-tech to continue their education at the height of the pandemic, and of this group, over 90 per cent were using only television or radio as a portal to learning.[102] Nationally, less than 1 per cent of students were engaged in online courses, despite the fact that Senegal, like Kenya, has better-than-average technology infrastructure relative to other countries in the region.[103] Human Rights Watch observed that many African children received no instruction, feedback or interaction from their teachers, regardless of technology platform. This dire reality was also documented in interviews with students, parents, teachers and education officials across Burkina Faso, Cameroon, the Democratic Republic of the Congo, Kenya, Madagascar, Morocco, Nigeria, South Africa and Zambia.[104]

These findings contradicted the idea that low-tech options, such as radio and television, would fill the gap when digital technology was unavailable for education. While these older technologies helped some students continue their education, they too failed to provide a sturdy bridge to formal learning. Nor were these technologies universally accessible. According to World Bank estimates, only 30 per cent of the poorest households in Africa have a working radio and just 4 per cent have a television. Less than 1 per cent of these households have a computer.[105]

Even when technology was available in households, this did not automatically mean it was available to students or even teachers. During periods of lockdown and less onerous restrictions on movement and social gatherings, connected technology was in high demand. Parents and other adults in a home often needed to use a limited number of family computers and mobile phones for work. And adults, often men, accustomed to having control over internet-connected technology and even lower-tech devices such as televisions or radios, did not always cede control of them so they could be put to use to access remote education. As a result, children and youth, particularly girls, were often unable to use technology shared by a family for educational purposes.

Expectations that a single laptop, tablet computer or television shared by a family would be deployed for educational use by children proved wildly optimistic.

In India, teachers regularly offered different time options for classes in recognition that their students might not be able to access devices at only one prescheduled time. Other teachers tried to find optimal times for classes by determining when their students were most likely to be able to use a family device.[106] Expectations that a single laptop, tablet computer or television shared by a family would be deployed for educational use by children proved wildly optimistic. Even for households that were categorized as 'connected', access to technology for educational purposes was not necessarily ensured.

These ed-tech access gaps, especially pronounced in many settings in Africa, played out around the world, including in middle- and high-income countries, particularly as they concerned internet-connected technology.[107] In December 2020, the World Bank estimated that half of the people in Central Asia were "not digitally connected" and that opportunities for distance education were widely unavailable.[108] According to a 2021 digital inclusion index developed by the consultancy firm Ronald Berger, around one-third of the adult population in Southeast Asia was estimated to be fully "digitally excluded".[109] Complementary reports suggested this percentage to be significantly higher for children.[110]

"We have one computer in the family. Both my wife and I are working from home, so we need it. Now, both children have classes, so they need to be on the computer. How can we afford to buy another laptop? So, one child is missing class."

– Father, India[xxi]

> Teachers expressed alarm at government expectations that education might seamlessly shift to ed-tech; they understood how severe the access gaps were in households.

Connectivity divides posed serious barriers to distance learning even in the wealthiest countries. In Western Europe and North America, for example, at least 1 in 7 students did not have internet access at home when the pandemic hit.[111] But even these baseline connectivity figures likely overstate the actual ability of learners to take advantage of technology-mediated distance learning. Detailed analysis of digital learning divides in the USA – one of the few countries where fine-grained data are available – indicated that one-third of students in kindergarten through Grade 12 (around 16 million learners) were cut off from education during the pandemic in 2020 due to inadequate internet connections and/or a lack of suitable hardware.[112] Similarly, an early 2021 study from the United Kingdom of Great Britain and Northern Ireland (UK) found that only 5 per cent of teachers in state schools reported that all their students had access to an appropriate device for remote learning at the beginning of school closures.[113] Teachers were often the first groups to express alarm at government expectations that formal school-based education might seamlessly shift to ed-tech; they understood how severe the access gaps were at the household level.

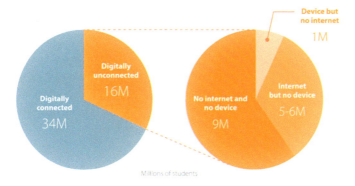

Figure 3:

Connectivity among K–12 students in the USA

Source: Adapted from Common Sense and Boston Consulting Group, 2020

As school closures stretched on as a result of the intensifying pandemic, education leaders began to realize that students and families classified as 'connected', according to government surveys and other records, were often unable to make use of this connectivity to learn due to inadequate

> Many students who had access to some form of in-person, school-based education prior to the pandemic found themselves cut off completely when ed-tech became the primary interface for formal learning.

internet connections or hardware and software shortages. This problem was observed in countries around the world and revealed the limitations of relying on dichotomous 'connected' or 'unconnected' categorizations to reliably assess how many learners could, in practice, access remote learning opportunities.

Globally, the COVID-19 crisis exposed connectivity and technology chasms that prevented home-based digital learning. Many students who had access to some form of in-person, school-based education prior to the pandemic found themselves cut off completely when ed-tech became the primary interface for formal learning.

TECHNOLOGY BARRIERS MIRRORED AND WIDENED EXISTING DIVIDES

While country and regional data showed gaping ed-tech divides, they tended to obscure details about the sociodemographic groups that were locked out of education due to limited access to technology within countries. With rare exceptions, existing inequalities in place well before COVID-19 drew the lines of ed-tech inclusion and exclusion during the pandemic. According to United Nations estimates, of the hundreds of millions of students from pre-primary to upper secondary school that did not have any access to remote learning, three-quarters lived in poor households.[114] More nuanced data showed finer disparities. Learners from ethnic and cultural minority groups were more likely to be disconnected from distance learning opportunities than those from majority groups. This also held true for girls and women, speakers of non-dominant languages, students with disabilities, students that lived in rural areas and students with parents with low levels of education.[115] While these learners often faced educational disadvantages prior to the pandemic turn to ed-tech, many of them had been attending school and accessing formal education.

"The [government's online] platform works well, but not everyone has access! A lot of kids have smartphones that they bought themselves, but what good is a phone if they don't have internet?"

– Teacher, Ecuador[xxii]

When schools shut down, limitations in access to technology-enabled remote learning put education out of reach for most students. This functioned to replicate and intensify social divides that education usually

Reliance on ed-tech subverted the notion that education might serve as a social equalizer and instead, given the severity of technology access gaps, guaranteed that education would be exclusionary.

aspires to bridge, however imperfectly. As explained by researchers at the Austrian Foundation for Development Research, "The key lesson to draw from the pandemic regarding digitalizing education comes down to the fact that layering digital technologies over existing inequality patterns will only exacerbate these patterns."[116] This did not, however, discourage governments from leaning heavily on technology-first approaches as the crisis prolonged. In May 2020, UNESCO observed that a majority of national remote learning solutions were largely dependent on online access and, by extension, expensive connectivity plans and costly devices.[117] The World Bank labelled the trend a "remote learning paradox" to highlight the futility of prioritizing the use of online solutions to minimize learning loss when "the students who are most at risk of learning losses cannot access online solutions".[118]

Across the world, the reliance on ed-tech subverted the notion that education might serve as a social equalizer and instead, given the severity of technology access gaps, guaranteed that education would be exclusionary.

"Access to the technology and materials needed to continue learning while schools are closed is desperately unequal.… A learning crisis already existed before COVID-19 hit. We are now looking at an even more divisive and deepening education crisis."

– Robert Jenkins, director of education and adolescent development, UNICEF[xxiv]

HEIGHTENED DEMAND FOR CONNECTIVITY AND DEVICES PUT A STRAIN ON POOR FAMILIES

The right to education, as defined by the United Nations and international agreements, stipulates that primary education is free while secondary and higher education are to be made free progressively. But when education moved from schools to technology-enabled remote learning, students and their families often incurred the connectivity costs needed to access formal learning content and, in some instances, participate in synchronous classes and sit for high-stakes exams. These costs, encompassing connectivity fees as well as hardware and software expenses, proved prohibitively expensive for many poor families and were a serious financial burden even for middle-income families.

"Poor people like us fight every day to keep the stove burning. Tell me how and where we will afford the money for mobile phones?"

– Parent, India[xxiv]

Smartphone affordability as a factor of income varied enormously across countries, ranging from 4 per cent in Botswana to over 600 per cent in Sierra Leone.

As the pandemic stretched on, households were unsettled to discover that every family member needed or wanted a connected device when forced to stay at home due to pandemic-related restrictions. Families that had been getting by with a single radio, for instance, suddenly needed a second one. Parents that were not planning to buy a mobile phone or tablet computer for adolescent children changed their minds and used savings or credit to purchase devices. But the cost implications were often prohibitive. Prices for hardware were often higher than usual due to soaring demand and dwindling supply stemming from pandemic-related slowdowns in the production and transportation of everything from internet-connected mobile phones and computers to radios and televisions. Even as sales of technology skyrocketed as a result of the pandemic and school closures in particular,[119] ed-tech hardware remained out of reach for poor families. Examining data from 70 countries in 2020, the Alliance for Affordable Internet found that "nearly 2.5 billion people live in countries where the cost of the cheapest available smartphone is a quarter or more of the average monthly income" – a price level that generally puts hardware out of reach. Smartphone affordability as a factor of income also varied enormously across countries, ranging, at the low end, from 4 per cent to 6 per cent of the average monthly income in Botswana, Costa Rica, Jamaica and Mexico, to – at the high end – 206 per cent of the average monthly income in India, 221 per cent in Burundi and as much as 636 per cent in Sierra Leone. In Sierra Leone, people earning an average wage would need to spend half their annual salary to purchase a low-end smartphone.[120]

Figure 4:

Smartphone affordability as a percentage of income in three countries

Source: Adapted from Alliance for Affordable Internet, 2020

These often immense cost barriers translated into a shortage of connected devices for students and a de facto stop to formal education for huge numbers of young people and adults when teaching and learning became dependent on these devices.

"I am a lower middle-class person and want to give my children the best education that I can afford, however I cannot afford multiple devices . . . This is not fair. Anyone who can afford faster internet connections and multiple devices will have a significant advantage over my children."

– Father, Pakistan[xxv]

Students who had devices often encountered major barriers when they tried to get access to the connectivity they needed to continue their education. The pandemic quickly exposed the limits of public investments to bring or improve internet connectivity in schools, championed by consortia like Giga, an initiative led by UNICEF and the ITU. During the crisis, connectivity needed to extend all the way to households and individual learners to effectively enable access to education. In this situation, hard-won progress in bringing schools online was of little assistance when schools were forced to close. Connected schools were generally prohibited from allowing learners to cluster together in computer labs or around wireless hotspots. In many countries, students resorted to unconventional strategies to find free connectivity – sometimes climbing to the top of hills or even trees;[121] travelling long distances to parks, school parking lots or other outdoor facilities known to have working Wi-Fi;[122] or sitting directly outside businesses that had password-free networks.[123] In response to this limitation, a few countries repurposed school buses into mobile Wi-Fi hotspots and sent them to neighbourhoods where many families lacked connectivity.[124]

"I have to take my motorcycle and go to [another village] about 12 kilometers from home. I usually went there four times a week to get phone signal."

– 17-year-old student, Indonesia[xxvi]

Act 2: FROM PROMISES TO REALITY | 73

State assistance to secure ed-tech hardware and software was virtually non-existent in poor countries and insufficient in many rich countries.

Hardware was another barrier. Governments occasionally made efforts to subsidize laptops, tablets or smartphones for education, but gaps and bottlenecks left many people without a realistic means to access remote learning opportunities.[125] State assistance to secure ed-tech hardware was virtually non-existent in poor countries and insufficient in many rich countries. For example, in France and Belgium, countries where social support for education tends to be strong, programmes to purchase and distribute ed-tech to disadvantaged students regularly fell short of meeting demand and had to be complemented with private donations.[126] Across the world, schemes to distribute connected devices to the most disadvantaged learners tended to be slower and less efficient than similar schemes to reach more privileged learners. As one illustration, a *Los Angeles Times* survey of 45 Southern California school districts revealed major delays with public programmes to buy and distribute technology in low-income communities. Some students who were promised devices at the onset of the pandemic did not receive them for the duration of the academic year that ended in June 2020. According to the survey results, nearly 1 out of 3 students in low-income school districts lacked devices for at least three weeks after campuses closed, while many waited much longer.[127] But from a global perspective, such students were fortunate as most unconnected learners around the world never received state-subsidized devices to continue formal education.

Even when hardware was successfully provisioned, it was sometimes insufficiently equipped to facilitate distance learning. In the USA, a survey conducted by the US Census Bureau indicated that while some schools provided computers to households that needed them, only "a small fraction were supplied with devices to access the internet", such as SIM cards or internet routers.[128] This forced families to either fill connectivity gaps with personal funds – a burden that fell hardest on economically disadvantaged families – or remain disconnected from education.

Poor families that had taken government-issued devices for education during periods of school closure were reluctant to send their children back to school if a device had been lost or stolen, on an assumption that they would be required to pay for it.

In poorer countries, evidence emerged that families sometimes declined offers of state-provisioned ed-tech due to concerns that they would be held liable for costs if the technology was broken or stolen. Many of these concerns were justified. Government schemes to provide devices did not always come with insurance or other guarantees that families would not be forced to pay for missing or damaged equipment. Reports from the Bolivarian Republic of Venezuela revealed that parents who had taken government-issued devices for education during periods of school closure were reluctant to send their children back to school if a device had been lost, stolen or was not in good condition for return, on an assumption that they would be required to pay for it.[129] Beyond this, evidence from studies predating the pandemic sometimes showed that valuable ed-tech could put learners and their families at heightened risk of theft, including violent robbery. For these reasons, programmes to provision 'free' technology to enable distance learning were not always successful and often carried unanticipated repercussions.

In addition to governments, some commercial connectivity and technology providers offered assistance to learners at the height of the pandemic, often in the face of mounting public pressure. There were instances of leading mobile network operators waiving data charges through 'zero-rating' tariffs to enable access to specified education and knowledge-focused websites such as the Khan Academy, Wikipedia and government-sanctioned learning platforms.[130] However, more generic websites, including YouTube, which is widely considered to house the world's largest and most language-diverse repository of educational content, were usually excluded from these discounted connectivity initiatives.

> While zero-rating schemes were sometimes genuine efforts by corporate entities to help people stay connected to education via ed-tech, they could also be interpreted as marketing ploys to pick up a new user base of school-age learners.

Beyond this, fragmentation and limited communication about programmes to offset connectivity expenses for education tended to hinder their use. Many families did not realize that accessing certain online learning materials would not count as billable data use and therefore did not use these materials as freely or as often as they might have done with this knowledge. Because the programmes varied from operator to operator, end users were often confused over what connectivity portals were zero-rated or discounted in some other way. Specific mobile network operators, such as Orange, for example, were likely to have different zero-rating offers than a competitor, such as Vodafone. Also, if the zero-rating did not work for whatever reason, families had little recourse. Contesting charges for connectivity use is a typically complex process, often with slim chances of success. These processes can be difficult to navigate for people with strong literacy skills and advanced levels of education. For those with low literacy and education levels, it is usually impossible. Finally, it is worth observing that while zero-rating schemes sometimes reflected genuine efforts by corporate entities to help people stay connected to education via ed-tech, they could also arguably be interpreted as marketing ploys to attract and onboard a new user base of school-age learners, many of whom had been unconnected prior to the pandemic.

Zero-rating schemes were not always initiated by connectivity providers. They often traced back to educational content providers that struck deals with connectivity providers to zero-rate access to their specific content. So instead of connectivity providers absorbing expenses for consumers to access educational content on a particular platform or charging consumers directly, the educational platform would pick up the bill. This was the digital equivalent of a business paying the transportation costs of shoppers who travel to its stores. Again, while this was sometimes a form of organizational or corporate philanthropy, it could also reflect less altruistic strategies to enlarge user bases, which could in turn increase the valuation of commercial educational content providers or increase revenue being generated from online advertisements. These ulterior motives were rarely disclosed, with zero-rating schemes often veiled as gifts or special offers to users. Unsurprisingly, the educational content providers most likely to strike these types of deals with connectivity providers tended to be for-profit ed-tech companies. What this meant on the ground was that financially stretched families looking for affordable means to access learning content were often directed to for-profit ed-tech platforms and content. Furthermore, zero-rating schemes were rarely indefinite; they would typically phase out after a period of months. This added yet more complexity and often expense for families trying to access education via technology during periods of school closure.

In some countries, private connectivity providers, in addition to providing zero-rated access to educational and other online content, also put temporary freezes on service terminations for reasons of non-payment, often in response to directives from government regulators. Governments justified this incursion into private sector affairs by highlighting the importance of maintaining internet portals for distance learning as well as to other essential services. The freezes rarely cancelled or forgave dues but simply postponed them. When the freezes ended, families, many of them under financial strain due to job loss or reduced working hours, faced a backlog of connectivity bills.

> Efforts to subsidize connectivity for educational purposes during the pandemic rarely benefited the most disadvantaged because they did not have existing connections that could be subsidized.

The ability to remain connected while not making payments applied mainly to families with post-paid connectivity subscriptions – in other words, families that pay for connectivity services after they are delivered, usually at a fixed monthly rate. The privilege rarely extended to families that access connectivity through prepaid or pay-as-you-go plans. In countries around the world, economically disadvantaged families tend to rely heavily on prepaid services, and as such, these families did not benefit from the freezes on connectivity blocks. When prepaid connectivity credits fell to zero, poor families generally had no way to continue accessing internet services, including those used for distance education. Overall, efforts to subsidize connectivity for educational purposes during the pandemic rarely benefited the most disadvantaged because they did not have existing connections that could be subsidized. Just as, for example, rental subsidies rolled out during the crisis missed homeless families and families living with relatives, so too did many efforts to offset or postpone connectivity expenses to assure the continuity of education.

Some countries recognized the problem with prepaid connectivity plans and made regulatory efforts to allow families to continue receiving service even when their pay-as-you-go credits were exhausted. Maintaining family

> When public education migrated to mobile and other digital networks, it moved outside public control and into the business logics of connectivity providers.

access to education was often cited as a primary rationale for government interventions of this type. India was one country that pursued this approach. At the end of March 2020, India's telecom regulatory authority required all mobile network operators to extend the validity period of prepaid mobile subscriptions to help low-income families maintain uninterrupted service during the pandemic.[131] The operators claimed to comply, announcing free, if time-limited, talk time and mobile data. In a letter to the regulator, the operators estimated that they supported the continuation of services for 280–300 million subscribers at a cost of approximately USD 80 million. The operators said that they had extended the benefits as they "deemed fit" and tailored them to target "truly needy" customers, rather than all prepaid subscribers.[132] The regulatory authority questioned the selective approach used by the operators and requested that they provide continued service for *all* prepaid users during the national lockdown. The operators, detecting that the authority had limited legal basis for its request, objected, stating that it was unsustainable and financially unviable to provide free connectivity indiscriminately. They argued that such an action would "amount to an unjustified subsidy" for customers that did not need assistance and would "dissuade" customers who were paying to recharge their connectivity credits, whether used for education or otherwise. The operators stated that a continuation of free or discounted connectivity to end users should be paid for using public resources and proposed that the telecom authority draw funds from the Indian Universal Service Obligation Fund and disburse them to operators to offset the costs of providing free connectivity.[133] According to an Oxford University paper, the Indian regulatory authority stopped pursuing the issue after receiving the letter, and Indian mobile operators went back to charging customers for service at standard rates.[134] This action, regardless of its basis, almost certainly cut off educational access for families relying on the free or subsidized connectivity service the telecom authority was trying to maintain. It also showed that governments had limited options at their disposal to keep connectivity intact for learners and teachers in need. When public education became fully remote and migrated to mobile and other digital networks, it moved outside public control and into the business logics of connectivity providers that are dependent on paying customers.

> Connecting to education via a mobile device was 15 times more expensive as a percentage of income for people in very poor countries than for those in rich countries.

Assistance gaps aside, structural inequalities in technology diffusion meant that the cost of using ed-tech tended to be highest for the people least able to afford it and lowest for the people most able to afford it. ITU data show that although the average cost of mobile data as a percentage of gross national income is 4.3 per cent, it is over 12 per cent in the least developed countries and under 1 per cent in developed countries.[135] This means that connecting to education via a mobile device during the pandemic was 15 times more expensive as a percentage of income for people in very poor countries than for those in rich countries. When the WHO declared COVID-19 a global pandemic, over one-quarter of the world's countries, many of them with large populations, did not meet the Broadband Commission's threshold for internet affordability, defined as entry-level broadband services costing less than 2 per cent of monthly gross income per capita.[136]

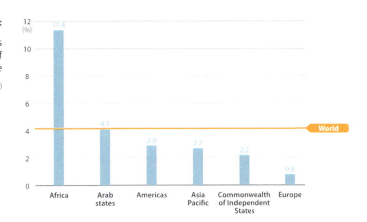

Figure 5:

Mobile data prices as a percentage of gross national income

Source: Adapted from ITU, 2020

UNICEF and other organizations documented instances of girls and young women trading sex for mobile phone credit and data.

Even when connectivity costs are expressed as an absolute figure, not accounting for average family income, they still vary dramatically: one gigabyte (GB) of mobile data costs about USD 0.27 in Italy, but USD 1.52 in Madagascar, USD 2.23 in Bolivia (Plurinational State of), USD 10.52 in Namibia and USD 16.98 in Yemen.[137] Huge disparities can exist not just between countries in different regions but across a single border. In mid-2020, mobile data connectivity was nearly 15 times more expensive in Turkmenistan than in the neighbouring Islamic Republic of Iran, for instance.[138] These differences mattered immensely as the pandemic wore on and schooling as well as other spheres of life became increasingly or entirely reliant on connectivity. UNICEF and other organizations documented instances of girls and young women trading sex for mobile phone credit and data in the Democratic Republic of the Congo,[139] a country where the cost of mobile data is very high as a percentage of median income. Long-running claims that connected technology would help equalize educational opportunities, often emanating from organizations based in North America and Europe where connectivity is inexpensive in both absolute terms and as a percentage of income, tended to gloss over the variability of fees to access the internet across countries and regions, as well as questions of who might pay these fees. During the pandemic, the burden fell hardest on disadvantaged families and often presented an insurmountable obstacle.

"Girls ... were willing to 'give' themselves to the boys in exchange for phone credit, mobile data, money for transportation or food."

– Teenage girl, Democratic Republic of the Congo[xxvii]

Digital users in wealthy countries are, on average, using 35 times more data than those in poor countries.

Given the massive price differentials, it is unsurprising that overall connectivity use in poor countries is far lower than it is in rich countries. In many places, because connectivity is an expensive service, it is used in moderation. Experts have estimated that the average data consumption in low-income countries is just 0.2 GB per month compared with just over 7 GB per month in high-income countries.[140] Put another way, digital users in wealthy countries are, on average, using 35 times more data than those in poor countries. This carries serious educational ramifications. Good digital learning content tends to incorporate videos, rich graphics, interactive lessons, synchronous sessions with teachers and peers, games and other features that require significant data usage. While students who use only 0.2 GB of data learning via ed-tech in a month are still classified as 'connected', their educational experience will be much different from that of students using 35 times that amount – and likely of diminished quality as well as quantity.

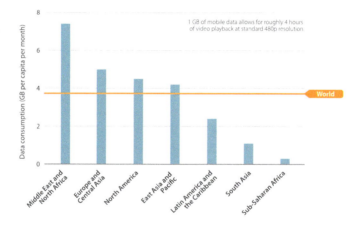

Figure 6:

Data consumption per month across regions, in gigabytes (GB) per capita

Source: Adapted from World Bank, 2021

The pandemic made it clear that the cost of connectivity varies widely from country to country and that this, in turn, affects educational uses (and non-uses) of digital ed-tech. Prior to the pandemic, however, pricing inequity for connectivity had not been a hard barrier limiting access to formal education. For most families, schooling had been largely free of tuition. And even in cases where schooling required expenditures, there were more established and functional schemes to help offset or subsidize costs for underprivileged families that could not afford them. Globally speaking, internet connectivity was not assumed or expected by educators, even if such expectation was gradually shifting. The pivot to full reliance on ed-tech during school closures changed this assumption and functioned to make education, a human right and a public good, more expensive and often inaccessible to those in the most precarious financial positions.

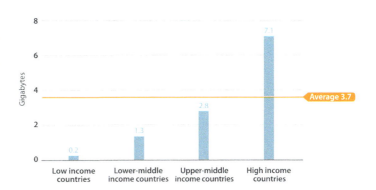

Figure 7:

Mobile data consumption across country income groups

Source: Adapted from World Bank, 2021

A DEARTH OF DIGITAL SKILLS PREVENTED TEACHING AND LEARNING

The success or failure of technology approaches to education rests as much on people as on networks and devices.

Although access to connected technology is a necessary prerequisite for digital distance learning, by itself it is insufficient to ensure educational continuity. The success or failure of approaches rests as much on people as on networks and devices. During the crisis, the varied human dimensions of distance learning were routinely overlooked, limiting the effective utilization of technology for educational purposes in contexts where this technology was available. These dimensions included everything from the ability of teachers and learners to use digital tools for pedagogical purposes, to the administrative capacities of education officials to procure and scale up digital learning solutions, to the technical know-how needed for parents and caregivers to play a supportive role.

"For students who are brand new to the country or had interrupted schooling, one big issue is that they weren't proficient in using the technology before the pandemic... Just getting a computer – that's step one in equity. Having access to the content is the way bigger issue."

– Teacher, USA[xxviii]

Globally, most people lacked the digital skills required to leverage connected technology for educational and other empowering purposes when the pandemic struck. UNESCO data clarify the severity of digital skills limitations, particularly in poor countries. For example, the proportion of youth and adults who could send emails with an attachment was estimated to range from 65 per cent in high-income countries to 34 per cent in upper-middle-income countries, to 20 per cent in lower-middle-income countries, and to just 3 per cent in low-income countries. Across all country income groups, only a minority of youth and adults knew how to prepare electronic presentations – a skill that is sometimes understood as a baseline ability for using technology for teaching and learning purposes, particularly for instruction. Within upper-middle, lower-middle and low-income country groups, most youth and adults lacked the digital skills required to: copy and move files, find and download software, and connect new devices to the internet.[141] These skills underlie the ability to learn at a distance with ed-tech. Within individual countries, digital skills gaps tended to be huge between rich and poor populations. In Mongolia, for instance, 39 per cent of adults from the richest quintile but just 1 per cent of their peers from the poorest quintile had the ability to use a basic arithmetic formula in a spreadsheet.[142] Within and across countries, ICT skills tend to be more unequally distributed than basic literacy and numeracy skills are.

Findings from cross-national skills assessments indicated that skills deficits were more likely to disadvantage women and girls than men and boys. As one illustration, UNESCO found that women in numerous countries are 25 per cent less likely than men to know how to leverage ICT for basic purposes and four times less likely to have advanced skills.[143] UNICEF analyses based on data from eight sub-Saharan African countries (the Democratic Republic of the Congo, Gambia, Ghana, Lesotho, Madagascar, Sierra Leone, Togo and Zimbabwe) similarly found that fewer girls than boys between 15 and 18 years old possess ICT skills, and that adolescent boys use computers and the internet considerably more frequently than girls in a majority of the countries.[144]

"Many people have a phone but don't know how to use it. Some people who do know how to use a phone borrow someone else's."

– 17-year-old girl, India[xxix]

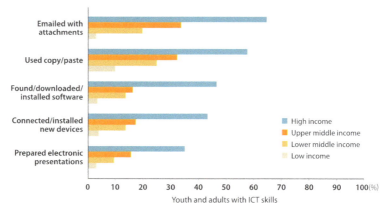

Figure 8:

Major digital skills gaps, especially in lower income countries

Source: Adapted from UNESCO Global Monitoring Report, 2023

Other multi-country studies reveal that women tend to have dramatically reduced access and exposure to the internet-connected technologies that would allow them to establish and build the digital skills needed to benefit from remote and technology-mediated learning.[145] Oxford University found,

Twice as many girls report needing to borrow a mobile phone for digital access than boys.

for example, that in Ethiopia young women are twice as likely as men to have never used a smartphone.[146] In India the chasm is even wider: while more than 80 per cent of young men have used a smartphone at least once, fewer than 20 per cent of young women have done the same.[147]
According to global research published by Vodafone, twice as many girls report needing to borrow a mobile phone for digital access than boys. Vodafone also found that even when both girls and boys have good access to internet-connected mobile devices, boys are far more likely to use them to access digital platforms and services and tend to use them for a much wider range of activities than girls.[148] Technology access and usage gaps of this type are major contributors to digital skills gaps. It is, of course, far easier for young people to develop digital skills with a personal device than without one and when use of digital technology is encouraged and a social norm.

Because of these digital skills gender divides, girls and women were often unable to participate in formal education when it suddenly shifted from the physical sites of schools to technology-enabled remote learning. Gender imbalances in digital skills proved especially problematic because women are often primary caregivers and were more likely to be tasked with helping children access and productively use technology for learning during the pandemic. When they could not do this skilfully, as was often the case, children lost out on educational opportunities. Moreover, in many countries, women are also far more likely to be teachers than men. Their limited digital skills vis-à-vis men and male teachers meant that they tended to have difficulty supporting the learning of students via unfamiliar technology. A UNESCO 2021 study on the gendered impacts of COVID-19 school closures indicated that gaps in perceived or actual digital skills had much stronger negative impacts on female teachers compared with male teachers and contributed to higher levels of stress.[149]

Re-engineering education systems to migrate learning onto digital platforms requires new skills, outlooks and competencies from everyone involved, be they learners, caregivers, teachers, administrators or policy-makers. The skills that are needed tend to go well beyond basic digital skills. Navigating powerful course management systems or logging into synchronous video classes are hardly intuitive tasks for people with limited experience using connected technology. Even advanced technology users experienced problems orienting themselves to a new normal of virtual classes and online-only communication during the pandemic. Previously unknown software had to be downloaded, installed and set up. Users had to register themselves on unfamiliar platforms and systems, processes that often required sophisticated digital competencies. Many learning applications could only be accessed via proprietary mobile operating systems, such as Google's Android or Apple's iOS, that in turn required their own registrations. The processes proved too complex for large numbers of users who did not yet possess intermediate or even basic digital skills. Ultimately, a lack of digital skills locked many learners, teachers and families out of education during school closures, and girls and women in particular.

TEACHERS WERE UNPREPARED TO SUPPORT REMOTE LEARNING

In all countries, large numbers of teachers, both men and women, lacked the digital skills and training needed to successfully facilitate distance learning – as was the case with parents. Indeed, a majority of teachers worldwide had no experience using connected technology for pedagogical purposes when schools started to close en masse in 2020. Even in wealthy countries, principals of secondary schools reported that only about half of working teachers had the necessary technical and pedagogical skills to integrate digital devices in their instruction.[150] And far fewer were practised in teaching at a distance with technology. What little training teachers might have received for technology integration prior to the pandemic, whether as part of pre-service training or continuing professional development, tended to focus on strategies for using digital tools to enrich learning in classroom settings, not as a means of provisioning and facilitating distance learning.[151]

Millions of teachers lacked prior training or experience using technology for instructional purposes.

Troubling inequities presented other barriers. Teachers' abilities to use technology skilfully were far from evenly distributed. Across countries, teachers serving privileged learners usually had much stronger digital skills for pedagogical purposes than teachers serving underprivileged students. Surveys of school principals in Sweden, for example, indicated that nearly 90 per cent of teachers working in schools serving socio-economically advantaged students possessed strong technical skills and competencies for education, compared with only about 50 per cent of teachers working in schools serving socio-economically disadvantaged students.[152] Sweden, it is worth noting, boasts one of the best-trained teacher workforces in the world and has a particularly equitable education system. Arguably, the deep inequity observed in Sweden was likely deeper still in other countries. Overall, these realities paint a bleak picture: when the pandemic hit, millions of teachers lacked prior training or experience using technology for instructional purposes in any form, let alone for fully remote learning. The realities also meant that underprivileged students were most at risk of having teachers that did not possess the technical and pedagogical skills to guide student learning from a distance with ed-tech.

"The government didn't provide any tools for [online learning] . . . It was a bit as though they said, 'You just need to cope.'"

– Teacher, Poland[xxx]

While some countries rolled out web-based training in a rushed attempt to help teachers support distance learning with technology, many did not. Surveys of ministries of education conducted jointly by UNESCO, UNICEF, the World Bank and the OECD at the height of the pandemic found that many countries offered "no support at all at the national level to help teachers transition to remote learning".[153] That this result emerged from self-reported survey questions reveals the dearth of options available to teachers to prepare for digital-first modes of education. Even when trainings were offered, they tended to focus on important but surface-level technical skills. They were, in effect, crash courses in doing rather than understanding and cultivating reflective practice. Typical training offered step-by-step tutorials on how to start video classes and log attendance using proprietary software. Efforts to acquaint teachers with advanced digital pedagogies and help them make independent judgements about the quality of different ed-tech tools at their disposal were rare. In the sink-or-swim educational environment of the pandemic, teachers used whatever techniques kept them afloat, regardless of pedagogical soundness. In some cases, this calcified bad habits, such as teachers delivering long lectures with digital slides via Zoom. The suddenness of the pandemic and the countless urgencies it triggered in education and other areas of life meant that there was little time and capacity for adequate professional development centred on ed-tech. Beyond this, restrictions on in-person gatherings meant the face-to-face trainings that would have helped teachers navigate ed-tech and practice instructional techniques for distance learning in a supportive environment with peers were off-limits. For teachers with very low baseline digital skills or those without connectivity, web-based trainings, no matter their relevance or quality, were fully unavailable. Teachers with no knowledge of technology could not make use of technology-based training. A few countries such as Saudi Arabia set up hotlines for teachers to call when they wanted assistance supporting distance learning and using new ed-tech tools and platforms, but supports of this sort were the exception globally.[154]

> In Brazil over 80 per cent of teachers reported that they were unable to teach remotely with technology.

Teachers were keenly aware that their skills limitations with technology, along with the limitations of technology itself, would diminish the educational experiences of students compared with what was possible in classrooms and schools. In a 2020 survey conducted by Education International, teachers overwhelmingly ranked "managing and orchestrating the use of digital technologies in teaching and learning" as the most "urgent" of all their training needs, with a strong majority saying these needs were either "insufficiently met" or "not met" at all.[155] This was corroborated by country surveys, such as one in Brazil in which over 80 per cent of teachers reported that they were unable to teach remotely with technology.[156] In addition to preventing teachers from helping students when schools closed, this dearth of preparation adversely impacted teachers' sense of professional self-worth and also their personal well-being. In the Brazil study, 2 out of 3 teachers reported they felt anxious following the switch to ed-tech, and less than 10 per cent reported feeling happy or satisfied.

Interestingly, research emerged to suggest that among teachers who had good baseline digital skills, educators with many years of experience appeared to better weather the switch to fully remote learning through ed-tech than younger and less experienced teachers. This contradicted popular notions that newer and younger teachers, those of a 'digital-first' generation and with supposedly more malleable habits, would excel with ed-tech. A 2021 global survey by T4 and EdTech Hub found that the most experienced teachers taught more classes online and deployed more sophisticated and creative types of remote teaching, such as recording videos or audio messages for their students, than less experienced teachers. The study revealed that more experienced teachers appear to have been "better able to transfer their long-honed skills of in-person classroom management to the direction and coordination of remote learning, allowing them to focus on the digital resources and techniques they needed to deploy".[157]

> While solid digital skills are a prerequisite to successfully supporting technology-dependent education, strong pedagogical skills are equally vital.

The takeaway was that while solid digital skills are a prerequisite to successfully supporting technology-dependent education, strong pedagogical skills are equally vital. Beyond digital skills shortages, factors such as long-standing deficits in standard teacher training and structural issues, including low pay, insecure contracts and poor working conditions that disincentivize teachers from staying in the profession and building experience, all contributed to problems leveraging ed-tech to facilitate remote learning. In education, as in other sectors, high levels of professional training and experience helped people transition to technology-first modes of working. The fact that these high levels of training and experience were often in short supply came into stark relief when teachers needed to exercise flexibility and resilience during the pandemic.

Inequalities were supercharged

Ed-tech had long promised to equalize educational opportunity and give all students, regardless of poverty, ethnicity, caste, gender or geography, a fair shot at learning. It was hailed as a tool that could bring high-quality education to the furthest corners of the globe and untether schooling from exclusionary and high-cost institutions. There was hope that the digital futures of education – and remote learning in particular – would be more equitable than education that revolved exclusively around in-person schools.

Reliance on families to supplement and guide technology-based education placed extra burdens on caregivers, most often women, with negative impacts on gender equality in the workforce.

Yet during the pandemic, even when learners had access to some form of ed-tech, their educational experience varied considerably depending on the type and quality of the technology and connectivity used. This tended to provide substantial advantages to already privileged students. Countries around the world invested heavily in internet-connected solutions for education, even though these solutions commonly reached only a minority of students, resulting in a bifurcation of educational opportunity.[158] Major efforts to build the digital skills and competencies of teachers, parents and students to ensure technology could be used productively for learning tended to benefit only those with intermediate to advanced skill levels, leaving people with lower skill levels or no previous technology experience behind. Additionally, the evidence indicates that reliance on families to supplement and guide technology-based education placed extra burdens on caregivers, most often women, with negative impacts on gender equality in the workforce.

Full reliance on technology as a response to the educational disruption of the pandemic demanded new practices, rules and norms that few in the education community had time to carefully consider. In many instances, education leaders were unprepared to address the challenges ed-tech reliance had introduced, particularly as they concerned educational equality. Many of the challenges confronting them had not even been considered, let alone deliberated or resolved. It was often unclear if the challenges even fell under the remit of education authorities. Haphazard and ad hoc measures were adopted to fill the void and patch problems, some of them of dubious utility and other with questionable legitimacy or even legality. Scores of lawsuits are pending in countries that allow families to sue the state for failure to follow its own legislation pertaining to equal access to education.[159]

Whereas schools often helped mitigate social inequities, technology-enabled remote learning seemed only to widen them.

Dividing lines between the haves and the have-nots are not new to education; they existed long before COVID-19. But the technology-first responses to the educational challenges of the pandemic placed heavy burdens on families and tended to exacerbate existing social inequities compared with in-person schooling. In schools, there were teachers who could facilitate formal learning and provide support, regardless of the quality of technology and connectivity or the availability and capacities of parents and other caregivers. Whereas schools could – and often did – help close disparities, the process of shifting site-based education to technology-enabled remote learning seemed only to widen them.

LEARNING BY RADIO VERSUS REAL-TIME, TEACHER-LED VIDEO

The types of connected hardware used by students during school closures fell across a wide spectrum from high-tech to low-tech devices. At one pole were latest-generation laptops that could seamlessly connect to powerful online learning platforms and were equipped with high-quality video cameras, speakers and microphones. At another pole were analogue radios that could play only unidirectional audio broadcasts.

The technologies that most learners and their families used or tried to use for education during the pandemic largely reflected their country's development status. Students in poorer countries were more reliant on lower-tech solutions, while students in richer countries often enjoyed access to higher-tech solutions. Analysis from the Brookings Institution, a public policy think tank, indicates that at the height of global school closures in April 2020, around 90 per cent of high-income countries were providing some form of online remote learning, while only 25 per cent of low-income countries were doing the same.[160] UNESCO monitoring of responses to the COVID-19 educational disruption clearly shows that, as the crisis stretched into the second half of 2020, a growing number of countries rolled out some type of online learning option and often invested heavily in it. This said, these remote online learning options were never universal, not even by late 2021 or 2022. Significant numbers of students in Africa, South-East Asia, Latin America and the Caribbean were never serviced with a robust digital option for public education during periods of school closure. At times, this reflected sober recognition that access to internet-dependent education would only reach a fraction of learners due to hardware, connectivity and digital skills limitations and was therefore not worth the investment. But more often it reflected a lack of resources and capacity to migrate learning content aligned with national curriculum online.

"The government did something resembling courses on national television. But since some neighborhoods experience electricity shortages all seven days of the week, it's complicated."

– Father, Cameroon[xxxi]

It is important to emphasize that learners accessing education through radio or television had vastly different educational experiences than learners accessing education through a computer with broadband internet. Connected computers generally allow students to search and access large digital repositories of interactive learning materials on demand, in addition to opening possibilities to communicate in real time and attend

In-person schooling had helped guarantee that modes of education provision were reasonably similar for students from different backgrounds and income groups. The switch to remote learning with ed-tech caused these modes to segregate.

synchronous online video classes run by teachers and attended by peers. While schools did not offer equal educational opportunities prior to the pandemic, the shift to different types of ed-tech generally widened already troubling pre-pandemic disparities. At both global and national levels, privileged students tended to take advantage of more expansive and more engaging digital learning content via connected mobile devices and personal computers. By contrast, underprivileged students were more likely to have either no options to connect to remote education or have only radio or television technologies. In-person schooling had helped guarantee that modes of education provision were reasonably similar for students from different backgrounds and income groups. The switch to remote learning with ed-tech, however, caused these modes to segregate. Even for learners living in the same geographic region, ed-tech learning experiences could be completely different depending on the hardware available to learners and their families.

DIGITAL ASPIRATIONS AND INVESTMENTS FAVOURED THE PRIVILEGED

During the pandemic, most countries aspired to provide rich, interactive learning opportunities to students at a distance, and this led them, largely regardless of development status, to elevate digital tools as a preferred technology. Attempts to mobilize synchronous or asynchronous online learning platforms to support distance education were observed across countries, even in many poor countries where relative few people have connectivity or devices that are capable of connecting to the internet. This appears to have had a knock-on effect of demoting lower-tech television and radio solutions, when available, to backup or last resort choices. Indeed, in many instances, these second-tier options received very little government support, thereby constraining educational options for learners who did not have internet-connected technology of any kind.

Nearly half a billion learners who had been attending in-person schooling were suddenly excluded because of the pivot to ed-tech.

In May 2020, UNESCO observed that 60 per cent of national distance learning alternatives relied exclusively on online platforms.[161] Given the scale of connectivity and equipment divides, this amounted to de facto exclusion of many from distance learning. Indeed, UNESCO projected that as many as 465 million children and youth being targeted by national online learning platforms did not have access to the internet at home.[162] This meant that nearly half a billion learners, approximately 50 per cent of all primary and secondary students globally, who had been attending in-person schooling were suddenly excluded because of the pivot to ed-tech.

Act 2: FROM PROMISES TO REALITY | 89

Because digital technologies were understood to be future-oriented and superior for learning, they enjoyed an elevated status, even if their potential to benefit large numbers of learners on the ground was very small.

The tendency of countries to treat internet-connected technologies as primary and first-choice options for distance learning often translated into greater investment and support for these technologies. Governments were, in effect, improving educational offerings available to only a minority of learners who had access to internet-connected technology and were often privileged in other ways as well. This heightened inequity and exclusion. Some countries, such as Mexico and Pakistan, broke from the status quo and poured energies and investments into supporting lower-tech offerings, such as educational television.[163] But this tended to be the exception rather than the rule. According to a 2020 UNESCO-UNICEF-World Bank survey of ministries of education, only two-thirds of low-income countries were using radio to reach primary students at the height of the pandemic, despite the relatively wide availability and ownership of radios compared to televisions and internet-connected technologies in these contexts.[164] Because digital technologies were understood to be future-oriented and superior for learning, they enjoyed an elevated status, even if their potential to benefit large numbers of learners on the ground was very small.

EFFORTS TO LEAPFROG PROGRESS SKIPPED OVER DISADVANTAGED LEARNERS

Ed-tech initiatives were often presented as efforts to leapfrog standard educational development and achieve accelerated improvement.

In early 2020, when the scale and duration of the crisis was still uncertain, a number of countries announced ambitious plans to deploy frontier technologies – those superior to existing and widely owned technologies – for educational purposes. These ed-tech initiatives were often presented as efforts to leapfrog progress; that is, to reduce steps in standard educational development, increase efficiency, lower costs and accelerate the rate of desirable change. In wealthier countries, this intent often found expression in calls to deploy AI, blockchain technology and virtual reality solutions for teaching and learning. In the context of developing countries, leapfrogging efforts were regularly associated with attempts to transition to digital modes of learning through mobile phones and other connected technologies. When applied to the global South, the term tended to signal implicit understandings that traditional school-based education was fundamentally broken and unfixable. In these contexts, new technology would largely bypass schools.

The Brookings Institution was one of many organizations to call the pandemic a "leapfrog moment". In September 2020, it announced that "it is now more important than ever to invest in innovations such as education technology and leapfrog progress – both during COVID-19 and beyond".[165]

Webinars and white papers on the subject were proposed by various groups, sometimes with financial backing from technology providers, and promoted using Twitter hashtags such as #TransformingEdu. This work drove a clear message: countries were not only supposed to meet the urgent educational needs of students during the crisis but should also lay foundations for more modern educational systems that would take root in the context of the pandemic and then blossom when it subsided.

"By turning the problem of poverty into a problem of technology, [public service organizations] reframe their own problems into something more manageable for their frontline staff and more legible to the politicians, donors and others who might offer support."

– Daniel Greene, professor of information studies, University of Maryland[xxxii]

The pandemic was considered a leapfrog moment precisely because it forced an unprecedented reliance on technology. (Few close observers doubted, for instance, that a different type of crisis, such as a prolonged and global shutdown of the internet, would have triggered commentary about leapfrogging educational development through non-technological means, such as improving the physical infrastructure of schools, reorganizing classroom-based instruction and changing face-to-face pedagogies.) The very notion of skipping steps and precipitating exponential educational improvement with similar or even decreased financial investment was and remains firmly attached to technology. The belief that the pandemic presented a leapfrog moment hinged on underlying convictions that ed-tech could provide much needed boosts to struggling education systems. Technology was seen as representing a more promising route to improvement than more established approaches that relate, for instance, to investments to reduce class sizes, improve teacher training or reform curricula. Rather than pursuing the more modest gains expected through conventional measures, leapfrogging was perceived to offer additional benefits and a higher return on investment. In this way, the process aimed to skip over standard steps for educational reform to deliver faster and bigger desired results.

Widespread calls to leapfrog educational progress during the COVID-19 pandemic were problematic because they tended to be interpreted by national and local authorities as recommendations to insist on digital-first futures for education, even though many learners, teachers and families could not afford and did not know how to use internet-connected technologies for educational or other purposes. Beyond this, leapfrogging steps were to be taken in the midst of a global health crisis that had triggered unprecedented social disruption and ushered in a host of economic uncertainties.

Act 2: FROM PROMISES TO REALITY | 91

A 2020 webinar hosted by the Brookings Institution exemplified a strain of thought, particularly pronounced early in the health crisis, that school closures would catalyse desired technological transformations to education. The title of the webinar – "Beyond reopening: A leapfrog moment to transform education?" – contained a question, but it was largely rhetorical. It advanced the idea that the pandemic disruptions would help countries move more quickly and resolutely into digital futures than they otherwise would. The webinar featured, among other speakers, authors of a 2020 publication titled, *Realizing the Promise: How Can Education Technology Improve Learning for All?* The webinar host summarized the publication as "targeting" ministers of education around the world, "especially those in low and middle income countries" in order to "to help them really think differently about how they can employ technology to accelerate student learning, leapfrog, and really close the gaps that we observe today between low-income children and youth in poor countries, and in high-income countries".[166] Facilitators asked an education leader from a West African country several questions about the various technology-forward actions his country was taking to respond to the educational disruption of the pandemic, even though fewer than 6 per cent of families in his country had a computer and only 14 per cent could access the internet through a connected device at home, according to research and analysis from EdTech Hub.[167]

> According to leapfrog thinking, radio and television solutions to support remote education signalled a type of backtracking rather than a jump towards the future.

Leapfrog thinking of the type on display in the Brookings webinar and many other discussions hosted by leading think tanks and development organizations held that radio and television solutions to support remote education were outdated – they signalled a type of backtracking rather than a jump towards the future. Programmes to print and disseminate paper-based learning materials were similarly viewed as unwelcome returns to an analogue age of education that countries were eager to leave behind in their aims to move closer to what they saw as the digital future of education.

While the language of leapfrogging was routinely couched in promises to improve educational inclusion and equity, the real-world application of the concept rarely advanced either. Instead, it was understood as licence and advice to move up a rung on the technology ladder of ed-tech. On the ground, this meant that in affluent communities where learners were well equipped with powerful personal computers and mobile devices, schools would sometimes push for the adoption and application of virtual reality technologies. In middle-income communities, efforts were made to move education to newer tablet and laptop computers with online learning applications requiring steady broadband internet connections. In poor communities and across many developing country contexts, efforts were made to transition education to affordable digital technologies,

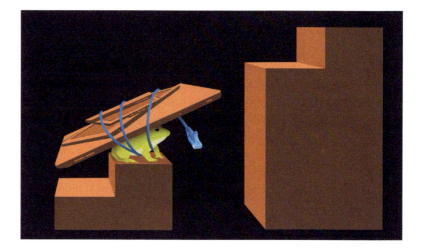

often low-end smartphones, rather than strengthening investments reliant on television and radio technologies or printed materials. The logic of leapfrogging held that the pandemic was a 'golden opportunity' to move education to future-oriented technologies and hope that these technological advances would, in turn, result in improved education and other positive outcomes, such as a more digital-ready workforce.

"Look before you leap. The notion of leapfrogging poor infrastructure in Africa needs to come back down to earth."

– The Economist[xxxiii]

These programmes, unfortunately, had the perverse side effect of leaving huge numbers of learners behind. Most people were simply not prepared to move up the technological ladder, nor were they typically supported to do so. The pandemic was, if anything, an inappropriate time to try to skip steps. It froze families and communities in place. Even when families had means to upgrade technologies and purchase a good-quality tablet computer in place of a low-quality smartphone to help dependants better follow distance learning and participate in virtual classes, these devices were often unavailable because of increased demand and constrained supply for connected hardware, itself a side effect of the pandemic.[168] Purchases aside, instruction and support to use more advanced devices were also in short supply due to restrictions on movement and gatherings. People who might have called on a tech-savvy relative, friend or neighbour to request in-person assistance could not do so easily, and many technology problems demanded on-site interventions.

Overall, attempts to leapfrog progress during the pandemic tended to do very little to centre the most marginalized groups. More often, they centred

Faith in leapfrogging disincentivized many governments and school systems from meeting students and their parents where they were by providing non-technical means of educational support.

the most privileged learners and families, who were well-positioned to leap technologically despite the myriad challenges imposed by the pandemic. Faith in leapfrogging disincentivized many governments and school systems from meeting students and their parents where they were by providing non-technical means of educational support in the form of, for example, paper-based learning materials or by enlarged investments to expand and enrich educational programming tailored for radio or television. Actions to leapfrog to digital education, although generally well-meaning, had an unintended consequence of putting distance education out of reach for large numbers of young people and adults who had been attending schools and benefiting from non-digital modes of formal learning. Belief in leapfrogging seduced many education leaders into assuming that technology could somehow catalyse major educational improvements and offer a silver lining in a crisis that had very few.

VARIABLE CONNECTIVITY QUALITY AND NEW FORMS OF DIGITAL EXCLUSION

When internet connectivity was available, its quality was variable, which carried major repercussions for education. Faster and more reliable connectivity corresponded to expanded possibilities for learning, while slower and less reliable connectivity limited access to education and constrained learning opportunities.

During the pandemic, millions of students who were designated as 'connected' were connected via networks and technology poorly suited to sustain remote online learning.

Internet connectivity is often understood as a binary concept, such that people are either 'connected' or 'not connected'. In practice, however, connectivity falls across a wide gradient, ranging from fast and seamless to slow and irregular. Looking only at speed, a 5G mobile network can, for example, accommodate extremely fast 10 gigabit per second downloads. A 4G network, by contrast, usually only supports up to 0.2 gigabit per second downloads.[169] And a modern 3G connection allows plodding speeds of just 42.2 megabits per second.[170] This means that a 1 GB educational video – approximately 60 minutes of standard video content – would take one second to download with a 5G connection, but over three minutes with a 3G connection.[171] Google research has indicated that 53 per cent of mobile website users will leave a web page that does not load within three seconds.[172] This variation in connectivity quality meant that millions of students who were designated as 'connected' were connected via networks and technology poorly suited to sustain the type of remote online learning that was rolled out during the pandemic. Much of the digital content that countries advised students and teachers to access during the pandemic was optimized for users with fast and reliable internet connections, usually 4G or better. Low-bandwidth solutions were generally an afterthought in country responses, if they were offered at all.

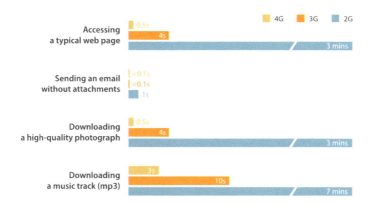

Figure 9:

How download times compare across different data networks

Source: Data from Ken's Tech Tips, 2018

Variable levels of connectivity heightened existing educational inequities during periods of remote learning, because the connectivity many learners and teachers used to access online education was far from ideal. According to ITU's global data published in 2021, approximately 88 per cent of people with mobile internet connections use 4G networks or better, about 7 per cent use 3G networks, and 5 per cent use 2G networks. In Africa, however, the percentage of 4G users falls significantly to under 50 per cent.[173] ITU data from the pandemic period did not usually indicate the percentage of 5G users, since the technology was so new, but Ericsson reported that over 1 billion people, about 15 per cent of the global population, were covered by a 5G network by the end of 2020.[174] Yet this coverage tends to only boost the connectivity speeds of people who already have a fast mobile connection. Maps of where 5G networks are being deployed correspond, with almost surgical precision, to maps of wealthy areas – both across countries and within them.

"While the whole country is shifting to the learn-from-home, we are still waiting for a Google page to open up in our phones."

– Rudrani Gupta, journalist, India[xxxv]

Higher and lower quality networks commonly exist side by side even in the confines of a single city, such that higher income neighbourhoods enjoy higher quality connections than lower income neighbourhoods, despite their geographic proximity. This practice is sometimes referred to as 'digital redlining'. The term traces to practices employed in the USA in the 1950s

A lot of digital redlining seems to stem from a cold financial calculus that ensures the best-quality connectivity services blanket the richest areas first and poorer areas second.

and 1960s to deny loans and mortgages to people, usually minority groups, living in particular neighbourhoods, regardless of their loan eligibility according to more relevant criteria such as income and credit history.[175] According to scholars, there are concerning parallels between those now-banned discriminatory financial practices and the policies, practices and investment decisions that result in the exclusion of specific groups from good-quality connectivity services.[176] Angela Siefer, executive director of the National Digital Inclusion Alliance, has highlighted data to show that majority black communities in the USA often receive lower quality internet services than majority white communities, even when they are paying the same fees and have similar connectivity plans. She asks: "Is it intentionally race? One doesn't know intentions. But one knows the outcome, which is the majority of the neighbourhoods that have slower speeds from providers … are lower income neighbourhoods, and they tend to be communities of color."[177] Some experts have argued that digital redlining can be "more insidious" than overt prejudice or exclusion because it is often difficult to detect but still confers serious disadvantage.[178] If a family with a 4G mobile internet plan living in one part of a city receives connectivity that is significantly slower and less reliable than a family with the same 4G plan living in another part of the same city, it equates to unequal opportunity. This was particularly true during the pandemic when reliance on connectivity for work, education and other purposes peaked.

Pernicious actions to block internet connectivity prevented students from exercising their right to education.

While a lot of digital redlining seems to stem from a cold financial calculus that ensures that the best-quality connectivity services, including services in a fixed tier like 4G or 5G, blanket the richest areas first and poorer areas second, the practice can be more targeted and more malignant. Increasingly, governments and other powerful groups, often in collaboration with commercial internet service providers (ISPs), redline specific groups and geographic areas intentionally, effectively gumming up digital links as a means of exercising power. This can take the form of purposeful internet slowdowns or, in more extreme cases, full internet shutdowns. Access Now, a non-profit organization dedicated to digital rights, documented 159 internet shutdowns in 29 countries in 2020 alone. Shutdowns were even more frequent in 2021, with a total of 182 across 34 countries, and appear slated to continue. Data from 2022 suggest it was the worst year on record for intentional internet shutdowns.[179] Villages, towns, cities, states and territories that are purposefully cut off from the internet are sometimes referred to as 'broadband deserts'. Such deserts have been observed in countries across the world. The practice of blocking connectivity as a means of controlling or gaining leverage over opposition and out-groups is often seen in places where there are conflicts or territorial disputes.[180] Frequent internet shutdowns during the pandemic have sometimes been referred to as "lockdowns within lockdowns" and as a form of "digital apartheid".[181]

Internet shutdowns were also de facto attacks on education. While pernicious actions to block internet connectivity may have been less visible and perhaps less taboo than attacks on physical education facilities, the result – due to the heightened reliance on connectivity – was the same: they prevented students from exercising their right to education. Existing intergovernmental agreements and commitments to protect education from attack, such as the Safe Schools Declaration, tend to make little or no mention of digital infrastructure, which may have muted international criticism of internet slowdowns and shutdowns on educational grounds.[182]

> Learners in wealthier communities could largely count on connectivity to function well, while learners in lower income contexts rarely had this luxury, even when they were paying for a service that was supposed to be of similar quality.

While intentional internet blocks prevented some students from accessing connected learning opportunities, unintended technical problems were more common and more widespread obstacles to connectivity. These technical problems were by no means evenly distributed; they disproportionately affected learners that were underprivileged in other ways, thereby widening inequity. Students living in countries served by multiple ISPs with excellent human and technical capacities, for example, tended to have more reliable and often less expensive internet connectivity than students living in countries serviced by only one or two ISPs that are poorly run and have only rudimentary technical expertise. When the pandemic struck and schools closed, families became acutely aware of the quality of their internet service.[183] Learners in wealthier communities could largely count on connectivity to function seamlessly, while learners in lower income contexts rarely had this luxury, even when they were paying for a service that was supposed to be of similar quality. Internet connections that cut out or slowed down dramatically tended to be more common in countries plagued by other challenges, such as poverty, corruption and weak public and private sectors.[184]

The capacities of ISPs mattered immensely during the pandemic because networks were strained when internet traffic soared as a result of lockdowns. Education was a significant source of stress on overburdened networks as millions of learners that would normally be at school and mostly offline were suddenly online and for long periods of time. BT, a leading British telecom company, reported that internet data usage increased around 50 per cent in daytime weekday hours during the first month of the pandemic.[185] Similar school-hour jumps were noted by large providers in other countries, including by Telefonica in Spain.[186] This heavy use affected internet connectivity, and speeds sometimes slowed dramatically across the world, including in countries with robust digital infrastructure. In Hubei Province in China, for instance, mobile broadband speeds fell by more than half.[187] Similar speed reductions were noticed in Germany, the USA and Spain, among other countries. In Italy, home use of the internet increased 90 per cent compared with usage levels before the pandemic and caused the

internet to slow to paces that people had not experienced since the early 2000s.[188] These slowdowns made online education frustrating or unfeasible. Video lessons were hard to follow, resources were difficult to access, files took significant time to upload, and systems that were supposed to provide immediate feedback provided delayed feedback instead.

"My colleagues and I often stayed awake at night waiting for files to take a lifetime to upload to email and student WhatsApp groups. … I felt that our technically impaired online classes … were simply a futile exercise. These dysfunctional classes consistently made me feel like a talking head in a dark room."

–Arif Hussain Nadaf, assistant professor, Kashmir[xxxv]

Wealthier countries with strong regulators and nimble ISPs were able to roll out solutions to accommodate the rush of internet users and bring connectivity speeds back to pre-pandemic levels. This often required complex technical adjustments, financial investments, government assistance and regulatory interventions.[189] Companies, including AT&T, China Mobile, Comcast, Deutsche Telekom and Vodafone, scrambled to add cellular sites and fibre-optic connections to networks as well as improve routing and switching equipment to fortify bandwidth capacity.[190] A leading French ISP, Orange, upgraded undersea internet cables.[191] On the regulatory side, the European Union demanded that companies, such as Netflix and YouTube, reduce the large size of video files that were dominating scarce internet bandwidth. In the USA, the Federal Communications Commission granted leading telecom providers temporary access to more airways, a move that helped relieve pressure on mobile broadband.[192]

This coordination and investment moved quickly in wealthier countries and yielded results: internet reliability and speed improved. In lower income countries, though, solutions, when they came at all, tended to be slower and less effective.[193] Connections that had slowed or stopped working due to pandemic surges in use were not necessarily upgraded or upgraded quickly. ISPs with limited business and technical experience did not always understand how to buttress overstretched networks, particularly in the midst of a pandemic.

With teaching and learning having largely shifted online, the quality of connectivity became a key determinant in the quality of educational experiences. Connectivity quality in higher income countries was rapidly restored to pre-pandemic levels and sometimes even enhanced, paving the way for digital learning. However, in lower income countries, connectivity service that had been subpar before the pandemic sunk lower still, rendering digital learning unreliable and unusable. From 2020 to early 2023, there were countless testimonials about the ways in which low-quality networks caused challenges for students in developing countries, including for those who owned first-rate hardware. Frustration with connectivity for education was also expressed in various surveys. A Gallup poll of higher education students in Pakistan was illustrative: over 80 per cent of learners said they had problems with internet connectivity during online classes. These problems regularly made education inaccessible or, at best, frustrating to access.[194] A separate survey of higher education students attending Delhi University in India found that the vast majority lacked fixed-line broadband connections at home, and two-thirds did not have the stable mobile internet connectivity needed to follow education remotely. This prompted the student union to launch an #EducationWithoutExclusion campaign to protest the university's decision to move forward with online examinations.[195]

"Every three seconds [my teacher is] like, 'Rachel, you're glitching. Rachel, you're not moving.'"

– 17-year-old student, USA[xxxvi]

Learners in wealthier countries also endured significant connectivity challenges. A 2020 government survey of students in 118 higher education institutions across Australia helped shine a light on the pervasiveness of connectivity issues in rich countries. The accompanying report identified the most frequently mentioned issues that students reported about their experiences with remote online learning: first among them was "IT problems", above "lack of/ inadequate academic interaction" and "lack of engagement". Many students complained of having slow internet speeds at home compared with the speeds that would have been available on campus without university closures. Close to half of the survey respondents reported that connectivity and other IT parameters simply "did not work well".[196] Globally, while connectivity problems may have been less severe and less frequent in rich countries than in poorer countries, they presented challenges everywhere, especially for underprivileged students and teachers.

Pandemic changes also disrupted strategies students – often students from poorer households – used to establish free links to the internet. For example, learners that relied on public Wi-Fi hotspots of the type found in schools, libraries and community centres or those offered by private businesses, such as mall operators, restaurants or coffee shops, were suddenly without access as many of these centres and businesses closed during lockdowns. This, however, did not necessarily stop students from trying to get online. Media accounts relayed how learners, sometimes in violation of stay-at-home orders, roamed through neighbourhoods in search of homes or businesses still beaming out an unlocked internet connection, a sort of turn-of-the-century digital nomadism. Young people hoping to follow education online would sometimes make their way to parking lots in front of fast-food restaurants to piggyback on open Wi-Fi signals intended for employees and customers.[197] Some governments tried to outfit school buses so they could be used as mobile Wi-Fi hotspots,[198] but these efforts, usually limited in scale and duration, only patched deep connectivity inequities that surfaced during the pandemic.

> Variations in connectivity quality gave rise to a bifurcation of educational opportunity that was unique to the shift to ed-tech.

Viewed from a global level, variations in connectivity quality gave rise to fast and seamless channels to education as well as slow and unreliable channels, a bifurcation of educational opportunity that was unique to the shift to ed-tech. While in-person, school-based education was hardly equal prior to the pandemic, there were not fast and slow lanes, at least not in a literal sense. In a physical classroom, the body and voice of a teacher never froze, and printed education resources did not pixelate or disappear because of a faulty wireless connection. This was a consequence of moving education to digital environments. It reinforced disparities in the quality of educational experiences of disadvantaged learners and out-groups.

> The promise of connectivity to help equalize education tended to rest on the faulty premise that connectivity itself was equal.

The experience further revealed that the promise of connectivity to help equalize education for underprivileged learners tended to rest on the faulty premise that connectivity itself was equal (or might quickly be made equal). The pandemic disruptions highlighted the many ways connectivity was profoundly unequal, even when it was available. Its reliability and speed varied between learners in different geographical areas and those with different connectivity plans, hardware and providers. These divisions accelerated and intensified existing inequities and made education less fair than it had been before the pivot from schools to fully remote digital learning.

EFFORTS TO PROVIDE DIGITAL SKILLS TRAINING LEFT LOW-LEVEL USERS BEHIND

Inadequate digital skills and competencies ranked as the greatest barriers to technology use for education, and this was true across countries at different levels of development.

Ministries of education were quick to recognize digital skills deficits as a central challenge to scaling up technology-mediated learning during the pandemic, and this was true across countries at different levels of development. An Oxford University Press survey of English teachers in 92 countries found that inadequate digital skills and competencies ranked as the greatest barriers to technology use for education, just behind poor digital access.[199]

But options to build the digital skills of these groups were limited during the pandemic. Restrictions on movement and gatherings meant that any training efforts had to be conducted at a distance. Despite the physical limitations caused by the pandemic, many governments attempted to support digital skills building. There was recognition that gains in digital literacy would help education reach more learners during the pandemic and also likely improve its quality by eliminating capacity barriers that inhibited the productive use of connected technology for learning.

Courses in digital pedagogy were hastily organized for teachers and parents, almost always through an online platform of some type. How-to guides for ed-tech, and digital technology more generally, were disseminated

electronically. But digital guides and training of this sort could not reach people who did not use or know how to use connected technologies and navigate the internet. It was the digital equivalent of searching for non-literate people in library aisles stacked high with books.

Like teachers and parents, students also needed help building their digital skills. At the global level, not all or even most young people were 'digital natives' in the sense that they grew up surrounded by connected technology. Many of them were as unfamiliar with ed-tech as older adults when the pandemic hit, and young children often lacked the literacy skills and general knowledge that provide important foundations for digital skills. Even students that were dexterous with technology still needed time, practice and assistance to familiarize themselves with new online tools and hubs for education. They often looked to teachers and parents for IT support. This was convenient for children in regular contact with adults who possessed advanced technology skills and a serious disadvantage for students who could not easily receive or request technical assistance. In the Oxford University Press study, 1 in 2 teachers said a lack of parental understanding of digital tools and online platforms limited the effectiveness of support available to students.[200]

> Online seminars commonly offered during the pandemic on how to use ed-tech productively excluded, by definition, people who did not already have the requisite skills to go online to find and attend them.

Conventional modes of teaching basic digital skills in physical settings, including computer labs staffed with on-site instructors, tended to be off-limits due to COVID-19 restrictions. This blocked the hands-on, over-the-shoulder training commonly used to help digital novices become more autonomous users of technology. The online seminars commonly offered during the pandemic about how to use ed-tech productively excluded, by definition, people who did not already have the requisite skills to go online and navigate digital spaces to find these seminars. This meant that people with nascent digital skills – and often those most in need of education or with children most in need of education – tended to be left behind. It also rendered schemes to distribute connected devices to teachers and caregivers with very low-level digital skills dubious in value. For hardware provision programmes to serve an educational purpose, they needed to be accompanied by training on how to use these devices for teaching and learning.

As the pandemic wore on and education became increasingly dependent on digital spaces, it was hard to avoid the conclusion that the digital upskilling programmes that countries and education systems rolled out in response to the pandemic were serving more advantaged learners and households. Programmes to develop the digital skills and capacities that underlie learning with ed-tech generally failed to reach those who needed it most.

TECHNOLOGY PRIVILEGED FAMILIES WITH TIME TO SUPPORT EDUCATION AT HOME

In practice, country efforts to assure educational continuity at a distance through technology were dependent on the active engagement of families. This involved considerable time commitments. Parents and other caregivers had to help children navigate digital learning portals and establish schedules and routines for technology-mediated instruction – tasks that were previously fully or largely managed by teachers and schools. Language skills also took on outsized importance: parents with limited command of the official languages of instruction could not easily facilitate technology-based learning from home.

Ed-tech had long been presented as an equalizer that would allow children with different home environments and varying access to parental support to participate without constraints. Yet families quickly discovered that often ad hoc models of remote technology-based education rolled out during the pandemic required lengthy and regular time commitments – in addition to financial obligations and digital competencies. Media accounts and academic studies described how parents felt exhausted and perpetually 'on call' when school closures moved formal education into the home.[201]

"I can't keep doing this. Please open the schools. The idea that I might have to continue to work while facilitating another subpar semester of virtual learning is almost too much to bear."

– Nicole Russell, writer and mother, USA[xxxvii]

A 2020 study from China attempted to quantify the time primary caregivers, usually mothers, spent assisting children with learning tasks. It found that caregivers dedicated approximately 50 to 60 minutes per day supporting distance education, often by troubleshooting connected technology.[202] One-third of the over 4,000 families surveyed for the study said that this time obligation hindered them from doing other work or searching for a job. The study estimated that this time loss translated into an expected income loss of roughly two months of an average worker's yearly salary. Given this reality, it was unsurprising that poor and rural caregivers, unable to easily dial back work obligations, spent considerably less time on their children's education than wealthier urban caregivers who tended to have more flexibility to support home-based learning. In addition to the costs of time, the China study found that a strong majority of families had to independently bear the costs of technology purchases to keep children connected to distance education. These outlays of time and money led to reductions in household incomes and placed a disproportionate burden on poor households that had less of a margin to absorb new costs associated with the switch to ed-tech. Separate research observed that these strains resulted in decreased spending on food and health as well as on education in poor rural households in China, a factor that put underprivileged children at further educational disadvantage.[203]

> Parents unable to carve out several hours a week to help their children navigate and stay focused on digital education tasks sometimes fretted that they were 'bad parents'.

Studies from the USA similarly indicated that caregivers were spending extensive time mediating technology-dependent education. A household survey conducted in California suggested that parents logged an average of 6.5 hours *per child* to support learning activities in a typical week.[204] This amounted to close to 80 hours per month for a family with three children – hardly, in effect, the seamless and minimally time-consuming experience parents had hoped remote learning with ed-tech might deliver as they struggled to meet work obligations that did not always change with the closure of schools. There was often a sense of obligation associated with the time demands of distance education. Parents unable to carve out several hours a week to help their children navigate and stay focused on digital education tasks sometimes fretted that they were 'bad parents'.

The children that lost out in this arrangement were those who could not lean on family members with sufficient time to support ed-tech modes of distance learning. These learners commonly came from immigrant or refugee families, single-parent households or families with two working-class parents. By contrast, children who had caregivers with sufficient availability to help mediate technology-reliant remote learning enjoyed significant advantages that often reflected other socio-economic privileges.

> Education could be – and regularly was – interrupted because parents were not at home or unavailable to resolve problems that often arose with ed-tech.

While parental ability to support children's education was not a new barrier to learning, the shift to remote learning made it a hard barrier, one that could halt formal education altogether. When children attended schools staffed by professional teachers, they generally received education regardless of how available or unavailable parents might be at home. Many school systems even had strategies and protocols in place to provide extra educational services to children that had overstretched caregivers. School closures and the recourse to ed-tech changed this. Education could be – and regularly was – interrupted because parents were not at home or unavailable to resolve problems that often arose with ed-tech. This carried particularly high stakes for younger children who were less likely than their older counterparts to be able to learn autonomously with ed-tech.

WEALTHY FAMILIES FOUND ALTERNATIVE SOLUTIONS

When privileged parents could not spend time supporting the remote learning of children or were concerned about the quality of distance education being offered by public institutions, they often found alternative solutions. So-called pod schools or learning pods, for example, became popular with parents living in wealthy enclaves. This education model, prevalent in the USA but observed in other countries as well, established informal microschools for small groups of students who lived in close proximity. Pod schools commonly involved in-person instruction provided by paid educators who also helped ensure the facilitation of distance learning provided by accredited schools.[205] These models often amounted to an outsourcing of the time and labour needed to manage and facilitate ed-tech learning.

> A cottage industry of companies and consultants emerged to help high-income families organize pod schools – sometimes precipitating a mass flight from public schools.

Pod schools also afforded families the possibility of bypassing technology-only modes of learning in favour of in-person instruction and peer-to-peer interaction, despite lockdowns and school closures. Fees for these alternative educational arrangements tended to be prohibitively expensive for poor families. In wealthy countries, costs could exceed USD 2,000 per child per month.[206] This, however, did not slow their growth. In the first half of 2020, a cottage industry of companies and consultants emerged to help high-income families organize pod schools – sometimes precipitating a mass flight from public schools. In some affluent areas in the USA, pod schools became so widespread that public school leaders felt compelled to express their concerns that these unofficial and unsanctioned schools would widen access and equity gaps in education.[207] Critics picked up on these concerns and accused families participating in pod schools of "opportunity hoarding" and directing energy, resources and advocacy away from public schools at a moment of crisis by constructing pay-to-use solutions for

their own children, thereby heightening exclusion.[208] Some pod schools also violated quarantine restrictions on movement and gatherings and were condemned on the grounds of jeopardizing health as well as equity. Ironically, these shadow education institutions tended to germinate in online spaces and through the efforts of internet-savvy parents intent on insulating their already advantaged children from the online learning that was being rolled out, often chaotically, by public schools. It was, at root, a case of families using connected technology to shield young learners from the perceived weaknesses of ed-tech as a primary medium for learning. Families without the connectivity and digital skills needed to find and organize pods were doubly disadvantaged: they could not access the formal remote and online education being offered by public institutions nor could they easily access alternative non-public options for education.

"When parents with privilege open their checkbooks and create private one-room schoolhouses for their children, they follow a long pattern of weakening the public education system they leave behind."

– Valerie Strauss, education reporter[xxxviii]

Apart from pod schools, privileged families also turned to high-priced private schools that were sometimes assumed to offer better education in the face of the unique challenges posed by the pandemic. Student enrolment in private schools declined globally for much of 2020 and 2021 due to high unemployment and other disruptions that decreased household income, as witnessed in India and other high-population countries.[209] However, enrolment in private schools often increased among wealthier families that did not experience large reductions due to the pandemic. In numerous countries, well-off parents decided that public schools were unable to satisfactorily manage the transition to ed-tech and opted instead to pay tuition to privately run schools with more experience and/or resources to support learning at a distance. In Canada, for instance, private schools advertised smaller classes and a greater ability to adapt to the disruptions of the pandemic, attributes that prompted many rich families to pull children out of public school and enrol them in private institutions.[210] In the USA, high-income and white parents of young students were much more likely to exit public education systems in favour of private school alternatives compared with low-income families.[211] In the Republic of Korea, the pandemic and associated school closures led numerous upper-class families to enrol their children in for-profit 'cram schools' that commonly touted more intensive, autonomous and exam-centred remote learning experiences than those being offered by public schools.[212]

The marketing surrounding such schools tended to use the pandemic as an opportunity to draw students from public schools to private ones.

Advertising by private education institutions commonly targeted parents and students with messages highlighting pandemic uncertainties and promising to provide 'certainty' – for a price.[213] Around the world, private schools and universities flaunted their ability to offer boutique ed-tech experiences that would demand less parental oversight and intervention and be of higher quality than experiences and services provided by public institutions.[214] A survey of teachers conducted by McKinsey in eight countries (Australia, Canada, China, France, Germany, Japan, UK and USA) suggested that private schools – which often had superior resources overall and better technology capacities compared with public schools – might indeed have been better at managing the pivot to ed-tech. Findings revealed that teachers who taught at public schools gave remote learning – as assessed on a scale 1 to 10, with 1 being abysmal and 10 being superb – an average global score of 4.8, while their peers in private schools averaged a rating of 6.2. Perhaps even more telling was the finding that teachers working in schools with high levels of poverty found virtual classes to be "especially ineffective", rating them 3.5 out of 10, and, as the report authors put it, "bolstering concerns that the pandemic has exacerbated educational inequalities".[215]

> The elite flight from public schools further segregated education and, in many instances, diverted vital funds away from public institutions at the moment they were most needed.

The tendency to switch to private schools was not only prompted by a concern for higher quality technology-first education. It was also driven by recognition that in some countries, private institutions, not always subject to the same rules and regulations as public institutions, were able to reopen sooner and exercise greater agility in doing so. At the start of the 2020/21 academic year, numerous affluent parents in the USA turned to private schools because those schools often offered in-person education, while many public schools continued to rely on distance learning with ed-tech. In mid-2020, the National Association of Independent Schools in the USA noted that its network of high-priced schools had reported a 58 per cent increase in interest from families from before the pandemic. Some of these member schools cost over USD 60,000 per year to enrol a single student.[216] Parents with more limited means, enticed by guarantees of in-person schooling, also switched their children to non-public institutions. For these families, it was often a simple dollar-and-cents calculation: even after paying new tuition bills, parents could break even or make more money if they could work longer hours by avoiding the labour and interruptions of overseeing technology-centric distance learning from the home.[217] Enrolling children in schools open for in-person instruction was therefore a way to minimize or try to minimize exposure to technology-based distance learning from home. This elite flight from public schools, observed most distinctly in the USA, further segregated education and, in many instances, diverted vital funds away from public institutions at the moment they were most needed.

Another side effect of this movement was a boom in enrolments at private religious schools. For instance, the Association of Christian Schools International, one of the largest networks of evangelical schools in the USA, recorded student growth of over 10 per cent in its global network of over 3,500 schools between the 2019/20 and 2020/21 academic years. Ray Moore, founder of the Christian Education Initiative, called the growth a "once-in-100-year moment" for the expansion of religious education.[218] Like other private schools, religious institutions regularly publicized the availability of in-person classes and manageable ed-tech.

These alternative options for education were usually outside the reach of poor families, who had to contend with the non-boutique options available. Private schools often proved more adept, at least initially, at making changes to adapt to the disruptions presented by the crisis and were therefore able to offer better quality distance education that could be easier for learners and their families to use and follow. Notably, this 'premium' provision of education tended to make use of mixed modes of learning that included a range of tech and non-tech strategies. In the final analysis, the shift to ed-tech, particularly in high-income countries, prompted an exodus of privileged learners from public institutions to private institutions that promised to ensure a smoother switch to distance education or allow in-person instruction.

SOCIOCULTURAL DIFFERENCES PUT POOR FAMILIES AT A DISADVANTAGE

Beyond the capacity, time and resource limitations that led to increased disadvantages for poor families, negative self-perceptions of academic ability – disproportionately observed among underprivileged parents and caregivers – likely further impeded the learning of poor students when education moved from in-person schooling to remote ed-tech. A major review of research conducted prior to the pandemic found that low-income families consistently report feeling less able to support their children's education than middle- and upper-income families and also give lower rankings to their sense of academic self-efficacy. The review argued that these negative perceptions likely intensified among underprivileged caregivers during the pandemic, when families were unexpectedly thrust into the role of facilitating education at home.[219] Separate studies conducted during the pandemic corroborated that working-class parents felt considerably less comfortable and capable of supporting technology-mediated distance learning for their children than wealthier parents.[220] This could, in turn, trigger stress and anxiety because families worried that their limited capacities to support home-based learning with technology would hurt the chances of their children to succeed academically.

Social science research has shown that underprivileged families tend to place greater trust in and reliance on teachers to make good decisions concerning education. For this reason, they take a relatively hands-off approach to formal education, whereas more privileged families are more likely to carve out a role for themselves in educational processes and engage more actively with schools and teachers.[221] Privileged families are generally more reliant on *independent* cultural norms, whereas families that are less well-off tend to rely more on *interdependent* cultural norms, both by necessity and learned experience.[222]

These differences put underprivileged families at a sharp disadvantage when education moved outside of schools. Distance education with ed-tech was distinct from school-based learning in that it almost always required active facilitation by adults at home. The solutions were typically new and untested at scale and, for these reasons, uncertain and often prone to glitches or outright failure. Their successful implementation demanded regular oversight and intervention from families. Without in-person schooling, education was not an external responsibility that families could entrust to professional educators. In this changed context, hands-off family approaches to education were no longer sufficient. Remote digital learning with ed-tech demanded that caregivers directly oversee and facilitate the learning of children. Obligations previously fulfilled by schools, such as ensuring that students moved from one class to another, stayed on task and were able to access educational resources, were outsourced to parents.

Wealthy families tended to make this transition with relative ease, as it conformed to their earlier orientations towards education. Poorer families

had more difficulty with the transition, largely because it did not fit their existing expectations of education. As was documented in Pakistan during the pandemic, as well as in other countries, underprivileged parents were sometimes criticized by their children's teachers for not being more involved in supporting education that had become reliant on ed-tech in the home environment.[223] Yet from the perspective of these parents, teachers and schools were not providing necessary services. Many parents did not deem it their role or within their capacities to support education being provisioned over connected technology in the home.

> The turn to fully remote learning demanded that families exercise proactive, ad hoc and informal strategies to establish contact with teachers or other authorities who could answer questions or provide guidance.

The pandemic also increased the stakes for productive and regular communication with schools and teachers. Such communication was often the only available means for families to unblock the many problems that arose with the overnight shift to remote learning with ed-tech, problems that ranged from the trivial (optimizing user settings on the operating system of school-issued devices) to the essential (finding, accessing and uploading assignments and examinations). Normal and more established modes of communication with families, such as report cards or pre-planned meetings with teachers, were less feasible with the closure of schools. The turn to fully remote learning demanded that families exercise proactive, ad hoc and informal strategies to establish contact with teachers or other authorities who could answer questions or provide guidance. Underprivileged families tended to be less comfortable and also less familiar with such strategies.

Moreover, the modes of getting in touch with education professionals also changed. Like education itself, communication with teachers relied almost exclusively on connected technology, often involving proprietary messaging apps, such as Apple's iMessage, Tencent's WeChat, Facebook's Messenger or WhatsApp. Teachers often encouraged parents to contact them directly at a personal mobile phone number. While this was well-meaning and arguably a commonsense solution to provide support during a major education disruption, poor families were less likely than wealthy families to feel entitled to contact teachers at their personal numbers, especially outside of normal working hours. More privileged families had fewer qualms about this. Research conducted for this publication found numerous examples of teachers complaining about relentless messaging from parents who enjoyed socio-economic advantages. The research also surfaced evidence to show that teachers serving underprivileged children often had the opposite complaint: parents almost never messaged them.

These overlapping cultural factors put underprivileged families at a triple disadvantage: (1) Low self-perceptions of academic ability and capacity to help children with academic tasks caused stress and likely resulted in

The academic achievement of disadvantaged learners was considerably lower than would have been expected were it not for the pandemic and reliance on home-based remote learning with ed-tech.

low levels of assistance. (2) Belief in and respect for interdependencies and the separation of formal education from home life was poorly suited to the successful uptake of ed-tech, which often required vigilant parental facilitation and oversight. (3) Trust in educators to do their work autonomously and without proactive family interventions resulted in reduced communication with teachers at a time when this communication was especially necessary. The combination of these factors likely contributed to the underachievement of disadvantaged children observed during the pandemic. Studies from Belgium,[224] France,[225] the Netherlands,[226] South Africa,[227] the USA[228] and other countries with reliable data found unambiguous evidence that the academic achievement of disadvantaged learners was considerably lower than would have been expected were it not for the pandemic and reliance on home-based remote learning with ed-tech.

SCHOOL-BASED INEQUITIES WERE AMPLIFIED IN THE TRANSITION TO REMOTE LEARNING

Prior to the pandemic, there was a sense that digital learning could be disassociated from schools. Popular thinking held that, on the internet, geographic constraints melted away. The physical space of the school that contained – and did much to shape – educational experiences prior to the pandemic no longer existed when teaching and learning suddenly shifted from classrooms to virtual spaces accessed from home. For some, this shift signalled the arrival of deep and presumably permanent transformations to education. In digital spaces, schools would no longer be the principal arbitrators of educational exchange, and, in their stead, new and superior pedagogies could emerge. These changes, it was often assumed, would enable more effective, efficient and innovative means of organizing learners and teachers in education.

The shift from in-person schooling to fully remote virtual learning was less an exercise in transformation than an exercise in replicating traditional school education in digital environments.

During the COVID-19 educational disruption, however, the school, as an institution, remained the locus and principal arbitrator of virtual education experiences. In virtual spaces, just like in physical spaces, schools continued to organize what teachers and students did, when they did it and how. Around the world, models of digital learning mirrored, with remarkable uniformity, school-based models. In online spaces, students entered virtual equivalents of the schools and classes they had attended prior to the pandemic. These virtual schools and classes were usually led, maintained and taught by the same people that led, maintained and taught them in person and at school. When digital learning worked, students typically found themselves in a synchronous virtual class with the same instructor and classmates that they had been working with prior to the pandemic. In practice, the shift from in-person schooling to fully remote virtual learning was less an exercise in transformation than an exercise in replicating traditional school education in digital environments.

Such an approach largely guaranteed that the quality of a student's online learning experience would be determined by the school that he or she had attended prior to the pandemic. This led to predictable results: well-resourced schools managed the digital transition far more smoothly than their poorly resourced counterparts. The inequities that had marked in-person schooling were, in effect, projected into the remote virtual experience.

"I have colleagues in schools in the center of [the nearby city of] Antigua, who do meetings on Zoom or send assignments through [Google] Classroom. Those of us from the villages don't have access to this technology."

– Teacher, Guatemala[xxxix]

This projection often entailed amplification. Inequities did not merely remain the same with the transition to remote learning with ed-tech, they rather enlarged and became more severe. The digital transition was so complex and demanding of resources as well as new technological and pedagogical capabilities that many low-performing schools struggled to provide any educational services online. And even when they could, they often had trouble delivering synchronous learning opportunities where learners could interact with teachers and peers in real time. High-performing schools, by contrast, generally managed the digital transition with greater ease and provided a reasonable approximation of school- and class-based instruction online. These schools also tended to do much more to support offline modes of learning by, for example, sending physical learning packs to homes or sometimes establishing mechanisms for families to request and receive hard copies of books from school libraries. This meant the learners served by schools providing good-quality ed-tech services were, ironically, the most likely to have access to learning resources not dependent on ed-tech. The inverse was also true: learners most likely to need physical learning materials because their schools did not provide suitable ed-tech services were the least likely to be able to get them from schools. Only in rare instances were resources (technological, physical and financial) shifted to underperforming schools to help them support distance learning.

"The quality and quantity of pedagogical support received from schools varied according to the social class of families."

– Researchers studying the effect of the pandemic on the achievement gap[xl]

Children from upper- and middle-class families in the UK were more than twice as likely to attend online lessons everyday than those from working-class families.

Research conducted in the UK detailed these new digital forms of school inequality. Studies found that schools serving poor students were less likely than schools serving better-off students to provide online classes, online video conferencing and online chat functions and more likely to support home-learning through passive means, such as assigning learning tasks.[229] Likewise, a majority of wealthy households reported receiving active help from schools in the form of online teaching, private tutoring and online chats with teachers. Yet only a minority of poor households received similar support. Another UK study suggested that children from upper- and middle-class families were more than twice as likely to attend online lessons everyday than those from working-class families.[230] Whatever the metric, schools serving wealthy students, at least in the UK, seemed to provide greater ed-tech services and support. These schools were more likely to message students and their parents, broadcast lessons and provide technical assistance.

In the USA, research found that schools serving minority students did very little to support digital learning. A national review of educational data conducted by McKinsey suggested that only 60 per cent of black students and 70 per cent of Hispanic students were regularly logging into online instruction, meaning between 30 per cent and 40 per cent of black and Hispanic students received *no* online teaching, compared with only 10 per cent of white students.[231] The review further estimated that when black and Hispanic students did receive remote digital instruction, it was likely to be of low quality. The McKinsey researchers concluded that these and other discrepancies would result in twice as much "learning loss" for students attending schools serving low-income students than for those in schools serving average-income students.

"Schools have responded to the crisis by offering markedly different packages of home-learning materials. This has led to substantial inequalities along socio-economic divides."
– Researchers studying inequalities in children's experiences of home-learning during school closures[xli]

Some social scientists have suggested that the varied school support evidenced during the pandemic may have been heightened by low expectations held for underprivileged students – a bias that had been well documented prior to the pandemic.[232] An important examination into why distance learning during the COVID-19 pandemic likely increased social class achievement gaps in the USA found that differences in perception may have influenced the behaviour of teachers during school closures, such that teachers in privileged neighbourhoods provided more information to students and their families because they expected more from them in terms of effort and achievement. The authors wrote: "The fact that upper/

middle-class parents are better able than working-class parents to comply with the expectations of teachers may have reinforced this phenomenon. These discrepancies echo data showing that working-class students tend to request less help in their schoolwork than upper/middle-class ones, and they may even avoid asking for help because they believe that such requests could lead to reprimands."[233]

"Schools set the terms for whether students can mobilize their playful digital pursuits for achievement, and they do so differently by student class and race. At schools serving primarily working- and middle-class youth of color, teachers communicate to students that their digital play is not valuable for learning. At a school serving wealthy and white youth, teachers communicate to students that their digital play is integral to learning and achievement."

– Matthew H. Rafalow, author of *Digital Divisions*[xlii]

> Schools serving underprivileged students were often slower to reopen than schools serving more advantaged students.

Schools were the pivotal on-off switch for technology-reliant remote learning. When schools closed, ed-tech was essential for continuity of teaching and learning; when they reopened, education was less reliant on technology, if at all. It did not take long for a near-global consensus to emerge that remote ed-tech modes of learning were far less effective than school-based modes, even if they were still deemed necessary for health reasons. Just a few weeks into the crisis, parents, teachers, learners and policy-makers stood united in their opinion that traditional in-person schooling was strongly preferable to fully distance education, and this view usually hardened as the crisis stretched on. Yet around the world, schools serving underprivileged students were often slower to reopen than schools serving more advantaged students. The disparities could be particularly striking in countries with decentralized education systems. In the USA, for example, a RAND Corporation study found that while only one-third of schools nationwide were using fully remote instruction in October 2020, half of schools with high levels of poverty were doing the same. When it came to US schools serving student populations that were under 25 per cent white, this figure shot up even higher: nearly two-thirds were using fully remote instruction.[234] This meant that poor and minority students, those most likely to be disadvantaged by technology-reliant remote learning, had to contend with this mode of education for longer durations than more privileged students. It was a compounding of disadvantage: the forced transition to remote ed-tech resulted in an exacerbation of inequality, and so did the often delayed transition back to in-person schooling.

As school closures stretched beyond 2020 and deep into 2021, 2022 and, in rare instances, early 2023, it became increasingly apparent that the quality of schools determined, to a considerable extent, the quality of digital learning experiences. This contradicted the promise of what ed-tech was

The quality of schools determined, to a considerable extent, the quality of digital learning experiences.

supposed to deliver. Before the pandemic, many education experts saw connected technology as a means to circumvent lower quality schools and provide learners and families direct channels to first-rate instruction and educational content residing online. Ed-tech, the thinking went, should open portals to high-quality education, regardless of the capacities of local schools and educators. But in the response to the COVID-19 school closures, schools shaped and mediated experiences with ed-tech for remote learning. Unsurprisingly, low-performing schools provided poorer experiences (or none at all) while high-performing schools provided better experiences. The ideas widely circulated before the pandemic that ed-tech could be parachuted into communities with broken education systems and provide cost-effective alternatives to schools proved illusory in practice throughout the crisis. Even when schools were closed, they still influenced ed-tech modes of learning, and, in many instances, exacerbated inequity in the educational experience.

NO ROOM FOR ANYWHERE LEARNING AND FIXED TIMES FOR ANYTIME EDUCATION

Virtual learning was not placeless learning. The corporal bodies of students did not disappear.

Distance learning during the pandemic was not placeless learning. It rather moved the physical location of education from the communal and publicly supported social space of schools to the private space of homes. This shift carried insidious repercussions for education and educational equality, commonly resulting in disadvantages for underprivileged families.

Technology-mediated education, despite its 'online' and 'virtual' labels, still required a physical learning space for students, whether in the home or elsewhere. The corporal bodies of students did not disappear; they had to be somewhere to learn with a screen or other technology. In a best-case scenario, a learning space might include a private room for study; protection from wind, rain, snow and heat; quiet or manageable levels of sound; a desk or table; a comfortable chair; adequate lighting; and physical resources to support study such as pencils, pens, notebooks and paper books. Globally, very few students, especially poor students, had home-learning environments that provided such conditions.

"It is not easy to study in these conditions because we do not have enough space at home to do so and she is often disturbed by her brothers and family members."

– Father, Democratic Republic of the Congo[xliii]

Schools were created to facilitate education, and their architecture, design and physical organization usually reflected this function, even if imperfectly. Students' homes, in contrast, tended to be busy, shared spaces that served multiple functions – places for sleeping, washing, cooking, eating, working, entertaining, relaxing and caring for children or older people. Few were optimized for learning, even if the accommodation of study and learning was one of their many purposes. This meant that when schools shut down and learning moved to the home, students occupied spaces that were not intended to be a principal location for formal education. Families did what they could to repurpose their homes to accommodate distance learning, but these efforts quickly ran into material constraints: a quiet space was not always available, tables and chairs had to be shared with others, paper was hard to come by or there was little or no money for books or other educational resources.

Schools normally play a vital role in equalizing imbalances in home-based spaces. Prior to the pandemic, the physical space of education was quite consistent for students attending the same school, regardless of a student's home situation. These spaces tended to support education in ways that homes did not or could not. The best-resourced schools had amenities that were rare in even the wealthiest households. These could include science labs and technical equipment, music rooms and instruments, art studios, workshops for carpentry, theatres, sports fields, gyms and other specialized spaces to support physical education. Under-resourced schools offered far fewer options but nonetheless tended to provide basic amenities often unavailable in the homes of the children they served, including running water, toilets, playgrounds, desks and textbooks.

For many students the physical home environment was often a place that made technology-dependent modes of distance learning difficult and, in some instances, impossible.

These realities meant that the closures of schools and the shift to home-based learning entailed a change in physical environment that was less conducive to education. This was observed across income groups in and across countries. Extremely wealthy students that had been attending high-priced private schools may have found, for example, that they could no longer take advantage of sophisticated laboratory equipment, libraries or media centres that had previously supported learning, even if they encountered few obstacles learning from home with ed-tech. Yet these students still had private rooms, equipped with doors they could shut, desks, comfortable chairs and other material amenities to support study. Their physical home environment may not have been as educationally enriching as their school environment had been, but it was still highly conducive to learning with connected technology. The same could not be said for less privileged learners. For them, the physical home environment was often a place that made technology-dependent modes of distance learning difficult and, in some instances, impossible.

"These children … they often don't have electricity – not even a lamp to study. So, the [distance learning] classes benefit only children in … the big cities."

– Teacher, Burkina Faso[xliv]

Extensive data, mainly from high-[235] and middle-income countries,[236] highlighted the ways spatial and material constraints at home heightened disadvantage for underprivileged learners. A 2020 European Commission policy brief on fairness, for instance, found extensive evidence of home environments poorly suited for formal learning with technology. Across all 21 European countries studied, over 94 per cent of advantaged students had access to reading material at home, but this figure fell to as low as 76 per cent for disadvantaged children.[237] The policy brief also noted that, on average, 25 per cent of young children in European countries do not have their own room and "miss out" on a quiet learning environment, ranging from a low of 9 per cent of fourth grade students in Denmark to a high of 49 per cent in Italy. In the USA, a nationwide survey indicated that only 70 per cent of fourth grade students with low performance in mathematics reported having a quiet place to do their schoolwork during the 2020/21 school year, compared with 90 per cent of high-performing students.[238] A study conducted in China found that a significant proportion of students lacked a desk, while large numbers of students, especially in rural areas, did not have an isolated room, a quiet study environment or access to basic learning tools. The study concluded that "students in rural schools had categorically worse learning conditions than their urban peers".[239] A UK study found that 1 in 5 children in low-income households spent lockdown in an overcrowded home, while children from black, Asian and minority ethnic backgrounds were significantly more likely to experience poorer indoor conditions than white children and have less access to outdoor spaces.[240] Separate research in Australia concluded that children living in low socio-economic areas were 12 times as likely to be living in an overcrowded situation. These realities presented major barriers to home-based digital learning during school closures.[241]

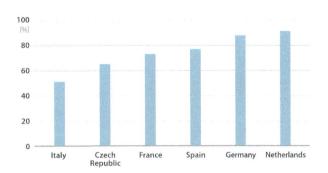

Figure 10:

Percentage of fourth grade students with their own bedroom in European countries

Source: Adapted from European Commission, 2021

Prior to the pandemic, connected mobile devices were commonly hailed as tools that could untether learning from specific physical locations (generally assumed to be schools) and enable 'anywhere and anytime learning'. This quality was supposed to assuage educational inequalities by empowering learning at times and in spaces selected by students. But during the pandemic, the anywhere of 'anywhere learning' was almost always the home. Students could rarely leave their homes to find more conducive learning environments, regardless of the quality of their connected mobile technology or the comfort or discomfort of their physical environment. Governments restricted movement due to the risks of the pandemic. But there were other restrictions that kept ed-tech modes of learning tethered to the home: Wi-Fi signals with limited range, the need to regularly recharge batteries and parents that did not want children and youth wandering away, even if the home environment was poorly suited for learning. Also, in the context of the pandemic, the places that students might have typically gone to find a better learning space, whether libraries, community centres, cafes, parks or even the homes of friends or relatives, were often closed or otherwise off-limits.

The challenge of finding appropriate physical learning spaces was particularly acute for homeless students for whom schools had previously been sanctuaries of stability and physical comfort.

The challenge of finding appropriate physical learning spaces was particularly acute for homeless and home-insecure young people, for whom schools had previously been sanctuaries of stability and physical comfort. Solutions for these students to secure spaces to participate in remote learning with ed-tech tended to be extremely limited. Recognizing the special disadvantages of homeless students, some municipalities experimented opening spaces where students could access and use ed-tech in comfortable and sanitary environments. The city of Baltimore in the USA, for example, piloted "small group in-person learning sites" hosted at schools and with strict social-distancing procedures. The sites gave homeless and other vulnerable students places they could go to participate in virtual classes without interference.[242] The sites appear to have been successful, but they benefited only 200 learners in total, a small fraction of Baltimore's homeless student population.[243]

"There was no table for two kids to study, therefore, I had to send my daughter to her grandmother."

– Mother, Kyrgyzstan[xlv]

Just as the 'anywhere' aspect of 'anywhere and anytime learning' with ed-tech was largely illusory in practice, so too was the 'anytime' aspect. This was largely because many schools and teachers ran synchronous classes with exact start and end times or otherwise insisted on rigid time schedules for home-based remote learning. Class schedules that had been in use at schools before the pandemic were sometimes transferred wholesale into the digital environment. In communities where ed-tech was plentiful and distance learning was 'working', the times for education were not normally freed from prescribed timetables and schedules. In some instances, bureaucratic prescriptions for class times became stricter with remote learning: choices of start and end times for learning that had existed at schools or universities were often stripped away, such that timings were specified unilaterally. While some families welcomed clearly structured schedules for virtual learning, others were frustrated by them and perceived a missed opportunity to rethink the centrality of timekeeping to the organization and processes of education.

> Young people from poorer households were far more likely than those from wealthier ones to have domestic obligations such as caring for siblings or older family members who were also stuck at home during the pandemic.

Many of the negative repercussions of strict, inflexible scheduling for home-based distance learning seemed to fall hardest on disadvantaged students who were more likely to be saddled with time conflicts in the form of home or work obligations. Students who might have had time for fixed learning schedules when schools were open were not as available when schools closed and other routines and expectations arose. Young people from poorer households were far more likely than those from wealthier ones to have time-inflexible domestic obligations such as caring for siblings or older family members who were also largely confined to the home during the pandemic. They were also more likely to be working paid jobs, often to supplement family income that had been depleted due to widespread unemployment and other economic disruptions of the pandemic.

Moreover, students were commonly prevented from using connected devices at allocated learning times because the devices were needed by

<aside>Older family members tended to take priority if there were competing needs for limited technology, space or sound, as was common in small homes.</aside>

other family members at the same time. Academic participation regularly overlapped with virtual or physical engagements that were important for other family members. Older family members tended to take priority if there were competing needs for limited technology, space or sound, as was common in smaller homes. Teachers grew accustomed to seeing messages in class chats such as 'Have to go now, dad needs the computer'. They also learned that one of the reasons students might refuse to speak in an online class when called on was not because they were unprepared or did not want to intervene, but because they were sitting near adults in a closed space and were not free to speak out. Families regularly complained that student participation in virtual classes was noisy, as students did not always have or use headphones, and oral participation required breaking silence at times that could be inopportune for adults sharing the home. Bandwidth was yet another finite resource that tended to become scarce in crowded homes at peak hours for educational participation, and family allocation of it did not always favour education. Parents would ask children to disable internet connections that were supporting education in order to preserve a different connection – perhaps a mother or father in a video call with an employer or an older sibling in a separate online class preparing for a high-stakes examination. The time and spatial problems that presented obstacles for online education applied to low-tech devices as well. Children relying on television or radio as a link to education rarely exercised full or even partial control over these unidirectional technologies.

<aside>During the pandemic, the lived reality for many students with connected technology bore no resemblance to the 'anywhere and anytime learning' that is often presented as a strength of ed-tech.</aside>

None of these obstacles had been an issue when schools were open. The time challenges of distance learning arose largely because homes had typically become the *only* space for formal learning. During the pandemic, the lived reality for many students with connected technology bore no resemblance to the 'anywhere and anytime learning' presented as a strength of ed-tech. The promise of ed-tech to make learning more flexible and equitable, particularly for children with challenging home environments, was largely unrealized in practice. Ed-tech learning was not 'anywhere', nor was it 'anytime', even if this was theoretically feasible.

VIDEO CLASSES MADE INEQUITY JARRINGLY VISIBLE

Reliance on new digital technologies to maintain the continuity of formal learning during school closures demanded new practices, rules and norms that presented unique and often under-anticipated challenges for disadvantaged learners. Perhaps no place was this more evident than in the embrace of synchronous video classes. Through the use of video and audio capture, these classes allowed teachers and students to see each other in organized digital environments and in real time, thereby approximating school-based modes of instruction. Software such as Google Meet, Microsoft Teams, Skype and Zoom typically mediated the virtual experience.

"Mom! My classmates can hear you! Mooooom! The teacher . . . The teacher can hear you!"

– Teenage girl, Mexico[xlvi]

Video classes were widely presumed to offer a best-case scenario for technology-first approaches to education, and schools, school systems and ministries of education elevated them as a preferred or sometimes singular way for students to remain connected to formal learning opportunities. Teachers also tended to like video classes because they felt familiar. The technology enabled them to observe student reactions and expressions just as they had done in brick-and-mortar schools. The classes further accommodated, even if awkwardly, pedagogies that had been used in traditional classroom environments. Furthermore, research conducted mostly prior to the pandemic had suggested that synchronous video lessons could be more effective for distance learning than non-video or non-synchronous options and appeared to promote interactivity and engagement,[244] foster community building[245] and counter feelings of loneliness.[246]

When video classes were first rolled out following the sudden and often chaotic closure of schools, media accounts and survey data indicated that many teachers and students were happy to see each other in online spaces. Familiarity in all forms was welcomed in the isolating context of the pandemic, and for many young people, nothing was more familiar than being in a formal learning environment with teachers and peers. The video aspect was important; it made ed-tech modes of remote learning seem 'normal', and it carried emotional weight. Media accounts relate that some teachers recalled tearing up upon seeing the faces of their students in virtual meeting rooms for the first time. Although video calls are over a decade old, the 'magic' of technology that allows people in different locations to clearly see and hear each other felt fresh again.

Many students had equally warm responses; they were thrilled to see both their teachers and their classmates again. When video classes worked, there was a sense that the pre-pandemic learning community had been reassembled. The software supporting these virtual gatherings tended to bring strong visual attention to whoever was speaking by making this person appear larger on the screen, but everyone in the class was usually visible. In some ways, it was very similar to school: a teacher at the front of the 'room' and students facing the teacher, with everyone able to see everyone else. There was a catch however: students and teachers were not in the public space of the school but in the private space of the home.

> With video lessons, information students had not previously disclosed or did not want teachers and peers to know was exposed, often without intent or warning.

The hazards of video capture outside the space of school became immediately apparent. Just beyond the face of a student or teacher was the previously intimate space of the home. Its sights and sounds became a backdrop for participation in education. While some of this was relatively harmless (the questionable decor of a teenager's bedroom) or even humorous (a pet jumping into the lap of an unsuspecting teacher), some of it was a source of embarrassment or indignity. A tilt of the camera could spark recognition that a student was living in an overcrowded house with multiple relatives, in a dilapidated space or in a place that signalled homelessness – a car, a shelter or a tent encampment. Young people would catch glimpses of a classmate's home life and see realities that had never been shared or discussed: a disabled family member, religious icons, people of different ethnicities and cultures, adults in unconventional dress or even signs of drug or alcohol use. Household life, from the banal to the unusual, shot into view. Information students had not previously disclosed or did not want teachers and peers to know was exposed, often without intent or warning, by cameras that mediated participation in education.

More worrying was the fact that the new video mediums of ed-tech opened entirely new tributaries for bullying, harassment and privacy violations, much of it aimed at girls and young women as well as other learners facing sociocultural disadvantages. Media accounts relate how teachers and principals were sometimes taken aback by how casually students would capture and circulate images and videos, typically taken surreptitiously, of their classmates in unflattering poses, often with commentary intended to degrade. Students could be brutal in their interpretations of what they saw: somebody's mother seen in the background of a video called a sexist name; somebody's disabled sibling labelled with a slur; and someone's same-sex caregivers berated with homophobic barbs. While bullying is hardly new to schooling, the windows into students' homes gave bullies, and those abetting them, more opportunities for denigration, privacy violations and harassment.[247]

The new video mediums of ed-tech opened entirely new tributaries for bullying, harassment and privacy violations, much of it aimed at girls and young women as well as other learners facing sociocultural disadvantages.

There were concerning gender aspects to this phenomenon. In the new screen-based space of education, girls and young women participating in classes could be easily photographed or video recorded without their knowledge or consent. In the physical setting of school, this secretive capture would have been much more difficult and perhaps presumed to be more invasive. But online, young people, accustomed to norms that anything in a digital space is fair game for replication and distribution, took screenshots without compunction and distributed them.[248] It was not uncommon for education authorities to learn that photos of girls and young women speaking in Zoom-type video classes were being bounced around public or semi-private social media channels maintained by groups of boys or men. These photographs could quickly be pulled into darker corners of the internet. Concerningly, the images often carried the name of the student photographed or recorded, as the software used by schools for video lessons commonly affixed a student's full name to his or her video feed. In some instances, technical options were available that harboured the potential to mitigate some of the risks associated with malicious video and image capture. Zoom and similar applications, for example, tended to offer functionality that could make student video feeds visible only to teachers and not to other students. Separate technical features could help block unapproved image capture, but these options were almost never fail-proof.[249]

But even when features that could help mitigate cyberbullying were available on videoconferencing platforms,[250] teachers were often unaware of them or did not know how to successfully activate or test them. Controls of this type commonly resided deep in settings that teachers did not know how to use or sometimes could not access because they did not have the necessary administrator privileges and controls. To best protect a Zoom virtual classroom, teachers would ideally understand options to lock the meeting, control screen-sharing, enable the 'waiting room', lock down the chat, remove participants, report users, suspend participant activities and rename participants – in addition to several other non-standard options.[251] For many instructors, simply getting through a single video class in default settings was difficult enough without having to navigate features that were challenging to activate and took practice to use. Beyond this, students often objected to school actions to block learners from seeing their classmates, and indeed, there were good reasons – pedagogical, cultural and social – for allowing students to see each other as well as a teacher in a synchronous lesson. Many assumed a class with all video cameras on was more participatory and helped establish coherent – and seen – communities of learners.

Virtual backgrounds and filters offered by some of the applications supporting video calls helped to obscure the homes and personal spaces of students.

This technology would keep objects in the foreground of the video clear and in focus, usually the face and body of a student or teacher while obscuring the background. Software supporting synchronous classes commonly offered options that allowed students, teachers and other users to select backgrounds that made it seem as if they were, for example, participating in a meeting from a beach, mountain landscape or alien planet. Media accounts from the lockdown period suggest that some students delighted in expressing themselves with these new virtual tools and often designed their own backgrounds rather than selecting from default options offered by platforms such as Microsoft Teams. Teachers would surprise and humour their students by appearing to teach from, say, the Moon one day and an undersea submarine the next. But just as it took white-collar professionals time to discover these virtual blurring and obscuring tools, it also took time for educators and students to find them. Many students used unfiltered video capture for weeks before they started to make tentative and then sometimes more regular use of virtual backgrounds. Norms often took hold that discouraged unreal backdrops on the grounds that these distortions were often perceived as obnoxious or distracting.

Students' self-expression with virtual backgrounds could also raise questions of appropriateness for formal academic settings. A student showing up to class with a brand name behind them, a picture of a celebrity, or a political slogan presented problems for teachers and administrators. It was unclear whether schools should be or were allowed to regulate these expressions. Given the hazards introduced by virtual backgrounds, some education systems established norms that students should keep their video feeds unaltered with no virtual background. This sometimes developed into an unspoken position that there was 'nothing to hide' and was seen by many educators as the ideal setting as it allowed them to see students *and* their surroundings, as they had been able to do in physical classrooms.

> Like the physical school setting itself, virtual backgrounds helped equalize – or at least disguise – inequities that existed beyond the school.

In countries around the world, numerous schools appear to have prohibited or strongly discouraged the use of background filters. In other contexts, schools appear to have mandated the use of specified filters, such as a simple blurring tool or backgrounds that did not leave room for self-expression. Required use of virtual backgrounds was, arguably, the digital equivalent of school uniforms and may have helped students with difficult home situations feel more comfortable participating in video classes. Like the physical school setting itself, virtual backgrounds helped equalize – or at least disguise – inequities that existed beyond the school. (Interestingly, there were anecdotal accounts that very wealthy students, like their disadvantaged peers, preferred options to obscure their background surroundings in video classes. This may have been because they were self-conscious about the opulence of their surroundings – a potential sign that even highly privileged youth recognized educational spaces as deserving of at least surface-level expressions of equality.)

However, despite these filters, the realities of home life could pop into view unexpectedly, often posing challenges or causing embarrassment to students.[252] In select instances, requirements to use video capture for academic participation may have blocked a child's access for reasons unrelated to technology or digital skills constraints. Media accounts included testimonies from teachers who noted that some of their most underprivileged students never attended video classes but participated in other forms of digital education. Some speculated that this non-attendance might trace back to caregivers prohibiting students to join classes that showed the insides of homes where marginal, unsafe or possibly even illicit activity was taking place, such as drug use. Indeed, it is not hard to imagine that a family might have uniformly barred students from turning on video cameras to participate in education for any number of reasons.

> It was unclear whether schools should or could require uniforms for academic participation in virtual spaces. In some countries there were brief experiments with virtual school uniforms.

While filters may have served as a virtual stand-in for school uniforms by equalizing views and expressions of family wealth or poverty, complications arose with actual school uniforms. Schools and school systems that had required students to wear uniforms discovered that young people often had no interest in wearing these uniforms to join video classes from home or that parents were opposed to the idea. In some countries, such as Thailand, there were brief experiments with virtual school uniforms – a visual effect that made it look as if a student was dressed in traditional school clothing, regardless of what the student was actually wearing.[253] These experiments, however, often resulted in a distorted appearance and were abandoned. With the physical space of the school shut down, it became unclear whether schools should or could require uniforms for academic participation in virtual spaces. Students were at home, after all. This issue became especially fraught in highly conservative societies where the dress of young people, especially of girls and young women, tended to be carefully monitored by schools. There were also other cultural complications. Female students who would typically wear a hijab in the public space of the school, for instance, would not, under normal circumstances, wear this covering garment in the private space of the home but often felt obliged to do so when joining a video class because it implied entering a public space.[254] This had the effect of blurring the separation of the private and public, even in the space of the home.

Around the world, the suddenness of the school closures during the pandemic meant that video classes became a reality for millions of learners and teachers in the absence of rules and norms to guide educational practices in the new virtual spaces made possible by ed-tech. In many contexts, answers to even the most rudimentary questions were lacking: Uniform or no uniform? Virtual background or no virtual background? There were a host of other questions too. Many students and families, for example, were unsure whether they could video record a synchronous online lesson. Lacking guidance from school administrators, media accounts suggest that teachers sometimes established their own guidelines, but these could differ from instructor to instructor, such that students at the same school and in the same class cohort might be encouraged to record their science class but be prohibited from recording their mathematics class. Yet with the technical capability to record or take a picture of anything happening on a computer screen rarely more than a few clicks away, privacy was never assured. Many educators believed that an advantage of the new digital medium was the ability to record lessons so that students could replay them to review content and strengthen understanding. Yet, this 'commonsense' functionality posed problems because the recordings typically included video footage of minors, and the legality of putting the content online was unclear, even in a password-protected location intended for school use. In some instances, issues around permissions and consent became paralysing and arguably prevented some of the unique and perhaps advantageous features of ed-tech from being fully realized.

> Public and private providers felt enormous pressure to roll out options for education, and rule books and statutes that might have been consulted or established in a non-emergency context were commonly swept aside.

Governments as well as private providers of education felt enormous pressure to roll out options for distance learning, and rule books and statutes that might have been consulted or established in a non-emergency context were commonly swept aside. Pandemic school closures were commonly understood as crises, and they were met with quick and often top-down decision-making that attempted to maintain educational continuity and avoid learning loss. The crisis framing often prevented teachers, students and families from voicing misgivings about video classes and other new educational practices that emerged during the pandemic.

"No one knows what the punishment is to have our video turned off. I guess the professor is going to reduce our participation grade, or maybe they'll call us out during lecture."

– University student, USA[xlvii]

For much of 2020, 2021 and into early 2023, schools and universities around the world made video participation in classes obligatory during periods of school closures. Data on video requirements for educational participation are difficult to find; however, a rare survey on the topic conducted by *Education Week* in the USA helps shine a light on practices at the school level. It found that "more than three-quarters of teachers, principals and district leaders whose schools or districts provide live remote instruction say that if students have working cameras on their devices, they must keep

Being seen on camera became the digital equivalent of school attendance.

them on during class". Of this group, a strong majority said students would "face consequences" if they turned the cameras off during class. The most common consequences were "parental notification", followed by "losing participation points" or "facing a lower grade", followed by "being marked partially or fully absent".[255] These requirements clearly put students with patchy Wi-Fi and other connectivity and bandwidth issues at a disadvantage. It also arguably put students without a camera at a disadvantage, as they were literally unseen during online classes. Interestingly, the survey found that 88 per cent of elementary school educators required that students kept their cameras on compared with only 60 per cent of their high school counterparts. It is possible that this reflected beliefs that young children are less likely to stay academically engaged off camera than teenagers, or beliefs that it is more important for elementary school teachers to see students than it is for teachers of older students. Regardless of the reasons for the disparity, the sudden shift to remote learning during the COVID-19 school closures normalized technology-dependent models of education that replicated classroom-based instruction and established understandings that being seen on camera and in Zoom-like digital environments was the equivalent of school attendance. This held true across education levels, from lower-primary through tertiary education.

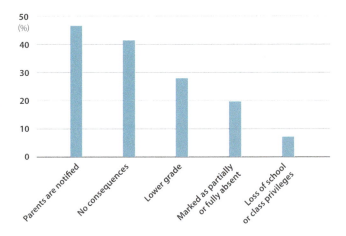

Figure 11:

Consequences to students for turning their cameras off during online classes in the USA

Source: Adapted from Education Week, 2020

Even schools and school systems that did not mandate student camera use during classes often required that students quickly turn their cameras on during online roll calls or other forms of attendance taking. Media accounts reveal that these visual checks were common at the beginning of classes as well as at the end of classes. In many contexts, they were conducted unexpectedly in the middle of classes to verify students were indeed following the class and catch learners who logged into a class but then left the screen. Seeing a student's name or profile in a list of digital participants was, for many, insufficient; education authorities insisted on seeing the actual student, even if only momentarily. Notably, the *Education Week* survey found that US educators in majority non-white school districts were twice as likely to require students to use cameras, no exceptions allowed, than educators in majority white school districts.[256] Sight-based digital attendance-taking practices tended to be agonizingly slow and struck many families as unnecessary, given that students were in their homes.

> Educators in majority non-white school districts in the USA were twice as likely to require students to use cameras, no exceptions allowed, than educators in majority white school districts.

Vigilant attendance checks had arguably been necessary when school education was conducted in physical locations outside the home. Brick-and-mortar schools, unlike virtual ones, serve a protective function as well as an educational one, and families and other community members understandably expect schools to account for young people and notify families of absences. But in the ed-tech-enabled home-learning environment of the pandemic, it was not clear why visual confirmation of attendance was necessary. If there was one onerous administrative task that virtual classes were supposed to ease, it was the taking of attendance. Like many ed-tech practices, though, the habit was simply transported, without much introspection, from the physical environment of schools to the virtual environment of remote education. Arguably, school leaders and teachers felt they could continue to fulfil a protective function, or some approximation of it, even at a distance. Whatever the reason, the shift to ed-tech in school systems across the world clouded once-clear meanings of attendance and absence, sight requirements and non-requirements, and often in ways that could disadvantage underprivileged learners, including those who faced difficulty joining video classes or those who were reluctant to do so.

"We have students who are parents, whose children need homeschooling. We have students who don't have a room in which they can close the door. We have students who are couchsurfing, or students with very personal home environments, and students across the world ... who would wake up their family if they talked."

– Carleigh Kude, assistant director for disability advising, Stanford University[xlviii]

Many students, families, teachers and school and university administrators were unwelcoming of rules and norms to turn on video feeds during classes. Petitions seeking to make video participation voluntary rather than a requirement were common in high-income countries where these rules tended to be in effect. Even students at elite universities felt the video classes could be invasive and inappropriate, more an attendance- and behaviour-checking mechanism than one to meaningfully improve teaching and learning.[257] A rare US study of student reasons for objecting to video classes found that the main concerns included judgements from other people, the physical space of homes being seen in the background and having a weak internet connection. The study suggested that these concerns were likely to "disproportionately influence underrepresented minorities".[258] It was significant that the study included only undergraduate students at Cornell University, an Ivy League research university in New York that charges annual tuition rates of over USD 60,000 per year[259] and has a considerably more privileged student population than most universities. If these well-off students were concerned about their homes being seen and about poor-quality internet connections, less privileged students were likely facing similar hesitations and challenges. And indeed, at other universities requiring video participation, administrators in accessibility offices were flooded with letters requesting formal permission to turn cameras off during class.

A key takeaway from the questions and problems surrounding the use of video classes was that the shift from in-person education to remote online learning affected norms and practices that extended well beyond the learning per se. While video classes may have helped assure the continuity of formal learning in some contexts, they also provided unexpected and often uninvited windows into student realities. These realities varied significantly across students' home and living conditions. The camera aspect of video classes unmasked deep inequalities reflected in home environments that the physical space of the school had kept hidden. The cameras students switched on at home beamed jarring reminders that the physical space of a school was a sanctuary for many students, one that afforded them dignity despite home situations that sometimes provided very little.

A consequence of the shift to remote, technology-facilitated education during the pandemic was the blurring of lines that had previously delineated the private space of the home from the public and shared space of the school, in ways that not only exposed, but also heightened inequalities.

> The cameras students switched on at home beamed jarring reminders that the physical space of a school was a sanctuary for many students, one that afforded them dignity despite home situations that sometimes provided very little.

HARDSHIP AND HEIGHTENED EXCLUSION FOR STUDENTS WITH DISABILITIES

Ed-tech was widely presumed to carry advantages for students with certain disabilities vis-à-vis school-based education. It was thought that powerful connected technology, matched with appropriate digital content and pedagogies, might better assure educational inclusion for the nearly 100 million children and youth estimated to have moderate to severe disabilities worldwide,[260] 80 per cent of whom live in developing countries.[261]

Prior to the pandemic, it was widely understood that students with disabilities faced acute challenges in accessing and successfully completing school-based education and were among the most left behind in education systems worldwide. A UNESCO study of ten low- and middle-income countries found that children with disabilities were 2.5 times more likely to *never* attend school than their peers without disabilities. When they did attend school, they were nearly 20 per cent less likely to achieve minimum proficiency in reading.[262] Similar gaps existed at the level of higher education. Data from the USA indicated that only 1 in 3 students living with disabilities graduated from four-year institutions within eight years. This fall-off rate is very high, even when compared with rates for students facing other disadvantages such as poverty.[263] The fact that these data come from a rich country that has and enforces laws to help assure the educational inclusion of students with disabilities, suggests that such non-completion rates might be even higher in other countries.

"It's difficult to manage a child with a disability full time on your own. [The pandemic] is exposing all the cracks, the stress of raising a child with a disability."

– Eileen Costello, paediatrician and clinical professor, Boston University[xix]

Beyond issues of access and inclusion, multi-country studies have routinely found that learners with disabilities tend to receive inferior-quality education, especially when they are separated from peers that are not disabled.[264] And disability challenges are, unsurprisingly, commonly compounded by other disadvantages, including those that might stem from income, gender, language or geography. The World Bank, for example, has documented how girls living with disabilities complete schooling at lower rates than boys with disabilities.[265]

Against this backdrop of existing disadvantage, the early decision to meet the educational disruption of the COVID-19 pandemic with connected digital technology was interpreted by some as a potentially hopeful sign regarding the inclusion of students with disabilities. Ed-tech had long been seen to carry considerable potential to help make education more accessible than it has historically been in schools. For learners with physical disabilities who could not easily move to, from and around brick-and-mortar schools, an option to learn remotely from home was sometimes viewed as a welcome development.[266] The same could be true for students with vision and hearing impairments who were pleased at the prospect of shifting educational content from paper-based mediums to digital devices with text-to-speech functionalities and options to seamlessly resize text and other visual media. For students with cognitive learning disabilities, ed-tech promised to help tailor learning to meet specific needs and enable greater repetition and review if desired.

These promises, however, were rarely realized during COVID-19 school closures,[267] even if there were a few bright spots, particularly in universities where technology integration in education was already well established.[268] Available evidence indicates that students living with disabilities faced heightened disadvantages during the pandemic-related school closures and the reliance on ed-tech for remote learning. In May 2020, a UN policy brief on responses to COVID-19 announced that learners with disabilities were being "disproportionately impacted" by the pandemic disruption to education and the heavy reliance on connected technology.[269] Data on the extent of this impact became increasingly available as the crisis stretched on for months and then past one- and two-year marks. In December 2020, UNICEF reported that over half of the 157 countries it surveyed about educational responses to the pandemic had not adopted *any* measures aimed at facilitating learning at a distance for children with disabilities.[270]

Around the world, accommodations for students with disabilities were regularly overlooked in the rush to deploy technology-enabled remote learning to ensure education during school closures. As school systems worked, often under enormous pressure, to digitalize learning materials for students, basic accessibility requirements for digital learning content – such as embedding text descriptions in digital files of images, which are essential for visually impaired students, or including transcriptions with audio files and caption options with videos, which are essential for hearing impaired students – were commonly ignored. Skipping these steps – which would have been required or at least more standard under less hurried circumstances – rendered much of the digital learning content developed for use during the pandemic difficult or impossible for students with disabilities to use. Moreover, heavy reliance on third-party learning platforms and apps tended to compound these problems. Many commercial solutions did not have strong accessibility options for students with different types of disabilities because of the expenses involved to develop them.

In addition to facing unique learning challenges, many students living with disabilities have health vulnerabilities that made the need to avoid social contact during the pandemic particularly imperative. Indeed, young people with disabilities were nearly twice as likely as peers without disabilities to have acute respiratory infection symptoms, increasing their risk of mortality from infectious diseases such as COVID-19.[271] Because of these heightened risks, students with disabilities were particularly dependent on screens and internet platforms to open portals to learning and interaction with peers and adults beyond the home. Yet far too often, these screens and platforms were either not provisioned or not appropriately accessible. When students with hearing impairments were directed to educational videos without captioning, learning was no longer possible. Learning also came to a standstill when blind students who had been learning using Braille books at school were told to navigate to educational websites without features and functionality to help them perceive, understand or otherwise interact with the digital content.

"I remember sitting, watching the school's presentation of how they want to handle COVID-19 [on Zoom] … But most of the presentation was on athletics. There was five seconds on special education [for students with disabilities]."

– Mother of a child with autism, USA[l]

More specific evidence of the ways in which the pivot from schools to remote learning with ed-tech exacerbated inequality for students with disabilities comes from individual countries. In the USA, for example, *none* of the 15 school districts' distance learning plans reviewed by the US Government Accountability Office (GAO) included details on how specialized instruction or related services for students with disabilities would be provided. This was less a case of insufficient planning than an absence of planning altogether. The only evidence the GAO could find of planned

Physical therapy required by many students with disabilities could not be provisioned online no matter how good the technology.

support were occasional notations that "parents of students with disabilities would be contacted individually by a special education teacher".[272] But even this practice was rare during the pandemic. Special education teachers were often supporting numerous students often across different schools and did not always have contact information for students under their care, nor had they been trained in how to provide support at a distance, assuming this was even possible. The physical therapy required by many students with disabilities, for example, could not be provisioned online no matter how good the technology. By June 2021, the US Department of Education, like many other national ministries of education, was clear-eyed that school closures and the move to technology had "significantly disrupted" the education and related aids and services students with disabilities "need to support academic progress and prevent regression". The Department of Education acknowledged that these disruptions were inflaming "longstanding disability-based disparities in academic achievement".[273]

"I am a barrier to my own daughter's education. I am unable to support her when she is studying because I am unable to read Braille materials. My daughter feels jealous when I am assisting other children who use print. … It is as if I am not interested in her schoolwork, which is not the case. I wish I knew Braille."

– Mother of a visually impaired daughter, Malawi[ii]

Although some governments launched websites on how to support the care and learning of children with disabilities,[274] this type of guidance was uncommon. In 2021, a study on the pandemic experiences of parents of children with autism found that investing in strong support systems for parents was the best way for authorities to help autistic children struggling with educational and lifestyle changes brought on by the pandemic.[275] But testimonies from parents with children with disabilities indicated that this support was lacking or non-existent. Ed-tech-reliant learning thrust parents of children with disabilities into the role of teachers and therapists, and parents did not always know how to fulfil these roles. In many cases, this work had been previously undertaken by trained professionals at schools. A survey conducted in Malawi found that 99 per cent of parents of children with disabilities reported "overwhelming dissatisfaction" with the educational experiences of their children during periods of school closure. Approximately 85 per cent of the parent respondents said that they had not received *any* support from a school or teacher. In interviews, they stressed that technology-based educational resources such as educational television tended to be inaccessible to their children, assuming it was even available at all. The Malawi parents also voiced frustration that they were not better able to assist the learning of their children on their own.[276]

Moreover, students living with intellectual or developmental disabilities such as Down Syndrome or autism are often more sensitive than others to changes in educational routines. These changes were relentless during the pandemic and the switch from school-based learning to technology-based remote learning. The unfamiliarity of government officials, schools and teachers with ed-tech tended to result in a steady flow of new directives, schedule alterations and other changes that could frustrate and disorient even the most flexible learners and families. Reliable routines took months to establish and sometimes never took hold, even as school closures extended deep into 2021 and 2022. These changes tended to carry special challenges for students with disabilities and the caregivers supporting them.

Around the world, the voices of learners with disabilities were largely unheard during the hasty switch to remote and technology-reliant education. Evidence shows that involving people living with disabilities and the organizations representing them is key to the successful planning of inclusive and accessible distance learning solutions.[277] Yet, in 2020, UNICEF found that civil society organizations advocating for learners with disabilities were almost never consulted in the design, implementation and monitoring of national COVID-19 educational response plans. Seeking input of this sort would have been more routine in a non-emergency context and provided clearer ideas about how to accommodate this group via distance digital learning.[278]

As school closures became prolonged, evidence mounted that, with rare exceptions, the deployment of ed-tech was resulting in severe educational exclusion for learners with disabilities. The Global Partnership for Education noted that ed-tech solutions routinely lacked the most "basic and necessary" accessibility features to render them usable for children with disabilities. It further observed that students with disabilities are uniquely dependent on the human care and support commonly provided by schools, and this support evaporated when schools closed and education moved online.[279] UNICEF found that over 80 per cent of countries in Eastern Europe and Central Asia reported prolonged disruptions in access to disability-related health and education services in late 2020.[280] In countries around the world, the shift to remote learning through ed-tech marked the end of actions and programmes to support students with learning and physical disabilities that had been active when schools were open. This could be catastrophic for, as one example, deaf students learning sign language who lived in families where no one else was able to teach or communicate in this language.

While the physical space of schools had often been inadequate for learners with disabilities before COVID-19, the virtual spaces of ed-tech commonly proved even more inadequate. Although the pandemic may have helped clarify the potential to provide new forms of accommodation for students with disabilities, perhaps particularly for students with physical disabilities that made travelling to and from school challenging, it only rarely delivered on this potential. More often, the shift to ed-tech resulted in further hardship and heightened exclusion for a group that had already been experiencing disadvantage with in-person schooling.

AN AMPLIFICATION OF DIGITAL GENDER DIVIDES

The pivot from school-based education to remote learning was commonly handled in ways that arguably replicated or reinforced existing digital gender divides. These divides as well as their origins had been well documented before the pandemic. A 2019 UNESCO study identified several factors that explain why girls are less likely than boys to use connected technology and develop the knowledge and practical experience needed to use it productively for learning and other tasks: differential access to connectivity and hardware, cultural and financial barriers, disparities in digital skills and capacities, and low self-confidence.[281] The study highlighted the persistence of digital skills gender gaps, noting that over a decade of national and international efforts to close them had accomplished very little. Indeed, data collected by the ITU indicate that these gaps are widening in many regional and national contexts.[282]

The pandemic rush to roll out distance learning solutions largely overlooked these digital gender divides. A review of the massive deployments and uptakes of ed-tech that were mobilized as a response to school closures reveals very little evidence of gender-responsive or gender-transformative strategies. Few countries used the pandemic context and its heavy reliance on connected technology as an opportunity to address the gender biases and exclusions that are at the root of digital gender divides. The many campaigns and trainings launched to build or reinforce the digital skills of parents so that they could better support ed-tech modes of learning with children during the pandemic generally disregarded gender. The audience envisioned for these campaigns was a generic adult, even though the target recipients were far more likely to be mothers and other women between the ages of 20 and 50 years old who tended to be apprehensive about helping children use technology as a portal to education. Some of these programmes even seemed to imply that fathers would troubleshoot technology problems, while mothers would simply monitor and encourage students to spend time on ed-tech learning tasks. A review of stock photos

that accompanied parental guidance regarding ed-tech-dependent education tended to feature pictures of men standing over the shoulder of a child working on a digital device of some sort. These assumptions and images further entrenched gender stereotypes about technology proficiency.

"If parents give their son a mobile phone, the community doesn't say anything, but when parents give a girl a phone, the community asks questions."

– 17-year-old girl, India[i]

> Girls tend to be far more reticent than boys to use unfamiliar technology.

Training aimed at teachers was similarly problematic. Reviews of crash courses developed to help educators improve their digital skills and establish foundations for digital pedagogies during the pandemic found that they almost never included instructions or ideas about how teachers might seek to break down gender stereotypes concerning technology. Nor did they recommend specific actions to help include and encourage girls to participate in the digital environments used for education. Yet this encouragement would have been warranted. Numerous studies have shown that girls are far more reticent than boys to use unfamiliar technology, post in online forums, make changes to default settings or experiment with the advanced functions of devices they already own.[283] In some countries, girls and women who have mobile phones only know how to answer voice calls – typically received from male family members.[284] As education moved into digital spaces, there was abundant evidence that girls were likely to be excluded or marginalized. Yet despite this, special provisions to ensure their equal participation seem to have been rare.

Teacher practice could also reinforce troubling gender stereotypes. During the pandemic, media accounts indicate that many classroom instructors designated select students to provide remote tech support to classmates during lessons. This allowed teachers to focus on the content of their instruction. While perhaps a useful strategy, the students chosen to provide this support were usually reported to be boys. The consistent designation of boys to fulfil technology roles arguably reinforced assumptions that boys are more likely to be 'natural' users of technology than girls.

Related to this, long-standing gender divides in digital skills meant that female teachers were often considerably less prepared to support technology-based learning than their male counterparts. Studies conducted in 2020 showed that female teachers consistently reported higher levels of stress using digital technology for instructional purposes and lower self-perception of their digital competencies compared with male teachers.[285] Large multi-country studies have found that women are between 1.5 and 2 times more likely than men to report a lack of skills as a primary barrier to internet use.[286] Practically speaking, this meant that synchronous classes with male teachers tended to run more smoothly than classes with female teachers. When education largely went online during the pandemic, these disparities only reinforced existing gender divides in digital skills. For instance, students might see first-hand examples of male teachers exhibiting their dexterity with technology by setting up online breakout rooms for small group discussions or being willing to use other complex technology features in new digital environments. Similarly, they might watch female teachers struggle with the technology in ways that could be embarrassing. For female students, often already lacking confidence in their digital skills, this arguably fuelled an unfortunate cycle, reinforcing rather than dispelling their self-doubt.

Testimonies indicate that with teachers and peers around, students often perceived unfamiliar online learning environments as carrying high stakes, reputational as well as academic. Digital skills are best developed when students feel comfortable that they can make mistakes, and this tends to be particularly true for girls.[287] But the newly established virtual learning environments were hardly locations for experimentation. Schools and other organisations rolling out ed-tech solutions tended to assume that users already possessed basic to intermediate digital literacy, which was not always the case, especially for girls. Tasks such as uploading a graded assignment, successfully logging into an online platform and completing a problem set or downloading a school-specified app were neither simple nor intuitive. Testimonies from the pandemic suggest that girls struggled more than boys to complete these processes and often felt overwhelmed. This could result in girls disengaging from education, including girls that had been excelling when learning was school based and less technology dependent.

> Subtle and overt signals that men and boys have special or innate aptitudes for technology compared with women and girls, however baseless in reality, were common in ed-tech spaces.

Subtle and overt signals that men and boys have special or innate aptitudes for technology compared with women and girls, however baseless in reality, were common in ed-tech spaces. For example, whenever a female teacher asked a male student, her junior in age, for help with a technology issue during online classes, this could reinforce a problematic belief among students that boys are superior technology users even to their adult female teachers. Similarly, online classes and trainings offered to help children as well as youth and adults make productive use of technology for learning during pandemic lockdowns tended, in reviews conducted for this publication, to be led by male instructors, again reinforcing views that men, and not women, understand technology. These realities point to missed opportunities to deconstruct and discard problematic gender expectations related to technology.

Research conducted prior to the pandemic found that girls' and women's interest in technology is significantly higher when technology subjects are taught by female teachers, while boys' and men's interest is unaffected by a teacher's gender.[288] The pandemic offered a unique opportunity to elevate female technology experts as role models and mentors. When girls see and interact with women and other girls who are highly proficient with technology, it inspires them to develop interest in technology and nurture beliefs that they can use it as well or better than their male counterparts.[289] But, based on reviews conducted for this publication, such female role models were often missing in digital spaces dedicated to education during the pandemic, and the myths around gender and technology were likely perpetuated.

Device distribution efforts could be equally insensitive to gender. Specialists in educational technology know that when connected devices are given to families, they are often monopolized by male members. Special actions and checks are needed to ensure girls and women are actually the end users of devices. An Oxfam project in South Asia, to cite one example, had so much trouble deterring men from appropriating mobile phones intended for women that it started procuring and distributing pink phones, assuming that the colour would help dissuade men from using them.[290] Significant bodies of research detail how cultural and family practices bestow digital hardware with strong male associations.[291] Families are more likely to purchase and provide digital technology to boys than to girls, tablets and smartphones are often marketed as gifts for boys and young men, parents are more likely to place a family computer in a son's room, and fathers are more likely to help and encourage boys to develop computer skills than girls.[292] Despite widespread knowledge of these trends, a review of the large and typically expensive technology distribution projects undertaken during the COVID-19 pandemic indicates that very few targeted girls specifically, even though it was well known that girls are less likely to have technology than boys – a trend that extends across developed and developing countries alike, albeit with less severity in wealthier countries.

"Girls in our [TechEnabled Girl Ambassadors] sample across Africa say that a quick way to access phones is through romantic or sexual relationships with more affluent boys and men, who will give them a phone."

– Girl Effect and Vodafone Foundation[iii]

Corroborating global research that documented major digital gender inequities before the pandemic, a study by Girl Effect in partnership with Vodafone suggested that boys are 1.5 times more likely to have a mobile phone than girls.[293] Similarly, multi-country research by UNICEF found that girls aged 15 to 19 are significantly less likely than boys to have used the internet in the preceding 12 months.[294] Gender differences in frequency of internet use can be staggering. In Nepal, for instance, rates of internet use among boys are double that of girls. In Pakistan, internet use is four times greater for boys than for girls.[295] The Girl Effect study found that girls are more than twice as likely as boys to need to borrow mobile phones from family members – often male family members – to gain digital access, a situation that tends to turn girls into technology supplicants.[296]

> Moving education to technology was not a neutral change: it carried distinct disadvantages for girls.

As these statistics clarify, moving education to ed-tech was not a neutral change: it carried distinct disadvantages for girls, and there appears to have been limited action to minimize these disadvantages. Given these realities, it is not particularly surprising that female students reported significantly higher increases in education-related stress than male students during the pandemic.[297]

With more careful planning and better sensitization, the education sector's embrace of ed-tech during the pandemic could have helped 'un-gender' technology as male. The educational disruption and its uncompromising – rather than voluntary – reliance on technology arguably offered an opportune moment to close digital gender divides by helping women and girls understand that they have the same right to use technology as boys and that they can be equally or more skilled technology users. Yet, evidence reviewed for this publication suggests that this did not happen. On the contrary, it seems that problematic gender stereotypes about technology that disadvantage women and girls intensified. In the rushed attempt to keep learning opportunities intact following abrupt school closures, women and girls rarely received special attention to counterbalance known digital inequities. This is not to say that girls and women did not, in some contexts, gain new levels of access to technology during the pandemic or improve their digital skills as a result of the shift to ed-tech; this almost certainly did occur. But it seems wishful thinking to imagine that this was enough to close skills and confidence gaps with boys and men, who also advanced digitally during the pandemic. Pre-existing gender skills and confidence gaps with boys and men were rarely accounted for, if at all. Future research will allow for more precise determinations regarding whether and to what extent digital gender divides widened during the pandemic recourse to distance learning. ITU data published in late 2022 provided an early, if incomplete, indication. According to the organization, "while women account for roughly half of the population, they account for a disproportionate – and increasing – share of the global offline population: women now outnumber male non-users by 18 per cent, up from 11 per cent in 2019".[298]

A STEP BACKWARDS FOR THE LABOUR PARTICIPATION OF MOTHERS

As schools closed and children spent their days at home, large numbers of women left the workforce, heightening gender inequalities in employment. The disproportionate deterioration of women's labour-market participation compared with men's was sometimes referred to as a 'she-cession' to highlight the gendered aspects of the COVID-19 recessions that swept the globe beginning in early 2020. A study conducted by the International Monetary Fund in 38 advanced and emerging market economies corroborated steep declines in women's employment. It found that between 2019 and the second quarter of 2021, women's employment declined 2.5 per cent, while men's employment fell significantly less by only about 2 per cent.[299]

"I am all by myself educating and taking care of my children. My husband doesn't help me at all as he has to work. Sometimes I don't have time to sleep."

– Mother, Kyrgyzstan[liv]

While declines in female employment during the pandemic trace to a variety of factors, the time commitments required to facilitate technology-first modes of remote education with children appear to have been a significant contributor. Detailed 2020 analysis of employment and economic data in the USA, for instance, showed that a 10 per cent rise in school closures was associated with a 1.5 per cent reduction in workforce participation for mothers compared with women without children. Across the USA, this translated into 1.6 million fewer working mothers than would have been expected without school closures. By contrast, the labour-force participation for fathers was not any more sensitive to school closures than it was for men without children.[300] These declines continued in relative lockstep with school closures. A US Labour Department report in October 2021 found that the number of working women aged 20 and older had declined by roughly 2 million since February 2020 – double the number of men in the same age bracket.[301] This report linked school closures to a female exodus from the labour market by showing that unemployment for women tapered off in parallel with school reopening.

Similar trends showing the adverse impact of COVID-19 school closures on women's participation in the workforce were observed in other countries, as highlighted by the Peterson Institute for International Economics. In Japan, for instance, labour-force participation by men barely changed as schools closed en masse in the first quarter of 2020. By contrast, 1 million women left the labour market in this first quarter, despite a government policy that sought to offer paid leave to parents unable to work due to childcare obligations tied to school closures.[302] While some countries, especially those that implemented programmes to support day care and other child services during the crisis, saw less backsliding on gender equality in workforce participation than others, globally the pandemic and the forced retreat to home-based and technology-facilitated learning disproportionately affected women's participation in the workforce and exacerbated gender inequalities in the labour market.

"My kids had nowhere to go, nowhere to be, no outlet. I found a job, and they were angry at me because I'm leaving and they can't."

– Mother, USA[iv]

Data released by the International Labour Organization (ILO) at the end of 2020 showed how fallout from COVID-19, and school closures especially, were "squeezing" working mothers out of the labour force globally. Noting that "women's labour-force participation is shaped by domestic and caregiving responsibilities in ways that men's is not", the organization cited evidence to show that in Brazil, Chile, Costa Rica and Mexico partnered women with children were experiencing much sharper pandemic-related drops in labour-force participation than men. It further explained that according to data from 55 high- and middle-income countries, nearly 30 million women aged over 25 lost their jobs between the fourth quarter of 2019 and the second quarter of 2020 and linked these job losses to school closures.[303] A later ILO report from March 2022 showed dramatic declines in women's labour participation rates across all regions. It explained: "In 2020, the pressures of juggling work and family, coupled with school closures and job losses in female-dominated sectors meant even fewer women were participating in the workforce. About 113 million women aged 25–54 with partners and small children were out of the workforce in 2020 [globally]." The ILO called this figure "astonishing" when contrasted with the comparable figures for men. For men with partners and small children, only 13 million were out of the workforce, 100 million fewer than women.[304]

> Mothers often noted that the shift to technology-based distance learning made schooldays more demanding in terms of oversight and obligations than days without school.

When schools began closing en masse, ed-tech was initially held up as a solution that might help parents, and mothers in particular, continue work unrelated to childcare. This 'benefit', however, rarely seems to have been realized in practice. Anecdotal evidence reviewed in media sources suggests that, in fact, the opposite may have been true: ed-tech modes of learning increased parental and caregiving obligations. Mothers often noted that the shift to technology-based distance learning made schooldays *more* demanding in terms of oversight and obligations than days without school. They lamented that they needed to be constantly on hand to assist technology-dependent learning. Where in-person schooling had freed up hours of uninterrupted time for parents to work and pursue professional goals, remote learning with ed-tech was, by contrast, consuming large amounts of parental time and focus, a burden that fell disproportionately on women. This deepened inequalities in gender labour divides and chipped away at global progress to establish more gender-equal workforces.

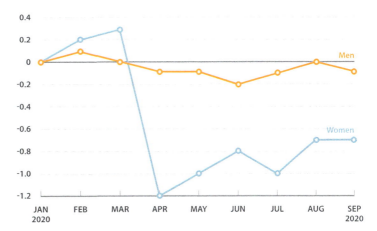

Figure 12:

Percentage change in Japan's labour force participation by gender in 2020

Source: Peterson Institute for International Economics, 2020

SCHOOL CLOSURES CONTRIBUTED TO INCREASES IN CHILD LABOUR

The inaccessibility, unreliability and poor quality of technology-first learning from home appears to have prompted many families, especially economically distressed families, to give students who had previously been attending school new or increased work obligations. In places where the connectivity, devices and capacities needed to leverage technology for education were scarce, students were regularly put to work.

"My father is a farmer. He sometimes asks me to help him in the field. But he didn't ask me to join him when I had school. But now I do not go to school, so I go to the fields to help him with his work."

– 17-year-old boy, Bangladesh[iv]

Global progress to end child labour had stalled for the first time in two decades during the first year of the pandemic.

In June 2021, the ILO reported troubling data indicating that global progress to end child labour had stalled for the first time in two decades. In a major publication, the organization, in partnership with UNICEF, noted that 160 million children globally were working, a disconcerting rise of 8.4 million from the last time global data were published in 2016. The report highlighted that children between 5 and 11 years old made up half of the total figure, and that the number of children aged 5 to 17 engaged in hazardous work – defined as work that is likely to harm their health, safety or morals – had jumped by 6.5 million to 79 million since 2016. Not all of these rises could be reliably attributed to particular disruptions and hardships imposed by the pandemic, including increased poverty and sharp declines in social services, but the ILO and UNICEF were careful to identify school closures and limited access to remote learning as contributing factors, particularly for children in vulnerable situations.[305]

Qualitative research conducted in 2020 and 2021 indicates that families that might have kept children in formal education had it been accessible via physical schools or remote learning instead pushed children into work when it was not accessible. Although various data limitations make it challenging to draw straight causal lines between the absence and limitations of ed-tech and spikes in child labour, considerable evidence suggests that these lines do exist. A 2021 ILO article about the acceleration of child workers into the construction sector in Uganda, for instance, noted that "education has been an important solution to combat child labour".[306] When links to formal education broke, families often saw children as idle and pushed them into jobs and labour that had no connection to curricular learning.[307]

Testimonials from children regularly supported this view. Children interviewed in West Africa as a part of a World Vision research project said that the cessation of school-based education and limited availability of remote learning alternatives precipitated their entry into labour.[308] Separate reporting from Burkina Faso found examples of parents who worked in granite mines bringing their children with them to support often hazardous mining activities, because the children had no means of continuing their studies with prohibitively expensive connected technologies when schools were closed.[309]

"There are some instances where parents ask children to go out to work to earn some income to support the household expenses. These incidences have become common due to the closure of schools during this period of coronavirus."

– 17-year-old girl, Ghana[vii]

School closures and the limited reach and effectiveness of ed-tech also seem to have led to meaningful upticks in unpaid domestic work completed by children, especially for girls. Analyses of the gendered impact of school closures found that when girls spent increased time at home, they were often burdened with new domestic chores and responsibilities – work that had been done by someone else when schools were operational. This change was documented almost exclusively in contexts where ed-tech modes of education reached relatively few families and learners, including in Bangladesh, Ethiopia, Niger and Pakistan. Burdens of care, such as cooking, cleaning or helping young siblings or older relatives, also fell heavily on girls in poor contexts where technology options to access education from home were typically non-existent during periods of school closure.[310]

The global takeaway from this evidence is clear: if voids left by school closure could not be filled with remote learning or other means to assure the continuity of learning, they were often filled with work. This meant the problems associated with access to ed-tech ran deeper than stalled learning – they could increase the likelihood that vulnerable children and youth would make a transition from education to labour. While some of these transitions proved temporary and reversed with the opening of schools, others did not. Early shifts to work are often permanent, especially for underprivileged children. As noted by the ILO: "When children leave school and enter paid employment, it can be very difficult for them to resume their education."[311] A defining characteristic of the pandemic and school closures is that when ed-tech alternatives were unavailable or failed, as was common globally, families put children to work, and some of these children did not have opportunities to return to education.

Learners engaged less, achieved less and left state-provisioned education

A central promise of ed-tech was that it would enable more engaging, more effective and more relevant learning that would, in turn, improve educational outcomes. There was also an assumption that ed-tech would make learning more instant and seamless by removing previous restrictions on when and where education could happen. Such developments would improve the quality and accessibility of education in ways that would accelerate academic progress.

However, the available evidence suggests that leaning outcomes declined dramatically when schools closed and remote learning with ed-tech was deployed as a replacement during the pandemic. This trend was observed in contexts where access to ed-tech was limited as well as in contexts where the availability of devices and connectivity was not a barrier to education. Around the world, technology-mediated remote instruction proved to be of considerably lesser quality than face-to-face education.

As teachers struggled to adapt their pedagogical approaches to facilitate teaching and learning in digital environments, student achievement either stalled or regressed. Students participating in remote learning rarely had opportunities for educational experiences beyond academic learning tasks. The socialization and non-academic experiences that were typical in school-based learning environments tended to vanish in the new virtual-only spaces. As a result, many students became disengaged. While some took up work, a large number remained idle – not engaged in education, employment or training. The closure of schools and universities and the shift to technology-facilitated remote learning also caused many students to abandon formal education altogether, sometimes with little prospect of returning when schools reopened.

TIME DEDICATED TO EDUCATION DECLINED DRAMATICALLY

One largely overlooked outcome of the pivot to fully remote learning during school closures was that students spent dramatically less time on formal education, even in places where devices and connectivity were plentiful. This trend, which appears to have been consistent across countries, contributed to slowdowns in learning and developmental progression, particularly for children and youth who did not have strong opportunities for educational progress at home.

Studies conducted in numerous countries indicate that the number of hours per day and per week that students participated in formal learning tasks routinely fell by 50 per cent or more when schools shut down and education moved to technology-mediated platforms. Research from the UK, for example, revealed that up to three-quarters of students attending state-run schools received just one or no daily online lessons after schools were first closed, despite a government policy of distance education.[312] In Ecuador, a

2020 World Bank rapid-response telephone survey of 1,500 secondary school students between the ages of 14 and 18 found that a majority of students were spending either no time or between 0.5 and 4 hours per day on educational tasks. Even the high end of this range is considerably less time than students would normally spend on education at in-person secondary schools in Ecuador.[313] Similar drops were found in developing countries. In Bangladesh, study time fell from ten hours to two hours per day, a decline of 80 per cent.[314] Data from Ghana indicated that approximately one-third of students were spending no time on education, and of those who were spending some time, 35 per cent were dedicating less than 30 minutes per day.[315]

> Ed-tech was being used more often, in more productive ways, and for longer durations with students that had enjoyed educational and other social advantages prior to the start of the pandemic.

Education researchers have long observed that time spent on education is not always of equal value. Live and direct instructional time with teachers is generally considered to be especially beneficial to improving learning achievement. But during the shift to remote learning, this time was almost always curtailed. A 2020 survey of households in California, USA, revealed that in a typical week, students had only three hours of live contact via phone or computer with their teachers, a fraction of the time that would have been standard at an in-person school. These averages, as bad as they were, obscured alarming disparities across lines of class and race. The California survey showed that children in high-income families typically had one more hour of live instruction per week than children in low-income families, and approximately 40 per cent of black students reported *no* live contact with educators.[316] Similar evidence accumulated in other countries to suggest that when ed-tech was available, it was being used more often, in more productive ways, and for longer durations with students that had enjoyed educational and other social advantages prior to the start of the pandemic. The disparities were often considerably more pronounced than they had been when education was conducted in person and at schools.

Furthermore, in some contexts, student time spent on education continued to decline as the crisis extended into mid and late 2020 and throughout 2021, a period in which reliance on ed-tech often deepened. This was a reversal of early expectations that students and their families would quickly overcome learning curves associated with the switch to ed-tech and fall into routines that allotted appropriate time to learning – durations that would approximate instructional time at schools. A 2021 UK study found that the amount of time students spent on formal education declined significantly between the outset of the crisis in early 2020 and the end of the school year in June. The decline was estimated at nearly 40 minutes per day for primary school learners and almost 50 minutes per day for secondary school learners. These were significant drops, especially considering that the time spent learning was already much lower than it would have been at a typical in-person school. This led the researchers to remark, "We find little evidence that students in aggregate adapted to the school closures; indeed … learning time fell substantially for children [as the lockdown progressed]."[317]

In places where connected technology was plentiful, students often shifted time that would have been spent learning in a school setting to the passive consumption of digital media. In Germany, a survey of parents showed that the time children spent on school-related activities dropped by half – from 7.4 to 3.6 hours per day – when schools closed because of the pandemic. The same survey also showed a corresponding rise in the time German students spent on other technology-mediated activities, such as watching television, playing computer games and scanning social media on mobile phones – from 4 to 5.2 hours per day.[318]

"Throughout the Zoom meetings, I personally didn't feel comfortable with it. I get distracted easily, so it was not possible, and I gave up. I stopped showing up and I didn't finish the last semester."

– University student, USA[lviii]

Remote education via ed-tech resulted in significantly less frequent and less sustained learning than would have been expected in a traditional school environment.

Research conducted for this publication could not find any evidence to suggest that students spent more time on formal education activities after the shift to technology-dependent distance learning than before the shift. And even instances of comparable time were very rare. At some level, this was surprising. Given that so many other activities were off-limits during the pandemic, a retreat into schoolwork did not seem implausible. Indeed, many businesses noticed that employees, even those on fixed salaries, worked significantly longer hours during the lockdown than they had before the pandemic.[319] This sometimes led to improved productivity, and, as a result, a number of firms moved quickly to make remote working arrangements more permanent. In the education sector, however, these sorts of 'successes' were unheard of, even in the best-resourced schools. Across countries, the evidence indicates that the amount of time students dedicated to studying never matched the durations governments expected and was sometimes drastically below official recommendations. While time spent on education activities is an imperfect proxy for learning achievement, the correlation is almost always positive: more time spent on education generally corresponds with improved educational achievement.[320] During the pandemic, the global trend was that remote education via ed-tech resulted in significantly less frequent and less sustained learning than would have been expected in a traditional school environment.

LOWER AND SLOWER LEARNING GAINS WITH ONLINE LEARNING

Beyond changes to time spent on education, much of the available research indicates that the switch to remote learning with ed-tech resulted in learning progress that was lower and slower than what would have been expected had school-based educational models not been disrupted by the health crisis. One of largest and most comprehensive US studies of the impact of technology-dependent modes of learning during the pandemic found that "remote instruction was a primary driver of widening achievements gaps" and that there were "profound" and uniformly negative consequences for student achievement vis-à-vis in-person schooling.[321] In areas where students were reliant on technology the longest, achievement growth was low for all subgroups that were studied but especially low for students who normally attended high-poverty schools. These findings correspond with pre-pandemic studies of online-only schools that found large, negative effects in learning achievement compared with achievement in brick-and-mortar schools.[322]

While a more precise global picture of the learning that occurred – and did not occur – during the pandemic will continue to come into fuller focus with the full resumption and analysis of large-scale local, national and cross-national learning assessments, the existing data paint a discouraging picture.

One of the earliest indications that remote learning through ed-tech was not facilitating academic gains came from a detailed analysis of data collected from an online mathematics platform used by nearly 1 million elementary school students in the USA as part of the regular school curriculum. The study observed meaningful learning declines linked to COVID-19 school closures and the ensuing reliance on technology for education.

The declines were particularly pronounced in children from lower income communities who, on average, scored 50 per cent below levels that would have been expected without school closures. The study concluded that although the mathematics platform captured only one aspect of education, it provided an early warning of the ways the switch to remote learning was amplifying inequality in the long run by hindering human capital development, especially for lower income children.[323] Poor results in mathematics, detected early in the USA, were soon observed in numerous other countries. Researchers in Germany, for instance, found that fifth grade students showed significantly lower competence levels in mathematics in 2020 than in previous years.[324] Later investigations corroborated these early findings. Numerous studies published in 2021 and 2022 indicate that learning progression in mathematics stalled when teaching and learning was conducted remotely through connected technology.[325]

"What happened in spring 2020 was like flipping off a switch on a vital piece of our social infrastructure. Where schools stayed closed longer, gaps widened; where schools reopened sooner, they didn't. Schools truly are, as Horace Mann famously argued, the 'balance wheel of the social machinery.'"
– Thomas Kane, faculty director of the Centre for Education Policy Research, Harvard University[ix]

Evidence of slow learning progress in mathematics is particularly troubling because mathematics instruction has long been considered an area where technology-first approaches might result in learning achievement that is superior to that observed in traditional in-person instruction. Prior to the real-world experiences of the pandemic, dynamic applications used on smartphones or computers were thought to be well-suited to organizing and pacing problem sets for students and showing them how to derive correct answers. Automatic and continuous assessment held the promise of helping learners quickly identify and fill gaps in understanding, much like a private tutor might do.[326] The thinking was that interactive images, animations and videos could complement content and bring abstract concepts to life in a way that is impossible for textbooks to do. Technology could also, in theory, help students better appreciate real-world applications for everything from basic arithmetic to advanced calculus. Finally, because of the universality of mathematics, good-quality content was assumed to be easily shared across different communities and even countries, and hence more readily accessible than content for other more text-heavy and context-dependent subjects, such as history. Yet studies on learning achievement during the pandemic showed that ed-tech gains in mathematics were considerably lower than what would have been expected with standard school instruction.[327]

A 2021 study of 700 mathematics educators in France, Israel, Italy and Germany offered insights into why teacher-led education delivered online was producing substandard results.[328] The main finding was that teachers were unprepared for the shift to digital pedagogy and had trouble supporting student learning in virtual environments, even as they worked to find solutions to problems they had not encountered before. The researchers identified four specific areas of difficulty vis-à-vis distance learning during the pandemic: (1) supporting student learning through specific methodologies, (2) developing assessments, (3) supporting struggling students such as those living in difficult situations, and (4) exploiting the potentials of technology to foster mathematical learning. They also found that teachers had trouble developing inclusive teaching methods in unfamiliar digital environments. Overall, the study illustrated just how difficult it was for teachers to shift mathematics education to technology-dependent environments, even in cases where good-quality technology and connectivity were widely available. The study notes that many teachers wanted to better assure fairness and equity for low-achieving students and were disturbed that they could not achieve "educational justice". The shift to ed-tech was, in this way, frustrating for teachers as well as students. The study concluded: "Among the challenges that this situation has brought, a central role is played by the contrast between the potentialities provided by digital resources in fostering the creation of effective interactive environments for teachers and students and the risk that the actual situation could amplify the social gap that exists in the world."[329] This risk became a reality throughout the COVID-19 pandemic.

> Over 90 per cent of primary school students examined as part of an educational study in India lost at least one language ability due to school closures and the failure of remote learning to forestall this unfortunate result.

Early indications that the switch to remote learning and ed-tech went hand in hand with poor learning progression in mathematics and other subjects were quickly corroborated in other countries where studies were available. In the Netherlands, researchers examined test scores following pandemic school closures and concluded that students made "little or no progress" when learning at home with technology-mediated instructional approaches.[330] Students from disadvantaged households made the least progress. The authors of the study presented the Netherlands as a best-case scenario for mitigating learning loss given the country's short lockdown, equitable school funding and world-leading rates of broadband access and technology ownership. The study suggested that learning loss might be equally bad or worse elsewhere, a concern that was quickly corroborated as more data became available. In late 2020 and early 2021, various researchers highlighted data indicating that school closures and full reliance on technology for education were slowing or stopping standard academic learning progression. Beyond academic losses, school closures also triggered cultural loss. Research in India, for example, found that over 90 per cent of primary school students examined as part of an educational study lost at least one language ability due to school closures and the failure of remote learning to forestall this unfortunate result.[331]

In December 2020, studies in the USA, often the first country to release large and reliable quantitative data sets, showed unmistakable signs of underachievement when learning was remote and largely or fully reliant on ed-tech. The consulting company McKinsey analysed results from curricular and diagnostic assessments used by nearly 30 per cent of kindergarten to Grade 8 students across the country, for instance, and found that students learned only 67 per cent of the mathematics and 87 per cent of the reading that would have been typical at their grade level without the pandemic disruption.[332] This equated to students losing three months of formal education in mathematics and close to two months in reading over the approximately four-month period when most schools shut down and learning was delivered remotely through technology platforms. The authors of the study noted that some students did not learn *any* new material once the pandemic hit and "may have even slipped backward". Curriculum Associates, the organization that generated the raw data for the McKinsey study, confirmed these trends, arguing that "the shift to remote learning has magnified already pervasive inequities for millions of school children".[333] The organization's follow-up research observed that Grade 1 and Grade 2 students finished the 2020/21 academic year further below expected levels in reading than in any previous year, sometimes two or more grade levels below expectations, a deficit that is projected to almost certainly hamper future education progression.[334]

> Regardless of socio-economic status, the more time students spent relying on technology as a primary means of education, the more their learning suffered.

These early findings of widespread declines in academic performance in the USA were harbingers of national testing results that were to come. Results reported by the National Assessment of Educational Progress (NAEP) in late 2022 – the first national test results since the start of the pandemic – showed that the reading abilities of 9-year-olds in the USA fell by the largest margin in over three decades, and that mathematics performance had the sharpest drop on record.[335] Only 36 per cent of fourth grade students and 26 per cent of eighth grade students were considered proficient in mathematics, down from 41 per cent and 34 per cent, respectively, in 2019.[336] As alarming as these national figures were, they obscured huge equity gaps.[337] The NAEP, commonly referred to as 'America's report card', showed performance in mathematics falling by 13 points for black students compared with 5 points for white students.[338] And for both mathematics and reading, the lowest-performing students had steeper declines than the top-performing students, compounding pre-pandemic inequities and perhaps reflecting the longer school closures in poorer communities.[339] Studies that sought to examine the specific links between poor academic performance and ed-tech modes of learning (rather than wider pandemic disruptions) strongly suggested causality instead of mere correlation.[340] Regardless of socio-economic status, the more time students spent relying on technology as a primary means of education, the more their learning suffered.[341] The director of the Centre for Education Policy Research at Harvard University summarized the situation in plain language: "Distractions, technical glitches, and the many other pitfalls of online education made it far less effective than in-person school."[342]

Such declines were hardly limited to the USA. In late February 2021, South Africa's Department of Basic Education announced a drop in Grade 12 pass rates, a setback in a country that had previously seen year-on-year improvements.[343] A study of the impact of pandemic-related school closures on learning outcomes in Colombia compared student achievement on national assessments in the five years preceding the pandemic (2015–19) with student achievement in the two years after the onset of the pandemic (2020–21). The study noted a decrease in overall results from the previous years and highlighted that learning losses were highest in areas of the country where school closures were longest.[344] Similar analysis of 2021 academic results in Chile showed that 43 per cent of students were below the expected level in mathematics, and 60 per cent were below the expected level in reading.[345] A study from Mexico found large pandemic-related learning loss in both reading and mathematics by comparing the survey data from 2019 and 2021 and interviewing over 3,000 children.[346] Research from Brazil estimated that during periods of remote learning with technology, test scores were "as if students had only learned 27.5 per cent of the in-person equivalent".[347] A longitudinal data study from Italy found significant changes in student achievement due to school closures and reliance on remote learning. Interestingly, the changes were minor for younger children but significantly adverse for older children. The study speculated that the result reflected the fewer number of days schools were closed for young children than older children. The finding was further evidence of associations between remote learning and heightened learning loss.[348] Studies and data from developing countries are challenging to find, but anecdotal evidence suggested that learning loss during periods of remote learning had been steep. A remark made by Kassaga Arinaitwe, head of the NGO Teach for Uganda, was typical of leaders of other civil society educational organizations in the global South: "Many [children] are so behind, we will need an entire year to bring them back up to speed."[349]

"The pandemic has exacerbated educational inequalities between children from different socio-economic backgrounds, which were already large before the pandemic"
– Bastian Betthäuser, Anders Bach-Mortensen and Per Engzell, authors of a multi-country review of learning outcomes during the COVID-19 pandemic[ix]

Teachers ranked the effectiveness of distance learning only slightly better than skipping school completely.

In a rare multi-country examination of the effectiveness of technology-mediated distance learning, McKinsey surveyed teachers in eight countries (Australia, Canada, China, France, Germany, Japan, the UK and the USA) to gauge their sense of student progress during periods of school closure. Teachers were asked to rank the effectiveness of remote learning on a scale of 1 to 10, with 1 being fully ineffective and 10 being comparable or better than learning that would normally occur in a classroom. Teachers who taught at public schools gave remote learning an average score of 4.8. Those working in schools with the lowest resources and with poorer students found virtual classes to be "especially ineffective", with a rating of 3.5 on average. These teachers also reported the greatest estimated learning losses for their students, in some instances nearly double the losses observed by teachers working with more privileged students. A majority of teachers in the USA and Japan, countries where the lowest scores were given overall, ranked the effectiveness of distance learning only slightly better than skipping school completely.[350]

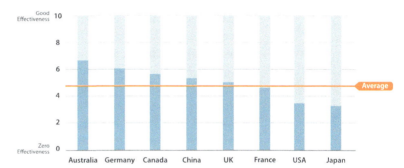

Figure 13:

Effectiveness of remote learning as reported by teachers in eight countries

Source: Adapted from McKinsey & Company, 2022

While few in education expected the switch to remote learning and reliance on ed-tech to result in learning gains the same as or similar to in-person school instruction, the size of the gap was daunting. Preliminary research reveals that overall learning achievement was far lower than it would have been without a switch to remote learning, even in contexts where ed-tech was widely accessible. In late 2021, a World Bank simulation suggested that in low- and middle-income countries, the number of children living in so-called learning poverty – generally defined as those unable to read and understand a simple text by age 10 – will "rise sharply, potentially up to 70 per cent" from pre-pandemic levels of around 55 per cent.[351] And by June 2022, the World Bank had reviewed sufficient evidence of stalled learning progress to state conclusively that global learning poverty had indeed "surged" to the 70 per cent level, according to its modelling.[352]

By some measures, nearly a full academic year of learning achievement was lost during the two years when reliance on ed-tech spiked because of school closures.

In 2022, McKinsey, drawing on UNESCO data, projected that students were, globally and on average, eight months behind where they would have been absent the pandemic.[353] This translates into nearly a full academic year of learning achievement lost during the two years of school closures, when reliance on ed-tech spiked. By late 2022, it was clear at the global level, and even in contexts where technology was widely available, that remote learning alternatives during school closures had produced poor learning gains compared with what would have been expected had in-person schooling continued without the pandemic disruption.

Perhaps the clearest global picture of the effects of pandemic school closures and prolonged recourse to remote learning with ed-tech was contained in a January 2023 meta-analysis of studies from 15 countries (Australia, Belgium, Brazil, Colombia, Denmark, Germany, Italy, Mexico, the Netherlands, South Africa, Spain, Sweden, Switzerland, the UK and the USA). The study estimated that students across these countries, many of which had very short school closures by global standards, lost on average about 35 per cent of learning compared to a normal school year. It found that learning deficits were largest for children from disadvantaged socio-economic backgrounds, a finding that held steady irrespective of different timepoints during the pandemic, countries, grade levels and learning subjects. The study indicated that learning deficits appeared to be particularly severe (based on the limited number of studies available) in the middle-income countries included in the review (Brazil, Colombia, Mexico and South Africa). It further noted that "learning deficits are likely to be even larger in low-income countries, considering that these countries already faced a learning crisis before the pandemic, generally implemented longer school closures, and were under-resourced and ill-equipped to facilitate remote learning", adding that a dearth of evidence from these countries made estimations difficult.[354]

DISENGAGEMENT AND DROPOUT FOLLOWED THE SHIFT TO ED-TECH

Beyond the learning losses and diminished academic performance, overall engagement with education declined with the transition to distance learning during the pandemic, sometimes leading students to drop out of education altogether. When schools close, especially for prolonged durations, some students do not engage in alternative education offerings – even in instances where these are offered – and do not return to schools when they reopen. The reasons vary but can often be traced back to students working, having children, getting married or being saddled with domestic obligations. In 2021, UNICEF estimated that 10 million more girls are at risk of becoming child brides before the end of the decade as a result of pandemic shocks such as school closures and increased economic insecurity.[355]

"Survive school or survive life? I can't blame the students – a lot of them choose work."

– Upper secondary school dean, USA[x]

Many youth who disengaged from schooling during the pandemic did not immediately transition to work, as might have been expected without a global health crisis on the scale of COVID-19, but rather appear to have remained idle, entering a demographic category all countries seek to minimize: youth who are not in education, employment or training (NEET). Data collected by the ILO highlighted troubling increases in NEET rates around the world and noted that "the rise in inactivity has not – in general – been offset by a return to education".[356] This signalled that student departures from education, which greatly accelerated during periods of school closures and full reliance on remote learning, did not always reverse after schools reopened. In other words, the disengagement and dropout prompted by school closures and remote learning alternatives were proving permanent.

"I loved going to school … I was good at it too. I even wanted to go to the university someday. No one asked me if I wanted to marry."

– 15-year-old girl, Afghanistan[x]

A primary goal of ed-tech during the COVID-19 crisis was to preserve the habit of formal learning. While remote learning with ed-tech kept links to formal education intact for some students, teachers and families, there is strong evidence that these links routinely failed, even in instances where technology was plentiful and people had the requisite skills to use it for educational purposes.

Arguably, this shortfall was predictable in light of considerable previous research demonstrating that students are far less likely to follow and complete technology-mediated education than in-person education. Prior to the pandemic, studies had documented dramatically higher dropout rates in virtual settings than in physical ones. As one example, analyses of online-only charter schools in the USA – one of the few countries to allow secondary school students to attend full-time virtual schools – found that many failed to matriculate their students on time and that a high percentage of students dropped out completely.[357] Similarly, massive open online courses (MOOCs) – a widely used model of technology-reliant education that is almost always exclusively virtual – had also been shown to have very poor retention rates. It is not uncommon for just 1 out of 10 students who start a MOOC to finish it.[358] While (normally) optional online university courses such as MOOCs cannot be easily equated to government-mandated distance learning during the pandemic, they illustrate that learners – even motivated adults who voluntarily sign up for classes and typically already have high levels of education completion – do not have a strong track record of following online education for extended periods of time. This is particularly true for younger learners who tend to quickly lose interest in digital learning content and are more stimulated in in-person learning environments. Where ed-tech had shown promise was when it was used in schools and by teachers. This promise was considerably dimmer though when technology served as a singular interface for education with no in-person component.[359]

Despite this evidence, many people held that children and youth were inherently interested in technology and maintained that it could make education more stimulating and rewarding. Educational researchers tended to be wary of these claims. They underscored that empirical evidence of ed-tech's effectiveness, especially as it related to engagement and retention, was "severely lacking".[360] While careful not to discount ed-tech's potential, scholars observed that the available research had failed to conclusively prove many of the widely assumed benefits of technology-centric learning.[361]

When COVID-19 flared into a global pandemic, little was known about ed-tech's effectiveness overall and even less about its ability to facilitate and motivate educational advancement over sustained periods of time in diverse learning and cultural contexts.

Studies extolling the virtues of ed-tech tended to be narrowly concentrated in the USA or other rich countries and often used questionable methodologies.[362] Others came from developing country contexts and compared the outcomes of ed-tech interventions to traditional schooling that was widely known to be failing, often due to severely under-resourced institutions and underqualified teachers. Education-focused 'tech4dev' (technology for development) projects, for instance, tended to be small-scale experiments and often came with resources and support that went far beyond what was typically available in mainstream school systems. In these scenarios, it was difficult to determine if the technology was the key factor when improved student learning was detected or whether such improvements stemmed from more support, encouragement and oversight to learners and teachers. In either case, the studies rarely produced conclusive evidence of improved retention and engagement. More often, the focus was on learning achievement as measured by standardized testing. When COVID-19 flared into a global pandemic, little was known about ed-tech's effectiveness overall and even less about its ability to facilitate and motivate educational advancement over sustained periods of time in diverse learning and cultural contexts.

"I hate those days when we were not able to go to school, not able to meet our friends or go out to play. We are ready to wear masks and maintain social distancing but I hope that schools do not ask us to sit at home and attend online classes again."

– Secondary school student, India[xcii]

There is, however, a greater consensus around factors that do sustain student engagement, achievement and school completion. The learning environment is of paramount importance. A 2021 review of more than 130 studies stressed that efforts to maximize student retention and interest in learning hinge on learning environments that (1) help students develop identities and relationships that positively promote academic expectations; (2) allow teachers to listen, use humour, foster dialogue and show interest in students; (3) maximize opportunities for active and problem-based learning; (4) support learners at key moments of transition, particularly between grades and schools; and (5) offer courses and schedules aligned with student needs and interests that encourage work in small interdisciplinary groups.[363] Such learning environments were challenging to create in schools and classrooms, and they tended to be far more challenging to establish in virtual spaces, given their many limitations vis-à-vis physical environments and face-to-face socialization. Few people had carefully considered how ed-tech might forge and strengthen the relationships, dialogue and group learning that help motivate academic completion. And far fewer had considered how this might be accomplished at a distance, in physical isolation and over long periods of time, as was suddenly needed with the arrival of COVID-19. It had long been assumed that schools would establish the principle learning environments for children and that digital spaces would be decidedly secondary. Prior to 2020, ed-tech offerings were largely constructed around microlearning – short-term engagement with a particular topic or subject – not the macro application of ed-tech that the unusual conditions of the pandemic demanded.

> Four out of every five students reported lower overall engagement and academic performance as a result of technology-only modes of learning.

These realities did not bode well for the rapid transition to fully remote ed-tech. Almost immediately, data emerged from different parts of the world to indicate that disengagement from technology-facilitated distance learning was severe. National and international surveys of students routinely found large spikes in disengagement and anecdotal evidence of decreased motivation and effort. One multi-country survey of students from nearly 90 different universities was typical: 4 out of every 5 students reported lower overall engagement and academic performance as a result of technology-only modes of learning.[364] A separate survey of over 10,000 secondary school

students in the USA saw a significant decline in the percentage of learners reporting that they were fully engaged in education.[365]

More troubling still were signs that students were dropping out of education altogether. Mexico's Interior Ministry, for example, reported that 5.2 million students under the age of 18, approximately 14 per cent of all school-age children, did not register for classes at the start of the 2021/22 academic year,[366] an unprecedented exodus from formal education compared with pre-pandemic enrolments.[367] While such a large-scale departure from education cannot be attributed purely to the shortcomings of distance learning, they were very likely a contributing factor. Mexico instituted large-scale shifts to distance education beginning in March 2020 and relied heavily on educational television broadcasts, in part due to the country's uneven internet connectivity. In the following months, testimonies from learners indicated disillusionment with such remote learning education delivered by television. Many decided to drop out and enter the workforce, sometimes to help their economically strained families.[368] A similar trend was observed in Pakistan, which also relied on educational television to replace in-person schooling. The Center for Global Development found that the proportion of children from low-income households watching educational television programming dropped from 1 in 5 to 1 in 7 during the pandemic.[369] Many of the programmes amounted to little more than teachers reading lessons aloud with no attempt at sustaining student engagement. While online environments offered more opportunities for engagement, the pedagogical model was often very similar to the dry television programming: an instructor merely reciting a lesson and only rarely, if ever, inviting virtual interaction.

Disillusionment and fatigue with ed-tech modes of remote learning were observed across the world. In general, the longer the reliance on ed-tech for remote learning due to school closures, the greater the rates of disengagement and dropout from formal education. A scan of news stories from 2020 to 2022 brought specificity to this blunt reality. In Bangladesh, experts estimated that more than 45 per cent of secondary-level students were at immediate risk of dropping out in mid-2020 and that the risk would grow higher if reliance on remote-only modes of learning remained in place due to continued school closures.[370] In Canada, 5,500 children in the country's largest school district expected to return to in-person classes in 2021 did not, following a lengthy period of distance learning.[371] In France, teachers in 2020 claimed that 30 per cent of their students were fully disengaged from online learning.[372] In Colombia, the World Bank estimated in mid-2020 that if distance education was maintained, 76,000 students were likely to abandon their studies.[373] In Hungary, experts calculated that up to one-fifth of children disappeared from the education system during periods of remote learning in 2020.[374] In Ireland, schools in disadvantaged areas reported disengagement rates of 25–50 per cent among students participating in online learning in 2020.[375] In Peru, the national high school dropout rate surged from 11.8 per cent in 2019 to 17.9 per cent in 2020 when the country was reliant on distance learning with ed-tech.[376] In the Philippines, school enrolments dropped in the 2020/21 academic year, with a 9 per cent decline compared with the previous school year.[377] In South Africa, over 300,000 children were estimated to have dropped out of primary school during the first year of COVID-19.[378] In Spain, the government estimated that up to 12 per cent of schoolchildren had not followed distance learning during the 14 weeks of confinement.[379] In the USA, nearly 50,000 Los Angeles students were reported absent on first day of the new school year in 2022.[380] At the global level, UNESCO released a study in 2021 projecting that 24 million children and youth were likely to drop out of school as a result of the pandemic.[381]

The longer the reliance on fully remote learning with ed-tech, the greater the rates of disengagement and dropout from formal education.

By late 2021 and 2022, it had become obvious that a prolonged reliance on remote learning often coincided with fewer students showing up for school, even when schools reopened. In the USA, a country that experienced especially long school closures, researchers noted in July 2021 that enrolment in public schools had dropped by 3 per cent nationally and by 13 per cent among preschool and kindergarten students, an unprecedented decline.[382] In a separate study, researchers noted that among students who remained enrolled in school, absenteeism increased dramatically.[383] Available data showed alarming rises in the number of students reported as chronically absent, defined as being away from school for more than one out of every three days.[384] Some countries reported that twice as many schools saw rises in chronic absenteeism compared with years before the pandemic.[385] Increases in absenteeism were documented for teachers as well. The National Center for Education Statistics in the USA, for instance, found that 3 out of every 4 schools reported increases in teacher absenteeism in 2021, a percentage that was far higher than what had been recorded in the years before the pandemic school closures and the deployment of remote learning.[386] By mid-2022, researchers were drawing a direct line between student dropout rates and prolonged reliance on technology-facilitated remote learning as a substitute for in-person schooling. The American Enterprise Institute, a public policy think tank, stated that the COVID-19 pandemic had caused "the largest enrolment declines in the history of American public schools" and that school districts provisioning instruction remotely "saw more students leave" compared to those that returned to in-person learning.[387] These trends, quantifiable in the USA due to frequent and reliable data reporting, were also observed in other countries.[388]

"The COVID-19 pandemic caused the largest enrolment declines in the history of American public schools."

– Nat Malkus, deputy director of education policy studies, American Enterprise Institute[lxiv]

Patterns of heightened dropout were evident in tertiary levels of education as well as in basic and secondary levels. Many universities, colleges and technical and vocational institutions reported significant declines in enrolment after in-person education moved online. In countries where national data were available, significant declines in post-secondary enrolment followed the shift to remote digital learning. The National Student Clearinghouse Research Center (NSCRC) in the USA reported that undergraduate enrolment was down approximately 4 per cent one month into the fall 2020 semester compared with the same period in 2019.[389] The June 2021 numbers from the NSCRC were even worse, showing the largest and most sustained decline in college enrolment in a decade – a drop of over half a million students nationally.[390] Students from less advantaged groups were the most likely to drop out. Especially sharp declines were reported for US students of Latin American origin or descent. Across the USA and in other countries, students spanning all demographic groups cited difficulties with online learning as a reason to leave higher education. In April 2020, a survey of college students found that three-quarters of them were unhappy with the quality of online classes.[391] A separate survey found that 35 per cent of respondents were considering withdrawing from their current school if it only offered a remote e-learning option in the following academic year.[392]

Similar enrolment declines were observed in other countries, including in Japan, where large numbers of students dropped out of universities and other higher education institutions,[393] and in Australia, where tertiary enrolments for 20- to 24-year-olds were down by 66,100 students in December 2020 compared with 2019 numbers.[394] In Latin America, surveys of undergraduate students found a strong preference for classroom-based education following the move to online learning. The main concerns expressed by respondents were not being able to focus during virtual classes and not being able to interact and engage personally with professors. Low- and mid-tier higher education institutions in Colombia, Mexico and Peru braced for major declines in new student enrolments.[395] A survey of officials at more than 50 public and private universities in 14 Latin American countries found that a majority of respondents expected enrolments to continue dropping until schools resumed in-person instruction.[396] Globally, reports warned that secondary school graduates will "probably think twice" before starting college as a virtual experience and either wait to get the "full college experience" or enter the workforce full-time[397] – predictions that proved true as the pandemic stretched into 2021, 2022 and 2023.[398] The global takeaway is that the switch to ed-tech-dependent education resulted in less demand for this type of education and fewer students completing formal education, especially at tertiary levels.

"Universities should not be allowed to charge students full price for remote learning!"

– Third-year university student, USA[lxv]

Students felt technology-based education was not as valuable as education that was less technology reliant.

Students in higher education were often vocal in their belief that the switch to ed-tech was falling short of their expectations and driving them to disengage and to drop out from education. Many students, when it was permitted, took leaves of absence to avoid technology-centric education. Proof that students were disillusioned was perhaps best corroborated by widespread demands for tuition reductions and refunds – evidence that students felt technology-based education was not as valuable as education that was less technology reliant. These demands and complaints sometimes crystallized into legal action. In the Republic of Korea, for example, the National University Student Council spearheaded a class action lawsuit against the Ministry of Education to seek partial refunds for educational fees that were paid, the students argued, with an understanding that attendance would involve more than logging into classes through a computer.[399] The suit involved over 3,500 students across 42 universities.[400] Similar lawsuits were filed in other countries, including against elite institutions such as Harvard University. Like most universities, Harvard contested the student allegations, and in June 2021 Harvard won the legal dispute when a judge ruled that the student plaintiffs failed to establish that the university had "contractually promised them in-person instruction and access to on-campus facilities".[401]

Universities regularly argued that their own costs had increased due to the sudden switch to ed-tech, so expense reductions were out of the question. Even so, student complaints about tuition appears to have been effective in some instances. In 2020 and 2021, a number of private and public educational institutions in various countries did reduce fees or, less commonly, extend refunds. The discounts tended to be modest. For example, John Hopkins University in the USA announced a 10 per cent reduction in undergraduate tuition for a semester in which all classes were conducted online.[402] Tuition freezes were also offered, but these only pushed students' educational expenses into the future and rarely signalled a concession that ed-tech modes of distance learning were problematic. The freezes were issued under the rationale that students and families were facing economic hardship, not that the remote learning experience was substandard.

> Student backlash against fully remote digital learning was widespread and sometimes spiralled into outrage as the health risks of in-person schooling were increasingly called into question.

Regardless of whether fees were reduced, frozen, left unchanged or sometimes hiked upwards, student backlash against fully remote digital learning was widespread during the pandemic. The backlash sometimes even spiralled into outrage as the health risks of in-person schooling were increasingly called into question, particularly as the WHO and other groups released guidance on how to safely resume face-to-face education. While protest was most visible at higher education levels, younger students also found the shift to remote digital learning disengaging and substandard. However, owing largely to their young age and limited experience with political engagement, their voices tended to remain unheard.

While numerous factors drove student decisions to discontinue formal education, the limitations and problems with ed-tech modes of learning seem to have been a strong contributing factor. Had the shift to technology-reliant remote learning largely succeeded in offering students a viable and attractive option to continue their studies during the pandemic, arguably this might have prevented the widespread decline in engagement and large-scale flights from education that were seen around the world. As it was, there was a shared impression that the quality of education had been reduced in the migration to remote learning at the same time that economic insecurity rose in many households. The choice left to families was either to accept the shortfalls of technology-dependent remote learning and stay enrolled in school or to drop out of education entirely, either temporarily or permanently. Many students, especially at tertiary levels where education is voluntary, chose the latter option. One legacy of the deployment of digital remote learning in response to the COVID-19 will be the many students that left formal education when it pivoted from in-person schools to online and broadcast platforms.

A FLIGHT FROM PUBLIC EDUCATION TO HOME-SCHOOLING

Aside from the sharp increase in student dropout rates, another type of fall-off from state-provisioned education documented during the pandemic was an increase in home-schooling. While the choice to home-school children has numerous motivations, there is evidence that large numbers of families made this transition due to concerns and complications stemming from the pandemic. For some families, the decision was based on health grounds. Parents pulled children out of mainstream education because they feared that schools open or reopened for in-person instruction would put their children at higher risk of contracting COVID-19. Families sometimes feared not only for the health of their children, but for other family members who might be at greater risk of death or serious illness if a child became infectious. But for many other families the decision to home-school children traced to exhaustion and disillusionment with technology-first modes of remote learning. These families felt they could do a better job providing instruction at home than educational authorities were doing at a distance with ed-tech.

Although solid data on home-schooling trends tend to be imprecise even in countries with well-resourced education systems and robust data-collection mechanisms, a number of reports signalled that school closures and the switch to ed-tech corresponded with significant growth in home-schooling rates. Research conducted in the UK, for instance, estimated that the number of children being home-schooled in England increased by nearly 40 per cent between 2019 and 2020.[403] While the total number of home-schooled children in England remains relatively modest in absolute numbers – about 75,000, slightly under 1 per cent of all school-age children[404] – this was nevertheless a significant uptick. Similar rises were observed in Australia and New Zealand. In Australia, all states and territories apart from Tasmania reported an over 19 per cent increase in home-school registrations between 2019 and 2021.[405] By 2022, in the most populous state, New South Wales, which includes Sydney and the federal capital, Canberra, the jump was nearly 30 per cent.[406] In New Zealand, the increases were more dramatic. In October 2022, the number of children being home-schooled was estimated to have increased by 80 per cent since the start of the pandemic. While the absolute numbers remained relatively small, in the low thousands, it was, nevertheless, a distinct trend without recent precedent. Israel was yet another country that saw a dramatic increase. In 2022, national data showed that requests to home-school children surged fivefold between 2020 and 2021. News sources reporting these figures quoted families expressing exasperation with school closures and remote learning and citing these concerns as factors in their decision to file the request.[407] This trajectory could also be detected in India with media calling attention to ways the pandemic was ushering in confidence in a "culture of home-schooling"[408] and pamphlets labelling home-schooling a "rising trend".[409]

Expressed in absolute numbers, perhaps the steepest pandemic spikes in home-schooling were observed in the USA. An October 2020 Pew survey found that an unprecedented 7 per cent of US parents were formally home-schooling their children, up from around 3 per cent before the pandemic and the transition to technology-dependent remote learning.[410] This massive growth was corroborated by surveys conducted by the US Census Bureau[411] and supported by academic work accounting for limitations with raw survey data.[412] The academic work suggested that over 3.7 million school-age children were home-schooled during the 2020/21 academic year, or 6.7 per cent of the school-age population. The doubling of home-schooling in the USA seems to have been triggered, at least in part, by families disillusioned with the technology-first approaches to education adopted in response to the pandemic.

In the USA, black households saw by far the largest increases in home-schooling, rising from 3 per cent of households to 16 per cent of households nationwide – an unparalleled jump. This rise was arguably fuelled to some degree from the reality that black families were often the least likely to benefit from technology-dependent modes of learning when schools were closed and commonly experienced low-quality provision of remote digital learning. During the pandemic, members of the National Black Home Educators organization rose from 5,000 to 35,000. The programme director of this 21-year-old organization attributed the rise to the numerous difficulties black families experienced with virtual learning, including limited internet access.[413]

> Growth in home-schooling appeared to signal a spiralling lack of faith in government-provisioned education.

Across the world, jumps in home-schooling rates corresponded to pandemic school closures. Many parents drew a straight line between their decision to home-school their children and their dissatisfaction with government-provisioned remote learning with ed-tech and, sometimes, concerns about excessive screen time. Many parents saw what was happening on their children's devices and felt they could do a better job directing learning through a use of online and offline modalities. Overall, the growth in home-schooling appeared to signal a spiralling lack of faith in government-provisioned education. Available evidence indicates that the failures of ed-tech modes of education, perhaps combined with previous and wider reservations about state-provisioned education, marked a breaking point for some families, prompting them to remove children from formal systems of education altogether and assume the responsibility of educating them at home.

Education was narrowed and impoverished

A central promise of ed-tech was that it would open new and exciting horizons for education, unencumbered by the many physical limitations of schools. In digital spaces, students could traverse the world with clicks and scrolls, tour the insides of cells and explore subterranean spaces – experiences that would be impossible or prohibitively expensive outside of screen-based mediums. Virtual environments would further enable language acquisition and help learners who are new to a community become more familiar with its norms and cultural traditions. Ed-tech proponents also spoke of the ways technology could help link education to other social services, providing teachers and schools more holistic understandings of their students and paving the way for superior support. For teachers, ed-tech was supposed to expand pedagogical possibilities and help better focus their human energies on teaching, while streamlining or automating laborious administrative tasks. It would ease the work of teachers, rather than add burdens, and make teaching more impactful and ultimately more rewarding. In the popular imagination, ed-tech was seen as a tool to finally break the factory model of education and facilitate learning that was more diverse, personalized and effective – and, in doing so, pull education into the modern and digital age.

These enthusiastic visions, however, were rarely realized in the hurried implementation of technology-enabled distance learning in response to mass school closures. While ed-tech allowed some learners to follow curricula that guided them through academic content in various subjects, many discovered that the educational experiences it enabled were flat and monotonous – a daily routine less of discovery and exploration than traversing file-sharing systems, moving through automated learning content, checking for updates on corporate platforms and enduring long video calls.

More importantly, student well-being was routinely overlooked in the jump to remote learning with ed-tech. Various social services available to young people converge at schools, ranging from psychosocial support to free school meals, and when physical schools were shut down, the education sector had difficulty providing for students' needs beyond academic learning. The many and varied functions of education – physical and social development, civic learning, fostering communities, assuring safety and building generational cohorts – were largely lost in the pivot to online learning. So too were understandings that education should fulfil public and shared societal goals as well as private ones.

> As huge numbers of students became reliant on just a handful of educational platforms, the factory models of education became global instead of merely local or national.

Moreover, despite the promise of ed-tech to democratize education and personalize learning, unshackling students from the school-based systems that ed-tech proponents considered constraining or oppressive, the reality of its implementation during the pandemic was often characterized by further automation and homogenization of the educational experience. As huge numbers of students became reliant on just a handful of educational platforms, the factory model became global instead of merely local or national. The pedagogical choices of teachers were often dictated by digital systems. Digital learning applications tended to employ behaviourist pedagogies that could accommodate huge numbers of students without reliance on teachers, and this stripped education of its human touch.

Education mediated by technology also moved into virtual spaces that were owned and controlled by private and often for-profit providers. These providers, despite offering services that hundreds of millions of students depended on to access education, tended to view education as one branch of much wider business interests, rather than a core area of focus. Overall, the myriad roles school-based education had fulfilled prior to the pandemic were often narrowed to corporate-controlled, screen-based experiences that provided a continuation of academic learning to some degree, but not the wider and more varied social learning that is typical of in-person schooling.

ENGINES OF SOCIALIZATION AND ACCULTURATION SLOWED

The rich school and community traditions that give expression to a wide range of cultural practices largely vanished in digital spaces.

The shift of formal education from in-person schooling to fully remote learning through digital mediums heightened awareness that human contact and social interaction lie at the heart of education. Much of the learning that takes place in the physical and social spaces of schools, such as interaction with others through play, sports, art and extracurricular activities, is not purely academic and is poorly suited for remote delivery through technology. Even in instances where distance learning worked smoothly, it tended to gloss over important social and civic learning. Survey data as well as first-hand accounts indicate that teachers and students alike found technology-enabled distance learning to be a largely insufficient substitute for the experience of being in school with person-to-person exchanges and communication. Many of the extracurricular activities that revolve around schools, from sports to social events to clubs of various types, came to a halt with the closure of schools and could not be replicated or easily moved online. The rich school and community traditions that give expression to a wide range of cultural practices largely vanished in digital spaces. These non-academic educational pursuits often provide students with a sense of purpose and belonging that helps them engage with curricular study and assimilate into societies and cultures.

Lost opportunities of this type tended to disadvantage immigrant, refugee and other students unfamiliar with community norms, which include accepted greetings, dress, etiquette and hygiene. Schools and universities have long prided themselves on modelling and developing appropriate social behaviour, and these functions, largely dependent on face-to-face interaction, whether in the classroom or on the playground, did not transfer easily to screens. Ultimately, remote learning with ed-tech did very little to help students understand or take part in sociocultural practices that have historically centred around school as a physical location where people meet and to which they belong.

"Latent functions of education like childcare aren't less important; they are just spoken about less explicitly. And when we kneecap them, their importance becomes clearer."

– Zeynep Tufekci, associate professor, University of North Carolina[lvi]

Considerable evidence indicates that these limitations posed acute challenges for speakers of minority languages. These learners quickly discovered that digital learning alternatives to schools severely limited their immersion in non-native and often majority languages used at school. Specialists in language acquisition highlight the many ways minority language speakers depend on schools to connect new words and sounds with meaning by observing the facial expressions of teachers and peers in hallways and playgrounds as well as in classrooms, and seeing how other students respond to spoken and written language.[414] The many low-stakes opportunities people had to practice an unfamiliar language at school largely disappeared when schools closed, putting language learners at a considerable disadvantage.[415] While students from linguistic and sociocultural minority groups might have still been able to pursue remote digital learning, including courses dealing with language and culture, the space of the school itself – a wider and arguably more important site of language and cultural learning – was inaccessible when in-person education was replaced by technology portals. Even well-off exchange students in higher education expressed dissatisfaction with distance learning during the pandemic. A study of international students, many of them non-native English language speakers, enrolled in post-secondary schools in Ireland found that only 1 in 10 respondents reported positive experiences with ed-tech as a primary mode of learning.[416] Such challenges led speakers of minority languages to abandon distance education in much higher numbers than speakers of majority languages. These negative effects were also apparent at lower levels of education. In the USA, for instance, research conducted at the end of 2020 found that English language learners in Connecticut were deemed "second only to homeless students in their drop in attendance in virtual and in-person classes".[417]

"For English-language learners, if you're not having those casual, informal, low-stakes opportunities to practice English, you're really at a disadvantage."

– Sita Patel, clinical psychology professor, Palo Alto University[lxvii]

> While the home is a rich site of social and cultural learning, schools open young people to experiences not available in the home.

The shift to home-based distance learning with technology also led to a dramatic reduction in synchronous interactions with peers and adults outside the home. These interactions help young people learn to live with others and experience different world views and opinions. While the home is a rich site of social and cultural learning, schools open young people to experiences not available in the home. The balancing of these two influences is widely understood as advantageous, especially when the cultural practices of the home are different from the cultural practices outside the home.

STUDENT WELL-BEING AND PROTECTION WAS NEGLECTED IN DIGITAL SPACES

Technology was poorly suited to attend to student needs beyond academic study.

In many countries, school closures and the shift to remote learning with ed-tech marked the suspension of crucial social services that complemented or were prerequisites for education. This included safety, health care, nutrition and counselling provided by schools or in cooperation with them. In countries around the world, the remote learning experience tended to elevate academic learning over a more holistic concern for child and youth well-being. While the medium of technology could help assure learning continuity, it was poorly suited to attend to student needs beyond academic study.

"Every day out of the classroom brings the most vulnerable children closer to dropout, gang violence, abuse or human trafficking."

– Jean Gough, UNICEF regional director for Latin America and the Caribbean[lxviii]

The economic costs and benefits associated with different responses to the 2009 influenza pandemic found that the economic cost per death prevented for school closures was over three times more expensive than the next most expensive intervention.

Various studies of school closures show that they often carry devastating health consequences, including increased exposure to violence and exploitation, rises in childhood pregnancies and sexual violence, and stunted mental development due to reduced social interaction.[418] These consequences, in addition to learning loss, can be exceedingly costly to societies. A 2017 review of scientific publications examining the economic costs and benefits associated with different responses to the 2009 influenza pandemic found that the "economic cost per death prevented" for school closures was over three times more expensive than the next most expensive intervention and over 4,000 times more expensive than the least expensive interventions, which included contact tracing and face masks.[419]

In January 2021, UNICEF and the World Food Programme estimated that 39 billion school meals had been missed globally since the start of the pandemic, leading to spikes in hunger and malnutrition.[420] Earlier studies of school feeding programmes had found that they provided dramatic benefits for poor families. The Midday Meal Scheme in India, for instance, decreased calorie deficits in children by 30 per cent.[421] A 2018 World Bank study found that school-provisioned meals resulted in important cost saving for poor families; these meals could represent as much as 15 per cent of a family's daily income.[422] But when schools closed, free or reduced-cost meals were no longer available.

Similarly, important mental health services for children and youth that were centred around schools were unavailable during school closures.[423] A March 2021 WHO report stated that the pandemic was disrupting or had halted critical mental health services for students in 93 per cent of countries worldwide at a time when demand for these services was peaking.[424] Experts observed that the closure of schools often severely compounded and complicated public health crises triggered by the spread of COVID-19, rather than mitigating them as intended.[425]

The disruption of key school-based services that help assure the well-being of young people was largely overlooked during the pandemic when the focus was on leveraging ed-tech to assure the continuity of teaching and learning remotely. There is extensive evidence of schools doubling and tripling budgets to purchase ed-tech hardware and software during the pandemic, but less evidence of schools making similar investments to ensure meals were delivered to children in need or to strengthen the provision of counselling in virtual spaces. A joint UNESCO-UNICEF-World Bank survey conducted in low-income countries, for example, found that only a very small number of countries – fewer than 10 per cent – took significant measures to reinforce school nutrition or make it more flexible during the pandemic, even though young people in these countries tend to be highly dependent on school meals for daily nutrition and calories.[426] Arguably, the focus on maintaining learning continuity and avoiding learning loss through remote learning diverted attention and investments away from efforts to protect and preserve some of the vital non-academic functions of schools.

> Arguably, the focus on maintaining learning continuity and avoiding learning loss through remote learning diverted attention and investments away from efforts to protect and preserve some of the vital non-academic functions of schools.

Around the world, dedicated teachers attempted to attend to the mental and physical health of their students despite the lack of physical proximity. They used technology to provide support outside the bounds of academic learning but with limited success. Online teacher forums were full of concerns that interacting with students through screens and on virtual platforms, typically as part of large groups, made it difficult to support the mental and physical health needs of students. The hashtag #MaslowBeforeBloom began trending in educator circles on Twitter, a reference to Abraham Maslow's hierarchy of basic human needs and Benjamin Bloom's taxonomy of educational objectives. The 'before' was sometimes written in all capital letters to stress the idea that the basic human needs explained by Maslow, encompassing physiological needs (food, rest, warmth), safety needs (security), and belongingness and love needs (friends and relationships), must be prioritized before the narrower learning processes explained by Bloom.[427]

> Online teacher forums were full of concerns that interacting with students through screens and on virtual platforms, typically as part of large groups, made it difficult to support the mental and physical health needs of students.

"I cannot demand much from these children … They live the daily violence within their home … School is a place where children go to protect themselves from their reality."

– Primary school teacher, Chile[ix]*

Remote learning also posed challenges in detecting abuse. The in-between moments that had been routine in the physical space of the school, such as when students left and entered classrooms, during breaks, over lunch and between extracurricular activities, were missing. Students did not linger in digital classrooms to share feelings or talk through fears and anxieties. Norms often developed around synchronous technology learning platforms such that teachers were the first ones to exit and end online lessons. This was a reversal of practices that were typical with in-person schooling. At schools, teachers generally remain in their classrooms after the completion of lessons and often make a point of being available to meet with students who might want to talk to them. Evidence captured in media suggested that many students were too intimidated to set up private online meetings with teachers due to the formalities this required in digital spaces – often the circulation of an electronic calendar item and the creation of a meeting link. In digital mediums, meetings tended to be either fully private or fully communal. The semi-private hallway and open-door chats that were possible in schools and often preferred by students had no parallels in digital spaces, and likely limited possibilities for sensitive conversations about mental and physical well-being.

The standard protocols to deal with situations of endangerment did not transfer easily to digital-only interfaces.

Despite these obstacles, students often did reach out to educators about problems that went beyond learning. Teachers in various national contexts reported receiving unsettling messages from students such as 'I don't feel safe in my home'. Replying to these online calls for help was rarely straightforward. The standard protocols and to deal with situations of endangerment did not transfer easily to digital-only interfaces. Established procedures tended to assume the physical presence of teachers and students and in-person involvement from social workers and other supportive adults.

"[When schools closed], we no longer had that window into children's lives. The screening … for trouble at home; the observation that a child is falling asleep at their desk or seems hungry or lacks an appetite."

– Lauren Bauer, education and safety net policy researcher[lxx]

These barriers were significant because teachers are often the first and primary reporters of abuse and other forms of child and youth endangerment. Given this reality, it was perhaps unsurprising that, in many countries, the closure of schools and the shift to home-based remote learning corresponded with what was almost certainly a sharp under-reporting of abuse. To illustrate the scale of this problem, a survey of children's advocacy centres across the USA reported serving 40,000 fewer children between the first half of 2020 than in the same period in 2019, a drop of over 20 per cent. The executive director of the group that organized the survey said, "We have absolutely no reason to believe the actual incidence rate has declined. What we really believe is that there are 40,000 fewer kids that haven't been saved from abuse."[428] By 2022, it was increasingly clear that, if anything, abuse appears to have increased during the pandemic. A nationwide government-led survey in the USA found that over half of upper secondary school students said they suffered emotional abuse, defined as swearing, insulting or belittling, from a parent or another adult in the home while schools were closed, and 1 in 10 said they experienced physical abuse.[429] These figures were much higher than they had been when comparable research was conducted in 2013.[430] The National Director of Adolescent and School Health called the study findings "beyond worrisome".[431] This data mirrored equally concerning findings trickling in from smaller studies in other countries.[432] When connected with learners only through technology, teaching personnel could not detect and flag potential abuse at home as vigilantly as they had done when students were in school.

During periods of remote learning, there were also fewer options to assist students experiencing homelessness. For this group, estimated to include around 150 million children globally, the physical space of school is often

> Schools are often places where children experiencing homelessness are first identified. But when schools closed and education largely moved online, this identification step collapsed and consequently so did the initiation of support offered to students and their families.

a sanctuary and pillar of stability.[433] When schools closed, this sanctuary evaporated and the academic participation of students experiencing homelessness plummeted well below pre-pandemic levels. This was hardly surprising given that these students were far less likely than students with homes to have the connectivity and devices needed to make productive use of digital learning. They were also less likely to have access to physical spaces conducive to learning via technology. For many learners, school is attractive because it provides a comfortable and enriching place to spend the day. Experts have observed that the community aspects of physical schooling, including the routine of seeing friends and receiving support and encouragement from adults at a fixed location, holds particular importance and value for students living through homelessness. Schools are also often places where children experiencing homelessness are first identified. But when schools closed and education largely moved online, this identification step collapsed and consequently so did the initiation of support offered to students and their families. In the USA, a report by SchoolHouse Connection and the University of Michigan estimated that 420,000 children and youth experiencing homelessness who might have been identified and enrolled in schools in pre-pandemic times simply vanished from educational institutions when learning transitioned to technology.[434] This amounted to a major reduction in the ability of schools to find and support children, youth and families experiencing homelessness and prioritize their education and well-being in public systems of care. The head of SchoolHouse Connection summarized the report's findings this way: "There is nothing equitable about distance learning for children and youth who are homeless. The cost of keeping everyone safe is costing some children much more."[435]

"I am concerned they are getting lost in the 'masked' shuffle, or in the virtual void. … I just fear kids experiencing homelessness will become even more invisible than they already are."

– School district homeless liaison, USA[xx]

Around the world, the move to technology-enabled remote learning was interpreted as an endeavour to preserve academic learning. What was less commonly acknowledged was that this singular focus, which oriented so much action and investment in education, tended to place student well-being, more broadly defined, in a secondary position. UNESCO worked to reassert the need for education, and teachers in particular, to prioritize students' physical, psychological and social-emotional well-being *over* academic obligations,[436] but much of the ed-tech deployed during the pandemic tended to sideline these fundamental needs. The overriding aim was to maintain academic progress.

A VOID OF SUPPORT TO NAVIGATE BEREAVEMENT

Just as online modes of education struggled to support students experiencing abuse or homelessness, it also provided limited options to assist students who lost a parent or other close relative during the pandemic. A research team writing in *The Lancet* medical journal estimated that over 1 million children globally lost a primary caregiver, either a parent or custodial grandparent, to COVID-19 between March 2020 and April 2021, and many more experienced the loss of a secondary caregiver, an older relative or co-residing grandparent.[437] Although schools typically have protocols in place to assist students grieving the loss of caregivers as well as processes to link them to support outside of schools when necessary, these processes and links were generally unavailable via the remote learning technologies during periods of school closure.

The authors of *The Lancet* article clarified that providing adequate support to grieving children carries high stakes: "Ineffective responses to the death of a parent or caregiver, even when there is a surviving parent or caregiver, can lead to deleterious psychosocial, neurocognitive, socio-economic, and biomedical outcomes for children", including increased risk of post-traumatic stress disorder, depression, domestic abuse and suicidal behaviours as well as sexual, emotional and physical violence. Another report from 2021, entitled *Hidden Pain*, affirmed the various ways the traumatic loss of a caregiver is associated with depression, addiction, lower academic achievement and higher dropout rates and noted that these associations tend to be especially pronounced for young children.[438]

> On ed-tech platforms, there was no 'app' for helping a child cope with the loss of a parent or caregiver, and schools and teachers were often unaware when a parent of a student died.

Schools had often been sites where adults outside a family were first made aware that a student's parent or caregiver had died. And the school was commonly the institution that initiated effective bereavement approaches, including psychosocial support, empowering surviving caregivers to facilitate adaptive grieving, open communication and trauma-focused therapy. However, the movement of education to technology-only platforms made it difficult for schools to fulfil these obligations. There was, simply said, no 'app' for helping a child cope with the loss of a parent or caregiver, and schools and teachers were sometimes unaware when a parent of a student died. Young people did not always feel comfortable sharing this information in digital spaces geared for academic learning.

The authors of *The Lancet* article observed, "Throughout this pandemic, children have been falling under the radar." Teachers have long functioned as this radar, and schools have long provided bridges to essential social services for children. The *Hidden Pain* report called in-person schooling "the most convenient location to identify and serve bereaved youth" and lamented the way pandemic school closures made it more difficult for children and families to receive in important social supports. Ed-tech, at least as it was implemented during the pandemic, generally lacked the mechanisms to detect student needs, including those that were arguably more important than learning such as support with bereavement.

"My art teacher literally emails us that we need to do the work and when someone in our class's family member died w corona he was like idk if i believe u and even if it's true she still needed to turn everything in 'on time.' no one cares abt their students' mental health."

– @sophia, TikTok post[lxxii]

TECHNOLOGY STIFLED PEDAGOGICAL POSSIBILITIES AND THE AGENCY OF TEACHERS

Remote digital learning tended to homogenize teaching practices due to the various limitations of electronic media, the design decisions of software developers and teachers' unfamiliarity with digital platforms as a primary vehicle for teaching and learning.

Pedagogical practices that teachers had developed and refined over years in classrooms rarely transferred easily to digital spaces. The way instructors monitored student work, used body language to assure classroom management, elicited interest in subject matter and provided support and encouragement to students often had no analogue in online spaces. There was no way to hold eye contact, no way to place a hand on the desk of a student who was losing focus and no real way to invite spontaneous reactions.

A lot of ed-tech was geared towards behaviourist pedagogies, not more modern pedagogical approaches such as constructivism or liberationism. Pavlov's bell rang loudly in education apps.

Modern pedagogical approaches – such as constructivism, which draws on ideas from Jean Piaget; social constructivism, which draws on ideas from Lev Vygotsky; and liberationism, which draws on ideas from Paulo Freire – tended to collapse in digital environments. Much of ed-tech was geared towards behaviourist pedagogies, reflecting ideas from thinkers such as Ivan Pavlov and B.F. Skinner. As an example, synchronous video apps commonly elevated teachers to principal figures of authority. Other ed-tech platforms encouraged teachers to lecture, model, demonstrate and engage students in recitation and repetitive tasks. Pavlov's bell rang loudly in ed-tech apps. Distinctive teacher strategies to co-construct knowledge with students, place students at the centre of group learning exchanges and collaboratively decide directions for education, for example, were rarely accommodated by technology that was built for hierarchical control and generic 'everyone and no one' users. Technology tended to be heavily tiered with permissions clustered according to groups, such that systems owners had expansive privileges while administrators, users and participants had respectively fewer privileges. The systems reflected a logic of top-down control and were, many observed, anti-democratic, making the practice of democratic and emancipatory pedagogy difficult or even impossible.[439]

"Edtech is not its own pedagogy. Instead, it needs to be used in accordance with sound pedagogy."

– Matthew Lynch, founder of The Edvocate[xxiii]

Numerical scoring systems that might have been optional or even discouraged in school and classroom environments were suddenly mandated by digital systems.

While the physical setting of schools and classrooms had certainly imposed pedagogical constraints before the pandemic, teachers were accustomed to them and, more importantly, knew how to navigate them. They knew their instructional practice had to account for rooms with particular layouts and resources, reflect various sociocultural norms and accommodate fixed schedules. But many teachers found that ed-tech introduced considerably more limitations, even if it occasionally opened new possibilities for teaching and learning. Teachers discovered they could not, for instance, work with students in small groups because of the way a particular piece of software had been designed. Other educators learned that preferred methods for providing student feedback had been forced into templates and rubrics that could not be altered. Numerical scoring systems that might have been optional or even discouraged in school and classroom environments were suddenly mandated by digital systems. Around the world, technology, often developed with little or no input from teachers and other education professionals,⁴⁴⁰ shaped teaching methods in profound ways.

"I like seeing students, learning their names, seeing their style, talking to them. It is very hard to teach to names in a black box."

– Digital art teacher, USA^xxiv

In digital environments, systems tended to exercise considerably more power and control than their human users. Various settings were locked or required administrator permissions that teachers did not always possess. Ways of working and communicating with students were often strictly prescribed and dictated by workflows. Students might, for example, upload assignments that would then appear on a teacher dashboard of some sort. The dashboard would instruct teachers to take specific and often narrow actions to grade or 'respond' to the assignments, which were then automatically sent back to students. These workflows were typically unidirectional: action, reaction, action – a conveyor belt rather than an open exchange. Electronic systems also made pedagogical interactions more time bound than they had been in the past. The buffers and breaks that allowed instruction or conversations to go overtime at physical schools often had hard stops in digital learning environments. Apps would sometimes transport teachers or students to new digital locations automatically. This teleporting often cut conversation short.

Additionally, bureaucratic procedures and forms that teachers had previously disregarded because they did not find them practical or beneficial could no longer be ignored when they moved to electronic systems. A computer would insist on their completion as a prerequisite for submission and continuation. Teachers regularly voiced frustration on social media that digital platforms were forcing them to spend more time filling out surveys of various sorts and different evaluations of students than actually teaching. And indeed, many systems reflected the wishes of administrators and policy-makers to accumulate data, instead of the learning needs directly observed by teachers. Much of the early commentary on the shift to ed-tech in 2020 celebrated the large amounts of data that would be produced about learning interactions when they moved from unseen and unrecorded offline spaces and into spaces that were easy to record, log, document and surveil. But for many educators and students, it was far from evident how these data were improving education or might do so in the future. The data were also very rarely available to teachers to study, synthesize and use in their practice. Most often information was piped directly to private sector technology companies who used it for purposes that were not always clearly understood or communicated.⁴⁴¹

"Only a handful of apps are designed with an eye toward how children actually learn."

– Hirsh-Pasek, K. et al., authors of a research paper about digital technology and child development[lxxv]

Beyond this, ed-tech systems developed by small technical teams, often located in a handful of North American or European cities, arguably privileged Western pedagogical practices and norms – even when learning content could be adapted. Many teachers were dismayed to find software suggesting that they respond to student work with grinning emojis or GIFs laden with references to Western popular culture, a visual shorthand that was, depending on the cultural context, sometimes assumed to be lazy, unserious, non-academic or even insulting.

Despite these constraints, many teachers went to extraordinary lengths to adapt to the new digital environments and find workable pedagogical approaches. In some instances, governments provided support in the form of crash courses that served as primers to orient teachers to technology-dependent instruction.[442] But these efforts tended to narrowly target technical skills and helped teachers enter and use systems rather than build the sophisticated competencies and experiences needed to implement effective digital pedagogies in virtual spaces. Some of the habits teachers developed during the pandemic, such as lecturing for long periods of time during synchronous classes and without visual learning aids, were arguably bad habits, even if systems invited or sometimes encouraged these approaches.

In best-case scenarios, teachers received only around ten days of training about how to teach and support students through remote digital technologies, a skill that can take years of education and experience to cultivate.

In the context of the pandemic and school closures, whatever was good enough pedagogically was usually assumed to be better than nothing. When teachers found approaches that worked reasonably well, they tended to stick with them. Time and head space for creative experimentation was a luxury few teachers had when they were forced to adapt learning to technology platforms with little training and for large numbers of students. A global survey of over 20,000 teachers from 165 countries conducted by T4 Education found that in best-case scenarios, teachers received only around ten days of professional development to help them navigate the transition from in-person education to remote digital learning.[443] To put this in context, many of the world's best teacher training colleges and universities advise at least a full year of education and training to prepare novice teachers to skilfully harness online technologies to improve student learning.[444] These institutions also tend to treat teaching and learning in digital environments as distinct from teaching and learning in physical classrooms, as they involve uniquely different outlooks and competencies. Abilities honed for teaching offline were not always transferable to teaching online, even if they may have provided a useful point of departure and reference. The pedagogical possibilities and limitations were distinct.

Early expectations that the pandemic would open doors to breakthrough pedagogical innovations and assurances that "necessity is the mother of invention"[445] were rarely fulfilled in practice. The reality for schools and teachers was more often a hurried search for basic, often behaviourist instructional approaches that worked passably well in digital spaces. Innovation tends to thrive when there is stability, collaboration, time to incubate and refine ideas, and the freedom to test and make errors, among other factors that were in short supply when teachers were asked, practically overnight, to practice their profession in an entirely new medium and with children's futures at stake.

CORPORATE AESTHETICS AND LINGUISTIC HEGEMONY REPLACED THE VIBRANCY OF THE CLASSROOM

Beyond contributing to the standardization and automation of learning processes, the spaces where this learning happened also changed with the shift to ed-tech. For many students, synchronous distance learning unfolded in one of just three digital locations: Google Meet, Microsoft Teams or Zoom. For the most part, these locations bore no sign of local communities; they were corporate and placeless and could, as transnational digital services, move relatively seamlessly over school, district, county, state and country lines that had once defined educational experiences.

"Even under optimal conditions, virtual school meant flattening the collaborative magic of the classroom into little more than an instructional video."

– Fourth grade teacher, USA[lxxvi]

Sometimes the full breadth of the digital educational experience – encompassing virtual classes, digital reading and writing, assignment completion and submission, and online communication and collaboration – unfolded in or around these platforms. For much of 2020 and 2021, and even into early 2023, Google Classroom, complemented by a wider array of Google G Suite apps, and Microsoft Teams, complemented by a wider array of Microsoft Office apps, became de facto classrooms for entire countries during the pandemic.[446]

> In place of science classrooms with animal skeletons, botanical illustrations, drawings of insects, photographs of planets and posters of the periodic table was the minimal corporate aesthetic of Google.

Accounts related in online forums and in media indicated that school leaders, teachers and students tended to experience these virtual spaces as significantly less versatile or customizable than the four walls of traditional classrooms. Teachers could not place maps, diagrams and other learning supports on walls, nor could they, in many instances, alter the look and feel of interfaces – not even their colour schemes. The design, controlled by professional teams in faraway locations, placed a corporate veneer over a school's or a teacher's aesthetic idiosyncrasies. The visual diversity and messiness of schools – sometimes overflowing with objects containing cultural, historical and community meaning – were replaced with the clean lines and logical efficiency of modern user interfaces. In place of science classrooms with animal skeletons, botanical illustrations, drawings of insects, photographs of planets and posters of the periodic table, was the primary-colour pop and minimal aesthetic of Google, the bubble-filled universe of Skype or the blue and teal hues of Lark, a collaboration platform used for educational purposes in China and other parts of Asia. While some open-source systems such as Drupal and Moodle gave educational institutions substantial control over platforms used for learning, many other providers kept their products largely locked and offered only limited personalization options, even for large institutions.

"I found the interface boring a bit. The colors used are a bit plain, and I don't see much of an option for us to maybe personal message a classmate because I don't know who is online. So, for me the interaction is a bit boring as it is only one-way communication with teachers."

– University student, Malaysia[lxxvii]

> The hegemonic position that the English language and the Latin alphabet assume within modern information-processing systems grew stronger still with the turn to global digital learning.

This also applied to language. Many ed-tech utilities were only available in a dominant language, even in communities that had been using a minority language for in-person school instruction. According to many commentators, the English language and the Latin alphabet assume a hegemonic position within modern information-processing systems. This language hegemony grew stronger still with the turn to global digital learning,[447] as many of the ed-tech solutions deployed during the emergency had been engineered and developed in English by anglophone teams, often based in North America. This domination meant that a reliance on ed-tech often entailed a forced embrace of English language educational content or navigating various English language portals to find digital content in other languages. Even if a digital 'skin' changed the appearance of an app and its outward-facing language, the typically English language original was often just underneath and would sometimes surface due to incomplete translations or technical glitches. After conducting a workshop in December 2020 with teams from ten countries, the EdTech Hub, a global non-profit research partnership, reported that "language created barriers in accessing technology" and explained that "learners, parents and teachers who did not speak English, or the dominant national language, were unable to use platforms and online resources designed in these languages".[448] In some regions of the world, ed-tech entrepreneurs and venture capitalists saw this as an opportunity to cater to non-English users by funding, developing and propagating digital ed-tech in vernacular languages. This was especially the case in multilingual areas such as India,[449] the Middle East and North Africa[450] and sub-Saharan Africa,[451] but also in countries where English is the dominant language, including the USA.[452] However, because many of these vernacular ed-tech solutions were deployed in a rushed manner, the English language versions often functioned more smoothly because the vernacular language version had not been as thoroughly error tested. Thus the sudden turn from in-person learning in schools and classrooms towards fully remote ed-tech was, for many students, a turn away from their native tongues towards the hegemonic lingua franca of digital spaces: English.

> Many teachers called on Zoom to spin off a stand-alone app exclusively designed for educators.

It is also significant that many of the digital spaces that served as a nexus for education during periods of school closure were not, in fact, expressly designed for education. Google Meet, Lark, Microsoft Teams and Zoom all classify themselves as generic communication, collaboration and productivity tools, rather than dedicated educational tools. This generic nature gives the platforms versatility, but it also means that functionalities that would be beneficial in a teaching and learning environment are often missing. In 2020, many teachers called on Zoom to spin off a stand-alone app exclusively designed for educators, requesting better functionality to break students into subgroups, more robust chat functions and richer ways of presenting lessons, among other education-targeted upgrades.[453] Zoom, however, remained a largely multifunction utility, even if it did, in some instances, respond to specific requests from large educational systems, such as when it shored up its privacy features after New York City's education department, encompassing over 1,800 schools, banned the use of the platform.[454] While many in education perceived Zoom's platform to be a nucleus for education during the pandemic, it was less clear whether Zoom and similar providers saw education stakeholders as a principal client group, despite the fact that Zoom was supporting virtual classes for over 90,000 schools across 20 countries in April 2020.[455] Media organizations reported that Zoom's platform was, at the same time and across all sectors, serving over 300 million meeting participants per day, meaning that schools, teachers and students represented just one client group among many for the company.[456] The education sector's importance may have been further diminished because Zoom provided pro bono or discounted prices to some educational institutions during the height of the pandemic. Schools and educators were not, therefore, necessarily the strongest customer base in terms of paying customers. The CEO of Zoom stated in a company blog post that the platform had been "built primarily for enterprise customers

– large institutions with full IT support [ranging] from the world's largest financial services companies to leading telecommunications providers, government agencies, universities, health care organizations, and telemedicine practices".[457] Conspicuously missing from this list were primary and secondary schools. When under pressure, commercial technology representatives sometimes noted that their tools and platforms had not been developed to stand in for schools, even if they were being propelled into this role and their companies were, in many instances, benefiting financially from an expanding user base of young new users.

Even relatively mature online platforms that had been purpose built for education were not usually intended to carry the full weight of schooling and had generally assumed a school-based experience for most teaching and learning. Google Classroom for instance, a platform that became something close to an all-purpose distance learning hub for large education systems and tens of thousands of schools during the pandemic, had not originally been built for this purpose. Rather, it had been designed as a digital extension for in-person schooling, a place where teachers could upload handouts and remind students of upcoming assignments. Google made a series of adjustments to the platform during the pandemic so it could better accommodate virtual class meetings through improved integration with Google Meet, Google's video meeting utility that, itself, had not originally been developed with education in mind.

During the pandemic, the digital spaces and platforms that supported learning proved to be largely fixed, unchangeable and corporate.

While schools as physical locations are often criticized as being poorly optimized for learning, they are, in most instances, designed and built expressly for education and not alternative purposes. They provide principals and teachers at least some margin for personalization and alteration to accommodate community and pedagogical goals for learning. Virtual spaces are sometimes described as more malleable than brick-and-mortar schools. They are widely imagined as blank slates where anything is possible and options to add educational functionality are plentiful and ever-expanding. But during the pandemic, the digital spaces and platforms that supported learning proved in practice to be largely fixed, unchangeable and corporate. In many respects, they were the opposite of blank slates – teachers, school leaders and sometimes even education ministers had little control over how they worked and appeared. And because many of the corporations that provided ed-tech during the pandemic were headquartered in countries far away from where their devices and services were used, even regulation or ensuring compliance with existing rules could be difficult. Staff at education ministries around the world were quick to learn that multinational technology companies were not as responsive as their domestic network of schools. Control of the digital spaces of education lay largely outside their reach and oversight.

AUTOMATION, STANDARDIZATION AND HOMOGENIZATION OF THE LEARNING PROCESS

Although internet-connected digital technology had long been positioned as an antidote to a perceived factory model of education, its practical application during the pandemic was arguably no more than an entry into vastly enlarged virtual factories.

Although internet-connected digital technology had long been positioned as an antidote to a perceived factory model of education, its practical application during the pandemic was arguably no more than an entry into vastly enlarged virtual factories. Many of the technology-dependent learning platforms and apps adopted during the crisis made students feel as though they were anonymous and interchangeable units being directed by unprecedented levels of automation. This was especially true for asynchronous apps where learning was guided by algorithms instead of teachers. But even in more human-mediated digital learning spaces, a student's membership in a particular community, family, school and class was often irrelevant. Affiliations that had organized learning in physical spaces, such as age and geography, tended to melt away in the new virtual learning environments. While some ed-tech solutions had appealing user interfaces and carried labels like 'AI-enabled', 'smart', 'adaptable', 'agile' or 'personalized', the learning experiences these solutions facilitated tended to be rote: a linear progression through machine-dispensed learning content with limited, if any, possibilities for interaction with peers and teachers.

Many students' experiences of remote online learning amounted to little more than logging into a video call and watching a teacher lecture and overview slide presentations. Other students were directed to watch educational videos, and indeed for the hundreds of millions of students without access to connected technology who were reliant on television broadcasts for ed-tech, this was the only option that existed.

Automation was a key ingredient of many ed-tech utilities used during the pandemic, especially those that served underprivileged learners who lacked options to follow synchronous teacher-led lessons in virtual spaces. Systems that did not require human intervention had a substantial advantage over systems more reliant on teachers and other human operators. Once established, they could quickly realize economies of scale, such that the cost difference of provisioning education to 1 or 100 or 100,000 learners was often very small.[458] This seamless scalability, reflecting a pursuit of cost-efficiency through 'bigness' that has guided the development of many digital services in use today, allowed educational platforms to rapidly expand the number of learners they accommodated – a feat that would have been unimaginable with brick-and-mortar institutions.

"It would be nice to put actual faces to names, or should I say dots."
– Eighth grade maths teacher, USA[lxxviii]

While this efficiency may have helped propel the uptake and use of digital learning content, it often had the side effect of stripping education of a human touch. In fully automated digital spaces, learning was guided by algorithms and bots, not human instructors that students knew and could see. The novelty of these systems tended to wear off quickly. Learners recognized that they were being tugged through worlds of algorithmically controlled and often gamified educational content. Encouragement from bot guides was often generic and came at the same predictable intervals. Learning was commonly structured in an identical unit-to-unit and module-to-module manner. This repetition caused students to grow exhausted and bored, and they regularly reported that learning journeys in virtual spaces felt less like knowledge explorations than treadmills of completion.[459]

"Something is lost when alternating periods of passivity and activity are compressed into interactivity, until eventually education becomes a continuous cybernetic loop of information and feedback. How many keystrokes or mouse-clicks before a student is told they've gone wrong? How many words does it take to make a mistake?"
– William Davies, sociologist and political economist[lxxix]

The tedium felt by students was not necessarily a failure of content design. Many of the learning applications and systems deployed during the pandemic had not been intended for prolonged use; they assumed instead a user who might engage with educational content for short and irregular periods of time – not extended durations, as was sometimes tacitly or explicitly advised in order to fill time that had previously been devoted to in-person schooling. Similarly, some of the software put forward as core educational tools had been developed to supplement rather than replace classroom-based learning. As the pandemic and its reliance on ed-tech wore on, media accounts relayed that students and their caregivers complained about the automation and lack of variety that defined many technology-mediated educational experiences.

> The digital pedagogies enabled by ed-tech felt fixed, flat, homogeneous and rooted in logics of machines.

The pandemic also pulled back a curtain on much of the software that promised to deliver personalized learning. Students and teachers found that a lot of 'personalized' content was little more than simple 'if A, then B' decision trees hard-coded by software engineers. The learning was personalized only insofar as a deck of questions or flash cards changed depending on whether input provided by a student was deemed correct or incorrect. Systems that were supposed to 'know' students did not know them at all, outside the narrow bounds of tracking various metrics about their use of unidirectional software, including, for instance, time on task, progression and right-or-wrong answers. These systems tended to ask students to demonstrate knowledge and understanding by answering fixed multiple-choice questions. Gone were the open discussions, spontaneity and human-controlled feedback that had often defined in-person classroom experiences led by professional teachers. For many learners, the digital pedagogies enabled by ed-tech, far from being emancipatory, innovative or imaginative, felt fixed, flat, homogeneous and rooted in the logics of machines. It was education stripped of humanity – learning calibrated to wire brains to answer question correctly rather than open hearts and minds to new knowledge, concepts and ideas.

"The virtues of men are of more consequence to society than their abilities, and for this reason the heart should be cultivated with more assiduity than the head."

– Noah Webster, lexicographer[lxxx]

> With the deployment of ed-tech, the former role of educators to direct student learning was regularly reduced to monitoring dashboards and ensuring the completion of units, sessions and assignments selected by autonomous systems – more proctoring than teaching.

Many teachers expressed that they felt sidelined by the automation and standardization of learning processes that tended to accompany the shift to ed-tech. A global survey by Education International found that ed-tech rolled out during the pandemic was regularly selected and deployed without teacher input or consultation. The organization argued that the emergency context resulted in a proliferation of "a unilateral top-down decision-making structure that overtly disregards the professionalism and experience of teachers and education support personnel".[460] Regardless of how technology was selected, educators were surprised to learn that their former role directing student learning was regularly reduced to monitoring dashboards and ensuring the completion of units, sessions and assignments selected by autonomous systems – more proctoring than teaching. Many teachers voiced a loss of control and autonomy when technology supplemented schools as the primary interface for formal education.

"Automated interventions in education are expanding fast and often with limited scrutiny of the technological and commercial specificities of such processes."

– Morten Hansen and Janja Komljenovic, education researchers[lxxxi]

Immersion in technology was unhealthy

The impetus to close schools and transition to remote learning with ed-tech was the protection of health. It was understood that school closures and remote learning would slow the spread of COVID-19 infections and minimize illness and death for learners, teachers, families and wider communities. There is evidence that these measures helped accomplish this goal, particularly early in the pandemic when infections were peaking and health facilities were overwhelmed.[461] But the intense focus on minimizing the immediate risk of COVID-19 transmission often obscured the reality that decisions to close schools and the associated transition to technology-mediated distance learning carried numerous and often damaging health consequences, both mental and physical, that transcended the immediate dangers presented by the novel coronavirus.

Prior to the pandemic, the impact of ed-tech on student and teacher health was not typically a question of particular concern. The overriding assumption was that technology's effects would be neutral, in part because few people foresaw it displacing schools and schooling entirely. There was a sense that technology-centric learning routines and activities, mixed with other social, recreational and developmental activities, including schooling as an in-person experience, did not pose any special health hazards. Existing studies of ed-tech tended to look for evidence of improved learning outcomes and greater educational efficiency. Health repercussions were rarely a focus of inquiry, even if there were some notable exceptions emanating from medical research – research that did not always find its way to education leaders and practitioners.

When the pandemic triggered school closures, apprehensions that remote learning with ed-tech might represent a threat to health were widely dismissed as anachronistic, especially early in the crisis. Few alarms were raised as millions of young people immersed themselves in screen-based learning experiences, sometimes for several hours each day, in addition to spending more time online for communication, entertainment and leisure. Debates over screen time that had burned hotly in the early 2000s were considered démodé and dismissed as the worries of a generation still uncomfortable with the idea that smartphones had already transformed societies, and young people especially who were assumed to move seamlessly between online and offline worlds.

> Few alarms were raised as millions of young people immersed themselves in screen-based learning experiences, sometimes for several hours each day, in addition to spending more time online for communication, entertainment and leisure.

These conceptions, however, were gradually exposed as incomplete and unmethodical, less the result of empirical research than of conjecture. The health repercussions of the often dramatic increases in the time young people were spending in front of screens, for education as well as other purposes, were soon documented in media and later, more systematically, by various medical experts and associations. Research clarified that the switch to education delivered remotely through technology was having discernible negative impacts on physical health, such as increased levels of physical pain reported by children due to the repetitive movements needed to traverse digital spaces. Evidence further pointed to unhealthy weight gain as a result of sedentary behaviours associated with the retreat into technology.

The mental health repercussions were even more worrisome. Rises in technology use corresponded with spiking levels of stress and anxiety, upticks in eating disorders and new feelings of isolation and alienation.

When learning routines became dependent on connected technology, time spent with digital devices soared, changing family dynamics in adverse ways and leaving many young people feeling adrift. Always-on internet connections that promised to help maintain social bonds sometimes seemed to accomplish the opposite – metastasizing feelings of disconnection that were already pronounced because of the multilayered restrictions of the pandemic.

Around the world, children as young as 4 and 5 years old were placed in front of screens, ostensibly for educational purposes, despite evidence that screen-based media does very little to advance learning for young children and may even slow cognitive development. Many children and youth were unprepared to navigate online content safely and with appropriate self-regulation. Anecdotal evidence showed that learners routinely encountered age-inappropriate material when ed-tech opened portals to the wider internet without the filters and teacher oversight that are customary in school settings.

> Fully remote digital learning largely neglected to help students learn to live together, a primary objective of formal education. Indeed it may have driven them further apart, given the tendency of the internet to draw like-minded people into digital silos and provoke polarization.

Young people also had trouble finding digital substitutes for the socialization, unstructured play and physical interactions that are mainstays of in-person schooling. Conversation diminished and people experienced being 'alone together'. Family members were near each other physically but immersed in separate screens and traversing metaverse-like spaces in search of entertainment and cyber-companionship as well as education. This immersion – sometimes consuming most waking hours of the day – left learners unfulfilled and drained. Fully remote digital learning largely neglected to help students learn to live together, a primary objective of education, and may in fact have driven them further apart, given the tendency of the internet to draw like-minded people into digital silos and provoke polarization. As evidence of the adverse physical and mental health consequences associated with the pivot from schools to technology came into sharp relief, many medical groups advised that the health risks of opening schools during the pandemic were eclipsed by the health risks of keeping them shut and maintaining exclusive reliance on ed-tech for formal learning.

NEGATIVE IMPACTS OF INCREASED SCREEN TIME

Without question, the decision to move education to technology increased the amount of time young people spent, almost always alone, in front of screens. Such a rise is meaningful, as it tends to correlate with poorer mental and physical health and greater perceived stress. Conversely, social support and coping behaviours are generally associated with lower total screen use.[462] Numerous organizations, including UNICEF, have rightly observed that screen time is a crude indicator of digital behaviours, which can be healthy or unhealthy given the wide variety of engagements possible in digital realms.[463] Nevertheless, excessive screen time remains closely and persistently linked with troubling health outcomes ranging from moderate to severe.[464] And researchers continue to discover new and often adverse health effects associated with the seemingly ever-rising amounts of time young people spend using connected digital devices, a trend that is still a very recent global phenomenon.

The negative health consequences of excessive screen time include physical pain, eye strain, alteration of sleep patterns, increased levels of stress and anxiety, depression and lower self-esteem, among other maladies.[465] However, despite long-held concerns about the dangers of excessive screen time, education authorities commonly advised or, in many instances, mandated students to spend several hours a day in front of digital devices for educational purposes during periods of school closure. This almost always added more screen time to daily routines that were often already dominated by online activities for connected children and youth.

> In the USA, children between the ages of 12 and 13 were spending twice as much time in front of screens during the pandemic than before the pandemic, from approximately four hours per day to eight hours per day.

An academic review of various studies on screen time from multiple and mainly highly developed countries found that overall digital device usage across various age groups increased by up to five hours a day during the pandemic, compared with usage before the pandemic.[466] The authors of the review estimated that heavy users were spending an average of 17.5 hours per day using digital technology, or close to the entire waking day, while non-heavy users were spending closer to 30 hours per week or around 4 hours per day. In countries with high digital penetration and affordable connectivity, children and youth seem to have been at the higher ends of this spectrum. One of the most comprehensive nationwide studies on screen time in the USA found that children between the ages of 12 and 13 were spending twice as much time in front of screens during the pandemic than before the pandemic, from approximately four hours per day to eight hours per day, *excluding* school-related work.[467] When educational engagement was considered, total screen hours jumped higher still. This heavy use gave rise to new nomenclature to call attention to youth immersion into virtual spaces. In the USA, for example, teenagers were being referred to as "screenagers",[468] and Generation Alpha, children born after 2010, were recast as "Generation Glass", an unironic attempt to label an entire demographic group according to their fixation with the glowing glass screens of digital technology.[469]

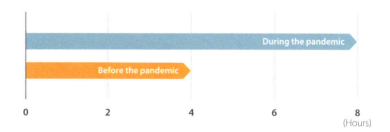

Figure 14:

Average increase in screen time during the pandemic among 12- and 13-year-old children in the USA

Source: Data from *JAMA Pediatrics*, 2021

"Though social media and video chat can foster social connection and support, we found that most of the adolescents' screen use during the pandemic didn't serve this purpose."

– Jason Nagata, assistant professor of paediatrics, University of California[lxxxii]

Qustodio, a Spanish research group focused on digital safety, conducted a multi-country study of the digital habits of children between the ages of 4 and 15 to shine a light on the constituent activities of increased screen time. It found that in 2020, children spent 25 per cent more screen time on online video than in 2019, 76 per cent more time on social media, 23 per cent more time on video games, 54 per cent more time on education and 49 per cent time more on communication.[470] These large jumps in screen time, typically far surpassing guidelines recommended by experts, were detrimental to health and development.

While screen time generally increased for all students, it increased significantly more for students from low-income families.

Other studies corroborated a dramatic rise in the amount of time children spent using screen-based media and showed particularly steep rises for children from poor families. Research encompassing Australia, China, Italy, Sweden, the UK and the USA found increases of nearly one hour per day among 3- to 7-year-olds and observed that children in households of lower socio-economic status spent the most amount of time in front of screens, a troubling result given the correlation of screen time to poor health[471] and lower quality relationships.[472] This evidence mirrored findings from pre-pandemic studies that had also revealed substantial disparities in screen-based media use based on family income. For instance, data collected in the USA by Common Sense, a research and advocacy organization centred on children's use of digital media, found in 2019 that 8- to 12-year-olds from wealthy families watched screens nearly two hours less per day than children of the same age from low-income families.⁴⁷³ This trend was observed in developed countries around the world during the pandemic such that, while screen time increased for all students, it increased significantly more for disadvantaged students with access to connected technology.

"You see a rapid screen time increase starting from when they are only 1–2 months old, and that really took our breath away and made us triple-check our figures."

– Leigh Tooth, principal research fellow, University of Queensland's School of Public Health^lxxxiii

When the pandemic hit, screen time also appears to have leaped for infants and toddlers. A 12-country study of 8- to 36-month-olds found that they too were exposed to more screen time during lockdowns than before lockdowns.⁴⁷⁴ Pre-pandemic studies had indicated that in many highly developed countries, children under 2 years old were already spending an average of up to three hours per day in front of screens,⁴⁷⁵ despite recommendations from the WHO and numerous national medical groups that children under 24 months old spend *no* time with screens and that 2- to 4-year-olds spend "no more than 1 hour per day, less is better".⁴⁷⁶

> Around the world, students were given connected technology to engage in formal learning activities, and this often afforded them wider allowances to use this technology for longer durations and with less oversight than would have been permissible prior to the pandemic.

With the overlapping disruptions of the pandemic, it is difficult to estimate the extent to which the turn to ed-tech in response to school closures contributed to ballooning screen time beyond direct educational tasks. One multi-country study suggests that the educational portion of the increase was approximately one-third, while the other two-thirds were associated with entertainment.⁴⁷⁷ But the education contribution was likely both direct and indirect. Around the world, students were given connected technology to engage in formal learning activities, and this often afforded them wider allowances to use this technology for longer durations and with less oversight than would have been permissible prior to the pandemic. Children instructed to engage in formal learning activities through a screen often remained in digital environments when formal education ended. Anecdotal evidence indicates that parents who asked their children to set down digital devices were often rebuffed by children who protested that they were doing schoolwork even if they were engaged in other online activities. Parents in Indonesia responding to an online survey about digital media use by young children reported that while they were deeply worried about screen time and recognized the importance of limiting it, they found it difficult to prevent their children from using online devices because of home-based learning.⁴⁷⁸ This finding was widely corroborated as parents across countries registered feeling more concerned about their children's excessive screen time but also less able and less confident about limiting it when teaching and learning moved online.⁴⁷⁹

Prior to the pandemic, school had often been one of the only places where young people in developed and digitally advanced settings were not regularly immersed in digital worlds for extended periods of time. Engagement in formal education was, in effect, the most offline part of their day. This reversed entirely during the pandemic and carried significant negative health impacts.[480]

PAINS, WEIGHT GAIN AND MALNUTRITION

Data from China suggested that the shift to online schooling had caused a threefold increase in the prevalence of short-sightedness among 6- to 8-year-olds in 2020.

Anecdotal and research evidence of the physical consequences of the turn to fully remote digital learning began to appear almost immediately. Children and youth using digital devices and watching television for hours a day regularly complained of pain emanating from fingers and wrists, eye irritation, neck and back aches, fatigue, headaches and trouble sleeping. The workstations children had at home, if indeed they had them at all, were rarely ergonomic. A survey of university students in India found that around 80 per cent of respondents reported experiencing discomfort in their head, neck and eyes due to the switch to online-only learning. And more than 40 per cent reported symptoms found in musculoskeletal disorders.[481] Ophthalmology experts warned of an acceleration of a "myopia epidemic" that was already closely associated with increased screen time.[482] A study of 120,000 Chinese schoolchildren suggested that the shift to online schooling had caused a threefold increase in the prevalence of short-sightedness among 6- to 8-year-olds in 2020.[483]

"[Electronic devices are] the No. 1 sleep enemy."

– Adiaha Spinks-Franklin, developmental behavioural paediatrician[lxxxiv]

Unhealthy weight gain was another common problem for screen-immersed youth. The sedentary nature of learning with technology decreased physical activity, and ad-saturated digital spaces often encouraged the consumption of unhealthy food and beverages. Spikes in obesity did not come as a particular surprise. Pre-pandemic health studies had identified a correlation between screen media exposure and obesity in children and attributed this to a number of factors: increased eating and snacking while viewing media; decreased physical activity; exposure to high-calorie, low-nutrient food and beverage marketing; and reduced sleep duration.[484] As school closures stretched deep into 2021, paediatricians began documenting weight gains of as much as 20 to 30 pounds among children participating in primary education through remote learning.[485] Alarming rises in type 2 diabetes in children were also widely documented, with cases sometimes doubling between pre-pandemic periods in 2019 and comparable times in 2020.[486]

"Screen time lends itself to more sedentary time and less physical activity, snacking while distracted, eating in the absence of hunger, and greater exposure to food advertising."

– Jason Nagata, assistant professor of paediatrics, University of California[xxxv]

A strong predictor of childhood obesity during the pandemic was the duration of home- and technology-based learning.

Instances of weight gain appear to have been particularly pronounced in many Western countries but were detected in countries throughout the world and closely corresponded to school closures and the shift to ed-tech.[487] For many young people, getting to and from school as well as navigating inside schools was an important form of exercise. School was also traditionally a hub for play and sports that helped children maintain a healthy body weight. Increased technology use usually caused a decline in exercise and often invited overeating and increased consumption of high-calorie foods and beverages. Health studies remarked that a strong predictor of unhealthy weight gain in children during the pandemic was the duration of home- and technology-based learning, with longer durations foreshadowing an increased prevalence in obesity.[488]

While weight gain was common in wealthy countries where ed-tech was widely available, malnutrition was a significant risk in low- and middle-income countries during periods of school closure. Across the world, many students relied on schools for regular and nutritious meals. In Thailand, for instance, experts estimate that school feeding programmes provide between 30 per cent and 50 per cent of daily nutritional requirements for some children and tend to offer healthier meals than those prepared at home at the same price. Children's nutrition was therefore often compromised when home-based learning with technology became the norm. Research from Thailand found that children residing in rural areas who missed school meals during the 43-day period of national school closures in 2020 could be expected to lose between 5 per cent and 10 per cent of their total body weight. The study further estimated that nearly 270 million meals had been missed countrywide as a result of school closures.[489]

Although food insecurity during the pandemic was most pronounced in low- and middle-income countries, it was hardly contained to them. Research in the USA, for instance, found that food insecurity tripled for families with children during the initial wave of COVID-19 lockdowns and school closures.[490] The pandemic provided a powerful reminder that the effective and widespread provision of meals and other services that benefit children and youth are largely dependent on schools that are operational as physical infrastructure. These services were not well supported or maintained when education became fully remote and digital.

PHYSICAL EDUCATION ONLINE AND IN ISOLATION

The spiral into digital worlds during the pandemic was so complete that attempts to mitigate the sedentary effects of technology use were commonly met with yet more technology.

The spiral into digital worlds during the pandemic was so complete that attempts to mitigate the sedentary effects of technology use were commonly met with yet more technology. To avoid youth weight gain, for example, many countries turned to digital apps designed to motivate and guide at-home exercise routines.[491] Across the world, physical education classes moved online, along with subject matter classes in reading, mathematics and other disciplines. Students were often told to complete workouts and stretching following an instructor's lead either online or via a television programme. Others were asked to video record the completion of jumping jacks, sit-ups and push-ups and then send them electronically to an instructor as proof of completion.

Many teachers as well as students expressed disappointment with technology-guided modes of exercising. A study from Spain, for instance, found that "sadness" and "anger" were the dominant feelings of physical education instructors surrounding the shift of physical education from in-person to virtual environments.[492] Families also expressed concern that screen-facilitated physical education would normalize exercise in isolation and in homes, rather than as group activities conducted outdoors or in communal indoor spaces. In-person physical sport and exercise can increase feelings of belonging and cultivate friendship and teamwork, but these feelings were much harder to replicate when sport and exercise were conducted at a distance through digital mediums.

Some educators further worried that conducting exercise and other physical education routines exclusively over remote technology might cement understandings that all forms of physical contact and touch are rare or forbidden in education contexts, even when the subject matter is the healthy maintenance of the physical body for sport and life. Research conducted prior to the pandemic indicated that, in some contexts, physical education teachers, coaches and others had grown increasingly concerned about the habituation of limited physical contact and expectations that education is – or should be – fully touchless.[493] Pandemic school closures and remote learning made 'no touch' and 'no contact' education – even physical education – more common and widespread than it had been previously.

TOUCHLESS WORLDS

As lockdowns and school closures prolonged, medical experts expressed worry about 'touch hunger' or 'touch starvation', the condition of increased stress, depression and anxiety, among a "cascade of negative physiological effects", brought on by reduced positive human touch.[494] The hugs, handshakes, arms around a friend, high fives, handholding, locked arms, playful punches, hands on shoulders and pats on backs that had been commonplace at school were gone in the world of remote learning with ed-tech.

The need for touch often overrides other physical needs, including even those for food and drink.

This was troubling because tactile communication is, according to experts, "absolutely vital" to our physical and mental well-being,[495] particularly for children. Skin is the largest organ in the human body, and people are wired both to touch and to be touched.[496] Touch is widely considered to be a primordial human sense, foundational to individual and communal selves. In the book *Touch: Recovering Our Most Vital Sense,* the author and philosopher Richard Kearney notes that the need for touch often "overrides" other physical needs, including even those for food and drink. Friendly touch catalyses processes that are well-understood to improve feelings of trust, strengthen emotional bonding and social connection, lower blood pressure, help with sleep and digestion, and bolster the immune system, all while minimizing fear and anxiety.[497]

Large multi-country studies have corroborated these benefits and found that people with positive attitudes towards touch have significantly higher levels of well-being and feel less lonely than those who claim to dislike touch.[498] Participants in studies reported feeling better about themselves and others if they had been touched recently. Touch has also been shown to have implications for academic achievement. Researchers have demonstrated, for instance, that touch appears to improve attentiveness and quantitative performance in mathematics, improving student speed and accuracy solving problems.[499]

"Touch is a crucial corrective to our fixation with control."
– Richard Kearney, philosopher and author of *Touch: Recovering Our Most Vital Sense*[xxxvi]

Academic learning is generally considered the principal objective of schooling, and, for this reason, it was the main, if not singular, focus of ed-tech solutions to school closures during the pandemic. While touch is typically commonplace at school, its importance is almost never counted as an 'aim' or 'goal' of schooling per se. Thus, when parents were told to have children sit in front of screens so they could follow academic instruction, little to no attention was paid to touch. Messaging to families about technology-based education rarely included mention that children, no longer with their friends or participating in groups, sports or play, were likely missing touch and that this could carry adverse repercussions for both physical and mental health.

> The remote and usually technology-tethered learning experiences common during the pandemic engaged learners' senses of sight and sound, but provided almost no tactile stimuli.

Such oversight may have reflected pre-pandemic observations that touch is, as experts have argued, undervalued in education and other fields, stemming from "deeply rooted beliefs that favour the cerebral over the corporeal".[500] According to Sushma Subramanian, the author of *How to Feel: The Science and Meaning of Touch*, touch is "maligned" in many societies and dismissed as being "dirty or sentimental, in contrast with supposedly more elevated modes of perceiving the world".[501] Remote learning with technology tended to privilege these assumed 'more elevated' modes of perception and placed a premium on touchless modes of learning through reading, lectures, videos, writing and speaking. Learning that involved tactile experiences – laboratory experiments, physical education, different types of art – was awkward, if not impossible, to move into digital environments. The remote and usually technology-tethered learning experiences common during the pandemic engaged learners' senses of sight and sound, but provided almost no tactile stimuli beyond, for example, haptic feedback from a mobile device or the touchpad on a laptop.

Beyond reducing touch in education, technology-only modes of distance learning rarely stimulated two other human senses – smell and taste. Both senses, like touch, can support learning and make it more interesting and rewarding. Chemistry, for example, often captivates students by demonstrating the molecular and chemical underpinnings of commonly encountered smells and tastes. Smell, in particular, has long been understood to enhance memory and recall, such that the scents of different spaces, educators, materials and peers can help differentiate experiences and reinforce recollection.[502] Even the senses ed-tech could engage – sight and sound, primarily – tended to lack the nuance and sophistication offered by the physical world, which is three-dimensional and contains vibrant images, light and noise that technical equipment can approximate but fails to fully replicate, despite steady advances. Due to these constraints, the predominately virtual learning spaces of technology tended to offer reduced and arguably degraded stimulation to human sensory organs that have evolved over millennia. This digital depletion of sensory experiences appears to be detrimental to health over long periods of time and may have limited the effectiveness and retention of learning as well as inadvertently reducing student motivation.

"Bodies, with all the risk, danger, limits, mortality and vulnerability that they bring, are part of our deepest humanity, not obstacles to be transcended through digitization."

– Tish Harrison Warren, priest and author[lxxxvii]

> With fully remote learning, the body was not of particular interest or concern.

The contactless and other sensory-reduced modes of learning that became commonplace during the pandemic and helped mitigate the risk of disease transmission normalised non-touch modes of learning with technology. Prior to COVID-19 numerous ed-tech solutions were premised on understandings that learners would work in close human proximity and many facilitated interactions that engaged students senses of touch as well as smell and taste. But these solutions were shelved during the pandemic in favor of ed-tech modes of learning that largely disregarded the human body. With fully remote learning, the body was not of particular interest or concern. While new virtual and augmented reality technology may point to options to engage the corporal body more fully in digital simulations, this hardware was functionally and financially out of reach for all but the most privileged families during the pandemic. For these reasons, students and teachers experienced the move to ed-tech as largely bodiless and touchless experiences. This was a radical departure from pre-pandemic learning experiences based at schools (including those involving technology), which had, however imperfectly, stimulated both the mind *and* the body. What prevailed and became dominant was virtual stimulation and experiences that were 'synthetic' to the extent that they existed beyond the tactile and physical world.

"We don't need to swap out our bodies with holographs and avatars. We need to nurture our sense of touch."

– JoAnna Novak, author of fiction and poetry[lxxxviii]

> The move to fully remote learning with ed-tech resulted in disembodiment. It ushered in a mode of education that many students and teachers experienced as a disassociation from their bodies and the bodies of others.

These virtual experiences were made possible by digital technologies that open new horizons for experience and exchange, but, at the same time, are often blamed for ushering humanity, and children and youth especially, into unnatural and unsatisfying realms that ignore human bodies and their diverse sensory organs. This trend had been apparent before the pandemic but accelerated with its arrival. Said differently, the move to fully remote learning with ed-tech took some students to new extremes of disembodiment. It activated, with little debate or deliberation due to the emergency context, modes of education that many learners and teachers experienced as a disassociation from their bodies and the bodies of others. Evidence suggests that the retreat *away* from education that included and accounted for the corporal body and *towards* incorporeal virtual education was detrimental to well-being and to learning, and researchers are still deciphering the full scope of its harmful effects.

A RETREAT INTO GAMES AND PROTO-METAVERSES

When governments closed schools and enforced wider restrictions on in-person social gatherings and activities such as sports during the pandemic, young people commonly turned to digital gaming and metaverse-like platforms to find community and interact with others. While this trend was not directly related to ed-tech, it illustrates how deeply youth immersed themselves in virtual environments peripheral to digital learning when schools were not operational and lockdowns peaked. It further shows how games and social media platforms aimed at youth enabled digital modes of socialization and cooperation that were often missing from the pedagogies, platforms and content upholding distance education. Dramatic upticks in gaming and time spent on social media caused overall screentime to rise far beyond the additional time students spent on digital devices for formal learning – with concurrent and sometimes adverse implications for health. Despite the popularity and appeal of digital experiences adjacent to ed-tech and sometimes overlapping it, there is little evidence that they meaningfully advanced education and learning.

As the pandemic spread across the world, video game play experienced "explosive" growth, much of it driven by games that involved competition or cooperation with other human players.[503] In June 2021, Statista estimated that the total time people spent playing video games globally had increased by 40 per cent since the start of the pandemic, with young people fuelling most of this gain.[504] An April 2021 Accenture report announced that the

The rise in social gaming corresponded with education becoming significantly less social as it moved to digital environments. Young people wanted an outlet for connection and found it most readily in video games.

global gaming market had "surpassed movies and music – combined" and "just keeps getting bigger".[505] The report stated that there were 2.7 billion gamers worldwide and estimated the direct and indirect value of the global gaming industry at over USD 300 billion. Accenture highlighted the growing appeal of social gaming – games played in real time with others – and noted that young people were drawn to games that prioritized connection and cooperation with other people. It called social interactions one of the "key drivers behind online gaming's impressive growth". Accenture surveys covering numerous countries found that three-quarters of gamers said that more of their social interaction took place on gaming platforms as a result of the pandemic and school closures. Accenture further noted that the "distinctions between playing a game and social interaction are blurring, if not completely disappearing".[506] This rise in social gaming was significant because it occurred when education becoming arguably less social as it moved to digital environments. It seems that young people wanted an outlet for connection during the pandemic and found it most readily in video games.

Video games provided many young people with a versatile and entertaining outlet for socialization. Stuck at home and often under quarantine, young people no longer just played video games: they watched others playing them, joining a surging community of e-sport spectators, and spent considerable time communicating in game forums and communities (the digital equivalent of athletes chatting on the side lines of a competition). Accenture estimated that during the pandemic the average gamer was spending 16 hours a week playing games, 8 hours a week watching games played by others and 6 hours a week interacting in community forums hosted in or adjacent to games. The massive growth of Discord, a social media platform widely used by gamers during the pandemic exemplified this blurring between playing online games and social interaction.[507] Outwardly it was a communications platform, but it enabled seamless incorporation of games.

"We experimented with every feature of our games to see which versions allowed us to extract the most time and money from our players. For us, game addiction was by design: It meant success for our business."

– William Siu, mobile gaming developer[xxxix]

Considerable evidence suggests that the move into virtual games and e-sports often came at the expense of physical games and sports[508] and unstructured play.[509] This trend had been in motion before the pandemic. According to a large study in the USA, for instance, the percentage of children aged between 6 and 12 regularly playing a physical team sport, whether basketball, football or track and field events, fell from 45 per cent in 2008 to 38 per cent in 2018.[510] This decline was assumed to have two main sources: first the increasing digitalization of societies and rising interest in e-sports, and second the growing costs associated with sports as well as their increasingly competitive nature.[511] Some families found e-sports less stressful and less costly, and many parents welcomed the idea that their children were unlikely to be injured playing virtual games, even if excessive gaming is associated with physical harm (for example, repetitive stress injuries on hands and wrists) and mental harm (for example, depression, impulsivity and anxiety).[512] Since 2018, the WHO has classified "gaming disorder" as an addictive behaviour that can "result in significant impairment in personal, family, social, educational, occupational or other important areas of functioning".[513] Regardless of the specific reasons, school closures, wider pandemic restrictions and the concurrent turn to digital spaces appears to have greatly accelerated a flight from physical sports to virtual ones, for boys and girls alike. A large survey of families in the USA by the Aspen Institute helped quantify the scale of change. It found that while only 19 per cent of parents said their children were not interested in playing physical sports in June 2020, this figure rose to 28 per cent in September 2021, a period in which e-sports experienced unprecedented growth.[514]

> China prohibited children and youth from playing video games on schooldays and permitted only one hour of play a day on weekend and holiday evenings.

Available evidence indicates that spikes in gaming were global. Video game play soared to such a degree in China during the pandemic and school closures that the government enacted restrictions to moderate the time young people spent gaming. In the second half of 2021, China prohibited children and youth from playing video games on schooldays and permitted only one hour of play a day on weekend and holiday evenings.[515] The rules tightened earlier restrictions on video game play and other digital activities that policy leaders deemed unhealthy, such as online platforms that encouraged celebrity veneration.[516] China was one of the few countries that passed measures during the pandemic to stem digital activities such as gaming that attracted large numbers of children and youth and may have distracted them from education that was also unfolding on screens for significant periods. The government's interventions appear to have been welcomed in many quarters but were perceived in others as a heavy-handed clampdown on new forms of digital leisure and entertainment accessible to minors.

"[Online video games have grown into] spiritual opium worth hundreds of billions."

– Chinese state media[xc]

The commercialization of gaming and interlinked data surveillance practices can strip play of its most beneficial qualities such as self-choice and inventiveness.

The growth of gaming had implications for play. An article in the *International Journal of Children's Rights* expressed concerns about the "platforming of play" during the COVID-19 pandemic. The article observed that, on the one hand, gaming offered a digital avenue for children to "realise their rights to play, socialise and express themselves" at a time when there were few opportunities for them to do so. However, the article warned that children who spend more time engaged in digital forms of play tend to be "exposed to sophisticated business models and other potentially harmful practices which may lead to them being exploited".[517] It further lamented the way that the commercialization of gaming and interlinked data surveillance practices can strip play of its most beneficial qualities such as self-choice and inventiveness.

"With all of its success, our technology has greatly diminished our direct experiences with nature. We live mediated lives. We have created a natureless world. … For 99 percent of our history as humans we have lived close to nature. … We are at war with our ancestral selves."

– Alan Lightman, physicist and author[xci]

As platforms supporting communication, social media, games, e-sports and other digital experiences became increasingly immersive and central to people's lives, they were sometimes referred to as metaverses – virtual and simulated worlds where users can 'live' and undertake work and leisure. Instead of entering and leaving apps with narrow functionalities, children and youth were increasingly traversing singular platforms offering varied experiences for extended periods of time. Facebook rebranded itself as Meta in October 2021. At this time over 3.5 billion people – nearly half the global population – used one or more of its applications, including WhatsApp and Instagram.[518] This ecosystem hosted many young people for five or more hours per day through much of the pandemic. One of the primary commercial goals was to recruit more young people to Meta's proprietary virtual spaces and keep those already there for longer durations. Internal Facebook documents leaked in 2021 showed that the company had a corporate target of holding teenage users for three to four hours a day on Instagram alone.[519] Similarly, WeChat – a 10-year-old China-based social media app sometimes referred to as a '2D Metaverse' – used the pandemic, like its Western counterparts, to expand its sprawling digital ecosystem and provide young people with a one-stop platform to shop, date, create, make payments and communicate, among other activities.[520] WeChat was commonly used for education during the pandemic and saw its user base grow considerably, both in total users and in time spent in the app. In 2021, WeChat was being used by over 1.2 billion active users every month, and the average WeChat user was opening the app, usually from a mobile device, over ten times per day, with around 25 per cent of users opening it over 50 times a day.[521] Because of the app's popularity, it was a go-to space for a lot of teaching and learning activities in China, especially at the beginning of the pandemic when people tended to resort to familiar software and tools for educational purposes.

Meta and WeChat were hardly the only corporate platforms drawing students who were out of school and equipped with connected technology towards metaverse-like spaces – spaces that some commentators consider a "successor state" to the mobile internet.[522] The video game Fortnite, for example, added new metaverse-like functionalities during the pandemic and, according to a global study, was being played by children and youth between the ages of 4 and 15 for over 90 minutes per day on average.[523] World of Warcraft was another video game with metaverse characteristics and extensive social functionality. It was being played by the same youth demographic group for over 140 minutes per day on average.[524] Minecraft, a Microsoft-owned video game where users construct virtual worlds and interact in them, and Roblox, a gaming platform where users create avatars and move through virtual worlds to perform tasks as varied as building hotels and fighting aliens, also became wildly popular during the pandemic. Both were sometimes lauded as 'educational' because they invited creativity, collaboration and problem solving. In the first quarter of 2021 when many schools remained closed, more than 42 million users, half of whom were under 13 years old, logged into Roblox each day and spent a cumulative 10 billion hours on its platform.[525] The company went public in March 2021 with a valuation of USD 45 billion and was worth approximately USD 70 billion as 2021 came to a close.[526]

One major study estimated that children in Spain, the UK and the USA were logged into Roblox for 96 minutes per day on average.[527] To put this in perspective, the longest time young people spent continuously in education-specific applications, according to the same study was under 20 minutes per day. Only two educational apps logged average daily time durations of over 15 minutes: the Khan Academy, a platform offering numerous educational resources and videos in various languages, and Kahoot, a game-based learning platform. This indicates that the dramatically increased time young people were spending in front of screens did not appear to be dedicated to education but rather involved traversing parallel virtual spaces, especially those mixing entertainment, socialization and communication.

What had once been a 5-hour window of heavy gaming and social media use was replaced with a continuous 13-hour period of use.

The shift to ed-tech almost certainly accelerated the embrace of gaming and metaverses. In wealthy countries where connected technology is widely owned, school-based education had been one of the last frontiers of sustained offline, non-virtual experiences. Moving education to screens assured more screen time overall and, beyond this, seems to have increased digital engagement for other purposes – particularly, gaming, social media use and passive viewership of videos. YouTube is arguably another proto-metaverse, and its use by children increased substantially during the pandemic. In the USA, for example, people between the ages of 4 and 15 spent nearly 100 minutes a day on YouTube in March and April 2020, up from 57 minutes in February before the pandemic and the shift to technology-based learning.[528] Similar dramatic increases in the time young people spent watching videos on online platforms were observed in other developed countries. Tellingly, the time of day students spent watching videos shifted during the pandemic. Before the health crisis, young people generally used video apps between 3 p.m. and 8 p.m., or during after-school hours. But with school closures and the move to ed-tech, these habits changed radically. Young people began spending the entire day watching videos, from 10 a.m. to 10 p.m. A similar shift was noticed in the time of day students played video games and used social media. What had once been a 5-hour window of heavy gaming and social media use starting in the mid-afternoon was replaced with a continuous 13-hour period of use.[529]

While many commentators speculate that youth might someday live in simulated worlds, the pandemic experience indicated that, by some measures, that day may have already arrived. No previous generation has spent close to as much time living behind screens.

Many people thought and hoped that screen time would taper off or decline quickly as the pandemic and school closures stretched on, but the opposite may have been more common: usage of digital devices and time spent in metaverse-like spaces often went up among young people as time passed – a trend that some labelled "the COVID-19 effect".[530] When full reliance on ed-tech ended with the reopening of physical schools, screen time for non-educational uses generally did decrease, as did screen time for education, unsurprisingly.[531] This provided perhaps the clearest indication that the pandemic, school closures and the movement of education to screens catalysed an overall rise in screen time across the board. The embrace of remote learning with ed-tech appears to have had a peripheral effect of pulling many young people into proto-metaverses where they spent a majority and sometimes a heavy majority of their waking days. While many commentators speculate that youth might someday spend nearly all their time in simulated worlds, the pandemic experience indicated that, by some measures, that day may have already arrived. No previous generation has spent close to as much time living behind screens. The physical, cultural and psychosocial effects of this trend are still only just coming into focus, with early signs pointing to concerning adverse outcomes, including loneliness, withdrawal, antisocial behaviour and depression.

> The digital spaces where students spent the most time were rarely emancipatory in the way education aims to be, but instead appear to have been the opposite: constraining, controlling, redundant, corporate and manipulative.

It is further significant that children around the world took refuge in games with social elements and in various social media platforms. Arguably they were seeking social connections that were severed with the closure of schools and that remote learning generally failed to approximate. While some video games are considered or marketed as educational – and some studies have cautiously suggested specific domains where they may facilitate superior learning outcomes than the use of conventional educational media and approaches[532] – they remain, at least given the limitations of current technology, touchless worlds with a strong tilt towards entertainment. For instance, although the video game Fortnite sometimes wins praise for honing teamwork, collaboration, strategic thinking, spatial understanding and imagination,[533] it is, at core, a commercial, corporately controlled game where the primary objective is to be "the last one standing" by killing all the other players.[534] During the pandemic, learners spent most of their time in digital spaces adjacent to education that allowed for narrow and often prescribed forms of interaction that doubled as entertainment. These spaces – and metaverses – of the pandemic were rarely emancipatory in the way education, at its best, aims to be. Indeed, sometimes these spaces appear to have been the reverse: constraining, controlling, redundant, corporate and manipulative.

A SUBVERSION OF LEARNING TO LIVE TOGETHER

The digital spaces that played host to education and so many other activities during the pandemic were poorly suited to advance important social and civic learning goals for education. Education has multiple interconnected academic and non-academic, personal and collective functions that schooling, as an in-person experience, has worked to fulfil, albeit imperfectly. UNESCO's seminal 1996 report *Learning: The Treasure Within* held that education should uphold and advance four pillars of learning: learning to know, learning to do, learning to live together and learning to be. Moving education to digital spaces via remote digital learning during the pandemic had the effect of weakening all these pillars, particularly the 'learning to live together' pillar, which seeks to foster tolerance, mutual respect and productive civic and social engagement.

The shift of education from in-person and school-based environments to digital and online spaces risked not only ignoring the community-building objectives of education but, more worryingly, subverting them. Since the 2000s, social scientists have documented strong correlations between increased time spent online with digital media and rises in community polarization.[535] Shifting the backbone of the educational experience from the social space of the school to the internet, as occurred in many countries, brought education much closer to the content and logic of the internet. This content and logic tend to place a premium less on building social cohesion and well-being, as education aspires to do, and more on generating adhesion – an action and technique of maximizing the time users spend online. Even when digital education content was not itself explicitly designed for adhesion, it was usually in close proximity to content that was.

> The objective of adhesive content is to keep users scrolling, searching, texting, browsing, liking and swiping, whatever ensures that people remain connected to platforms and immersed in screens.

Adhesion is a by-product of internet business models reliant on data extraction and advertising. It increases the potency, frequency and duration of exposure to advertising and hence profitability, while also revealing strategies to extract data that makes advertising more effective and more lucrative. The objective of adhesive content is simply to keep users – be they children or adults – scrolling, searching, texting, browsing, liking and swiping, whatever ensures that people remain connected to platforms, immersed in screens and feeding data into complex predictive systems that yield profit. Writer Shoshana Zuboff went so far as to call this digital loop "the dominant economic institution of our time".[536]

"There are a thousand people on the other side of the screen whose job it is to break down the self-regulation you have."

– Tristan Harris, technology ethicist[xxx]

This so-called dominant economic institution works by extracting data about humans and assembling the data into predictions of human behaviour – expectations for how people will respond to advertising and other digital stimuli that are forever tested and perfected. A Facebook document leaked in 2018 exposed the sophistication of digital machinery to influence human behaviour in ways that maximize profit. The company used secretive AI systems to scan trillions of behavioural data points each day to yield 6 million behavioural predictions every second. As AI systems learn and improve, their capacity to manipulate people, and young people in particular, grows. This manipulation can be exterior and interior. Digital platforms routinely manipulate people's dealings with others (exterior). They also manipulate the consciousness and cognition of individuals (interior). As playwright Ayad Akhar explained in a November 2021 essay about the internet: "The automation of our cognition and the predictive power of technology to monetize our behavior, indeed our very thinking, is transforming not only our societies and discourse with one another, but also our very neurochemistry. … This technology is no longer just shaping the world around us, but actively remaking us from within."[537]

Too often, this remaking has been in opposition to educational goals, catalysing processes and reactions that seek not to teach, expand knowledge or facilitate encounters with alternate world views and opinions, but rather to reaffirm existing biases, often by sowing distrust, arousing intolerance and entrenching opposition to unfamiliar ideas. Producers of online content have realized that burrowing deeper into existing predilections and hardening personal opinions is what makes internet content 'sticky', and 'stickiness' is the basis of adhesion. As Akhar notes, the internet has morphed into a force that constructs "gathering places for various camps of confirmed bias" and "agglomerations of outrage" incited by "slogans of belonging and creedal statements".[538] This outrage functions to accelerate social splintering: the antithesis, in other words, of learning to live together and a formidable obstacle to the other three pillars of education: learning to know, learning to do and learning to be.

> When teachers and learners became fully dependent on online environments as a result of the pandemic and school closures, education entered a space with currents hostile to many educational ideals.

Ed-tech, of course, did not build these logics and problems into the digital space of the internet. But when teachers and learners became fully dependent on online environments as a result of the pandemic and school closures, education entered a space with currents hostile to many educational ideals. Whereas a great deal of internet content tends to calcify and strengthen existing ideas and opinions, education, in the best cases, has different aims: to increase exposure to new ideas, to invite reflection and to moderate certainty. Building these habits of mind underpins the cooperation of diverse societies, nurtures social cohesion, fosters innovations and can prevent social division.

"Social scientists have identified at least three major forces that collectively bind together successful democracies: social capital (extensive social networks with high levels of trust), strong institutions, and shared stories. Social media has weakened all three."

– Jonathan Haidt, social psychologist[xciii]

Discomfort with the logics and sticky content of the internet may be one of the reasons so many education professionals, prior to the pandemic, were reluctant to embrace it as a primary interface or medium for learning. But the emergency of the pandemic unravelled these compunctions, and the internet, despite its myriad problems, was cast, in many contexts, as the only option to ensure the continuity of formal learning.

Students commonly experienced this shift as disorienting. Education's objectives to expand, deepen and diversify thought did not easily align with what many young people had come to expect from the internet, namely the affirmation of existing beliefs, moral positions, political persuasions and personal tastes. On the internet, it was easy for students to turn away from

> On the internet, it was easy for students to turn away from what much of education demands – processes of critical reflection and the interrogation of beliefs – and instead to retreat into information flows carefully curated to reflect and uphold certainties that they already possessed.

what much of education demands – processes of critical reflection and the interrogation of beliefs, however closely held. All it took was a click or a swipe for learners to retreat into information flows carefully curated to reflect and uphold certainties that they already possessed. Researchers and teachers alike were vocal that many young people lacked the self-regulation needed to resist opening apps and tabs that are less demanding than educational tasks. Once online, it was easy for learners to retreat from formal education and into ideological echo chambers and personalized 'infotainment'.

Anecdotal evidence of this behaviour was abundant. Teachers complained that students could not stay focused in digital environments and were spending more time scrolling algorithmically controlled social media accounts tailored for adhesion. The dopamine hits triggered by an Instagram like, a new notification or humorous 30 second video made certain content and platforms hard to resist. Teacher-produced slide presentations, lectures and even synchronous discussions about academic subjects such as science and literature had trouble competing with more familiar and less demanding digital feeds and routines.

The shift to digital learning was so sudden that many education systems that made the internet the primary or only gateway to education following school closures had been prohibiting its frequent or unencumbered use in educational settings just days or weeks before. Digital content that had been strictly off-limits in formal learning contexts – TikTok videos, YouTube channels, Snapchat feeds, Twitter notifications, among others – were now just one or two clicks away. Content that had previously been restricted in classrooms was suddenly in learners' hands. Teachers and other authorities were physically remote and rarely able to see when learners' attention drifted away from educational content and into other websites or apps on the open web.

Many hoped that moving education online might help recast the logics that give shape, form and purpose to the architecture of the internet – the platforms and apps that compete for attention and adhesion. But this architecture ran deep and was linked to financial interests far beyond education. In the end, it was less a case of education authorities bending the internet to support the aims and values of humanistic education and more a case of various commercial companies capitalizing on the sudden uprooting of in-person education that brought more and younger users to the internet. Without question, the shift to ed-tech during fully remote learning increased student exposure to digital spaces beyond those expressly dedicated to teaching and learning.[539]

"Modern [people] now seek camaraderie online, in a world defined not by friendship but by anomie and alienation. … Instead of entering a real-life public square, they drift anonymously into digital spaces where they rarely meet opponents; when they do, it is only to vilify them."
– Anne Applebaum and Peter Pomerantsev, authors of "How to put out democracy's dumpster fire"[xciv]

> The internet spaces hosting students, teachers and families during the crisis tended to have an orientation that was calibrated less for education than for its inversion: a turn inward to repetition and self-gazing.

Student exposure to digital content and spaces where opinions and prejudices are often endlessly confirmed and reconfirmed matters for education. Algorithmically optimized, AI-enhanced validation of what is already known or believed is not conducive to learning or to the generation of new knowledge and ideas. Moreover, these echo chambers have been shown to reduce empathy, induce quick judgements and provoke intolerance. Shifting learning into online spaces was not, therefore, a neutral decision. Physical schools, however flawed, are guided by different logics than the internet and stand at considerable distance from its oceans of sticky, adhesive content. Ultimately, the internet spaces hosting students, teachers and families during the crisis tended to have an orientation that was calibrated less for education than for its inversion: a turn inward to repetition and self-gazing. While digital environments can certainly facilitate intellectual exploration and learning, they are, because of the commercial logics that drive them, more typically engineered for interiority and self-valorisation. Seen from a wide angle, education's jump from in-person school environments to the contemporary internet appears to have weakened the 'learning to live together' objectives of education and may have even undermined them by exposing students to discourses, behaviours and actions that have a track record of fragmenting social and civic life and reducing respect for difference and diversity.

ZOOM DYSMORPHIA AND DIGITAL EXCARNATION

Beyond aspects of physical health, excessive time spent online and in simulation sometimes distorted the ways learners saw themselves and could lead to unhealthy and obsessive behaviour. Researchers noticed that with the turn to screens for fully remote learning many young people, especially image-conscious teenagers, were developing a negative self-image, in part because they were seeing and studying their physical features far more often in the digital environments of remote learning than they would have in brick-and-mortar schools. The applications used to attend online classes, whether Google Meet, Microsoft Teams, Skype or WeChat, commonly subjected students to hours-long exposure to their own appearance, a process that led many users to critically interrogate their features and fixate on perceived flaws. Default app settings would utilize self-facing cameras on laptops or mobile devices to prominently show student users how they appeared to others, and students rarely adjusted these default settings. In many instances, teachers and other education authorities required students to keep their cameras turned on during class, presenting students with an always-on view of themselves, as well as teachers and classmates, even if this self-reflection was unwelcome.[540] The result, if transferred to a physical school setting, was not entirely dissimilar to educational authorities affixing a vanity mirror to every student's desk.

Numerous studies have found that people of all ages will look most often at their own reflection in a virtual class or meeting when it appears, and teenagers most of all. Many disliked what they saw. The term "Zoom dysmorphia" began appearing in academic articles about the health consequences of the shift to online learning. The term helped encapsulate the way rises in the use of video-based communication and platforms correlated with increased reports of body dysmorphic disorder, a mental health condition most common in teenagers and young adults, in which people obsessively worry about flaws in their appearance.[541] A survey conducted for the UK Parliament in 2020 showed that self-perception was declining for many young people. It found that nearly 60 per cent of respondents under the age of 18 reported feeling "worse" or "much worse" about their physical appearance during the pandemic than before the pandemic, a percentage considerably higher than older respondents.[542]

"The digital is a medium of hyper-objectification. ... The digital is a set of technologies that mediates, intensifies, abstracts, reproduces, and generalizes existing forms of domination."

– Scholars and activists, Precarity Lab[xcv]

The least common video manipulation behaviour was 'hiding self-view' followed by 'turning the camera off'.

Further evidence of the uptick in the number of people experiencing negative body image began pouring in from countries soon after the first lockdowns and school closures. A study from Poland found that the stress and anxiety resulting from the pandemic was "exacerbating symptoms of eating disorders and negative body image and that women with excess body weight were particularly at risk".[543] Research from Spain highlighted that rises in social media use observed during lockdown were linked to "increased drive for thinness and eating disorder risk among adolescent and young women".[544] A study from Australia further found that video-based communication, an integral part of the shift to ed-tech, increased "appearance dissatisfaction in healthy individuals" as well as in people "with pre-existing body image concerns", and also sparked increased interest in cosmetic products and procedures. The authors of the Australian study noted that over 40 per cent of the study participants who had recently taken part in a video call reported "noticing a new aspect of their appearance that they disliked". They further documented the ways many young people engaged in appearance manipulation behaviours during video calls, including strategies to use flattering camera filters, adjust room lighting and change camera angles. The least common video manipulation behaviour was "hiding self-view" followed by "turning the camera off".[545]

"The age of video conferencing opened up a Pandora's box of physical insecurity."

– Ashely Abramson, health and psychology journalist[rcvi]

In addition to the prevalence of body dysmorphic disorder associated with video calls, moving education platforms online risked increasing student interaction with internet advertisements optimized to respond to body anxieties. In 2021, whistle-blower Frances Haugen explained how this

Figure 15:

From a survey on appearance dissatisfaction in video calls during the pandemic

Source: Data from *Aesthetic Surgery Journal*, 2021

worked at Instagram, a picture-sharing social media platform owned by Facebook. She said Instagram used algorithms that promoted pages that "glorified" eating disorders to teenage girls,[546] sometimes accompanied by paid content for commercial solutions to lose weight and improve one's appearance. In a media interview, Haugen noted that as "young women begin to consume eating disorder content, they get more and more depressed. And it actually makes them use the app more. And so, they end up in this feedback cycle where they hate their bodies more and more".[547] This feedback cycle, as destructive as it may have been for individuals, generated profits for Facebook by increasing user engagement with the company's Instagram app and, crucially, its advertisements.[548] Following Haugen's disclosures, Facebook paused development of Instagram Kids, a service that was in the works for use by children aged 13 or younger.[549]

The fashion and cosmetics advertisements common in online spaces used for education tended to normalize Western notions of beauty – norms that could lower the self-image of young people who did not conform to these standards.

Around the world, advertisements and tutorials featuring beauty products were common in social media and other online spaces used for education because of business models that make 'free' content and platforms financially dependent on advertising. These advertisements, often heavily tilted towards fashion and cosmetics, tended to normalize dominant Western notions of beauty, norms that could lower the self-esteem of young people who did not conform to particular aesthetic standards, whether because of ethnicity, body type or other factors. Regular exposure to idealized notions of beauty has long been problematic for people across demographic groups, and young people in particular. For some it can trigger unhealthy eating and exercise regimes and lead to dangerous disorders, including bulimia and anorexia. Evidence from a major review of 50 studies in 17 countries indicated that social media usage leads to "body image concerns, eating disorders/disordered eating and poor mental health via the mediating pathways of social comparison, thin/fit ideal internalisation, and self-objectification".[550] While these problems are not directly connected to ed-tech, moving learning into advertising-laden digital spaces made repeated exposure to idealized bodies and beauty advertisements hard to avoid. Unhealthy obsessions with physical appearance were likely exacerbated, trapping young people in what Naomi Wolf described in *The*

Beauty Myth as "an endless spiral of hope, self-consciousness and self-hatred" as people try "to fulfil society's impossible definition of 'the flawless beauty'".[551]

"There is no way, no tweak, no architectural change that will make it OK for teenage girls to post photos of themselves, while they're going through puberty, for strangers or others to rate publicly."

– Jonathan Haidt, social psychologist[xcvii]

Thinkers, including philosopher Richard Kearney, have noted that the extended time young people spend on video calls, viewing digital advertisements and generally deepening their immersion in online spaces is inverting long-held understandings of the body. The largely digital existence experienced by many young people during the pandemic meant that a primary purpose of their bodies was not for physical interaction, socialization and traversing the 'real world' but rather for representation in digital spaces. It prompted people to view their bodies in ever more disembodied ways. Kearney has termed this phenomenon "excarnation" or "flesh becoming image", the opposite of "incarnation" or "image becoming flesh". He explains: "Incarnation invests flesh, excarnation divests it."[552] As young people spent more and more time online for education and other purposes, they came to understand their own bodies as objects to represent digitally. This view of the body appears to have sparked anxiety not only about physical, real-world appearance, but also and especially represented appearance. For much of 2020 and 2021, the body as it appeared to others on screens carried as much if not more meaning and significance for identity as actual appearance. Previously and outside the unique conditions of the pandemic, most people understood their bodies as objects firmly anchored in the physical world, an anchoring that schooling as an in-person experience helped reinforce.

We are seeing more body dysmorphia than we've ever seen. People are more dissatisfied with their bodies, and unfortunately the pandemic has magnified that further with Zoom dysmorphia."

– Gemma Sharp, psychiatrist[xcviii]

Kearney's observations about the societal impacts of bodily representation in digital spheres include the ways in which sex is also increasingly mediated through online portals. While pornography consumption, including by young people and minors, has risen dramatically with the expansion of the internet and connected technology, researchers observed "an unprecedented increase in internet use and consumption of online pornography during the pandemic, and possibly even directly caused by it."[553] Data from relevant sources show jumps in pornography use in different countries worldwide during COVID-19 lockdowns. At the same time, significant declines in actual sex, especially between young people, a so-called sex recession, documented before 2020 and often associated with rises in screen time and increased immersion in digital experiences, became more pronounced during the pandemic.[554] These trends pointed to a pandemic reality in which sex was increasingly virtual and mediated by digital portals. This new reality – heavy with simulation and light with physical intimacy – was often considered to carry adverse health impacts. Consumption of online pornography is, for instance, regularly linked to lower self-image and increased rates of anxiety and depression.[555] Declines in healthy, physical, non-virtual sex can have similar deleterious health consequences, both physical and mental. Changes documented in the frequency of physical sex on the one hand and increases in digital pornography consumption on the other, stood as yet another example of the ways the pandemic lockdowns appeared to be moving people from physical and bodily experiences to virtual screen-based experiences, even for sexual intimacy.

While these trends are rooted in sociocultural changes much wider and deeper than ed-tech or education, the shift of schooling to virtual spaces likely contributed to the dysmorphia, 'excarnation' and touchless existence that peaked during the pandemic and has carried concerning health implications. The transition from largely offline education to fully online education catapulted students out of physical worlds and into virtual ones, thereby elevating the prominence and frequency of digital interactions to a point where they often eclipsed physical interactions and diminished the primacy of the body and bodily experience. These changed norms and behaviours, triggered by the pandemic and standing as a perhaps unavoidable response to the many social and physical restrictions it imposed, appear slated to ripple well beyond school closures end of the health crisis.[556]

ISOLATION, INVISIBILITY AND ALIENATION IN SCHOOL-LESS SCHOOLDAYS

Learning is a human experience rooted in social interaction and processes. When these processes moved from face-to-face settings, whether schools, libraries, community centres or places of worship, to virtual-only environments, students reported feeling heightened isolation and depression, a trend observed across countries. Radio, television and even dynamic online spaces could not begin to approximate the togetherness and camaraderie students felt in the physical and social space of the school. Uprooted from networks of non-family peers and supportive adults, learners reported feeling that they were on their own in ways they had not experienced previously. This dislocation tended to intensify a broader sense of unease that attended the pandemic. While the health crisis with its mortal dangers and unpredictability unnerved people of all ages, children and youth reported feeling particularly vulnerable, in part because of their dependence on adults who were themselves under increased strain.

"It doesn't do me any good to not go to school. I feel like something in me is missing."

– 15-year-old girl, Central African Republic[xcix]

The isolation experienced by young people due to the closure of schools and other pandemic restrictions was rarely short-lived. In March 2021, UNICEF estimated that over 330 million children had been stuck at home for a period of nine months or more since the onset of the pandemic a year earlier, heightening feelings of fear, loneliness and anxiety.[557] In select countries and communities, these durations were much longer, sometimes as long as 20 continuous months, as was the case in Uganda, which closed schools in March 2020 and tentatively reopened them only in January 2022.[558]

"The more virtually connected we are, the more solitary we become. We 'see' brave new worlds but 'feel' less and less in touch with them. ...Technology overcomes distance, but it does not always bring nearness."

– Richard Kearney, philosopher and author of *Touch: Recovering Our Most Vital Sense*[c]

In this context, ed-tech was seen not just as a learning tool but as a digital lifeline to social contact beyond the home. Families had hoped that educational uses of connected technology would break cycles of isolation, even if they observed that heavy technology use for other purposes, such as entertainment or scrolling social media feeds, seemed to contribute to withdrawal. People wanted digital learning to facilitate academic advancement, but they also wanted it to help young people feel less caged in and more socially alive. There was a desire to see technology at least approximate the human-to-human interactions, peer bonding and generational identity formation that characterized the in-person school experience. But technology rarely delivered on these goals. When it was available and worked, a rarity for most learners globally, it tended to provide little more than lonely portals to academic learning. Only in rare instances did ed-tech open spaces for unstructured conversation, play, levity and sustained opportunities for caring and reassurance that had been more common in schools.

> Software architects and other technology shapers generally saw their creations as complementary to in-person schooling, not as substitutes for a holistic educational experience.

Some of these limitations likely stemmed from the fact that nearly all of the ed-tech deployed to stand in for education during the pandemic had not actually been developed for this purpose. Software architects and other technology shapers generally saw their creations as *complementary* to in-person schooling, not as substitutes for a holistic educational experience. Even powerful school and classroom management systems tended to assume a strong face-to-face schooling component and therefore did not include features that might, for example, easily allow students to interact during or between lessons via chat functions. Indeed, many education apps had designs that actively blocked or discouraged student-to-student exchange that was not focused on strictly academic tasks. On many platforms, teachers could send chat notices to individual students, but students could not send messages to peers, only to the teacher or the entire class. As the pandemic stretched on, educators as well as parents voiced complaints that ed-tech systems gave low priority to socialization.

Even platforms that accommodated synchronous learning, such as Zoom, rarely allowed students to interact with peers inside or outside of a class meeting for extended durations. The software was often customized to prevent learners from seeing each other as they had been able to do in school classrooms. In this way, technology was effectively a social blinder, as it prevented students from looking at their classmates, even though these classmates were often in close digital proximity. Technology tended to dictate an orientation that restricted a student's field of view to an instructor or some type of educational media, often a slide presentation. Sometimes students could see the faces of peers on small tiles, but this 'room-facing' view was, in many contexts, often reserved only for teachers and required administrator permissions to change. Students almost never had these permissions and teachers often lacked them as well. Teachers with advanced digital skills occasionally managed to set up breakout rooms in digital classes that enabled students to meet, work and talk in smaller group settings. And some teachers held individual calls with students where more open and natural conversations were possible. But these practices were rarely incentivized and were technically or logistically challenging to arrange, assuming the functionality was even supported by available systems and software. They also tended to place additional burdens on teachers who were already overstretched trying to move teaching and learning to unfamiliar digital spaces.

"My daughter hasn't spoken to [friends] in over a year."
– Mother, USA[ci]

Features and restrictions like this meant that the experience of using ed-tech was usually one of anonymity. Rampant absenteeism suggested that students rarely felt that they were missed when they skipped a digital class.[559] Anecdotal evidence showed that students quickly learned that they could be marked 'present' in online classes without actually being present. Young people could log into a digital class so their name appeared on a list then slide their device under a pillow or navigate to other online spaces. Systems to actively track online attendance commonly relied on technologies, often billed as 'AI-powered', that students could easily trick by, for example, hitting a key or moving in front of a camera from time to time. The non-human technologies policing attendance tended to reinforce a sense that attendance did not matter to actual people. This was a marked contrast to physical classroom settings where teachers and students alike noticed empty seats, often with concern and follow-up actions.

Hardware and connectivity limitations could further increase feelings of invisibility. Learners regularly reported that they had 'no idea' what their teachers looked like. Often this was because video classes were not available, but sometimes it was because devices issued to or owned by teachers or students did not have cameras or had a camera that faced away from the screen, a layout typical for inexpensive mobile devices with a single camera. With this hardware arrangement, users could not both observe a class and be seen in the class. There were testimonials of students propping up mobile phones with front-facing cameras against mirrors so they could be captured on camera while still being able to see the screen of their phone. Other learners had connected devices with speakers but no microphone or a broken microphone, effectively muting them and foreclosing opportunities for dialogue. Students reported that when they were unable to respond to teacher prompts due to a malfunctioning microphone, teachers and classmates simply assumed that they were not present. And, of course, any time connectivity was lost during a synchronous class, the educational experience ended. Teachers remarked that students behaved like ghosts in online classes, appearing and disappearing for unknown reasons and for unpredictable durations. When a teacher fell out of a class, the class often collapsed entirely. Collectively, these experiences meant that connected education often had the paradoxical effect of making students and teachers feel less connected and more alone.

> Connected education often had the paradoxical effect of making students and teachers feel less connected and more alone.

For many students, the isolation and loneliness they experienced during the pandemic peaked when they started a new academic year of remote learning due to ongoing restrictions on in-person schooling. For children and youth following a September to June academic calendar (approximately two-thirds of the global student population), September 2020 and September 2021 often entailed entering unfamiliar classes or schools remotely and exclusively via technology. These learners did not have any in-person experiences or rapport to build upon to help establish a supportive learning community in digital spaces. This was a marked contrast to the 2019/20 academic year. When the initial pivot to remote learning happened in early 2020, most students had attended five or six months of in-person schooling. They had met and interacted with their classmates and teachers in person. This prior contact helped ease the transition to remote learning.

Students who began academic years when schools were closed did not necessarily know each other or their teachers, and ed-tech, by and large, did not enable them to get to know each other, and certainly not to the extent that would have been possible in in-person environments. The result was social alienation. Learners felt more disconnected from formal education than they had in previous school years. Given these realities, it was perhaps unsurprising that dropout and disengagement surged as the 2020/21 academic year – the first school-less school year – got underway via remote learning with ed-tech.[560] These trends were observed again at the beginning of the 2021/22 academic year in systems where schools remained closed.[561] As reliance on ed-tech stretched on for months and sometimes across academic years, learners and teachers lost sight of what had been a vibrant school community prior to the pandemic – a place where people gathered, met and shared in-person experiences that etched themselves into memory more clearly than staid online interactions.

> Ed-tech could not easily build the relationships, comity, trust and goodwill that had helped sustain the 2019/20 academic year and the years before the outset of the pandemic.

The beginning of the 2020/21 and 2021/22 school years clarified just how isolating digital learning spaces were compared with in-person school experiences. Ed-tech could not easily build the relationships, comity, trust and goodwill that had helped sustain the 2019/20 academic year and the years before the onset of the pandemic. The isolation experienced by many students being schooled remotely was a poignant reminder that education is, at its core, a social experience built on social interactions. Despite considerable efforts, remote digital learning was not able to facilitate these nurturing experiences and interactions as effectively as in-person learning, even if ed-tech might carry this potential in theory.

A PARALLEL MENTAL HEALTH PANDEMIC AMONG YOUNG PEOPLE

During the pandemic, research indicated that, globally, 1 in 5 people aged 15 to 24 regularly felt depressed.

As the pandemic dragged on, the mental health of young people suffered. In October 2021, UNICEF and Gallup published research indicating that, globally, 1 in 5 people aged 15 to 24 regularly felt depressed.[562] The report noted the strong impact of COVID-19 in young people's lives, stating that the increased stress and anxiety experienced by children during the pandemic was caused in part by "uncertainty over lockdowns and school closures". UNICEF linked lockdowns and school closures to children getting "less exercise, more screen time and disrupted sleep", all of which are associated with "increased psychological distress".[563] The elevated use of technology among children and young people, exacerbated by lockdowns and the shift of education into online spaces, may have also contributed to or amplified depressive feelings during the pandemic. A pre-pandemic review of studies on the effects of screen time and the well-being of children found evidence that higher levels of screen time are associated with a variety of health harms, including depressive symptoms and lower quality of life.[564]

Other research observed correlations between increased loneliness among teenagers and smartphone and social media use.[565] The *Journal of Adolescence* published a study in 2021 that sought to understand why teenage loneliness remained relatively stable from 2000 to 2012 but then increased dramatically, such that the percentage of secondary school students reporting high levels of loneliness doubled in Europe, Latin America and several English-speaking countries and rose by approximately 50 per cent in East Asian countries. Looking at data from 37 countries, the authors examined various global trends that might have impacted teenage loneliness, including declines in family size, changes in GDP, rising income inequality and increases in unemployment, as well as more smartphone access and more hours of internet use.[566] The results, the lead authors explained in a *New York Times* article, were unambiguous: "Only smartphone access and internet use increased in lock step with teenage loneliness. The other factors were unrelated or inversely correlated." They went on to strongly recommend returning to children and youth "a long period each day when they are not distracted by their devices: the school day".[567]

"Adolescents spending a small amount of time on electronic communication were the happiest."
– Jean Twenge, Gabrielle Martin and Keith Campbell, authors of a study on psychological well-being in adolescents and screen time[GT]

During the COVID-19 crisis, several countries documented increased rates of suicidal thinking and behaviour among young people and children, inflaming a mental health issue that makes suicide among the top five leading causes of death for 15- to 19-year-olds globally.[568] In Japan, for instance, a record number of school-age children committed suicide in 2020,[569] and the number of suicides committed by people under 20 rose 10 per cent over the previous year, despite a decrease in the overall number of suicides across all demographic groups.[570] In the USA, researchers found that by the summer of 2020, a few months into the pandemic, emergency department visits for suspected suicide attempts among 12- to 17-year-old girls began to increase dramatically. The rate remained elevated, and by the end of 2021, it was 50 per cent higher than the same period in 2019.[571] Other research from the USA showed that overall suicide rates among youth rose during the pandemic, particularly for those experiencing disruption to school and mental health care.[572] A detailed study of youth suicide during the first year of the pandemic, published in the journal *Pediatrics* in 2023, called attention to increases in death by suicide among adolescents and also discussed the impact of school closures. It noted that while the exact relationship between youth suicide and school closures is unclear, "the lack of live instruction has been associated with impaired academic progress, decreased physical activity, lower levels of social and emotional support, and greater emotional distress and exposure to in-home conflict."[573] School closures also meant that school-based suicide prevention programmes to increase mental health literacy, enhance awareness about suicide risk, and decrease the incidence of suicide attempts and suicidal ideation ground to a halt. So too did other place-based and in-person mental health services offered beyond schools. The WHO noted that the crisis had disrupted or stopped critical mental health services in a vast majority of countries and these services could be slow to restart even when countries began reopening them.[574]

In many countries, suicide presented a higher risk of death for children and youth than COVID-19. In a number of national contexts, school-age children accounted for less than 0.1 per cent of all COVID-19 deaths. In the USA and according to the data from national Centers for Disease Control and Prevention, fewer than 1,000 children between 5 and 18 years old died of COVID-19 in the over two-year period from the beginning of the pandemic in March 2020 to November 2022.[575] To put this figure in context, the *New England Journal of Medicine* stated that in the 12-month calendar year in 2016, suicide killed at least 2,300 children and youth (aged 1 to 19) in the USA, while motor vehicle crashes killed over 4,000.[576] These data, along with evidence that opening schools according to recommended protocols did not appear to significantly increase community transmission of COVID-19, led the WHO and many national medical groups to argue that schools should be opened and remain open on health grounds.[577] The preservation of mental health was cited as one of the most powerful rationales for school reopening. The American Academy of Pediatrics asserted that lengthy time away from school resulted in social isolation and placed adolescents at "considerable risk of morbidity and, in some cases, mortality".[578]

> The prevalence of child and adolescent depression and anxiety was estimated to have doubled during COVID-19 when compared to pre-pandemic levels.

As 2020 and 2021 passed, countries, some of them with schools that were still shuttered, began reporting unassailable evidence of spiking mental health problems, particularly among children and youth. In a meta-analysis of 29 studies that included approximately 80,000 youth globally, the prevalence of child and adolescent depression and anxiety was estimated to have doubled during COVID-19 when compared to pre-pandemic levels.[579] Data from individual countries showed similar results. A large study in the Netherlands found a significant rise in severe anxiety as well as in sleeping disorders among children during periods of school closure.[580] A study in the UK showed the mental health problems of 5- to 16-year-olds nearly doubling between a control period in 2017 and a study period in 2020, with young women showing a significantly higher prevalence of reported problems than young men.[581] In the USA, nearly half of upper secondary school students reported persistent feelings of sadness or hopelessness that prevented them from participating in normal activities in the first half of 2021. As 2021 drew to a close, UNICEF, citing mental health challenges among other health and well-being concerns, labelled COVID-19 the "biggest global crisis" for children in the organization's 75-year history.[582]

"COVID-19 has interrupted essential mental health services around the world just when they're needed most."

– Tedros Adhanom Ghebreyesus, Director-General of the World Health Organization[CIII]

> A number of pandemic and pre-pandemic studies observed correlations between screen use of more than two hours per day and depressive symptoms among children.

It is impossible to pinpoint the exact role that remote learning with ed-tech might have played in the deteriorating mental health of young people, but this does not mean its impact was neutral. Considerable bodies of research have observed connections between increases in digital media use and "depressive symptoms, suicide-related outcomes and suicide rates" among adolescents,[583] and that "moderate or severe" depression levels are closely associated with additional time spent watching television and using computers.[584] Likewise, a number of pandemic and pre-pandemic studies observed correlations between screen use of more than two hours per day and depressive symptoms among children.[585] Research on the impact of screen-based media on suicide rates has noted that social media in particular can adversely affect feelings of self-worth and confidence in young people. In some countries, adolescent use of social media tracks closely with rising rates of suicide, particularly for women and girls.[586] UNICEF, noting that "clusters of suicide" are much more common among young people than among adults, observed that social media can contribute to this clustering and bind victims through "digital connections".[587]

Closing schools during the pandemic undoubtedly increased the isolation and levels of stress experienced by children and youth and contributed to a deterioration in their mental health. Moving education to the digital spaces of ed-tech may have further increased the prevalence of mental health issues among learners. Given the volume of research showing negative mental health repercussions arising from elevated exposure to screens, the uprooting of education to online environments likely carried unique mental health risks.

A DIGITAL CONVEYOR BELT OF PERSONALIZED LEARNING AND THE NORMALIZATION OF LEARNING ALONE

Students' feelings of isolation were arguably heightened by the reliance on 'personalized' learning systems enabled by ed-tech. Before the pandemic, these systems had been used to complement school- and class-based learning that was experienced collectively. But the pandemic and school closures meant that technology-mediated personalized learning was routinely elevated to the main educational solution, while teacher-led and class-based instruction became secondary. Algorithms guided students down different learning pathways, ostensibly according to their unique needs and competencies, such that young people were not only learning in physical isolation but were sometimes following an individual learning trajectory that was fundamentally different from their peers. In theory, this meant students were being offered a bespoke learning journey that accommodated their personal interests, aptitudes and challenges. In practice, however, the experience could be lonely, especially given the already isolating conditions of the pandemic. Students sensed that they were encountering new knowledge alone rather than as a group or generational cohort.

Interestingly, anecdotal evidence suggests that students following distance learning through television or radio programming rather than through digital portals sometimes voiced feelings of togetherness. There was perhaps a perception among these learners that they were part of a wider community of peers because the educational content they received was identical to that received by others in their age group. In Mexico, for example, students at the same grade level were expected to watch the same educational television programmes on the same days and at the same time of day, resulting in a sense that pandemic learning was a shared experience rather than an isolated and individual exercise. Similarly, according to educators in Mali, Honduras, the Democratic Republic of the Congo and Zambia,[588] as well as in Nigeria, Chile, Colombia, Peru and Ecuador,[589] radio broadcasts, podcasts and other fixed educational content accessed by large numbers of learners appears to have connected learners within and across age, gender and geographic groups, while also engaging wider communities in learning and education.

"The path of educational progress more closely resembles the flight of a butterfly than the flight of a bullet. … Trying to accelerate learning by ramping up technology is like putting rockets on butterfly wings. More force does not lead linearly to more progress."

– Justin Reich, education researcher and author[civ]

Much of the digital educational content that went under the rubric of personalized learning was, in fact, fully automated learning. The learning was only personalized to the extent that a machine cued preselected educational material, according to responses to particular questions or prompts. An algorithm, not teachers, peers or other humans, sequenced activities for learners. But these algorithms, however 'intelligent' or 'AI-powered' they were purported to be, simply relied on very large data sets that automated the selection of content shown to individuals in ways that are assumed to improve student engagement or achievement.[590] The learning was personalized in the same way search engines are personalized. In essence, algorithms made assumptions about individual preferences based on the selections and behaviour of large groups and according to criteria deemed relevant by the maker of the algorithm, such as age, gender, geography, residence or other factors. Collective preferences and habits give rise to content that is assumed to be relevant to individuals.

Despite expectations that personalized learning systems deployed during the pandemic might untether education from industrial models of learning, many students felt more encumbered and more constrained. Instead of learning in school, a physical 'factory' of many, students found themselves instead inside something closer to a digital factory of one, often with narrower and more unidirectional passageways. Students would log into personalized learning apps to answer questions and complete sessions, modules, units or levels, following learning routes that had been mapped out by software engineers in faraway places. Sometimes these routes were gamified so that various animations would offer answers, explanations or encouragement as if there were a teacher present. Learning platforms offered 'leader boards' and various comparisons or competitions with other users, often people unknown outside of a username and icon. But even with these traces of other people, the learning space experienced by students was not usually populated with other sentient humans. It was, rather, a space built and controlled by a machine tracking inputs and reacting in preprogramed ways, according to predetermined paths.

"It's people who personalize learning, and people not technology must be at the centre of education."

– Paul Emerich France, teacher and literacy specialist[cv]

Almost without exception, these learning systems were easily scalable. They could accommodate 100,000 students with only marginally more investment than was required to accommodate 1,000. This aspect was critical for profitability as well as scalability. As schools closed en masse at the start of the pandemic, automated, profitable and scalable platforms that could be pitched as personalized solutions were in peak demand, and unsurprisingly, many experienced exponential growth in 2020. As one example, the user base for Duolingo, a personalized language learning app, grew as much in a single month – March 2020, the first month of global school closures – as it had in the previous nine years combined.[591]

After adjusting to the novelty of learning outside collective and cooperative school environments, many students reported feeling as though they were on a digital conveyor belt. In place of the discussion and conversation that had often accompanied classroom-based instruction, there was linear progression: another unit, more points, a different playlist and more predictable and largely repetitious sequencing. For some young people, these changes were an improvement from school-based learning, especially for students that had attended under-resourced schools staffed by underqualified teachers. But for many more, it was a diminished form of education that occurred largely in isolation.

"There is something wonderful in being in contact with other humans, having a human who tells you, 'It's great to see you. How are things going at home?'"

– Fernando Reimers, professor of education, Harvard University[cvi]

Some students confronted this digital education isolation with technological means. For example, the pandemic saw a rise in the creation and viewership of *gongbang* or 'study-with-me' videos, largely unedited footage of a solitary student studying for hours at a time. The videos are widely thought to have originated in the Republic of Korea as a form of virtual companionship and camaraderie. Although the genre can be traced to 2007, it soared in popularity with school closures. YouTube reported that videos containing the hashtag #withme in the title, of which #studywithme videos are a subset, increased by 600 per cent at the outset of the pandemic and lockdowns in March 2020.[592] Some of the #studywithme videos have over 8 million views,[593] and the genre, despite its outward simplicity, is vast. Videos can either be live or recorded, with or without music, filmed during the day or at night, animated or live action and have such specificities as the view outside the window or options to have rain or snow falling. Many videos employ specific study methods, such as the Pomodoro Technique, a time-management method that recommends short breaks at fixed intervals and is intended to increase focus and concentration.[594] Particularly popular videos seem to feature tidy, quiet and sometimes spacious workspaces. Others are filmed in semi-communal spaces, in a library for instance, and give viewers a sense that they are with other learners in a studious yet public space. The videos stand as testimony to the ways learners used technology to feel less isolated while completing personalized learning and other technology-centric educational tasks. In recognition that many learners were studying using internet-connected computers, study-with-me content creators commonly advised viewers to keep the video open on a corner of their desktop as a reminder that they were not alone in their ed-tech modes of study. Sometimes, after two or even three hours of footage, the study-with-me video 'companion' would look into the camera and say, "Good work. Thanks for studying with me."

"Just knowing someone else is studying with me made these two hours more tolerable. Whenever I have a 'study buddy' with me, it really helps me keep focused on what I'm doing."

– Commentator on YouTube[cvii]

FRUSTRATION AND STRESS MARK THE TRANSITION INTO UNFAMILIAR MODES OF DIGITAL LEARNING

Students, teachers and families often reported stress and frustration when using or trying to use ed-tech, much of it entirely new or otherwise unfamiliar. For many, technology-first modes of learning seemed to present as many obstacles to education as they did pathways to successfully access it.

Some of this frustration stemmed from inexperience using technology for purposes of teaching and learning. People in rich and poor countries alike struggled to navigate new devices, systems, connectivity options, platforms and software required for education, typically without assistance or training. Apps had to be downloaded, usernames and passwords had to be established, email accounts had to be created and verified, terms and conditions running across multiple pages had to be accepted and memberships had to be initiated to access online 'suites', 'studios', 'workplaces', 'collaboration hubs' and other proprietary and commercial systems. This was not technology bending to accommodate education, as many families and teachers had expected, but the inverse: education and its many constituent groups contorting to the logics of digital technologies and the business models that finance them. People around the world experienced the jump from school-based, in-person learning to remote, technology-based learning as an exasperating and often unsuccessful exercise in trying to unlock digital learning opportunities.

Technical assistance was sparse, and parents and caregivers with low-level digital skills found the processes especially taxing. Many were intimidated by prompts that asked them to consent to lengthy terms and conditions for digital services. New technology users were sometimes unaware that people

> Educational experiences that had been local – and had offered local and human networks to troubleshoot problems – were suddenly corporate and international, and human intermediaries were scarce or non-existent.

with advanced digital skills routinely click through consent pages and barely glance at the legal fine print. Others needed help getting past registration systems with CAPTCHA (Completely Automated Public Turing test to tell Computers and Humans Apart) and other unfamiliar verifications designed to differentiate human users from automated ones. While experienced internet users are accustomed to prompts asking them to, for example, select the images with a stop sign, inexperienced users found these tasks baffling. Password requirements posed more obstacles. Many users did not know, for example, what keystrokes met 'special character' requirements, and password management is an area that can befuddle even digitally savvy users. Adults rarely knew how to get support from tech companies, and some were unaware that these companies can be very difficult to contact directly. Educational experiences that had been local – and had offered local and human networks to troubleshoot problems – were suddenly corporate and international, and human intermediaries were scarce or non-existent.

The frustration that many families experienced as they scrambled to understand and use unfamiliar digital learning systems for education contrasted with the sometimes celebratory discourse that greeted the massive deployment of ed-tech and was projected by various think tanks and international organizations. A June 2021 OECD report was illustrative. It argued that the pandemic experience had "catapulted education systems, traditionally laggards when it comes to innovation, years ahead in what would have been a slow slouch towards smart schooling".[595] Proponents of ed-tech often welcomed the pressure that was placed on parents, teachers, students and the wider education community to embrace or at least learn how to use technology for teaching and learning purposes. But the stress this entailed for many families and learners was acute, and many millions were excluded, despite their considerable efforts. Ultimately, 'catapulting' was not what families or educators wanted in the midst of a global pandemic. They wanted support and straightforward ways to help young people continue their educations. The sink-or-swim approaches to ed-tech that proliferated due to the suddenness of school closures and changed modes of learning caused many to sink.

Technology novices were not the only ones who struggled. Expert technology users sometimes chaffed at the complexity and barriers they encountered trying to continue education in digital spaces. Parents in the USA and other countries occasionally posted screenshots of inscrutable instructions they received from education authorities explaining how to find and use disparate online learning resources. In digital learning environments, students frequently had to attend and navigate between multiple virtual locations, many of them behind digital barriers. This was a sharp contrast from school-based education where learning was typically

The predictable schedules and other organizational structures that had characterized in-person schools, whatever their flaws, often evaporated in digital spaces.

housed under a single roof and directions to parents and students readily available. The predictable schedules and other organizational structures that had characterized in-person schools, whatever their flaws, often evaporated in digital spaces. Many students at basic or secondary education levels confronted a mix of synchronous and asynchronous educational experiences that were often staggered irregularly throughout the day, a significant departure from the back-to-back, morning-to-afternoon scheduling that had been typical of in-person schooling. These disruptions to routines created further aggravation. Overall, educational reliance on ed-tech introduced new forms of unpredictability that could shorten tempers and create discord in the new home-learning environments.[596]

"Routine is really important for young children's sense of stability in the world and is known to be important for healthy development in kids, so when routine gets disrupted, that creates additional stressors."
– Anna Gassman-Pines, professor of public policy, psychology and neuroscience, Duke University[cviii]

Adding to the sense that learners were being catapulted into ad hoc ed-tech solution was the fact that very few countries had established public, free and open digital platforms for education prior to the onset of the pandemic. Even when countries did have publicly available digital spaces and content for learning, they were not always easy to find, navigate or use. In the early weeks of the pandemic, one of the most viewed pages on UNESCO's website was one that contained a simple list of links to respected providers of digital learning content, an indication of the confusion that accompanied the pivot to ed-tech. People were looking to an international organization, rather than local, regional or national education systems, for guidance on where to find day-to-day learning resources.

Given these contextual factors, it is perhaps unsurprising that words like 'chaotic', 'messy' and 'dizzying' were frequently used by parents as well as students to describe the new technology-dependent educational experience. Frustration with fully remote learning found various outlets. Popular and usually un-inflammatory parenting blogs contained articles under all-capitalized headings such as "F*** COVID SCHOOL".[597] Entrepreneurial online vendors marketed T-shirts and coffee mugs emblazed with the words "Operation enduring clusterf**k", to frustrated teachers, families and students.[598] This and other anecdotal evidence from around the world revealed that learners and their families were often uncomfortable with the unfamiliarity of digital learning and frustrated by the limited support they received.

Many parents noted that the seemingly endless technical demands of ed-tech degraded the quality of the time they spent with their children.

Parental energies were commonly directed at trying to troubleshoot ed-tech for children, rather than discussing ideas, knowledge and values with them.

Questions about why a piece of hardware or software was malfunctioning seemed to be dominating conversations and interactions that could have been more human, educative and joyful. Testimonials suggest that much of the time caregivers and children spent together was dedicated to providing technology support. When web pages did not load, log-ins failed, connections cut out, software froze, navigation went astray, files got lost and apps closed unexpectedly – occurrences that could be commonplace – parents became IT support workers. In addition to the time obligations, this demand influenced the ways parents and children spoke to each other during the pandemic. Parental energies were often directed at trying to troubleshoot broken technology portals for children, rather than discussing ideas, knowledge and values with them. Many parents wrote posts on social media to lament that they were spending limited time with children rebooting problematic devices, re-entering Wi-Fi passcodes, restarting routers and otherwise trying to fix technical problems and equipment. This was not, many of these parents observed, an especially judicious use of time. Time spent servicing digital technology could come at the expense of other more desirable work and hobbies that could have been shared with children, whether cooking, gardening, listening to music, reading books or any number of other pursuits that can carry educational value.

Sometimes caregivers put technology aside out of frustration and simply started engaging children in family tasks and educational activities that were not screen based or otherwise technology dependent. Tablets were put in drawers, and non-digital tools and toys – crayons and paper or wooden blocks, for instance – were pulled out and put to use, regardless of whether a teacher, school or ministry of education had called for this type of activity. The practice of abandoning ed-tech because it was perceived to be a source of stress and provided modest educational benefits appears to have been more common among highly educated and wealthy parents than lower educated and lower income parents, who often reported feeling a great deal of pressure to keep their children using and following ed-tech lessons offered by schools and teachers, lest their children fall behind.[599]

While the aggravations associated with fully technology-dependent remote learning subsided somewhat as teachers, parents and learners developed new competencies and routines, the rapid pace of change meant that the sites and systems required for education were rarely static. This was especially true early in the pandemic as educational authorities experimented with different approaches. Regular changes required learners and their families to download new software, create more accounts and accept new permissions. For millions of learners and their caregivers, remote technology-dependent learning remained frustrating and anxiety-provoking for weeks and months into school closures.

THE HIDDEN DANGERS OF RUSHED ONLINE IMMERSION

The usual steps to acclimate learners to online spaces and prepare them to mitigate risks and ensure healthy and positive experiences were scuttled in favour of a push to prevent learning loss.

Family and government efforts to equip learners with internet-connected devices such as mobile phones or tablet computers did not usually encompass training to help them develop the skills and competencies needed to use these devices safely. Just as learning via reading requires basic reading ability, learning via technology requires basic digital skills. Rushing to move underprepared learners into digital spaces without strong digital skills carried risks. For example, UNICEF noted that the rush to move learning to online environments likely placed many children at heightened risk to sexual exploitation, cyberbullying, unsafe online behaviour, exposure to harmful content and inappropriate collection, use and sharing of personal data.[600] The National Crime Agency in the UK issued a warning in April 2020 stating that "with children spending more time online to do school work or occupy themselves while parents and carers are busy, they face an increased threat from offenders who are also online in greater numbers".[601] Across the world, the usual steps to acclimate learners to online spaces and prepare them to mitigate risks and ensure healthy and positive experiences were scuttled in favour of a push to prevent learning loss. During this confused time, hashtags such as #KeepLearning emanating from ed-tech providers[602] were competing with hashtags such as #OnlineSafetyAtHome, emanating from law enforcement or child protection authorities.[603]

A 2020 study published in the medical journal *Pediatrics* used online tracking and parent reporting to provide a rare glimpse into the ways young children unaccustomed to digital spaces used technology and connectivity during the pandemic. The authors documented numerous instances of preschool children (aged 3 to 5) using apps that are classified for teenagers and adults, including general audience apps such as YouTube and Candy Crush, but also gambling apps such as Cashman, violent apps such as Terrorist Shooter and Flip the Gun, and horror apps such as Granny. The authors noted the serious implications for child privacy because "general audience apps and platforms may not place restrictions on the data they collect or distribute to third-party advertising companies".[604] The research also found that parents did not accurately estimate the duration of time their children spent on devices.

"That would always really stress me out – if the Wi-Fi would go, because I'd be like, 'oh my god, I don't know what [my students are] doing, there's no adult overseeing the call.'"

– Preschool teacher, UK[cix]

Advertising, ubiquitous in online spaces, presented other risks as education moved into digital spaces during the pandemic. Work to track advertisements seen by children online and on television indicated that children encountered large numbers of advertisements overall, but of particular concern was the exposure of young children to age-restricted advertising content, such as for alcohol, gambling and other products and services inappropriate for children.[605] Research has highlighted that children are particularly vulnerable to advertisements and often have trouble differentiating between advertising and content.[606] Interestingly, this capacity is lower in online mediums than on television. Experts have documented that while children can identify television advertisements from about 5 years old, they struggle to consistently identify internet advertising on web pages below the age of 12.[607]

> On the instruction of ministries of education and school authorities, students entered virtual worlds to access remote learning, but often they did not have the attendant digital literacy skills needed to safely navigate the internet.

During the pandemic lockdowns and confinements, large numbers of young people came online, sometimes for the first time, with limited orientation and guidance. On the instruction of ministries of education and school authorities, students entered virtual worlds to access remote learning, but often they did not have the attendant digital literacy skills needed to safely navigate the internet. Technology-enabled remote learning entailed substantial risk for these students given the sometimes dangerous currents of disinformation, advertising, conspiracy theories, hate speech, pornography and calls to radicalization, violent extremism and polarization on the web. Many parents found it difficult to carefully monitor the digital behaviour of children or to install filters that could block forbidden software and websites on personal devices, while also allowing access to educational content. In a school environment, these filters would usually be in place and well maintained, but at home, they tended to be largely absent. As a result, the rush to move education online often resulted in many young people finding and engaging with inappropriate content.

A CURTAILING OF CONVERSATION

During the pandemic, technology was commonly celebrated for helping young people maintain bonds with others beyond the home. Messaging, video calls, social media and emails enabled connections that could and certainly did facilitate education and make space for interactions that underlie learning. But young people and adults also reported that the quality of these digital interactions often left them feeling empty or scattered. Hardware and software used for education tended to privilege communication that was fast, frequent and brief rather than deep and textured. There was a sense that technology was truncating conversation and creating barriers to rich and prolonged exchanges that might allow people to be heard as well as to hear others, actions that are essential for education and departure points for the development of empathy and other types of socio-emotional learning.

"Smartphones and social media don't just affect individuals, they affect groups. The smartphone brought about a planetary rewiring of human interaction. As smartphones became common, they transformed peer relationships, family relationships and the texture of daily life for everyone – even those who don't own a phone or don't have an Instagram account."

– Jonathan Haidt and Jean M. Twenge, psychologists[cx]

Social scientists have observed that communication conducted through digital technology tends to be more controlled than face-to-face communication. It usually requires less vulnerability and entails fewer risks and disappointments.[608] By providing a means to avoid the often challenging yet rewarding demands of dealing with others, technology-mediated conversation short-circuits the intimacy that provides a foundation for trust, cooperation and friendship. During the pandemic, heavy reliance on screen-based communication for education and other purposes arguably inhibited the cultivation of deeply felt human relationships that normally grow out of educational exchange conducted in the physical and social space of schools. Screens were, simply put, poorly suited for forging thick interpersonal bonds that can give purpose and meaning to education and other pursuits and also help motivate perseverance and achievement.

Prior to the pandemic, scientists studying the psychosocial effects of the digital revolution had noticed that technology use was conditioning people to expect more from digital tools such as smartphones and less from each other.[609] This trend arguably accelerated when education, once an almost entirely human-to-human experience, became critically reliant on technology. Students were quickly habituated to see devices as principal educational companions and guides, and to perceive other people involved in education, whether teachers, peers or administrators, through devices, often in disembodied forms. In several landmark books, including *Stimulation and Its Discontents*, *Alone Together* and *Reclaiming Conversation*, sociologist Sherry Turkle explains how this type of reliance, distance and distortion can, without vigilance, reduce human relationships to mere connections and falsely recast these connections as intimacy. Indeed, during the pandemic, many students participating in remote-only education reported feeling 'connected' to teachers and classmates they did not really know, in the same way they might feel connected to a celebrity they follow on social media. The relationship had the trappings of closeness, familiarity and rapport, but it was not actually close, due to the distance of the digital medium of interaction and communication. This pseudo-intimacy, easy to attain through screens and without risking vulnerability, was ultimately psychologically dissatisfying and precipitated feelings of isolation and emptiness. Turkle explained this as cyberintimacies sliding into cybersolitudes.[610]

"We are increasingly connected to each other but oddly more alone."
– Sherry Turkle, sociologist and author[cxi]

> Educational interactions that had once been conversational, with all the frustrations, surprises and rewards that attend discussions about ideas and learning, withered into mere utilitarian communication.

Students and teachers around the world experienced this sliding into cybercultures as full remote learning stretched on first for weeks and then months, semesters and, in some instances, a full year or longer. Remote learning platforms were places of communication, yes, but rarely of conversation. Sometimes there were not even human interlocutors. Systems were instead managed and run by chat bots or cartoon figures that provided feedback and encouragement but could not sustain enriching conversations the way a peer could have done on a playground or a teacher speaking directly with a student. And even when there was human-to-human exchange, technology tended to deform it. Where there had previously been synchronous and in-person talking at school, there was instead asynchronous and remote messaging inside digital platforms. Educational interactions that had once been conversational, with all the frustrations, surprises and rewards that can attend discussions about ideas and learning, often withered into mere utilitarian communication. Nominally, there was still enriching content and information, sometimes far more of it than had existed at school, but it was content and information stripped of personality, untethered, as it were, from human discourse that made it memorable and gave it greater meaning. Many learners experienced this technology-driven pivot as education losing its humanity.

Live video classes promised to open up spaces for more human-centred conversations via technology. But these classes tended to unfold in digital spaces that were overflowing with distractions. Various notifications, chat

The busy and distraction-prone space of online video classes tended to undermine an irreplaceable ingredient of successful conversation and learning: careful listening.

threads, reminders and so forth flashed on screens, breaking student and teacher attention. The busy and distraction-prone space of online video classes therefore tended to undermine an irreplaceable ingredient of successful conversation and learning: careful listening. Various media accounts and surveys showed that teachers frequently found it challenging to keep students attentive during remote video classes.[611] Even teachers who had prided themselves on facilitating good discussions in physical school settings reported major barriers trying to replicate the humanistic qualities of classroom exchanges in digital environments.[612] The problem, they said, was not the pedagogy but the medium itself.[613]

"Teaching in a classroom is a sensory deluge, and experienced teachers know how to track students' verbal and non-verbal cues about their understanding, engagement, and affect. Much of that visual and aural information gets lost during virtual instruction."
– Justin Reich et al., authors of a report on the lived experiences of teachers during the COVID-19 pandemic[cxii]

Conversation could also be scuttled by software that pushed teachers and students to communicate and participate using short messages. Many applications used for education made it technically difficult to send messages containing more than a few lines of text. Microsoft Teams, for instance, provided users only a very small space to compose messages that were then posted anytime a user hit the Enter key. This design and functionality discouraged communication longer than a handful of words, let alone full sentences and paragraphs. In the case of Microsoft Teams, the system itself prevented users from easily formatting text to demarcate separate ideas or paragraphs with line breaks. While this may facilitate speedy information exchange inside businesses, it is less conducive to helping students come to understand complex ideas and practice articulating them in an educational context.

Teachers felt obligated to help students use well-chosen words and thoughtful sentences and paragraphs to convey meaning, rather than pictorial images.

Communication was also arguably degraded and, to some, dumbed down by systems that encouraged or even forced the use of emojis, GIFs and other pictorial representations in place of words. Teachers and students from countries accustomed to formal spoken and written language in educational settings were frequently taken aback to discover that an ed-tech platform, often originating from North America, prompted users to click on, for example, a smiley face emoji or a thumbs-up symbol as a response to a human comment or other substantive input. This messaging was sometimes viewed as vapid – less meaningful feedback than shallow signalling.[614] While not ruling out new and inventive forms of communication, teachers tended to feel an obligation to help students use well-chosen words and thoughtful sentences and paragraphs to convey meaning, rather than pictorial images. The platforms of ed-tech did not always easily accommodate these formal modes of communication though, and, in some instances, seemed to discourage them by prompting students and teachers alike to use word-light and image-heavy forms of exchange.

Anecdotal evidence further suggests that many ed-tech users chafed at the way learning platforms seemed to insist on an endless stream of excessively upbeat and enthusiastic feedback and communication. Digital worlds filled with smiling faces and exclamation marks affixed to various prompts and commands (expressions like "Get ready!!!" and "Let's go!!!!!") were considered childish and the antithesis of serious education in numerous contexts. Yet during the pandemic these super-positive, colour-bursting digital spaces were sometimes elevated as principal hubs for formal learning. Such systems and platforms framed – and could constrain – educational conversations that many had perceived as more mature when they existed outside of the boundaries of select ed-tech applications.

The pandemic showed that while the often automated digital spaces of education were, in some ways, optimized for engagement via clicks and various other unilateral commands and selections, this engagement was a long way from conversation. Ed-tech tended to make student-to-student and student-to-teacher educational exchanges shallower and more fragmented than they had been at in-person schools. The digital systems and platforms supporting education through the pandemic did not usually demand careful listening and navigating the uncertain, emotional and empathic aspects of communication – hallmarks of genuine conversation. In their place was a digital culture characterized by distraction, multitasking, signalling and self-presentation – one click 'like', 'laugh' and 'love' emojis and other pictorial stand-ins for human emotion and expression.

"Emoji convey a message, but this breeds laziness. If people think, 'All I need to do is send a picture', this dilutes language and expression."

– Chris McGovern, chair of the Campaign for Real Education[citation]

DIGITAL ADDICTION AND BEING ALONE TOGETHER

During the pandemic, many people voiced concern that they were becoming perniciously attached to digital technology and that self-regulation over time spent online and in front of phones and other screens was caving. While feelings of excessive and detrimental attachment to devices and apps had been documented well before 2020, the pandemic marked an inflection point: never before had connected technology been

Stay-at-home mandates led to the formation of new digital habits and triggered unhealthy relationships and behaviours with technology and the internet – cravings, preoccupation, unsuccessful efforts to cut back on device use and feelings of irritation and restlessness when not online.

so central to communication, work, education and leisure than during COVID-19 restrictions. Stay-at-home mandates led to the formation of new digital habits, intensified existing ones and triggered, for some people, unhealthy relationships and behaviours with technology and the internet – cravings, preoccupation, unsuccessful efforts to cut back on device use and feelings of irritation and restlessness when not online.

While clinicians debate the appropriateness of describing people's perceived loss of control and autonomy in their relationships to digital devices as an actual addiction, the notions of 'phone addiction' or 'internet addiction' have certainly entered the vernacular.[615] Book titles such as *Digital Detox*, *How to Break Up with Your Phone*, *Untethered*, *Digital Minimalism*, and *The Phone Addiction Workbook*, frequently catalogued next to titles about dieting or strategies to stop drinking or gambling, were hard to miss even before the pandemic.[616] Apps that block social media and other 'addictive' digital content commonly rank among the most downloaded productivity software in widely used app stores – an instance of deploying technology to ease technology use. A 2018 survey by the Pew Research Center found that a majority of teenagers between the ages of 13 and 17 in the USA said they felt anxious, lonely or upset when they did not have a smartphone on their person,[617] a phenomenon that has given rise to the recognition of a new anxiety disorder – 'nomophobia', shorthand for 'no mobile phone phobia'.

"The design of modern technologies is purposefully habit-forming and programmed with the sort of variable rewards that keep humans engaged."
– Jenny Radesky, professor of developmental behavioural paediatrics, University of Michigan[xiv]

Even prior to the uprooting of in-person schools to technology-mediated education, many teachers and parents were concerned that students were spending too much time engaging with devices and in online spaces instead of in face-to-face conversation with other people or finding quiet moments for reflection or creativity. It was not only parents and educators who worried that technology was monopolizing too much of students' time and attention; students were also concerned. In the 2018 Pew survey, a majority of teenagers expressed that they felt they spent too much time on their phones,[618] a sentiment that was by no means exclusive to the USA.[619]

The habitual and poorly regulated use of connected technology carried social repercussions. The title of Turkle's 2011 book, *Alone Together*, encapsulated the experience of many people during the pandemic. Family members and friends found that despite being in close physical proximity with each other, they were often mentally apart because of their immersion in personal digital devices. Turkle's descriptions of families sitting around a dinner table with each individual staring into a separate mobile phone,

friends devising strategies to maintain each other's attention and keep eyes from slipping away to screens, parents neglecting children to finish scrolling social media feeds and never-ending news updates, spouses pleading with each other to put the phone or laptop down and listen, and children throwing tantrums when digital devices were taken away from them were unsettlingly familiar during lockdowns – a period in which people's reliance and time spent on screens for education and other purposes shot upwards, often from already high levels.

> The powerful role that schools had played in providing spaces for sustained offline and non-digital experiences in highly digitalized societies was lost.

When schools and universities closed during the pandemic, it became apparent that these institutions had played an important role placing young people in physical proximity and, in many instances, encouraging or enforcing offline interaction, creating conditions that could help young people express feelings and vulnerabilities face-to-face, and in doing so, forge friendships and emotional connections with others. But when education moved to digital-only realms and closed off opportunities for human-to-human exchange, many young people reported finding that it was newly difficult to build strong interpersonal relationships or to sustain those that had been in place before lockdowns.[620] Deeper immersion into technology, in part to fulfil educational obligations and owing to the unique restrictions of the pandemic, disrupted the equilibriums many young people had carved out between online, offline and blended experiences. Students who believed that they had exercised a more or less balanced relationship with technology prior to the pandemic reported that school closures and the shift to ed-tech made this relationship feel unbalanced and unhealthy.[621] Around the world, the powerful role that schools had played in providing spaces for sustained offline and non-digital experiences in highly digitalized societies was lost, and young people noticed themselves spending excessive time in virtual environments, often in ways that felt unwanted.

"Time in simulation gets children ready for more time in simulation. Time with people teaches children how to be in a relationship, beginning with the ability to have a conversation."

– Sherry Turkle, sociologist and author[cxv]

Virtual environments tend to provide illusions of control that rarely exist in offline worlds.

Research continues to clarify that excessive time spent in digital realms makes it difficult for people, children and teenagers especially, to learn how to contend with other people and their unpredictable ways outside the confines of digital worlds.[622] Virtual environments tend to provide illusions of control that rarely exist in offline worlds and to downplay the mutual dependence and reciprocity that provide scaffolding for strong human relationships.[623] Prolonged periods of time in digital simulations of reality undermine the development of empathy, an ability that develops through feedback on how actions affect others. This feedback is often missing in digital spaces or delayed to degrees that cause distortion.

Many ed-tech apps designed for education relied largely on asynchronous communication – communication that slows the instant feedback vital to the development of healthy social skills and emotional response. Posting written comments in an asynchronous group chat is a very different and often less fluid exercise than participating in an oral conversation face-to-face at school. The conversational and non-verbal feedback received through direct, in-person interaction is educative to the extent that people see, in real time, what their words and actions do to others. The ephemeral nature of face-to-face interaction also tends to make it more forgiving – and more trusting – than the communication that unfolds in digital mediums and tends to be much more permanent. These distinctions all have implications for the cultivation of sensitivity, sympathy, rapport and other important interpersonal skills. As the author Adam Alter explains, the more that young people disconnect from real-world interaction in favour of virtual interfacing, the more the development of empathy stalls and atrophies.[624] Yet for millions of students this is what ed-tech demanded: virtual interfacing in place of real-life interacting. This is not necessarily to suggest that there were ready alternatives, given the sudden realities of the pandemic and disease transmission, but rather to observe that the move from in-person education to fully remote learning carried distinct, and often overlooked, repercussions for the development of important social skills and emotional intelligence.

"We are learning to live with the jeopardy that even when we are physically together, we can be socially, emotionally or professionally alone."

– Daniel Miller, anthropology professor and lead author of *The Global Smartphone*[cxvi]

Ultimately, the suspension of more challenging and more enriching conversations that would have happened at schools had they been open, as well as those that were arguably diminished due to digital dependencies, stand as a significant social change brought about by the pandemic. Arguably, there might have been more frequent and better human-to-human conversations during the pandemic without education's pivot to technology – and indeed in contexts where connected technology was unavailable, there was anecdotal evidence of increased and higher quality conversations between people living together. In the absence of technology, people were, to borrow Turkle's evocation, more likely to be 'together' than 'alone together'. Even if these technology-free conversations were unlikely to be explicitly educational or aligned with a curriculum, they nevertheless likely played a role fostering socio-emotional learning and development, strengthening social and family bonds, and building interdependence by helping people come to understand themselves and others. These are all aims of education. In some contexts, digital interactions of the sort enabled by ed-tech may have, paradoxically, reduced conversation by disconnecting and distracting young people from the people nearest to them in favour of connections to learning content that was often static or automated and to communication that was asynchronous and remote.

ED-TECH IS POORLY SUITED FOR YOUNG CHILDREN

Debates about the uses and misuses of screen-based technology for education during the pandemic tended to ignore the reality that its relevance and effectiveness hinges on the age and development levels of learners. When technology was selected as the go-to tool to offset school closures, it was widely framed as something that would help *all* students. The idea was that devices such as smartphones and laptops were capable of accommodating a wide range of pedagogies appropriate for learners of all ages, from adults to children at primary and even pre-primary education levels.

"You get genius learning from a live human being, and you get zero learning from a machine."

– Patricia Kuhl, brain scientist[cxvii]

For young children, the medium of content was the problem, not necessarily the content itself.

Decades of research, however, have clarified that very young children receive few, if any, educational benefits from screen-based media. For children under the age of 5, screens have been shown to hijack attention spans, deteriorate the capacity for concentration and focus, curtail impulse control, hinder imagination and motivation, inhibit the ability to read faces and learn social skills, detract from play, and stall emotional development, among other deleterious effects.[625] These effects have been observed regardless of what is happening on the screen. For young children, the *medium* is the problem, not necessarily the content.

Numerous studies have demonstrated that screen-based media is the technological equivalent of junk food for the minds of very young learners. Like junk food, this media carries a strong pull for children but can be unhealthy, especially when consumed frequently and in excess. Before the pandemic, a major longitudinal study found that the more time children between 2 and 3 years old spent looking at screens, the less well they performed on tests for behavioural, cognitive and social development. Tellingly, the researchers did not find evidence of associations in the other direction: developmental problems leading to more screen time.[626]

> While children 3 and under can see and hear a video shown on a screen as well as adults, they do not understand that these sights and sounds represent the real (off-screen) world.

Other studies have shown that screen technologies are poorly suited to facilitating the language development of young children. A 2018 experiment, for example, examined how well children from 24 to 30 months old learned the name of a new object in four different conditions: responsive live (a live person interacting in person with a child); unresponsive video (a recorded video of a speaker reading from a script); unresponsive live (a live person reading the same script as the person in the video); and responsive video (a speaker interacting with the child through a video chat similar to a Zoom or FaceTime call). Researchers found that children were unable to learn the name of the object from either of the video conditions, and only the oldest children in the experiment, those nearing 3 years of age, reliably learned the new word in the unresponsive live condition. The only condition in which all the children learned the name of the object was responsive live, the interactive human-to-human scenario that most closely approximated interactions that take place with human caregivers or teachers.[627] The researchers concluded that content shown on screens presents conceptual rather than perceptual challenges to children under 3 years old.[628] While children in this age cohort can see and hear a video shown on a screen as well as adults, they understand these sights and sounds as unconnected and irrelevant to real life. Only at later stages of development do they grasp that content on a screen can and often does represent the real world.[629]

The practical implication of the finding was clear: screen-based content, no matter how beneficial or educational it might seem to an adult, is unlikely to confer educational benefits to very young children.

Emerging research further indicates that, beyond stalling learning, screen-based technology may present neurobiological risks to growing brains. A 2020 study examining the brains of very young children with MRI scans found evidence that increased screen time appears to cause significant

physiological changes to the brain itself. Heavy use of screen-based media was linked to lower amounts of brain white matter, a microstructural tissue that supports the acquisition of language and literacy.[630] The study concluded that screen use appears to affect young children's brains in ways that are potentially harmful for cognition.

> The rise of digital reading has increased people's abilities to access information at the expense of their ability to convert it into conceptual knowledge.

Other scholars have noted that moving reading and reading instruction to screens carries non-trivial consequences for learning and education.[631] In *Reading in a Digital Age*, David Durant explains that when text is read in digital environments it encourages reading that "focuses on either reading short pieces of text or browsing or skimming texts in search of specific pieces of information", a process known as tabular reading. Tabular reading is distinct from linear reading, a reading that is continuous and facilitated by offline and off-screen paper-and-ink mediums. Durant underscores that the more people read on screens in tabular fashion, the more their brains rewire themselves to facilitate this activity and the harder it becomes for them to engage in deep print reading. For Durant and other reading experts, format does matter; text is not seamlessly interchangeable across mediums.[632] While Durant acknowledges that e-reading certainly has advantages, he stresses that it is not the same as reading from the printed page: "It fosters a different set of cognitive skills and a qualitatively different way of thinking." Durant concludes that the rise of e-reading has caused tabular reading to eclipse linear reading, and this has, in turn, increased people's abilities to access information at the expense of their ability to convert it into conceptual knowledge. Stunting the ability to convert information into knowledge is anathema to education. The essence of literacy, as understood by many educators and families, is linear reading, even if tabular reading is an important skill. Linear reading enables deep rather than surface entry into text and the ideas and worlds text contains. It is the reading that allows people to read and savour full-length books.

Nicholas Carr, the author of *What the Internet Is Doing to Our Brains*, carries these arguments further to observe that digital screens are usually engines of distraction, with an ability to "seize our attention only to scatter it".[633] Similarly, reading expert Naomi Baron and the author of *Words Onscreen* highlights the ways screen-based reading devices, especially those loaded with applications and buzzing with notifications, consistently disrupt the focus required to draw meaning and nuance from text.[634] They are a trampoline for attention, propelling readers from one place to another and straining sustained concentration.

> Moving reading instruction to screens, especially when learners are young and not yet skilled readers, may result in the formation of reading habits that short-circuit the development of more cognitively demanding comprehension processes.

Most reading experts recommend that children learning to read begin with text printed on paper, a medium that helps foster the development of linear reading skills. According to the Association for Supervision and Curriculum Development, moving reading instruction to screens, especially when learners are young and not yet strong linear readers, may result in the formation of reading habits that "short-circuit the development of the slower, more cognitively demanding comprehension processes that go into the formation of deep reading and deep thinking".[635] During the pandemic, a great deal of reading moved to screens, despite an emerging consensus among experts that learning to read on screens involves costly trade-offs. Although the paper-to-screen transition was, in many contexts, well under way prior to 2020, full reliance on ed-tech due to school closures accelerated this process considerably and made screens a primary reading medium for formal education, even for young children.

"What are the three most critical drawbacks to reading onscreen? Distraction first, distraction second, distraction third."

– Naomi Baron, linguist and author of *Words Onscreen*[CXVIII]

Maryanne Wolf, who has dedicated her career to studying what she calls the "reading brain", called special attention to ways reading on digital devices can compromise the development of creativity and social-emotional intelligence that reading usually entails, especially for children. She details how slow, immersive, linear reading, facilitated by paper books, is important not only for academic learning but for the formation of crucial cognitive processes such as critical thinking, personal reflection, imagination and empathy. Wolf does not see digital reading as a cause for despair though. She argues that humanity now possesses both the science and the technology to understand how digital and non-digital reading mediums change the way people read and think, and that education systems can act on this valuable knowledge before changes in reading habits and reading instruction are "entrenched in the population" and accepted without "comprehension of the consequences". Societies and educators, she explains, need to improve "technology to redress its own weaknesses, whether in more refined digital modes of reading or the creation of alternative, developmentally hybrid approaches to acquiring it".[636]

The global rush to move reading and reading instruction to digital mediums due to school closures entrenched tabular screen-based reading on devices swirling with distractions as an educational norm, including for young children. This transition occurred without the systematic examination of the cognitive, linguistic, physiological, and emotional impact of different mediums on the "acquisition and maintenance of the reading brain" envisioned by Wolf and others. As a result, the embrace of ed-tech in response to school closures propelled screens from a secondary to a primary reading medium for children. And this medium was poorly suited to developing deep-reading abilities and forging the reading-brain circuits that help young readers build their own storehouses of knowledge and learn to think critically for themselves.

Beyond slowing the development of linear reading skills, education's wholesale transition into screen-based learning limited children's opportunities to play and develop gross and fine motor skills. Prior to their closure, primary schools were places where children developed coordination and control over their bodies by engaging in physical learning activities in groups, including building with blocks, writing with crayons, cutting with scissors, manipulating clay into shapes and navigating playgrounds. Schools also helped facilitate structured and unstructured play for children, thereby cultivating their abilities to work cooperatively, establish and enforce rules, compromise and arbitrate conflicts.[637] The advantages of play for children cannot be overstated. Work by psychologists like Peter Gray show that play is the "major means" by which children develop intrinsic interests and competencies; learn how to make decisions, solve problems, exert self-control and follow rules; practice regulating their emotions; make friends and treat others as equals; and experience joy.[638] Thinkers like Steven Horwitz have linked unsupervised and unstructured play in groups of peers, to democracy, tolerance and liberalism. As Horwitz explains, play that happens in person and outside of digital spaces and is usually encouraged at primary and pre-primary schools is the "key way" that children practice cooperating socially and solving conflicts without resorting to violence. He warns that losing or delaying the skills learned through play makes coercion more likely by threatening the human ability to "create and sustain the rule-governed relationships that are at the core of liberal societies".[639] The benefits of play are so profound and so well established that a 'right to play' was inscribed in the 1989 United Nations Convention on the Rights of the Child.[640]

Yet despite the importance of play, the virtual and screen-based realities of distance education, commonly accessed by children individually, had few options for supporting the social and physical play that is essential for the development of children. While digital technology and content can open frontiers for different types of digital play, this type of play is generally less relevant, engaging and beneficial for young children – such that leading paediatric groups recommend no or heavily moderated and supervised technology use by very young children. In some instances, ed-tech modes of learning appear to have distracted from play. Throughout 2020 and into 2021 and 2022, parents of first, second and third grade students were regularly advised to have their children log into synchronous learning platforms or asynchronous educational apps in place of playing with siblings and other relatives. The time children spent staring at screens was time not spent playing with others in their household or manipulating toys and other physical objects that can build understanding as well as enhance physical dexterity and strength.

"I'm eager to be proved wrong, but I suspect that for [my son] and for my family, Zoom kindergarten might be worse than no school at all."

– Author and parent of a 5-year-old, USA[cxix]

> Before the pandemic, kindergarten was widely viewed as the antithesis of online activity – it was a real-world experience that many considered undigitizable.

Prior to the pandemic, researchers had already observed declines in the total amount of time children spend in physical play, a trend that was speculated to trace to the growing popularity of digital entertainment and childhood becoming more circumscribed overall.[641] Fully remote digital learning during school closures likely amplified this trend. Despite the limitations of ed-tech to encourage play that boosts cognitive, emotional, social and physical development for young children, many schools and school systems advised or mandated digital learning for early-grade learners. Parents in regions across the world reported receiving emails and other notifications instructing them to enrol their children in online kindergarten and early primary school grades. This was understood by many experts in childhood development as a surreal contradiction. Kindergarten was widely viewed as the antithesis of online activity – it was meant to be a hands-on, in-person, play-centric and social experience that many considered undigitizable. Yet the educational switch from in-person schooling to fully remote learning cast a wide net and caught various grade levels, even those serving young children for whom digital technology was of questionable and perhaps deleterious utility.

"The basic pattern that has been found in dozens of studies is that children learn better from a person who is with them face-to-face than from a person on a screen, even if it's the exact same person doing the exact same thing."

– Georgene Troseth, psychologist[cxx]

Families were rarely advised to minimize screen time for very young children.

The normalization of technology use for education during school closures appears to have carried over to toddlers, despite there being few explicit mandates for the continuation of preschool learning during the pandemic. One of the rare multi-country studies to examine this issue found that toddlers experienced "increased exposure to screens during lockdowns". The study found that the increases in screen time appeared to be related to the duration of the lockdown period, such that "children from countries who enforced longer lockdowns had increased screen time relative to children from countries with shorter lockdowns".[642] According to pre-pandemic studies, one of the overriding reasons cited by parents for allowing or instructing young children to watch screen-based media is a desire to support education.[643] In the context of the pandemic and countrywide efforts to shift formal education to ed-tech mediums, and amid widespread concerns that children of all ages were 'falling behind', it is easy to see how some parents absorbed a message that educational content presented on digital technology holds value for learners of any age, even toddlers and babies. While some countries were careful in their communications about ed-tech to include warnings about the importance of minimizing screen time for very young children, these notices appear to have been the exception rather than the rule.

Compared to studies of screen time for toddlers, research about the effects of digital media on children over 4 or 5 years of age presents a more mixed picture: risks remain but real educational gains are also possible. This research, however, tends to come with caveats on how exactly screens should be used and for how long. For example, various studies showing that good-quality educational television programming can help children improve their vocabulary and language skills usually observe that learning gains are greatest if an adult watches the content with the child and helps reinforce the material through talk and interaction. The learning gains from exposure to this content are significantly weaker without the same mediation from parents or caregivers.[644] But this social mode of technology-based learning with young children was hard to apply in practice during the pandemic. Working adults had little capacity to interact with children while they watched educational content for long stretches of time. As school closures were extended, families quickly interpreted that it was acceptable to have young children watch screens alone. This practice did not, however, conform with evidence that using screen-based media is most beneficial if done with others and in ways that maximize opportunities for person-to-person exchange. The move to fully remote ed-tech during the pandemic unfolded in ways that normalized the use of screens as first-order learning tools for young children outside of social contexts.

"That anyone – a parent, a first-grade teacher, a school principal, a journalist – would expect a six-year-old to have the self-control, motivation, and attention span to participate in remote instruction is strange – yet typical of our extraordinary expectations for the power of learning technologies."

– Justin Reich, education researcher and author[xx]

Some parents took to social media to voice their incredulity that school leaders were calling for children younger than 10 years old to spend as long as six hours per day on screen-based education.

Besides encouraging the use of screen-based media for children, remote digital learning routines and recommendations commonly disregarded WHO guidance concerning maximum screen time durations for different age cohorts. Early in the pandemic especially, many schools and education leaders tried to keep class schedules intact despite the transition to technology. This meant, for example, that second grade students who had five-hour schooldays when schools were open were supposed to spend five hours per day in front of screens. While fifth and sixth grade students could sometimes muddle through screen marathons like this, it simply did not work for younger learners. Many parents reported that the instructions coming from schools defied common sense: of course, a student under 10 years old was likely to have problems following hours of screen-based instruction and educational content. In April and May 2020, some parents took to social media to voice their bewilderment and incredulity that school leaders were calling for as much as six hours of technology-based instruction per day. Unsurprisingly, young children were rarely eager or able to comply with these guidelines. (Indeed, many adults and university students with strong self-regulation skills found it challenging to sit through five or more hours of online learning day after day.) Even after some of the more excessive time recommendations were dialled back, many education systems continued to insist that young learners follow screen-based lessons or other educational content for two, three or more hours per day. Experts voiced warnings that durations of this sort, still consuming large chunks of the waking day, could be detrimental to learning and development, not just for very young children but also for students in upper primary and lower secondary schools. Correlational studies compiled by child and adolescent health researchers have shown, for example, that 8- to 11-year-olds who exceed screen time recommendations score lower on cognitive assessments than peers who follow the recommendations.[645]

Viewed holistically, the available evidence strongly suggests that the way technology-first modes of learning were deployed during school closures were insufficient and perhaps even harmful for young and very young learners. Ed-tech was not equally relevant or usable for students in different grade levels and of different ages. There were good reasons why technology-dependent modes of teaching and learning were more common at the level of higher education than at the level of primary school. Yet governments across the world turned to screen-based technology as a response to the educational disruptions of COVID-19 regardless of the age of learners.[646] While school leaders may have been quick to say that the content of ed-tech was not one-size-fits-all for different grade levels and students, the screen-based mediums and delivery methods for this content very much was.[647] These mediums and delivery methods, all reliant on technology, were not equally beneficial to all age cohorts.

"Our daughter has never set foot in the classroom. She thinks the mobile phone is her school. … What we are giving our children these days is not education for overall development but trying to keep them busy, knowing very well this is bad for their future."

– Parent of a 5-year-old girl, India[cxxii]

There is some evidence to suggest that the myriad challenges young children faced learning through digital portals and the frustrations this entailed for parents prompted some families to pull their children out of formal education or decline to enrol them. For example, in the USA, the drop in enrolments for kindergarten students was so severe that the *New York Times* called it a "kindergarten exodus". Data experts estimated that national kindergarten enrolment levels dropped by nearly 10 per cent between 2019 and 2020.[648] This equated to over 340,000 young children exiting formal education, even if only temporarily. More severe declines were observed in poorer countries. A survey of households in the western Indian cities of Mumbai and Pune found, for instance, that enrolment in preschools dropped by between 30 per cent and 40 per cent in 2021 compared with pre-pandemic enrolments.[649] It is uncertain if family disillusionment with the transition to screen-centric modes of learning for preschool age children was a strong driving factor of the exodus, but considerable qualitative and anecdotal evidence suggests that it was likely a contributing factor. Parents around the world seem to have realized that there were few good options to teach young learners remotely through screen-based technologies. Given this reality, these parents sometimes concluded that there was little reason to keep their children enrolled in schools resorting to technology-centric modes of distance learning, especially if these schools charged tuition that stretched families financially during a period of immense uncertainty.

Environmental tolls multiplied with the ed-tech boom

Apart from the promises of ed-tech to improve teaching and learning by making these processes more engaging and efficient, ed-tech was widely promoted as a means to make education more environmentally sustainable. Proponents announced that ed-tech would gradually reduce the education sector's reliance on physical learning resources and infrastructure, most immediately paper – the millions of textbooks, workbooks, notebooks and handouts that flow to schools and learners – and, in time, perhaps schools and their innumerable material assets – roofs, tiles, paint, desks and auditoriums.

Images of trees crashing down in pristine natural environments, logs travelling in dirty trucks to emissions-spewing paper mills, and crates of educational books being distributed across long distances in gas-guzzling ships and trucks – all to feed the education sector's voracious appetite for paper – were vivid in the minds of people inside and outside of education. This imagery, sometimes packaged for maximum emotional impact by education institutions seeking to reduce paper use and its associated costs, could be so powerful that teachers and administrators sometimes recounted feelings of guilt standing in front of printers and calling up yet another 30, 50, 100, 500 or 5,000 copies of a document to distribute to students. People higher up in educational hierarchies quietly voiced similar laments when boarding another flight to another conference in another city. And bureaucrats overseeing the physical maintenance of schools and universities knew the considerable material needs of these institutions were, due to limited budgets and short-term planning, commonly met with large orders for inexpensive goods manufactured in faraway places and constructed from inexpensive plastic and other non-renewable materials that had limited longevity. There was a sense that education was not living up to its aspirations to practice as well as teach sustainability.

Technology, as is so often the case, was positioned as the antidote. With laptops, tablets and smartphones in wide circulation, the need for paper would plummet and the trees and other raw ingredients needed to make it could remain undisturbed. Pencils, a centuries-old instrument of education and, indeed, a common visual shorthand for education itself, would become redundant in the paperless future of learning, replaced by touchscreens and electronic styluses. And with distance and remote learning via ed-tech, there was a promise that the environmentally straining materiality of education could, in time, melt away entirely: digital clouds instead of schools, invisible wireless connections instead of buses, video conferences instead of in-person ones. The green future of education would, according to this narrative, be a digital future. Ed-tech companies pushed these ideas, such that their slide decks for sales pitches to would-be buyers invariably included reminders that ed-tech was a financial outlay to protect the environment as well as to enhance learning.

But assumptions that ed-tech would transform the education sector into an engine and model of sustainability were simplistic at best. The experiences of the global turn to technology to continue education during the pandemic revealed the fissures and fictions of the narrative that the digital transformation of education would be a green transformation. The environmental strains of surging demand for hardware and connectivity were evident across global supply chains. The beginning and end points of this process – resource extraction and device disposal – caused serious environmental scars and likely took a heavy toll on a wide range of life forms. Before and during the pandemic, people, especially children and youth living in fragile and mineral-rich developing countries, were recruited to either mine raw materials for digital devices or scavenge technology

Rather than facilitating a cleaner and greener future, growing reliance on ed-tech hardware and connectivity infrastructure appears to have placed added stress on ecological and climate systems already under pressure.

dumps for materials that could be sold and reused, often to make more of the digital devices that education suddenly required. Huge upticks in technology production and use for education required power, and much of this power was sourced from fossil fuels. During the pandemic, digital technology-related greenhouse gas emissions stemming from the education sector rose across the planet. Rather than facilitating a cleaner and greener future, growing reliance on ed-tech hardware and connectivity infrastructure appears to have placed added stress on ecological and climate systems already under pressure from other areas of human activity. Ultimately, remote digital learning depended on products derived from non-renewable resources and processes that contribute to pollution, greenhouse emissions, and other degradations of the environment.

NEW MATERIAL AND ENERGY NEEDS

The global effort to shift from classroom-based education to technology-reliant distance learning was widely understood as entailing a move from physical infrastructure that is visible and tangible to digital spaces that are assumed to be ethereal – 'in the cloud'. But the technology supporting distance learning had a sprawling physical presence and tangible energy needs. It is far from clear that ed-tech is – or might be – a greening force in the education sector, as many claim.[650]

"For all the breathless talk of the supreme placelessness of our new digital age, when you pull back the curtain, the networks of the Internet are as fixed in real, physical places as any railroad or telephone system ever was."

– Andrew Blum, author and journalist[cxxiii]

Throughout the pandemic, governments and families alike purchased hundreds of millions of devices for educational use. These devices are resource-intensive to manufacture and typically have very short life cycles. They are made of metals, chemicals and plastics that are challenging to mine, fabricate and source. Their use also increased demand for data processing and storage. Digital operations related to education spiked, as did energy requirements to power these operations. The infrastructure necessary to make ed-tech functional is not nebulous, but made of things, albeit things that are largely out of sight: data centres, servers, cell towers, switches, buildings, offices, modems, lasers, routers, cables and wires. Although ed-tech is commonly thought to enable efficiencies that have environmental benefits – less frequent transportation and reduced use of physical learning materials – a realistic net balance has yet to be calculated.⁶⁵¹ Many of the most adverse and long-term environmental effects of ed-tech, such as production and disposal, are routinely overlooked. And because ed-tech remains so new, these effects are still only just coming into focus.

The total cost of technology ownership, including maintenance and disposal, tends to greatly exceed the cost of devices alone.

In many countries, ministries of education set ambitious targets of equipping every learner and teacher with a connected device of some sort. Governments and public bodies initiated huge procurements of laptops, tablets and smartphones. Various loaning schemes and subsidies were put in place to help families buy devices that they would not have purchased otherwise. From 2020 through early 2023, school systems in developed and developing countries alike spent billions of dollars of public money to purchase digital devices, almost always from for-profit technology companies.⁶⁵² These expenditures were often financed with non-reoccurring stimulus funds directed towards education, raising questions about the sustainability of investments in technology. Considerations about the upkeep, maintenance and recycling of new ed-tech hardware were afterthoughts, if they were contemplated at all. Education leaders with experience in ed-tech implementations voiced alarm, noting that the total cost of technology ownership, including maintenance and disposal, tends to greatly exceed the cost of devices alone. Huge device purchases made good headlines, sometimes scoring political points for leaders, but they introduced longer term challenges and liabilities: How would the devices be serviced when problems arose? Who was responsible for theft, loss and damage? How would operating systems be kept up to date? How would software be licensed and installed? While many sectors of the economy increased reliance on digital technology during the pandemic, the education sector saw some of the largest increases in terms of volume and sales.

"What most school districts did was they dropped everything, and they bought ed-tech whether they had budget for it or not."

– Keith Krueger, CEO of the Consortium for School Networking[cxxiv]

Education sales of digital hardware such as laptops and tablets reached all-time highs in 2020, with growth slowing down only towards the end of 2021.⁶⁵³ Some school systems doubled or tripled the number of devices they had before the pandemic, while other schools started buying devices for the first time. Orders placed for Chromebooks, low-cost laptop computers that run on Google's proprietary Chrome operating system, exemplified the surge in education sector demand for devices. Unlike other types of connected devices that can serve a variety of purposes across a range of industries, Chromebooks are closely associated with the education sector.

They are specifically marketed to governments, schools and families as simple and affordable devices for educational use. The technology research firm Gartner observed an unprecedented 90 per cent increase in the sale of Chromebooks in the third quarter of 2020, compared with the previous year.[654] Expressed in absolute terms, 17 million Chromebooks were sold globally in 2019. This figure leaped to 31.8 million in 2020 and to 37.3 million in 2021,[655] suggesting that more than twice as many Chromebooks were produced and distributed in 2020 and 2021 than would have been expected, were it not for the pandemic and its disruption to school-based education.

Schools in the USA bought about 30 million laptops and tablets in first academic year of the COVID-19 crisis.

While fine-grained global data on hardware purchases for education use are not well-tracked, the national estimates that were available showed that tens of millions of devices flowed from factories to teachers and students. Futuresource, a market research consultancy, estimated that in the first academic year of the COVID-19 crisis, schools in the USA bought about 30 million laptops and tablets while parents bought 2.2 million directly, a trend mirrored in other high-income countries during the pandemic.[656] Demand was so high for ed-tech hardware in 2020 that inventories were often depleted to zero, and newspapers published stories of school systems trying to outmanoeuvre and outbid other school systems to secure the devices they needed, sometimes within a single country or state.[657]

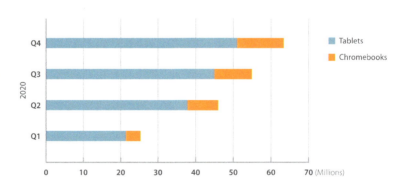

Figure 16:

Growth in worldwide shipments of digital devices during the first year of the COVID-19 pandemic

Source: Adapted from International Data Corporation, 2021

The energy and resources required to make so much new ed-tech hardware are immense. The hardware is constructed from several raw and often non-renewable materials that are mined, transported, cut, purified, moulded, welded, assembled, packaged and shipped as part of complex supply chains. A widely cited life cycle assessment – an analysis that evaluates the ecological impact of a product from its earliest creation to its disposal and decomposition – found that approximately 33 pounds of minerals

> Approximately 33 pounds of minerals and 79 gallons of water are required to make a single e-reader.

and 79 gallons of water are required to make a single e-reader, such as an Apple iPad or an Amazon Kindle, compared with less than one pound of materials and just two gallons of water to make a standard paper book.[658] While computers and smartphones operate with relatively small amounts of energy compared with other power-consuming technologies, the industries required to produce these electronics tend to be energy intensive. For example, the production of an e-reader requires 100 kilowatt-hours of fossil fuels, compared with only 2 kilowatt-hours to produce a paper book. In 2018, the global carbon footprint of manufacturing mobile phones was estimated to equal or exceed the carbon emissions of the Philippines, a country with a population of over 100 million.[659] Studies comparing the output of greenhouse gases required to make an e-reader versus a paper book found that the production of an e-reader releases 100 times more greenhouse gases.[660] This means that for an e-reader to have a net-positive effect on greenhouse gas emissions, it would have to result in 100 fewer paper books being produced. While digital devices such as e-readers have long promised radical reductions in paper use and production, these reductions have yet to materialize. According to the International Energy Agency, global paper production reached a record peak in 2021, a year in which pandemic restrictions were in full force in many countries and reliance on digital technology for schooling and other purposes was especially pronounced. Paper and pulp production are expected to continue increasing through 2030, in large part because of growing demand for wrapping and packaging stemming from increases in e-commerce shipments from vendors like Amazon, itself an outgrowth of digitalization.[661] Cardboard production hit all-time highs in 2021, and the international market for corrugated packaging is expected to equal the GDP of New Zealand or Greece by 2025.[662]

Beyond their production, connected devices consume energy and place energy demands on the internet infrastructure that provides the piping of online learning. Even though important steps have been made to improve the energy efficiency of data storage and processing,[663] the networked data centres that help power the internet and online education nevertheless account for more than 2 per cent of global energy use, a figure that is growing every year.[664]

While many experts assume that ed-tech and internet infrastructure will become more energy-efficient over time, this is far from assured. Many of the blockchain technologies proposed to improve privacy, data protection and transparency, for example, are extremely energy intensive. The blockchain that powers Bitcoin, the world's most recognizable cryptocurrency, is estimated to consume 110 terawatt-hours per year, roughly equivalent to the annual electricity consumption of Malaysia.[665]

Adding generative AI to internet search technology increases the computational power needed for each search by a factor of five.

Some future forms of ed-tech anticipate much higher rates of energy consumption. The computational and electrical power required to run virtual reality educational apps, those that are claimed to be just around the corner for many teachers and students, can be exponentially higher than the power needed to run an app on a standard laptop or smartphone. Similarly, educational apps that make heavy use of AI commonly require large amounts energy. *Wired* magazine reported that adding generative AI to internet search technology increases the computational power needed for each search by a factor of five.[666] Training AI models is also, according to the Stanford University AI Intelligence Index, "incredibly energy intensive".[667] So too is everyday use of these models. One expert estimated that the cumulative electricity consumption of ChatGPT, a popular AI chatbot developed by OpenAI, may have been as high as 23 million kilowatt-hours in January 2023. This is roughly equivalent to the monthly energy use of 175,000 people living in Denmark.[668] The data centres that power ChatGPT and other generative AI apps further require large amounts of cooling water. Just training the GPT-3 large language model consumed an estimated 700,000 litres of freshwater, which is about the same consumption as the cooling tower of a nuclear reactor. Industry observers have equated an average user's conversational exchange with ChatGPT with "dumping a large bottle of fresh water on the ground".[669]

The global ICT industry is on track to account for over one-sixth of total greenhouse gas emissions by 2040, and education constitutes a rapidly growing slice of this industry.

These figures suggest that even if the energy efficiency of frontier technologies improves, the increasing computational demands of the education sector will likely cause net energy and other resource use to continue to rise. Although ChatGPT was only released in November 2022 and after COVID-19 school closures and full reliance on remote digital learning had crested, millions of students and teachers were using it by 2023. Globally, emissions associated with ICT are climbing steadily higher, despite international commitments to reduce emissions overall. Experts have estimated that the global ICT industry is on track to account for over one-sixth of total greenhouse gas emissions by 2040, and education constitutes a rapidly growing slice of this industry.[670]

THE MOUNTING SCOURGE OF E-WASTE

Perhaps the most daunting environmental challenge associated with ed-tech in the near term is electronic waste, or e-waste. Even before the pandemic, e-waste – discarded electronic devices, such as computers, televisions, mobile phones and tablets – was the world's fastest-growing trash stream.[671] According to the United Nations University's monitor on global e-waste, the world generated 53.6 million tonnes of e-waste in 2019, the latest year for which global data are available.[672] This is equivalent to 82 times the number of jumbo jets ever produced or the combined weight of all of the adults in Europe. Just one tonne of e-waste equates to about 8,000 mobile phones.[673]

Figure 17:

Global annual production of e-waste

Source: Data from United Nations University, 2020

53.6 million metric tons = Combined weight of all the adults in Europe

> Buyers, including those making large educational purchases, have been conditioned through marketing and experience to see ed-tech hardware as reaching expiration dates much earlier than other educational purchases.

To a significant degree, the enormous volume of e-waste traces to the very short life cycles of consumer electronics. Many ed-tech devices, including mobile phones and laptops, are used on average for around three years,[674] a period so brief that a typical device would not see a student through a full cycle of primary, secondary or higher education. While this is partly due to consumer demand for newer and better devices, it also reflects persistent structural problems: new software is often not compatible with hardware that is more than a few years old, and much of the hardware is difficult or impossible to repair. Buyers, including those making large educational purchases, have been conditioned through marketing and experience to see ed-tech hardware as reaching expiration dates much earlier than other educational purchases. Hardcover printed textbooks, for example, are assumed to have a lifespan of around ten years, while chairs, desks and chalkboards can be used for over half a century when they are cared for and well made. Even other electronics purchased by schools, such as televisions and projectors are generally assumed to have lifespans that will hover closer to five or ten years rather than the three or four years of tablets and laptops. Apple, the world's most valuable corporation, received accolades when it announced in late 2021 that it would make parts, specialist tools and repair manuals available to help consumers maintain and repair its flagship product, the iPhone, estimated to be used by about 1 in 7 people globally.[675] That this announcement came nearly 15 years after the release of the first iPhone and was considered to be a pioneering step by industry standards illustrates the dismal state of repair options for these devices as well as similar hardware used to power ed-tech.

Some recent government initiatives, such as the European Commission's campaign for a 'right to repair' and the introduction in France of a 'repairability index' for laptops and smartphones, seek to steer manufacturers towards making devices that are easier to repair, thereby increasing their lifespans.[676] New commercial options, such as Fairphone, a smartphone built with parts that are easy to replace, carry a potential to create consumer demand for expanded maintenance and repair options for digital hardware.[677] Other consumer electronics companies are regularizing designs to use modular parts that can be easily upgraded if technology components become outdated, in an effort to 'future-proof' and extend their life.[678] Additionally, third-party verifications such as the Cradle to Cradle certification – an assessment of product sustainability across a variety of environmental stewardship, social justice and material safety categories – seek to establish new standards for assuring electronics are safe, circular and responsibly made.[679] Yet these developments aside, the pace of market and regulatory changes needed to extend the life of electronics remains slow and offers little confidence that sustainability efforts can keep up with rapidly rising global demand for electronic devices. The WEEE Forum, a global leader in the management of waste from electrical and electronic equipment (WEEE), projected that over 5 billion mobile phones would be discarded in 2022 alone.[680]

"In a near-future of rising sea-levels, climate mass migration and low-carbon restrictions, much of the current hype that surrounds EdTech is likely to quickly seem inappropriate if not obscene. Demands for 'One Device Per Student', unlimited data storage, live streaming and the expectation for everyone to be 'Always-On' will seem as anachronistic as twentieth century attitudes toward smoking cigarettes and burning fossil fuels."

– Neil Selwyn, professor, Monash University[cxxv]

With limited lifespans and options for repair, ed-tech hardware quickly travels from the hands of students and teachers into waste streams. In 2019, only 17.4 per cent of global e-waste was properly collected and recycled, leaving more than 44 million metric tons to find its way into landfills, illegal disposal sites or black markets of illegal trade.[681] Such a poor recycling rate is particularly concerning given the value of materials that are discarded. The United Nations University has estimated that unrecycled e-waste contains USD 57 billion worth of recoverable materials, including gold, copper and other valuable metals, which are routinely dumped or burned instead of collected for reuse. This practice stems from business and regulatory environments that incentivize mining rather than recycling and reuse. The education sector is a major and growing contributor to e-waste trash streams that wind up in dumps. While there have been some legislative efforts to mandate or encourage appropriate disposal and recycling of e-waste, including the Electronic Waste Recycling Act enacted in California in 2003[682] and the 2012 EU directive on waste from electrical and electronic equipment, known as the WEEE Directive,[683] the global volume of e-waste continues to climb ever upwards.

"Preventing waste and recovering important raw materials from e-waste is crucial to avoid putting more strain on the world's resources."

– Virginijus Sinkevičius, European Commissioner for the Environment, Oceans and Fisheries[CXXVI]

An unfortunate legacy of the pandemic will be the hundreds of millions of devices purchased by the education sector that were constructed and sold with little regard for how they might be repaired or recycled.

An unfortunate legacy of the pandemic will be the hundreds of millions of devices purchased by the education sector that were constructed and sold with little regard for how they might be repaired or recycled. Without dramatic action to assure more sustainable practices, ed-tech is likely to constitute a growing portion of e-waste flows as hardware purchased during the health crisis breaks, becomes outdated and is discarded. Indeed, the massive volume of ed-tech purchased from 2020 to 2022 will likely reach trash cans and dumps starting in 2024 and 2025 and stretch on into the decade.

ED-TECH FOR SOME, MINES AND LANDFILLS FOR OTHERS

Ed-tech production, disposal and unregulated recycling can directly endanger human health. When improperly discarded, electronic hardware releases toxic substances that contaminate air, water, dust, soil, plants and animals. These substances also come into contact with adults and children. E-waste is commonly dumped in the poorest regions of the world,[684] and children as young as 5 years old are recruited or forced to scavenge dumps for valuable parts and metals, many of them dangerous to handle without protective equipment.[685] This means that while many children and youth experience digital technology as a dynamic portal to learning, others experience it as labour and a health hazard.

E-waste 'recycling' activities are creating health risks for up to 18 million children and youth globally.

A 2021 report by the WHO specified that e-waste 'recycling' activities are creating health risks for up to 18 million children and youth and 13 million women globally.[686] (To put these figures in perspective, Brazil, the seventh most populous country in the world, has a total primary school population of approximately 14 million students.) Insufficient education about the hazards of unsanctioned recycling and limited access to health care compound these risks. Recycling vendors routinely set up operations adjacent to the sites where e-waste is dumped, magnifying the environmental dangers confronting the adults and children who complete the arduous work of separating and sorting materials that can be resold. The risks are particularly acute for children, who, due to their smaller size, less developed organs and rapid rate of growth and development, are more vulnerable than adults to the toxins released from e-waste.[687]

The production side of technology hardware can put children at risk, particularly in poor countries where manual labour is used to physically extract non-renewable resources from mines.

Like the health hazards of unregulated dumping and recycling, the production side of technology hardware also puts adults and children at risk. Human labour is required to physically extract non-renewable resources, such as rare earth metals and chemical elements, that provide the raw materials needed to fabricate digital devices. This labour is often conducted in hazardous mining sites and with minimal regulation or safety oversight. Several materials essential to the manufacture of sophisticated components used in hardware such as smartphones and laptops are only found in a few parts of the world, sometimes in extremely poor countries and those with weak human rights protections. The low cost of labour can also be a draw for mining companies pursuing higher profit margins for raw materials and lead to an expansion of mining operations in low-income countries.

Efforts to extract cobalt, a valuable chemical element used in the manufacture of lithium batteries, which power various types of digital devices, including ed-tech hardware, provide a specific example of the ways mining can undermine the rights of children, including their right to education. Over 70 per cent of global cobalt mining occurs in the Democratic Republic of the Congo, which has more than half of the world's cobalt reserves.[688] An estimated one-fifth of cobalt mines are small-scale enterprises that rely heavily on child labour. Reports from different international organizations have detailed dangerous working conditions faced by children, sometimes as young as 3 years old, recruited to work in the mining sector for extremely low pay.[689] Of the over quarter million Congolese people mining for cobalt, 40,000 are estimated to be children.[690]

In 2019, several Congolese families launched a lawsuit against some of the world's largest technology companies, including Apple, Google, Dell and Microsoft. The suit alleged that the companies aided and abetted in the death and serious injury of children who were working in cobalt mines that the defendants claim are part of these companies' corporate supply chains.[691] *The Guardian* newspaper called the case a "landmark legal case", explaining that it is the first time that such a legal challenge had been brought against any of the technology companies involved. In court papers, one of the plaintiffs asserted that her nephew, a child who died when a mine tunnel collapsed on him and other workers, was forced to seek work in the cobalt mines when he was a minor because his family could not afford to pay his monthly school fees of USD 6.[692] In November 2021, the judge who heard the case in a district court in the USA said that while the complaint listed "tragic events", the suit could not trace a clear link back to the US technology companies. The judge dismissed the case, stating that "the only real connection is that the companies buy refined cobalt" and that a "long chain of contingencies creates mere speculation, not a traceable harm".[693] The organization that brought the lawsuit on behalf of the Congolese child miners, International Rights Advocates, has appealed the decision, declaring its position that the technology companies named in the suit "have failed to take responsibility for their supply chains, despite claiming to have policies that allow them to monitor for and enforce their prohibition on child labour".[694]

"Children work for at least 12 hours a day without protective equipment in deep underground shafts around 10 metres long, which they have often dug themselves. With no mask or helmet, they go down into the shafts unprotected and put their lives in danger to bring mineral-encrusted rocks to the surface. They are only paid 1 or 2 USD a day."

– Eleonora Tria, blogger for the children's rights NGO Humanium[cxxvii]

> Appeals to quickly and drastically expand digital learning need to consider how supplying some children with digital devices may put other children halfway around the world at heightened risk of exploitation.

This lawsuit has helped highlight some of the ways the rush to secure the raw material needed for ed-tech and other electronics at minimum cost can present mortal risks for vulnerable children. At the global level, appeals to quickly and drastically expand digital learning need to consider how supplying some children with digital devices may put other children halfway around the world at heightened risk of exploitation. Current projections suggest that worldwide demand for cobalt, for instance, is on track to increase 60 per cent in the period from 2017 to 2025,[695] in part due to stepped-up production of consumer electronics – an increasing share of which are being used in the education sector.

The child labour and health and environmental hazards associated with technology production and disposal cast a dark shadow over the massive deployment of ed-tech during the COVID-19 pandemic. Yet this shadow is rarely acknowledged or discussed. As schools around the world closed in response to the pandemic, some children traded seats in classrooms for hazardous work scavenging for e-waste or working in mines to source the raw materials needed to produce the hardware that powers ed-tech.[696] And as demand for ed-tech continues to outpace just labour practices, there is every indication that more children are likely to be put at risk due to stepped-up production.

The private sector tightened its grip on public education

Well before the pandemic, many people were convinced that looser government control and greater autonomy for private actors would strengthen education. When education was unexpectedly uprooted from schools and moved to the cloud, people on both sides of privatization debates understood that education conducted digitally would be far more exposed to market logics. Although a handful of countries had robust public digital platforms and content to help sustain state-controlled education, the majority had nothing in place or were faced with offerings that were still

Although a handful of countries had robust public platforms and content to help sustain state-controlled education, the majority had nothing in place and were presented with a menu of solutions provided by non-public entities, many of them for-profit companies.

embryonic and incapable of upholding formal education for huge numbers of students and teachers. What was immediately available was a menu of solutions provided by non-public entities, namely for-profit companies. Countries turned to them en masse in an attempt to assure the continuation of learning. Enormous corporations that had business interests in education prior to the pandemic became principal mediators of formal education with remarkable speed. They controlled the schools of the digital realm and much of the pedagogical experience.

This development was welcomed by some, particularly at the outset of the crisis. Growing involvement of the private sector seemed to promise faster and bolder innovation along with superior efficiency and expanded choice for learners and their families as well as for teachers and schools. Companies competing for business, the thinking went, would be forced to offer high-quality educational services or risk learners and educators walking away from them. Beyond this, it was imagined that private sector actors would help wrestle education from the slow-moving bureaucracies of public school systems that some perceived to be stuck in a non-digital era and frustratingly dismissive of the transformational potentials offered by increasingly ubiquitous connected technology. There was a sense that when education was propelled into digital spaces because of school closures, the market would be able to deliver high-quality digital education experiences that could meet the diverse needs of learners and help better personalize education. The incentive of financial rewards would fuel a rush to build superior quality products.

Many people also placed significant trust in the technology companies that were thrust into the role of education facilitators and providers during the pandemic. Global technology brands had grown spectacularly throughout the 2000s and released various tools and services that changed day-to-day life and sometimes seemed to have power, utility and the attraction of novelty that bordered on the miraculous. Technology companies also invested heavily in marketing and were, on the eve of the pandemic, household names throughout the world. Their products were seen as more modern, better designed and more exciting than anything coming out of the public sector and especially ministries of education, which were widely perceived as slow to innovate.

Various surveys have found that private sector technology companies enjoy significantly more social trust than educational institutions, whether schools or colleges and universities.[697] In the USA, for example, Amazon and Google ranked as the second and third most trusted institutions in the entire country, according to 2018 research led by scholars at Georgetown and New York University. A January 2020 survey found that

In the USA, Amazon and Google ranked as the second and third most trusted institutions in the country.

major technology companies enjoy significantly more trust than teachers, local police, the government and scientific studies.[698] And a separate June 2020 study, undertaken to gauge how the pandemic was impacting trust in different organizations, found that four of the top five most trusted organizations were technology companies: Amazon, Google, YouTube and Zoom.[699] According to the survey, people were about three times as likely to say they trusted these companies than to say they trusted the federal government. While these findings were specific to the USA, multi-country investigations similarly suggested that people around the world found technology corporations highly trustworthy and capable of offering more reliable services than those provided by the government. A January 2022 Ipsos study encompassing 29 countries in various regions revealed that technology companies constituted the most trusted sector globally, ahead of banks, governments, public services and the media.[700] Interestingly, the USA was not among the countries indicating the most trust in technology companies, suggesting that even though trust levels were high in the USA, they were considerably higher in other countries, including Malaysia, India, Saudi Arabia, China and the Russian Federation.[701] These data help explain some of the high hopes and enthusiasm that accompanied the extensive engagement of private sector technology companies in the provision of education during the pandemic.

However, despite the dynamism and innovation that was expected from technology corporations, many learners and teachers were disappointed with their solutions and services. The company offerings often made education feel constraining and overly rote. This is perhaps because education, even conducted remotely and with technology, remains a social endeavour, an act of preparing people to participate productively in local communities and wider society. Continuing education during the pandemic school closures was, then, primarily a social challenge, rather than a technical one. A better messaging system, a new tool for sharing inside an app, improved AI recognition of patterns and slicker user interfaces could improve the technology hosting education, but it rarely made the holistic education experience feel complete. What technology companies offered was, unsurprisingly, technology – not a solution for education itself, even if some people thought well-financed and professionally run corporations staffed largely by programmers and engineers might somehow deliver it.

Perhaps the most lasting influence of heightened private sector involvement in education during the pandemic was the way it reframed education, to a large extent, as a private and commercial good and a sector ripe for business expansion and profit generation. This could – and, in the eyes of many, often did – endanger the special status of education as a human right and public good. By any analysis, the pandemic elevated the influence of private

> The most lasting influence of private sector involvement was that it reframed education as a private and commercial good and a sector ripe for business expansion and profit generation, endangering its special status as a human right and public good.

ed-tech actors and made them important players in what had traditionally been a tightly regulated, state-controlled public service. It turned the education sector into a site of intense financial activity and speculation that, in many instances, provided large monetary returns for small groups of ed-tech founders and shareholders. Governments commonly found themselves brokering deals with private and often for-profit ed-tech entities to help provision education remotely, rather than managing and steering the continuation of education themselves. These changes engendered and normalized consumer behaviour in education and hardened beliefs that teaching and learning are services that can be bought and sold largely outside government oversight and according to a logic that the quality of educational services hinges principally on what a family is able to pay. Globally, the turn to connected technology for remote learning resulted in an acceleration of privatization trends that were already under way in many countries and marked the entry of new and powerful commercial companies in the education sector whose influence is likely to ripple well beyond the pandemic.

UNPRECEDENTED GROWTH AND LUCRATIVE INITIAL PUBLIC OFFERINGS FOR COMMERCIAL ED-TECH PROVIDERS

A defining characteristic of educational responses to the pandemic was the creation of new and valuable market spaces for commercial ed-tech companies. The unanticipated rush to remote learning was identified as a once-in-a-lifetime paradigm shifting disruption in the normally staid education sector, and investors bet on a digital future for education. There was a sense that the conservatism typically associated with education, especially its cautious stance towards commercial models of technology integration, would melt away with the hard realities and limited options presented by the pandemic. Rules and norms were being rewritten to allow private providers to play more foundational roles in education. The providers also began to employ more aggressive marketing tactics, including selling services directly to students and teachers.

Money rushed in and powered corporate ambitions to monetize education's pivot into digital spaces. While investment can help assure healthy functioning of commercial firms and promote growth and innovation, the capital flowing to ed-tech was largely speculative. The main objective was not sustainability and innovation per se but rather an attempt to capture financial returns stemming from government and family reliance on ed-tech. The financial inflows were also a means for corporations to gain users and capture markets that would pave the way for longer term profit generation. Conventional wisdom held that there would be no looking back – the technology shift would become permanent. The post-pandemic 'normal' would not be pre-pandemic 'normal'.

Venture capital flowing into ed-tech more than doubled between 2019 and 2020, swelling from USD 7 billion to 16.1 billion and increasing again in 2021, topping USD 20 billion.

One illustrative barometer of the leap in spending was global investment of venture capital in ed-tech. Funding more than doubled from USD 7 billion to 16 billion in 2020.[702] It spiked again in 2021, topping USD 20 billion.[703] This rush of investment made October 2020 to July 2022 a fertile period for ed-tech unicorns – start-up companies with valuations over USD 1 billion – which increased in number from 20 to 36, according to tracking by HolonIQ.[704] The ed-tech sector was projected by some to continue this vertiginous financial ascent. Estimates held that the sector was on pace to be worth over USD 400 billion in total global expenditures by 2025.[705] While broad market pull-backs that started in mid-2022 moderated some of these soaring projections, ed-tech remains widely perceived as a sector primed for growth. In 2023 large sums of money flowed into ed-tech as interest in generative AI technologies such as ChatGPT added new fuel to promises of an imminent inside-out digital transformation of education.

Across the world, the technology-centric educational responses to the pandemic positioned largely for-profit digital and online learning utilities as a new core for education rather than a menu of complementary services on the periphery. Given the unique constraints of the health emergency, the responses also tended to privilege commercial ed-tech solutions that minimized dependence on physical schools and human teachers. Speculators understood that if these largely school-less and teacher-less ed-tech solutions were successful, they would likely become more permanent and trigger a tectonic reallocation of resources towards technology companies.

The global nature of ed-tech deployments during the pandemic also strengthened beliefs that commercial technology providers might be capable of transforming education systems in underdeveloped countries.[706] COVID-19 was perceived by some as the catalyst needed to break cycles of traditional education provision that were deemed to be failing in low-resource contexts. It gave concrete expression to views that low-income countries should stop trying to replicate education systems common in high-income countries and instead embrace a shift to technology-first modes and models for education. Although the global South had not historically been a primary geographic focus for large, for-profit private providers of digital education, the pandemic helped recast it as a booming and largely untapped market. Many ed-tech investors came to see middle- and lower income countries as more financially enticing than rich countries, given their often very large youth populations and perceived receptivity to radical changes to education provision. In national and local contexts where public funding for education was under pressure and conventional actions to improve faltering systems of public education were deemed too slow or too expensive, market-driven ed-tech was seen as an antidote, both during school closures and, in many places, well after they reopened. With the arrival of COVID-19, the large sums of money that moved into ed-tech generated considerable financial gains for the private sector actors involved. Beneficiaries were not limited to established technology companies already involved in education but extended to a proliferation of ed-tech start-ups and multipurpose technology companies, many of them with limited experience and expertise in teaching and learning.[707]

> Education was running headfirst into digitalization, and the primacy of school and other place-based models of public education was slipping. New paradigms seemed to be forming around digital ecosystems that were mostly private and for-profit.

Across the world, narratives that had been in wide circulation before COVID-19 about the inevitability of digital transformation led by commercial entities became a blueprint for action during the pandemic.[708] As schools closed in quick succession, the entire enterprise of education moved, to a large extent, from publicly owned, controlled and managed schools to privately controlled networks, platforms, applications and content. This process sometimes unfolded in a matter of weeks or even days as a response to the health crisis. Students were instructed to use a device of some sort to connect to distance learning via the internet, where and if it was available. Investors and speculators were watching this process, and for many, it signalled a tipping point: education was running headfirst into digitalization, and the primacy of school and other place-based models of public education was no longer assured. New paradigms seemed to be forming around digital ecosystems that were mostly private and for-profit.

"Crises lead to accelerations, and this is the best chance ever for online learning. … Companies are better positioned to see where the jobs of tomorrow will be and prepare people for them than universities."
– Sebastian Thrun, co-founder and chair of Udacity[cxxviii]

The shift to digital and remote technology during the pandemic exposed a system of complete or near-complete reliance on privately held and for-profit companies. The categories and corporations listed on the following pages help illustrate just how much of the educational endeavour moved towards corporate entities and services as COVID-19 swept the world. The list contains businesses located in the global North, many of them with global reach. In other parts of the world, China and India in particular, some of the central ed-tech actors were different. These companies, like the ones based in the global North, were also private and for-profit enterprises.

Central corporate entities in the digital shift to ed-tech

Devices: The devices used by students and teachers were manufactured and sold by a handful of technology corporations, including giants such as Apple, Asus, Dell, Huawei, LG, Samsung and Sony.

Operating systems: The operating systems used on digital devices typically came from one of just three technology corporations: Apple, Google or Microsoft. Only a minority of learners and teachers used open-source operating systems, such as Linux or Ubuntu.

Networks: The networks needed to connect devices and operating systems to the internet were controlled by large private service providers such as Airtel, China Mobile, Comcast, Orange, MTN, Ooredoo, Telcel, Vodafone and Verizon.

Platforms: The platforms and learning management systems students and teachers relied on to provision education remotely were typically controlled by for-profit companies, including Blackboard, BYJU'S, Edmodo, Google Classroom and Schoology. The use of the non-profit and open-source Moodle platform was more limited. Although many governments appeared to offer publicly provisioned distance learning platforms, this was often a practice of white-labelling corporate software and systems that were leased or purchased on a subscription basis, such that governments did not actually own or exercise strong control over the platforms.

Apps: The tools and apps used for educational purposes in digital spaces were similarly for-profit and managed by private entities. Providers included Adobe (Creative Suite), BYJU'S, Google (Workspace), Microsoft (Office) and Remind, among others.

Video classes: Leading software that enabled synchronous video interaction and instruction for education was privately held and included commercial services such as Google Meet, Lark, Microsoft Teams and Zoom.

Learning content: A great deal of the educational content used on digital devices was corporately produced, hosted or controlled. For example, YouTube was a primary portal to educational videos. Pearson offered digital learning resources, including a wide range of digital textbooks. And companies such as Duolingo, Udemy and various MOOC companies, including Coursera, provided dedicated online lessons and courses. Non-profit organizations, such as EdX and Khan Academy, were also active in the content space but, like for-profit alternatives, remained outside public control and accountability.

General communication: General purpose communications systems widely appropriated for educational purposes were owned and run by private firms. Gmail, Outlook, Skype, Slack, WeChat and WhatsApp became essential digital infrastructure for education in countries around the world. All of these systems are run by for-profit companies accountable not to the general public but rather to small groups of private shareholders.

Learning data: The companies storing and processing learning data were almost exclusively private companies and included Amazon, Microsoft and Google.

The shift to remote digital learning amounted to a near-complete handover of education to a relatively small number of interlocking corporations experiencing massive growth in usership, market share and reach.

While this list does not capture all the branches and levels of learning at a distance with ed-tech, it sheds important light on how the technology-based education systems forged during the pandemic relied heavily on a few companies driven by private and usually profit-oriented interests. The only central actors and players in this ed-tech ecosystem that were not corporately controlled were teachers, whose salaries and assignments tended to come from public institutions. If, however, teachers had been removed from the system, the shift to remote digital learning would have amounted to a near-complete handover of education to a relatively small number of interlocking and, in many instances, already powerful corporations experiencing massive growth in usership, market share and reach due to the circumstances of the pandemic.

The UN Special Rapporteur on the right to education from 2016 to 2022, Koumbou Boly Barry, called strong attention to this trend in a July 2022 report entitled "Impact of the digitalization of education on the right to education". The report noted that the Special Rapporteur "regrets" the way education technology companies, many of them "global businesses without interests in or a deep understanding of the contexts in which they operate", perceive education as a market in which they can profit, "embedding private logics and actors in public institutions and decision-making spaces" dedicated to education. The report further flagged the symbiosis between the digitalization and marketization of education as "particularly problematic" for countries in the global South due to their heightened risk of becoming "subordinated to corporate providers". The report lamented that, with rare exception, representatives from the global South were "missing from the discussion and development of digital solutions for education".[709]

"The use of privately provided services and platforms also creates a harmful dependency of Governments in relation to private companies. … Governments end up not developing their own tools, giving control over data, decisions, privacy and autonomy."

– Koumbou Boly Barry, UN Special Rapporteur on the right to education[CXIX]

Google Classroom grew from 40 million to 150 million users between February 2020 and February 2021.

An in-depth examination of the widely used Google Classroom app helps illustrate how instrumental the pandemic was in thrusting private ed-tech providers into central roles in education, not just in a single country or region, but globally. Google Classroom was a tool originally designed to provide teachers with a virtual extension of in-person classrooms. During the pandemic, it saw exponential growth as it was rapidly repurposed as a stand-alone distance learning platform. In February 2021, Google stated that its user base had grown from 40 million users to 150 million users in a single year, an increase of 375 per cent.[710] To put this figure in perspective, 150 million users is more than double the entire school-age population of the European Union.[711] The pandemic was undoubtedly the trigger. Downloads of the app soared to 580 per cent the week of 22 March 2020, compared with the same week in the previous year.[712] And rapid growth continued well into 2022. In January 2022, there were over 600,000 downloads of the app, the largest-ever number of downloads in a one-month period, showing the ways the pandemic was fuelling long-term gains in market share. These leaps and jumps were a deviation from the far more gradual growth recorded by the app prior to the pandemic.

Figure 18:

Increase in the number of people using Google Classroom in the first year of the COVID-19 pandemic

Source: Data from Google, 2021

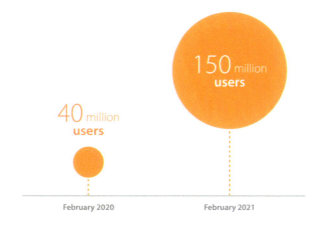

Google had aimed its sights on education well before the pandemic. In 2017, *New York Times* technology reporter Natasha Singer explained that starting in the early 2010s, the company began "[enlisting] teachers and administrators to promote Google's products to other schools", a method she notes helped "upend" traditional practices used by businesses to place products in classrooms.[713] The effort bore fruit. In the USA, the country where Google's endeavours to expand its footprint in education were most concentrated, Singer noted in 2017 that more than half of all primary and secondary school students were using at least one Google service, such as Gmail for a school email account or Google Docs for collaborative academic projects. In the same year, approximately half the mobile devices shipped to schools were Chromebooks, effectively laptop computers with a Google operating system optimized to run Google apps. The company's interest in education may be multifaceted, but the value of habituating learners to use Google products as children cannot be overstated. Students who use Google apps as part of their schooling are more likely to use these applications after graduation. As Singer noted in 2017, educational institutions often facilitated this transition by, for instance, telling students to "make sure" they convert school email accounts "to a personal Gmail account".[714] These practices benefit Google owing to business models constructed around data extraction and advertising. The company is adroit at monetizing users and use of its services, including – and perhaps especially – those that are outwardly offered for free. The title of Singer's 2017 article, "How Google took over the classroom", presaged, in many ways, a trend of incremental corporate capture that went into overdrive during the pandemic.

"[Google] has extraordinary power to affect what happens in classrooms, to monitor children through the interface, to intervene in the labour of teachers, to generate class performance data, to select content and knowledge, and to introduce AI and automation into schools through mundane feature upgrades. It markets its services as 'magical' but they are really technical, social, economic, and political interventions into education systems at enormous scale around the globe."

– Ben Williamson, education scholar[lxxx]

In many instances, the uptake of Google Classroom and complementary Google applications was not offered as a choice during COVID-19 school closures. Rather, teachers and learners had no option but to use these corporate services to stay connected to education; no alternatives were offered. This occurred even though Google Classroom, the only Google app designed expressly for education, had very low user ratings compared to other widely used educational apps. In September 2022, for example, Google Classroom had an aggregate user rating of 2.4 stars (out of a maximum rating of 5 stars) from approximately 2 million user reviews in Google Play (Google's app store) and an aggregate rating of just 1.5 stars (out of 5 stars) from an additional 2 million user reviews in Apple's app store.[715] For comparison, the average user rating across the millions of apps offered on the Google and Apple app stores is above 4 stars – 4.5 stars for apps in the Apple store, and 4.1 stars for apps in the Google store.[716]

Dissatisfaction with Google Classroom was expressed in other ways during the pandemic. Students, for example, mobilized campaigns on social media platforms like TikTok to flood the app with low ratings in the hope that it might be removed from app stores.[717] This practice had been observed earlier in China when students 'review bombed' DingTalk, a leading communication app, with negative ratings when it was appropriated for education purposes in the earliest wave of school closures.[718] While these actions were sometimes dismissed as part of a time-honoured practice of students' trying to escape schoolwork, a closer look at the actual reviews showed articulate and genuine critiques of the learning software that was imposed on young people and teachers during the pandemic. Commentary suggesting that students giving the app one-star reviews were "procrastinating" or "lazy",[719] or that they were being "little brats",[720] was hard to square with tens of thousands of narrative reviews highlighting how specific functions (or the lack of functions) made participating in education difficult and, moreover, distracted from learning.[721] Other comments belied a broad disillusionment with technology-reliant distance learning. Applying a low user rating was one of the few ways students could express frustration with ed-tech modes of learning.

"The team that made this [app] has barely touched it since it came out, this app has been unusable for years and continues to get worse as the hardware in my phone slows down. As a 14 year-old I can't afford to buy a new phone every few years."
– Student review of Google Classroom[CLXXI]

Despite the millions of terrible reviews, however, Google Classroom remained in app stores, even though other apps are investigated and sometimes removed when ratings are consistently low. (In the case of Google's app store, this was hardly surprising – the company controlling the store opted not to purge its own app and service. And Apple may have been reluctant to remove the app of a competing technology giant out of concern that the practice would be considered anti-competitive, an area of sensitivity for both Apple and Google, companies that wield extraordinary influence over mobile operating systems and applications.) It is significant that the negative reviews continued well after the 'review bombing' campaigns lost momentum. The action signals that people were dissatisfied enough with aspects of the Google Classroom utility to independently give it a low rating. The fact that the number of people using Google Classroom increased dramatically during a period when user ratings were very low signals that use of the service was compulsory. And indeed, for large numbers of students, use of the app was the only option for connecting to formal teaching and learning.

Google Classroom was hardly an outlier in terms of growth stemming from practical necessity. Similar user spikes were reported by other ed-tech providers, including hardware manufacturers, organizations offering learning management systems and small companies providing single-purpose learning applications. The e-learning platform Coursera, a privately held MOOC provider that had been struggling financially prior to the pandemic, provides a case in point. In August 2020, the company reported that it had seen global usage increase by 640 per cent between March and April 2020 when education institutions closed globally in response to the pandemic.[722] Coursera, like other commercial ed-tech companies, used the COVID-19 surge in usership to seek additional financing and take the company public. According to Bloomberg, Coursera priced its initial public offering (IPO) at "the top of the range" to raise over USD 500 million in early 2021.[723] After less than two weeks of public trading on the New York Stock Exchange, shares in the company had nearly doubled in price, providing a handsome return for founders and early investors. A headline from *Insider Higher Ed*, an education news outlet, announced "Coursera IPO seized on the right moment".[724] In April 2021, the market valuation of the company was over USD 7 billion. To put the size of this valuation in perspective, the combined government expenditure on *all* levels of education in the 28 countries classified as low-income economies[725] (home to over 700 million people[726]) was estimated at USD 12 billion in 2021.[727] While Coursera's stock price was doubling in value, UNESCO and other international organizations were documenting severe declines in public funding to education. In late February 2021, five weeks before Coursera's IPO "windfall",[728] UNESCO and the World Bank published a press release under the title "Two-thirds of poorer countries are cutting their education budgets at a time when they can least afford to".[729]

"This was a perfect time to go out and do an IPO to raise a significant amount of capital for [Coursera] and garner a really healthy valuation."

– Paxton Riter, CEO of iDesign[cxxxii]

The stratospheric growth both in user numbers and market capitalization seen at Coursera was typical of ed-tech companies in 2020 and 2021, including at non-Western companies. As the pandemic gathered steam in 2020, it was possible to find private and for-profit ed-tech companies

> While Coursera's stock price was doubling in value, UNESCO and other international organizations were documenting severe declines in public funding to education.

reaping financial benefits from the sudden shift to remote learning in most countries, often with a boost from governments that were recommending or even mandating the use of for-profit digital utilities providing education services and content. For instance, the India-based firm BYJU'S, sometimes considered the most widely used learning app in the world, added 13.5 million users in March and April 2020 and raised nearly USD 1.12 billion from private investors in the first three-quarters of 2020. The company garnered headlines by crossing the unicorn threshold – a valuation of USD 1 billion or higher – and becoming a rarer decacorn – a company with a valuation of over USD 10 billion. In early 2022, BYJU'S ranked among the most valuable private sector companies in India and employed over 9,000 people.[730] It was also considered by some to be a de facto national learning platform for public education during much of the pandemic.

Other examples from Indonesia, Kazakhstan, Pakistan, the USA and China help clarify the speed and scale of the growth experienced by private sector ed-tech companies. The following case studies provide illustrative snapshots of the rapid wealth, power and influence capture that was without historical parallel in education.

Indonesia spotlight – Ruangguru

In Indonesia, the country's most visible digital learning content provider, Ruangguru, saw downloads of its mobile app balloon by 44 per cent between the three months immediately before the COVID-19 pandemic (509,185 downloads from December 2019 to February 2020) and the first three months of the health crisis (1,077,096 downloads from March to May 2020).[731] The company's marketing partner, Dentsu, annouced that school closures and targeted advertising had helped Ruangguru achieve a "double-digit conversion rate" from free trial subscriptions to paid premium subscriptions.[732] During the pandemic, Ruangguru accelerated expansion into other countries, especially Thailand and Vietnam, and launched new products, including an English Academy and an AI-powered homework solver. In April 2021, at a moment when large numbers of schools in Asia and beyond remained closed, Ruangguru reported that it had secured a USD 55 million investment led by Tiger Global Management, a blue-chip technology investment firm based in the USA.[733] This funding secured its position as the largest education technology company in Southeast Asia and kicked off various acquisitions that extended into 2022. In June 2022, the news outlet Tech in Asia reported that the service was being accessed 200 million times a month and had 38 million users in total, making it a powerhouse digital property regardless of sector.[734] The company CEO and co-founder served as a special adviser to the president of Indonesia on innovation across various sectors, ministries and government bodies in 2020, exemplifying the mounting influence of ed-tech business leaders in the highest echelons of political leadership. Ruangguru provides an example of the way the pandemic propelled relatively modest commercial ed-tech enterprises into household names with national and regional reach.

Kazakhstan spotlight – Daryn Online

> During the COVID-19 crisis, commercial ed-tech services were awash in paid advertisements, and profits flowed to private owners and investors.

In Kazakhstan, Daryn Online, an educational platform established in 2019 offering digital classes for students in Grades 1–12, saw a surge in new users when schools closed in late March 2020. In April alone, the platform added 1.5 million new users in a country with 3.6 million primary and secondary school students.[735] The government facilitated this growth by working with telecommunications companies to zero-rate access to the website and its complementary app, such that no data fees were incurred by users accessing the service.[736] The company founder, 27-year-old Aibek Kuatbaev, credited the "explosive" growth of Daryn Online to the "support of the state" in an interview with Forbes.[737] He explained: "Thanks to the government, a huge increase of subscribers didn't cost us anything. Marketing and public relations which would have cost USD 8 million (KZT 3.5 billion) were not required, in the end."[738] This public sector assistance did not, however, stop the company from taking aggressive actions to monetize its surging user base of children and youth. Like other commercial ed-tech services during the COVID-19 crisis, Daryn Online was awash in paid advertisements and required users, typically minors, to consent to privacy policies that allowed the company to track and share personal information with third-party "partners and advertisers". Tracked information included fine-grained data related to search history, messages to teachers and classmates, and notes attached to homework.[739] Profits generated from these actions flowed to private owners and investors.

Pakistan spotlight – Taleemabad and public-private divisions

In Pakistan, Taleemabad, a for-profit app aligned with the national curriculum that uses cartoons and games to teach young children, reported a 660 per cent rise in use of the platform between the start of school closures in early 2020 and July 2020. In the same period, MUSE, another privately held digital education content provider in Pakistan, posted a 200 per cent rise in growth.[740] The government, like other governments in countries that did not have extensive public digital learning content, recommended these private ed-tech platforms and steered learners and their families towards them.[741] It is worth noting that the government of Pakistan also rolled out a public education television broadcast called Teleschool that was beamed to televisions nationwide.[742] As a state-controlled and state-provisioned broadcast, Teleschool's learning content was not reliant on advertising, nor was its development heavily steered by growth or profit motives. Rather, the guiding motivation was to facilitate learning. But when education was conducted over internet technologies, Pakistan, like many other governments, turned to commercial providers. It was a situation private sector entrepreneurs welcomed and took steps to sustain and enlarge. In July 2020, for instance, the British Broadcasting Corporation (BBC) reported that ed-tech "experts" were advising the government of Pakistan to invest in private sector partnerships and allow wide-scale testing of largely commercial digital solutions in Pakistan's nearly 200,000 public schools.[743]

> Learning content shared on radio or television broadcasts was commonly public, whereas online digital learning content was commonly private.

Pakistan was hardly unique in offering a public television broadcast for education and pointing people to a privately controlled digital learning platform during COVID-19 school closures. In many national contexts, the public-private division was distinguished by the type of technology used to provision remote learning – learning content shared on radio or television broadcasts was commonly public, whereas online digital learning content was commonly private. This appears to have reflected the reality that while many governments had on-the-shelf educational content for radio and television – or were able to create it quickly and in the midst of a pandemic – this was not the case for internet-based offerings. Digital education options were, in many cases, not public for the simple fact that there was no public digital learning content. Alternately, there may have been some digital content available, but, due either to its low quality, nascent nature or disorganization, it was not widely taken up or promoted by public authorities. Understandably, governments were not keen to steer people to public digital learning resources they knew were lacking in significant ways. It was, arguably, easier to steer them to higher quality commercial options – and also options that the government would not have to answer for because, at the end of the day, the provider was a private company.

USA spotlight – Chegg

In the USA, Chegg, a California-based company offering a wide range of education services, including homework assistance, exam prep, learning content and writing support, saw year-over-year revenues increase by 57 per cent in the first year of the pandemic. This equated to about USD 200 million in new money on a total revenue of USD 644 million. The company's subscriber base rocketed by 67 per cent to a total of 6.6 million global subscribers in the same period.[744] In a 2021 note to investors, Chegg's CEO stated that because the company was "built to scale online" it was able to meet the increased demand for online learning stemming from the pandemic "without missing a beat". Mirroring statements made by other ed-tech business leaders, the CEO clarified that the changes brought by the pandemic had accelerated efforts that "weren't on our roadmap at the start of the year". Such changes included increasing investments in e-commerce infrastructure for education, developing new content aimed at international markets and improving technology to stop users from sharing paid accounts. The company's chief financial officer summarized the 2020 earnings results: "By any measure, 2020 was our best year as a company. We far exceeded our initial expectations for revenue."[745] The company's share price soared from about USD 30 per share in mid-March 2020 to peaks of USD 110 per share in February 2021, an over threefold gain. Chegg's market valuation briefly exceeded USD 11 billion, making it another ed-tech corporation that morphed from a unicorn into a mightier decacorn during the pandemic.[746] The company's revenue growth continued in 2021, rising an additional 20 per cent to exceed USD 775 million in total.[747]

In a May 2022 podcast, titled "Educational technology in the age of COVID-19", Chegg's vice-president of engineering noted that globalization has made it easier for Chegg and other commercial ed-tech companies to enter new foreign markets quickly with scalable learning platforms and content. When prompted to provide guidance to entrepreneurs, he noted that the conditions brought about by the pandemic provided the right kind of set-up for "hypergrowth", adding, "My advice – now is the time to open an educational technology company."[748] In statements, Chegg has noted that, as an ed-tech firm, it is driven by a desire to "provide services that create overwhelming value for academic and professional learners". In the same statement, however, it added that its top priority is to "deliver on financial goals".[749] This guiding monetary obligation is not unique to Chegg. It is shared by commercial ed-tech firms regardless of their location, areas of focus, size or reach. It is simply the logic of any for-profit firm – the creation of value for investors. This commercial logic stood in opposition to the community and human rights objectives that usually guided public education offline.

China spotlight – private sector growth and subsequent regulation

Perhaps ground zero for soaring private sector growth in ed-tech was in China, home to approximately 340 million learners between pre-primary and tertiary education levels, most of them locked out of physical education institutions as the pandemic spread in early 2020 and periodically after this as the virus flared in different localities into 2022.⁷⁵⁰ Ed-tech was a growth sector in China before 2020, but the health crisis launched it to new heights. Between 2018 and 2020, the ed-tech market grew close to 120 per cent, from a USD 22 billion industry to one valued at USD 48 billion.⁷⁵¹ The school closures triggered by COVID-19 caused the number of daily active users of educational applications to increase by nearly 50 per cent between 2019 and 2020, a jump that commentators called "staggering" and "a windfall rarely seen in any industry".⁷⁵² Indeed, massive investments poured into ed-tech firms. Venture capital firms such as Sequoia and Softbank, sovereign wealth funds such as Singapore's Temasek, multinational technology corporations such as Tencent and Alibaba, private equity firms such as Jack Ma's Yunfeng Capital, hedge funds, small-operation financial speculators and individual investors alike directed money into ed-tech companies serving the Chinese market.⁷⁵³

CompassList, a market research firm focused on technology start-up companies, estimated that nearly CNY 50 billion (approximately USD 7.7 billion) flowed into the Chinese K–12 ed-tech sector in 2020 alone.⁷⁵⁴ This amount was estimated to be more than the cumulative capital inflows of the past decade.⁷⁵⁵ Analysis by CompassList indicated that over 80,000 ed-tech start-ups were launched in China in 2020.⁷⁵⁶ As in other countries, ed-tech companies, boasting soaring user numbers and other impressive metrics of growth, such as page views, monthly visits and so forth, attracted unprecedented investment. Yuanfudao, an established online education platform that provides tutoring services primarily to Chinese primary and secondary students, raised over USD 2.2 billion after ten months of the pandemic.⁷⁵⁷ Near the end of 2020, the company was estimated to be worth USD 15.5 billion, making it the most valuable ed-tech firm in the world at the time, according to PitchBook, a financial data company.⁷⁵⁸ Other powerhouse Chinese ed-tech companies also used the pandemic to fuel fundraising. Zuoyebang, a company offering online courses, live lessons and homework assistance, raised nearly USD 3 billion in 2020 on an estimated value of USD 10 billion.⁷⁵⁹ According to the company, the service was reaching 170 million active users monthly, and 50 million people were using the service each day. In late 2020, Zuoyebang's paid live stream classes reached more than 10 million users – the equivalent of the entire K–12 student population in Germany. Near the end of 2020, 8 of the top 14 highly capitalized and privately held ed-tech companies in the world were based in China.⁷⁶⁰

Soaring valuations of Chinese ed-tech companies did not, however, always signal profitability. In fact, it almost never did. Industry researchers estimated that the ed-tech start-ups reliably generating profit represented just a sliver of the market, only 5 per cent of all ed-tech companies. Yu Minhong, an ed-tech investor and founder of the New Oriental Education and Technology

Ads for commercial ed-tech firms were ubiquitous in China starting in 2020. They appeared on billboards, in popular television shows, on social media feeds and in a wide array of other digital and online environments. One large ed-tech company was a sponsor of the 2022 Olympic Games.

Group, told CompassList, "I still haven't seen a sustainable business model in the online education sector. To earn one cent, companies have to spend two cents first."[761] Much of the money raised by these companies was funnelled into advertising. Ads for ed-tech firms were ubiquitous in China starting in 2020. They appeared on billboards, in popular television shows, on social media feeds and in a wide array of other digital and online environments. Yuanfudao, for example, doubled marketing expenditures between 2019 and 2020, from CNY 500 million (USD 77 million) to CNY 1 billion (USD 155 million).[762] The company also became an official sponsor of the 2022 Winter Olympic Games held in China, joining long-established companies like Intel, Toyota, Air China, Samsung and Coca-Cola. Sceptical observers called the advertising juggernaut a "cash-burning competition" and documented signs of a speculative bubble.[763] Education professionals noted that money pouring into advertising was money that did not fund the development of improved learning content or new resources and technology to support students and teachers. It was instead money that flowed out of the education sector at a time of major educational disruptions. Nevertheless, money kept rushing into – and quickly out of – Chinese ed-tech firms into 2021.

In mid-2021, the Chinese government – concerned about the influx of financial speculation in ed-tech and the rising cost of digital education amid widespread perceptions that supplemental education, often delivered via ed-tech, was necessary for academic success – made a major policy change. Authorities banned companies and other entities that teach school curriculum subjects from making profits, raising capital, listing on stock exchanges worldwide or accepting foreign investment.[764] This policy shift, announced by the General Office of the country's Central Committee and the General Office of the State Council, effectively forced ed-tech firms to operate on a not-for-profit basis. The restrictions appear to have enjoyed strong public support and were, according to the government, designed to control the often excessive out-of-pocket costs parents incurred to supplement the education of their children. According to a 2018 estimate, Chinese parents were spending an average of USD 17,500 per year on extracurricular tutoring intended to confer competitive advantages to their children, and some were paying as much as USD 43,500 per year.[765] A separate 2020 report estimated that the average Chinese family spent 11 per cent of annual family expenses on education services, much of it offered by for-profit ed-tech providers.[766] This outlay was assumed to create disincentives for families to have children at a time when the Chinese government was expressing concerns over declining birth rates. Government officials explained the new policy as an attempt to bring education costs under control and "reduce the [financial] burden of students enrolled in compulsory education".[767] The legislation was widely referred to as the Double Reduction policy, a shorthand for the longer policy name: "Opinions on Further Reducing the Workload of Students in Compulsory Education and the Burden of Off-Campus Tutoring".[768]

Ed-tech business leaders and entrepreneurs called the policy U-turn a "worst-case scenario" and heavy-handed intervention that would stifle innovation and paralyse a nascent industry that was gaining momentum.[769] But the government was resolute, rationalizing its intervention as a mechanism to tame an out-of-control shadow education industry that had been "severely hijacked by capital" and was threatening "the nature of education as welfare".[770] Commentators supporting the government action noted that the government's "strike" against the ed-tech industry was designed to rein in unscrupulous practices.[771] These included false advertising and complex schemes companies used to attract new users, such as offering learners heavily subsidized subscriptions to online classes on a trial basis and making the fees excessively expensive once the trial period ended. Ye Liu, a sociologist who studies educational inequality in China, interpreted the policy shift as an instrument, however blunt, to "respond to the concerns of the poor" burdened by the perception that they need to spend large sums of money to provide educational advantages to their children. Michael Norris, the leader of a consumer and technology research organization focused on China, saw the "crackdown" as strategy to eradicate "tech-mediated harm" in education.[772] By any analysis, the decision had immediate and sweeping financial consequences. Many of the country's largest ed-tech firms saw their market values plunge by around 75 per cent, more or less overnight.[773] Analysts at Goldman Sachs quickly adjusted their valuation of China's largely ed-tech-based private education market from USD 100 billion to USD 24 billion.[774] The policy action in China was a rare instance of government intervention to pump the breaks on the privatization of education services that accompanied the forced switch to digital modes of teaching and learning during the pandemic.

The Double Reduction policy action in China was a rare instance of government intervention to pump the breaks on the privatization of education services that accompanied the forced switch to digital modes of teaching and learning during the pandemic.

"The surge in EdTech spending brought on by COVID-19 is expected to recalibrate to a longer-term integration of digital technologies, and transition to much higher adoption of online education over the coming years."

– Patrick Brothers, co-CEO at HolonIQ[xxxiii]

The unprecedented growth experienced by private sector companies featured in the country spotlights were far from outliers. Almost every country saw select ed-tech corporations boom during pandemic school closures, even if the unique regulations instituted by China dramatically curbed financial speculation and investment in the sector.

Act 2: FROM PROMISES TO REALITY | 279

The year 2021 provided regular reminders that the ed-tech industry was continuing to rocket to new financial height. Following Coursera's example, numerous ed-tech firms listed on public stock market exchanges. Examples included Duolingo,[775] PowerSchool,[776] Nerdy[777] and Instructure,[778] among others. A November 2021 headline in PitchBook, a broker of financial data and insights, read: "Edtech backers rewarded as IPO pipeline heats up". PitchBook estimated that so much venture capital had flowed into the sector that the number of ed-tech unicorns, had nearly doubled between 2020 and 2021.[779]

> When the MOOC provider Udemy completed its IPO, this single commercial ed-tech company was worth more than the world's largest fund dedicated to supporting under-resourced education systems globally for the next five years.

Larger technology companies that counted schools and ministries of education as customers also saw ballooning growth and profit throughout 2020 and 2021. Zoom, for example, documented a thirtyfold profit increase in a single year of the pandemic, from USD 22 million in 2019 to USD 672 million in 2020.[780] Several MOOC providers, in addition to Coursera, experienced comparable "exponential growth".[781] Class Central, a MOOC aggregator, had 9 million users visiting the site at the end of April 2020 compared to just 500,000 at the end of February 2020, the last pre-pandemic month in most countries.[782] Udemy, a for-profit MOOC provider offering a large repository of learning and training courses, saw its consumer base grow by 425 per cent in the weeks following the start of the COVID-19 crisis.[783] New users came onto the platform faster in India, Italy and Spain than the USA, where the company is based, exemplifying the global reach of ed-tech providers.[784] In late 2021, Udemy completed, according to Bloomberg, an ambitious and successful IPO, raising over USD 420 million at a valuation of USD 4 billion.[785] This USD 4 billion valuation figure was approximately the same amount governments and corporations cumulatively pledged to the Global Partnership for Education during its 2021 fundraising summit.[786] This meant that a single commercial ed-tech company was worth more than the world's largest fund dedicated to supporting under-resourced education systems globally for the next five years.

"We believe for-profit businesses in the education industry are well-positioned to benefit from the global theme of rising demand for advanced education."
–Pedro Palandrani, director of research, Global X Education ETF[CXXXIV]

Apart from enriching individual companies, the pandemic cemented ed-tech as a distinct branch of financial markets and one ripe for speculation and growth. Soon after the start of the COVID-19 crisis, two different exchange-traded funds (ETFs) dedicated to ed-tech were launched: Global X Education ETF (EDUT) was listed on the Nasdaq Exchange in July 2020, and Rize Education Tech and Digital Learning ETF (LERN) was listed on the London Stock Exchange a few months later in September 2020.[787] These funds came on the heels of an earlier ed-tech fund, Edutainment Equity Fund, launched by Credit Suisse in September 2019, which saw its share prices double between March 2020 and early 2021.[788] These financial instruments were noteworthy because they offered investors an easy way to bet on ed-tech without having to select individual corporations. The funds further provided financial professionals tools to consolidate interest in the continued growth and proliferation of the ed-tech industry. The prospectuses and market materials announcing the new ed-tech ETFs were not shy about identifying the pandemic as a catalyst for short-term growth as well as attractive long-term gains. A company brochure on the Global X Education ETF called COVID-19-induced school closures "the most immediate use case" for ed-tech and projected that "social distancing will remain a consistent theme even after the pandemic runs its course". The brochure further elaborated an investment case for ed-tech on the grounds that education expenditures might gradually shift away from schooling as a place-based experience and towards digital experiences. It stated that virtual classrooms were a promising business opportunity because they "remove the costly physical aspects of some education mediums" and would "exclude high-cost budget items like room, board and transportation". The brochure concluded that the global education industry was "ripe for transformation" and offered unique "opportunities for for-profit companies" that investors could "access" through the ETF.[789] Ben Williamson, a scholar of education, highlighted the significance of ed-tech ETFs in his *Code Acts in Education* blog. He explained that because ETFs act as "gatekeepers" and define which companies from the wider ed-tech sector are eligible for inclusion in the funds, they are "shaping the edtech market". With the ever-increasing influence of ed-tech, Williamson argued, ETFs such as Global X Education and Rize Learning have, to a significant degree, "positioned themselves to reshape education itself".[790]

> COVID-19 created a split screen view of financing directed to education – on one screen, capital was flooding into commercial and profit-oriented ed-tech corporations, while on the other, public sector financing of education was slowing and, in some countries, collapsing.

The rapid rise in financial gain and power for private and for-profit ed-tech companies during the pandemic stood in stark contrast to the chronic underfunding of public education globally. COVID-19 created a split screen view of financing directed to education. On one screen, capital was flooding into profit-oriented ed-tech corporations. On the other, public sector financing of education was slowing, and in some deeply indebted and low-income countries, it was collapsing. In 2020 and 2021, as the pandemic spread unsparingly, emergency spending to prop up various sectors and services rarely supported education. UNESCO estimates that less than 1 per cent of public money in COVID-19 stimulus packages was directed to education.[791] Simultaneously, however, massive sums of private investment poured into commercial ed-tech companies, such that many of them doubled or tripled in value, generating large profits for financial speculators and other investors.

> At the beginning of 2022, the market valuations of just two of the largest publicly traded technology companies, Apple and Microsoft, exceeded the annual expenditure on education and training for the entire world.

It is difficult to overstate the financial power that technology companies involved in ed-tech amassed during the pandemic, even if investments cooled considerably as the pandemic and government stimulus spending wound down starting in 2022. At the beginning of 2022, the market valuations of just two of the largest publicly traded technology companies, Apple and Microsoft, exceeded the annual expenditure on education and training for the *entire world*, projected at USD 5.4 trillion or around 6 per cent of the global GDP. In early 2022, Apple became the first-ever company to reach a market valuation of USD 3 trillion.[792] It took Apple 42 years to reach a USD 1 trillion valuation (1976 to 2018), an additional 48 months to add another USD 1 trillion (August 2018 to August 2020), and a mere 16 months during the COVID-19 pandemic (August 2020 to January 2022) to add a further USD 1 trillion.[793] According to the World Bank, only six countries in the world have GDPs over USD 3 trillion: the USA, China, Japan, Germany, the UK and India.[794] Apple and other technology companies with trillion or multibillion USD valuations have openly identified education as a growth market and a driver of future revenue. Their financial influence is without comparison.

CORPORATE DEPENDENCIES AND REDUCED GOVERNMENT OVERSIGHT

> The rapid adoption of ed-tech deepened the education sector's reliance on private providers of technology whose growing influence was undermining education as an inclusive and equitably distributed public good.

Across countries, the rapid adoption of ed-tech for remote learning during the pandemic deepened the education sector's reliance on private providers of technology products and services. School closures pushed education into corporately controlled ed-tech ecosystems, accelerating the privatization of teaching and learning. As remote, technology-first learning models stretched from early 2020 into 2022 and, in rare instances, early 2023, it became increasingly evident that the growing influence of private providers in education was, in many contexts, undermining education as an inclusive and equitably distributed public good guaranteed by the state.

In 2016, Kishore Singh, the then UN Special Rapporteur on the right to education, cautioned that a growing reliance on digital technology risked pushing education towards heightened or even exclusive reliance on corporate for-profit providers. In a 2016 report to the Human Rights Council, he observed that the education sector's mounting and misguided faith in the ability of technology to solve complex educational challenges quickly, cheaply and easily was catalysing the commercialization of education. The report warned that mainstream models of online learning would, if left unchecked, "weaken public provision of education" and, in lockstep, "promote the privatization and commercialization of public education". The report went on to advise that digital changes to education should not be "allowed to erode the concept of education as a public good". The Special Rapporteur recommended more "prescriptive, prohibitive and punitive regulations on the use of digital technology in education" in order to prevent education from becoming another consumer good dictated by market logics. While Singh expressed worries that "distance education formats" might "undermine human values in education" and chip away at commitments to assure free and high-quality public education for all, he imagined that this would be a gradual process.[795] Little did he imagine that a global pandemic, lurking just around the corner, would vastly accelerate and give global scope to the privatization trends he foresaw.

The ascent of private and for-profit ed-tech providers during the pandemic was met with deep concern in the education community. Many school leaders, teachers and education scholars felt that new technology-first and technology-dependent models of teaching and learning were dismantling norms that place education beyond market logics of services, products, profit and loss. These models, they worried, were subverting education's special status as a public good and a human right and risked contorting teaching and learning into commercial services and products that would ebb and flow according to the whims of markets. The UN Special Rapporteur on the right to education in 2020, Koumbou Boly Barry, warned early in the pandemic that "the massive arrival of private actors through digital technology should be considered as a major danger for education systems and the right to education for all in the long term".[796] In a 2022 report on the impact of digitalization on education, Boly Barry again concluded that the privatization dangers she had flagged at the outset of the pandemic were no longer on the horizon but were rather a here-and-now reality. She observed that education technology companies were "embedding private logics" in public institutions of education. She further noted that public education was likely to face increasing pressure from large technology corporations and rich philanthropists that "aim to find ways of combining education and profit".[797]

Academics, too, were quick to sound the alarm about the tech industry's "pandemic profiteering", claiming it was "morally unjustifiable for tech companies to walk away from the pandemic with massive profits while schools are burdened with debt".[798] Ben Williamson observed that commercial actors were leveraging the health crisis to "actively reorganize public education as a market for its products, platforms and services" with a view to reshape public education around private providers and consolidate gains in market share resulting from the shock of school closures.[799] On occasion, even ed-tech business leaders expressed similar views. The former CEO of a multinational technology services and consulting company based in India, for instance, called for a halt to celebrations of value creation in the ed-tech industry by asking: "Is it right to start seeing education as a business for people to invest in for huge returns? Are the days of 'Education for Good' getting replaced by 'Education for Profit'?"[800]

"In many cases, the beneficiaries of the digitalization of education may well be businesses, not students or society."

– Koumbou Boly Barry, UN Special Rapporteur on the right to education[cxxxv]

> Governments sometimes established formal contracts with private providers of digital education services, but more often, they cleared regulatory pathways to provide ed-tech companies permissions and allowances that afforded them wide access to students, teachers and families.

In some countries, the turn towards the private sector for ed-tech services threw into question the role of states and governments to assure the right to education in the context of the pandemic. While some governments kept a steady and controlling hand on the provision of education by rolling out public, free and open online learning supports for students and teachers while simultaneously developing plans to reopen schools quickly, others found themselves stepping back from direct provision and towards new roles as brokers for large companies. Governments sometimes established formal contracts with private providers of digital education services to help fulfil right-to-education obligations, but more often, they cleared regulatory pathways to provide ed-tech companies permissions and allowances that afforded them wide access to students, teachers and families. In many countries, the shift to online learning amounted to little more than ministries of education instructing students and teachers to start using 'free' commercial services provided by private sector businesses. A study conducted by Human Rights Watch identified 163 ed-tech products and services formally recommended by 49 countries, the vast majority of which were created and controlled by non-government entities, usually for-profit businesses.[801]

This established dependencies that linked the right to education to the operation and health of private businesses. When control over education exchange was offloaded to corporations such as Microsoft, Google, Facebook (Meta) and Zoom, problems with these providers could – and did – disrupt the learning of millions. This was seen, for example, when Zoom ceased to work temporarily when students in the northern hemisphere returned to distance learning after the summer break in 2020. The outage, associated with a surge in educational use of the utility, prevented students around the world from accessing synchronous instruction.[802] While the issue was quickly resolved, it demonstrated the hazards of building so much educational infrastructure around a single privately controlled platform. Zoom declined to specify the cause of the outage, an option that would not have been available to most public providers of essential services.

Similarly, in October 2021, Facebook and its multiple subsidiaries, including Messenger, WhatsApp and Instagram, went dark for multiple hours, momentarily cutting off millions of learners from education services that relied on these products as a technical backbone.

Around the world, careful public sector oversight was often missing when teaching and learning moved online. Many governments simply hoped private service providers would be able to support the weight of public education, and when these providers encountered problems, there was little governments could do beyond hope they would become operational again quickly. Recognizing their precarious reliance on commercial ed-tech companies, some governments actively assisted them by, for example, brushing away regulatory barriers or adopting flexible interpretations of existing legislation intended to assure the online safety and data protection of children. In the UK, laws passed to ensure that commercial interests do not outweigh children's interests, as well as rules and agreements to prevent children from receiving marketing and advertising messages during their learning, were not rigorously applied to ed-tech providers during the pandemic, according to analysis by the Digital Futures Commission. The commission found that while it was generally thought that the rules, packaged in a statutory code of practice, "would apply to all EdTech", there was "ample leeway for EdTech providers to judge their products out of scope" of the relevant legislation.[803] It is telling that many governments did not announce until 2022, after schools had largely reopened, that powerful commercial ed-tech providers such as Google and ClassDojo were out of compliance with legislation that existed before 2020, such as the General Data Protection and Regulation (GDPR) laws active in Europe since 2018. Citing GDPR violations, regulators in Denmark, for example, issued a ban on the use of Google products in public schools in July 2022, well after the peak of educational disruptions wrought by the pandemic.[804]

Countries came to recognize that their heavy or sometimes singular reliance on private providers introduced risks that were challenging to regulate in educational contexts. Reports that commercial online learning platforms were being flooded with inappropriate advertising, featuring, in some instances, violent or pornographic content, soared in lockstep with the pandemic-era shift to digital learning.[805] So, too, did privacy breaches. But because private providers of educational content were often shielded from the rules and regulations that would normally apply to digital services providers, they rarely faced government scrutiny over privacy controls. Learners remained connected to these services, despite their problems, because there was rarely a viable public alternative.

"We don't monetize the things we create. We monetize users."

– Andy Rubin, creator of Android[cxxvii]

If governments were paying for an ed-tech solution, they might rightly expect to have some say over its design, use and terms of service, but because many of these services were free to use, governments found themselves in a weak negotiating position.

Countries' reliance on 'free' ed-tech services, such as Google Classroom, often weakened public control over them. If governments were paying for an ed-tech solution, they might rightly expect to have some say over its design, use and terms of service. Yet because many of these services were free to use, governments found themselves in a weak negotiating position. Requests directed to ed-tech providers, often enormous multinational companies, tended to be framed as favours rather than directives. The only real stick governments had was regulation, but rules proved difficult to enforce even when governments were motivated to do so. In some instances, this was because ed-tech companies operated from outside the countries where their services were being used, complicating issues of liability and compliance. In other instances, it was because existing regulations were years, if not decades, behind the new technologies that were being deployed during the pandemic for educational purposes. Compounding this challenge, corporations devised terms and conditions and adopted other practices to skirt existing regulations.

In instances when school systems did pay for services, they often found themselves buying credits, licences and subscriptions rather than digital products they could own, alter and use for unlimited durations. They were, in effect, renters and not owners and, as such, they had limited options to modify or optimize the technology, platform or content being used for education. Customization features that did exist, often enabled little more than cosmetic changes, alterations to a colour-scheme for instance. The subscription payments, or 'rent', due at regular intervals, had to be indefinitely paid or the service could be shut down with a flip of a switch. Prices were often assessed per student, giving ed-tech companies financial incentives to grow quickly and lock in existing customers.

Calls for Zoom to build a separate education-focused product using its core technology went unheeded.

Private companies that supported education for much of the pandemic frequently resisted making major structural and design changes to adapt widely used products and services to better accommodate teaching and learning. Educators often had clear ideas about what extended functionality and options would make general purpose applications more supportive of synchronous instruction at a distance. As one example, early in the pandemic, teachers and other educational stakeholders pushed Zoom to build a separate education-focused product using its core technology.[806] While Zoom could support remote instruction, its design and functionality tended to reflect the needs of white-collar businesses rather than schools. The requests coming from the education sector went largely unheeded. Anne Keehn, Zoom's global lead for education, told the publication *Fast Company* that the corporation's core priority was to educate teachers on the features Zoom has, not to develop new software for specific use in educational contexts.[807]

Even when companies showed a willingness to make changes that would strengthen the educational utility of products and services, this was not always possible due to the multiple layers of technology and corporate dependencies. During the pandemic, huge numbers of ed-tech providers relied on a single company for the cloud computing and data processing that powered their respective services: Amazon. While many people think of Amazon as an online retailer, its primary profit engine is a subsidiary called Amazon Web Services (AWS). In 2020, AWS generated 60 per cent of Amazon's operating profits even though it accounted for only 12 per cent of the corporation's total revenue.[808] The dominant position that AWS holds in the education sector is, according to education scholars Ben Williamson, Kalervo Gulson, Carolo Perrotta and Kevin Witzenberger, akin to a state-like corporation that influences education through a connective architecture of cloud computing, infrastructure and platform technologies.[809] These scholars detail how AWS, aided by the education sector's increased reliance on digital services triggered by the pandemic, cemented itself as an "essential technical substrate" of teaching, learning and educational administration. Because AWS provides the technical backbone for most ed-tech solutions, even those that might not seem to have any outward connection to Amazon, the company has asserted itself as a "cloud landlord for the education sector" capable of "governing the ways schools, colleges and edtech companies can access and use cloud services and digital data, while promoting a transformational vision of education in which its business interests might thrive".[810]

While the ways that public education was platformed by private and for-profit ed-tech companies during the pandemic has been well documented, what is less discussed is that many of these companies were themselves platformed by AWS. Amazon controlled the hosting, storage, processing and analytic tools necessary for smaller companies to operate. This established, as Williamson and his co-authors explain, new types of reliance and technical lock-ins, whereby functionalities offered by third-party education platform companies could "only exist according to the contractual rules and cloud capacities and constraints of AWS".[811] These rules, capacities and constraints, while capable of accommodating education, were hardly optimized for it. AWS provides foundational digital services to organizations across a wide range of sectors and is therefore not honed for education specifically. Yet because AWS provides the technical foundations for so much ed-tech, it exerted enormous influence on education during the pandemic and is in a commanding position to continue influencing the digital futures of education beyond the pandemic. According to Williamson and his co-authors, the "infrastructural rearrangements" that thrust AWS into a central role in the education sector have solidified to such an extent that they would be extremely expensive and challenging to reverse, making AWS "the default digital architecture for governing education globally".[812] Never before has a for-profit corporation, often operating outside the authority of schools, universities, ministries of education and sometimes even states, played host to so many services and so much of the data that make education possible in digital spaces. As recently as 2010, schools and universities commonly controlled their own digital architecture – the servers, hard drives and processors that supported websites, student databases, learning management systems, teacher portals and so forth. But these services were outsourced to AWS via a constellation of commercial and consumer-facing ed-tech solutions before and especially during the pandemic. Education quite literally slipped out of the hands of public authorities and into the laps of technology corporations accountable to private investors.

"The governance of public sector and its institutions is becoming increasingly dependent on the standards and conditions set by multinational big tech corporations like Amazon and Google."
– Ben Williamson, Kalervo N. Gulson, Carlo Perrotta and Kevin Witzenberger, education scholars[lxxxvii]

Due to their outsize influence, large ed-tech companies tended to have an upper hand over governments in shaping the legal terms and agreements that facilitated the rapid deployment of remote education services in response to school closures. School systems tended to have limited familiarity purchasing digital products and services and would often sign a template agreement provided by a corporate provider rather than insist on their own agreement. Typically, government contracts with outside and private sector vendors would contain various protections and restrictions including, for example, carefully worded clauses concerning issues such as accessibility, data protection, safety and liability. But public authorities commonly lacked pre-prepared agreements for digital education services. These agreements tended only to cover the provision of material goods that schools and universities were more accustomed to bidding and purchasing. Unsurprisingly, when a corporate ed-tech provider provided the base contract for a legal agreement, it tended to afford the company generous privileges and protections, including limited responsibility for problems such as privacy breaches.

But more often, institutional contractual processes were bypassed altogether, due to the time pressures imposed by the pandemic. In their place, individual students and their families were asked, if not explicitly instructed, to enter into direct agreements with private ed-tech providers and other general-service technology companies. According to research conducted by Human Rights Watch, these agreements commonly included language that required users to forfeit their data and privacy.[813] This put students in the unusual of position of having to consent to legal agreements to continue their education, including students who were too young to have sufficient reading skills to comprehend multiple pages of terms and conditions of use.

> As education systems became more and more reliant on the decisions and designs of ed-tech providers, the public authorities were left with very little control over what education could or should look like for students in digital environments.

With large volumes of student and teacher data moving into various proprietary and private systems due to prolonged school closures, it became harder for schools to break away from using them. Education systems around the world became more and more reliant on the decisions and designs of ed-tech providers, and public authorities were left with very little control over what education could or should look like for students in digital environments. These decisions increasingly rested with corporate executives working to generate value for private investors as a first-order priority. While profit motives can – and within the context of the pandemic, almost certainly did – motivate companies to innovate and build superior ed-tech products beneficial to learners and teachers, these were motives that had, in most national contexts, been kept at arm's length within the education sector. It was a sector where, historically, cooperation, public investment and trust, rather than the logic of business competition, had been the main engine of national efforts to assure and expand the human right to education. The closure of schools and the shift to ed-tech during the pandemic turned this dynamic on its head.

> *"New kinds of technical arrangements, introduced as temporary emergency solutions but positioned as persistent transformations, have affected how teaching is enacted, and established private and commercial providers as essential infrastructural intermediaries between educators and students."*
>
> – Ben Williamson and Anna Hogan, education scholars[cxxxviii]

CULTIVATING CONSUMER BEHAVIOUR IN STUDENTS, FAMILIES AND TEACHERS

Among the most profound impacts of the pandemic shift to ed-tech was the amplification and normalization of consumer behaviour in education. Around the world, students, schools, teachers and families were positioned as customers or providers of educational goods and services operating in a competitive marketplace. Education that had been previously understood and treated as a largely collective and community endeavour, sustained with public resources and services that were shared and managed at national, state and local levels, was often recast as a private commercial good when it moved online. Corporations marketed and sold a wide variety of 'solutions' to support learning and knowledge development in order to generate profit. As this occurred, community control and stewardship over education were weakened and, in some instances, evaporated completely.

The strong associations between the digitalization of learning and the entry of commercial logics in education were well documented before the start of the COVID-19 pandemic. Observers noted that when education moved into digital spaces, it often took the form of a transactional client-consumer relationship. Many for-profit ed-tech providers were accustomed to seeing digital education as a marketplace where buyers and suppliers negotiated terms and prices, like other digital marketplaces, such as those for entertainment. Albert Hitchcock, the chief operating and technology officer at Pearson, one of the world's largest corporations focused on education, explained in 2018 that the company's main mission was to "transform education through the digital medium" and that this would be accomplished by delivering "a competitive digital experience" to "consumers" and "institutional customers", where 'consumers' meant learners, and 'institutional customers' meant schools and universities. Inspired by other platform businesses such as Netflix and Spotify, Pearson, along with many of its competitors, sought to develop a "highly scalable" and "global" digital destination to provide education to millions of learners on a fee basis.[814]

With these business plans unfolding in plain sight, human rights advocates called critical attention to the cosiness between the digitalization of education and its commercialization. In 2016, for instance, the UN Special Rapporteur on the right to education Kishore Singh warned that the use of digital technologies in formal learning was cultivating "more consumer-oriented attitudes" towards education. He further explained that the global ed-tech actors were treating teaching and learning as profit-driven activities.[815] These trends accelerated greatly when schools closed globally due to the pandemic and pushed education online, often exclusively. Technology-mediated education was no longer a choice. Largely unregulated digital spaces, predominately controlled by corporations and governed by market logics, suddenly went from merely supplementing or complementing public education to upholding it. With little warning, education lurched away from a known and usually trusted public institution – a local school – and into a space that felt more like a chaotic shopping bazaar than a tightly regulated service guaranteed by the state. By mid-2022, Koumbou Boly Barry, the UN Special Rapporteur who succeeded Kishore Singh, explained that the digitalization of education had become so closely linked to the marketization of education that, for many observers, the two could no longer be separated.[816]

"Education policy and education reform are no longer simply a battleground of ideas, they are a financial sector, increasingly infused by and driven by the logic of profit."

– Stephen Ball, professor of education, University College London[cxxxx]

The commercialization and consumerization of education during the pandemic was facilitated by a presumption that the ideal model for digital learning was each student using a unique device, one that would not be shared with others. Scheduling for online distance education reinforced this view. Start times for synchronous online classes routinely overlapped for students in different grades, effectively forcing families to have unique devices for children in different grade levels. If there was only one device and classes were running concurrently, at least one child would be unable to participate. This contrasted with the staggered schedules that were characteristic of television and radio broadcasts of educational content, such that content targeting primary grade level students played at a different time of day than content targeting secondary grade level students, a scheduling arrangement that allowed children at different grade levels to share a single television or radio and still participate in remote learning. The pedagogies of digital distance learning also tended to buttress understandings that every student should have a unique device. The instruction offered in applications, platforms and synchronous learning spaces used during the pandemic almost always took it for granted that one learner was using a device, rather than two or more learners, even though there are digital pedagogies to support multiple learners that are using a single device or screen concurrently – pedagogies that can reinforce notions that learning is a social process, relational and most effectively conducted with others.

Reflecting these assumptions, governments around the world launched huge procurement programmes to equip school-age children with dedicated devices, such as Google Chromebooks. The one-to-one ratio of students per device helped turn learners into individual consumers that could be tracked, profiled and ultimately targeted with marketing and advertisements, if not necessarily inside learning spaces, then outside of them, where students invariably navigated. This arrangement formed the basis of a complex global ecosystem of digital advertising that, across industries and sectors, was estimated to be worth over USD 375 billion in 2020 and over USD 450 billion in 2021.[817] It established profit incentives for ed-tech providers to attract as many users as possible and keep them engaged for the longest possible durations. Quite predictably, this in turn led to a rush of marketing to get learners to sign up for and start using commercial ed-tech apps. Money spent on marketing, educational professionals were quick to observe, was money not spent on improving digital education offerings. It flowed instead to companies that sold digital advertising.

> In the digital space, purchasing education had never been easier, with families around the world in possession of devices connected to app stores that were seamlessly linked to bank accounts and credit cards.

The shift to connected technology further presented families ways to instantly purchase learning content and services outright for individual children, an activity that had certainly been possible offline but tended to require significantly more time and effort, such as finding, engaging and scheduling an in-person tutor. In the digital space, though, purchasing education had never been easier, with families around the world in

possession of devices connected to app stores that were linked to bank accounts and credit cards. A click and a swipe could initiate a paid education service or, alternately, a free service that generated profit through data harvesting and targeted advertising.

Since at least the 1990s, the organization and technical architecture of the internet has been gradually optimized to treat users as consumers and to spin off profit from their online activity. It should not have come as a surprise, then, that when the internet played host to education at a global scale during the pandemic, learning became governed by logics and technical processes that tended to view students as 'commodities' that could be monetized. Although there were sites and platforms that offered something akin to a digital commons for education and knowledge dissemination, Wikipedia being perhaps the most prominent example, these were outliers. The default ed-tech experience tended instead to treat learners as individual consumers and to extract profit from them in exchange for services.

This model for digital education stood in contrast to broadcast modes of remote learning also used during the pandemic. The broadcast model tended to anticipate collective use of hardware, such as televisions or radios, and presented fewer options to commercialize and profit from education. The challenges of individualizing users and treating them as distinct consumers meant that education delivered via broadcast technology tended to be less commercial. While education broadcasts on television and radio sometimes featured advertisements, these were targeted to a general audience and not aimed with laser precision at individuals whose personal data had been harvested, as was typical in many online education environments.

Similarly, when education is conducted in face-to-face settings, students are rarely treated as consumers. Brick-and-mortar public schools – both public and private – usually have rules in place to prevent actors, whether those embedded in education or outside of it, from overtly treating students and their families as consumers and submitting education to the full force of business logics. Even the most market-oriented for-profit schools do not, for example, affix screens to the desks of individual students and intermittently play personalized advertisements, as YouTube and other commercial online platforms hosting learning content do routinely.

"'Personalized learning' on a machine is an oxymoron."

– Diane Ravitch, education historian[cxi]

With masses of learners newly in possession of connected hardware during the pandemic, ed-tech providers seized an unprecedented opportunity to market and provide services to students and their families directly, bypassing schools. This represented a shift from standard pre-pandemic modes of operation. Before COVID-19, ed-tech companies, especially the bigger and more established ones, largely transacted with institutions, namely schools, school districts or national ministries of education. While institutional agreements helped ed-tech firms secure large deals and sometimes for long durations, the agreements tended to be hard to negotiate and routinely encountered cumbersome approval processes and hurdles related to budget uncertainties and compliance issues. Many companies wanted to circumnavigate these processes and adopt a direct-to-consumer business model. The pandemic provided the tipping point. With schools closed and students learning from home, ed-tech providers sensed it was an optimal time to pivot their business away from institutional relationships with public education authorities and towards individuals. Pandemic disruptions also tended to suspend the authority of schools as intermediaries to connect young people to education services. Schools could be slow to act to lay institutional foundations for remote learning, and teachers and students found intermediate and ad hoc solutions on their own. Ed-tech providers launched direct marketing, outreach and advertising campaigns to pick up student and teacher users in the vacuum created by school closures. This process repositioned learners and families as stand-alone consumers and subtly encouraged them to develop consumer behaviours and attitudes as they sought to continue education.[818] Business and marketing models targeting individuals yielded results and proliferated in 2020 and 2021 and remained widespread in 2022 and 2023. They often catalysed more significant rises in user growth and profit than older approaches of selling ed-tech products to schools and school systems.[819] Although the change promised to carry some benefits for learners, such as expanded choice, it also left families vulnerable to commercial exploitation and interference while they pursued knowledge and the right to education.

"Everyone that has a direct-to-student outreach is reporting a huge growth."
– Paul Freedman, CEO and co-founder of an education consulting firm[cxli]

Consumer protection and human rights groups recognized these new vulnerabilities as education became more and more reliant on commercial ed-tech providers. In April 2020, as school closures were peaking globally, a consortium of around 30 civil society organizations, including Campaign for a Commercial-Free Childhood, Consumer Action, Corporate Accountability, Digital Rights Foundation and Parents Together, penned an open letter calling on governments to safeguard education from corporate overreach and shield learners from actors "who see them only as consumers".

The authors implored public authorities to "procure and recommend only those technologies which openly demonstrate that they uphold children's rights" and further called on them to offer secure online spaces for children to access knowledge "without commercial interference". The letter included an appeal to private ed-tech providers asking them to refrain from "[misusing] the additional power that the [pandemic disruption to schooling] conveys on them, to further their commodification and use of children's personal data, for their own purposes and to extract profit".[820]

"States must take all effective measures, including particularly the adoption and enforcement of effective regulatory measures, to ensure the realisation of the right to education where private actors are involved in the provision of education."
– Overarching principle 4, Abidjan Principles[cxlii]

With governments ceding control of education to ed-tech providers in the face of massive school closures, various civil society groups and public education advocates evoked the Abidjan Principles to demand that governments more forcefully regulate private ed-tech companies to ensure the universal and equitable provision of education.[821] Adopted in February 2019, the Abidjan Principles compiled and unpacked existing legal obligations that countries have regarding the delivery of education, with a particular focus on the roles and limitations of private actors in the provision of education. The principles were widely interpreted as an attempt to, if not compel, at least encourage governments to rein in the growing power and influence of commercial education providers. The very existence of the principles demonstrates that international education experts were worried enough about an acceleration of consumerization trends and the encroachments of non-state entities in education to devote a three-year consultative process to the topic and, ultimately, ring alarm bells calling for more vigilant public oversight. It is significant that the Abidjan Principles were formulated *before* the pandemic. Had states been satisfactorily regulating private and often for-profit entities, there would have been less need for the principles and the various advocacy campaigns organized around them. They stand as an implicit admission that many governments were not doing enough to provide free and public education or to regulate private education providers that were, in many contexts, filling the gap, even before COVID-19. As the pandemic took hold and greatly elevated reliance on private ed-tech providers, this failure to act to protect against rapid consumerization tilted education further into the hands of private actors and exposed learners and families to new risks.

A lot of the most important rules to protect consumers from bad actors had been shaped in a pre-digital era and were difficult to apply to ed-tech providers.

Recalling the Abidjan Principles and other frameworks, human rights groups noted that although students would seem to warrant expanded consumer protections when education was conducted digitally with commercial providers, these protections were often poorly defined and, in some instances, less robust than protections afforded to consumers of more established digital services, such as online banking and online shopping. A lot of the most important rules to protect consumers from bad actors had been shaped in a pre-digital era and were difficult to apply to ed-tech providers that were not operating classes or tutoring services conducted in person and at fixed geographic locations. Beyond this, the nascent legal frameworks that did exist to provide protections and recourse for consumers of digital goods and services rarely differentiated between adult and child consumers, a distinction that was meaningful when it concerned ed-tech providers. Prior to the pandemic, children had not historically been regular 'consumers' of digital services, even if this had been changing with the rapid expansion of inexpensive mobile connectivity and growing acceptance of child and youth participation in social media and other digital realms.

Vacillating responses to ed-tech regulation during the pandemic belied confusion about how education, once moved to digital spaces and mediated by commercial providers, was to be regulated and what regulations applied. Standard practices to protect consumers, including transparent disclosure about products and services, detailed information about companies, accuracy of marketing and advertising materials, and obligations to allow and redress grievances, were not always applied to ed-tech companies. In India, for instance, courts in the country, prior to the pandemic, had taken a conflicting view on whether educational institutions provide a 'service' and are, therefore, governed by the provisions of national consumer protection laws. In 2020, India reinforced consumer protection rules for e-commerce to rein in fraud and poor-quality providers at a moment when ed-tech and other technology companies were growing rapidly during the pandemic.[822] Yet the applicability of Indian e-commerce rules depends on the specificity of the business model that a particular company follows and therefore requires a case-by-case analysis to ascertain whether or not they apply.[823] This establishes a grey area that limits the legal protections afforded to learners and teachers accessing services offered by ed-tech companies. Numerous voices in India have called for greater efforts to shield students and their families from the deceptive and unethical practices used by some private ed-tech providers, particularly concerning payment methods, refunds and advertising.[824]

"We're turning to the profit-driven internet as a tool to educate our children. We're asking the internet of Netflix and TikTok, Verizon and Comcast, Amazon and Apple – a realm optimized for pleasure and productivity and commerce, at the expense of privacy and sanity and equity – to help us develop the minds of our young."

– Will Oremus, technology reporter[cxlii]

The cultivation of consumer behaviour in education also heavily targets parents and caregivers who are encouraged to think and behave as consumers in a new market-driven education economy. This was especially the case for those who found themselves responsible, during periods of lockdown, isolation and quarantine, of supporting the remote learning of children and keeping them occupied and mentally stimulated. Families that were unable to access publicly provisioned online learning, because it was either not up and running or of low quality and reliability, took matters into their own hands, directing their children to use learning apps marketed directly to consumers. They could access these services for free, establish paid subscriptions or pay one-time fees to unlock ed-tech content. Ed-tech marketing strategists took advantage of the added sense of responsibility felt by parents and caregivers to assure the continuity of education. Parents were described by companies as a "new key audience" to drive the growth of ed-tech products.[825] EdSurge, a news outlet devoted to ed-tech and the future of learning, observed that BYJU'S, the provider of India's most widely used commercial learning app, was effective at picking up new subscribers by ensuring marketing was "attuned to the psyche of parents" and by "creating whimsical and, at other times, emotionally compelling commercials that tap into both parents' worries about whether their kids are learning and kids' passion for handheld devices". This tailored and direct-to-consumer advertising would help ensure, as EdSurge phrased it in July 2021, that the "next wave of edtech will be very, very big – and global".[826]

Ed-tech providers often offered free content or provided a temporary suspension of fees during the pandemic, usually as part of wider strategies to pick up users that they could later transition to paid services.

Some ed-tech providers offered free content or provided a temporary suspension of fees during the pandemic, usually as part of wider strategies to pick up users that they could later transition to paid services. But many providers required payment to access content. The fee structures were rarely simple. Families discovered that there were tiered packages to select from, such as platinum, gold, silver and bronze offerings, each unlocking different functionalities, layers of content and customization options. Other providers, following a software-as-service business model, offered subscriptions of various durations with different prices for one-month, six-month, one-year and lifetime subscriptions. Even distinctions between free and paid content were muddied by apps that offered free access to some content but required payment to unlock 'premium' learning content. Internet parenting forums delineated strategies to jump to and from different apps that offered

time-limited free trials to avoid incurring costs. Much of this paid content, and some of the free or 'freemium' content as well, promised to give learners a competitive advantage over their classmates. Accompanying advertising typically framed learning as an individual good and service, not the more pluralistic community good and service that school-based learning tended to emphasize.

Around the world, many caregivers felt compelled to pay for commercial solutions when it took governments time to roll out or scale up free public systems. In many countries, a freely accessible digital space to support public education never materialized, even two years or more into the pandemic. Pressure to produce public learning platforms on the internet often dissipated with the reopening of schools, and projects to develop public learning platforms in service of public education were shelved due to budget limitations and reduced urgency. This, in turn, helped ensure that the digital spaces of education would remain under the control or heavy influence of private and commercial providers.

"There are entirely too many education platforms to keep track of – my children work with 11 different types of software."

– Mother of five, USA[cxliv]

Furthermore, paid ed-tech applications were often deemed by many families to be of higher quality than free options, whether provided by the government or a non-state entity. Early in the crisis, many government-established and government-run ed-tech platforms experienced problems, ranging from glitch-prone software to hard-to-navigate interfaces and slow speeds due to overwhelmed servers. The platforms sometimes failed outright or were compromised by cyberattacks – problems that, in some instances, were never fully resolved. Deep into 2020 and 2021, bugs in public learning platforms posed obstacles for the teachers and learners that were reliant on them. As one example, when France ordered a second round of school closures in April 2021 when COVID-19 cases spiked throughout

> Public portals for distance and technology-based education were sometimes so error-prone and disorganized that families often found them unusable.

the country, many people signing into the government-endorsed remote learning platform Ma classe à la maison (My class at home) experienced the same problems they did during the first round of school closures a year earlier.[827] Teachers and learners struggled with lag time navigating the system, and some users experienced a total inability to access the platform for up to three consecutive days due to repeated cyberattacks. Significant cybersecurity measures were undertaken by public authorities to improve the platform, but users on social media continued to report technical difficulties that could interfere with education.[828] It is significant that these problems occurred in France, where the government dedicated considerable energy and investment to assure the public provision of education extended to digital spaces. Government-supported online learning platforms crashed in other wealthy countries, too, such as in Australia.[829] In poorer countries, public portals for distance and technology-based education were sometimes so error-prone and disorganized that families often found them unusable. At the end of 2022, UNICEF reported that one-third of nationally developed platforms to support remote digital learning during the pandemic were not functional.[830] Without other options, families often took educational matters into their own hands and came to rely on commercial ed-tech providers that promised a more seamless and orderly remote learning experience. Frustration with the sometimes very low quality and unreliability of free digital learning platforms and content gave validity to a view that commercial ed-tech options were superior. Tiered price options offered by commercial providers further supported perceptions that more expensive offerings were of a higher quality than less expensive options, reinforcing implicit and explicit messages that families can and perhaps should purchase education services according to their means, a view that is anathema to the principles that underlie the right to education.

Services provided by teachers regularly benefited commercial ed-tech companies and sometimes in opaque ways. For example, various ed-tech firms encouraged educators to record lessons that could be disseminated without their presence indefinitely and, in some instances, without their explicit approval. Compensation tended to be modest, if it was offered at all. Recordings of human teachers, complemented with other automated and on-demand learning resources, including AI 'tutor' chatbots and other dynamic tools, were bundled together as courses, units or modules and marketed to learners as stand-alone products that did not require the intervention or involvement of human teachers. In digital environments, the temporal and geographic remove of teachers could be so extreme that students were not always sure they were dealing with a live human teacher. This was poignantly exemplified in 2021 when a student at a university in Quebec, Canada, discovered that his art history professor, the assumed instructor of a class being conducted remotely during the pandemic, had, in fact, died two years earlier. The university was using the professor's recorded lectures, originally developed for use as complementary teaching tools, as the centrepiece for a distance education class. Writer Tamara Kneese noted that while the incident in Quebec was particularly egregious, it raised "questions about copyright and control over faculty members' online course materials and the various ways faculty labour within higher education is degraded and devalued".[831] The case further illustrated the ways that full reliance on remote digital learning could enable new means of appropriating teachers' labour. Educational institutions and ed-tech firms alike had an expanded set of tools to separate human teachers from education services aimed at learners, a practice that almost always reduced costs by minimizing the expert involvement of teachers and the compensation this required.

"HI EXCUSE ME, I just found out the prof for this online course I'm taking *died in 2019* and he's technically still giving classes since he's *literally my prof for this course* and I'm learning from lectures recorded before his passing."

– University student, Canada[cxiv]

Large technology companies regularly sought to educate teachers about how to leverage their products for educational purposes, often emphasizing the utility of using a suite of propriety applications or using integrated hardware and software solutions. Apple's Distinguished Educator (ADE) programme is one such example. Established in 1995, this programme, according to its own promotional literature, aims to "recognize K–12 and higher-education pioneers who are using Apple technology to transform teaching and learning". Educators selected for the programme through a competitive application process are described by Apple as being "active leaders from around the world helping other educators rethink what's possible with iPad and Mac to make learning deeply personal for every student". Numbering nearly 2,000 individuals across 43 countries, ADEs fulfil roles as "trusted advisors" who "work closely with Apple to foster innovation in education" as well "passionate advocates" and "global ambassadors" for leveraging Apple products to "develop and promote powerful ideas for improving teaching and learning worldwide".[832] While Apple's ADE programme and others like it, including Google's Certified Educator programme[833] and Microsoft's Educator programme,[834] can create dynamic communities of practice and are often appreciated by teachers, they are tightly anchored to massive corporations. The outward quest for better education and improved pedagogy is, in effect, viewed through a branded lens.

"A few exceptional teachers may become major contractors or part-owners of an education business, but the majority may become less and less important in the edtech space. Marketing managers and sales professionals are much more important to get new subscribers."

– V. Santhakumar, professor, Azim Premji University[CXlvi]

Commercial ed-tech providers were fast to roll out flash trainings for teachers. These trainings facilitated and accelerated user uptake of proprietary ed-tech tools.

Recognizing that the pandemic was forcing greater and more prolonged exposure to various digital tools, commercial ed-tech providers large and small were fast to roll out flash trainings for teachers to explain the educational functionalities of different services and products. These trainings facilitated and accelerated user uptake of proprietary ed-tech tools. Google's Teach from Anywhere website, for example, launched at the peak of school closures in 2020, promised to give teachers and families "the tools and tips they need to help keep students learning", yet on close inspection, all the tools recommended to accomplish this task were Google products. The site contained detailed guidance on how to use Google Meet, Chromebooks and Google Workspace for educational purposes as well as a video series to help teachers "solve key teaching and learning challenges with Google Classroom". Under headings with questions such as "How do I manage a virtual classroom?"; "How do I make lessons accessible to all?"; "How do I keep my students engaged?"; and "How do I keep in touch with other teachers?" were links to tutorials on how to use various Google products. Much of the language contained in the Teach from Anywhere website was unabashedly promotional. The resources on Chromebooks, for instance, described the hardware this way: "Running on the fast, secure, and intuitive Chrome OS, Chromebooks are powerfully simple devices that help students and teachers be more productive and creative – whether they are at school, at home, or anywhere in between".[835]

Google was hardly the only corporation to feature the ways its products could be deployed for education as schools closed globally. An article published on the Microsoft 365 blog in March 2020, authored by the corporate vice-president, was titled "Helping teachers and students make the switch to remote learning" and, unsurprisingly, explained how to use Microsoft products for education.[836] Apple encouraged educators in the USA to schedule free, one-on-one virtual coaching sessions with company-employed and affiliated learning specialists early in the pandemic.[837] These sessions, like other training resources Apple developed for educators, were effectively guides about how to leverage Apple's hardware and software offerings for distance learning. Technology companies recognized that if teachers started using proprietary products and systems, they would, in many instances, use them with students and sometimes recommend them for bulk purchase by schools or universities. A teacher using a particular ed-tech app with just one single class might mean 30 or more students gaining exposure to that app from a young age.

"Don't have a Google Workspace for Education account? Check out the schools tab to learn how your administrator can sign up for our suite of tools for no cost."

– Google's Teach from Anywhere website[clxvii]

As the pandemic stretched on and reliance on technology deepened, evidence emerged that teachers were developing more comfort and expertise with ed-tech. One UK study, for instance, found that close to two-thirds of teachers reported feeling "more confident" using technology for teaching and learning several months after school closures.[838] But these expanded skill sets often boiled down to narrow knowledge on how to use proprietary and for-profit platforms to connect with students. This is not to suggest that such skill sets were without value, but they arguably contributed to a branding of teaching and learning such that digital pedagogies were tightly bound to products from a particular corporation. UNESCO and other educational organizations have long advised that teachers learn to deploy technology for education in ways that are, to the extent possible, brand agnostic.[839] An end goal is to help teachers independently assess the attributes and limitations of a wide range of commercial and non-commercial products to make expert determinations about what products to use (and not use), in dialogue with and reflecting guidance from school and ministerial authorities.

Teachers rarely had opportunities to develop advanced and brand agnostic digital pedagogies during the rushed transition to distance learning.

Facilitating teaching and learning with technology, especially from a distance, requires extensive training and hands-on experience. It demands unique competencies and technical skills that are often quite separate from the competencies and skills required for teaching in an in-person setting, even if there is some overlap. The *UNESCO ICT Competency Framework for Teachers* report recommends the development of 18 distinct skills to support knowledge acquisition, knowledge deepening and knowledge creation across various areas, including curriculum and assessment, pedagogy, administration and professional learning, a process that normally unfolds over months, if not years.[840] These complex and layered skills cannot be taught overnight, nor are they easily compatible with corporate training modules that elevate the promotion of proprietary ed-tech products. Few teachers had opportunities to develop advanced and brand agnostic digital pedagogies during the rushed transition from in-person instruction at schools to distance learning using ed-tech. This lack of teacher experience put ed-tech providers in an influential position. Their utilities often mediated the bulk of the education experience, sometimes bypassing public school instructors entirely and sometimes using teachers to drive new users to their services. Both scenarios rightfully alarmed people concerned about the encroachment of commercial interests in public education.

Surveillance, control and machine processes marked the move to ed-tech

When the pandemic prompted a transition away from in-person schooling and towards remote learning with ed-tech, many observers held high hopes for the vast amounts of data that education would generate when it was conducted in digital spaces. With computers as educational intermediaries, the practices, interactions, progress, learning and behaviours that had been ephemeral in the physical environment of schools would be easy to track, log and analyse. What had previously been obscured would become visible.

Ed-tech companies advanced claims that the data they collected – the clicks, page views, right answers, wrong answers, changed answers and time-on-task metrics – could be woven into intelligence that would guide educational interventions, both at classroom and system levels. The assumption was that information recorded in digital mediums would flow into powerful computer systems that would find previously unseen correlations, causations and other patterns that would then direct actions to improve education and personalize it to better support the learning of individual students. This thinking further held that unbiased machines would manage this direction and personalization with greater accuracy and objectivity than teachers and other humans involved in education.

The tracking and processing of learning data in real time promised something close to educational omniscience.

Before and during the pandemic, technology's capacity to generate real-time data was also regularly elevated as a rationale for transitioning more of education into digital environments. For proponents of ed-tech, tracking and processing learning data in real time promised something close to educational omniscience: teachers could glance at a screen and see, moment to moment, how students were learning. This tech-enabled knowledge would be complemented by computer-generated instructions specifying what interventions were needed for which students and when. The data collected and generated by ed-tech would therefore direct teaching and learning in machine-mediated input-output feedback loops. At school, district and national levels, real-time data would flow into automated monitoring systems tirelessly analysing teacher, school and system effectiveness. This analysis would, in turn, ensure the selection of superior supports for individual learners, place better information at the fingertips of teachers and parents, and clarify the policies and investments needed to strengthen schools and wider education systems.

Pairing the big data bounties of ed-tech with the prodigious processing power of modern computers would, it was assumed, unlock the many mysteries of education.

The data streams of ed-tech further promised to help clarify research questions about what teaching approaches, content, prompts and incentives are most impactful in different contexts, thereby turning the art of education into a more data-driven science. Many believed that as teaching and learning moved into digital spaces, technology would reveal optimal ways to teach different concepts and subjects. Just as dynamic digital maps can show the quickest way to travel, step by step, from one physical destination to another, even after accounting for complex variables like weather and traffic conditions, ed-tech would, in the popular imagination, manage similar feats with learning – it would guide students and teachers, step by step, to desired learning outcomes. Even questions about how to foster complex and desirable behaviours like kindness, empathy and tolerance through education could, it was imagined, be answered with new certitude in the data-rich spaces of ed-tech. With technology watching and recording learning, there would be fountains of raw and ideologically untainted data to facilitate knowledge breakthroughs. Machines would help vastly enlarge the small sample sizes of traditional educational research, while minimizing the risk of human error or bias tarnishing research findings. Pairing the big data bounties of ed-tech with the prodigious processing power of modern computers would, it was assumed, unlock the many mysteries of education.

"Big data purports to provide a basis for technological innovation that promises progress and disruption, and analyses of these data influence both the smallest and the most consequential decisions made by individuals and organizations."
– Kalervo Gulson, Sam Sellar and P. Taylor Webb, education scholars[cxlviii]

Greater reliance on ed-tech also promised to make education fairer. Subjective assessments of student performance, so often stained by cultural, ethnic, language, gender and socio-economic biases held by teachers and schools, would be replaced by machines programmed to see beyond these markers. Technology would power better and more meritocratic assessments of student work. It would measure learning progress more objectively and pinpoint student aptitudes, directing attention to areas of strength and intervening in areas of weakness. Ed-tech would, in sum, be immune to biases that so often confront students, and minority students especially, in human-led classrooms.

These visions, however vivid and desirable, were rarely realized in the actual implementation of ed-tech during the pandemic. Instead, the shift from in-person education to digital-only learning environments introduced considerable risks stemming from increased data capture, surveillance and machine processes in education. Ed-tech generated data, no doubt, but these data tended to wind their way to people and parties less interested in knowledge expansion and improved learning than in placing advertisements, policing ideas and shaping beliefs and behaviours for commercial or political gain.

Evidence suggests that, around the world, teachers, learners and others involved in education often had trouble deciphering the relevance of data presented to them on digital dashboards. Additionally, teachers, as well as school officials, tended to have only limited understandings about what information was tracked by ed-tech, who controlled it and how, exactly, it could be used for pedagogical purposes.[841] When information was analysed and presented to learners, teachers and others involved in education, it tended to give outsized importance to easily quantifiable indicators of learning – time spent in a learning app, for example – but had less to say about how well or poorly students were comprehending and generating ideas or productively applying new concepts. Just as a step counter on a smartwatch provides a narrow, if intriguing, indicator about health and fitness, the information tracked, measured and analysed with ed-tech had *something* to say about learning, but its relevance was often questionable. And it could obscure other measures that were more important but less visible to technology because they were contingent on human observation and judgement.[842]

> Corporations often treated student data as a commodity – assets that could be extracted and auctioned for profit.

Behind screens and in online environments, teachers and students commonly became unwitting targets of complex data capture operations. While many of these processes were typical of business models that underlie 'free' digital services, they had not previously cast a wide net around children and youth involved in formal education. As the pandemic stretched over the one-year and two-year marks, ed-tech corporations took on new roles as ad hoc education authorities, assuming functions that were historically the responsibility of public sector organizations. Many of these corporations treated student data as a commodity – assets that could be extracted and auctioned for profit. Illicit hackers also flocked to education, seeking to exploit security loopholes and hijack sensitive educational data that could be ransomed for financial gain. During the pandemic, education was, far and away, the sector most likely to be targeted by malware attacks.[843]

At the level of classrooms, it became apparent that a side effect of data- and machine-driven processes was that pedagogical tasks could become dictated by what could be digitally performed and measured. Educational relationships became less human and less personal when they were mediated by automated systems and corporately provisioned platforms hosting education. In these new learning spaces, surveillance was ubiquitous, and student mistakes, questions, behaviours, ideas and opinions were regularly crystalized in permanent digital footprints that could shadow students for life. Essays authored by teenagers and linked to them with fixed markers such as birth dates, school-issued identification numbers and other unchanging identifiers routinely leaked out of ed-tech utilities and into the wider internet, where they were quickly indexed by machines for seamless retrieval via search engines. Opening the classroom to out-of-context scrutiny also provoked new clampdowns and constraints on what teachers felt conformtable doing, saying and teaching. Politicians as well as parents could hover over education and log ideas and practices that they did not like, dismantling long-held norms that treated teacher-student relationships as privileged and warranting protection from the unnecessary scrutiny of outsiders.

> Students and their families signed away their privacy and submitted to new extremes of surveillance and control.

Existing educational governance was largely unprepared to guide an orderly transition to remote learning with ed-tech that upheld the right to privacy as well as the right to education. There was a belief that governments should step out of the way and refrain from imposing regulations that might hamper the technological progress that suddenly seemed vital to the provision of education during the health emergency.[844] But this step-aside mindset all too often brought students face-to-face with educational utilities designed to monetize users and small print, click-here-to-accept agreements drafted to advance the financial interests of corporations and private investors. Opting out was not a realistic option when ed-tech provided a singular link to compulsory education. Around the world, students and their families signed away their privacy and submitted to new extremes of surveillance and control in order to pursue education in digital environments. This was an affront to the right to education, a human right intended to expand and reinforce other rights, including the right to privacy and to freedom of opinion and expression.

NEW DATA GOLD AND THE MANY EYES OF ED-TECH SURVEILLANCE

The shift from school-based education to distance learning with technology enabled new and invasive forms of surveillance that regularly violated student and teacher privacy. Ed-tech could watch educational exchanges with unprecedented levels of detail. Every selection, sound, click and gesture could be tracked, logged, analysed and fed to various education stakeholders – usually teachers, but also parents, school leaders, district administrators, policy-makers, employees at ed-tech firms and others. This information, however, routinely moved outside of education. It was sold to third parties, often for advertising purposes, and in some contexts, it was used to detect political dissent and flag ideas that were deemed dangerous by schools or other government authorities.[845]

Surveillance is hardly new to education. Schools have long been spaces of supervision and monitoring, and these actions help schools assure protection, especially for younger children. Everything from teacher observation of students and management of classroom behaviour to informal assessments of learner comprehension and high-stakes standardized examinations can be classified as forms of 'watching'. But moving education activities to digital technology vastly expanded what actions could be watched, as well as by whom.

"The actual benefits of EdTech and the data processed from children in schools are currently not discernible or in children's best interests. Nor are they proportionate to the scope, scale and sensitivity of data currently processed from children in schools."

– Digital Futures Commission[cxlix]

Also, with tens of millions of students learning on a handful of proprietary platforms – whether learning management systems such as Blackboard,

Act 2: FROM PROMISES TO REALITY | 307

With tens of millions of students learning on a handful of proprietary platforms, the traditional boundaries of schools, districts, states and even countries and regions were largely erased.

Canvas and Google Classroom or more multipurpose communication utilities such as WhatsApp – the traditional boundaries of schools, districts, states and even countries and regions were largely erased. In digital spaces, the actions of students and teachers scattered across the globe were quickly codified as views, clicks and time spent on pages and then beamed to faraway locations and used for various purposes. This gave the owners of these spaces – mainly multinational technology corporations – unprecedented powers of surveillance. They had views of learning that could toggle from the micro (e.g. specific behaviours of individual students) to the macro (e.g. transnational trends related to learning activity). It was a data-rich view of education that could rival and surpass the views available to national governments and intergovernmental organizations.

Information about data generation and use was buried in the fine print of agreements that even skilled readers had trouble comprehending.

Data in the digital age are a commodity, often lauded as the 'new gold', and data collected and generated by ed-tech are no exception. During the pandemic, educational data were routinely sold to different parties, some involved in education and some not. Without regulation, ed-tech data tended to flow to the highest bidders and traders who used the data to generate returns that surpassed the purchase price. The data trails of learners and teachers were scraped from applications used for distance education and mined for information about users' behaviours and responses to stimuli – information that could be used to make ed-tech more effective but that was also valuable in sectors beyond education, such as marketing, advertising, politics and other spheres. Teachers and many education leaders usually had only a blurry sense of how data captured by ed-tech utilities were or could be harvested, by whom and to what ends. A major 2022 study conducted by the Digital Futures Commission in the UK, for instance, found that school officials often had trouble answering basic questions about why educational data were collected in the first place, let alone about the particularities of what data were collected.[846] Information about data generation and use was buried in the fine print of lengthy agreements written in legalese that even skilled readers had trouble comprehending. People around the world most often clicked 'I agree' and hoped for the best.

The effortless portability of data captured in digital learning environments during the pandemic was a marked departure from school-based learning spaces, where words and actions did not normally travel beyond the four walls of a classroom. Ed-tech companies operating under loose regulations not necessarily intended for education or to protect minors commonly bundled this information in ways that maximized its value to parties outside education – parties that were willing to pay. Bundling data for educational purposes could be a secondary priority. The 2022 study by the Digital Futures Commission on education data realities in UK schools found, for instance, that teachers and school staff could only present "modest examples" of beneficial uses for education data in schools. The researchers noted that the two vital components needed to make data valuable for educational purposes were largely missing: "the ability of staff to manipulate the data appropriately, and their critical knowledge that data provide only indicative information that requires further detailed, often sensitive, investigation to ensure that the child's well-being is considered as well as performance". The report concluded that the data benefits touted by ed-tech companies are "simply not there – or not there yet". While it acknowledged some benefits, the report continued, "the technology typically does not generate data that solely illuminate or inform educational decisions", noting that the data are "used for a host of other purposes, not all of them apparent to the school".[847] In effect, the data were used to benefit parties and interests beyond education and educators and not necessarily in the best interests of children and youth.

"Continuous surveillance in education has become so deeply naturalized that the question of whether personal educational data should be collected in the first place is rarely asked. Data collection is increasingly built in the educational process as a basic requirement, leaving no room to question whether or not data should be collected at all."

– Marko Teräs, Juha Suoranta, Hanna Teräs and Mark Curcher, social science scholars, Tampere University[cl]

Even skilled data scientists found it difficult to decipher how the mountains of data collected by technology were actionable for the purpose of improving education.

Teachers and school leaders were not the only ones who had trouble understanding and manipulating the volume and nature of data generated by ed-tech. Even skilled data scientists found it difficult to decipher how the mountains of data collected via technologies facilitating and surveilling education were actionable for the purpose of improving learning – or how this data might generate insights that were not already apparent to skilled human teachers beyond providing more fine-grained analysis about student behaviour that was easy to quantify such as attendance and task completion.[848]

Quandaries about how to productively use education data are not new. In the 2010s, several major projects in the USA that aimed to improve if not reinvent education with more expansive, centralized and coordinated data collection fell flat. For example, inBloom, an ed-tech initiative to help personalize student learning and improve education through streamlined data collection and sharing, collapsed after just a few years amid pushback from parents concerned about their children's data privacy.[849] Although its promoters claimed that inBloom ran into unfair "mischaracterizations" and "misdirected criticism" before it had a chance to show the value of standardized and consolidated student data collection,[850] the system never demonstrated meaningful educational improvement despite funding of USD 100 million from powerful philanthropic organizations, including the Bill and Melinda Gates Foundation and the Carnegie Foundation.[851]

"Modern education reform has been driven in large part by wealthy amateurs, convinced that their expertise in other areas can be translated into reform, rebirth and revival."

– Peter Greene, education author[di]

A perhaps more prominent and cautionary example was AltSchool. Founded by a former Google executive, AltSchool sought to analyse fine-grain data collected from a network of high-cost private schools to personalize learning and gather insights to transform education.[852] AltSchool campuses used in-house learning apps, cameras and microphones to monitor words, fidgets, facial expressions, clicks and social interactions for insights that might pave the way to improved instruction.[853] The founder aspired to establish systems that would incorporate wearable devices to track everything from students' heart rates to the exact time between meals.[854] This information, derived from both digital and non-digital teaching and learning experiences, moved from AltSchool classrooms to computer systems where it was studied by data scientists – often recruited from sectors far removed from education – for meaningful patterns.[855] Proponents of AltSchool spoke of the ways in which better data collection and analysis had triggered major changes to established practices in other fields, from how professional athletes were scouted to the ways department stores were designed and organized, and said similar data-driven changes were overdue in education.[856] Yet the much-anticipated transformations and exponential improvements in learning never came to pass.[857] AltSchool's most novel offering was a 'playlist' of learning tasks and resources that were, in theory, personalized for each student and presented on a tablet or laptop computer. These playlists directed the learning content and trajectories of children in preschool and early primary grades as well as older students up to Grade 8.[858]

"Former Googlers and I are thinking about what big thing do we dedicate ourselves to next? Where is our background in technology and personalized technology relevant? What can we work on for the long term? Because you don't leave a place like Google to do something hokey and small."

– Max Ventilla, CEO and founder of AltSchool[dii]

Although AltSchool attracted around USD 175 million in capital from prominent Silicon Valley investors, including Mark Zuckerberg, Peter Thiel, Marc Andreessen and Laurene Powell Jobs, it folded in 2019 after just six years of operation.[859] A primary cause was parents pulling their children out of AltSchool campuses because they felt their children were falling behind academically. Other parents came to believe their children were being enlisted as beta testers or guinea pigs to facilitate the development of educational software that could be marketed and licensed to large numbers of educational institutions. They expressed frustration that AltSchool leaders seemed to be beholden first to the organization's influential investors and second to the families and children enrolled in its schools. Parents and teachers alike expressed disillusionment with attempts to use technology to personalize learning and came to question the value of pervasive data collection to improve education.[860] One AltSchool teacher told a technology news outlet that at AltSchool: "There's this assumption that every kid needs a different activity to meet their needs, and that by applying tech, one can simply send them individualized content through a video or activity card. But that's not necessarily true. It's not best for kids to learn only through a video or other content that's sent primarily for consumption. And tech that operates under this assumption really undermines educators and the value of good teaching."[861] When AltSchool shut down, its number of campuses had contracted from seven to four, and the remaining campuses were sold to a for-profit operator of Montessori Schools.[862] AltSchool recast itself as a "technology-enabled service organization" and installed a new leadership team.[863]

> Education has multifaceted aims and objectives that have proven perennially difficult to advance and analyse with data generated by ed-tech alone.

AltSchool and inBloom exposed some of the limitations of attempts to improve education quickly and definitively by corralling large and complex data sets and making them readable by computers. This is not to suggest that these two initiatives did not produce valuable, if very expensive, lessons, but they strongly indicated that technology-enabled data mining and analytics did not apply as neatly or effectively to teaching and learning as they did to other problems and sectors. Education is not a sports game with narrow statistical metrics, rules and objectives; nor is it a retail shopping experience, where a seller's overriding goal is to induce consumers to spend money. It is also not a digital platform in need of eyes to profit from advertisements. Education, by contrast, has multifaceted aims and objectives that have proven perennially difficult to advance and analyse with data generated by ed-tech alone.

The well-funded AltSchool and inBloom initiatives further provide reminders that data derived from education are not natural or essential elements extracted in neutral ways.[864] As Williamson has argued, "Data may be big, but at the same time, often tend to erase complexities, context, meanings, and causal factors, so producing highly partial and incomplete renderings of reality".[865] It is telling that although many countries are 20 or more years into a digital revolution, attempts to transform education with expanded data collection and superior analytics have yet to yield the massive changes that have seized other sectors. The search to generate new answers with data, while necessary and admirable on the one hand, can obscure what existing data say very clearly about education, such as the importance of retaining rigorously trained and well-supported teachers, maintaining manageable class sizes and ensuring well-resourced schools. Arguably, the turn to big data is often a search for shortcuts around well-understood and time-proven solutions to educational challenges. As inBloom and AltSchool demonstrated, there is no assurance that new and technology-driven modes of data collection will pave the way to better education and superior learning outcomes. These lessons, however, were not front of mind when in-person education was replaced by remote education that was easy to surveil during the pandemic. Ed-tech providers and enthusiasts were once again hailing that deeper, wider and more frequent data collection would pave a straight road to improved learning outcomes. More data were assumed to signal better data, and the increased collection of data was often mistakenly conflated with knowledge and intelligence.

"Children shouldn't be compelled to give up their privacy and other rights in order to learn."

– Hye Jung Han, children's rights and technology specialist, Human Rights Watch[865]

> Ed-tech providers routinely allowed learner data to be sold or tracked by outside entities for marketing and other purposes far removed from education.

If the data collected by ed-tech providers carried minimal use and benefit to teachers and school leaders concerned with education, the data collected by outside entities were almost never used for educational purposes. These entities siphoned educational data from digital spaces and mined them for commercial purposes. In countries around the world, ed-tech utilities, including those formally recommended by governments for distance education, commonly threw open doors to third-party surveillance.[866] Large studies of leading ed-tech software and platform providers found that an overwhelming majority of them allowed learner data to be sold or tracked by outside entities for marketing and other purposes far removed from education.[867] Human Rights Watch titled its 2022 report documenting extensive privacy and children's rights violations by leading ed-tech firms *How Dare They Peep into My Private Life?* The title sought to give expression to the anger felt by students and teachers who were surveilled by an "invisible swarm of tracking technologies" while trying to exercise their right to education.[868]

In addition to known and intended actors surveilling student and teacher activity, ed-tech vulnerabilities allowed unknown and malicious actors to track and observe ed-tech users with the application of malware, spyware, viruses and ransomware. While the education sector was developing online learning strategies, cybercriminals were working out ways to access, breach and steal educational data. In early 2021, the US Federal Bureau of Investigation reported that schools had become the leading targets of ransomware attacks. Hackers repeatedly held educational data controlled by a particular school, university or system of education institutions hostage for up to millions of dollars.[869] The data in question were deemed so sensitive and valuable that institutions often – and usually quietly – paid the ransoms, which solved an immediate problem but incentivized further attacks. Laws concerning the disclosure of educational data breaches were often non-existent, suggesting that the alarming number of reported attacks was likely a significant undercount. In the USA, the State of California sought to address this problem of disclosure by passing a law in October 2022 mandating schools to report cyberattacks impacting 500 users or more.[870]

"If you're a bad student and had disciplinary problems and that information is now out there, how do you recover from that?"

– Joe Green, cybersecurity professional[div]

> During the pandemic, malware attacks launched against ed-tech users surpassed attacks against technology users in all other sectors combined.

At the international level, tracking by Microsoft indicated that education as a sector was far more likely to be targeted by malware than any other sector. Troublingly, during the pandemic, malware attacks launched against ed-tech users surpassed attacks against technology users in all other sectors *combined*.[871] During the switch to distance learning, individual teachers, learners and their families became much more susceptible to data theft at the hands of hackers. They were required to quickly download new software and create accounts with little to no online security training or advice, making the contents of their devices vulnerable to phishing and other schemes used to steal data and hijack systems. When cybercriminals took control of devices remotely, they could search for financial information, track a user's locations, record keystrokes and even commandeer camera and microphone controls. The proliferation of ed-tech apps, many of them requiring usernames, credentials, accounts and passwords, created scattered digital outposts for education that individuals often needed to manage and protect, sometimes with very little assistance or guidance.[872] This established new vulnerabilities that cybercriminals were quick to exploit.

In countries around the world, ed-tech introduced heavy technological surveillance and various online risks to a population who, until then, had not typically had extensive experience with them: the millions of children that were plunged, often with little or no preparation, into the world of digital learning. Despite the vulnerability of these new users – all of them under the age of maturity needed for consent to legal agreements and some as young as preschool age – laws and regulations largely failed to keep pace to assure adequate privacy protections and, in some cases, were absent entirely.[873] Many schools and school systems relied on outdated policies that effectively gave ed-tech providers carte blanche to collect and use student data. These data were uploaded to proprietary ed-tech systems during the pandemic, either by school administrators or by learners and parents complying with instructions from schools.[874] Much of the data were sensitive and included information that extended beyond teaching and learning, such as notes about a student's home life, medical conditions, behaviour and overall welfare. The information provided deep insights into the lives of learners and was intended only for professionals close to students working to promote good-quality education, health, development and holistic well-being.

"We collect basically everything you can about a student … you can even collect down to things like the doctor's contact details … then you have to have information about their parents and their careers, so you get personal information on other people as well. And it's information you have to have."

– School vice principal, UK[clv]

> Google included clauses in its user agreements to classify the company as a 'school official'. This definitional sleight of hand was a technique to conform to laws in the USA that restrict the sharing of student data and educational records to school officials.

When ed-tech providers found that wide-net data-collection techniques might run afoul of policies concerning the treatment of children's personal records, they often devised creative ways to circumnavigate them. Google, for instance, included clauses in its user agreements to classify the company as a "school official".[875] This definitional sleight of hand was a technique to conform to laws in the USA that restrict the sharing of student data and educational records to school officials. Objections that the authors of these laws almost certainly did not have a huge corporation in mind when they specified that only school officials should handle student data were brushed aside. Google was a school official because the legal fine print said Google was a school official. The corporation was, therefore, able to function as a steward of student data like a teacher, school principal or someone else close to learners in a particular community. These hops and skips around existing regulations were common during the pandemic. In many cases, they were not even needed. Government regulations and protections concerning digital education data tended to be nascent at best and absent at worst when schools began closing en masse. The laws that did exist had largely been formulated at a time when regulators never expected that digital platforms might one day function as schools and provide singular repositories for information related to education. This gave ed-tech companies considerable latitude to set their own standards and self-monitor compliance.

"Data processed by edtech platforms, whether generated from children, teens, or adults, deserves special protection and care. It does not always receive this care."

– Joe Jerome, policy director, Common Sense Media[clvi]

Figure 19:

Google G Suite for Education agreement

Source: Google, 2020

(c) Opposition. Recipient will comply with the other party's reasonable requests opposing disclosure of its Confidential Information.

7.4 **FERPA.** The parties acknowledge that (a) Customer Data may include personally identifiable information from education records that are subject to FERPA ("FERPA Records"); and (b) to the extent that Customer Data includes FERPA Records, Google will be considered a "School Official" (as that term is used in FERPA and its implementing regulations) and will comply with FERPA.

8. Intellectual Property Rights; Brand Features.
8.1 **Intellectual Property Rights.** Except as expressly set forth herein, this Agreement does not grant either party any rights, implied or otherwise, to the other's content or any of the other's intellectual property. As between the

> The expansive powers of surveillance enabled and utilized by ed-tech providers during the pandemic largely benefited parties outside or peripheral to education.

While governments were largely unprepared to regulate the privacy implications the switch to ed-tech entailed, the technology companies at the centre of the transition were well-practised at gathering large amounts of personal data and using the data to expand market share, tailor applications, steer new development and, overall, generate value for shareholders. Companies such as Google and Facebook (Meta) had spent years meticulously building robust networks with sophisticated tracking tools. When learning activities moved online due to the pandemic, they were able to follow student's digital footprints across the internet, both in their own proprietary applications and often beyond. Apps used for educational purposes, and especially those offered for free, generated monetizable data, in addition to familiarizing users with company-specific offerings. In summary, the expansive powers of surveillance enabled and utilized by ed-tech providers during the pandemic largely benefited parties outside or peripheral to education and provided only limited advantages to learners and teachers.

FORCED CONSENT AND NEW LEVERS OF CONTROL

When data agreements are aimed at consenting adults, people commonly tolerate the 'my data for your services' trade-offs that underlie many online services and platforms. This arrangement, however, was more complicated when it involved minors pursuing education during the COVID-19 pandemic. As school closures swept the world, children and adolescents, many of whom had been barred from signing up for accounts with large internet companies like Google or Microsoft just months before, were

assigned usernames and passwords to access services connected to these companies. Methods for establishing more anonymized means of accessing education services were commonly overlooked. Huge numbers of children and youth were instructed to set up email accounts and other profiles on systems not designed for children or education but rather for adults operating in professional workplaces. Sometimes it was up to schools to determine the default settings for how students might be tracked using identifying information such as birth dates and genders. There were rarely, however, options *not* to have a user-specific profile, and this block on anonymity greatly facilitated digital tracking and data harvesting aimed at individual students as opposed to classes, schools or other group cohorts. Apps hosting content, including those serving primary school children, routinely required unique user log-ins to access learning materials. This practice was akin to, say, Wikipedia refusing to show internet users the content of an encyclopedia entry unless they entered unique identifying credentials. Learning resources that were extremely low cost to share widely and anonymously in digital environments commonly resided behind gates of this sort.

Migrating an entire school or school system onto digital platforms such as Google Classroom effectively bypassed the typical agreements and permissions that individuals consent to in exchange for the ability to use software and join platforms. Parents were seldom consulted or properly informed about decisions made on behalf of children. Schools were likewise not always aware of the range of online privacy and security implications that they agreed to. According to the Digital Futures Commission, schools faced major data protection challenges as a result of "the power imbalance between schools and major EdTech providers, the complexity and opacity of EdTech data processing, and the paucity of guidance on EdTech decision-making and procurement from government".[876]

New users of ed-tech services rarely understood the particulars of the trade-offs presented to them in the small print of long and challenging-to-understand agreements.

The power imbalance between providers and users similarly disadvantaged learners and families when they were tasked with accepting terms and conditions set by ed-tech companies. Approaches to offload consent to individuals tended to reflect a perspective that end users were well-placed to decide whether the benefits of a digital service were worth its costs and trade-offs concerning data collection, compromises that sometimes supported the business models of ed-tech companies. But this was not usually the case in practice. Numerous studies have found that very few people read terms and conditions for services, young people especially.[877] In one experiment, 99 per cent of users agreed to ridiculous permissions such as surrendering the right to name their first-born child when this and other outlandish clauses were inserted into terms and conditions.[878] Researchers found that participants tended to view the terms as a nuisance and ignore them in order to "pursue the ends of digital production, without being inhibited by the means".[879] Additionally, users have an "inner feeling" that even if they read through an agreement, they can "neither raise their voice to oppose, change, or even refuse to accept" the terms.[880]

Educational continuity depended on clicking 'I agree'.

The long length of terms and conditions introduces another burden. As one example, in November 2020 users in the UK who wanted to sign up for Microsoft Teams, an app widely used for educational purposes, were asked to agree to over 18,000 words explaining the privacy policies and terms of service, a document length that would take a typical person 2 hours and 30 minutes to read carefully.[881] (By comparison, William Shakespeare's *Macbeth* contains just over 17,000 words.) Agreements approaching or exceeding 10,000 words are hardly outliers and include WhatsApp, Messenger and Zoom, among other apps.[882] According to one estimate, a typical American, for instance, would need to spend 250 hours a year reading digital contracts to use a standard assortment of online services.[883] The complexity of these agreements present another barrier. Analysis by Reboot, a digital marketing firm, found, for instance, that TikTok, an app widely used by teenagers, had among the most complex terms and conditions of leading apps. Although users as young as 13 are allowed to sign up for the service, Reboot estimated that complexity of the terms of service would require reading skills typical of a 20- or 21-year-old.[884] During the pandemic, this created a reality in which new users of ed-tech services rarely understood the particulars of the trade-offs presented to them in the small print of long and challenging-to-understand agreements. When the provision of core educational services depended on agreeing to ed-tech conditions, users could not easily behave like discerning customers – they were forced to accept the associated terms. Educational continuity depended on clicking 'I agree'.

Once these agreements were in place, the data collected by ed-tech utilities tended to reside in digital repositories off-limits to individual students and

Ed-tech organizations often had policies in place granting them wide control over the user data they collected and, as such, were under limited or no obligation to share this data with the individuals who generated it.

their families, and sometimes to teachers and schools as well. Control of the data shifted to the developers and providers of ed-tech. During the pandemic, parents often ran into obstacles when they asked to review digital data collected about their children.[885] Students, including those who were not minors, encountered similar difficulties accessing their own data records held by entities beyond their educational institutions.[886] Ed-tech organizations often had policies in place granting them wide control over the user data they collected and, as such, were under limited or no obligation to share this information, even when requested by the individuals who generated it. Requests that were made could also be slow-walked or outright ignored with little recourse. In other instances, ed-tech providers only granted institutions permissions to view, use, correct, delete or share data collected from learners on their platforms.[887] For example, the September 2021 version of Zoom's K–12 privacy and security policy stated that students and parents must contact their school districts for any request to access or delete data, which commonly included students' profile information, contacts, calendars, settings, video recordings, messaging content and device and location information, among other data.[888] Many families had never been in contact with educational bureaucracies beyond the level of the school and did not know how to reach them, let alone successfully submit a request concerning data collection and use.

When requests, often originating from parents, did reach educational authorities, it was not always clear what data could and could not be shared, removed or altered in line with requestor demands. Action to successfully fulfil a data request also assumed that educational authorities understood the processes of how to access and manipulate data held on proprietary platforms that schools were, in most instances, either leasing from an outside ed-tech organization or using for free. This action sometimes required a school administrator to fill out extensive forms that were, in turn, submitted to commercial ed-tech providers. Operators at the school level did not always have strong or even passing knowledge of the steps needed to honour data requests; others were too overwhelmed with more pressing demands to follow up on requests. A seemingly simple request from a parent to delete, say, posts a young student made on a communication platform like Zoom or Microsoft Teams could initiate a labyrinthine and time-consuming process that was not necessarily assured to achieve the desired action of erasure. And even when an erasure request was reported as fulfilled by an ed-tech company, it could be challenging for students, parents and schools to verify. Although leading ed-tech companies usually granted schools the right to audit the data they held, this was generally far too costly for schools to realistically contemplate.[889] As a result, schools tended to blindly accept that ed-tech companies fulfilled requested actions pertaining to learner data.

"The reality is that schools are outmatched. They not only need more resources and personnel to devote to privacy and information security, but they need more help overseeing and monitoring edtech companies generally."

– Joe Jerome, policy director, Common Sense Media[clvii]

Given these obstacles, it appears that schools and ed-tech providers tried to discourage data requests from students or parents.[890] Requests that did reach ed-tech firms were commonly redirected to schools or wider school systems. These deflections amounted to a de facto data policy in lieu of more established rules and regulations. They arguably shaped and entrenched understandings that ed-tech companies, despite their considerable resources, were outside the reach of educational end users – namely, students and parents. Their accountability traced, instead, only to the school authorities who set the dials on a given ed-tech product, whether a learning management system, software to track and filter web searches, or a subject-specific learning app.

Schools commonly struggled to effectively identify, control and limit what types of personal data were collected, how they were used and to what ends.

The Digital Futures Commission examined this problem in the context of the UK and found that while national regulations held schools responsible for children's education data, ed-tech companies "undermine schools' control over education data processing, along with children's and parents' ability to object to data processing or manage children's data".[891] It argued that UK rules were deeply flawed because they gave schools the responsibility but not the power to control ed-tech data processing. The commission's detailed examinations of the data policies and practices of Google Classroom and ClassDojo, both leading ed-tech providers, found that the corporate power of ed-tech and its "ethos of data maximisation (rather than minimisation), and commercially motivated policies and designs place a near-impossible burden on any school, parent, caregiver or child wanting to manage how data processed from children are used".[892] These impossible burdens were not specific to UK schools. Around the world educational institutions were thrust into an uncomfortable intermediary position, trying to relay specific requests concerning learner data to ed-tech providers, organizations that often required the submission of proprietary forms to address non-standard requests related to data. For the duration of school closures and heavy reliance on ed-tech, schools commonly struggled to effectively identify, control and limit what types of personal data were collected, how they were used and to what ends. Expectations that schools would suddenly be able to successfully navigate the thicket of complexities surrounding the collection and use of education data by managing outside providers proved to be overly optimistic. The reins largely stayed with the ed-tech providers, while schools, broadly speaking, did their best to stay out of the way and ensure compliance with the incomplete rules and limited guidance that existed when educational processes moved into heavily surveilled digital spaces during the pandemic.

It is hard for learners and their families to understand, with confidence, what data collected about them carries low and high stakes.

Some of the ed-tech solutions rolled out during the pandemic previewed a future in which technology might permanently log and seek to quantify nearly all educational interactions and assessments, starting from the earliest grades through secondary and tertiary education levels. Technology that tracks the minutiae of educational performance over students' lifetimes – etching every step and misstep in a digital dossier – could give outsize importance to banal assignments and tests, potentially diminishing students' future opportunities in ways that are not necessarily foreseen today. Professional-level employers routinely demand detailed educational transcripts and test scores from prospective employees. Given this existing norm, it is easy to imagine that employers in the future would want to review the most detailed educational dossiers available. Much of the ed-tech rolled out during the pandemic expanded the volume and type of educational data collected and recorded from pre-pandemic levels, and these data might, down the road, expose learners to information requests from prospective employers that look well beyond markers that are currently considered significant. Because it is challenging to anticipate what techniques future employers might use to comb through educational data and what data they will deem more and less important, it is hard for learners and their families to understand, with confidence, what data generation is low stakes and what is high stakes. In this context, assurances that an assignment, quiz or examination logged in a database and linked to an individual are 'no big deal' can be difficult to take at face value given the many uncertainties surrounding how these data might be used 10, 15 or 20 years in the future. Simply said, educational data that are recorded – and incorporated into digital dossiers of the kind that exploded in popularity during the pandemic – may end up conferring advantages or, conversely, disadvantages to learners in ways that are not fully known today.

Recent digital era regulations allowing EU citizens the right to demand that social media and other internet companies delete compromising posts and other information tagged to them (known colloquially as the 'right to be forgotten') were occasionally held up as a promising blueprint for thinking about students' right to their personal data on ed-tech platforms. Although this legislation points to regulatory solutions that might minimize harm from undesirable data and, in theory, affords individuals more control over the permeance of digital information, in practice, it is limited in scope. As an example, in 2019 Google won a court case against a French privacy regulator when a court ruled that while the "request for de-referencing made by a data subject" could be upheld within the European Union, there was no legal obligation for Google to delete the data from all versions of its search engines. This meant that the data that the individual petitioned to have deleted could still be retrieved and seen in other parts of the world.[893] The ruling was a reminder that digital data rarely respect national boundaries and, as such, can be challenging to regulate effectively with domestic laws alone and only limited regional and international coordination. Overall, the pandemic showed the extent to which rules and guidance about data privacy, particularly as it concerns education and the special sensitivities associated with educational data collected from and generated by children, remain loosely formed, even though the near-, medium- and long-term stakes for learners can be very high.

"We will need to envision privacy as a collective social good in need of collective solutions: strong public regulation that systematically reins in the parties who trample it."

– Sarah Elizabeth Igo, author and historian[clviii]

In addition to students, teachers were regularly asked to consent to digital tracking and other forms of surveillance in the virtual spaces that hosted education during the pandemic. While teachers are adults who can agree to terms of a user agreement, their consent was often expected and, in some cases, an unstated condition of employment. Teachers had little room to negotiate. Education International and other groups representing teachers called attention to the coercion inherent in these arrangements.[894]

The permanent monitoring and surveillance that characterized a lot of ed-tech apps – usually implemented with little analysis of the impacts on teachers' rights – created new workplace pressures on teachers already struggling for professional autonomy. Surveillance capabilities tended only to get stronger as reliance on ed-tech was prolonged. The extensive research conducted for this publication was unable to identify a single example of an ed-tech company rolling back surveillance functionalities during periods of school closures. Upgrades Google made to its Google Classroom utility in 2021 provided an illustration of the type of stepped-up surveillance that confronted teachers in online environments. The software changes allowed school administrators to generate "audit logs" that detailed teacher actions on the platform and flagged "instigating events".[895] These flags would document everything from mundane tasks like teacher archival of classes to more dramatic actions like teacher removal of a student from a digital class. The system also produced adoption and engagement insights and visualizations, allowing administrators to see which teachers were – and were not – using different Google education tools. It also provided teachers feedback about which students were using Google applications and to what extent. The major takeaway was that the systems of ed-tech were watching, recording, organizing, curating and sharing large volumes and types of information about teacher actions and practices, even though the utility of these data to improve teacher oversight in ways that might prompt better instruction was contested.

> A lot of ed-tech established a digital architecture to enforce strict hierarchical controls. This ran counter to goals embraced by many education systems to model egalitarian societies.

Combing through the small print about surveillance options available on mainstream digital education platforms, layers of panoptic control were easy to detect: teachers watching and controlling students; administrators watching and controlling teachers; ministry of education officials watching and controlling administrators. While these hierarchies were not new, the extent of the powers of surveillance and control that ed-tech enabled were often without precedent. Ed-tech permissions could create a rigid system of power with administrators enjoying numerous options and levers to watch and control educational interactions. Teachers, by contrast, would have fewer surveillance and control options, and learners fewer still. This was, in many respects, a digital architecture tailor-made to enforce strict control at different levels, and it ran counter to goals embraced by many education systems to model egalitarian societies.

PRIVACY AND PERSONAL DATA SLIP AWAY IN THE DIGITAL ENVIRONMENTS OF EDUCATION

Incursions on student and teacher privacy grew significantly when learning became largely mediated through technology and digital platforms, rather than in in-person schools. Regulations governing how ed-tech companies collect, store, use, sell and share data collected on their platforms were embryonic prior to the pandemic, if they existed at all. And during the COVID-19 health crisis, governments did very little to step up privacy rules, mainly because they were inundated with other concerns, but also because they were reluctant to disrupt operational ed-tech practices and business models at a time when the continuity of education was largely dependent on them.

Careful evaluations of how leading ed-tech organizations treated data collected in their respective systems found that an overwhelming majority had limited privacy protections. Data generated through educational tasks were routinely passed to other parties for purposes unconnected to education, such as advertising. As one striking example, the digital advocacy organization Common Sense found that only 20 per cent of 150 ed-tech products it evaluated received a 'passing grade' for acceptable privacy practices. The methodology used by Common Sense examined each ed-tech product according to three basic privacy criteria: first, whether the product had a publicly available privacy policy; second, whether it supported and used encryption when users were logged in; and third, whether it used online trackers. In the review, performed in 2019 (before the beginning of the pandemic), 20 per cent of the applications looked at failed to meet even the most basic privacy and security standards, while 60 per cent of ed-tech apps were flagged for caveats and concerns.[896]

Disappointing assessments of this sort likely reflected a regulatory reality that asked ed-tech companies to self-monitor their data privacy practices. Even when relatively robust regulatory frameworks existed (at least by global standards), there was typically lax enforcement or punishments for offences. In the USA, for example, as late as 2021, no state had announced a public investigation against any ed-tech provider under existing student privacy laws.[897] Regulators in Europe have been similarly slow to police the privacy violations of technology corporations, including those involved in ed-tech. As of mid-2020 and two years since the passage of the EU-wide GDPR, only a single technology company, Google, had been penalized under the law. The GDPR fine assessed to Google totalled slightly over EUR 50 million, a figure that amounted to just one-tenth of Google's daily sales revenue at the time.[898] This tepid action can be traced to resource limitations that curtailed the formation and prosecution of legal cases needed to hold privacy violators accountable. A 2020 survey of European technology privacy regulators found that over two-thirds felt their budgets were insufficient to fulfil their responsibilities.[899] Since the pandemic has wound down, however, Europe has brought more – and more punitive – cases against technology corporations for privacy violations, including those that concern children's privacy. In 2022 and early 2023, for example, regulators in Ireland prosecuted a series of successful cases against Meta (previously Facebook) for failing to adequately handle and safeguard user data.[900]

"Regulation designed to protect children's education data, their privacy, and other rights is undermined by EdTech companies' complexity and lack of public scrutiny about these companies, rendering it less effective."

– Digital Futures Commission[clix]

Perhaps because of the limited regulation and lack of clear privacy rules related to ed-tech, providers of digital learning services regularly shared, sold and traded the data they collected. Indeed, many commercial ed-tech providers depend on business models that require collecting and tracking user data in an effort to maximize engagement and sell targeted advertising, a process that almost always involves passing information to third parties.

> Human Rights Watch called third-party data tracking on ed-tech utilities 'dizzying' and noted that a child logging into a typical commercially provisioned ed-tech platform 'could expect to be followed by an average of six third-party trackers'.

Evidence of the ways data generated by ed-tech moved outside education is abundant. In September 2020, the International Digital Accountability Council investigated the privacy practices of global ed-tech applications spanning 22 countries. Of the 123 applications the council manually tested, 79 were observed to be communicating user data to third parties, defined as "any entity that is not the developer of the app or a parent company of it".[901] A separate and later study conducted by Human Rights Watch found that the majority of ed-tech products endorsed by governments during the pandemic "put at risk or directly violated children's privacy and other children's rights, for purposes unrelated to their education". The Human Rights Watch study called the third-party tracking "dizzying" and noted that a child logging into a typical commercially provisioned ed-tech platform "could expect to be tracked by an average of six third-party trackers".[902] The prevalence of these practices was corroborated again by a detailed study conducted by the Digital Futures Commission on educational utilities offered by Google and ClassDojo, two of the largest private ed-tech providers in many countries. The commission found that both companies were "collecting children's educational data and processing and profiting from that data for advertising and other commercial purposes – often in ways that are likely non-compliant with data protection".[903]

Available evidence suggests that the already poor data privacy practices of ed-tech providers worsened during the pandemic. Since 2018, Common Sense has been evaluating the way leading ed-tech utilities treat data. The share of utilities exercising data practices that the organization classifies as 'worse' rose substantially between 2018 and 2021. Over this four-year period, it documented a 600 per cent increase in the share of ed-tech providers selling data, a 62 per cent increase in the share of providers using behavioural advertising, a 290 per cent increase in the share of providers that create advertising data profiles, and a 130 per cent increase in the share of providers that track users. More modest increases were also observed between 2020 and 2021. Common Sense cautioned that some of the changes observed between 2018 and 2021 reflect a decrease in the number of unclear data and privacy policies, which enabled superior classification of 'better' and 'worse' practices. The organization explained that the decrease in unclear policies is commendable because it means that privacy policies are more transparent, even if they reveal worse data practices.[904] Nevertheless, it is hardly reassuring that improved transparency revealed worse data privacy practices.

Figure 20:

Percentage increase in adverse data practices in ed-tech applications from 2018 to 2021

Source: Data from Common Sense, 2021

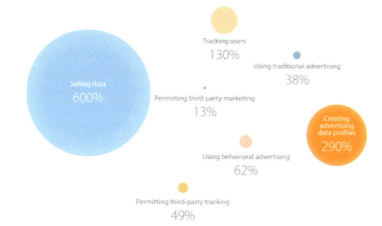

"Children are disadvantaged by the power imbalance between them and school authorities under normal circumstances. But this imbalance is only made worse in the current circumstances [of the pandemic], as some States Parties choose to impose surveillance, and allow commercial companies into children's home life without consent."

– Open letter to policy-makers by children's advocacy organization Fairplay[cix]

In addition to letting ed-tech companies mine student data for purposes related to advertising and other non-educational aims, the loose stewardship of student data that characterized many ed-tech provisions during the pandemic opened the door to malicious hacks. This was exemplified by a 2022 cyberattack on Illuminate Education, a large ed-tech company that offers student-tracking software. The data breach compromised the personal information of well over a million students across various districts in the USA. The information that was stolen included names, birthdays, ethnic classification and test scores. In some instances, it also included information about disabilities or citizenship status, as well as disciplinary actions and tardiness records.[905]

Hacks such as the one targeting Illuminate Education are concerning because the data collected by ed-tech can be deeply personal. For example, the pandemic saw a proliferation of utilities that track student activity in digital environments, regardless of platform or software. These new tools record every internet search, every page viewed and every app opened, providing schools and teachers extensive surveillance and filtering capabilities. Major providers include GoGuardian, Gaggle.Net, Securly and Bark Technologies, among others. The software is usually loaded on computers provisioned to students by educational authorities, runs 24 hours a day, seven days a week, and is active whether a student is at home or at school. This type of personal tracking – and the logging of all internet searches especially – creates dossiers that are, understandably, highly sensitive. If these data are leaked or stolen, they could expose individuals to embarrassment or even blackmail, depending on the nature of the information in question.

"The software that many school districts use to track students' progress can record extremely confidential information on children: 'Intellectual disability.' 'Emotional Disturbance.' 'Homeless.' 'Disruptive.' 'Defiance.' 'Perpetrator.' 'Excessive Talking.' 'Should attend tutoring.'"

– Natasha Singer, technology and education reporter[clx]

DATAFICATION OF LEARNING AND HUMANS

Datafication is a process of rendering things and activities into quantitative data that enable analysis, particularly by computers. The shift to remote learning technology greatly accelerated datafication practices in education, a trend that was well under way prior to the COVID-19 pandemic. Digital ed-tech translated people and educational experiences into numerical data that were piped into databases and used for a wide variety of tasks, from measuring learning progress to making analytic predictions about student aptitudes, challenges and learning preferences. Turning technology-reliant educational exchange into number-based data was relatively seamless because binary systems underlie digital processes. Digital ed-tech therefore spoke a language of numbers by design and by necessity. No matter what was happening on the screens, platforms and software of ed-tech, it was, at a base level, a string of numbers, ones and zeros – commands of 'on' or 'off'.

> There is nothing natural about representing students, teachers, learning or knowledge as chains of numbers that enable computer operations.

The process of turning the inputs, outputs and actions of education into numerical data is synthetic. There is nothing natural about representing students, teachers, learning or knowledge as chains of binary numbers that enable computer operations, even if this process can greatly facilitate educational tasks and improve the scope and accuracy of record keeping. While binary digital data are, of course, a tool that underlies powerful analytics that can help represent and make sense of a wide range of human activity, they do not necessarily represent what occurs in education and other spheres of life easily or neatly. They can morph and twist the lived experience of education and give it entirely new presentation.

Datafication can also involve highly subjective decisions. There are many ways to 'data-fy' a particular educational actor or process, each with respective consequences reflecting different assumptions. Many ed-tech systems rolled out during the pandemic prompted teachers, for example, to assess students according to fixed categories such as engagement, performance and effort. Teachers would click boxes to mark the student as 'excellent', 'good', 'acceptable', 'poor' or 'failing' under each category. Different categories were assigned different weights such that some categories contributed more to a holistic assessment than other categories. These systems produced crisp and authoritative-seeming outputs about how individual students were faring educationally, but they were anchored in system-level assumptions about both what criteria to use to assess students and the mechanics of translating a marking such as 'good' into a numerical form. While rubric-based assessments that facilitated the translation of performance into qualitative data have long been a hallmark of education systems, ed-tech made these systems easier to apply and use. Importantly, ed-tech could also automate processes of this sort, taking them largely out of human hands. Instead of asking teachers to assess something like student engagement according to fixed option choices, ed-tech software found proxies to generate these rankings automatically. Proxies for assessing engagement might include numerical indicators of how long a student was logged into a particular learning platform, how quickly and frequently a student made inputs into a system, how much progress was made in a given learning module, and so forth. These individual pieces of data would be compiled and processed to make determinations about a student's engagement. The output information was then presented to teachers on dashboards, sometimes with recommended interventions. A system might, for instance, advise a teacher to instruct a student to repeat a module or spend more time and make greater progress inside certain learning software. In some instances, the system might even offer to send a template digital message of instruction to the student. The teacher would usually have the option to tailor the message or send it without personalization or alteration.

"Datafication introduces new regimes, routines and hierarchies into schools that not only change the values and beliefs of teachers and staff, but also the focus and priorities of curriculum and assessment"

– Luci Pangrazio and Julian Sefton-Green, education scholars[905]

> Teachers could be 'robotized' – conditioned to cede important decision-making to algorithms and prioritize the collection of data that is easy to feed into machines.

These practices – enabled by datafication – could dictate educational priorities in profound ways. For instance, knowing that the time spent inside a learning platform and the frequency of clicks made in the platform would positively influence assessments of student engagement, students would, understandably, take these actions regardless of whether or not they were conducive to learning. Stephen J. Ball, a professor of sociology of education at University College London, argued in *Governing by Numbers* that education stakeholders need to come to terms with the reality that "numbers do not simply represent", but, rather, "have real effects" on what is and is not emphasized educationally. He explains that what he calls the "tyranny of numbers" can sidestep difficult and important issues about education objectives and processes in favour of a myopic push to improve quantitative measures of educational progression.[906] Similarly, education scholars Kalervo Gulson, Sam Sellar and P. Taylor Webb advance an argument in *Algorithms of Education* that "the increased datafication of education … offers less and less control, as algorithms and artificial intelligence further abstract the educational experience and distance policy-makers from teaching and learning". They warn that data-rich ed-tech systems and practices are causing schools and school systems to rely on "synthetic governance – a governance where what is human and machine become less clear – as a strategy for optimizing education".[907] This synthetic governance was facilitated by the quantitative data generated by ed-tech, and it could create incentives for various education stakeholders, whether learners, teachers or school leaders, to give such data importance regardless of the value of what, precisely, was behind those numbers. Incentives of this type tend to devalue the expertise, judgment and experiences of subjective human teachers, establishing instead deference to the supposedly objective calculations of machines. In such a context, teachers could be 'robotized' – conditioned to cede important decision-making to algorithms and prioritize the collection of data that is easy to feed into machines.

Prior to the pandemic, scholars observed that datafication techniques were turning the physical and social sites of schools into data platforms – sites where various types of ed-tech hardware and software transformed

Full reliance on digital technologies for education helped normalize expectations that students and teachers would be subject to constant surveillance and the datafication this surveillance enabled.

educational processes and exchanges into numerical forms comprehensible to digital technology. When in-person schooling was interrupted and formal education became fully reliant on remote learning technology, this process accelerated considerably. With formal learning moved into digital environments almost exclusively, schools were not merely *like* data platforms; they *were* data platforms. This could make schooling and education feel less human. People and actions were inscribed into data that were then used to make inferences about what students could and could not do and what corresponding interventions should be taken in response. Many education stakeholders experienced the stepped-up datafication that accompanied remote learning with ed-tech not as something entirely new but as a more extreme version of datafication practices that were already familiar. In this way, full reliance on digital technologies for education helped normalize expectations that students and teachers would be subject to constant surveillance and the datafication it enabled. As one example, Blackboard, a learning management system popular in higher education, announced that it captured 25 billion digital interactions each week. These interactions were generated by surveilling complex educational activities and then distilling them into machine-readable data. According to the company, these interactions were used to establish and refine the largely automated nudges and reports that students and their instructors received.[908]

Ben Williamson, an education scholar who has dedicated his career to understanding the many ways new technologies are influencing and changing education, brought specificity to what datafication can entail in education. Writing in 2019 on the eve of the pandemic, he wrote:

> *To offer a simple example from the datafication of education, when a child enters a database, she is chopped up into data points, turned into bits, aggregated with other data, evaluated against norms and so on. Over time, as more data becomes available from the student's activity, it becomes possible to generate a data profile of her skills, progress, abilities, and knowledge—often known as a 'student model'—which can be compared with regularities in massive datasets. Sometimes these profiles are called 'data doubles,' as if they represent a digital shadow version of the profiled individual. But, importantly, the data can always be called up and arranged differently—data doubles are really data multiples. When one of these data multiples gets selected as the student model, it becomes a make-believe substitution which can then be used to inform how the teacher approaches that student, or how an algorithmically personalized learning program assigns her tasks. As such, the substitute profile built out of the data takes an active ontological role in shaping the*

'real life' of the student—a process that could always have been done otherwise, with different real-world results. The data play a part in 'making up' the student.[909]

Educational decisions were taken out of the hands of teachers and outsourced to computers that saw students only as numbers or bits.

Due to the pandemic shift to fully remote learning, huge numbers of students entered databases of the sort described by Williamson. While this was not necessarily problematic and could carry distinct educational benefits, it commonly resulted in educational decisions being taken out of the hands of teachers and outsourced to computers that saw students only as numbers or bits. It was, as Williamson explained, a case of computers educating a "digital shadow" of a student rather than the actual flesh-and-blood student who, even with advances in technology, remains more knowable to a skilled human teacher than to a computer algorithm.

Williamson stresses that datafication practices in education rest on assumptions that "patterns and relationships contained with datasets inherently produce meaningful, objective and insightful knowledge about complex phenomena". But these assumptions were hardly assured. Williamson cites an example in which 29 teams of data scientists reached different conclusions from their analysis of the same data set. This showed that "significant variation in the results of analyses of complex data may be difficult to avoid and that subjective analytic choices influence results".[910] The analysis offered up by ed-tech was similarly predicated on a range of subjective analytical choices. These choices were commonly taken outside any public oversight and then embedded in proprietary black box algorithmic engines. Although the techniques ed-tech systems used to collect, process and output information were often presented as definitive and objective, they were, in fact, molten and could be cast in a variety of different ways based on different assumptions about data and their relevance, meaning and connection to education. These assumptions were shaped by particular cultural contexts – how data are treated depends to a considerable degree on the teams that are processing them and on the worldviews they hold. Scholars have argued that datafication approaches in education commonly see data as decontextualized, universalistic and connected to individuals instead of groups. These approaches can elevate technocratic ideals originating in the global North. Scholars Kalervo Gulson, Sam Sellar and P. Taylor Webb have said that when data-driven rationalities of this sort are applied to education governance it can result in "anglo-governance models".[911] During the pandemic, ed-tech utilities reflecting such ideas and models about educational data spread around the world. This interjected (or could even impose) particular data practices on people and cultures that may have taken a very different view of uses and misuses of data in education had they been developing ed-tech utilities from scratch.

"Data do not pre-exist the practices and technologies that bring them into being. As such, data are products of social practices."

– Ben Williamson, education scholar[clxiii]

Ed-tech companies often claimed that their proprietary backend datafication processes could provide schools and teachers with intelligence about everything from students' day-to-day learning performance to warnings about which students are most likely to drop out. Some ed-tech utilities even purported to be able to determine students' emotional states by quantifying, corralling and crunching educational data, a process sometimes referred to as 'sentiment analysis'. As one specific example, GoGuardian – software that records and filters student internet searches and other digital activity – said that its machine-learning models could analyse the data it scraped from queries, clicks and digital posts to detect emotional distress such as suicide ideation and risk of self-harm. Although GoGuardian's system made determinations as consequential as assessing and flagging suicide risk, the company, according to reporting from Bloomberg, "declines to disclose the specifics of how its algorithms make determinations".[912] GoGuardian was not unique in this regard. Many ed-tech companies decline to provide detailed information about how data are collected and analysed to generate outputs that could carry major repercussions, from how students are scored to how teachers see students. While some major ed-tech providers, including Google Classroom and Class Dojo, provide schools rights to audit certain data processing practices, the Digital Futures Commission has dismissed this as unrealistic in practice because it would be "far too costly for any school to contemplate".[913]

"The machines that [man] has constructed now impose their own law on him: he must be made readable for the computer, and this can be achieved only when he is translated into numbers."

– Joseph Ratzinger, Pope Benedict XVI[LXIV]

Parents and students were understandably sceptical of datafication practices that marked learners as failing, disengaged, or likely to drop out when these practices and the raw data that fuelled them could not be explained or were held in secret.

It was this black box aspect of datafication that worried many educational professionals. Transparency about how educational processes were 'data-fied' and how the data were analysed to make determinations allowed various stakeholders to study them and, if necessary, contest either the analysis or a given determination. A clear view of datafication practices would make the many assumptions that underlie them visible. They would be revealed as they are: synthetic human inventions, however practical and useful. Ultimately, any effort to turn students and their actions into numerical data will be a by-product of the choices, processes, ideologies and technologies that enable this transmutation. But very often these choices, process, ideologies and technologies were out of sight or obscured, sometimes with claims that it was too complicated to grasp and required specialist knowledge of big data computation or AI. Parents and students were understandably sceptical of datafication practices that marked learners as failing, disengaged, or likely to drop out when these practices and the raw data that fuelled them could not be explained or were held in secret by a corporation licensing a product to a school or a school system.[914] Available evidence suggests that the stakeholders closest to education had only a muddy sense of how datafication worked and how it provided the basis for automated decision-making. In *The Datafication of Education*, Juliane Jarke and Andreas Breiter explain that the "underlying algorithms and the ways in which data are produced by data providers, statisticians as well as the role of software companies and educational technology providers are hardly understood".[915]

Because automation was, definitionally, data-based and derived from numerical representations of reality, it tended to carry a veneer of 'scientific' authority.

Despite being hardly understood, the automation of learning, enabled by datafication, was widespread during the pandemic. Also, because this automation was, definitionally, data-based and derived from numerical representations of reality, it could carry a veneer of 'scientific' authority that surpassed assessments made from more multifaceted human observation. During the pandemic, teachers observed ed-tech systems producing evaluations, warnings and sometimes blanket assessments of students that bore little relationship to the students they knew and worked with in schools before the pandemic and behind screens during periods of school closure.[916] One well-publicized example was the UK's reliance on supposedly unbiased datafication techniques to help determine grades in lieu of traditional end-of-term tests that were not administered because of COVID-19 restrictions. It was not a smooth process. According to reporting in *The Guardian* newspaper "bright students in historically low-achieving schools were tumbling, sometimes in great, cliff-edge drops of two or three grades, because of institutional records they had nothing to do with".[917] Teachers told reporters stories of being baffled to discover that students expected to receive the highest possible marks were deemed by the automated system to be barely passing.[918] The public outrage was swift and unsparing. *The Guardian* said the algorithm used to assign grades was perhaps "the first algorithm in the history of computer science to be condemned on the front page of every major British newspaper".[919]

Newer AI tools can generate outputs that are neither consistent nor knowable in advance.

As the reach and scope of educational datafication and algorithmic controls expand, they can become progressively harder to govern and control.[920] Educational utilities powered by AI have introduced modes of computation that can produce decisions and outputs that are not fully explainable even to the teams that built them. This is a significant change from ed-tech, which ran on conventional algorithms governed by if-then logic chains that generate consistent and knowable outputs from a given set of inputs. Newer AI tools, by contrast, can generate outputs that are neither consistent nor knowable in advance.[921] It is understandable that people in the education community might expect the recommendations, decisions, content, prompts and interventions specified by ed-tech to be 'explainable' but this attribute, once taken for granted, is no longer assured, as a new generation of AI technology is adopted by many schools and universities. UNESCO has called for international and regulatory frameworks to address the ethical concerns of AI, recognizing that AI increasingly runs unnoticed in ways that covertly affect societies and individuals.[922] In the European Union's 2021 Artificial Intelligence Act, schools and other educational institutions and service providers were identified as being especially high-risk users of AI.[923] Yet so far, ed-tech firms deploying AI at scale for educational use have been left unaccountable for the wide range of risks and consequences their products can introduce as they roll out automated tools that can shape children's futures.[924]

"At its most hubristic, data science is presented as a master discipline, capable of reorienting the sciences, the commercial world, and governance itself."

– Chris Wiggins and Matthew L. Jones, authors of *How Data Happened*[lxv]

EMOTION-RECOGNITION TECHNOLOGIES GAIN A TOEHOLD DESPITE FLIMSY SCIENCE

Special glasses developed at MIT sought to measure brain activity and eye movements to detect a lack of focus and nudge users to alertness with audio and haptic feedback.

Beyond capturing actions and behaviours measured through clicks and other digital activity, pandemic modes of learning – happening alone and with technology – appeared to trigger increased interest in technologies used to surveil learners' bodies. Just as datafication practices could be aimed at educational activities, the human body could also be 'data-fied' as part of attempts to, for example, detect and measure concentration, emotional states and other internal sentiments and feelings. Researchers had long postulated that surveillance technology such as user-facing cameras on laptops and microphones could be activated to scan faces and record voices for signs of learning and focus and package this information in ways that might be valuable to learners, teachers and others involved in education. These ideas gave rise to different types of "affect-aware" technologies that aim to identify, codify and interpret – and eventually respond to – students' mental and emotional states. One extreme example of this type of technology was a glasses prototype developed at MIT called AttentivU that could, according to its developers, measure brain activity and eye movements to detect a lack of focus and nudge users to alertness with "gentle audio or haptic feedback" when their attention wanders.[925] Such devices point to a new class of hardware that scans the human body for indicators of engagement and other corporal signals that can be related to learning in order to bring these signals to levels that improve knowledge acquisition and maximize receptivity to education.

Processes to render students' bodies as signal transmitters of data require invasive forms of surveillance, such as detailed video capture of facial and eye movements and even measurements of breathing, pulse and electrical activity in the brain.[926] Prior to the pandemic, these processes remained largely experimental. Some notable exceptions in China, however, foreshadowed practices that became more mainstream during the pandemic. In 2018, for example, a high school in Hangzhou installed surveillance cameras in classrooms to capture and record students' facial expressions for "performance analysis and improvement".[927] The school claimed that its "smart classroom behaviour management system" could be used to determine student concentration and that this would inform not only student performance but also teacher performance. The system gave students a "real-time attentiveness score" that was also shown to teachers on a digital dashboard, incentivizing students and teachers alike to maximize this score.[928] In 2019, similar systems were rolled out elsewhere in China, including in an elementary school in Shanghai. According to media accounts, the "AI+School" system used in the Shanghai elementary school was able to "automatically detect the behaviours and emotions of teachers and students" and "provide evaluation and suggestions in light of performance analyzed by the intelligent algorithm".[929] Although these developments received considerable international press coverage, they were understood to be small-scale pilots and limited largely to China where video and other forms of surveillance are increasingly commonplace. Even within China, it was not clear if intensive video surveillance in education and systems designed to algorithmically determine students' emotions and levels of concentration would be made permanent or expand outward.[930] In late 2019, the Chinese government, reflecting privacy concerns, announced plans to "curb and regulate" the use of facial recognition technology in schools.[931]

"Since the school has introduced these cameras, it is like there are a pair of mystery eyes constantly watching me, and I don't dare let my mind wander."

– High school student, China[clxvi]

Ed-tech modes of distance learning triggered an upsurge in interest in machines scanning students faces and bodies in order to gauge their levels of attention, focus and other signals associated with learning.

The pandemic though seemed to trigger an upsurge in interest in machines reading students in order to gauge their levels of attention, focus and other signals associated with learning, within as well as beyond China. The sudden elevation of online classes as a default mode of remote education and the ubiquity of user-facing digital cameras on computers and mobile phones both normalized the video surveillance of students and made data capture of students' bodies and facial expressions far less costly than it had previously been. Instead of installing expensive facial recognition cameras in classrooms, ed-tech companies could write software that activated the cameras built into the devices students were using to access education. The surveillance infrastructure was, in effect, student-controlled devices. In some cases, the hardware students used for digital learning offered state-of-the-art facial scanning technology. iPhones in production since 2017, for instance, come equipped with a TrueDepth camera and sensor system that uses over 30,000 invisible infrared dots to scan and build mathematical models of a user's face.[932] With scanning systems like these in wide use for educational participation, numerous companies, including technology giants like Intel, began accelerating the development of commercial software to detect the emotional states of learners participating in formal education.[933]

Proponents of this type of technology claimed that it could 'read the room' in an online synchronous classroom as well as or better than a human teacher instructing students in a physical classroom.[934] When the pandemic triggered massive growth in online learning, companies began marketing and selling the tools in different national contexts. As one specific example, a Chinese ed-tech company called Find Solution AI advertised products that it claimed could "detect and identify the learners' emotions and performance in real time to understand where [the learner] struggles on a particular subject".[935] The company's ed-tech platform, 4 LittleTrees, is described on its website as a "patented AI-driven motivation model" that "combines AI with emotional analysis" to "facilitate students' learning process and provide better teacher assistance".[936] During the pandemic the popularity of the platform, initially launched in 2017, exploded. The number of schools using it (with a price point between USD 10 to USD 49 per student) more than doubled in 2020. The company's founder claimed the software's evaluation of children's emotions was accurate about 85 per cent of the time, and even more accurate for detecting primary emotions such as happiness or sadness.[937]

While Find Solution AI and other firms offering emotion-recognition software projected confidence that student emotions are machine-readable, this confidence is not widely shared by the scientific community.[938] Peer-reviewed investigations into emotion-recognition technology tend to cast serious doubts on its value and reliability.[939] Researchers explain that attempts to draw assumptions about the internal mindsets and capabilities of learners from external appearances are fallible and based on dubious assumptions.[940] An important two-year meta-review of more than 1,000 different studies of emotion recognition, commissioned by the Association for Psychological Science and led by five distinguished scholars, found that emotion is expressed in varied and inconsistent ways. Published in 2019, the review concluded that facial expressions offer a specious window into emotional states. According to the authors, "How people communicate anger, disgust, fear, happiness, sadness, and surprise varies substantially across cultures, situations, and even across people within a single situation." They concluded that it is "not possible to confidently infer happiness from a smile, anger from a scowl, or sadness from a frown, as much of current technology tries to do when applying what are mistakenly believed to be the scientific facts".[941] This finding was, in effect, a rebuttal to the premise that ed-tech solutions could use face scanning and AI engines to assess emotions. A separate 2019 report from AI Now came to similar conclusions and advised researchers to pay greater attention to why so many organizations in education and other sectors are "using faulty technology to make assessments about character on the basis of physical appearance in the first place".[942] In mid-2022, Microsoft became one of the first large technology companies to publicly announce that it would cease work on systems that purport to use facial scanning to infer emotional states, citing "potential socio-technical risks" and "the inability to generalize the linkage between facial expression and emotional state across use cases, regions, and demographics".[943] Nevertheless, the value of the emotion detection and recognition market, which encompasses education and other sectors, was valued at over USD 23 billion in 2022 and projected to surpass USD 43 billion by 2027.[944]

"[Tech] companies can say whatever they want, but the data are clear. They can detect a scowl, but that's not the same thing as detecting anger."

– Lisa Feldman Barrett, psychologist and neuroscientist[clxvii]

Facial scans were not the only surveillance technology deployed to gauge student emotion. Companies based in Japan and the USA offered products that used audio capture to deduce emotion.[945] Hume.ai, for example, claimed that its technology could "measure 53 emotions reliably expressed by the subtleties of language".[946] Other companies marketed voice recording and processing technology to schools to use as aggression detectors, even though this technology was shown to have serious shortcomings such as equating the voice of a comedian telling a joke with aggression.[947] Yet with education exchange largely limited to digital mediums during the pandemic, voice was seamless to capture and process. Any synchronous class involved the translation of teacher and student voices into digital data. While voice is commonly understood to offer useful clues to emotional states, it is, like facial scans, an imperfect indicator. A voice that a piece of ed-tech software tags as 'frustrated' may not be expressing frustration at all, but rather a different emotion.

Utilities that purport to ascribe emotions to faces and voices risk giving outsize importance and credibility to automated and technology-dependent methodologies that many scientists find prone to inconsistencies and imprecision.[948] They can further cause teachers and other humans involved in education to distrust their own assessments.

Scientific studies have demonstrated the influence emotional labels can carry. Research has shown that providing people with preselected emotion words inadvertently primed them to detect certain emotions over others and thus skewed their human ability to read other people's emotional states by drawing on a multiplicity of essential contextual clues that are often invisible to technology.[949] Other studies have found that recognizing human emotions from facial expressions is highly culturally specific and that claims of universally recognized expressions should be approached with caution. For example, research conducted with the Himba, a remote tribe in Namibia, found that people from this tribe consistently labelled photographs of actors' faces differently than people from the USA. Facial expressions tagged as 'happy' or 'afraid' by US participants were tagged as 'laughing' and 'looking' by Himba participants. The authors concluded that the perception of emotion depends heavily on cultural and conceptual contexts.[950]

> Emotion-recognition technologies also expose ways that datafication can bluntly simplify a complex phenomenon filled with ambiguity and nuance.

Emotion-recognition technologies also expose ways that datafication can bluntly simplify a complex phenomenon filled with ambiguity and nuance. When deployed in schools, such technologies commonly use face scans to designate a single emotion to a student such as 'neutral', 'happy', 'sad', 'disappointed', 'angry', 'scared', or 'surprised'. But these single labels do not capture the complex interplay of emotions that students can feel. It is possible, of course, to feel happy *and* surprised or disappointed *and* sad. Almost any mixture of emotions is possible, and any single emotion may be fleeting. After assigning an emotion label to a student, an ed-tech algorithm typically makes an inference about what the emotion means for education. For example, an algorithm might deem that anger or disappointment is inconducive to learning, even though these emotions may not, in fact, be impediments or even present. Emotion-recognition technology offers a powerful example of the ways surveillance, datafication and automated decision-making could move teaching and learning onto tenuous ground: machine-assigned labels based on a questionable methodology matched with machine inferences about the meaning and significance of these labels to cue an educational intervention or recommendation.

"We can no longer allow emotion-recognition technologies to go unregulated. It is time for legislative protection from unproven uses of these tools in all domains – education, health care, employment and criminal justice."

- Kate Crawford, author of the *Atlas of AI*[clxviii]

SELF-CENSORSHIP AND CLASSROOM CONTROL

Ed-tech enabled a host of new, top-down and often illiberal controls over education.

Ed-tech deployed during the pandemic enabled a host of new, top-down and often illiberal controls over education. Software for synchronous video sessions, for example, often included teacher controls that bordered on the autocratic, such as 'mute all' buttons and other options to silence or eject individual students with a click of a mouse. Teacher-facing dashboards invited teachers to disable chat and video functionalities for classes as well as individual learners. Teachers and administrators had levers to prevent specific students from seeing their classmates, while allowing this view to other students. Teachers and administrators also often had buttons that allowed them to ping students on their personal mobile phones or other devices with instructions to join a class. These sometimes domineering controls – often unique to the virtual spaces of ed-tech – compelled students to learn which actions met standardized expectations for reward or punishment. More open and democratic forms of teaching and learning, although possible via ed-tech, were not characteristic of the technology and solutions that were rolled out during the COVID-19 school closures. Indeed, many of the most meaningful educational experiences, such as engaging in critical thinking, inquiry, debate, group work, play, collaboration, questioning, fieldwork and experimentation, often fell outside of what was possible with mainstream ed-tech apps and platforms.

Of equal concern was the high cost of taking risks in online settings, where momentary missteps could become part of a learner's or teacher's permanent record due to omnipresent surveillance, particularly video recordings of educational exchange. Although video recording classes sometimes provided new benefits to learners, such as the ability to rewatch lessons on demand, and to teachers, including the ability to observe and

reflect on their practice, it could also carry a chilling effect. On-camera teachers and students self-policed their ideas and behaviour, quelling the spontaneity, flexibility and changeability that good pedagogy can elicit. The off-the-record comments and personal asides that could enliven classes and facilitate learning and understanding, as well as build trust, were hazardous with constant video and audio surveillance. The 'slack' of education – the less formal moments and conversations between lessons that had been commonplace in schools – seemed to some to be a casualty of systems that recorded everything. The heavy surveillance that accompanied ed-tech modes of distance learning was often justified by explanations that classes should be accessible to students who missed them or wanted to see them again. Video recording made this re-playing possible, and lessons were routinely recorded, tagged, stored and made easily retrievable, by learners and teachers but also others less proximal to digital classrooms such as school administrators, parents and politicians.

> Many commentators likened the surveillance powers of ed-tech to a panopticon.

Citing the ubiquity of surveillance, many commentators likened the surveillance powers of ed-tech to a panopticon – a building with architecture that enables systems of watching and control. The infamous panopticon prison, designed by the social theorist Jeremy Bentham and regularly invoked in philosophy, is constructed around a rotunda so that each individual cell is fully visible to a watchtower in the centre. While guards in the watchtower can peer into each cell and observe each prisoner, the prisoners cannot see the guards. Because the prisoners have no way of knowing when they are being watched, they are compelled to regulate their own behaviour as if they are being watched constantly. For this reason, panopticon prisons do not necessarily need a guard in the watchtower – the *perception* of unbroken surveillance is enough to compel prisoners to self-regulate their actions. The pervasiveness of unique log-in credentials, cameras, timers, microphones, location tracking, facial recognition technology, and time and date stamps among other modes of surveillance in the new digital environments of education could create a similar perception of incessant watching – and engender a sense that any blunder might be captured, shared, made public, decontextualized and scrutinized by others, prompting self-policing and suspicion of others. The pandemic deepened this effect due to the increased reliance on virtual spaces – where surveillance was often ubiquitous. *The Economist* dubbed this phenomenon "the coronopticon" (a conjoining of the words 'coronavirus' and 'panopticon'), calling critical attention to "a brave new age of surveillance and data control catalysed by hasty tech decisions under COVID-19".[951] In education circles, careful readers of philosophy noted that Michel Foucault's famous explanation of a panopticon prison – a collection of cages or small theatres "in which each actor is alone, perfectly individualized and constantly visible"[952] – was a remarkably apt description of some Zoom or Google Meet classes. Administrators and teachers were in a watchtower, with considerable powers of surveillance, while students were in isolated digital cells where incessant visibility could be, as Foucault argued, a trap.

The panoptic effects of the transition to remote learning were widely discussed, and in some contexts there was clear evidence that video recordings and other, often passive, forms of tech-enabled watching were indeed triggering self-censorship among students. For example, according to a survey conducted in the USA by the Center for Democracy and Technology, a majority of students in K-12 schools in the USA agreed with the statement, "I do not share my true thoughts or ideas because I know what I do online is being monitored", and 80 per cent reported being "more careful" about what they searched for online because they were aware that they were being monitored.[953] When students pre-emptively muzzle closely held ideas or avoid internet searches to further knowledge about potentially sensitive topics because of heavy-handed technology surveillance, this surveillance can constrain educational exchange and limit learning. In higher education, professors at universities in the USA and Australia noted that students from countries with strict rules on freedom of speech and harsh punishments for slander seemed less willing to speak about sensitive topics following the shift to online education.[954] Human Rights Watch documented cases of students reporting other students to national authorities for comments or activism expressed online or during online classes, including students studying outside their home countries.[955] The ease of recording educational exchanges conducted digitally could heighten fears of reporting and reprisal. A video or audio recording of a class made available on a school or university platform offered authorities concrete evidence of opinions or activism expressed in an educational setting, instead of mere hearsay.

"Everything is monitored. We have to be careful to not lose our jobs or maybe life by being sent to jail. … Many prosecutions for free speech happen every day now."

– University professor, Lebanon[clxix]

Ed-tech surveillance also appears to have heightened the self-censorship of teachers. For example, a survey of professors in 17 Arab countries (Algeria, Egypt, Iraq, Jordan, Kuwait, Lebanon, Libya, Morocco, Oman, Palestine, Saudi Arabia, Somalia, Sudan, Syria, Tunisia, the United Arab Emirates and Yemen) found that 85 per cent of respondents reported that they were 'somewhat likely', 'likely', or 'very likely' to self-censor in online classes, in emails or over social media. Professors were less likely to report censoring themselves in traditional in-person classes. The survey was conducted from November

> Ed-tech provided a technical means to pierce the privacy and intimacy that had been a hallmark of in-person and classroom-based instruction.

2020 to March 2021, a period when many Arab universities were prohibited from holding in-person courses because of the COVID-19 pandemic and thus were reliant on ed-tech for distance learning. The surveillance features of ed-tech could make classroom instruction and discussion reviewable by people outside the class or even the educational institution. Respondents of the Arab-country survey indicated that they were more concerned about government authorities or university administrators finding the ideas they shared in academic settings objectionable than their co-workers or students.[956] Ed-tech provided a technical means to pierce the privacy and intimacy that had been a hallmark of in-person and classroom-based instruction that was standard prior to the COVID-19 pandemic and shift to remote learning.

"An expectation that each session will be recorded and made available online regardless of staff preference takes away from our autonomy as lecturers and makes us feel like cogs in a machine and not human beings. It will add to the rhetoric that we're disposable and accountable for literally everything we say and will take away from our freedom of speech and creativity within the learning space to have timely, challenging discussions."

– University educator, UK[clxx]

Qualitative research conducted at universities in Palestine provided a fuller picture of how the surveillance features of ed-tech were changing dynamics at the level of individual classes. The researchers found that students and teachers in literature classes sanitized and self-regulated their discussions of books when these discussions were recorded by ed-tech utilities during the pandemic. The authors explained that topics related to sexuality, politics, misogyny and religion in literary works were repressed in class discussions due to multilayered surveillance from students, parents and administrators who could easily watch the classes either live or via a digital recording. They argued that "panoptic surveillance" enabled by remote learning with ed-tech "arguably violates the human rights to freedom of educational practices" and compelled teachers to simplify the literary analysis they performed with students. The teachers' internalization of self-censorship led them to "detach texts from politics" and avoid free and discursive discussion about literature that might stimulate critical and creative thinking. The researchers did not mince words in their summary of their main findings: "Surveillance shatters the illusion of liberation many literacy educators thought they have gained in online education; indeed, the instructors' testimonies highlight their internalization of panoptic surveillance that derails the liberating purpose of education."[957]

"Education, even in-person education, is digital in the COVID-19 era, and staff members use a piece of software to watch everything students do on school-issued laptops and to keep them off banned websites. The kids are aware."

– Priya Anand and Mark Bergen, technology journalists[clxxi]

> Ed-tech's surveillance features have threatened the viability of learning spaces that should be safe spaces for students to grow, change their minds, think and truly learn in a process of identity formation.

Ed-tech's surveillance features have threatened the viability of learning spaces that should be safe spaces for students to grow, change their minds, think and learn in a process of identity formation. The ease of data capture, storage and surveillance in digital environments can make it risky for learners to experiment with new ideas and to try on different identities to develop and grow intellectually. Beliefs staunchly held by a student in one moment could ultimately prove embarrassing at a future time as ideas change, views soften and opinions become more nuanced. Many ed-tech utilities and digital technologies generally provide people with tools to easily capture a moment, take it out of its original and intended context, and put it in a new and often unflattering light. In a world where careers and reputations can be destroyed because of a single tweet or blog post, there is a risk that what a person does, says or writes in a virtual classroom, where surveillance and recording are often inescapable, can carry outsize consequences and shadow a person in adverse ways indefinitely. Few would argue that one ill-considered school essay should limit a student's job opportunities a decade later, but the permanence and permeability of ed-tech platforms where assignments are uploaded and tagged to individuals with birthdates and other fixed identifiers have made this a more distinct possibility. As students and teachers guard themselves against risks of this sort, education becomes prone to excessively cautious self-censorship that can narrow viewpoints and discourage the formulation or sharing of original ideas – the antithesis of the knowledge expansion that education is supposed to foster.

Beyond triggering self-censorship, ed-tech could be deployed in ways that fortify top-down government censorship of knowledge and ideas. Regimes around the world, and particularly those with vested interests in buttressing an official ideology or narrative and extinguishing alternative perspectives or accounts, found that when teaching and learning was conducted over connected technology exclusively (or near exclusively), they could often exercise firmer control over what was taught and how. Some governments welcomed ed-tech as a new repertoire of tools to tighten oversight of the ideas and information introduced through education. With class instruction and discussion being beamed into homes during the pandemic, public authorities sometimes encouraged parents and other adults to hover over educational exchange and report content and ideas they deemed objectionable or off-limits. Countries and localities established online and telephone hotlines so people could report violations of rules that sought

> Ed-tech could be leveraged to implement heavy-handed censorship, doctrinaire filtering of knowledge, and the policing and intimidation of institutions.

to, for example, sanctify a particular version of history, elevate a particular leader or designate certain topics and realities as off-limits for educational discussion.[958] Knowledge that parents and other adults who were not learners might be scrutinizing online classes could prompt teachers to sidestep sensitive topics, whether explanations of current events, the reality of a historical event, or scientific concepts that have become controversial due to the circulation of misinformation and disinformation.[959] Although ed-tech had long promised to expand access to knowledge for educational purposes and help it travel across borders and boundaries, it could – in the hands of dedicated government handlers – be leveraged to achieve the opposite result: heavy-handed censorship, doctrinaire filtering of knowledge, and the policing and intimidation of institutions and instructors that shared information which had not been explicitly sanctioned.

In digital spaces, blocks on information did not always have to take the form of outright censorship. Subtler approaches were available to public authorities exercising controls over internet traffic and content. Some governments, for example, use techniques to slow, rather than stop or redirect, internet traffic at specific websites they dislike. This practice can cause users looking for these sensitive websites to grow impatient and move to other, less objectionable websites, while also allowing public authorities to avoid accusations of fully blocking content.[960] During the pandemic, many governments, autocratic and otherwise, came to appreciate and more fully understand and exercise the surveillance features and top-down controls enabled by various ed-tech utilities. The technology supporting remote learning became a versatile means to help formulate beliefs and worldviews aligned with a particular ideology, while blocking access to alternative ones. This is not to say that connected technologies did not help certain learners and teachers circumnavigate blocks on information and expand their access to knowledge. Surely this occurred. Intrepid users of technology are often able to find leaks and holes in digital firewalls and access the unfiltered internet and see content that is ostensibly restricted or censored. But many ed-tech users, especially those new to digital technology, lacked this sophisticated technical know-how. And in regimes that tightly police technology use, this knowledge could be difficult or dangerous to obtain. For these reasons, the knowledge exchange that occurred with ed-tech could be far removed from the sometimes more private and more trusting space of physical classrooms where teachers and students may have felt freer to engage in education discourses that touched on sensitive matters that were not necessarily embraced by a ruling regime.

Full internet shutdowns are another mechanism to limit access to knowledge, ideas and learning available online. They have become concerningly commonplace, including during the COVID-19 pandemic when online access carried heightened importance for education and many other sectors. Access Now, a free speech advocacy organization, documented 159 internet shutdowns across 29 countries in 2020 and 182 internet shutdowns across 34 countries in 2021.[961] Remarkably, the power of governments to shut down the internet is sometimes exercised for 'educational' purposes. Authorities in the Middle East and North Africa, including Algeria, Jordan, Sudan and Syria, occasionally shut down the internet during national exams ostensibly to prevent cheating. This rationale is based on assumptions that students will use connected devices to share answers to standardized tests. Recently, this practice has come under heavy critique by citizens and human rights experts alike, citing its limited effects on preventing cheating at the cost of infringing on citizens' rights to information and communication.[962] Nevertheless, these practices show that numerous governments hold levers to bluntly – and sometimes with high degrees of precision – block digital information flows at will, including those flows that provide portals to education and knowledge.

Figure 21:

Global internet shutdowns in 2020 and 2021

Source: Data from Access Now, 2022

On their own, advanced technologies deployed in response to public emergencies do not pose an inherent threat to citizen control over education and the free flow of knowledge and ideas. The speed and extensive application of ed-tech in the pandemic, however, upset institutional balances and often circumvented civic discourse through blanket measures and top-down directives instructing students and teachers to use applications and platforms that were developed outside public oversight. This appears to have held true in democratic regimes as well as non-democratic ones. In both situations, the surveillance capabilities of ed-tech appear to have resulted in considerable self-censorship and changed relationships among learners and teachers, often in ways that threatened to inhibit intellectual exploration and introduced new risks to open and honest educational exchange.

TECHNOLOGY AIMED AT INDIVIDUALS TILTS EDUCATIONAL RESEARCH AWAY FROM GROUPS

Many ed-tech utilities reflected a view that education could be detached from many of the group dynamics that had characterized in-person learning in school.

During the pandemic the surveillance technology of ed-tech was often aimed at individuals instead of groups, and this had implications for educational research as well as practice. Researchers studying remote learning were confronted with data that looked closely at individual actions and behaviours but tended to be relatively blind to the wider social and environmental contexts in which this learning took place. Many ed-tech utilities were built to enable personalized learning and reflected a view that education could be detached from many of the group dynamics that had characterized in-person learning in school. This aspect helped make ed-tech scalable. If an automated system accommodated only individuals, it tended to be easier and cheaper to scale out than systems that accommodated regular and sustained socialization between students who knew one another. The surveillance apparatus around a lot of ed-tech reflected this individual-at-the-centre orientation. The data that technology collected and presented on dashboards and spreadsheets to different stakeholders in education, including researchers, often provided details about the actions and progress of individual learners, yet offered little insights into how this action and progress was influenced by social interactions. Such atomized information could be rich for research purposes, but it could also obscure the complex social and environmental relationships that underlie learning and help make education engaging and purposeful.

"The sheer amount of microlevel data make big data methods a powerful tool for analyzing learner processes, but that power can lead researchers to ignore broader and potentially more important patterns that cannot be measured at the microlevel."

– Christian Fischer et al., authors of *Mining Big Data in Education*[lxxii]

Outside the context of the pandemic, sociologists and anthropologists commonly observed learners studying and living in contexts far wider than that of an ed-tech platform. But these more panoramic views of education were difficult to obtain with learning happening in homes under lockdowns and in digital spaces catering to individuals, and, in many instances, regardless of any group affiliation. The review of the literature conducted for this publication identified relatively few studies in which researchers attempted sustained observations of group dynamics in Zoom-style video classes or other ed-tech utilities supporting human-to-human interactions, even though these observations would have been relatively easy to conduct with the appropriate permissions – and, in many contexts, these permissions were quite loose. (During school closures, video classes were routinely seen by people not actively participating in them, and, presumably, this extended ring of observers could have included researchers.)

Ed-tech surveillance zoomed in on individual students but largely ignored the dynamics of groups, classrooms and schools.

A lesser-observed side effect of the surveillance and datafication features of ed-tech was the way it could background the social relationships and interactions that influence and indeed fuel meaningful learning, while foregrounding the actions of individuals, observed without much attention to social context. The automated outputs of ed-tech software, while data-rich in volume, tended to offer a rather myopic view of education that could trickle down into education research. With the benefit of hindsight, it is worth considering what AI-powered and other ed-tech surveillance systems might have revealed if they had set their sights more squarely on the working of groups.

AUTOMATION AND MACHINE PROCESSES WEAKEN TEACHER AUTHORITY

Essential relationships between teachers and students were also recast during the transition to remote learning with ed-tech. Some teachers expressed feeling "dehumanized" and lamented that they were being treated like extensions of the technology and largely automated systems that dominated the new digital-only environments of education.[963] It could be an unwelcome jolt. Before the pandemic, in physical schools and classrooms, students had interacted with teachers in person and technology

A maxim popular in ed-tech circles holds that teachers should facilitate personalized learning with technology and function as a 'guide on the side' rather than a 'sage on the stage'. But technology was often reducing teachers' roles to 'proctors on platforms'.

was usually tucked away, preserving the centrality of human connections. Many schools, especially in the lower grades, routinely banned mobile phones and computers from classrooms to avoid distractions and maintain the primacy of non-digital learning and interactions.[964] This kept teachers, rather than digital tools, as captains of pedagogy. But when schooling moved to remote, technology-mediated platforms, some educators experienced their authority slipping away amid layers of technology. Technology could, for example, assert a particular pedagogy, automatically guiding and pacing instruction, thereby reducing a teacher's role to one of a technology facilitator. Teachers expressed alarm at realizing they were, in some contexts and instances, tasked only with prompting students to progress down paths prescribed by automated systems.[965] A maxim popular in ed-tech circles holds that teachers should facilitate personalized learning with technology and function as a 'guide on the side' rather than a 'sage on the stage'. But technology was often reducing teachers' roles to 'proctors on platforms'.

A few distance learning ed-tech systems were so awash with automation that it could be hard for students and parents to see or feel the presence of teachers. One university student in Canada expressed alarm at learning that the teacher of his online art history class had died two years before the start of the course, but the course kept running with various forms of automation and, according to the university, a human teaching assistant.[966] Many advanced ed-tech apps incorporated AI-powered 'teacher' chatbots capable of sustaining human-like conversations. On occasion, this aspect could make it challenging for learners and their families to immediately distinguish between what messages and content were machine-generated and what were generated by human teachers, a challenge that is likely to grow as large language model AI chatbots are incorporated into ed-tech apps. This may have carried repercussions for how teachers were treated. If technology dehumanized teachers or made them indistinguishable from the automated features of a particular system, students could come to see them as lacking influence, authority and expertise. There is anecdotal evidence of teachers observing shifts in the style and tone of communication from students in the digital spaces of ed-tech, such that the polite and formal manners that had marked face-to-face interactions, gave way to something more abrupt and unmannerly.[967] While the pandemic had innumerable external stressors that could explain a tilt to indecorous and even rude communication, some of this decline may be attributable to the nature of impersonal technology and the downgrading of teachers' authority. Instead of being subject matter experts with deep knowledge of pedagogy and their students' learning contexts, teachers were often relegated into lesser roles when education became more automated in the digital environments of remote learning.

"Decisions made by computer are not fundamentally more logical and unbiased than decisions made by people."

– Joan Donovan, Robyn Caplan, Jeanna Matthews and Lauren Hanson, authors of *Algorithmic Accountability*[clxviii]

Algorithms carried a veneer of unassailable objectivity and fairness owing to the consistency of their outputs in response to particular inputs.

In instances where computer systems were seemingly in charge of education, students learned to defer to them not only for instruction, but evaluation as well. Many learners completed assignments inside automated apps that generated clean, instant and predictable outputs and scores. Human assessment, by contrast, tended to be less clean and less predictable. Feedback and grades given by teachers were not dictated by the rigid rules underlying machine algorithms. Human evaluators tended to look for evidence of improvement and growth from different starting points rather than evaluating assignments according to a fixed barometer of achievement. In practice, this meant that a good paper from a low-performing student was more likely to warrant strong praise and encouragement than a good paper from an extremely high-performing student. Teacher assessments can, of course, be inconsistent and imperfect in their objectivity. But some degree of variation and subjectivity do not necessarily make feedback, instruction or recommendations any less valuable. Indeed, crafting individualized feedback aimed at unique students known to a teacher is vital to personalizing education. When done well, it is a world apart from the generic feedback pre-prepared for different hypothetical students that automated systems tend to employ as a matter of necessity. Understanding that people have different strengths, weaknesses and opinions and incorporating this knowledge in feedback and evaluation is an essential part of human-centred education. It entails learning how to interact and connect with others as well as how to cooperate despite views that can diverge and conflict. These important social skills, as much a part of education as knowing the minutiae of academic subjects, cannot be evaluated by automated apps. Human relationships and exchanges that had been an important part of both learning and evaluation prior to the pandemic were commonly sidelined in ed-tech environments. In their place were unfeeling and unknowing algorithms. These algorithms often carried a veneer of unassailable objectivity and fairness owing to the consistency of their outputs in response to particular inputs.[968] But they too were subjective and reflected human agendas and biases.

Seen from this angle, the move to ed-tech was, for many, a step towards machine-reliant evaluation and a step away from the human-centric evaluations that can help students learn to navigate the complexity of human relationships and grow comfortable with diverse input and feedback. Students' deferring to machines over teachers and other humans in educational contexts did not start with the pandemic-driven reliance on technology, but it appears to have accelerated during the shift to remote online learning. For much of 2020, 2021, 2022 and early 2023, ed-tech habituated young people and families to learning that was guided and assessed by machines, and some came to see these machines as holding authority similar to or even greater than human instructors.

FALLIBLE ALGORITHMS

The cessation of in-person schooling combined with new dependencies on ed-tech for educational administration as well as teaching and learning resulted in a rise in algorithmic decision-making during the COVID-19 pandemic.[969] Computers were called on to generate information that was previously reliant on human assessments.[970] Algorithm-based systems made determinations about educational admissions, retention, scholarships and grades.[971] While many of these systems had been developed and used prior to the pandemic, they tended to touch more learners and institutions with the move to distance learning and ed-tech. Experts and media organizations regularly called attention to the ways algorithms could – and, in many instances, did – unfairly disadvantaged certain groups educationally.[972]

Examples were numerous. The Markup, an investigative media organization, documented the ways that software used by more than 500 universities in the USA was four times more likely to label black male students as 'high risk' for dropping out than white male students.[973] Separate research conducted by the Brookings Institution revealed how higher education institutions use enrolment algorithms in a two-stage process to, first, predict how likely prospective students are to enrol in a given institution and, second, to decide how to disburse scholarships in an effort to convince more prospective students to attend the institution. Researchers concluded that such use of this type of algorithm likely contributes to greater debt burdens for students, higher student dropout rates and larger racial disparities. Brookings found it particularly troubling that public information about how proprietary enrolment algorithms are designed and work was rarely available and hard to find when it was available. The researchers advised policy-makers to demand more transparency in how enrolment algorithms are used.[974]

While algorithmic systems to flag students at risk of dropping out, drive enrolment decisions and determine scholarship levels were used during the pandemic as well as before it, the widespread use of algorithms to determine student grades was unique to the pandemic. Algorithmic grading systems were deployed in various contexts mainly because tests, including high-stakes examinations, that normally would have been administered in person and at schools were cancelled due to health concerns. In search of a solution to assign grades, many educational authorities turned to algorithms. The results were almost always contentious.

As one example, the International Baccalaureate (IB) programme, which has over 170,000 upper secondary students enrolled in schools around the world, cancelled its traditional end-of-term examinations and deployed an algorithm, developed by an unnamed educational organization specializing in data analysis, to assign grades. According to the IB, the algorithm used current and historical data to arrive at subject grades for each student. Although the details of the methodology were not disclosed, the IB shared that "predicted grades" would be an "active element" in determining the final mark each student received. The organization further noted that it was committed to ensuring that "overall outcomes will look similar to [the previous year's outcomes] unless there is clear evidence why the overall cohort has changed".[975] When the end-of-term grades were assigned, many students felt that their scores had been unfairly, and in some instances, dramatically downgraded. For some students, the unexpectedly low score assigned by the algorithm endangered their offer of admission or scholarships at universities. As of early 2023, more than 25,000 people had signed an online petition expressing disappointment in the IB's practice of algorithmic grading. Students and parents raised particular concern over the IB's use of historical results to set school-based boundaries for grades. The online petition, written by Ali Zagmout, a student in an IB programme, implored the IB organization: "DO NOT use historical data because how is that in any logical sense fair on the students who go to a school with

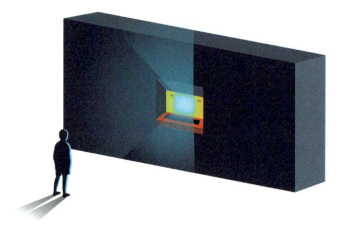

a considerably 'bad history.'"[976] Zagmout's argument captured a well-documented critique of algorithmic decision-making: its tendency to simply reproduce outcomes from the past, replete with their inequities and biases.

"We need transparency, we need an explanation ... We want our universities to admit us based on our coursework which outlines our capabilities in analytical, practical, and theoretical work rather than your skewed assessment of what your AI assumes our capabilities are."

– Author of an online petition protesting a 2020 exam grading algorithm[clxxv]

Problems and complaints observed with grading algorithms reached a national scale in the UK in 2020.[977] The UK government decided to use an algorithm to determine exam grades for students in upper secondary school. It was a major shift from traditional practice. The high-stakes, subject-based examinations known as A-levels (General Certificate of Education Advanced Level), normally taken in person and at schools, influence everything from university placements to alternative study, training or work opportunities. But because students were not able to sit for these examinations due to pandemic school closures, an algorithmic grading system was developed by the country's national examination regulation authority, Ofqual. According to reporting by *The Guardian*, Ofqual built 11 candidate algorithms to generate grades and tested them extensively, eventually determining one to be superior to the rest. But this choice of algorithm, like the others under consideration, weighted relatively sparse inputs to assign grades: namely, the historical grade distribution of the school, the predicted grade distribution of the class, the predicted grade distribution of the student and, lastly, the number of students for whom there was historical data.[978] Ofqual gained confidence in the selected algorithm because in trials it generated grades that were not excessively high or low compared with those awarded in previous years, and Ofqual considered that the close replication of past results was a primary indicator of fairness.

> The grading algorithm used in the UK gave considerable weight to the past performance of schools to determine students' final grades.

Ofqual did observe some anomalous results when it tested the algorithm, but these were estimated at less than 0.25 per cent of total results, a margin of error that was considered a palatable level of deviance. Officials were clear-eyed that any model would have imperfections, and Ofqual flagged that its algorithm had a concerning tendency to downgrade bright, high-performing students in historically low-performing schools. Like the IB algorithm, the one developed by Ofqual gave considerable weight to the past performance of schools to determine students' final grades. However, school performance is often a reflection of geography – schools in less affluent areas tend to perform lower (as measured by students' results on standardized exams) than schools in wealthier areas. Before the algorithm was deployed to assign grades to hundreds of thousands of students, Ofqual highlighted risks that "outlier students" might be disadvantaged and informed the government that "some students may think that, had they taken their exams, they would have achieved higher grades".[979]

When the algorithm was deployed at scale at the end of the 2019/20 academic year and computer-generated grades were communicated to students in August, reactions were immediate and explosive. The grading system was described as a "disaster", a "debacle", "like the sinking of the Titanic", "unfair", "harmful", "unethical", "a prejudice engine", and "cruel".[980] Nearly 40 per cent of teacher-assessed grades (around 700,000 in total) were downgraded by the Ofqual algorithm, sometimes by two grades or more.[981] Students protested across the country and were often joined by parents and teachers. They held placards with slogans such as "Your algorithm doesn't know me" and "Judge my work not my postcode".[982] While arguments have long existed in the UK about the appropriateness of assigning grades by high-stakes examinations alone, the tradition of using timed, school-administered and in-person tests was widely perceived as enabling an equal opportunity to all students. The algorithmic system developed by Ofqual was, by contrast, understood as a tool that stripped students of agency and responsibilities that they had previously exercised. At student protests held outside the UK Department for Education, students asked "How can I fail an exam I've never taken".[983] Various autopsies of the algorithmic grading system bristled in particular at the way the performance history of a student's school was used to determine grades. For many, it seemed "intrinsically unfair" that the grades assigned to students by the algorithm were "decided by the ability of pupils they may have never met".[984] The chair as well as the chief executive of Ofqual resigned, and the UK prime minister who initially supported algorithmic grading to prevent grade inflation and its knock-on effects attributed the grading fiasco to a "mutant algorithm".[985] In the face of public, media and parliamentary outcry, the government decided to drop algorithmic grading in favour of grades specified by teachers, a model that was applied again in 2021 in the face of extended school closures.[986]

Figure 22:

Algorithm developed to assign grades to students in the UK, in lieu of in-person examinations in 2020

Source: *The Guardian*, 2020

$$P_{kj} = (1-r_j)C_{kj} + r_j(C_{kj} + q_{kj} - p_{kj})$$

"Your algorithm doesn't know me."

– Slogan written on a sign held by a student in the UK protesting algorithmic grading[clxxv]

> The resistance to algorithmic grading in the UK clarified that even within the emergency context of the pandemic, there were limits to what decisions people were willing to offload to computers.

While "Trust teachers, not machines" was an oft-repeated slogan of students and parents protesting the results of the Ofqual algorithm, its defenders maintained that the dispassionate calculations of a computer could assign grades more objectively than human teachers. Ofqual's pre-COVID studies indicated that around half of grades issued to students by teachers year-to-year are aberrant in some way.[987] During a grilling by the UK Parliament's Education Committee, the chair of Ofqual was pressured to disown the grading algorithm, but he largely declined, even as he apologized to students who felt they had been hurt by it.[988] As reporter Tom Lamont observed in a detailed accounting of the UK's turbulent and short-lived experiment with algorithmic grading, Ofqual's creation was neither "mutant" nor "rogue". "The algorithm," Lamont wrote, "did what it was supposed to do. Humans, in the end, had no stomach for what it was supposed to do."[989] But the imbroglio revealed that people in the UK did have a stomach for teacher assessments – and, beyond this, they took to the streets to demand them when traditional testing practices were suspended. Despite the many imprecisions and inconsistencies of their grading, teachers could better see and account for the complexities of students' lives and contexts than a machine. They could see learners as people, humans with strengths, weaknesses, ambitions, struggles, interests, work ethics and imperfections – a messy whole difficult to distil into quantitative data. The resistance to algorithmic grading in the UK clarified that even within the emergency context of the pandemic, there were limits to what decisions people were willing to offload to computers. The Ofqual algorithm stands as an example of technology solutionism at work in educational assessment. A one-size-fits-all formula capable of crunching various bits of data available to a central authority was put forward as a clean, efficient, fast, technology-dependant and reasonably fair remedy to the thorny problem of assigning grades during pandemic school closures. Students and families, however, voiced a strong preference for keeping human teachers at the helm of grading decisions. Ultimately, they successfully prompted the government to reverse course on a technical and automated solution in favour of a more human-mediated interim solution.

"The question that the exam authorities and the politicians needed to answer was not: 'How do we create a fair assessment system to replace the exams?' but: 'What kind of fairness do we want and what kinds of unfairness are we willing to tolerate?'"

– Kenan Malik, writer and columnist[clxxvi]

Beyond resisting algorithmic grading, students and the public also pushed back against algorithms used to guide university admissions during the pandemic, perhaps reflecting increased awareness of the tendency of algorithms to simply replicate past results. In one notable example, the University of Texas, spurred by a series of crucial tweets in 2020, phased out a machine-learning system that helped admissions officers make determinations about which students to admit into the university's prestigious doctoral-level computer science programmes.[990] The system had been created by two people in 2013 to speed up applicant reviews and reduce the human labour of admission committees. To hone the automated system, the creators trained it to give a numerical ranking to each applicant using data from past (pre-2013) admissions decisions. When the system came under scrutiny, its critics voiced dismay that the university was relying on a machine process that had 'hard-coded' whatever patterns – and biases – the University of Texas selection committee possessed nearly a decade before. Even the creators of the system acknowledged that it had only been programmed to mirror what the admissions committee had been doing before 2013.[991] Yet lost in some of the media coverage about the system was research to indicate that the technology reduced the time needed to review candidates' applications by approximately 75 per cent, and separate data showing that the number of candidates submitting applications to the university's computer science doctoral programmes ballooned from 250 in 2000 to around 650 in 2012 to over 1,200 in 2020.[992] The time and cost efficiencies enabled by such algorithmic systems, combined with greater demands on educational institutions, made the systems understandably attractive to educational authorities.[993]

> In closing off various traditional processes reliant on in-person human exchange to make educational decisions, the health crisis hastened the introduction and wide-scale implementation of algorithmic substitutes.

Although the University of Texas admission algorithm and the UK grading algorithm were both ultimately abandoned, elsewhere, the trend of using algorithms and other automated systems to make important decisions related to education was on the rise.[994] In closing off various traditional processes reliant on in-person human exchange to make determinations related to everything from admissions and grades to counselling and teacher assessment, the health crisis hastened the introduction and wide-scale implementation of algorithmic substitutes. This was sometimes cast as matter of necessity, rather than a strategy to optimize efficiencies and reduce costs, as was typically the framing prior to COVID-19. Algorithms that had been optional prior to 2020 were often repositioned as only- or best-option choices to keep the machinery of education running in the context of pandemic school closures and the hard pivot to ed-tech. Because these systems were highly reliant on data inputs, they were almost exclusively deployed in countries where educational data were already plentiful. The volumes and types of data needed to, for example, compute student grades algorithmically in lieu of test scores or teacher assessments were largely unavailable in countries where datafication processes remained nascent. Algorithmic decision-making, in this regard, followed the trail of educational datafication. Both accelerated during the pandemic.

REMOTE PROCTORING, SUSPICION SCORES AND SOFTWARE SEDIMENTATION

While many educational institutions cancelled important tests during the pandemic, others attempted to keep them going by moving them online, thereby minimizing disruptions to standard practices and academic calendars. If students could take tests, these instruments could remain mechanisms to assess student achievement and assist various ranking, sorting and gate-keeping exercises. A lot of tests were not particularly difficult to digitalize and, well before the pandemic, testing had been moving out of paper formats and into digital ones. Ed-tech organizations offered extensive services and options to create digital tests. Various systems allowed students to answer multiple-choice questions, balance equations, type short answer responses and compose lengthy essays. Once a test was completed it could be passed onward to a teacher for review. In some cases, computers performed all or part of the review – a process that could make assessment nearly instantaneous, especially for tests with fixed-answer questions and other inputs that were easy for machines to read and mark. Computer evaluations of tests with open-ended questions requiring written responses tended to be less seamless, however, and often introduced problems. Researchers documented, for instance, the ways leading

language- processing AI systems used to score student essays, including on high-stakes examinations, could give high and even perfect scores to "complete incoherence" and "meaningless gibberish".[995] Other automated grading engines could be tricked into awarding high marks with simple hacks like writing a few long and grammatically complex sentences followed by a disjointed list of keywords.[996] The systems also did little to recognize and reward stylistic and other compositional creativity – concerns that the Australian government cited in 2018, among others, for abandoning plans to transition to an automated scoring system to mark standardized writing assessments.[997]

Regardless of who was doing the evaluation (teachers or machines), when assessments moved online during pandemic school closures, digital testing opened the door to various exclusions and inequities. Students without requisite technology or digital skills were cut off from examinations, and learners with slow internet connections or distracting home environments tended to be at a disadvantage. These problems were especially pronounced at basic and secondary education grade levels, and as a result, many examinations scheduled for K-12 learners were postponed or cancelled.

Institutions of higher education were more likely to adopt and require digital testing. Compared to learners in basic or secondary education, students in higher education were, on average, more digitally skilled and better able to access connected technology, in addition to being older and more independent. They could more reasonably fulfil digital testing requirements, and higher education institutions were more likely to adopt and require digital testing. Universities around the world decided to keep testing routines largely in place throughout pandemic lockdowns. What had previously been done in person and on paper would be completed digitally and remotely. The major challenge, as it was widely understood, was the prevention of cheating.

Educators and others assumed that cheating would be rampant if tests were taken outside of schools, in online environments and beyond the watchful gaze of teachers. A survey conducted by Wiley, a leading education publisher, found that over 90 per cent of instructors believed students were "more likely" to cheat in remote online learning environments than in standard non-digital testing environments.[998] However, research into online test-taking suggested that these suspicions had limited empirical evidence. Findings from a 2014 study indicated that the prevalence of cheating in online test modalities did not appear to vary significantly from traditional offline modalities.[999] A separate study from 2010 found that the percentage of students who anonymously self-reported dishonest behaviours during a

> The perception that cheating would spike in the distance learning and remote testing environments of the pandemic pushed higher education institutions to seek quick remedies to assure the integrity of examinations. Enter technology.

test was roughly the same in live and online settings, even though students reported that they were much more likely to get caught in a live setting.[1000] Research had also revealed that simple honour pledges were highly effective at curbing cheating, suggesting that a culture of mutual trust is among the most effective mechanisms to prevent cheating.[1001] Regardless, the perception that cheating would spike in the distance learning and remote testing environments of the pandemic pushed higher education institutions to seek quick remedies to assure the integrity of examinations. Enter technology.

Prior to the pandemic, a handful of start-up companies had already developed and sold software that 'watched' students taking examinations remotely. By giving human observers or AI systems access to a test taker's computer, including through screen-sharing and camera and microphone controls, the software was purportedly able to detect cheating. The products were bundled under a generic label of remote proctoring technologies. They had filled a relatively niche market before COVID-19, providing online-only universities and some professional schools a means to supervise examinations taken online and at a distance with, in theory, the same or greater vigilance that might be paid to students taking an in-person examination in a classroom setting.

Although very few students had direct experience with remote proctoring technology prior to 2020, this changed with the pandemic. Higher education institutions around the world instructed teachers to ensure online tests were overseen with remote proctoring utilities. A poll taken of higher education institutions in numerous countries found that over half (54 per cent) were actively using remote proctoring services as early as April 2020, just a few weeks into the global health crisis.[1002] A later and larger study of colleges and universities in Canada and the USA found that 63 per cent appeared to be using proctoring software in November 2020.[1003] By 2021, remote proctoring was anything but fringe. Commentary about it spilled from ed-tech focused publications like EdSurge to general interest newspapers and magazines with international readership, ranging from *The New Yorker* to *Teen Vogue*.[1004]

Online proctoring was marketed to educational institutions as a bundle of technology to "secure exam integrity" and "protect" institutional reputation.[1005] The implicit assumption was that institutions that did not use the technology were putting their reputations at risk and endangering the integrity of the diverse examinations administered by different departments and instructors. At its core, remote proctoring is surveillance. It conveys an explicit lack of trust to students because its only purpose is to try to prevent cheating and detect it if or when it occurs. While teachers and teaching assistants overseeing an in-class examination might also play a prevention and detection function, these are hardly the only ones. Teachers can provide clarifications, make needed adjustments, respond to requests and provide encouragement. They can also observe responses and hear student feedback to adjust future instruction. Many educators recoil at the idea of sternly policing examinations being taken by young adults attending universities on a voluntary basis and often paying for the privilege. They assume students will adhere to ethical standards and only intervene when there is strong evidence of deviation from these standards.

Remote proctoring technologies are different. They are purpose-built to root out any form of cheating: from extreme infractions (a student paying someone else to take a test) to minor rule-breaking lapses (glancing at a mobile phone that is supposed to be out of sight to check an incoming message). The starting point of proctoring technology is a view that all students are 'suspects' of cheating until they 'prove' themselves innocent by adhering to the rules and protocols – some of them kept in secret – surrounding a given examination.

"To take a test you need to let a stranger have a video recording of your room? Are you kidding me?"

– Bill Fitzgerald, researcher at Consumer Reports[clxxvii]

> The surveillance required for remote proctoring could verge on the Orwellian: unknown and unseen proctors transforming a student's computer into a watching and recording device that studied movements, noises, typing patterns and digital navigation for potential infractions.

The surveillance required for remote proctoring could verge on the Orwellian: unknown and unseen proctors transforming a student's computer into a watching and recording device that studied movements, noises, typing patterns and digital navigation for potential infractions. Students were often required to prove their identity by holding a government-issued photo identification up to a webcam. Sometimes they had to answer verification questions related to their place and date of birth, place of residence, student identification number and so forth. Identity might also be corroborated with technical proxies such as IP addresses or typing speeds. If a student's IP address or typing speed differed from one test to another, the system might flag the discrepancy to a human proctor for inspection. Additionally, students were regularly required to show their physical surroundings prior to the start of an examination by turning webcams 360 degrees and enabling close-up views of their immediate workspace, the table or desk where the laptop would sit.[1006] Some companies offering remote proctoring services guaranteed that a human proctor, often working from a country with low labour costs, would watch a student for the entire duration of the test, even though the student could almost never see the person proctoring the exam.[1007] Behaviour and actions deemed suspicious such as another person entering the testing room, sometimes a shared bedroom or common area in a student's home, might be escalated to an 'interventionist' who could demand that the student stand up or point the webcam in a particular direction. Prior to taking examinations, students would also have to download proprietary software that would lock their devices, preventing, for example, internet searches or blocking the use of other software, thereby compelling strict compliance with conditions specified by an educational institution.

Figure 23:

Step-by-step guide to start an exam overseen remotely by a human proctor

Source: ProctorU, 2023

1 **Log in** to your ProctorU account 2-3 minutes before your scheduled appointment and click Start Session when the countdown timer reaches 0:00:00.

2 **Pre-checks:** If you don't already have the ProctorU extension, you'll be prompted to download it. You'll be required to accept exam guidelines and terms of service. The browser will prompt you to share your screen, a required part of being proctored online. You'll be automatically guided through a series of equipment checks to make sure your system meets minimum requirements.

3 **Photos & Authentications:** You'll take a photo of yourself as well as your I.D. for identity verification purposes. Depending on the level of verification required by your institution, you may be asked to answer a series of randomly generated, public record challenge questions. You may also be required to type out a paragraph of text that will be checked against a pre-existing typing test that you would have been asked to complete prior to exam day. Both of these are optional measures selected by your instructor or institution.

4 **Chatbox download:** You will be prompted to download and run a LogMeIn Rescue applet file that will bring up a chat box allowing you to text with your proctor. If prompted, be sure to click "open" or "allow" to give the file permission to run. When the chat box says "waiting," it means that you are in the queue waiting for your proctor. TIP: If your status shows "waiting," do not re-download the applet file as that will put you back at the end of the queue. If you have issues with this applet file, view these troubleshooting tips.

5 **Proctor Connection & Confirmations:** Your proctor will greet you and confirm that you passed your identity verification steps. You'll review the exam rules with your proctor and they'll ask to see any permitted resources that your instructor has allowed you to use during your exam.

6 **Remote System Check:** Your proctor will ask to take remote control of your mouse and keyboard via the LogMeIn Rescue applet in order to make sure no unpermitted programs are running. You will be able to see everything that your proctor is doing during this step, and it is impossible for them to access any files without your knowledge.

7 **Camera Pan:** Your proctor will ask you to show the 4 walls of your room as well as your desk space via your webcam. You may or may not also be asked to show your computer monitor by using a mirror or cellphone camera. Lastly, your proctor will make sure your cell phone is out of reach.

8 **Navigating to the Exam & Password Entry:** Your proctor will then direct you into your LMS or exam delivery system so that he or she can unlock your exam with the password we've been provided by your instructor.

9 **Take Your Exam:** Your proctor will release control of your computer and you'll begin your exam when you're ready.

NOTE: Your webcam view and your screen will be recorded through the duration of your exam.

Remote proctoring systems typically required students to sign off on long user agreements that allowed for the collection of extensive personal identifying information. The March 2020 privacy policy of ProctorU, a leading provider of live human proctoring services, offered an example. The policy included a supplement disclosing, in accordance with a California state law in the USA, that information collected from test takers over the previous year included the following: "name, alias, signature, address, phone number, email address, driver's licence or other state identification card number, passport number, or any other personal identifier … age, race, color, height, weight, gender, gender identity, or gender expression … national origin, marital status, parental status, military status, or veteran status … citizenship, educational background and current employment … genetic, physiological, behavioral, and biological characteristics … fingerprints, faceprints, voiceprints, iris or retina scans … photographs, video recordings, or audio recordings".[1008] It was unclear how or why many of these identifiers might be necessary to uphold the integrity of an academic examination, but they were collected nevertheless. ProctorU later merged with another proctoring company to become Meazure Learning. The entity's updated privacy policy grants the company permission to share information with proctors at a student's educational institution and, in some cases, with unspecified "affiliates". The terms further state that the student data could be retained "for as long as necessary".[1009] Although the collected data were assumed to be secure, this was not always the case. In August 2020, ProctorU confirmed a data breach that compromised the user records of close to half a million people.[1010] A student newspaper in Australia reporting on the theft included a statement from the University of Sydney Students' Representative Council about the incident: "We consistently warned the University that this could happen. We demand the University immediately suspend the use of ProctorU, as that is the only way to guarantee that students are not exposed [to privacy breaches] again in the future."[1011]

Some remote proctoring companies opted for a fully automated approach to supervising exams, dropping human observers in favour of AI systems. Instead of hiring people to watch test takers through cameras, microphones and screen-sharing utilities, several ed-tech firms used algorithms trained via machine learning to flag suspicious activity that could be reviewed by humans after the exam. These solutions were sometimes billed as more efficient, cheaper, and less invasive than live human remote proctoring products.[1012] It was also a textbook example of technology solutionism – AI software was elevated as an expedient tool to solve or at least mitigate the complex human problem of cheating on academic examinations.

On close inspection though, fully automated remote proctoring systems did not actually identify cheating, but rather recorded and flagged "raw

> Remote proctoring systems used recorded activity to generate an overall 'suspicion score' for each student.

evidence of potentially suspicious activity".[1013] This activity was tagged and aggregated to generate an overall "suspicion score" for each student. The information was then presented on an instructor-facing or institution-facing dashboard, often with red, yellow and green icons to designate high, medium and low suspicion scores. The assumption was that a course instructor or perhaps someone else at the educational institution would review the suspicious activity and make determinations about which incidents, if any, constituted *actual* cheating. In practice, this required an instructor to wade through detailed information about potential computer-based abnormalities (designated with labels and headings such as 'navigating away', 'keystrokes', 'copy and paste', 'browser resize', 'mouse movement', 'scrolling', 'clicking'), environmental abnormalities ('audio levels', 'head and eye movement', 'leaving the room', 'multiple faces'), and technical abnormalities ('exam duration', 'start times', 'end times', 'exam collusion'). Abnormalities were defined as unusual behaviours "calculated with respect to the rest of the class". This meant that a student exhibiting behaviour identified by the automated system as being "slightly different" from the behaviour of other students taking the same exam was likely to be flagged for suspicion. Incident logs cued up information the system deemed warranting human review. Clicking through these incidents, instructors were shown video and audio replays of students taking tests along with other technical information. Depending on the settings specified before a test, a human reviewer could also check room scans (a 360-degree video of the exam environment, often a student's bedroom), screen recordings (footage of exactly what a student saw, second-by-second, on the computer monitor used to take the test), and location (where in a particular community a student took the test, usually a home address).[1014]

"It can be challenging to interpret a student's actions. That's why we don't."

– Spokesperson for leading provider of remote proctoring technology and services[clxxviii]

While the technology accumulated and presented evidence that could constitute cheating, it was ultimately left to instructors to determine if the evidence rose to the threshold of actual cheating.

Determinations about what behaviours constituted cheating were rarely straightforward. Was the detection of a student routinely glancing away from a computer screen proof of cheating? Was video evidence that a student looked at a mobile phone momentarily during an exam enough to fail a student or initiate more serious punitive actions? Were unsanctioned attempts to copy and paste information or resize a window or open multiple internet tabs signs that a test taker was trying to gain unfair advantage? Were high suspicion scores, designated by a computer, reliable indications of impropriety? Should students with exam logs containing numerous abnormalities be watched more closely than other students during future examinations? The automated systems would not say. According to the documentation of a major remote proctoring provider, the "software does not perform any type of algorithmic decision-making, such as determining if a breach of exam integrity has occurred. All decisions regarding exam integrity are left up to the exam administrator or institution".[1015] This meant that human instructors, people who typically had no previous experience using computerized proctoring systems of any sort, had to differentiate harmless behaviour from genuine misconduct. In most instances, they had to do this without any training in how to judiciously review evidence in the form of various playback functions and complex technical information presented on instructor-facing dashboards. While the technology accumulated and presented evidence that *could* constitute cheating, it was ultimately left to instructors to determine if the evidence rose to the threshold of *actual* cheating. This aspect allowed remote proctoring providers to deflect criticism that their technology was wrongly punishing students, because, officially, it was the instructor or institution that did this. The Electronic Frontier Foundation, an organization focused on civil liberties in the digital world, called this practice "blame-shifting". The organization highlighted the tendency of remote proctoring companies to "advertise the efficacy of their cheating-detection tools when it suits them, and dodge critics by claiming that the schools are to blame for any problems".[1016]

"Cheating is not a technological problem, but a social and pedagogical problem. Technology is often blamed for creating the conditions in which cheating proliferates and is then offered as the solution to the problem it created; both claims are false. Cheating predates the internet and will not be solved by a tool, a product, or an algorithm, even when that cheating happens online."

– Shea Swauger, librarian and instructor, Auraria Library[clxxix]

The problems with automated remote proctoring systems went well beyond outsourcing arcane exam security settings and integrity reviews to inexperienced teachers and administrators. The technology was widely reported to rely on facial recognition and facial detection tools that could disadvantage non-white students, even in countries and contexts where a majority of students are black or have dark skin. A student software researcher, Lucy Satheesan, demonstrated, for example, that a leading provider of remote proctoring services appeared to be relying on an open-source facial detection model that "fails to recognize black faces more than 50 percent of the time".[1017] This defect had long marred other automated systems and commonly disadvantaged non-white users, particularly women of colour.[1018] A major 2019 US government-funded study had found that even top-performing facial recognition systems misidentify black people at rates five to ten times higher than white people.[1019] If an automated proctoring system does not appropriately identify a test taker's face, the test taker is more likely to be flagged for suspicious behaviour. The systemic flagging of people of colour for possible infractions can, in turn, spark unconscious bias in teachers.[1020] During the pandemic students of colour in the USA and other places occasionally took to social media to vent frustration that machine proctoring systems were unable to recognize their faces. Several called critical attention to automated prompts to increase lighting, even though they were sitting in well-lit rooms.[1021]

"THIS! There's no reason I should have to collect all the light God has to offer, just for [remote proctoring software] to pretend my face is still undetectable."
– Twitter post from a student expressing frustration with an automatic proctoring service[clxx]

Like unreliable face detection, connectivity problems could also raise a student's suspicion score. Remote proctoring software was prone to designate breaks in connectivity, whatever the cause, as suspicious activity. In September 2020, a ruling by the Supreme Court of India resulted in the cancellation of a remote AI-proctored admissions exam at the National Law School because the software was deemed to have unfairly penalized students who did not have reliable, high-speed internet access or devices capable of supporting the hardware requirements to run the proctoring software.[1022] Sometimes it was not students' computers and internet connections that caused problems, but the technology used by the proctoring service providers themselves. In some instances, the proctoring service would go down and students would have to wait for it to come back online before they could continue taking a test, often losing exam time in the process or being forced to log back into the system, a process that typically involved various security and identification protocols.[1023]

> The inflexibility of remote proctoring technology often failed to accommodate the special needs of disabled students, such as extended examination time, frequent breaks or alternate testing environments.

Students who might require accommodations in exams could also be disadvantaged by the technology. By relying on AI algorithms and constant video surveillance, machine proctoring systems could exacerbate anxiety and discomfort for students with mental health issues or conditions like ADHD (attention deficit hyperactivity disorder). The systems were also prone to characterize atypical movements or behaviours associated with certain disabilities, such as physical tics like those expressed by individuals with Tourette Syndrome, as suspicious activity. Some remote proctoring software either did not have or blocked access to assistive technologies that help accommodate students with disabilities, such as screen readers and magnification tools for visually impaired students. Overall, the inflexibility of remote proctoring technology often failed to accommodate the special needs of disabled students, such as extended examination time, frequent breaks or alternate testing environments.[1024] The machine algorithms powering automated proctoring software were coded to treat deviations from average or ideal behaviour or movement as suspicious. But what is average for a student with ADHD or Tourette Syndrome was generally far from the average or ideal hard-coded in automated proctoring utilities.[1025]

"I try to become like a mannequin during tests now."
– Teenager accused of cheating after being flagged by AI proctoring software[cixxx]

A 2019 study found that heavy digital surveillance introduced by remote proctoring appears to exacerbate test-taking anxiety, resulting in lower overall exam performance.[1026] During the pandemic, students reported that they were afraid of being flagged for innocuous behaviours, such as looking at the floor or fidgeting, while other students worried that technical issues, such as sound made by an incoming email or an unstable internet connection, might raise their suspicion score and result in unjust disciplinary action.[1027] Researchers found that students were generally dissatisfied with remote proctoring and would not continue with it, if given a choice.[1028] Testimonials revealed the lengths students would go to in order to avoid appearing suspicious to remote proctors, human or machine. There was documentation, for instance, of students urinating in bottles or wearing adult diapers to avoid stepping away from screens to use the toilet in case this action caused the termination of their online proctored exam.[1029] One student told a *Washington Post* reporter that she asked a live human proctor permission to vomit without moving outside the view of a webcam to ensure that she would not be at risk of disqualification (permission was granted.)[1030] In a particularly extreme incident, a pregnant woman completing a high-stakes, remotely proctored exam stayed in view of the camera, finished answering questions and concluded the exam following official protocols, despite her water breaking and the onset of labour. She was aware that if she closed her computer, moved out of the screen or made sudden movements, the AI proctoring software watching her was likely to flag her for disqualification and perhaps unethical behaviour.[1031]

"Students have already spent the majority of this year stressed out and anxious about the state of the world. They shouldn't have to worry about whether they are doing enough to convince the robot proctor that cheating is not occurring."
– Editorial board of the University of Illinois student newspaper[clxxxii]

Remote proctoring technology also introduced additional stress and work for teachers. Systems prompted them to watch and listen to long queues of video and audio snippets taken from students sitting in isolation, typically in their bedrooms or in other rooms in their homes, scenes that could make instructors feel like trespassers. From these snippets, teachers were supposed to pinpoint what actions violated rules and warranted discipline. The incidents flagged as suspicious were commonly clouded in ambiguity. Teachers could find themselves watching a video replay four or five different times to determine if cheating had occurred. Remote proctoring systems, due to their singular function to flag potential instances of cheating, established an adversarial dynamic that could pit teachers against students. Teachers were cast as sleuths as they tried to decipher if a particular student was, say, illicitly glancing at a mobile phone at minute 00:36, or if the sounds detected between minutes 00:42 to 00:44 were made by someone reciting answers or were, rather, more innocuously, coming from someone speaking loudly in the same home. Remote proctoring organizations and affiliates produced videos and posted webinars to YouTube to sharpen teachers' skills at ferreting out unethical practice with titles such as "How examinees cheat and how to catch them".[1032] They could be over 45 minutes in duration.[1033] This policing and detective work diverted valuable time and energy away from instruction and constructive communication with students. Many teachers also felt uncomfortable being presented with hours of video footage of students taking examinations inside their homes.

> Teachers and students alike voiced concerns that personal privacy was being overrun by efforts to assure the integrity of examinations, and they pushed back against the new norms that were being erected around test-taking.

Teachers and students alike voiced concerns that personal privacy was being overrun by efforts to assure the integrity of examinations, and they pushed back against the new norms that were being erected around test-taking. Students at numerous universities created petitions to call on their educational institutions to stop using remote proctoring software.[1034] These letters commonly cited concerns about privacy, increased stress and the untrusting relationships the software introduced. Student petitions to cease use of remote proctoring software alternately labelled it as "legitimized spyware", "creepy and unacceptable", and disadvantageous to "students with limited access to technology or a quiet testing location".[1035]

Faculty associations sometimes joined students in communicating discontent and calling for a change of course.[1036] In some cases, activist organizations took direct aim at specific remote proctoring companies and their leaders. This was evident when the digital rights organization Fight for the Future created a website with the URL proctorioisworsethanaproctologyexam.com to target the CEO of Proctorio in no uncertain terms.[1037]

"I have heard from dozens of individuals who want to speak out about this technology but fear the repercussions."

– Albert Fox Cahn, founder and executive director of the Surveillance Technology Oversight Project[clxxxii]

Remote proctoring companies did not take criticism of their services lying down and sometimes brought legal threats and actions against detractors.[1038] In one incident, dubbed "an egregious case of legal bullying",[1039] lawyers for ProctorU, a provider of online proctoring services, sent an aggressive letter to the faculty association at the University of California Santa Barbara (UCSB) after the association sent a letter to the university chancellor and vice-chancellor urging them to discontinue UCSB's contract with the company. The association's letter, dated March 2020, stated: "We recognize that in our collective race to adapt our coursework and delivery in good faith, there are trade-offs and unfortunate aspects of the migration online that we must accept. This is not one of them. We are not willing to sacrifice the privacy and digital rights of our students for the expediency of a take-home final exam. That is a price too high and unfairly borne by our students." The faculty association asked the university to withdraw from its contract with ProctorU and to "issue a statement discouraging faculty to use this service or any other private service that either sells or makes students' data available to third parties".[1040] In their response, ProctorU's lawyers characterized the faculty's correspondence as "defamatory" and demanded an immediate "cease and desist from the continued misrepresentation and misstatement of ProctorU's privacy practices".[1041] ProctorU's attorneys demanded that the faculty association issue a retraction acknowledging its "errors and misrepresentations" and went so far as to prepare a letter for the faculty members to sign, which included a line stating: "I had no legitimate basis to interfere with UCSB's contract with ProctorU, or to request the University issue a statement discouraging faculty from using ProctorU's services".[1042] Public Citizen, a consumer rights advocacy organization, stated that ProctorU's demands had "little merit" and speculated that their "intended effect" was "terrifying the faculty group".[1043]

This was not the only time critics of remote proctoring companies were targeted with legal action. In a separate 2020 incident, Proctorio, a leading provider of automated remote proctoring services, sued Ian Linkletter, at the time a learning technology specialist at the University of British Columbia.[1044] His offence? Sharing links to internal instructional videos he found on Proctorio's website that detailed how the company's technology worked, including how it detected abnormal eye movement and how it performed room scans.[1045] Linkletter is fighting the charges brought by Proctorio, which his legal team has labelled a "strategic lawsuit against public participation".[1046] The same ed-tech company also requested extensive retractions of unflattering information and analysis contained in a peer-reviewed academic journal about remote proctoring services.[1047] The journal, *Hybrid Pedagogy*, declined. Proctorio further compelled a university student studying computer engineering to remove online posts that included a critical analysis of its software code.[1048] Proctorio argued that because the student's posts contained links to excerpts of its proprietary computer code, they were an infringement of the company's copyright. This action promoted the Electronic Frontier Foundation (EFF), a civil liberties organization focused on digital issues, to sue Proctorio on behalf of the student, stating in a press release: "Software companies don't get to abuse copyright law to undermine their critics. Using pieces of code to explain your research or support critical commentary is no different from quoting a book in a book review."[1049] This lawsuit prompted Proctorio to try to subpoena documents from Fight for the Future, another organization that had campaigned against the use of remote proctoring software and was active in defending the actions of the computer engineering student and Ian Linkletter.[1050]

> The use of heavy-hitting legal manoeuvres to muzzle criticism of commercial ed-tech products was seen by some observers as an aggressive corporate tactic planted in the more freewheeling, say-what-you-want world of education.

The use of heavy-hitting legal manoeuvres to muzzle criticism of commercial ed-tech products was seen by some observers as a troubling new development in education – an aggressive corporate tactic planted in the more freewheeling, say-what-you-want world of education. In many national and local contexts, students and faculty, particularly those at universities, were accustomed to having the freedom to speak out against actions, practices and businesses they did not like; indeed, the academic environment often encouraged this. But the entry of commercial ed-tech players with aggressive legal teams and lofty sales ambitions changed the dynamic. It raised the stakes for people voicing critiques and appears to have had a chilling effect on open exchanges about the place, appropriateness and functionality of new technology used to oversee examinations, sometimes with full automation. An "aura of litigiousness" surrounded the topic and had the effect of dissuading people from pointing out the limitations and flaws of the technology.[1051]

Privacy and litigation concerns aside, it was unclear whether remote proctoring systems were accomplishing their singular objective of preventing cheating. A group of researchers from the University of Twente in

Privacy and litigation concerns aside, it was unclear whether remote proctoring systems were accomplishing their singular objective of preventing cheating.

the Netherlands tested the efficacy of Proctorio as part of a 2021 experiment that involved 30 students. Six of the students were asked to cheat in various ways, while five were asked to behave nervously but take the test honestly. According to the researchers, the most important finding was that "*none* of the cheating students were flagged by Proctorio", but it did flag several students taking the test honestly or those acting nervously. This led the researchers to conclude that the use of the proctoring tool is "best compared to taking a placebo … not because it works but because people believe that it works, or that it might work".[1052] The problem of automated systems flagging innocuous actions as suspicious was documented outside experimental settings. In one well reported case, an automatic remote proctoring service offered by a company called ExamSoft flagged over one-third of nearly 9,000 test takers completing a high-stakes professional credentialing examination for possible cheating.[1053] Ultimately, around 90 per cent of the students initially marked for suspicion were cleared, while the other 10 per cent underwent further scrutiny.[1054]

Perhaps owing to the sometimes numerous false flags and the technology's limited reliability, many teachers, it seems, did not bother to review the videos and other evidence of potential impropriety the automated systems fed into instructor-facing dashboards. Beyond this, reviewing the incidents could be time-consuming (clicking through videos of students staring at a screen) and fraught with ethical dilemmas (was it *really* cheating?). The reviews could also trigger a cascade of administrative burdens if they resulted in formal accusations of cheating. ProctorU, a remote proctoring service provider that stopped offering fully automated options and provided only live human proctoring solutions, stated that according to its internal data, only about "11 percent of faculty members review the video" for students who are flagged by the fully automated tools. This was cited as a reason the company discontinued the fully automatic service.[1055] This finding was corroborated by a separate audit of automatic proctoring software used at the University of Iowa in the USA. The audit found that of the flagged incidents teachers were encouraged to manually review, only 14 per cent were actually accessed and seen.[1056]

The use of automated proctoring systems dedicated to spotting suspicious behaviour resulted in a proliferation of strategies to avoid being tagged as suspicious as well as more unethical advice on how to 'beat the machine', or more plainly, how to cheat on exams.[1057] Internet websites and forums were awash with tutorials outlining methods to gain unfair advantage and avoid getting caught. The strategies ranged from the crude (affixing sticky notes to a computer monitor or writing answers directly on the screen)[1058] to the creative (renaming computer icons with formulas, names and dates that would be of assistance)[1059] to the technically sophisticated (running a virtual machine during an exam, thereby turning a single computer into two – one being policed by proctoring software and another unencumbered).[1060] When high-stakes exams moved outside educational institutions and onto computers used in homes, it ignited, according to some students, a "digital arms race", pitting new ways of cheating against new types of software designed to prevent cheating.[1061] Cheating and deception of this sort extended beyond remote proctoring and spilled into run-of-the-mill online classes. In China, for instance, the pandemic was a boom for firms offering services to finish pre-recorded classes for students who did not want to watch them and respond to occasional questions designed to compel viewership. A representative of one of these companies said the costs assessed to students to attend one course on their behalf rose from 3 yuan (USD 0.40) in January 2020 to 10 yuan (USD 1.40) in early March 2020, after China had closed most schools due to the pandemic.[1062] Cat-and-mouse manoeuvres to facilitate cheating and a cottage industry of digital work to feign course completion were a long way from the educational benefits ed-tech like remote proctoring had promised to deliver.

> Regardless of how effective or ineffective remote proctoring systems might have been at protecting exam integrity, they were definitely lucrative.

Regardless of how effective or ineffective remote proctoring systems might have been at protecting exam integrity, they were definitely lucrative. The pandemic was, unsurprisingly, a bonanza for remote proctoring businesses.[1063] Like other providers of ed-tech, companies selling digital proctoring technology and services experienced unprecedented growth as schools and universities began closing en masse starting in early 2020. Proctorio's chief executive, Mike Olsen, told the *New York Times* that his business grew 900 per cent after lockdowns were implemented. In April 2019, his company proctored 235,000 exams versus 2.5 million in

April 2020.[1064] The company's list of clients grew more than 500 per cent between 2019 and 2021.[1065] Companies offering mostly live proctoring also experienced massive growth. ProctorU told *The New Yorker* it administered 1.5 million exams in 2019 and roughly 4 million in 2020.[1066] Similarly, Examity, another provider focused on live proctoring, was sailing past growth targets in 2020 and, like its peers, scrambling to keep pace hiring, vetting and training new proctors.[1067] The direct costs for remote proctoring services were hardly trivial, nor were the indirect expenses that included everything from system integration, staff time, training seminars and so forth. Sometimes universities transferred the direct costs to students.[1068] An exam requiring a remote live human proctor, regardless of location, typically cost more than USD 20 per exam and could be over USD 100, depending on the duration of the exam and selection of features such as rigorous identification checks.[1069] Services provided by fully automated online proctoring companies were typically cheaper. These providers commonly offered packages that presented students with a variety of payment choices. They could, for example, spend USD 5 to take a single examination, USD 20 to cover the costs of all examinations associated with a particular course, or USD 100 for a "lifetime subscription".[1070] These USD 5, 20 and 100 payments made by students or their institutions in countries around the world during COVID-19 lockdowns quickly added up to hundreds of millions. MarketWatch, a website offering financial and business analysis, estimated that the global market for remote proctoring services was worth slightly over half a billion USD by 2021 (USD 550 million).[1071]

> The use of proctoring software exemplified a certain kind of ed-tech solutionism that flourished in the pandemic.

Seen from a business perspective, the spectacular rise of proctoring software during the pandemic was an incredible ed-tech success story with a meteoric rise in customers and profits. The systems, especially the fully automated ones, had been built for scale, so administering double or triple or ten times the number of exams tended to result in only marginal increases in expenses.[1072] Viewed through an educational lens, however, the use of proctoring software exemplified a certain kind of ed-tech solutionism that flourished in the pandemic but that also had troubling effects that extend into the future. Increased use of remote proctoring services, driven by the pandemic, helped normalize practices that were once marginal and brought educational surveillance into people's homes, often via personal devices they owned and without realistic options to opt-out. The systems also offered no discernible investments to improve education as a whole, despite profiting extraordinarily from it. The revenue the digital proctoring firms generated was not usually reinvested in education but rather directed to company owners, investors and employees. Sometimes it went towards technology improvements to improve the detection of cheating or further enhance automation.

Although some educational institutions walked back guidance recommending or mandating use of the remote proctoring services for examinations and others discontinued contracts with service providers,[1073] the macro trend seemed to be growth, even as the pandemic abated. MarketWatch reported that the global market value for remote proctoring services continued to grow after the initial spike triggered by the pandemic, expanding from USD 550 million in 2021 to USD 678.34 million in 2022. It further projected that the value of remote proctoring technology and services will increase at a compound annual growth rate of nearly 20 per cent through 2028 at which time it is projected to be worth nearly USD 2 billion cumulatively.[1074] This sustained expansion indicates that the pandemic cemented remote proctoring as a mainstream practice for testing. A 2021 study by Educause sought to examine the staying power of remote proctoring software. It found that two-thirds of the major colleges and universities it surveyed in North America mentioned proctoring services on their websites, indicating use. The organization concluded that "proctoring tools and services are becoming increasingly ubiquitous among higher education institutions in North America—though more so in the USA than in Canada".[1075] Later that year and deep into 2022 news publications ran stories with headlines asking: "Is online test-monitoring here to stay?" But the question was mostly rhetorical; the evidence cited in the articles indicated that the answer is yes, remote proctoring has become an entrenched branch of educational ecosystems.[1076]

> The unintended consequence of software sedimentation is that teachers and others in education come to rely on technology products rather than adapting their pedagogies, assessments and relationships with students.

The way that remote proctoring systems have been integrated into education is an illustration of what ed-tech specialist Martin Weller has called "software sedimentation". Drawing on the ideas of futurist Jaron Lanier, Weller has defined software sedimentation as a process by which schools and universities invest so many resources in a software-based technology – money, expertise, processes and training – that they transform the technology into an integral part of their operations. The term sedimentation, borrowed from geography, refers to actions that make layers of sediment permanent. In education, the unintended consequence of software sedimentation is that teachers and others in education come to rely on technology products rather than adapting their pedagogies, assessments and relationships with students. Weller describes this phenomenon as "tool-focused solutionism", highlighting the way it elevates a particular ed-tech product over solutions that are process- or practice-oriented.[1077] Tool-focused solutionism leads educators to ask questions like 'How can surveillance software protect the integrity of examinations?' instead of 'How might adjustments to our teaching, assessments, academic culture and relationships with students better ensure the integrity of examinations and the wider educational environment?'

Once sedimentation occurs, it can become difficult for institutions to extricate themselves from specific and often proprietary technological tools. The internal processes designed to support these tools come to be considered long-term investments. Training hundreds, if not thousands, of instructors and other educational staff to use a particular remote proctoring software product creates a network of invested stakeholders that can be difficult to unwind or reverse. Even if serious flaws are found in the proctoring product, so much time and energy has been spent deploying it, training people how to use it and developing workflows to manage it that any attempt to change course looks like an admission of failure – backtracking rather than forging ahead. Even shifting to a different proctoring product, however functionally similar to the original one, will entail a significant learning curve. Additionally, universities and colleges typically sign multi-year contracts with remote proctoring companies. As the ed-tech researcher Jesse Stommel explained, once an educational institution has paid for a tool, it finds ways to rationalize using it, even if it is problematic and disliked.[1078] For these reasons, remote proctoring systems although novel when the pandemic began have become increasingly permanent fixtures in educational contexts, complete with proprietary software and embedded processes that would be challenging to change.

COMPLEXITY, POOR TRANSPARENCY AND LIMITED CAPACITY MAKE ALGORITHMIC AUDITS RARE

As remote proctoring systems began calcifying in education systems, many experts pushed back against the lack of transparency about the complex algorithmic and AI processes that powered them. While it was widely known that they weighted various actions and inputs to detect and flag suspicious activity, it was less clear what, specifically, constituted suspicious activity and why. Many instructors did not have a clear understanding of what behaviours a particular automated system treated as 'normal' and what behaviours the system treated as 'aberrant'. Its inner workings – how exactly the gears turned and how the scales were set – tended to be closely guarded secrets. The technology was proprietary and constituted a remote proctoring company's core commercial offering, especially for companies specializing in automated proctoring.

While companies assured educational institutions their remote proctoring products were reliable and would assist the detection of cheating and thereby help uphold the integrity of examinations, the practice of using complex data inputs and technology to automatically generate suspicion scores traced to a troubling history in other fields. Researchers had noted that excessive complexity in automated systems could make their weaknesses and biases especially hard to pinpoint and prove, and remote proctoring companies often highlighted the sophistication of their offerings.[1079]

Algorithms used for other sensitive purposes such as predicting recidivism and even setting prison sentences have been shown to have alarming biases.

One example of this came from a detailed study of an algorithm used in the Netherlands between 2017 and 2021. The study illuminated some of the ways attempts to corral various data inputs to help identify rule breakers, could go awry. The Dutch system used over 300 distinct data points to gauge which individuals were at higher and lower risk of committing welfare fraud. Extensive third partying testing of the system showed, however, that certain characteristics, including being a parent, a woman, young and not fluent in Dutch, substantially increased suspicion scores, even though none of these qualities should, either in isolation or in combination, suggest criminal behaviour.[1080] Careful studies of separate algorithms used for other sensitive purposes such as predicting recidivism and even setting prison sentences have similarly been shown to have alarming biases, such as tendencies to consider defendants with darker colour skin at far greater risk of recidivism than defendants with lighter colour skin.[1081] These system biases translate into real-world consequences for specific – and often already disadvantaged – groups of people in the form of longer prison sentences, extended parole and increased scrutiny for welfare fraud.

"The pattern of local and national governments turning to machine learning algorithms is being repeated around the world. The systems are marketed to public officials on their potential to cut costs and boost efficiency. Yet the development, deployment, and operation of such systems is often shrouded in secrecy. Many systems do not work as intended, and they can encode troubling biases. The people who are judged by them are often left in the dark even as they suffer devastating consequences."

– Matt Burgess, Evaline Schot and Gabriel Geiger, investigative reporters[lxxxiv]

Understanding and testing the workings of complex algorithms and other machine-guided processes used to make predictions about unethical behaviour can be exceptionally challenging. As a specific illustration, it took Lighthouse Reports and *Wired* magazine, the two organizations that led the investigation into the fraud-risk algorithm used in the Netherlands, two years and more than 100 requests under the Freedom of Information Act to decipher the particularities of how the system worked and document the numerous ways it "discriminates based on ethnicity, age, gender, and parenthood" and makes other "inaccurate" and "unfair" assessments.[1082] Time, labour and resource-intensive algorithmic audits of this type are difficult and expensive to perform and are, therefore, seldomly undertaken.

> Government entities involved in regulating processes and technologies used in education often lack the technical expertise required to thoroughly study, understand and quality control algorithmic and newer AI systems coming from private sector companies.

UNESCO research conducted for this publication failed to unearth independent audits of remote proctoring technology that came anywhere close to the rigour of the study conducted on the algorithm used in the Netherlands. The absence of system checks creates a climate that allows flawed algorithms to develop and spread outward with limited scrutiny or resistance. On top of this, ministries of education and other government entities involved in regulating processes and technologies used in education often lack the technical expertise required to thoroughly study, understand and quality control algorithmic and newer AI systems coming from private sector companies. According to the 2023 AI Index Report less than 1 per cent of new AI Ph.D. graduates in North America enter public sector jobs, a level that has remained relatively unchanged since 2018.[1083] During the pandemic, education systems placed extensive trust in technical systems that assigned suspicion scores to students taking high-stakes exams, among other consequential tasks, absent comprehensive government or other rigorous third-party audits.

CONTESTING SPURIOUS MACHINE JUDGEMENTS AND PRIVACY OVERREACH

When automated systems like remote proctoring apps generated suspicion scores that provided the basis for accusations of academic misconduct and corresponding disciplinary actions, students often had limited information about their assumed offences and narrow avenues to contest charges and defend themselves, even when they were adamant about their innocence. Evidence that machine proctoring systems could trigger false indications of unethical behaviour accumulated quickly. In one widely reported incident, the remote proctoring software used to ensure the integrity of the October 2020 California Bar Examination, an assessment used to credential attorneys, flagged over one-third of test takers (approximately 3,000 individuals) as potential cheaters, a proportion that strongly indicated excessive and erroneous detection. Nevertheless, flagged students learned that they were under a cloud of suspicion when they received formal notices from the California State Bar. These notices sparked anxiety and alarm, and justifiably so. The consequences for cheating on a high-stakes test like the bar exam can be severe and, in some instances, shadow individuals for years, derailing future academic and career prospects. Some of the formal notices sent to the test takers suspected of misconduct included a short summary of the supposed violation. These summaries could be hard to interpret and often appeared to conflate technical issues with integrity concerns.

They contained terse messages such as: "Facial view of your eyes was not within view of the camera for a prolonged period of time", "No audible sound was detected", and "Leaving the view of the webcam outside of scheduled breaks during a remote-proctored exam".[1084] Students had no ability to review the supposedly suspicious instances the automated system had observed and captured on video.

"Schools seem to be treating [remote proctoring] as the word of God. If the computer says you're cheating, you must be cheating."

– Cooper Quintin, technologist at the Electronic Frontier Foundation[clxxxv]

Test takers did not know how to respond to a charge that they had not sustained sufficient eye contact with a webcam.

Despite the lack of specificity about assumed offences, test takers were instructed to respond to the notices within ten days after receiving them. Understandably though, test takers did not know how to respond to a charge that they had not, for example, sustained sufficient eye contact with a webcam. Nor was it clear why these incidents were designated as potential offences. A test taker's eyes moving out of view of a webcam is not, of course, tantamount to cheating. Ultimately, nearly all the test takers notified of possible violations were cleared of wrongdoing, but the experience exposed the hazards of relying on automated systems to open investigations that can carry damaging long-term repercussions.

"What has happened to me in the last month, despite not cheating, has resulted in one of the most terrifying, isolating experiences of my life."

– Medical student accused of cheating on a remotely proctored examination[clxxxvi]

While the test takers in California did not have to mount a prolonged defence, other students were less fortunate and had to fight for months to insist that they had been wrongly flagged for unethical behaviour by technology and, on this basis, unjustly persecuted by human instructors or administrators. A specific example of this played out at Dartmouth College in 2021 when 17 medical students were informed that they had acted in violation of the college's honour code while taking remote examinations on a learning management platform and were at risk of expulsion. The college had used a technology platform to retroactively track student activity during testing and without the knowledge of the students. The digital rights organizations Electronic Frontier Foundation and the Foundation for Individual Rights in Education, citing extensive technical documentation, said the college had overreached and "likely turned random correlations into accusations of misconduct".[1085] Some of the accused students reported that they were given less than 48 hours to respond to the charges levelled at them and were not given the complete technical logs from the examinations. They also noted that they were advised to plead guilty even though they denied cheating, and that they were given only two minutes to make a defence during an online hearing about the accusations.[1086] The incident sparked campus-wide tensions and several members of the faculty wrote to the dean of the medical school to say that the cheating inquiry had created "deep mistrust" and advised the school to "make amends with the students falsely accused".[1087] Some students told media organizations they were so fearful of being unjustly targeted in a "data-mining dragnet" that they wanted the school to offer in-person examinations with human proctors, even though the pandemic was still in full swing.[1088] As the pressure and resistance mounted, the college eventually relented and dropped all charges against the medical students accused of misconduct during the remote examinations.[1089]

This outcome was, however, a perhaps rare instance of students successfully pushing back against shaky accusations of cheating. The students caught up in the investigation at Dartmouth College were adults in a professional school at a prestigious Ivy League institution. They had the endurance and means to push back against charges that they felt were wrong and unjustified and were assisted by influential voices and organizations. They were also members of a group – it was not just one or two students facing charges, but nearly 20. But other students faced charges alone and lacked the resources, experience and community mobilization that supported the Dartmouth students. It is impossible to tally the number of students who were given a zero on an examination because a teacher saw, for example, a high suspicion score on the dashboard of a remote proctoring system. Nor is it possible to know how many students were wrongfully subjected to more serious disciplinary measures that could leave permanent stains on an academic record. The accounts that did surface tended to expose a labyrinth of challenges students faced when trying to clear their names and contest accusations of misconduct that traced to automated technology systems.[1090] It is reasonable to assume that not all wrongly accused students bothered to fight. For low-achieving and low-status students, being labelled a cheater by an educational institution relying on machine surveillance and suspicion-score algorithms could be understood as nothing more than familiar unequal and unjust treatment in a new wrapping.

> A US federal judge ruled that room scans sometimes required by specific remote proctoring systems were 'unreasonable' searches and therefore violations of constitutional protections.

While the pandemic appears to have normalized and vastly expanded the reach of remote proctoring technologies in some countries, usually at the level of higher education, their continued entrenchment and growth may be curtailed or even reversed by legal objections to their use. In the USA various organizations brought lawsuits against remote proctoring companies, typically on privacy grounds. Students in Illinois, for instance, brought different suits against several commercial remote proctoring companies arguing that the companies' products and practices violated the state's Biometric Information Privacy Act.[1091] Illinois has some of the most robust biometric privacy laws in the USA and they have served as a blueprint for other states.[1092] Digital rights organizations such as the Electronic Privacy Information Center have also filed formal complaints against remote proctoring firms for violating students' privacy rights. In December 2020, concern about remote proctoring had reached the highest levels of the US federal government, and a group of six senators sent letters to the leaders of proctoring companies to inquire about ways they ensure accuracy of their tools, accommodate individuals with special needs, train human proctors, comply with student privacy laws, and respond to student complaints. The letter stated: "Students have run head on into the shortcomings of [remote proctoring]—shortcomings that fall heavily on vulnerable communities and perpetuate discriminatory biases." It further said that students had put a "great deal of trust" in remote proctoring companies and that these companies had an obligation to demonstrate that they are respecting students' privacy.[1093] While all three companies wrote extensive responses defending their products and practices,[1094] some of the lawsuits brought against them have advanced. In 2022 one of the companies settled a class action lawsuit brought against it in Illinois for USD 2.5 million in 2022.[1095] Other suits have continued to progress. In August 2022, a US federal judge ruled that room scans sometimes required by specific remote proctoring systems were "unreasonable searches" and therefore violations of constitutional protections. The ruling stated: "Though schools may routinely employ remote technology to peer into houses without objection from some, most, or nearly all students, it does not follow that others might not object to the virtual intrusion into their homes or that the routine use of a practice such as room scans does not violate a privacy interest that society recognizes as reasonable, both factually and legally."[1096] Legal challenges like these were not limited to the USA. In early 2023 a court in Montreuil, France, suspended a university's use of a proprietary remote proctoring system on the grounds that "permanent surveillance of bodies and sounds" is unreasonable and excessive for the purpose of preventing cheating.[1097]

Beyond lawsuits, the sudden uptake and use of remote proctoring systems sparked by the pandemic gave rise to new legislation in at least one instance. In September 2022, the State of California in the USA passed the Student Test Taker Privacy Protection Act (STTPPA). The bill explicitly prohibits businesses providing proctoring services used in education from "collecting, retaining, using, or disclosing personal information except to the extent necessary to provide those proctoring services".[1098] According to the Electronic Frontier Foundation, an organization that advocated for passage of the legislation, the STTPPA will help "right the imbalance that exists and give students the ability to protect their own private information … require proctoring companies to be more transparent about their data collection and usage … and allow courts to analyze the effectiveness of remote proctoring tools".[1099] The California law set guardrails around proctoring processes that many argued had gone overboard with surveillance and forced students to compromise their privacy. But the legislation, even in being perhaps the first of its kind, also demonstrated the ways legal frameworks and regulation are often catching up with new technologies. The STTPPA arrived over two years after the massive deployment and uptake of remote proctoring tools. And many countries and states still do not have clear regulations regarding remote proctoring services, even after three years of the pandemic and the changes it brought to traditional practices to assure the integrity of examinations.

Remote proctoring technology created hostile testing dynamics and could erode trust between learners and their institutions.

In the final analysis, the proliferation of remote proctoring tools and services was a prime example of the technology solutionism that characterized much of the education response to the challenges of pandemic school closures. At first glance, proctoring technology seemed to offer an efficient, easy and effective remedy to the problem of assuring the integrity of examinations taken online and from a distance. And many companies were ready to sell these remedies. According to them, universities and schools did not need to develop new tools in-house or make significant changes to assessment routines. Rather they just needed to purchase and stack the new technology on top of existing examinations. But on close inspection, these tools changed testing norms and dynamics in significant ways. They brought unprecedented surveillance into everyday academic settings. For many students, they also created hostile testing dynamics and could erode trust between learners and their institutions, even as they outwardly afforded new options and flexibility for the administration of assessments.

> Remote proctoring services did not attempt to contend with any of the broad and multifaceted factors – social, economic and academic – that give rise to cheating.

Remote proctoring systems also introduced practices that had previously been entirely foreign to many educational institutions, such as the algorithmic generation of suspicion scores for test takers. These tools further placed students in the fraught position of having to prove their personal integrity and intelligence in ways that computers could understand, and that their human operators would believe. It is not even clear that the problem remote proctoring tools aimed to address – cheating – was especially widespread or, more importantly, if the tools deployed at considerable expense successfully dissuaded cheating or facilitated its detection. Ultimately, the technology was solutionist, in the Evgeny Morozov sense. It did not attempt to contend with any of the broad and multifaceted factors – social, economic and academic – that give rise to cheating. Instead, it perpetuated an idea that the problem was technical and therefore the 'fix' could also be technical. Belief in this technical solution gripped huge numbers of educational institutions and directed money and resources to its for-profit providers, accelerating reliance on private and proprietary utilities, while normalizing student surveillance in ways that are likely to endure beyond the pandemic.

"We are much less Greeks than we believe. We are neither in the amphitheatre, nor on the stage, but in the panoptic machine, invested by its effects of power, which we bring to ourselves since we are part of its mechanism."

– Michel Foucault, philosopher[clxxxvii]

End of Act 2

Act 2 traced how school closures and the shift to remote learning with ed-tech during the COVID-19 pandemic resulted in exclusion, inequity, diminished academic achievement and the deterioration of physical and mental health. It highlighted how ed-tech modes of learning precipitated a rush of privatization in education and opened doors to new and invasive forms of surveillance and control. It also documented the considerable environmental impacts of the growth of ed-tech, from the energy and non-renewable materials required to manufacture ed-tech hardware to the short lifecycles of digital devices that contribute to streams of hazardous electronic waste.

> The pandemic tempered overly optimistic visions of what ed-tech might do and could do if it became the primary interface of education and instead left an indelible record of what it did do.

The pandemic tempered overly optimistic visions of what ed-tech might do and could do if it became the primary interface of education and instead left an indelible record of what it *did do*. Act 2 recounted this history. It juxtaposed ed-tech's promises with the realities of its implementation in various country and community contexts from 2020 to 2022 and documented what occurred when schools closed and connected technology was elevated as a singular portal to teaching and learning.

Overall, the evidence presented in Act 2 shows that ed-tech has numerous limitations, despite being a powerful tool that will almost certainly catalyse future innovation, reform and perhaps transformation in the education sector. With rushed and uncritical application, however, it can undermine the diverse and humanistic aspirations societies hold for education. Act 2 reminds readers that actions and investments to neatly solve complex problems with technology do not always go according to plan and, in many instances, introduce new problems. The pandemic experience with ed-tech stands as a case study of the myriad ways technology-solutionist thinking can blind people to the complications and adverse effects of utilizing technology as a shortcut.

Although schools have reopened globally, many educational systems have inherited new norms in the aftermath of extended reliance on distance learning technologies. Act 2 clarified how schools, students and families often extended goodwill to ed-tech actors, with tacit understandings that they would protect the best interests of learners and preserve education as a common good. During the health crisis there was a sense that the multiple collective and individual aims of education would be upheld by these technology actors and, ultimately, outweigh actions to consolidate power and maximize profits. Many stakeholders believed that digital and other forms of remote learning would be as accessible, inclusive, transparent and trustworthy as school-based education – beliefs that quickly unravelled when reliance on ed-tech peaked. There was also a sense that existing regulations would block business or government attempts to recast public education as a private and for-profit enterprise or use ed-tech as a means to assert ideological control and police ideas and knowledge flows. These regulations, however, often did not exist. And even when they did, they largely failed to prevent such perversions, exposing dated rules and measures that continue to be exploited as education changes because of digitalization.

> The technology solutionism that framed and guided responses to school closures has set education on a troubling trajectory and established problematic norms around digitalization.

The lens applied to the ed-tech experiences in Act 2 is a decidedly critical one, with various subsections specifying how ed-tech fell short of goals to assure educational continuity and quality for large numbers of learners during a health crisis. This is not to suggest that technology failed completely – it provided important benefits for significant numbers of students and teachers. But viewed from the global level, it is hard to make a serious argument that ed-tech 'saved the day'. It is harder still to drive an argument that the ed-tech solutions deployed during the pandemic meaningfully improved education or pointed it in a promising future direction. The technology solutionism that framed and guided responses to school closures has set education on a troubling trajectory and established problematic norms around digitalization – norms that continue to take root even as the shocks of the pandemic recede.

Act 3 will propose ideas and recommendations to make a course correction. It is preceded by an Inter-Act that considers alternatives to technology-first responses and puts forward several think pieces to problematize conventional thinking about education during the pandemic and in its aftermath.

Inter-Act

LOOKING BACK
TO SEE AHEAD

With attention shining so brightly on ed-tech during the pandemic, the education community almost never considered responses to school closures that did not centre technology. Around the world ed-tech was elevated again and again as the primary solution to the disruptions imposed by the health emergency.

The Inter-Act takes a step back from examining the reality of what happened and delves into questions, ideas and alternative scenarios that were either not raised or did not gain traction when schools were closed. Its subsections are think pieces intended to help readers re-examine and reassess the choices that led to technology-dependent educational experiences. An assumption running through them is that the actions countries took to sustain education during the pandemic were not inevitable and that different actions would likely have established different norms and precipitated different outcomes. Such an exploration allows policy-makers and a wide range of stakeholders in education to reconsider, refine and reformulate their takeaways from the widespread and prolonged embrace of ed-tech stretching from 2020 to 2023.

Just as the Inter-Act of a theatrical play invites audience members to pause and reflect on the action of a drama, so too do these think pieces. Collectively and individually, they encourage readers to think beyond the confines of what happened and to imagine what might have happened had different approaches to the educational challenges of COVID-19 been considered.

Looking Back

The regularity with which countries turned to technology-dependent distance learning as the primary response to school closures is remarkable. Barring few exceptions, the playbook to assure educational continuity was the same: provide educational content targeted to individual learners through a technology portal – the internet, television or radio – and require use of these technologies. On many levels, this was a commonsense response to school closures that were mandated by governments in an effort to slow the spread of COVID-19. But it may have also reflected limited creativity, a narrowing and homogenization of possible responses, or even an instance of near-global groupthink.

While governments closed schools almost uniformly in the early stages of the health crisis, the duration of the closures and recourse to remote learning varied enormously, ranging from a few weeks to nearly two full academic years. The years 2020 to 2023 were marked by intense and evolving debates about the utility of these drastic actions to protect public health. In many contexts, questions about closing or opening schools and pivoting to and away from ed-tech were among the most fraught of the pandemic.

Regardless of the basis for school closures or their durations, it is legitimate to ask whether the widespread recourse to technology-enabled distance learning was the best response to the disruption of schooling, particularly in light of the severity of technology and connectivity gaps. Many argued that there were no viable options beyond technology and that, while the deployment of ed-tech may have been imperfect, it still 'saved the day' and was certainly 'better than nothing'. Yet, as the exclusion, inequity and harms of full reliance on ed-tech have come into fuller view, this only-option argument has been called into question.

With critical distance, it is possible to reflect on alternative directions and possibilities to decisions taken during the pandemic, recognizing that policy-makers were regularly called upon to make difficult and time sensitive decisions with incomplete information. Much more is now known about COVID-19 and its myriad impacts, including the impacts of different responses to the health emergency, than was understood at the beginning of the health crisis. Revisiting and reflecting on choices taken during the pandemic and considering alternative scenarios carries a potential to help various stakeholders better prepare for future disruptions to education and respond to them with a more circumspect sense of possible courses of action.

School closures, the shift to remote learning and public health

The COVID-19 virus spread across the globe with unrelenting speed in early 2020, unleashing a dangerous new disease. Communities experienced dramatic spikes in the number of people requiring urgent medical attention, and health care systems working to save lives were quickly stretched to the limits of their capacities. In order to protect medical facilities from becoming overwhelmed by gravely ill people, countries instituted stringent measures to help slow community transmission of the virus. By minimizing social contact through lockdowns and quarantines, countries hoped to flatten the curve of infection, take pressure off strained health care systems and allow more time to improve treatments and develop vaccines. Initially, and with very rare exception, these measures included school closures.

Research conducted prior to 2020 suggested that school closures during the peak of an influenza pandemic could significantly reduce infection rates.[1100] At the height of the COVID-19 pandemic in 2020, nearly every school and university in the world closed for at least some duration.

Considerable evidence exists to indicate these closures were largely effective in flattening the curve of COVID-19 infections during the first wave of the virus and subsequently when there were jumps in transmission due to the emergence of new variants of the virus.[1101] But pre-pandemic studies about the effectiveness of school closures as a public health measure cautioned that their usefulness was in moderating dramatic upticks in infection rates during a pandemic and that they did not have a meaningful impact on *overall* rates of infection.[1102] In effect, they were understood to be a short-term measure to interrupt virus transmission alongside wider quarantines and other social-distancing restrictions. Mirroring this expectation, numerous studies conducted during the COVID-19 pandemic found that school closures provided only limited benefit once other stringent lockdowns were dialled back, as was experienced in countries around the world starting in mid-2020.[1103] These findings call into question the rationale for lengthy school closures and the concurrent reliance on remote learning via ed-tech as a singular means to access education beyond initial lockdowns.

The text that follows traces the chronology of research about school closures as a measure to protect health during the height of the pandemic. It highlights how the messaging of influential organizations evolved over the course of 2020 and 2021.

Just a few months into the pandemic and when most countries were enforcing regional or national lockdowns, some governments were beginning to question the value of school closures and the recourse to remote learning as effective measures to protect public health. In Europe, many governments moved quickly to reopen schools – instituting strict sanitary and social-distancing protocols – in May 2020, before the end of the 2019/20 academic year in the northern hemisphere. Sweden, an outlier, never fully shuttered its schools, opting instead to adjust in-person educational practices and facilities to minimize disease transmission. Since constitutional rules in Sweden made unilateral countrywide school closures difficult to implement, the country carved out a solution that relied on teachers, students and families to follow disease mitigation methods recommended by the nation's public health agency.[1104]

> *"Given the devastating consequences on children, youth and our societies as a whole, the decision to close schools should be a last resort and only at a local level in areas with intense transmission."*
> – Tedros Adhanom Ghebreyesus, Director-General of the World Health Organization[clxxxviii]

In the second half of 2020, international organizations started tentatively signalling that extended school closures were of questionable utility to protect public health, in part because of the adverse health impacts

International organizations started tentatively signalling that extended school closures were of questionable utility to protect public health, in part because of the adverse health impacts on children arising from widespread school closures.

on children arising from widespread school closures. These included children's increased vulnerability to domestic abuse, poor nutrition due to the cessation of school meals, and the negative mental health impacts of prolonged periods of isolation from peers and adults outside the pandemic. Entire cohorts of students began to fall behind on vaccination schedules for other deadly diseases routinely delivered or required at school, risking the resurgence of vaccine-preventable diseases such as measles and polio.[1105] An early stance of maximum precaution was ceding ground to evidence that extended school closures were causing significant harm to the health and well-being of learners and wider communities.

By September 2020, the WHO in partnership with UNESCO and UNICEF stated that "most evidence from countries that have reopened schools or never closed them, suggest that schools have not been associated with significant increases in community transmission [of COVID-19]".[1106] Among its sources, the WHO statement referenced an influential July 2020 article published in the *New England Journal of Medicine*, which found that schools reopening in the first wave of the pandemic had not led to increases in COVID-19 case counts in multiple countries, including in Denmark, Finland, Belgium, Austria and Singapore. The article explained that schools in these countries had opened under "strict social distancing rules" and took "substantial extra precautions" to protect health. The article's authors underscored the importance of adherence to sanitary and social-distancing measures in school reopening by noting that the reopening of secondary schools in Israel, where rigorous sanitary protocols were not observed, may have caused a resurgence in disease transmission. The authors concluded that "the fundamental argument that children, families, educators, and society deserve to have safe and reliable primary schools should not be controversial" and called for action to ensure full and swift school reopening.[1107] These findings, however, despite being anchored in empirical data and coming from experts in infectious disease transmission, did not trigger a wave of schools reopening. According to UNESCO monitoring, at the end of September 2020, approximately 582 million students, over a third of the global student population, were not attending school regularly due to closures and were expected to rely on technology to continue formal academic learning.

"Primary schools, preschools, and early childhood development centres are not high-risk settings for transmission, especially if the right safety measures are followed. Transmission levels in these settings have been found to reflect those of the surrounding community."

– Joint statement by WHO and UNICEF regional directors[clxxxix]

> Less than a year into the pandemic, the world's leading international health organization cited the inadequacy of distance learning to support child and youth well-being as a major reason to prioritize the resumption of school-based learning.

Guidance that schools should reopen grew more forceful as 2020 came to a close. In December 2020, the WHO made pointed statements to encourage a resumption of in-person learning: "If proper and consistent measures are in place, schools do not pose a greater risk of infection for children and teachers and other staff than any other public place."[1108] Significantly, the inadequacy of distance learning to support child and youth well-being was cited as a major reason to prioritize the resumption of school-based learning. The WHO was attuned to the ways ed-tech could engender exclusion, isolation and stress. The organization further recognized that existing models of remote education could not attend to the holistic health of children and youth in the same way as well-functioning schools. From late 2020 onwards, health and education organizations alike tended to reflect a view that distance learning via technology was an insufficient substitute for in-person, school-based learning. Experts were quickly adopting a position that replacing in-person learning with full reliance on ed-tech modes of learning did not achieve net health gains as intended and was, instead, leading to a net decline in health and well-being.

As evidence continued to build that schools could reopen safely and that full reliance on remote learning with technology carried adverse consequences, UNICEF labelled blanket shutdowns of national school systems "the wrong direction". In late 2020, the organization's global chief of education declared: "Evidence shows that schools are not the main drivers of this pandemic. Yet, we are seeing an alarming trend whereby governments are once again closing down schools as a first recourse rather than a last resort. In some cases, this is being done nationwide, rather than community by community, and children are continuing to suffer the devastating impacts on their learning, mental and physical well-being and safety."[1109] By the end of December 2020, the European Centre for Disease Prevention and Control declared that the decision to close schools to control the COVID-19 pandemic should be rare and used only after all other options to keep schools safely open had been exhausted. It noted that the negative physical, mental health and educational impacts of lengthy school closures on children as well as the associated economic costs warranted a swift return to in-person learning.[1110] The organization maintained and amplified this position throughout 2021, even with the emergence of the Delta variant of the virus, which posed greater risks to children than earlier strains of the virus.[1111] Yet despite this advice, large numbers of schools remained shuttered for prolonged periods.

Appeals to reopen schools became more frequent and more vocal throughout 2021, especially as vaccines became widely available in some regions of the world. At the international level, the non-profit foundation Insights for Education examined health data from 101 countries alongside

Appeals to reopen schools became more frequent and more vocal throughout 2021, especially as vaccines became widely available in some regions of the world and evidence mounted that schools were not amplifiers of community transmission.

UNESCO's global monitoring of school closures and found no clear association – positive or negative – between school status (open, closed or partially open) and community transmission of COVID-19. The organization challenged the "widespread assumption that there is an inevitable trade-off" between keeping schools open, protecting human health and ensuring the functioning of the economy.[1112] In February 2021, the journal of the British Medical Association announced that an "emerging consensus is that schools do not seem to be amplifiers of transmission, and that cases in schools simply reflect prevalence within the local community".[1113]

Throughout 2021, data from individual countries, in developed and developing regions alike, corroborated this consensus view. A March 2021 study looking at the unique case of Sweden, one of very few countries to never close lower grade schools, indicated that keeping schools open had only a "minor impact on the overall spread of SARS-CoV-2 in society".[1114] Research published in May 2021 from the Democratic Republic of the Congo strongly indicated that school closures were presenting more health risks than advantages.[1115] A separate study from Germany found that school closures did not seem to have a containing effect on COVID-19 infections in either the school population or older generations.[1116] And research from school districts in the USA similarly found that in-person instruction did not lead to noticeable spikes in community disease transmission.[1117] *Scientific American*, a widely respected publication in print since 1845, stated that "the benefits of having kids in school – with precautions in place – strongly outweigh the risks".[1118]

Research released in the second half of 2021 continued to buttress a view that school closures provided limited health benefits, especially when schools followed specific guidance issued by national and international medical groups. For example, a major study of the causal effects of school closures in Japan published in *Nature* "did not find any evidence" that closing schools had reduced the spread of COVID-19.[1119] Nevertheless, school closures and full reliance on connected technology for formal education remained a reality around the world. In October 2021, before the emergence of the Omicron variant, which sparked a resurgence in school closures, UNESCO estimated that over 53 million students remained shut out of schools, and 15 countries were still implementing blanket national closures.[1120]

One of the reasons school closures did relatively little to prevent the spread of disease over extended periods of time is that this measure, despite the disruptions it imposed, rarely resulted in a full cessation of social contact. In areas with high-density housing and limited access to basic sanitation, school closures may even have been counterproductive, as social interaction in domestic environments could be more varied and frequent than it had been in formal and controlled education settings. Although relatively few studies attempted to examine changes to the volume, frequency and duration of social contact during periods of school closures, some suggested that shuttering schools did not result in an overall reduction in human-to-human contact for young people and teachers.[1121] In these scenarios, social contact was not prevented by closing schools; it was merely uprooted and moved to other places and settings.

As the pandemic wore on, it also became clear that ed-tech infrastructure, like other consumer-facing digital services, were also not as clean, safe, efficient and 'contactless' as many presumed. Writing in *The Guardian*, Naomi Klein, an author who popularized the concept of disaster capitalism, explained that most supposedly 'pandemic-proof' digital services were actually held together by tens of millions of anonymous workers tucked away in warehouses, data centres, content-moderation mills, electronic sweatshops, lithium mines and other sites "where they are left unprotected from disease and hyper-exploitation".[1122] Indeed efforts to provision technology to students and families as well as to establish and maintain remote modes of education often relied on people coming into contact outside the orbit of school. Distance learning with ed-tech was not, in fact, a fully contactless solution, even if it may have involved fewer physical interactions than a typical pre-pandemic class or school experience.

> Efforts to provision technology to students and families as well as to establish and maintain remote modes of education often relied on people coming into contact outside the orbit of school.

By 2022, with lockdowns largely lifted, vaccine drives under way in some contexts, improved treatments and more knowledge of mitigation strategies, school closures were widely understood as an overly disruptive and largely ineffective measure to stem the spread of COVID-19. Most countries had resumed in-person schooling, but not all. School closures continued to persist and so did student and teacher dependence on ed-tech. In January 2022, full school closures remained in effect in six countries, impacting 44 million students, according to UNESCO monitoring. Millions more students were living in countries with partial and ad hoc school closures, which, like full school closures, make education reliant on connected technology in significant ways. COVID-19 related school closures became increasingly rare over the course of 2022, and by the time the WHO declared the end of the pandemic as a global health emergency in May 2023, they were fully in the past.

The evidence and chronology recounted here suggest that school closures played an important role mitigating the rapid spread of COVID-19 at the onset of the pandemic. In many contexts, school closures, as one part of broader social-distancing measures, helped flatten the curve of infections and prevented health care facilities from becoming overwhelmed at

Uprooting education from schools and moving it to technology appears to have done relatively little to protect public health during the COVID-19 pandemic.

dangerous moments of strain. But over long periods of time and once lockdowns were eased, school closures appear to have been ineffective measures to reduce the spread of disease. Countries that closed schools for very short durations often had comparable and sometimes significantly better health outcomes than countries that closed schools for very long durations. While the effects of specific actions to mitigate disease transmission can be challenging for researchers to isolate, studies that attempted to examine the impacts of school closures found that they provided limited protection from COVID-19. Beyond this, closing schools often carried adverse net or cumulative health impacts. Shuttering schools may have temporarily reduced social contact and therefore risks of contracting an infectious disease, but it came at a cost: the protection, nutrition, well-being and health functions played by schools came to a standstill. Additionally, moving learning to digital spaces as a response to school closures carried its own set of deleterious health impacts, physical as well as mental, as detailed in this publication. In the final analysis, outside of the initial emergency lockdowns to reduce high infection rates and cases of hospitalization, closing schools and transitioning to remote learning with ed-tech appears to have had very little utility as a measure to protect public health over extended durations.

Did technology-mediated remote learning contribute to the prolongation of school closures?

Education is a sector where visions of digital-only and digital-first modes of operation were already in circulation before the onset of the pandemic. In many contexts, distance learning with connected technology had long been positioned and understood as a durable and, sometimes, desirable alternative to education conducted in person and at schools. When the pandemic tore across countries, there was wide acceptance that ed-tech would offer a workable solution to the challenge of school closures, even if this solution had never been attempted at scale in practice or for long durations. As the pandemic moved beyond its initial phases of peak infections, is it possible that school closures lasted longer than they would have without the existence and endurance of perceptions about the viability of ed-tech to supplant schools?

> In 2020 and 2021, numerous countries kept schools closed and fully reliant on ed-tech even as other sectors and institutions reopened.

In 2020 and 2021, numerous countries kept schools closed and fully reliant on ed-tech even as other sectors and institutions reopened. Some countries and localities were criticized, for instance, for opening bars and restaurants while schools remained shut. When COVID-19 infections spiked at irregular times, schools were sometimes ordered to close, while businesses that were not easily classifiable as 'essential', such as hotels and furniture shops, remained open, despite carrying health risks similar to those presented by schools.

> People were receptive to the idea that connected technology might stand in for schools but rejected ideas that they might stand in for other in-person establishments.

Policies that allowed for the reopening of bars before schools particularly incensed many people in the education community.[1123] Parents wrote posts on Twitter and other social media platforms to voice their discontent using hashtags such as #closebarsopenschools and #schoolsbeforepubs.[1124] Editorial writers also vented that the policies exemplified "backward priorities".[1125] But such policies arguably reflected a less discussed reality: that is, connected technology was understood to offer a viable alternative for school closures, a technology fix to the education disruption of the pandemic. There were, however, no widely accepted technological alternatives for bars, pubs and restaurants, or at least none that garnered broad public support. Said differently, people were receptive to the idea that connected technology might stand in for schools but rejected ideas that they might stand in for other in-person establishments. These differing expectations may have functioned to increase the prolongation of school closures beyond what would have been the case without ed-tech.

Another way to consider the argument that ed-tech may have made school closures both more likely and more prolonged during the pandemic is to indulge a thought experiment: What if a health crisis similar to COVID-19 had occurred in 1980, when internet-connected digital technology was almost non-existent in homes, and other connected technology that played host to education during the 2020–22 emergency was far less prevalent in most national contexts?

A reflexive answer to this question is that it would have been an educational disaster. Without smartphones, laptops and broadband internet, there would have been no means to keep formal education intact during periods of school closures. This is, to an extent, undeniable. Connected technologies provided educational links to significant numbers of students during the health crisis, even if it left a global majority behind. But would the school closures have been as long or as frequent without this technological alternative? Might there have been more examples of countries that never fully shuttered their schools on a countrywide level, especially beyond the first months of the global health emergency when lockdowns were at their most stringent?

There is historical evidence to support a view that school closures might have been significantly shorter without the possibility of a recourse to connected technology.

The questions raised are counterfactuals, so they cannot be answered authoritatively. There is, however, some historical evidence to support a view that school closures might have been significantly shorter without the possibility of a recourse to connected technology. Experts from the National Bureau of Economic Research in the USA compared the durations of school closures during the COVID-19 pandemic to the ones ordered in response to the 1918–19 influenza pandemic – one of the most recent parallels to the global COVID-19 health emergency. They found that even though the 1918 influenza virus was much deadlier to young adults and children than COVID-19, schools closed for "many fewer days on average".[1126] The authors calculated the average length of school closures in 1918–19 in the USA to be 36 days. By contrast, UNESCO estimated that the average duration of full school closures globally was 126 days in September 2021, 3.5 times as long as the average 1918–19 duration observed in the USA. These findings raise the possibility, even if only tentatively, that the availability of ed-tech during the COVID-19 pandemic may have contributed to the longer duration of school closures compared with the 1918–19 influenza pandemic. In 2020, connected technology offered possibilities for remote modes of learning that were simply not available a century earlier.

Figure 24:

Average duration of school closures in the 1918 influenza pandemic and in the COVID-19 pandemic

Source: Data from National Bureau of Economic Research, 2020, and UNESCO, 2021

36 days
1918 influenza pandemic
USA average (no global data)

126 days
COVID-19 pandemic
Global average (February 2020–September 2021)

Perceptions that homes were largely safer, more sanitary and more controlled environments than schools for purposes of protecting health help explain the very long duration of school closures during the COVID-19 pandemic.

Historians have recounted that a major impetus for reopening schools quickly during the 1918–19 pandemic, despite its known dangers to children as well as adults, was a belief that schools were safe and controlled spaces compared with many home environments. Health and education authorities at the time also justified quick school reopening on grounds that schools would help keep children occupied and off the streets, where they were likely to have more incautious social contact than in the adult-supervised spaces of schools.[1127] The assumptions that attended the COVID-19 pandemic were, in many ways, a reversal of those from a century before. Public perception held that homes were largely safer, more sanitary and more controlled environments than schools for purposes of reducing social contact and protecting health. Also, worries that children not attending school would flood into public spaces and the homes of others for socialization were hardly acute in 2020-2021, even when sanitary measures allowed for movement of this sort. This historical comparison suggests that the unique capacities of connected technology to hold the attention of children and youth for long periods of time combined with the changing assumptions that homes were safer and more sanitary than schools may also help explain the very long duration of school closures during the COVID-19 pandemic versus the 1918-19 pandemic.

The perception that workable and palatable technological solutions existed to mitigate the challenge of school closures arguably functioned to prolong reliance on these solutions. The fixation with technology solutionism was so strong that it took repeated and high-visibility problems to spark recognition that connected technology could not realistically support education for extended periods in inclusive and equitable ways. Only when the flaws in the technology-mediated vision of education became unavoidable did pressure to reopen schools become sufficiently strong.

If not ed-tech, then what?

The explanations and justifications for the global pivot to technology-mediated education during the pandemic commonly boil down to the argument that there was no alternative solution. While this view can accommodate critiques of ed-tech, it also blunts them by failing to ask: What else was there?

If there were indeed no options beyond connected technologies to assure the continuity of education, then it holds that it made sense to try, however imperfectly, to leverage technology for this purpose, including in contexts such as parts of Africa and broad swathes of Asia where ed-tech remains scarce. According to this logic, even if large groups of students were left behind, significant numbers could be helped by ed-tech, and this warranted making the attempt. The severity of the crisis required hard choices, and it was understood that helping some young people with ed-tech was better than helping none.

Such a position purported to embrace a realist view of the pandemic: educational regression was unavoidable, and any slippage in terms of education equity, inclusion and quality would amount to collateral damage. The challenge, then, was mitigation – doing what was possible to simply keep education afloat.

With the power and prevalence of these assumptions in mind, it makes sense to examine what other options, outside of technology-first approaches, might have been possible within and across countries. Despite perceptions that online learning technology was an only-option solution, it should be seen, more accurately, as one option among others. The sections that follow outline three alternatives to help illustrate possibilities beyond technology that could have been considered — and in rare contexts were attempted — to address the educational disruptions of the pandemic.

> Despite perceptions that online learning technology was an only-option solution, it should be seen, more accurately, as one option among others.

ALTERNATIVE A: KEEPING SCHOOLS OPEN OR REOPENING THEM QUICKLY

The most obvious alternative to technology-dependent distance learning is school-based learning. In the early weeks and months of the pandemic, various strategies were identified to avoid full reliance on ed-tech and to maintain or restart in-person education in ways that could help assure the safety of children and teachers. Epidemiological studies indicating that opening schools and keeping them open did not directly exacerbate the severity of the public health crisis weakened the rationale for maintaining technology-first modes of distance learning. By the second half of 2020, health experts and medical journals published data showing that school closures were doing very little to slow the spread of COVID-19.[1128] Shuttering schools did, however, endanger student health by making young people more vulnerable to risks that schools often help mitigate, including malnutrition, abuse at home and psychological distress stemming from isolation, among other maladies. The vaccine rollouts that began in December 2020 helped schools reopen with greater safety. So too did improved knowledge of virus transmission that informed the ways that schools and other social institutions could function with social and sanitary measures to better mitigate the risks of disease transmission. Yet despite this knowledge, ed-tech continued to be upheld by governments, think tanks and policy-makers as a first-recourse solution to the educational challenges imposed by the pandemic.

> Epidemiological studies indicating that opening schools and keeping them open did not directly exacerbate the severity of the public health crisis weakened the rationale for maintaining technology-first modes of distance learning.

Guidance to facilitate the safe reopening of schools was issued by international organizations just a few weeks after COVID-19 began spreading globally. UNESCO, UNICEF, the World Food Programme and the World Bank published guidelines in mid-2020 detailing steps that schools could take to reduce disease transmission, safeguard essential services and supplies, and promote healthy behaviours. Recommendations included developing strict protocols concerning social-distancing and sanitary practices.[1129] By May 2020, numerous medical and educational organizations had released recommendations to keep schools operational while mitigating student and teacher risks of contracting or spreading COVID-19.[1130] In June 2020, a consortium of UN organizations again reiterated the importance of reopening schools and released a detailed framework to facilitate the resumption of in-person education.[1131]

While guidance to reopen schools could differ subtly between countries, regions and districts, the main recommendations were consistent. Medical authorities advised schools to require or encourage masking; improve ventilation in classrooms; move learning outdoors when feasible; adjust learning spaces, practices and schedules to maintain social distancing; make rapid tests easily and quickly available; and ask students and teachers to isolate at home if they test positive for the virus or have any COVID symptoms. After vaccine rollouts began, the guidance was updated to emphasize the importance of vaccines to increase the safety of school-based learning.

> Reopening schools was an ever-present alternative to remote and technology-dependent modes of learning.

By mid-2020, there was growing consensus that if schools followed the guidance of health authorities and implemented targeted measures and rules, they could safely reopen for in-person education.[1132] The recommended measures were often relatively simple and did not carry excessive costs. While some reopening plans involved ed-tech for select functions, learning no longer entailed full reliance on technology. When schools reopened, ed-tech was repositioned from a 'must-have' to a 'nice-to-have' for formal learning. It is important to note that the possibility of keeping schools open or reopening them quickly after the initial lockdowns was gaining traction as a viable option within the first few weeks of the pandemic. This meant that reopening schools was an ever-present alternative to remote and technology-dependent modes of learning.

"If buildings are too crowded, how about dividing the day into shifts, and having more outdoor education, drawing on the plentiful research that shows that time in nature enhances children's capacity to learn?"

– Naomi Klein, author[cxc]

Many commentators voiced their bafflement that government and education authorities were directing investments towards ed-tech instead of spending funds to improve the safety and sanitary conditions of schools. The tepid and sometimes sluggish actions of governments to direct resources and energy to prepare physical schools for reopening weakened confidence that schools would be – or could be – reorganized for safe teaching and learning. Families and teachers around the world observed

Teachers and opinion writers alike wondered aloud why COVID-19 did not catalyse and fast-track bold actions to improve educational facilities, many marred by neglect that predated the pandemic.

underfunded and undisciplined approaches to school compliance with public health guidelines, leading some to conclude that the education sector was taking a laissez-faire attitude towards the safe reopening of schools.[1133] Yet numerous voices continued to maintain that schools could and should be reopened and questioned ballooning expenditures on ed-tech to support remote learning. Teachers and opinion writers alike wondered aloud why COVID-19 did not catalyse and fast-track bold actions to improve educational facilities, many marred by neglect that predated the pandemic. Such actions could better protect student and teacher health in the near term and provide benefits for years into the future, such as superior ventilation and air purification. Well before the pandemic a growing body of research was revealing the adverse impacts of airborne pollutants on cognitive ability. One study from January 2020 examined the impact of installing inexpensive air filters in classrooms and found that academic achievement in mathematics and English improved by an increase in scores comparable to cutting class sizes by a third.[1134] The author of the study wrote that "air filter installation is a highly cost-effective policy to raise student achievement and, given that underprivileged students attend schools in highly polluted areas, one that can reduce the pervasive test score gaps that plague public education".[1135]

Author Naomi Klein, who has written critically about the speed with which technology-centric solutions were adopted in response to the COVID-19 pandemic, questioned why governments dismissed or were slow to take resolute steps to better guarantee the safety of schools by, for example, hiring more teachers and reducing class sizes, establishing half-day school shifts to minimize close physical contact, distributing free masks and making COVID-19 tests more widely available. She observed that in place of these actions education systems undertook large structural changes to support

Education systems undertook large structural changes to support a shift to ed-tech-enabled distance learning when simpler and perhaps more effective solutions were at hand to keep schools operational.

a shift to ed-tech-enabled distance learning.[1136] Throughout the pandemic, commentators argued that governments were missing opportunities to improve school buildings, allowing for superior air circulation among other upgrades that would make them safer for human health. While expensive technology was being purchased in bulk, only limited investments trickled into contracts to upgrade physical school infrastructure, ventilation, playgrounds and classrooms in ways that would reduce class size, improve sanitation and avoid overcrowding. These investments carried the potential to not only improve the health and safety of schools in an outbreak of transmissible disease but to advance education's wider goals of ensuring quality instruction, social interaction, protection and well-being.

"Stop asking whether schools are safe. Instead, acknowledge that in-person instruction is essential; then apply the principles we learned from other essential services to keep schools open."

– Leana S. Wen, professor of health policy and management, George Washington University[cxci]

Digital learning fuelled an illusion that it was possible for education to forever 'hide' from the pandemic, which in turn delayed action to figure out how to 'live with' the pandemic and lessen the risks of disease transmission in school environments.

Education was something of an outlier in terms of its prolonged shuttering of physical buildings and reliance on technology. COVID-related mitigation efforts of the type recommended for schools were commonly implemented in other sectors of the economy. No action was fail-proof, but every mitigation strategy helped reduce risk.[1137] Numerous institutions and businesses, from grocery stores and farms to hair salons and utility companies, took rapid steps to improve the safety of physical in-person facilities in order to stay open or reopen as quickly as possible while also protecting their staff, customers and communities. They rarely attempted to or were expected to uproot all or most of their operations to digital spaces. And, in many instances, this uprooting was unfeasible or impossible: hair could not be cut with connected technology, and food could not travel over fibre-optic wires to the kitchens of families. But around the world, education was commonly deemed movable to technology-mediated spaces, and because of this, resources poured into making this unprecedented transition work rather than implementing changes to keep physical schools at the centre of educational exchange. By 2021, some education leaders reflected that the prioritization of digital learning had fuelled an illusion that it was possible for education to 'hide' indefinitely from the pandemic, with students and teachers suspended in isolation at home. This arguably delayed action to figure out how to 'live with' the pandemic and lessen the risks of disease transmission in school environments.

"One might argue, again, that any risk is too great, and that schools must be completely safe before local governments move to reopen them. But this approach ignores the enormous costs to children from closed schools."

– Emily Oster, economics professor, Brown University[cxcii]

The 1918–19 influenza pandemic was met with major undertakings to retrofit schools with superior sanitation, more outdoor spaces for learning and play, and more spacious classrooms to minimize the spread of disease. It also sparked a movement to hire more school nurses.

Interestingly, numerous safety measures implemented during past health emergencies were directed towards physical schools. The 1918–19 influenza pandemic, for instance, was met with major undertakings to retrofit schools with superior sanitation, more outdoor spaces for learning and play, and more spacious classrooms to minimize the spread of disease.[1138] Schools ramped up investments to hire and retain school nurses, a group that was widely credited with helping improve the safety of in-person schooling during the 1918–19 health crisis.[1139] Some of these lessons appear to have been forgotten over the course of the century. In the 1918–19 pandemic, school nurses were in high demand, and education leaders envisioned a future in which every school would have a qualified health professional working alongside teachers and administrators.[1140] Yet in some national contexts the number of school nurses has been steadily declining for at least the past decade.[1141] Rather than meet the challenges of the COVID-19 pandemic with investments in the physical and human infrastructure of schools, as was done in the 1918–19 pandemic, many leaders instead made wholesale investments in ed-tech, prolonging the reliance of education on connected technology rather than moving quickly and decisively to reopen schools.

Historically speaking, the educational response to COVID-19 was unique because efforts to reinstate formal education following emergency school closures were not solely focused on reopening schools. Considerable effort was instead directed to establishing and maintaining technology-reliant alternatives. Even during relatively contemporary health emergencies that prompted school closures such as the 2002–04 SARS and 2014–16 Ebola crises, actions to maintain educational continuity were primarily directed towards reopening schools with only minor attention paid to supporting ed-tech alternatives. Regardless of how countries balanced the prioritization of remote learning and the resumption of school-based learning during COVID-19, in-person schooling, alongside efforts to assure it was conducted safely, was always a realistic alternative to technology-only modes of education. And while many countries relied on connected technology for long periods of time – perhaps reflecting the prioritization of this type of education – several countries reopened schools after just a few weeks of closure. In France, for instance, schools were fully closed for only seven weeks, according to UNESCO monitoring.[1142] Around the world, the most salient alternative to ed-tech was quickly resuming or never stopping school-based learning while making it as safe as possible for students and teachers.

Figure 25:
Average duration of school closures in different countries

Source: UNESCO, 2022

ALTERNATIVE B:
PAUSE FORMAL EDUCATION UNTIL THE RESUMPTION OF IN-PERSON SCHOOLING

A second viable, if controversial, alternative to technology-first modes of education during COVID-19 was simply pausing formal education. In this scenario, formal education would have been temporarily placed on hold when schools closed. Rather than trying to hastily move entire education systems from schools to connected technologies in the midst of a deadly pandemic, government leaders could have reassured families that, upon school reopening, education would pick up where it had stopped when schools closed. Learning by ed-tech still could have been encouraged, but framed as optional instead of compulsory in recognition that an unacceptable proportion of students lacked the hardware, connectivity and support needed to effectively access technology-reliant modes of learning.

Such an approach would not necessarily have foreclosed important roles for teachers. Instead of trying to keep up with the pace of covering a curriculum as if normal schooling were in session, teachers could have checked in on students over available communication platforms and perhaps even tried to see students through home visits, when feasible, following strict safety guidelines, such as meeting outdoors and standing a safe distance apart. This practice was already well established in some countries, such as Japan,[1143] and appears to have been practised in select contexts during the pandemic, such as in rural areas of Zambia.[1144] Such actions, if scaled outward, would have provided learners, including those without connected technology, with at least limited face-to-face human interaction with their teachers – supportive adults who are not family members – and modelled protocols for safe in-person exchanges. In addition, teachers could have perhaps organized optional online gatherings to provide young people opportunities to socialize and participate in educationally, socially and personally enriching activities, such as discussing a particular piece of art or writing that would not require prior preparation. In the exceptional circumstances of the pandemic, a teacher's role could have been reconceived to prioritize the holistic well-being of students and to reassure families that formal learning would resume when schools could safely reopen.

> The decision to pause formal education in Kenya reflected a recognition that too many students would be excluded from remote distance learning dependent on connected technology.

Very few countries appear to have attempted or experimented with this approach. A notable exception, however, is Kenya, with Bolivia as another example, although its policy fluctuated somewhat throughout 2020 and 2021.[1145] In Kenya, the government announced that portions of the 2020 academic year affected by school closures would be repeated when schools were expected to reopen for the next academic year in January 2021.[1146] The decision was communicated in July 2020 – three months into a hurried attempt to transition to distance learning – following the nationwide closure of schools in March as part of wider efforts to slow the spread of COVID-19. The Kenyan Ministry of Education estimated that the suspension of education, would affect 90,000 schools serving over 18 million students, ranging from pre-primary to upper secondary learners, as well as an additional 150,000 students in refugee camps.[1147] The country justified the decision on the grounds of guaranteeing equity and inclusion. So many students were unable to access remote education provisioned via connected technology that a pause was warranted. The government had, in effect, acknowledged that technology-reliant approaches were leaving too many students behind. It could not reasonably expect most learners to successfully complete their current grade-level studies from a distance. Bolivia used the same rationale when it announced the cancellation of the school year due to the pandemic's disruption.[1148] The decision sent the message that learning via ed-tech was not required or expected, and that students would pick up where they had left off when schools reopened.

"The 2020 school calendar year will be considered lost due to COVID-19 restrictions."

– George Magoha, Minister of Education, Kenya[1149]

This policy action appears to have made Kenya an outlier globally. Most other countries communicated that formal learning should continue regardless of school closures. In these places, education was not on hold; it had moved from schools to technology, and students were still expected to participate. The OECD was one of many international organizations advocating for the continuation of education regardless of pandemic disruptions. It published an influential essay in April 2020 entitled "Repeating the school year not the answer to COVID learning losses". Citing "analyses of grade repetition" in typical school years, the OECD argued that pause policies might amplify "social disparities". The OECD instead advised "redoubling efforts to help struggling students" through scaling up distance learning and remediation measures when schools reopened.[1149]

Many countries heeded this recommendation from the OECD and tried to keep formal education moving ahead during periods of school closure by relying heavily or exclusively on ed-tech. Cognizant that dependence on technology would trigger major learning divides, education systems also moved to expand and reinforce remediation programmes when schools reopened.[1150] For example, the Philippines[1151], Japan and the Netherlands offered summer and/or weekend classes,[1152] and countries as diverse as Ghana[1153] and the UK established tutoring programmes. These programmes sought to help students who had missed distance learning catch up with their peers who had benefited from it. Many of these programmes were expensive. As one illustration, the national tutoring programme launched in the UK had a GBP 350 million price tag and was part of a larger GBP 1 billion package to "support children and young people to catch up on missed learning caused by the coronavirus".[1154]

Other education systems made decisions to trim the curriculum to only a few academic subjects when it was provisioned remotely via ed-tech. It was surmised that curtailing the breadth of education would allow students who missed technology-reliant forms of instruction to catch up faster and more easily when in-person schooling ultimately resumed. It was an instance of education authorities limiting the scope of remote education, in part so that students unable to access it could realistically get back on track once they returned to school. Winnowing the curriculum also offered other perceived advantages. For example, countries and schools did not need to produce and disseminate as much digital learning content, and schools and teachers had fewer classes and subjects to support remotely.[1155]

> The education system had been set up in ways that guaranteed the need for remediation and often for large numbers of students.

The attention countries paid to various remediation and catch-up programmes indicated an awareness that many students had failed to progress academically when education was administered exclusively through technology. Remediation was needed because students were behind, and students were largely behind because they were unable to access distance learning via ed-tech. In effect, the education system had been set up in ways that guaranteed the need for remediation and often for large numbers of students. The academic deficits students faced when they returned to schools traced to structural shortcomings and not individual ones. Ed-tech, due to its limited accessibility, cemented inequities into

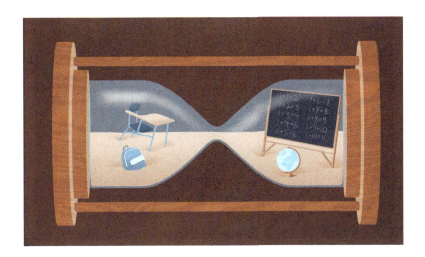

education systems that had been much less pervasive when schools were operational. Huge numbers of students fell behind through no fault of their own.

The policy to suspend education in Kenya illustrated an alternative possibility. Instead of assuming students would be able to progress academically during periods of school closure, as most countries did, Kenya acknowledged the wide inaccessibility of technology-dependent distance learning and decided that no progress should be assumed. Technology ownership and use did not, at least not overtly, determine which students would be 'behind' or 'on track' when schooling resumed. The pause in education also presented the possibility of removing or lessening the need for large-scale remediation when schools reopened. If learners were resuming their studies where they had left off when schools closed, they were less likely to be 'behind' and to require remedial classes or accelerated learning. This did not, of course, mean that there were no differences in educational progression when schools were shuttered. Some students advanced academically during lockdowns, while others stagnated or regressed, regardless of whether distance education was available or not, due to varying home situations and individual and family behaviours, among other factors. But because a pause policy did not expect educational progression while schools were closed, students without formal learning opportunities were not assured to fall behind.

> The pause in education presented the possibility of removing or lessening the need for large-scale remediation when schools reopened. If learners were resuming their studies where they had left off, they were less likely to be 'behind' and to require remedial classes or accelerated learning.

Kenyan authorities were clear-eyed that very few learners in the country would be able to follow education remotely through technology. A study conducted by the Population Council in four districts in Kenya clarified just how out of reach connected technologies were for most students.[1156] It found that in a best-case scenario, only 30 per cent of students were able to use any type of connected technology for distance education. This was observed in Nairobi, the capital and wealthiest city in Kenya. The worst-case scenario was found in Wajir, a rural district. Here, the study observed that technology access was limited to just 2 per cent of students. The authors of the research noted that even these very low figures likely overstated the actual ability of students to use technology for educational purposes due to limited electricity and various connectivity restraints. Of the minority of learners who said they had access to a mobile phone, nearly half reported that insufficient data credits hindered them from using the device to access educational content. It was also significant that the study included only adolescents aged 15 to 19, who are generally more likely to have access to connected technology than younger learners. The Kenyan policy of pausing education, rather than assuming students would progress with ed-tech during periods of school closure, seemed to account for these sobering realities.

Kenya began reopening schools for select grades in October 2020,[1157] ahead of its initial projection, with all grades beginning in January 2021.[1158] This was due to both public pressure from families anxious to get students back in school as well as an improving health situation. In line with the pause policy, students picked up where they had left off when schools had closed their doors.[1159] The learning that would have happened for, say, seventh grade students in March and April 2020 without the pandemic and school closures was shifted to early 2021.

The Kenyan plan was far from ideal in many ways, and its implementation was not without controversy. Many students and families were upset by the prospect of losing time and delaying academic progress. Other families and many teachers were worried about the health implications of children returning to school en masse at a preselected time, the beginning of the 2021 academic year, when the trajectory of COVID-19 remained highly uncertain. Some groups, arguing that the timing of school reopenings was premature, even took the matter to court.[1160] Many people experienced Kenya's policy as confusing, especially when, ultimately, the plan was implemented so that some grade levels resumed school-based instruction earlier than others. Adjusting the standard academic calendar also appears to have presented challenges. Some students resuming school in January 2021 were not starting a new grade, as would usually be the case, but rather continuing a partially completed grade. And even the equity justification for the pause was called into doubt, in part due to the country's growing reliance on private providers of education. In some instances, these providers were better able to provide distance learning during periods of school closure than public schools, creating a perception that private school students were advancing while public school students were not.[1161]

The Kenya experience highlights fraught questions of how societies should balance desires to facilitate academic progression via ed-tech with assuring commitments to access, inclusion and equity.

The Kenya case deserves attention, however, because it highlights fraught questions of how societies should – or could – balance desires to facilitate academic progression via ed-tech with assuring commitments to access, inclusion and equity. One question, for example, is whether broad educational inclusion is more or less important than assuring educational continuity for some learners, who may be privileged in other ways.

When schools closed as part of national strategies to mitigate the spread of COVID-19, it was well known that huge numbers of students would not be able to access formal learning that was dependent on connected technology. In numerous countries, national data suggested fewer than 20 per cent of school-age children could realistically follow education delivered through digital channels. Given the dizzying exclusion and inequity that reliance on ed-tech introduced, not to mention other problems with technology-first modes of learning, was it wise to mandate a transition to ed-tech? Pausing education was always a distinct possibility.

Pause policies were criticized early in the pandemic because the duration of school closures was highly uncertain in early 2020.[1162] Many believed it was better to move learning to ed-tech, no matter the availability of technology, because the closures might continue indefinitely. The prospect that a technology alternative to school-based education might be needed for long durations and perhaps years justified trying to construct this alternative system sooner rather than later, despite the exclusion it entailed. But school closures are rarely tenable over very long periods, and evidence indicates that the viruses that cause pandemics usually taper off and become less deadly over time.[1163] As such, governments had data to suggest, even from the outset of the health crisis, that a pause in education was unlikely to stretch on uninterrupted for a period of years. Should this have made pause approaches more widespread or at least more worthy of consideration?

"What this period has shown is that those that have resources will continue to flourish as they can access and engage with the different platforms. And those that are poor will continue to be left behind."

– Gugu Ndebele, former CEO of Save the Children South Africa[cxciv]

The compulsory nature of the shift to ed-tech as a response to school closures carried hidden costs. It tended to place pressure on families to buy expensive technology they might not have otherwise purchased. Sometimes government agencies supported these purchases, but in many cases, the responsibility fell to families, many of them already financially vulnerable due to pandemic disruptions to work and income. The compulsory nature also placed significant psychological stress on families at a time when fear and anxiety levels were already high. Families that did not have access to technology worried that their children would fall behind. Many felt their inability to buy a smartphone or top up connectivity credits was compromising the future of even very young children. Given these realities, should more countries have made distance learning with technology fully voluntary and adopted pause policies?

> Historical data suggest that pause policies might have been more equitable than those that expected learners to use unevenly available technology to progress academically.

Evidence from school closures that accompanied past pandemics indicates that pausing education did not result in the amplification of social disparities that the OECD and other organizations warned about in the context of COVID-19.[1164] Instead, it seems that pausing education for students when schools closed helped level the playing field when young people returned to school. For example, researchers from the US National Bureau of Economics Research studying the educational impacts of school closures during the 1918–19 influenza pandemic found "null effects of school closure length on 1920 school attendance" and little evidence of long or short-term impacts on educational attainment and future labour-market outcomes. Moreover, these results were observed "across student characteristics, including socio-economic status, race and parental nativity". The authors, writing in December 2020, went on to speculate that the absence of alternative means of accessing formal education in 1918–19 likely explains the homogeneous effect of school closures on students from different backgrounds: "The lack of effective remote learning platforms in 1918–19 may have put students on roughly equal footing when they missed school, unlike today, when there is substantial heterogeneity in access to online resources and parental support."[1165] The authors' implication is clear: total reliance on ed-tech, rather than school closures, amplified educational disparities. These historical data suggest that a pause policy might have been more equitable than policies that forced or expected learners to use unevenly available technology to progress academically.

It is significant that pause policies eventually became more widespread as the education responses to the pandemic evolved. For example, when governments closed schools in late 2021 and early 2022 in response to the Omicron variant, many simply treated the closures as an extension of school holidays and did not mandate a shift to online learning.[1166] Governments communicated a message that education would resume when schools reopened. This evolution reflected confidence that schooling would resume after a relatively short duration and kept education priorities focused on reopening schools. It also reflected a waning confidence in the value, equity and utility of fully remote distance learning.

ALTERNATIVE C:
FOCUS ON SUPPORTING CAREGIVERS AND PRIORITIZING NON-TECHNOLOGICAL LEARNING RESOURCES

A third alternative to heavy reliance on digital and online modes of remote learning was to support learning from a distance with low-tech and no-tech resources aimed primarily at caregivers. Rather than expecting teachers and school systems to use laptops and smartphones to interface directly with students online, education authorities could have mobilized outreach campaigns to share ideas and resources on how families might best support in-person learning opportunities in the home. This could have been done through a variety of communication channels and would not have necessitated internet-connected devices.

> The instructions given to caregivers generally boiled down to edicts to ensure young people were watching the right screen at the right time or logging into the appropriate online platform with the appropriate frequency.

During the pandemic, the instructions given to caregivers generally boiled down to edicts to ensure young people were watching the right screen at the right time or logging into the appropriate online platform with the appropriate frequency. The task was primarily framed as one of planning time with technology, and much of the advice stressed the importance of establishing and following rigid routines structured around ed-tech.[1167] Adults in closest proximity to children often lacked other recommendations to support education and turn the home into a learning environment. The common message from schools and governments was that formal education could and should progress in virtual environments, even in places where connected technology was known to be scarce. While learning might happen away from screens, this was not the learning that ministries of education tended to prioritize and encourage. The technology-centric approaches sent signals that serious and important learning, even for young children, would be delivered by technology, and learning that happened elsewhere was less important and less valuable.

It is not hard to imagine a different approach: one that supported and encouraged parents to find and embrace learning opportunities available in the home and not wholly dependent on ed-tech. These opportunities were numerous and included involving children in household tasks and teaching them non-academic skills, such as cooking, gardening or animal rearing. If technology was available and could assist learning processes, its use could be encouraged. But if technology was not available, messaging from the government could have signalled that this was fine too. Rather than placing full reliance on expensive and logistically complex efforts to support curriculum-based learning with ed-tech, while schools were closed, educational priorities could have shifted towards understanding education

and learning in ways that were broader and could be incorporated into family life.

<small>Paper brochures listing, say, ten ideas to support learning at home could have been printed and disseminated to millions of families, lessening exclusive reliance on ed-tech.</small>

Messages promoting the value of family- and community-based learning, along with advice and support to parents and caregivers, could have been disseminated through technology (TV and radio as well as the internet), but also through other channels such as teacher outreach, local community leaders or in printed brochures, in sober recognition that many families and communities did not have equal access to the connected technology. Paper brochures listing, say, ten ideas to support learning at home could have been printed in the millions and sent out by post or set out at food markets, pharmacies, government offices, places of worship and other institutions that often remained open during lockdowns. Guidance could have been prepared in multiple languages, with graphic illustrations for illiterate caregivers, and disseminated alongside health recommendations, which were rarely solely reliant on technological means of communication. Yet despite these possibilities, UNESCO observed few multimodal communication campaigns that encouraged informal and non-technology-reliant forms of learning during the pandemic.

<small>For young children, learning tools such as crayons, paper and storybooks can be as educative and engaging as expensive tablet computers or smartphones.</small>

Moreover, efforts to disseminate physical learning materials such as books, paper, and pencils appear to have been eclipsed by efforts to disseminate connected technology such as smartphones, tablets and laptops. This was often the case even in communities where electricity and connectivity were known to be unreliable. Announcements of government purchases of hundreds of millions of USD of ed-tech were common during the pandemic,[1168] while comparable announcements of purchases of non-electronic learning resources were hard to find. Physical learning resources are often cheaper and easier for governments to acquire than ed-tech, and easier to produce locally. Digital hardware, by contrast, usually has to be purchased from abroad and is contingent on complex global supply chains. Device orders were routinely delayed or never arrived at all during the pandemic due to disruptions to these supply chains.[1169] For young children, learning tools such as crayons, paper and storybooks can be as educative and engaging as a USD 500 tablet computer or USD 100 smartphone, but the overwhelming message that families received was that education should proceed via technology. Families routinely went to extreme lengths to secure ed-tech with personal funds when government provisioning was not available or insufficient, as was common.

> National campaigns to rapidly scale up and expand initiatives to bring printed books to households during the pandemic were a distinct possibility but appear to have been meagre and short-lived, if they existed at all.

Deprioritizing ed-tech and elevating more accessible and informal learning would have perhaps encouraged families to spend more time on games and cultural pastimes that are often enmeshed in centuries of history and rich with educational value. Whether boardgames or puzzles, puppetry or dance, numerous activities were within reach at homes and inviting of creativity and learning. A focus on physical learning materials could have prioritized book production and distribution, with funds flowing to local publishers, authors and printers and concurrent campaigns to encourage print reading. Given the importance of literacy, communities could have established special allowances and protocols for teachers to read to and with young people as well as neo-literate adults in communities where illiteracy is widespread. UN data indicate that only 5 per cent of poor families in developing countries have books in their homes.[1170] Such inequities are not limited to developing countries: a 2007 study found that in disadvantaged neighbourhoods in the USA, the book to child ratio is 1 to 300,[1171] and in 2020 the OECD stated that children from poor households are four times less likely to have access to a good supply of children's books at home than children from advantaged families.[1172] Physical books carry unique advantages for children and beginning-level adult readers,[1173] yet the pandemic shut off access to libraries, schools and other community centres where families, including many low-income families, had typically gone to read or borrow paper books. National campaigns to rapidly scale up and expand initiatives to bring printed books to households during the pandemic were a distinct possibility but appear to have been meagre and short-lived, if they existed at all. In their place were efforts to equip learners with digital technology, usually developed and manufactured by a handful of large corporations.

While lip service was sometimes paid to the importance of disseminating non-digital resources as a means of supporting learners without access to connected technology, such efforts tended to benefit more privileged families. For example, some schools and libraries set up systems to dispense physical books to people who requested them, however, these systems tended to use online portals, effectively locking out families without connectivity. Affluent and middle-income communities were more likely to organize sites where parents could pick up bundles of physical learning materials. The bundles would commonly contain notebooks, workbooks, pens, pencils and craft supplies such as markers, scissors, glue, paints, tape, coloured paper and clay. Like book check-outs, these bundles had to be reserved and scheduled for pick up through online systems. A more effective way to support poor families would have been with door-to-door drop-offs of learning supplies, but these appear to have been uncommon. In some instances, deliveries of this type were deemed unsafe because they risked increasing social contact. But this contact risk would not seem to surpass the risks presented by the deliveries of prepared food and commercial goods, fulfilled by companies like Amazon and Deliveroo, that were active during periods of school closure.

Many families with access to functioning ed-tech were attuned to its shortcomings to support education as a singular interface. Perhaps due to norms and perceptions of independence,[1174] wealthy families were more likely than lower income families to abandon ed-tech modes of learning in favour of less technology-reliant solutions, often in defiance of official educational guidance. These families were also arguably more equipped to support non-technology-reliant modes of learning because they had physical learning resources in the home, such as books, educational toys, art supplies and games, that provided educational alternatives to digital technology.

> The existence of learning pods highlighted that there was demand for educational solutions not solely dependent on technology and that numerous families were willing to self-organize these solutions.

Learning pods were a concrete example of an educational model that emerged during the pandemic that was less dependent on technology than school and government systems of remote digital learning. This model typically involved small groups of young people, often those already in close physical proximity, coming together in person to learn under the tutelage of a parent or a hired teacher.[1175] The pods were often organized despite rules preventing social gatherings. Scans of media sources suggest that learning pods were established and used predominately by privileged families, perhaps due to the time and resources required to get them up and running and the investments required to sustain what was effectively a shadow education system. The existence of learning pods highlighted that there was demand for educational solutions not solely dependent on technology and that numerous families were willing to self-organize these solutions.

Less affluent families and communities also found ways to continue their children's educational journeys without technological solutions. In the Central African Republic, some community schools drew from their experiences of sustaining education in times of civil conflict and applied what they had learned to adjust to COVID-19 disruptions. Early in the pandemic, teachers and administrators consulted with families to organize students into small, decentralized schools, such that small groups of children could continue learning together with the support of teachers and families. Since these schools were already village- and neighbourhood-based, they often complied with restrictions on travel and gatherings.[1176] Neighbour-to-neighbour communication and simple SMS messages were sufficient to announce the existence of the schools and encourage attendance. Creative use of technology in the form of webinars, videos, podcasts and teaching materials complemented some of these in-person learning approaches. The technology, however, was decidedly secondary; it was not the primary nexus of connection and educational exchange.[1177]

In order to accommodate the large numbers of learners lacking access to digital ed-tech, schools and educational authorities could have invested greater energy in and provided more resources to supporting offline and in-person learning both inside homes but also through community and neighbourhood initiatives that did not endanger public health. Teachers, for example, could have been encouraged or deployed to support and direct learners in microschools, and government messaging could have promoted and celebrated the ingenuity of families that found ways to continue educating their children without unilateral reliance on ed-tech.

> The pandemic may have helped solidify social perceptions that in-person and non-technology-reliant education is a marker of privilege in wealthy communities where ed-tech is plentiful.

Interestingly, the pandemic may have helped solidify social perceptions that in-person and non-technology-reliant education is a marker of privilege in wealthy communities where ed-tech is plentiful. To some extent, this is an inversion of conventional understandings of ed-tech. Through the 1990s and early 2000s, the use of connected digital technology for education signified advantage and wealth, but starting in the 2010s, as technology became more ubiquitous and less expensive, its cultural value decreased. Children in affluent communities would learn to use digital tools no matter what, so formal school-based education sought to cultivate interpersonal and other soft skills that are developed largely through in-person exchange and not easily taught in digital spaces or through virtual interaction. Many of the most elite private primary and early secondary schools in so-called tech hubs like Bangalore, London, Nairobi, San Francisco and Seoul, some costing over USD 20,000 per year in tuition, are marketing their limited use of technology as a selling point and signifier of excellence.[1178] For high-income students, ed-tech is a tool to be used sparingly in formal education, even as these students continue to have access to the most advanced types of learning technologies. For low-income students the trend is the inverse: ed-tech is being used with greater frequency and for a wider range of educational purposes, often in ways that makes education reliant on technology. This is exemplified by the rise of education models that require teachers and students in under-resourced countries to have connected devices to teach and learn in formal settings. For instance, Bridge International Academies, an educational company that operates low-cost private schools in countries such as India, Kenya, Nigeria and Uganda, has teachers deliver scripted lessons to students by following step-by-step instructions that are developed off-site and sent to a tablet computer.[1179]

Regardless of how this trend might develop in the future, the use of educational approaches and resources that do not depend on connected technology remained a constant alternative to technology-reliant approaches to remote learning during the pandemic. Yet despite the promise these approaches held to help underprivileged and marginalized learners without access to technology, as well as those who did have access, they were rarely employed during COVID-19 school closures.

Was COVID-19 an education crisis?

While COVID-19 was incontrovertibly a health crisis, it was widely referred to as an education crisis too. This transference of terminology influenced the response of the education sector to pandemic-related school closures and, arguably, made the rapid deployment of ed-tech appear more urgent and necessary than it might have been if the crisis designation had not been applied to education.

Rationales for crisis labelling varied. For some, the pandemic was an education crisis because schools were closed at times that they would normally have been in session, raising concerns over student well-being and the possibility of heightened dropout rates when schools reopened. Seen this way, the term 'education crisis' was a shorthand way of expressing alarm about unplanned school closures of uncertain durations.

For others, the cessation of formal academic learning was the root of the crisis, not necessarily school closures per se. Under this logic, disruptions to formal learning – regardless of the mode of learning – were alarming because students were not acquiring important knowledge and skills according to academic schedules. Learners were also assumed to be forgetting previously learned material while they were not engaged in curricular tasks. In this sense, unrealized or lost learning and the possibility of academic regression constituted an education crisis.

Still others employed the word 'crisis' to signal evidence and concern that funding to education would be reduced due to pandemic-driven changes to employment and tax revenue. This education crisis was about the slashing of education budgets or expectations of this outcome.

Finally, for groups and organizations that look at education through a primarily economic lens, including the World Bank, the OECD and the World Economic Forum, as well as a wide network of business and government consultancies such as McKinsey, the crisis label conveyed the ways that stalled education would reduce human capital and, by extension, slow economic growth and expansion. In late 2021, the World Bank projected that COVID-19 disruptions to education would cost a generation of students USD 17 trillion in lost lifetime earnings and presented this projection as the heart of the education crisis.[1180] A 2022 article published by the World Economic Forum in cooperation with the World Bank announced that "the global education crisis is even worse than we thought" and expressed alarm that "14 per cent of today's global GDP" could be wiped out in part as a result of school closures during the pandemic. The report estimated that the number of children living in "learning poverty" could reach 70 per cent in low- and middle-income countries as a result of the "relative ineffectiveness of remote learning", gravely endangering the future earnings of students.[1181] Here 'education crisis' meant the short-circuiting of skills development and the economic damage this was projected to inflict on individuals and national economies.

> When COVID-19 was framed as an educational crisis, ed-tech was quickly positioned as a lifeline of sorts – a rescue boat that could carry students through the treacherous currents of disruption.

The language of emergency was hardly limited to the use of the word 'crisis'. The COVID-19 pandemic was also framed as an 'educational disaster'. But even this was not peak doomsday terminology. In mid-2020, leading international organizations (including UNESCO) published a white paper called *Averting an Education Catastrophe for the World's Children*, as part of the Save Our Future coalition.[1182] Throughout 2020 and early 2021 there was a gradual ratcheting up of language used to discuss educational affairs and futures, even if there were some notable exceptions, such as UNESCO's 2020 publication *Education in a Post-COVID World: Nine Ideas for Public Action*.[1183]

Within this bleak framing, remote distance learning via ed-tech was quickly positioned as a lifeline of sorts – a rescue boat that could carry students through the treacherous currents of school closures and other educational disruptions. Technology, and digital technology in particular, is what would keep education afloat. Governments and schools rushed to purchase, support and deploy it. Families were instructed or mandated to use it.

"You never want a serious crisis to go to waste. And what I mean by that is an opportunity to do things you think you could not do before."

– Rahm Emanuel, politician, USA^{cxcv}

Indeed, the crisis view of the pandemic became so firmly ingrained in the educational imagination that it was almost blasphemous to question it throughout much of the pandemic. Yet despite this, alternative views remain possible and instructive, particularly as more panoramic understandings of the educational disruptions have come into focus and school closures have ended.

> Most academic calendars allow for planned, monthslong breaks in education, and these are almost never referred to as education crises.

Is an extended pause in academic learning really a crisis? Does a pause in formal school-based learning warrant major structural changes to the traditional practice and delivery of education? Most academic calendars allow for planned, monthslong breaks in education, and these are almost never referred to as education crises. In many countries, a year-long break in academic progress is typical for young adults nearing the end of secondary school for purposes such as mandatory military or volunteer service. And around the world, students, often while in universities or before entering higher education, take gap years to work, travel and pursue hobbies or sometimes just take a break and not do much of anything, yet these extended breaks in education are not called educational disasters.

While COVID-19 disruptions did affect all levels of education more or less simultaneously, many national education systems only closed schools for less than ten weeks in total from the beginning of 2020 to the end of 2022, and some for just five weeks, according to UNESCO monitoring. Was this disruption a crisis? Did this relatively short duration of school closure in select countries, even if only known with certainty after the end of the global health emergency, justify the enormous effort and expenditure required to move formal education into digital spaces? Might it have been more reasonable to simply announce that education would resume when schooling restarted and focus on strategies to reopen schools quickly and safely without the distraction of figuring out how to support learning over connected technology for all students – something that, in most contexts, had never been successfully accomplished or even attempted?

Upon close inspection, it seems the concept of a pandemic-driven education crisis derived from two main factors: (a) prolonged school closures and (b) the limitations or failures of ed-tech to satisfactorily patch the effects of these closures. Had schools been able to remain open without compromising safety, it is unlikely there would have been an education crisis. And had the transition to technology solutions for education helped all students learn and socialize in ways that at least roughly approximated

> The effectiveness or ineffectiveness of ed-tech is what determined whether school closures were education crises.

school-based methods, there similarly would not have been an education crisis. A handful of developed and often low-population countries, including Estonia, Singapore and Uruguay, which had spent decades carefully integrating digital technologies into their education systems before COVID-19, managed the transition to technology-reliant distance learning relatively seamlessly and without widespread exclusion or soaring levels of inequity. There was very little talk of an education crisis in these nations, even when schools were closed. Seen from this angle, the effectiveness or ineffectiveness of ed-tech is what determined whether school closures were education crises.

"In moments of crisis, people are willing to hand over a great deal of power to anyone who claims to have a magic cure."

– Naomi Klein, author[cxcvi]

It is reasonable then to ask whether elevating technological solutions as only-option remedies for school closures, and therefore a singular means of 'saving' education, gave traction to the concept of crisis and normalized its use in education circles. If ed-tech had not been positioned as a shield against an education crisis, would school closures, even those that stretched on for months, have necessarily carried the ominous crisis labelling? Would it have been possible for more education leaders and others to refer to temporary school closures resulting from a health emergency as exactly that: an unplanned break, a hiatus in formal learning similar to breaks that are occasionally necessitated by severe weather events or security concerns, rather than a calamity?

There is contemporary and historical evidence to support a view that a non-crisis framing was a distinct possibility. Contemporarily and in contexts where ed-tech is extremely scarce – in sub-Saharan Africa, for example, and countries in South Asia such as Bangladesh and Pakistan – the language of education crisis did not appear to be nearly as common on the ground and in local media as it was in reports coming from international organizations and NGOs with global reach. These groups were often voicing concerns over the repercussions of large digital and connectivity divides for education that had become largely reliant on connected technology. But inside low-income developing countries, the language of crisis did not appear to encompass education as readily as it did inside global organizations. In countries such as Chad, Mali and Niger very few people had access to connected technology before the pandemic, and this did not change during the pandemic. School closures in these areas affected nearly all learners and families similarly – it was not a case of some children making progress in formal education and others not making progress. Access to ed-tech was equal in the sense that almost no one had it. Without access to ed-tech, there was no promise or expectation of digital solutions to 'save' education. It had stopped for almost everyone, and there were strong understandings that it would resume in due time.

Around the world, the equity or inequity of ed-tech access seems to have been a significant driver of the language of crisis. In situations where ed-tech was ubiquitous and universally available for education, the crisis framing was less common. The same appears to have been true, if perhaps to a lesser extent, in situations where ed-tech was almost uniformly unavailable. This raises an intriguing question on whether the core of an education crisis is a sudden leap in inequality, as was experienced in many countries where ed-tech access and use was deeply uneven.

Further, it is significant that the word 'learning' rather than 'education' was commonly affixed to 'crisis', including and perhaps particularly when used in reference to contexts in the global South. Education literature rolling out of development organizations was awash with descriptions of a 'learning crisis' stemming from school closures, as well as concerns over 'learning loss'. The semantic nuance between 'education' and 'learning' could narrow or enlarge conceptions of what the crisis entailed. Where notions of an 'education crisis' might encompass student well-being, nutrition and protection as well as learning, notions of a 'learning crisis' zoomed in on problems stemming from stalled academic and curricular progress. A lot of the crisis language used during the pandemic seemed to have focused on learning rather than education as a whole. This may have been one of the reasons holistic student and teacher well-being sometimes seemed to be eclipsed by concerns over maintaining learning progress at a pace that would have been expected absent the pandemic disruptions.

Reviews of historical evidence conducted for this publication suggest that framing pandemic-necessitated school closures as an 'education crisis' or a 'learning crisis' is a relatively recent trend. For example, available descriptions of school closures implemented in response to the 1918–19 influenza pandemic, the last comparable global pandemic, indicate that the language of crisis was rarely applied to education. At that time, the preservation of health was the overriding concern in debates on whether to close schools and for how long. It also seems that there was no comparable discussion on the hazards of learning loss and vanishing GDP due to missed education. The twin focuses appear to have been avoiding disease and maintaining the well-being of students and teachers.

Revealingly, the language of crisis often lingered long after schools reopened. The learning loss that resulted from unscheduled disruptions and breaks in formal learning was commonly classified as a crisis. At the beginning of 2022, UNICEF announced in a press release that the scale of pandemic learning loss was "nearly insurmountable". The organization declared that "reopening schools is not enough" – students needed "intensive support" to recover lost learning.[1184] The crisis, in this estimation, had mutated from school closures to the failures of technology-reliant distance learning solutions to keep learning progressing at rates that would have been expected had schools been open. In actuality, much of the data on learning loss and learning poverty referenced in announcements such as the one at UNICEF existed well before COVID-19 school closures. Poor learning outcomes resulted from factors connected to the pandemic disruptions but also factors that predated the pandemic.

"It is one of the great ironies and sorrows of the present age that disasters have become prime fodder for the sort of laissez-faire economic development that aims mainly at the creation of private fortunes for well-connected corporations and individuals."

– Richard Kahn, professor of education, Antioch University[cxcvii]

> The learning loss born from the failures of ed-tech to facilitate learning progression during school closures was to be remedied by more ed-tech.

The staying power of faith in technology solutionism was evident when groups in and outside education began hoisting ed-tech as a means to mitigate learning loss crisis that had been exacerbated by school closures. When the 'old' education crisis of school closures melted into the 'new' education crisis of learning loss, digital technology was positioned as a first-option antidote to both. In numerous countries, stimulus money that had been earmarked to help students recover lost learning poured into ed-tech solutions and virtual tutoring.[1185] This reflected a strange circular logic: the learning loss born from the failures of ed-tech to facilitate learning progression during school closures was to be remedied by more ed-tech.

As various scholars have observed, the concept of crisis often functions to narrow the ways problems are interpreted and what solutions are proposed.[1186] Crises, as Naomi Klein and others have argued, tend to make market-based reforms feel 'natural' or 'inevitable'.[1187] Academic work to identify paths that facilitate the privatization of education systems have identified the "path of emergency" as among the most potent and rapid.[1188] In a paper exploring how education has become privatized through "crisis-making", scholar Hang Minh Le explains how the invocation of specific types of emergencies, such as a "refugee crisis", has been a crucial force in facilitating the privatization of education. She notes that the "urgency of crisis helps to naturalize private actors' participation in refugees' education as equal partners to host governments, multilateral agencies, and civil society". Published in 2019, Le's descriptions of the tendency of crises to carve out "new spaces" and "new markets" for private actors to infuse "market and business principles such as 'innovation' into all aspects of education" carried renewed relevance as the COVID-19 pandemic gripped the world.[1189]

These critical views of crisis should not, however, negate recognition that, regardless of whether an education crisis framing was appropriate or advisable at the outset of the pandemic, actions to respond to it with prolonged school closures and the application of technology-dependent solutions have precipitated outcomes that are of grave and urgent concern: large numbers of students unable to read; young people burdened with anxiety, depression and feelings of isolation; and increased numbers of students dropping out from education, among other factors. These unfortunate developments resemble the outcomes of crises, and perhaps unsurprisingly, numerous technology and market-based approaches are being flouted as solutions.

The language of crisis has become so saddled with notions of quick technocratic and private-sector-led fixes that the education sector might be well served with new concepts, diagnoses and terms to frame the havoc wreaked by COVID-19 on education – concepts that are less tethered to technology-first approaches and corporate entrenchment and that carry more potential to open alternative pathways for solutions and reforms.

Looking Ahead

This part of the Inter-Act describes and problematizes lessons drawn from the pandemic about the future of ed-tech.

The first section explains how connected technologies were quickly positioned as an essential – or the essential – ingredient of educational resilience in the context of pandemic-related school closures. Although improving educational resilience had not been a particularly strong selling point for ed-tech before 2020, the pandemic provided the conditions that galvanized a belief that complex and expensive technologies would allow education systems to respond with speed, agility and flexibility to COVID-19 disruptions as well as to future disturbances to schooling as a result of future pandemics, climate change, conflict and other challenges.

The second section examines the extent to which ed-tech actually improves educational resilience. Citing research and data from around the world, it shows that connected technologies have numerous points of failure as stand-alone educational solutions and in fact introduce considerable fragilities compared with conventional school-based approaches to teaching and learning.

The third and final section critiques arguments that the pandemic awakened recognition that education is under digitized and that going forward, connected technologies will invariably disrupt and transform the sector. The analysis challenges notions that investments in education are destined to shift away from expenditures on teacher salaries and the physical infrastructure of schools and towards ed-tech. While such a shift in financial allocation might bring education in closer alignment with other sectors that spend more proportionally on technology, education is a unique sector. It has long reflected a commitment to helping young people integrate into social communities, navigate relationships with diverse people in face-to-face settings, and develop skills and competencies that will help them make productive social contributions. These social and interpersonal goals are, however, often insufficiently supported by digital spaces and tools, especially when accessed and used in isolation.

Ed-tech finds a new rationale – resilience

Prior to the COVID-19 pandemic, the digital transformation of education was widely understood as a strategy to improve the quality, accessibility and inclusiveness of learning. The end goal of ed-tech was modernization in service of educational improvement, along one or multiple dimensions.

> 'Resilience' was the word marshalled again and again to explain why the uptake of ed-tech was necessary, unavoidable and desirable.

Yet following the widespread adoption of distance learning solutions during pandemic-related school closures, the concept of 'resilience' became the go-to rationale for ed-tech. This idea, perhaps more than any other, was used to explain and justify the unprecedented investments countries poured into ed-tech, financial as well as programmatic and pedagogical. Resilience was the quality that education systems needed to confront the immediate challenges of COVID-19 disruptions and, beyond this, lay more pliable foundations to meet future challenges, be they foreseen or unknown. 'Resilience' was the word marshalled again and again to explain why the uptake of ed-tech was necessary, unavoidable and desirable, and the concept of ed-tech providing resilience to education has remained a primary rationale for ongoing investments in ed-tech even after schools reopened in 2022 and 2023.

In the decades before COVID-19, research on ed-tech sought to compare technology interventions in education against non- or lower-technology controls of some sort in order to assess effectiveness. Findings from this research produced muddy and often contradictory results. Some research showed ed-tech integration could dramatically improve educational outcomes, while other research indicated no meaningful change or even regression.[1190] Ed-tech was deemed inappropriate if it failed to facilitate learning gains because of its considerable costs, both for the technology itself and the many human processes needed to ensure that it is appropriately leveraged to enhance education.

Perhaps the most comprehensive comparative analysis of ed-tech's impact on learning is the 2015 OECD report *Students, Computers and Learning: Making the Connection*. The work's central finding delivered a disappointing verdict: countries that invested heavily in ICT for education "show no appreciable improvements in student achievement in reading, mathematics or science". The findings further indicated that "technology is of little help in bridging the skills divide between advantaged and disadvantaged students".[1191] Whatever the limitations or flaws of the OECD study, its design reflected a belief that ed-tech *should* improve learning outcomes. The study's architects understood technology as a means to higher ends, not an end in itself. Other research reflected a similar orientation: ed-tech's value was the extent to which it furthered academic and social aims for education.

As the pace of digital transformation in sectors beyond education accelerated, some observers argued that technology integration was desirable even if it failed to facilitate learning improvement in reading, mathematics, science and other academic subjects. The rationale was that exposure to technology would help students develop a familiarity with tools and services that are shaping the future. It was also seen as a necessary starting point for building digital skills, especially for students who did not have access to technology in the home. Connected technology could also be its own field of study. Beginning in the 2000s, there were numerous movements to make subjects such as computer science part of core academic curricula in primary through upper secondary schools. Mandating computer science or narrower computer programming courses prompted educational purchases of computers and other ed-tech. Groups like Code.org, founded by technology entrepreneurs and investors and backed by donations from large technology companies, often pushed this agenda.[1192] Finally, many technology enthusiasts and entrepreneurs saw technology use in education as a field for experimentation. Although ed-tech might not show positive learning results early on, the thinking was that innovation and iteration would unveil positive changes. Pilots, tests and tinkering were therefore justified on the grounds that they would, in time, illuminate strategies to improve and perhaps transform education.

The pandemic, however, disrupted this widely shared view of what ed-tech should offer by elevating a separate and previously marginal rationale for its use and integration: educational resilience. From the moment schools started closing in early 2020, ed-tech deployments were framed around a new language of necessity and even survival. Concerns about its effectiveness to offer educational value shifted to the background. Technology was variously deemed a 'lifeline to learning', a 'must-have', a 'flexible' and 'adaptive' solution to crises, and a 'shield' or 'insurance policy' against future disruptions. Ed-tech was no longer understood as being on the offensive – pushing education to new and previously unreached heights – but rather it became a defensive strategy – providing continuity through disruption and helping preserve and protect what was already in place.

> Ed-tech was no longer understood as being on the offensive – pushing education to new and previously unreached heights – but rather it became a defensive strategy – providing continuity through disruption and preserving and protecting what was already in place.

Ed-tech's status as a pillar of educational resilience emerged for the simple reason that it could – when used by students and teachers at a distance and in relative isolation – support learning models that complied with the strict social-distancing stipulations and other restrictions on movement and gatherings precipitated by COVID-19. Although ed-tech had previously featured in discussions about education in emergencies, it was rarely, if ever, seen as an only-option tool. There were, it was understood, multiple pathways to resilience in most emergency settings: ed-tech was one among others and often complementary to more human-centred interventions.

The pandemic functioned to elevate ed-tech as a singular and largely undisputed bastion of resilience because other potential approaches to education entailed human-to-human contact and were therefore quickly dismissed. Resilience in this context meant maintaining education while minimizing disease transmission. As associations between ed-tech and resilience quickly solidified, so too did views that expanded investments in technology would make education stronger and more flexible in the future, lest there be another pandemic or some other shock that might again require schools to shut their doors. In a few short months, technology catapulted from a messy, makeshift, stopgap response to the educational disruptions of an unparalleled global health crisis to an essential ingredient of 'building back better'. Ed-tech was no longer an experiment but the foundation or backbone of forward-looking, resilient education systems.

> In a few short months, technology catapulted from a messy, makeshift, stopgap response to the educational disruptions of an unparalleled global health crisis to an essential ingredient of 'building back better'.

A July 2020 World Bank policy paper on education was illustrative of this new framing and typical of recommendations released by other multilateral and international organizations. Entitled *Building Back Better:*

The message was clear: investments in ed-tech were needed not only during the pandemic but also beyond it. Conspicuously absent were debates about the extent to which technology might introduce new risks.

Education Systems for Resilience, Equity and Quality in the Age of COVID-19, the World Bank paper put forward six policy recommendations. All of them implored governments to double down on ed-tech and digital transformation. The first three recommendations advised (1) "investing in emergency connectivity and IT infrastructure for education in emergencies", (2) "supporting digital content and pedagogy for safety and quality", and (3) "building better institutional capacity for education technology resilience".[1193] The message was clear: investments in ed-tech were needed not only during the pandemic but also beyond it. Technology was now a pathway to 'better' education systems based on the assumption that it would strengthen resilience. Gone were conversations on whether major investments in technology and increased reliance on technology were superior to non-technology or more limited technology approaches to education. Also conspicuously absent were debates about the extent to which technology might introduce new risks.

The World Bank was not alone in its insistence that technology assured educational resilience. In September 2021, UNICEF published a report entitled *Reopening with Resilience: Lessons from Remote Learning during COVID-19*. Its first recommendation, highlighted in bold, was: "Increase investment in remote learning programmes to build resilience into education systems."[1194] The other four recommendations, similar to the World Bank report, all put ed-tech front and centre. Although the UNICEF report regularly noted that "there is no replacement for in-person learning", its recommendations uniformly advised strengthening ed-tech-reliant systems to provision fully remote education. None of the recommendations suggested approaches to meet educational disruptions to schooling without technology, reinforcing the view that technology forms the nucleus of educational resilience. The report did, however, observe that "all forms of technology-enabled remote learning require electricity" and cited data to show that "only 47 per cent of the population has access to electricity in sub-Saharan Africa". The work did not clarify how technology- and electricity-reliant modes of education might help these students beyond calls to address electricity, connectivity and data affordability challenges. The message was unambiguous: even in the poorest communities on earth, the path to educational resilience depends on ed-tech and its demands for expensive and complex infrastructure that, quite plainly, does not yet exist in large parts of the world.

"The global school closures due to COVID-19 have shown the fragility of education systems and the need for accessible and effective remote learning modalities that can be relied on when schools are forced shut."

– UNICEF[cxcviii]

> In the context of the COVID-19 pandemic, ed-tech did not have to prove itself against other educational interventions. It was merely required to provide a conduit to learning that did not transmit a viral and airborne disease.

This shift in discourse positioned ed-tech as a non-negotiable necessity rather than a reasoned choice, best choice or experimental consideration. In the world before COVID-19, ed-tech interventions, even those deployed in emergencies, needed to prove themselves against other educational interventions less reliant on technology. In the pandemic context, though, this proof had a significantly lower threshold: ed-tech was singular and indispensable for the simple fact that it was not a conduit for transmission of a viral and airborne disease. This has hurt ed-tech innovation. Existing and often deeply flawed models of technology use in education have been labelled 'good enough' and are scaling up at a pace that would have been unimaginable outside of the pandemic.[1195]

The residual trauma of school closures has also, it seems, made policy-makers more hesitant to ask critical questions about the effectiveness and desirability of technology-first solutions for education. Expectations are high that countries will be better prepared for future pandemics and other disruptions that might result in widespread school closures. But disruptions to schooling are not guaranteed to not also entail disruptions to connectivity and digital services. Prior to the emergence of COVID-19, many people were more worried about the havoc computer viruses might bring to societies, including the possibility of a global internet shutdown, than they were about biological viruses. Yet education leaders who reject calls for larger investments in ed-tech to support learning from a distance are swimming against the current of popular opinion that has been forged by the recent experience of massive school closures. This will not, however, change the reality that greater investments in ed-tech typically require diverting funds away from other uses in education. These financial diversions are coming at a time when education budgets are expected to tighten in many countries due to debt stemming from large public expenditures made during the pandemic. Numerous countries have cut their total education budgets to below pre-pandemic levels.[1196] The heightened prioritization of ed-tech translates into lower prioritization of other efforts, whether the construction of physical schools, in-person training for teachers, purchases of physical learning resources or other educational expenditures that do not fall under the banner of technology. This outcome – the elevation of ed-tech, with its considerable flaws and risks, at the expense of more tried-and-true interventions – leaves a troubling legacy from the pandemic.

> The elevation of ed-tech, with its considerable flaws and risks, at the expense of more tried-and-true interventions leaves a troubling legacy from the pandemic.

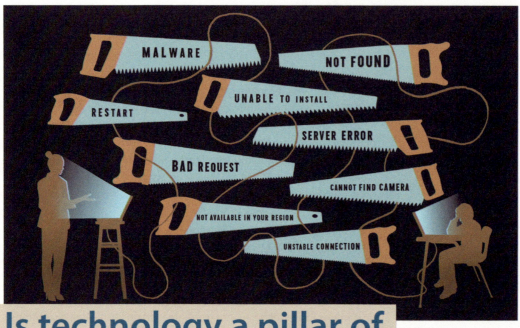

Is technology a pillar of educational resilience?

In education policy circles, a common and sometimes key takeaway from the COVID-19 disruption was that education systems need to build greater resilience by increasing investments in connected technology and capacities to use this technology to teach and learn from a distance. But is ed-tech a linchpin of educational resilience?

Since the onset of the pandemic, educational resilience has been framed as the ability to withstand major and sustained educational disruptions, including widespread and prolonged school closures of the type seen during the COVID-19 health crisis. The OECD's *Lessons for Education from COVID-19: A Policy Maker's Handbook for More Resilient Systems* was typical in its framing of resilience as an ability to "withstand and recover from adverse events". The handbook asserted that only resilient education systems that plan for disruption "will be able to fulfil the fundamental human right to education, whatever the circumstances, and foster the level of human capital required for successful economies and societies".[1197] Along with many other organizations, the OECD saw ed-tech as a necessary tool of resilience.

> A narrative took hold that traditional schooling was fragile and collapsed under the weight of the pandemic, while technology was tough and ensured learning never stopped.

The future envisioned by policy handbooks of this type tended to be many shades darker than it had been before the pandemic. New and severe crises were assumed to be on the horizon, and to prepare, ed-tech was commonly hailed as a first-order tool of resilience. A narrative took hold that traditional schooling was fragile and collapsed under the weight of the pandemic, while technology was tough and ensured learning never stopped. From these understandings, a logical next step was to urgently accelerate the digitalization of education and increase expenditure and reliance on ed-tech. It was often positioned as an only-option hedge against the spectre of future school closures.

But is ed-tech the straightest route to more adaptable and flexible education systems, capable of overcoming foreseen and unforeseen disruptions? Globally, the experiences of the pandemic suggest that this is far from assured. The sudden shift to technology was chaotic, grossly inequitable and often dissatisfying for the teachers, families and students who were able to access and use it for educational purposes.

> Ed-tech can only promote resilience where batteries can be charged.

The steps and expense required to make technology a more leak-free wall of educational resilience at the global level are staggering. The ITU has estimated the cost of connecting everyone in the world over 10 years old to the internet would be more than USD 400 billion.[1198] Adding suitable hardware to make productive use of this connectivity would push this figure up much higher. And all these scenarios assume that there is reliable access to the electricity needed to power digital devices. A recent nationwide survey of villages conducted by the Ministry of Rural Development in India shows just how wrong this assumption can be. It found that fewer than 50 per cent of Indian households receive more than 12 hours of electricity per day.[1199] These gaps can be more severe in Africa. According to World Bank data, fewer than 50 per cent of people in sub-Saharan Africa have any reliable access to electricity.[1200] Ed-tech can only promote resilience where batteries can be charged.

Ongoing connectivity and hardware expenses are also substantial. While more and more people come online each year, this upward trajectory obscures data showing that there is also substantial regression. Households and educational institutions that were connected often become unconnected, due to financial challenges or lack of technical expertise. Many schools that were equipped with hardware and internet connections in the late 1990s or early 2000s no longer are. The history of technology deployment for education is one of ricocheting progress littered with abandoned investments.[1201] One Laptop per Child, perhaps the largest and most hyped global initiative to transform and improve education with ed-tech, managed to bring computers to learners who did not previously have access to them in several countries, but many of these efforts were not sustained and students went back to studying without technology.[1202] One of the most influential books on educational technology is titled *Oversold and Underused*.[1203]

Connected technology also has many co-dependencies. Hardware requires compatible operating systems. These operating systems will only support specific software, and this software will only run seamlessly if certain hardware requirements are met. Anyone who has tried to get a new mobile app working on an older mobile phone can attest to the limits of backward compatibility. Connectivity introduces still more co-dependencies. Hardware supports certain types of connectivity but not others, therefore gadgets may work on Wi-Fi but not Bluetooth, or vice versa. SIM cards are often locked to specific devices and are compatible with some carriers and networks but not others. Securing SIM cards, mobile credit and other tools for connectivity can necessitate identification and financial requirements that many families do not have. The layers of dependencies to keep ed-tech operational make paper books, blackboards, chalk and lined notebooks look like remarkably versatile pieces of educational equipment.

Ed-tech hardware availability is reliant on complex manufacturing and distribution processes. In the early stages of the pandemic, many schools and families found that even when money was available to purchase technology for educational purposes, the technology was unavailable due to supply chain disruptions. Most countries lack the equipment or capacity to build their own digital technology and were therefore dependent on orders fulfilled by private sector companies based in other countries with factories in still other countries. In the first half of 2020, there were numerous reports of countries, states, school districts and even individual schools trying to outmanoeuvre each other for scarce ed-tech equipment.[1204] Most of the hardware that runs mobile networks is produced by just a handful of vendors that are themselves dependent on various subcontractors and external firms to fulfil orders. Sanctions can instantly close the door to needed technology imports across entire countries, while a tax or price change, can make once reachable technology unattainable. This is resilience as dependence.

Beyond supply fragilities, the hardware and connectivity that make technology useful for educational purposes are also fragile in a physical sense. Water, even in small amounts, can be fatal to electronics, as can dust and heat. Batteries stop holding power. Screens break. Buttons lock. Most of the digital hardware used for ed-tech is unfixable beyond replacing screens. Even simple components, such as the batteries and microphones in smartphones and laptops, cannot be easily replaced by end users.

> The layers of dependencies to keep ed-tech operational make paper books, blackboards, chalk and lined notebooks look like remarkably versatile pieces of educational equipment.

Internet connectivity is also prone to disruption, notoriously fickle in many parts of the world and far from a sure backstop for education. A connection that was fast one day can be slow the next. A reliable mobile signal can become unreliable due to something as trivial as a change in the weather. It takes daunting engineering and technical expertise to build and maintain mobile networks that provide the anytime, anywhere connectivity that a lot of ed-tech solutions assume.

Examples of accidental internet service outages are common, and while they are usually local, they can also be global. For example, on 4 October 2021, Facebook and its subsidiary companies, including Messenger, Instagram and WhatsApp, went dark for several hours, showing that even one of the most technically sophisticated companies in the world with a market capitalization more than the GDP of many countries can fall offline for unexpected reasons.[1205] The Facebook outage led to disruptions at other heavyweight internet services, including Twitter, Discord and Signal, due to the sudden flight of Facebook users to these other online destinations that were quickly overwhelmed by the spike in traffic.[1206] Similarly, in June 2019, a small error made by Verizon, another sophisticated and highly resourced company that provides internet service in North America, resulted in a "cascading catastrophic failure" that affected thousands of networks.[1207] In 2018, Mauritania, Sierra Leone, Liberia, Guinea-Bissau, Guinea and the Gambia were taken offline for days due to a severed undersea internet cable.[1208] In March 2022, a fire at the Telecom Infrastructure Company, which serves as a gateway for network operators in the Islamic Republic of Iran, caused major disruptions to internet connectivity across the country.[1209] These outages raise questions on the viability of the internet as an insurance policy for something as important as education. Prior to 2020, some internet experts imagined that a global disruption to education would be more likely to take the form of problems with internet services than a health crisis.

A cornucopia of threats, from botnets to spyware, can swiftly undermine digital learning and undercut its standing as a solution that can be trusted to help education persevere through adversity and uncertainty.

Malicious attacks present grave and ever-mounting risks to ed-tech. While the COVID-19 pandemic was caused by a biological virus, computer viruses have long crippled the digital tools of families, businesses and entire communities; they can stop or delay learning for millions of students reliant on ed-tech. Computer viruses, though, are hardly the only human-made maladies that can disable or disrupt ed-tech modes of learning. A cornucopia of threats, from botnets, rootkits, worms and malware to file infectors, ransomware, scareware, logic bombs, spyware and adware, can all swiftly undermine digital learning and undercut its standing as a solution that can be trusted to help education persevere through adversity and uncertainty.

Education was the most targeted sector for malware attacks during the pandemic by a significant margin. In one month in early 2022, Microsoft documented almost 7 million attacks on devices used for education.

The pandemic witnessed an unprecedented rise in debilitating cyberattacks against schools and colleges. Microsoft's global tracking of malware encounters indicates that education was the most targeted sector during the pandemic by a significant margin. Between mid-February and mid-March 2022, for instance, Microsoft documented 6.9 million attacks on devices used for education, accounting for 83 per cent of all malware incidents globally. The next most affected sector was retail and consumer goods, which accounted for just 8 per cent of attacks, followed by health care and pharmaceuticals, which accounted for only 4 per cent.[1210] The disproportionate number of attacks directed towards the education sector was consistent with earlier periods of the pandemic.[1211] An international survey of several hundred IT professionals working for schools and universities found that nearly half of them reported that their institutions had been targeted by ransomware in 2020 and that a majority of these attacks succeeded in compromising important data. Three-quarters of the respondents said that the rise in online learning since the onset of the pandemic had increased cybersecurity risks. The survey further found that the average cost of ransomware incidents to educational institutions was USD 2.7 million when factoring in ransom payments, downtime, repairs and lost opportunities. This was USD 300,000 more expensive than the average cost of ransomware incidents in the next most expensive sector, distributors and transportation companies.[1212]

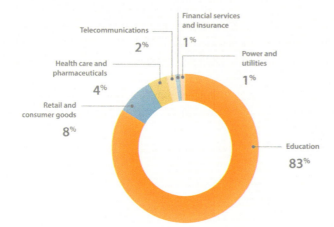

Figure 26:

Percentage of malware encounters in education compared to other sectors

Source: Adapted from Microsoft Security Intelligence, 2022

At the national level, the cybersecurity research website Comparitech found that an estimated 1.4 million students and 2,000 schools and colleges in the USA were impacted by ransomware attacks in 2020 alone.[1213] These figures reflected the rapidly increasing frequency and severity of cyber-assaults on education. The K-12 Cybersecurity Resource Center, an organization devoted to tracking cyber incidents in US schools, noted that hacking

> Hacking incidents aimed at schools increased approximately fivefold between 2016 and 2020.

incidents increased approximately fivefold between 2016 and 2020. In the introduction to the organization's 2020 *State of K–12 Cybersecurity* report, the authors wrote, "cybersecurity risks are now neither hypothetical, nor trivial".[1214] The frequency of hacks averaged at more than two per schoolday for the first academic year of the pandemic. The organization also noted that the disconcerting figures observed in 2020 during the pandemic were almost certainly underestimated, as many if not most incidents go unreported.

While attacks typically targeted individual schools and universities, they also debilitated companies and organizations providing digital services to educational institutions. As one example, in early 2022, when Finalsite, a private sector company that provides web hosting services, was hit by a successful ransomware attack in 2022, the websites of 5,000 schools and colleges went dark.[1215] A headline about the incident in *Education Week* read: "Thousands of school websites went down in a cyberattack. It'll happen again, experts say."[1216]

> The rationales to pay malware ransoms reflected a cold calculus – the cost of not paying was much higher.

Throughout the pandemic, various school districts, higher education institutions and technology firms servicing these institutions quietly paid malware ransoms, thereby increasing the likelihood of future attacks.[1217] The rationales to pay malware ransoms reflected a cold calculus – the cost of not paying was much higher. A statement from the University of California, San Francisco, about a June 2020 cybersecurity breach showed how unknown cybercriminals could drag an over 150-year-old research university into the mud of extortion. In explaining its decision to pay the ransom, the university wrote: "The data that was encrypted is important to some of the academic work we pursue as a university serving the public good. We therefore made the difficult decision to pay some portion of the ransom, approximately $1.14 million, to the individuals behind the malware attack in exchange for a tool to unlock the encrypted data and the return of the data they obtained."[1218] Evocations of the public good did little to abate the attacks; universities remained front-line targets.

Grade schools were also regularly in the cross hairs of digital criminals, and these schools, like universities, also forked over hefty ransoms to recover data being held hostage in order to resume services to support remote learning.[1219] When educational institutions refused to pay, hackers commonly followed through on threats to publish captured and confidential educational files that can harm teachers and students alike and diminish trust in educational institutions. A study found that ransomware gangs published data from more than 1,200 K–12 schools in the USA in the first nine months of 2021.[1220] These leaks contained deeply personal information, including medical conditions, immigration status, descriptions of disability, financial status, home language, national identification numbers, behaviour incidents, date of birth, home address, photographs, notes on addiction and drug abuse, grades, teacher comments and other sensitive information that can shadow students for their entire lives.[1221]

Check Point Research, an organization specializing in cybersecurity, drew a direct connection between education's growing dependency on technology-centric approaches and digital attacks, noting in mid-2021 that cybercriminals were seeking to "capitalize on the short-notice shift back to remote learning driven by the Delta variant, by targeting people of schools, universities and research centers who log-in from home using their personal devices".[1222] Nir Kshetri, an expert in cybersecurity management, detailed several ways the pandemic shift to ed-tech was creating new opportunities for cybercriminals to attack schools and colleges. These included institutions loaning devices to students that lacked important security updates, cybersecurity staff overwhelmed by IT issues and unable to focus intensely on security, the ease of baiting unfamiliar and inexperienced users into providing credentials or downloading malicious files during a period of disruption, and the use of new platforms that established vulnerabilities and entry points for cybercriminals.[1223]

While schools, students, teachers and others completing face-to-face education have, in rare instances, been targeted for ransom or taken hostage in brick-and-mortar schools,[1224] there is no equivalent in offline worlds of the regularity and scale of attacks that seek to criminally profiteer from education in digital spaces. The volume and frequency of attacks are particular to the hardware, software and virtual spaces that comprise ed-tech. Although legislation has been developed in a handful of countries to address this spiralling problem,[1225] thus far, new rules have shown limited effectiveness. The number of cyberattacks aimed at education continues to climb,[1226] and enforcement is difficult, as many attacks originate outside a particular country's national borders.

> As education's reliance on technology increases, so too do attacks that put education institutions as well as individual teachers and students at risk.

This evidence suggests that as education's reliance on technology increases, so too do the attacks that put education institutions as well as individual teachers and students at risk of extortion, damaging privacy breaches and other types of maleficence that carry real-world harm. Once again, these risks undercut claims that ed-tech can assure educational resilience.

In addition to rogue private actors, governments have also demonstrated a growing willingness to target the connectivity infrastructure of other countries, actions that can compromise the usability of connected technology for education. This is particularly evident in times of armed conflict, but it increasingly involves countries that are not engaged in on-the-ground fighting. There have been numerous accounts of state-led cyberattacks aimed at government ministries in other countries, including ministries of education.

Beyond attacking the digital and connectivity infrastructure of other countries, governments sometimes initiate internet blocks and shutdowns on their own populations. Human rights observers have long documented these practices and shown how such interference can bring remote, technology-reliant learning to a standstill. Access Now, an organization that tracks internet shutdowns globally, documented 155 internet shutdowns in 29 countries in 2020 and a further 182 shutdowns in 2021.[1227] Specific examples spotlight the severity of these shutdowns. Authorities in Myanmar, for instance, blocked mobile internet connections in a number of regions for prolonged intervals between June 2019 and June 2020, leading Human Rights Watch to call on the government to "immediately end what is now the world's longest government-enforced internet shutdown".[1228] In Cameroon, internet access was cut off to parts of the country for 230 days between January 2017 and March 2018. The longest of these internet blocks lasted 93 consecutive days and caused connected education to come to a standstill.[1229] In Sudan, a countrywide shutdown of mobile services was initiated in September 2020 during the pandemic for the sole purpose of trying to prevent students from cheating on national exams.[1230] Sudan is not alone in providing an educational rationale to switch off the internet. Access Now reported seven separate instances of internet blackouts in 2021 that were ordered for the secure administration of school exams.[1231] All of these attacks and shutdowns can block, sometimes with alarming ease, education that is provisioned purely through digital means.

Educational reliance on technology is also undermined by non-technical factors. UNESCO has long made the case that the technical aspects of connected learning – the wires, chips, signals and circuits that make digital learning possible – although very complex and fragile, are often simpler and faster to troubleshoot than the many human factors that limit the productive use of technology for learning.[1232] Even when the correct technical infrastructure is in place and working appropriately, people run into problems using it for academic learning: Wi-Fi passwords are forgotten, applications require updates, wires are not correctly attached. Ed-tech fails with alarming regularity due to banal issues, such as a poorly trained network technician working for a ministry of education, a family's limited knowledge of software settings, a learner's inability to find the right button to turn a microphone on and off, or a parent's lack of confidence to troubleshoot issues with hardware such as an internet router. Learning with ed-tech outside supportive environments like schools can be daunting. While ed-tech can facilitate learning with technology, it rarely, in isolation, teaches people how to start learning with technology. This reality further chips away at claims that ed-tech can provide across-the-board educational resilience.

Against this backdrop of technological fragility, cyberattacks and digital skills deficits, schools as physical spaces can seem like far sturdier pillars of educational resilience, even if their reliance on human proximity makes them hazardous during a pandemic. Compared with reliance on connected ed-tech, the age-old mode of learning with and from other people has fewer points of failure: it is not nearly as dependent on complex supply chains or sophisticated infrastructure and is arguably harder for malicious actors – whether individuals or government authorities – to shut down or disrupt. Teachers and students meeting in person can still communicate and make progress towards learning objectives even when internet connections fail, power goes out or digital devices stop working. School-based and other types of face-to-face learning have provided necessary agility to assure the continuity of education through a wide number of disruptions, including those that have knocked out essential connectivity infrastructure, such as natural disasters and human conflict.

Distance learning enabled by ed-tech certainly affords an expanded set of options to overcome crises, but its advantages as an enabler of educational resilience can look relatively narrow compared with in-person and school-based learning. Even with COVID-19 still circulating and presenting serious health risks, brick-and-mortar schools staffed with professional teachers have reappeared as societies' toughest and most reliable tools of educational resilience.

> Compared with reliance on connected ed-tech, the age-old mode of learning with and from other people has fewer points of failure: it is not nearly as dependent on complex supply chains or sophisticated infrastructure and is arguably harder for malicious actors to shut down or disrupt.

If ed-tech is the answer, what is the question?

Beyond resilience, another dominant rationale for stepping up investments in ed-tech is market analysis suggesting that, globally, the education sector is 'under digitized' compared with other sectors. This rationale is commonly presented as a business and financial opportunity. It is premised on a belief that education will or should follow in the footsteps of other sectors and increase spending and reliance on digital technology.

HolonIQ, a consultancy that produces market data and analysis on education aimed at investors, made this rationale explicit when it published a data visualization in 2021 that purported to explain the global education technology market in ten charts.[1233] The overarching message of the presentation is unambiguous: the digital future of education is inevitable and only just warming up. While this type of message is to be expected from a firm like HolonIQ, part of a new breed of organizations that build investment cases for ed-tech and drum up interest in the sector as a financial market, it is also one that is increasingly accepted as an article of faith, both inside and outside education circles. Assertions that ed-tech will undoubtedly 'boom' deserve scrutiny precisely because they have become so automatic in the aftermath of pandemic disruptions to education.

The basis of HolonIQ's pronouncement about the inevitability of ed-tech rests in a number of claims. The company puts forward arguments that education is "grossly under digitized" and that "current models" cannot deliver education at the scale, quality and speed required to accommodate a growing influx of students. It also states that advanced technologies will become "increasingly integrated into core education delivery and learning processes".[1234] It further observes that venture capital investments are pouring into ed-tech at unprecedented rates, signalling ed-tech's quickly solidifying influence and relevance. For HolonIQ, these developments all point towards a future of vastly accelerated digital transformation. The ideas advanced by the organization contain many of the usual tropes about education failure (claims that current models cannot deliver) and ed-tech momentum (assertions of increasing integration and more investment).

The notion that education is "grossly under digitized" stands as perhaps the most illustrative of popular arguments that ed-tech is somehow destined for continued and rapid growth. HolonIQ goes to lengths to establish that

The notion that education is grossly under digitized stands as perhaps the most illustrative of popular arguments that ed-tech is somehow inevitable.

education is, in the company's words, a "digital laggard". This label is warranted, in HolonIQ's 2021 analysis, because the education sector spends "less than 4 per cent of global expenditure on tech".[1235] In the company's presentation, this data point is illustrated visually with a large chart representing the multitrillion USD global education sector. A tiny section of the chart represents digital expenditures on "hardware, software and technology enabled services". The rest of the chart, almost its full volume, represents non-digital expenditures on "labor, physical equipment, analogue content, real estate and building works, utilities, etc.". This list is, upon close inspection, a rather elusive reference to teachers and administrators, schools, books and every other education expenditure that is not explicitly digital technology.

Figure 27:

Global expenditure on digital solutions for education as a proportion of total expenditure in education

Source: Adapted from HolonIQ, 2021

HolonIQ's chart communicates a premise that digital expenditures are insufficient and should increase quickly and dramatically. The design implies that the small section representing technology investments should grow, and the large section representing human and other non-digital investments should shrink. Tellingly, though, the rationale for increasing expenditures on ed-tech is less clear. Text next to the chart says that the low 4 per cent expenditure on ed-tech "[presents] a serious challenge given the scale of what's to come" – but "what's to come" is never clearly specified.[1236] The chart sets up a tautology of sorts – it does not allow room for questions on whether spending more on ed-tech is indeed an appropriate answer to whatever unstated development is coming.

Why ed-tech? Because something big is coming. Why is something big coming? Apparently because of technology.

Ultimately, the HolonIQ formulation of 'something is coming, and ed-tech is the answer' is circular to the point of being inscrutable. Why ed-tech? Because something big is coming. Why is something big coming? Apparently because of technology. Yet this circularity is not atypical. Many justifications for enlarging ed-tech expenditures, beyond ed-tech's utility during periods of school closure, are not much easier to pin down other than exhortations that 'something is coming, and ed-tech is the answer'.

The education and technology group at the World Bank has rightly advised that any government or other entity investing in ed-tech should always ask, "If technology is the answer, then what's the question?"[1237] But despite this recommendation, the question is rarely defined, even as technology is elevated time and again as the answer.

In the HolonIQ slide describing education as a "digital laggard", another sentence expands the rationale for increasing ed-tech investments. It asserts that "the knowledge economy and future skills require massive digital transformation, and, while accelerated through COVID-19, there is still far to go".[1238] This claim, put another way, suggests that ed-tech spending must increase because the "economy and future skills require massive digital transformation". The slide further adds that while the pandemic had nudged technology investments in the (presumed) right direction, these investments remain too small and should grow greater still.

Here again, an astute reader might wonder if "massive digital transformation" is indeed advisable, desirable or necessary for the economy and for future skills. And even if it is, does this warrant a large increase in education sector expenditures on digital hardware, software and services? Is spending more money on technology for educational purposes an appropriate response to digital and other transformations rippling through the economy and, by extension, the need to build skills and competencies to navigate this economy? Detailed analyses of job postings have concluded that various soft (human) skills, such as critical thinking, creativity, communication, analytical skills, collaboration and relationship building, are often the ones most vital in digitalizing economies.[1239]

> A metaphor commonly used to refer to ed-tech is that of a wave – an unstoppable force moved by celestial bodies.

What shines through the HolonIQ presentation is a message of urgency and inevitability that is typical of pronouncements on ed-tech. A metaphor commonly used to refer to ed-tech is that of a wave – an unstoppable force moved by celestial bodies. The HolonIQ analysis, like that put forth by other organizations including development organizations, effectively announces that the education sector should hurry up and digitalize already. Keep directing more money to technology. But the 'whys' behind these directives and recommendations tend to be left unexamined. Often, they emerge out of insinuations and vague assumptions that education will invariably digitalize because everything else seems to be digitalizing.

Perhaps the education sector should indeed direct more money to digital technology, as HolonIQ and other consultancies advise. But the rationale for this decision must be more than a chart showing that current digital technology expenditures are low compared with the proportion of education budgets spent on teacher salaries and the physical infrastructure of schools. Education is, at its core, about human development, so investments in salaries and training for teachers, administrators and other humans who help students face-to-face would seem warranted and in line with the humanistic aims of education. So too would investments in schools and other brick-and-mortar education facilities and spaces that allow young people to gather, interact and learn together socially in groups, classes and cohorts as well as individually. The basis for spending more money on digital technology must trace to reasons beyond references to unspecified changes and transformations that are supposedly coming. They should also be based on rationales that run deeper than the financial momentum trumpeted by data brokers like HolonIQ, companies that stand to profit with increased investment in ed-tech and greater identification of ed-tech as a distinct and profit-oriented sector of global financial markets. HolonIQ's analysis of the profit-making potential of ed-tech is, ultimately, what sells the company's USD 120,000 annual subscriptions to its full slate of ed-tech market commentary and data.[1240]

> Recommendations to increase spending on ed-tech should reconcile why so many of the most exclusive and best-performing schools often eschew ed-tech in favour of human-to-human education.

Recommendations to increase spending on ed-tech should also reconcile why so many of the most exclusive and best-performing schools often eschew ed-tech in favour of in-person, school-based and human-to-human education, particularly schools serving young children. If more education expenditure should be directed towards digital technology, why are so many technology and government leaders sending their own children to schools that spend relatively modest sums on technology and a lot on teacher salaries, small class sizes, first-rate physical facilities and other non-virtual educational resources?

It is reasonable to make arguments that spending on ed-tech should increase, but these arguments should come from educationalists, not from financial actors that have staked their futures in speculative pronouncements on the high probability of exponential ed-tech growth.

Education is how the future is made, and education is still very much under human control. No trend is destiny, not even technology trends. Choices about ed-tech and education expenditures on technology should be presented as such: choices, not certainties.

Act 2 of this publication detailed how the high hopes for ed-tech to facilitate more accessible, better quality, transformative and sustainable modes of education were largely unmet when technology became the primary medium of teaching and learning during the COVID-19 pandemic. In 2020 and significant portions of 2021 and 2022, huge numbers of students around the world were both locked out of schools and unable to access new modes of remote learning that were fully dependent on technology portals. This was especially true for vulnerable and disadvantaged learners most in need of government-assured educational opportunities. Even students who managed to access education via technology generally found the learning experience to be greatly diminished and spent less time learning and made far slower progress than they had before the shift to technology. This occurred despite massive investments of money and energy from the education sector to assure more successful results from ed-tech solutions.

While much can be learned from accounts of what worked with technology integration during the pandemic, there are, arguably, more valuable insights to be gained from understanding the numerous ways an unprecedented reliance on technology did not, in so many contexts, preserve or protect education, let alone strengthen it. Available evidence strongly indicates that the bright spots of the ed-tech experiences during the pandemic, while important and deserving of attention, were vastly eclipsed by failure. Any attempt to shine light on successes needs to keep the more sombre results and consequences in clear view.

Recognizing the shortcomings of ed-tech helps correct widely held and simplistic ideas that greater, faster and deeper technology integration in education is firm evidence of modernization and improvement. The data and experiences recounted in this publication suggest that the opposite is more likely to be true – that lighter, more considered and less automated models of technology integration in education are probably superior markers of educational progress.

Such acknowledgement clarifies that the transformations needed to reliably strengthen education are not necessarily digital or technological, or at least not primarily so, but rather social and human. Conversations around ed-tech are typically characterized by soaring ambition, but the evidence from the pandemic indicates that greater humility is a wiser approach going forward.

The ed-tech experience of the COVID-19 pandemic clarified the limits of current technology to perform the multifaceted and vital functions that societies expect from education. Whether societies recognize these limits and moderate expectations for technology is, however, an open question. While the global health emergency has ended, the reliance on ed-tech that grew out of the response to the pandemic looks to be nowhere near its end and may just be warming up. The extent to which this reliance on ed-tech should continue and perhaps grow is among the most important educational questions facing schools, countries and, indeed, the world. Questions have also been raised about what norms, principles and rules are needed to guide future digital changes to education. The pandemic has awakened people everywhere to the possibility of constructing education systems around digital technologies as a strategy to confront crises, but it has also introduced strategies to re-engineer the way education is conducted outside of crisis scenarios. The roles ed-tech should play in the future of education – and the ways ed-tech can alter the purposes set for education – demand careful contemplation.

Act 3 attempts to tackle the complex question of how ed-tech might be better conceived to reinforce educational inclusion, equity and quality in ways that help students, teachers, families and communities thrive.

It first examines how the objectives, design codes, business models and regulatory frameworks of ed-tech should be realigned to prioritize the best interests of students and teachers. It considers strategies to reposition school-based learning as a necessity that ed-tech can support, reinforce and enrich rather than circumvent. Next, Act 3 proposes strengthening digital connectivity, content and competencies in ways that support access to quality education for all, with special priority for the most marginalized learners. It wraps up with a discussion about the right to education, outlining ideas to safeguard this right at a moment when technology and remote learning are changing long-held norms about how education is conducted, where and for whom.

The education community needs to come together to draw coherent lessons and understandings from the shocks of the pandemic as they work to make ed-tech a more reliable enabler of inclusive and high-quality education. Acknowledging and understanding the adverse consequences of the hurried transition to ed-tech can lay the groundwork for a revival and renewal of human-centred and school-based education that is complemented and improved by digital and AI technologies.

Act 3 concludes with an invitation to continue the task of reflecting on the ed-tech experiences of the pandemic, welcoming the voices of the many groups that were affected, from students to school leaders and ed-tech developers to teachers. The actions and directions outlined here provide a roadmap to reorient digital changes to education towards inclusion, equity and quality in ways that advance public and common goals for education as well as individual ones.

Act 3: NEW DIRECTIONS FOR ED-TECH

Prioritize the best interests of students and teachers

Teachers, families and students bore the heavy load of adaptation to ed-tech; they made adjustments and conformed to the rules and logics set by the technology companies that largely guide the digital economy.

The COVID-19 pandemic required schools, teachers, families and students to adapt to new modes, standards and ways of working and learning. And adapt they did. Hundreds of millions of people learned to use new software, download assignments, search for online resources and join video calls. Education entered a digital world not of limitless possibility – as virtual spaces are sometimes promised to be – but of pre-existing norms and expectations. Teachers, families and students bore the heavy load of adaptation to ed-tech; they made adjustments and conformed to the rules and logics set by the technology companies that largely guide the digital economy. These contortions twisted educational processes and also, in many instances, purposes and possibilities for education. This experience raises a key question for future ed-tech practices and integration: Who should adapt to whose norms and interests?

Many of the ed-tech tools employed during the pandemic – file-sharing systems and video conferencing software – are tools that have been around for a long time and were developed primarily for business use. Certain default features that might make sense in corporate settings, such as assigning every user a dedicated email address and data profile, were applied in educational contexts, even though they were often inappropriate or introduced unique risks when applied to primary or secondary school students.

Teachers who work in physical classrooms are keenly aware of the effects that the built school environment has on opportunities to learn and interact – from the visual learning aids on the walls to the configuration of desks and furniture. Digital learning spaces are similarly important. But they tended to lack the flexibility afforded by schools. The systems and software deployed during the pandemic were largely unalterable and littered with features that teachers could not remove or adjust and that students and families had to use or try to work around. Additionally, once teachers and students left the boundaries of an ed-tech tool, perhaps to view an educational video or conduct online research, they were quickly forced to navigate digital design logics inappropriate for education: targeted advertising, behavioural manipulation, clickbait and content tailored for adhesion. Many of the online worlds that played host to formal education were not designed with learners' interests or formal education in mind but rather for monetization, whether through recruiting followers, growing subscribers, extracting data or maximising time spent looking at advertisements. The education community has only just begun the process of scrutinizing the environments, players and processes shaping the contours of online learning experiences. This section considers ways that ed-tech design and deployment might be reimagined to prioritize the best interests of users.

REDESIGN ONLINE ENVIRONMENTS TO CENTRE STUDENTS' NEEDS

During the pandemic, countless decisions were made for learners and without input from them.

Students' voices were rarely heard during the pandemic, even with regard to choices that affected them directly. Countless decisions were made for learners and without input from them. In many instances, decisions were taken at the expense of students in order to prioritize the interests of other groups. With schools being among the few social spaces expressly dedicated to children and youth, it is perhaps not surprising that students' voices became less audible and accessible to the public as a side effect of shuttering in-person schooling. Outside of school, students did find digital tools for self-expression and peer connection, encompassing social media, multiplayer gaming and private messaging apps, but these outlets tended to fragment young people into tight-knit groups centred around shared interests.[1241] In-person schools and universities help give students a collective and generational voice. When they closed, this voice did not carry over easily to the digital environments of remote learning, which tended to be far more atomized.

In cases where students *did* raise public opinions or express preferences, concerns and objections, they were frequently ignored. Universities in countries around the world, for example, flatly refused to decrease or reimburse tuition fees when in-person learning was halted, even while other sectors issued refunds for cancellations, waived change fees and worked with consumers to soften the financial blow of pandemic-imposed restrictions. Similarly, many changes students and teachers wanted in digital education environments were slow to arrive or never implemented. Digital platforms used for learning often reflected corporate interests first and accommodated needs that often cut across sectors as well as national and regional boundaries. Learners and teachers, scattered in different locations and often lacking decision-making power about technology systems, were rarely a primary constituency for the large technology companies and digital products that stood in for schools.

Separately, the academic passivity of students, widespread during the pandemic, was typically interpreted as laziness, rather than a legitimate expression of agency or protest. The dehumanization and isolation that many students reported feeling when participating in technology-only modes of learning contributed to the low engagement, falling academic achievement, chronic absenteeism and reluctance to opt in to future educational pursuits that was well documented during the pandemic.[1242] Withdrawing from educational pursuits was, in many contexts, a form of student rebellion against digital-only learning that could be rote and lifeless, even if it was not always registered this way.

"The [teacher] always asks me how I am, how is my grandmother and how I have been doing through this quarantine. I miss school a lot. It's not the same studying at home and I miss being with my classmates."

– 11-year-old student, Ecuador[x]

An important step towards forging new directions for ed-tech is making sure students are heard in digital learning environments. Too often these environments follow corporate interests first and students' interests second. Students accessing educational tools online are not markets to

> Students accessing educational tools online are not markets to be captured or data generators to be monetized.

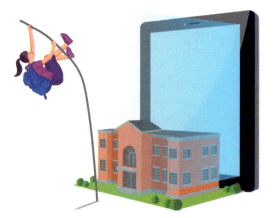

> Education was contorted to accommodate rules and norms prescribed by and beneficial to technology corporations.

be captured or data generators to be monetized. They are children, youth and adults who have agency, and grow and learn through relationships and relational processes – interactions with teachers, peers, caregivers, family members and communities. The pandemic experience of moving education into digital-only environments dislodged learning from schools and other places that are purpose-built for young people and, in doing so, exposed the limitations of ed-tech platforms to replicate the networks of guidance and support that exist in physical learning environments. While considerable effort was devoted to maintaining the continuity of formal education through the disruptions of the pandemic, the digital systems and processes utilized for this task did not always centre student well-being or advance students' best interests. Operating in the absence of regulations typical of services used by minors and possessing limited knowledge of the complexities of education, technology corporations generally had little external or internal motivation to change their existing systems and standards to meet the multifaceted aims of education that do not always reflect market logics. This was especially true when the existing systems and standards were highly profitable. As a result, the ed-tech utilities that dominated during the pandemic often followed the designs that characterize online experiences in non-educational settings. This is not, ultimately, technology serving education, but its inversion: the contortion of education to accommodate rules and norms prescribed by and beneficial to technology corporations.

Questions raised about ed-tech during the pandemic sit within debates concerning how children are regarded in online spaces more broadly. Ed-tech and online learning are a point of entry to the wider internet for many children, especially as teachers link to resources on platforms outside the confines of ed-tech software. The walls between the internet and education conducted online are deceptively porous or even non-existent. The distinctions between *learning* online and *being* online are rarely clear. Mixing and blending learning spaces with the wider and open internet may make sense for upper secondary and tertiary education students, but less so for younger learners in primary and lower secondary education. Currently, many popular online platforms are not explicitly designed for child well-being, and children confront numerous risks in digital worlds, from algorithmically recommended content and default surveillance to behavioural nudges and tracking and recording settings inappropriate for minors. Indeed, many digitally skilled adults struggle to traverse the thicket of behavioural manipulations and privacy compromises that have become normalized in online environments.[1243] These thickets, challenging for adults, can ensnare children. Going forward, regulators as well as ed-tech developers need to do more to safeguard children and youth from online risks, leveraging the power and versatility of technology to help achieve this aim.

The burden of ensuring student safety in digital spaces should not fall under the guise of digital skills and media and information literacy.

Historically, schools have aimed to accommodate children's holistic needs in terms of socialization, attention, nutrition and well-being, in addition to facilitating academic and curricular learning. Extending education into online spaces need not entail the casual disposal of all these walls of care and protection, as was the case in many contexts during the pandemic. In digital spaces, some of the aims of socialization are recast in unhealthy ways – amassing online followers, collecting 'likes', entering closed-minded groups that vilify others, and aspiring to idealized and curated images that distort perceptions of reality. Given the centrality of care, protection and well-being in education, online pedagogical spaces must be more tightly regulated to avoid these types of perversions. Education can and should promote healthier forms of socialization and interaction, steering clear of systems that, for example, inflate the importance of questionable indicators to quantify blurry concepts like 'influence'. The burden of ensuring student safety in digital spaces should not fall under the guise of digital skills and media and information literacy, and certainly not for students as young as 5 or 10 years old. While young learners, of course, need to develop skills and competencies that will allow them to navigate the wondrous and treacherous currents of the open internet, these skills develop gradually, as part of the educational process. Societies do not generally expect children to be able to protect themselves from manipulation and exploitation in offline spaces, and they should not expect this in online spaces either, particularly in the spaces developed to advance their education.

Increasingly, children have become valuable targets for advertisers and tech companies eager to encourage the early adoption of habits and brands.[1244] Technology companies work to establish and grow 'pipelines' of child and youth users who will become lifelong users of particular services, software or systems. This is exemplified by campaigns launched by competing companies like Instagram and TikTok to pick up younger and younger users.

> Future ed-tech design must account for the special vulnerabilities of children while also affording them agency.

Video game makers, metaverse developers and marketers of generative AI apps are also working to onboard children into proprietary digital spaces. Future ed-tech design must account for the special vulnerabilities of children while also affording them agency. Education, whether conducted online or offline, should assiduously avoid schemes intended to profiteer from children. Just as schools work to ensure that conditions are appropriate for the developmental and educational needs of children at different stages of growth, so too should the virtual environments of digital education. Physical and digital learning spaces can be better paired to reinforce one another to serve the wide range of interests, aspirations and capacities that students possess as valued members of society.

GIVE TEACHERS AGENCY IN ED-TECH PEDAGOGIES

> The rapid move of entire educational systems online involved little consultation with teachers.

Prior to the pandemic, a growing community of technology-savvy educators were eager to discover new digital tools and activities that they could add to their teaching repertoires. They often had existing expertise and opinions about ed-tech content and pedagogical practices in digital spaces. They shared these views with peers and school leaders, sometimes as part of formal or informal groups or inside professional organizations. The rapid move of entire educational systems online in the pandemic, however, involved little consultation with teachers. Teachers' roles in technological decision-making were narrowed, not only by what was physically unavailable to them due to school closures, but also by what technologies they were now required to use. Software design and learning management systems tended to circumscribe pedagogy far beyond what a standard lesson plan would do and forced teaching into inflexible moulds. This proved restrictive and even degrading for experienced educators accustomed to exercising greater control and autonomy. Learning platforms commonly dictated how long teachers could spend on certain tasks and prescribe whether and when teachers could organize students into small groups. Such pedagogical rigidity in lesson design tended to stem from the initial design of the ed-tech itself, which was commonly developed outside classroom contexts and did not necessarily reflect teachers' preferences.

Although teachers did not always welcome inflexible technology systems, they did value opportunities to teach remotely in order to assist students and protect themselves from health risks associated with the pandemic. The Responses to Educational Disruption Survey conducted jointly by UNESCO and the International Association for the Evaluation of Educational

Achievement examined the experiences of teachers and students across 11 countries in Africa, Asia, Europe and Latin America. The survey found that when the pandemic was at its height, teachers were highly concerned about catching COVID-19 at work and grateful to be able to teach from home and believed that this arrangement would minimize their risk of contracting disease.[1245]

The curiosity and enthusiasm many teachers held for ed-tech prior to the pandemic often gave way to disillusionment.

Yet at the pandemic stretched on, even digitally experienced educators who had approached the shift to online learning with optimism found themselves becoming burned out by the constant use of technology to interface with learners. In a survey of educators in the USA, conducted by *Education Week* in March 2022, nearly two-thirds of teachers, principals and district leaders said that they were experiencing technology fatigue during the pandemic.[1246] This sense of overexposure to technology, precipitated by the pandemic, extended beyond school closures in many contexts. Officials regularly instructed teachers to continue using the digital tools that schools had invested heavily in, even after students and teachers returned to the classroom and even after teachers said the tools had little pedagogical value outside the remote learning context of the pandemic. The curiosity and enthusiasm many teachers held towards ed-tech prior to the pandemic often gave way to disillusionment.

"Teaching on-line is a heck of a lot more work. You've got to plan for just about everything. You put the assignments on Google Classroom and set up the Zoom meetings and make your handouts into PDFs and try to digitize your books and figure out how classroom policies designed around a physical space can be revised for cyber space. You answer countless questions and concerns, videotaping your lessons for those who can't be there in person. You try to make things interesting with new apps, new software, new grading systems, new approaches to the same material you've been teaching for over a decade. And it never ends."

– Steven Singer, classroom teacher, USA[cc]

> Human educators should be firmly in the driver's seat – their decisions on what works and does not work for their students must shape how technology is used in education.

In rethinking ed-tech for the future, greater consideration needs to be given to the pedagogical implications of when, why, how and under what circumstances digital learning and ed-tech apps and devices are used. UNESCO's report *Reimagining Our Futures Together: A New Social Contract for Education* encourages education stakeholders to enact new and better futures for education by posing three key questions: What should we continue doing? What should we abandon? What needs to be invented afresh?[1247] Taking this line of thinking further, teachers and those who support them should ask similar questions about the future of ed-tech pedagogies: What works best online with the help of technological tools? What works only marginally well with technology and needs to be tinkered with and refined? What does not work at all in digital contexts and should be experienced primarily in person and free from technology? Ed-tech should not usurp teacher autonomy and instead should defer to teachers' expertise. Educators need to be able to learn about, experiment with, modify, adopt or reject future digital tools, systems, devices and platforms according to what best suits their pedagogical goals and meets the unique needs of their students. The pandemic model had educators making major adjustments to teaching practices honed over years to fit an ed-tech model that they did not ask for or choose. Looking ahead, human educators should be firmly in the driver's seat – their decisions about what works and does not work for their students must shape whether, when and how technology is used in education. Skilled teachers know their students better than even the most advanced AI software today. Elevating teachers to decision makers with agency over technology use also ensures that technology investments made by schools and school districts are most beneficial to the professionals who will use them most often.

"The teacher becomes a 'line operator' on a conveyor belt run by algorithms. The amassed data triggers algorithmic diagnostics from each application, carving up the curriculum, controlling students and teachers."

– Velislava Hillman and Molly Esquivel, London School of Economics[co]

> Now that the crisis implementation of ed-tech is over, the education sector needs to insist on a different approach from ed-tech developers, one that supports teachers' needs, agency and professionalism.

Beyond pedagogical questions, greater attention also needs to be paid to ed-tech's wider impact on the teaching profession and teacher identity. During the pandemic, teachers came under tremendous pressures adapting to remote digital teaching – they were forced to conduct their jobs in entirely new ways and without prior agreement. Ed-tech enabled this transition to occur, yet at the same time it often undermined the autonomy and professionalism of educators. Now that the crisis implementation of ed-tech is over, the education sector needs to insist on a different approach from ed-tech developers, one that supports teachers' needs, agency and professionalism. Teachers and educators must be allowed to influence the design and application of ed-tech; it cannot be a case of ed-tech dictating what teachers do, when and how, as was common during the pandemic.

With teachers testing, selecting, and using ed-tech tools that support their work, in collaboration with peers and school leaders, ed-tech is more likely to facilitate the human art of teaching rather than dictate it algorithmically.

"If today's ed tech amounts to a hodgepodge of tools, rather than an all-purpose Swiss army knife, that's no reason for despair. If technology isn't transformative, that doesn't mean it can't be useful. If we adopt a tinkerer's mindset, then we can learn important lessons from the pandemic."

– Justin Reich, education researcher and author[cix]

DESIGN CODES, REGULATION AND LEGISLATION TO PUT STUDENTS FIRST

Every major technological revolution has provoked the need for new laws, norms and rules to protect against abuse and promote wider social aims. The digital transitions under way in education are no exception.

Governments, leaders and lawmakers have important roles to play in creating regulatory environments that promote the best interests of students, teachers and schools as they navigate learning with new technologies. A positive outcome of the pandemic-induced shift to mass online learning is increased public awareness about the lack of regulations and guidelines for technology companies operating in the education space. Companies did not sufficiently self-monitor and self-govern products and practices when they played host to formal education during periods of school closures. Since schools have reopened, these same companies often continue to decline or delay adjustments needed to ensure that digital environments are safe, accessible and appropriate places for students. Frontier technologies such as generative AI can present novel risks to students' safety and well-being as well as new opportunities to help students learn. These risks cannot be brushed aside: Yet in the current environment major AI models used by millions of learners for formal education often undergo far less vigorous and transparent vetting and testing for pedagogical and child appropriateness than a standard school textbook. Every major technological revolution has provoked the need for new laws, norms and rules to protect against abuse and promote wider social aims. The digital transitions under way in education are no exception. Governments need to formalize clearer and stricter guidelines for services that will be regularly used by young people for educational purposes.

"For far too long, tech companies have treated their egregious privacy and safety issues as a PR problem to be addressed only through vague promises, obfuscations, and delays."

– Josh Golin, executive director, Fairplay[cx]

Progress to create more robust regulatory frameworks to protect young people online, in spaces for education and beyond them, appears to be gaining needed momentum. Governments are leveraging new and existing frameworks to better assure the digital well-being and educational needs of young people. In 2021, for example, the UK adopted the Age Appropriate Design Code as an amendment to the 2018 Data Protection Act.[1248] The legislation requires apps, games, websites and internet-connected toys that are likely to be accessed by children under 18 years old to follow standards that "put the best interests of the child first".[1249] These standards include terms of service that are easy to understand and settings that make the highest level privacy settings a default setting. The standards also mandate turning off geolocation and profiling technologies, disabling private messaging from strangers and avoiding nudge techniques that encourage children to dial down privacy settings or remain endlessly engaged on a particular platform due to features such as auto-playing videos.[1250] By setting the code to apply to users under the age of 18 – and not the age of 13 that has become the industry norm as a threshold for users to sign up for online accounts[1251] – the code also better complies with the standards and spirit of the UN Convention on the Rights of the Child.

In another example, in March 2022 the European Union took a major step in adopting the Digital Markets Act, which requires powerful technology corporations like Amazon, Apple and Google to loosen their grip over digital spaces and make room for new entrants, paving the way for competition that might change how data are collected and controlled, how privacy is managed and how users experience online and other virtual spaces, potentially in ways that distinguish children's experiences from adults' experiences.[1252]

Regulatory changes to increase digital protections for children have also been under way in the USA. For example, in September 2022, the State of California passed legislation aimed at protecting the well-being, data and privacy of children using online platforms for education and other purposes.[1253] The law is expected to provide a template for other states. Civil society groups such as the 5Rights Foundation and Fairplay are helping to catalyse legislation of this type by promoting children's digital rights and putting pressure on governments and corporate actors to prioritize young people's well-being in online as well as offline spaces.

As the pandemic has abated, authorities appear to be stepping up needed enforcement of digital protections for learners and other users.

In addition to formalizing new regulations and guidelines, some governments and regional bodies have shown an increasing willingness to enforce existing rules and legislation. Meek and delayed enforcement of rules pertaining to digital protection and privacy for children as well as adults were widespread both before and during the most turbulent phases of the COVID-19 pandemic.[1254] However, as the pandemic abated, authorities stepped up enforcement of protections provided by major laws such as the European Union's General Data Protection Regulation. For example, in September 2022 Ireland's Data Protection Commission fined Instagram, owned by the parent company Meta Platforms (previously Facebook), approximately USD 400 million for the mistreatment of children's data.[1255] The fine stemmed from a 2020 investigation into Instagram's handling of children's data, in particular the app's default setting that made the accounts of children between the ages of 13 to 17 years old public and permitted teenage owners of Instagram business accounts, often budding social media influencers, to make their email addresses and phone numbers public.[1256] The commission's regulatory action was cheered by advocates for stronger digital privacy protections for minors. Andy Burrows, the head of child safety online for the UK's National Society for the Prevention of Cruelty to Children, told the BBC that "the ruling demonstrates how effective enforcement can protect children on social media and underlines how regulation is already making children safer online".[1257]

Regulators in Ireland, who are of special importance in Europe because of the large number of technology companies with European headquarters located in the country, brought further fines against Meta in October 2022 for violations related to its WhatsApp messaging service and again in November 2022 for a data leak that exposed the personal information, including names, locations and birth dates, of over 500 million Facebook users.[1258] The October and November fines totalled over USD 550 million. The company was hit with an even bigger penalty in 2023 for breaching European privacy laws.[1259] National governments have also levied fines. For example, in December 2021 in France, the Commission nationale de l'informatique et des libertés assessed penalties to Meta and Google totalling more than EUR 200 million for reasons that included making options to refuse cookies, essentially electronic tracking tools, needlessly complex.[1260] These mounting penalties signal that some governments in Europe seem to be instituting more muscular enforcement of rules designed to protect children and other users in digital environments.

"We have allowed a situation to develop in which it is legal for a multibillion dollar industry to own, wholly and in perpetuity, the intimate and personal details of children."

– Beeban Kidron, children's rights advocate and member of the House of Lords[ccv]

While these are only initial and geographically limited steps in regulating some of the world's most powerful corporate actors and interests, they are indications that more youth-friendly and education-appropriate digital experiences are possible and that existing digital norms and business models can change. Going forward, regulations and standards should be aimed more squarely at the digital environments of formal education. Young people are rushing into these environments in huge numbers, and they demand the same vigilant care and attention that societies pay to the physical environments of schools and universities. Digital educational experiences and platforms should assure safety and prioritize the development of features and functionality that can help students maintain holistic well-being, including logging off and taking breaks from screen-intensive tasks. As ed-tech continues to expand and evolve, it can – and indeed must – be steered in ways that serve the interests of students, teachers and schools. Commercial interests should be decidedly secondary.

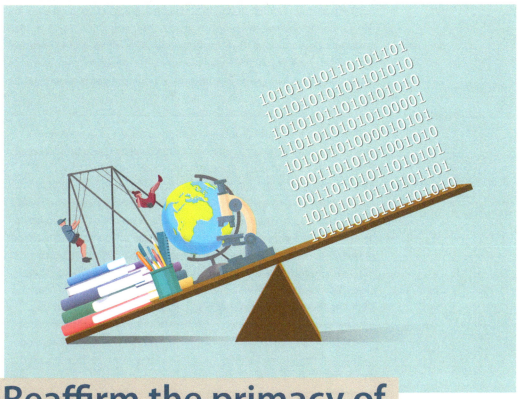

Reaffirm the primacy of in-person learning

A challenge in many education systems, due in part to their size, is that once certain structures and models are in place, they can be difficult to change or even question. For this reason, the jolting disruptions brought by the pandemic were viewed by some as a rare opportunity to reengineer education for digital age. Such reengineering could, in theory, confront the immediate challenges of school closures, while also laying foundations for a new type of education after COVID-19. The health crisis upended the educational status quo and made learning models constructed around powerful technologies seem achievable, and numerous voices hailed them as desirable. And without question, school closures, online learning and ed-tech solutions created new norms and new paths of dependency. Corporate contracts had been signed, device orders had been procured and on-site staff had been furloughed or let go. Even long after schools reopened, educators and students found they were operating in a new normal in which technology was playing a far more central role than it had prior to the health crisis.

Yet the particular models of online and remote learning adopted early in the pandemic were rarely best-case solutions for education. These models gave poor orientation to the digital transformation of education because they fully bypassed schools. They were a hurried means to retain some connection to teaching and learning and school routines in a world under lockdown.

> Digital modes of education that began life as a patch to confront the unusual challenges imposed by COVID-19 quickly morphed into a vision for the future of education.

When countries closed schools and instituted other restrictions on movement and in-person gatherings, ed-tech seemed a suitable lifeboat. But it was not intended nor appropriately designed to be seaworthy for a long voyage. Although the limitations and inadequacies of mass remote learning became increasingly obvious to those directly involved in education, there were few triggers to alert external decision makers to reverse course and push for a return to in-person schooling as a first-order priority. The initial idea that schools were being closed for the purpose of taking urgent steps to make them safe to reopen again was, in some cases, sidelined in the flurry of actions required to set up remote learning. Digital modes of education that began life as a patch to confront the unusual challenges imposed by COVID-19 quickly morphed into a vision for the future of education. Even as schools resumed in-person learning, technology dependencies that had rooted themselves in the education sector during the pandemic continued to hold or expand. Decision makers are only now beginning to consider how hurried and sometimes deeply flawed approaches to ed-tech integration, rolled out as an emergency measure, might be dialled back and recalibrated.

This section makes a case for the primacy of school-based learning and calls for a more critical and clear-eyed view of ed-tech's tendencies towards homogenization and reductionism. The 'new normal' of education remains malleable, and the elevated place connected technology has assumed vis-à-vis in-person schools and human teachers is not a foregone conclusion.

BUTTRESS SCHOOLS AS ESSENTIAL SOCIAL INSTITUTIONS

The dramatic expansion of in-person schooling over the past century is a momentous achievement, even if schooling remains far from universal. Schools around the world provide valuable services to young people, families and communities. Their quality, though, remains variable. Many schools fail to provide the safe and supportive environments that help children learn and flourish. The ed-tech modes of learning implemented during the pandemic were layered over pre-existing inequalities present in schools. But these modes of learning did not merely replicate inequalities, they widened them, often dramatically. Technology-reliant distance learning tended to achieve more equitable outcomes when the education provided by schools, prior to their closing, was more equal for learners and of high quality.

Success with ed-tech hinges, to a considerable degree, on school quality.

A key lesson, then, to draw from the pandemic experience is that success with ed-tech hinges, to a considerable degree, on school quality. Higher quality schools pave the way for more inclusive and equitable digital learning that in turn raises student achievement. Connected technologies can and should work symbiotically with in-person education, each one buttressing and enriching the other. To ensure ed-tech's effectiveness in the future, then, commitment to schools needs to be renewed and strengthened. Schools need to be positioned as essential sites of learning that utilize technology without submitting to it. The pandemic also reminded societies that schools provide benefits ed-tech cannot: schools are places where young people learn to socialize with others, navigate difference and cultivate empathy beyond the sterilized distance of a screen. Strengthening in-person schooling is not separate from or even complementary to ed-tech modes of learning, it is essential to them.

Educational experiences during the pandemic also illustrate the extent to which in-person schools consolidate an array of community services that stretch well beyond academic learning. Numerous activities take place at schools that enhance well-being, from providing students with nutrition, physical activity and social interaction to serving as hubs for cultural and artistic expression, technical and vocational training, adult education and community engagement. Schools are also important sites for community health, including vaccine administration and various health education campaigns that play a vital role in slowing the spread of transmittable diseases such as HIV. In 2021, UNICEF noted that vaccinations to protect children and youth against human papillomavirus, one of the most effective preventions against developing cervical cancer, fell further behind schedule than ever before because of school closures.[1261] The pandemic shut down other avenues of in-person supports as well, including parent and youth volunteering, clubs, performances and more.

In future health or other crises, the importance of schools as centres for individual and societal health should be recognized and reinforced. This was a key lesson that education leaders took away from the 1918–19 influenza pandemic, which drove them to equip schools with improved sanitation and nutrition as well as trained school nurses and other health

> Actions to make school closures unnecessary should carry more urgency and importance than determining what stack of technologies will allow for the continuity of education if and when schools close.

professionals. Schools should draw similar lessons from the COVID-19 pandemic. Questions about the actions, upgrades, services and preventative measures that will make school closures unnecessary in the face of foreseeable disruptions should carry more urgency and importance than questions about what stack of technologies will allow for the continuity of education if and when schools close. Strong attention to the latter question risks making school closures more frequent and perhaps more prolonged. Policy-makers and education leaders should create and invest in adequate measures to strengthen school quality and school resilience and redouble efforts to ensure schools effectively support children's physical, social and psychological well-being.

> *"Prioritizing connection over separation would require schooling practices that confront the traumas of childhood, not only those brought on by living through a pandemic but those that preceded and are exacerbated by COVID-19 because of social and economic inequalities."*
>
> – Julie C. Garlen, professor of early childhood education, Carleton University[cv]

GUARD AGAINST THE HOMOGENIZATION OF EDUCATION

Various technologies have demonstrated a troubling tendency to flatten diverse ways of thinking. Left unchecked, they can converge experiences into monopolies of hegemonic thought and action. Prior to the pandemic, a handful of corporations managed services and spaces that have become essential to many human interactions and transactions. During the move to remote schooling, education was likewise subsumed as Google Classroom, Microsoft Teams and a few other platforms became 'schools' and 'learning spaces' not just for a smattering of communities or a particular district, state or province, but for entire countries and regions.

The uncritical application of technology can accelerate the erosion of cultural, linguistic and epistemic diversity in education, and during the pandemic, ed-tech often played a bulldozing role, razing differences that support a multitude of cultures.

Educational diversity is not a trivial concern; it helps incubate a wealth of knowledge and a variety of ways of being, knowing and doing. Globalization has fostered valuable intercultural dialogue and cooperation, advanced consensus about human rights, and established networks and mechanisms to support international solidarity. At the same time, it has, in many instances, catalysed a loss of diversity – diversity of knowledge, experience, culture and expression – that is precious to humanity's heritage and vital to shaping its future. The uncritical application of technology can accelerate the erosion of cultural, linguistic and epistemic diversity in education, and during the pandemic, ed-tech often played a bulldozing role, razing differences that support a multitude of cultures. Homogeneity tends to deepen as dependence on large internet platforms and applications grows. Dominant languages, for instance, became considerably more dominant with the global turn to ed-tech, and future pairings of digital learning platforms with AI and language learning technologies carry more worrying implications for deforming and narrowing the structures of thought in education. For example, Google's efforts to incorporate the AI-powered Language Model for Dialogue Applications (LaMDA) into its educational platforms ignore the acute concerns that the company's own former ethical advisers raised over the biases and misleading information embedded in the company's AI models. These problematic models risk being legitimized and amplified through the near-global reach of Google's education services and tools.[1262]

"History has repeatedly demonstrated that control over information is central to who has power and what they can do with it. … Our future should not be left in the hands of two powerful companies [Microsoft and Alphabet/Google] that build ever larger global empires based on using our collective data without scruple and without compensation."

– Daron Acemoglu and Simon Johnson, authors of *Power and Progress*[ccvi]

Similarly, OpenAI's large language models, developed in partnership with Microsoft and outside public oversight, were quickly integrated into numerous mainstream education utilities, including the Khan Academy, Duolingo and various MOOC providers, in addition to OpenAI's proprietary ChatGPT app and various Microsoft tools, often just a few days after their initial release. While these AI models can simulate human fluency with language and demonstrate remarkable proficiency with various information and knowledge tasks, they reflect highly specific design choices by their creators and foreground certain processes of information generation and presentation, while backgrounding others. They are also trained on language corpora that further reflect particular types of information and knowledge. Unlike traditional web search engines that rank and curate numerous possible answers to user queries, AI models generate, through

fully automated processes, singular and therefore authoritative-seeming answers, lending them exceptional influence when utilized for teaching and learning purposes. Technology that behaves more like an oracle than a research assistant, it must be observed, is not particularly conducive to the development of independent thought.

> A real-world playground full of peers is a space of immense possibility and invention compared to the digital architecture of even the most dynamic ed-tech platforms.

Academic learning was not the only process central to children's development that risked homogenization as young people's activities moved increasingly to digital platforms throughout the pandemic. Free and self-chosen play is essential to fostering creativity, imagination, physical growth, motor skills, awareness and problem-solving skills. It is not yet possible to richly nurture these developmental skills when play is mediated by digital platforms, especially platforms that are developed around commercial logics that constrain and incentivize particular interactions and behaviours. For children, a real-world playground full of peers is a space of immense possibility and invention compared to the digital architecture of even the most dynamic ed-tech platforms. The increasing replacement of in-person, unstructured play with online gaming and social media platforms narrows the scope of creativity and imagination that children can themselves introduce.[1263] While video games and social media can offer unique kinds of visual, auditory and digital interactions, they are not an adequate substitute for the developmental benefits of open, in-person play. The kinds of social relationships facilitated in digital environments are dictated by the ideas, rules, designs and business imperatives programmed into them. While unstructured play outside of virtual spaces carries some danger of physical injury and social conflict depending on the activity, the navigation of acceptable risk through healthy play is itself integral to young people's learning, development and gradual understanding of the world and their place within it.

> Education is not a process of production where increases in efficiency are uniformly welcome. Any ed-tech intervention must enable skilled educators to operate with high degrees of flexibility, responsivity, trust and autonomy.

Reflecting lessons from the pandemic, education systems need to preserve and foster the diversity of teaching and learning both online and offline, reflecting the rich cultural diversity of humanity. No piece of software should be irreplaceable in education. As students, educators and schools use technology to support their work, they should be empowered to create and innovate rather than forced into narrow moulds and templates. In a way, a school can be seen as a kind of platform in support of education – one that has constraints, but not nearly as many as most of the ed-tech that was adopted during the pandemic. Good schools try to accommodate a wide and diverse range of teaching and learning; they are at their best dynamic platforms that can meet the needs of learners, teachers and communities. While some uniformity and consistency are required to achieve these outcomes, automation is never the end goal. With ed-tech however, automation is very often a primary objective. But education is not a process of production where increases in efficiency are uniformly welcome. Teachers and students are not widgets or inputs that are unknown to each other and involved in some transactional relationship to be mediated by a digital platform. The existence and quality of human-to-human relationships must be at the heart of the educational enterprise, and any ed-tech intervention must enable skilled educators to operate with high degrees of flexibility, responsivity, trust and autonomy.

There is an unsettling irony in calls to keep outsourcing education – arguably society's most humanist endeavour, and one that sustains and expands social and cultural diversity – to machines running the same operating systems and the same software in the name of efficiency and modernity. In-person schools should remain the primary platform for education because, despite their flaws, they help ensure humans remain at the centre of educational practice and allow for a wider range of interactions, including those that involve technology and those that do not. Debates about the future of ed-tech should involve questions of how to strengthen and improve school-based education with technology, rather than questions of how to utilise technology to bypass schools.

QUESTION THE LOGIC OF TECHNOLOGY SOLUTIONISM

COVID-19 pandemic school closures caused technology solutionism to spike in education. Laptops, wi-fi and automated software were positioned as quick and often only-option fixes to complex challenges imposed by the pandemic. This caused digital hardware and apps to become primary, while human relationships slid into the background. Students were directed to look at content on screens rather than at teachers and peers or at books and other physical resources that can function without the internet or even electricity. The technology solutionism that characterized educational responses to pandemic disruptions (and, very often, rippled beyond school closures and the health emergency) tended to obscure and sometimes foreclose alternative solutions that might have been more effective or carried fewer risks.

Students want breaks from the digital world.

Before the pandemic, schools were often the sole spaces of reprieve from the technology saturation prevalent in many parts of the world, where screens and mobile devices play a commanding role in the lives of children and youth and are being introduced earlier and earlier in childhood. Schools have an important role to play in providing opportunities for young people to more critically question, evaluate and reflect on their own relationships with technology. This can and should be done with technology, however, any reflection on relationships with technology also requires taking steps away from it, and research is increasingly showing that students want breaks from the digital world. Children and youth, arguably more than adults, need time and space to log off and exit screen-based experiences. Research from the USA, for instance, found that over one-third of teenagers report that they spend too much time on social media and that over two-thirds of children under 5 years old are far surpassing screen time recommendations by leading health and paediatric organizations.[1264] Studies have also found that children and youth increasingly want to spend more time away from digital and Internet technologies.

Societies should further recognize that not every feature that is desirable in the digitalization of other sectors or spheres – such as work or leisure – can translate appropriately to education. The flexibility of remote work in some professions has been an attractive feature to many adult workers, allowing employees greater autonomy in where and how they work, albeit with caveats and shortcomings. But children are not mini adults, and that same appeal to flexibility in education has translated, in many cases, to a harmful lack of structure and support needed to shape students' personal and shared educational journeys. Social contact and interaction are of particular importance to children, and schools provide some of the most essential contexts for nurturing social relationships with peers and adults. Students are still learning how to forge bonds, navigate socially and in groups, and build friendships. Adults engaging in remote working arrangements generally have other pre-established social outlets and relationships outside of those mediated through technology. Children, on the other hand, have more limited autonomy over initiating social relationships outside of school, so learning exclusively through remote technology poses barriers to their ability to form social relationships, friendships and interpersonal bonds.[1265]

"The recent spate of former social media designers and inventors who regret their contributions – e.g., as stealing attention, as fostering politically toxic filter bubbles and fragmentation, etc. – is telling; as is the now open secret that the top executives in Silicon Valley … send their own children to non-digital school environments (while happily continuing to sell devices to any [and] every educational institution around)."

– Charles Ess, professor of media and communications, University of Oslo[ccvii]

New ed-tech solutions should seek to supplement, expand and enrich in-person education, not replace it or dismantle its valuable societal role.

A key lesson of the ed-tech expansion during the pandemic is that the success or failure of digital learning rests largely on advancements in education as a whole. Digital learning must be anchored and reinforced by good-quality schools capable of drawing on the possibilities of ed-tech but also going beyond its limitations to more effectively reach all students and fulfil their learning and developmental needs. Additionally, because ed-tech implementations hinge, to a considerable degree, on teachers, the health of the teaching profession and teacher training programmes form a vital basis for efforts to leverage technology for teaching and learning.[1266] Education's many stakeholders should reject temptations to see ed-tech as a magic bullet to meet educational objectives. In practice this approach tends to siphon much needed support away from maintaining and improving schools and prioritizing the recruitment and training of teachers. A moral clarity also needs to guide the integration of technology in education: ed-tech should uplift schooling, and schools should not be seen as a 'ready market' for ed-tech. New ed-tech solutions should seek to supplement, expand and enrich in-person education, not replace it or dismantle its valuable societal role.

Educational goals must prioritize processes as well as outcomes. Education processes model ways to live and be together, conveying intrinsic values and purposes for why students learn as well as what they learn.

Finally, the extent to which the logic of efficiency governs and shapes education deserves scrutiny. Improved efficiency is a perennial selling point for ed-tech. But education cannot be reduced to mere task completion; rather, it is human development itself. Educational goals must prioritize processes as well as outcomes. Education processes model ways to live and be together, conveying intrinsic values and purposes for why students learn as well as what they learn. These processes also dictate how young people spend time. Many students will spend a sixth or more of their lives in education. Whether they spend this time interacting with others in the social and physical environment of a school or behind a screen traversing automated apps in relative isolation matters. Yet during the pandemic, the processes of education were often ignored. Obsessive attention was placed on outcomes and replicating academic achievement realized in pre-pandemic conditions, regardless of how. In the future, arguments touting ed-tech's efficiency and value in education need to be evaluated in terms of not only learning gains or losses but also the educational processes used to reach those outcomes.

Strengthen digital connectivity, capacities and content

No discussion of technology's future relationships with education can be complete without underscoring the vast inequities in global access to digital connectivity, content and capacity that denied many students opportunities to learn with ed-tech during the pandemic. In terms of connectivity, approximately two-thirds of children and youth were without internet access at home in 2020, undercutting efforts to use remote online learning to benefit a majority of learners.[1267] In terms of content, a dearth of free, high-quality digital education resources posed other barriers to learning and teaching remotely. The experience of the COVID-19 educational disruption revealed that large numbers of learners do not know where to go or have nowhere to go to access digital learning content necessary to pursue their studies. And in many instances, the content that does exist has not been quality assured, is inaccessible from widely owned devices such as mobile phones, is poorly organized or resides behind paywalls or in virtual spaces that inappropriately capture and sell student data. Finally, in terms of capacity, the ITU estimated in 2018 that one in three people lacked even basic digital skills, and for those who do have skills, very little training is available to help them use ed-tech with dexterity for teaching and learning purposes.[1268]

These deficits – which both frame and constrain any attempt to leverage connected technology for education – are well known and of deep concern. UNESCO and the wider United Nations family have advanced ideas to expand digital access and make technology a more reliable engine of educational inclusion and equity. In June 2020, the Secretary-General of the United Nations published a road map for digital cooperation that identified eight areas for action to achieve a safer and more equitable digital world. Acknowledging the ways in which the COVID-19 pandemic changed society's relationship with technology, the road map announced goals for digital development that included achieving universal connectivity by 2030, investing in the creation of public digital goods and strengthening citizens' digital skills.[1269] Subsequently, in December 2021, UNESCO released *The RewirEd Global Declaration on Connectivity for Education*. This publication drew on input from an international advisory group to identify three principles for prioritizing equitable, sustainable and humanistic digital futures for education: (1) centre the most marginalized, (2) expand investments in digital learning content and (3) facilitate pedagogical innovation in digital environments.[1270] Building on this work, UNESCO led the drafting of several documents for the UN Transforming Education Summit held in September 2022 as part of the United Nations General Assembly. Major outputs included a discussion paper on digital learning and transformation,[1271] which offered recommendations in support of the three principles from the *RewirEd Declaration* and a call to action to assure and improve the quality of public digital learning for all.[1272] This document, endorsed by numerous countries, established three 'keys' for unlocking the power of digital teaching and learning: content, capacity and connectivity.

Collectively, this work shows promising signs that the international community is committed to steering the digital transformation of education in more humanistic directions and without abandoning in-person and school-based teaching and learning. It also proposes ideas to re-engineer the logics and incentives that guide digital changes in the education sector so that they protect and reinforce education's unique status as a public good and a human right, regardless of whether it is conducted in online, offline or hybrid spaces. This section draws on lessons learned from the ed-tech experiences of the pandemic to further elaborate principles to steer digital changes and integration in education.

CENTRE THE MOST MARGINALIZED IN ED-TECH PLANNING AND DEPLOYMENT

Ed-tech deployments were designed to improve education for young people who were already attending school when the pandemic struck. Students out of school were almost never considered.

Inequality and exclusion shaped the context onto which the technology solutionism of the COVID-19 pandemic was superimposed. Before the pandemic, 258 million children and youth were already out of school, public education systems were largely underfunded and under pressure, and 771 million people were unable to read or write.[1273] Well before school closures, educational inequality was concentrated along lines of poverty, disability, gender, and social and cultural marginalization, with divides tending to deepen in situations of conflict and disaster. The educational responses to the pandemic largely exacerbated these pre-existing conditions. Ed-tech deployments were almost uniformly designed to improve education for young people who were already attending school when the pandemic struck. UNESCO found almost no evidence of major efforts to extend ed-tech to children that had been out of school prior to the health crisis. Arguably, this established a troubling precedent for ed-tech deployments: the rise of approaches exclusively targeting learners already served by formal education.

Despite the promise of ed-tech to expand the right to education and reach young people who are out of school and help bring them into formal education, this ambition was almost never attempted during the pandemic when reliance on ed-tech peaked. Instead, prolonged school closures and the transition to remote learning contributed to increases in the number of students who could not access education, largely due to device and connectivity deficits. This meant that full educational reliance on ed-tech shrunk the number of students benefiting from education well below the numbers that had been in place when schooling was an in-person and school-based experience. And children who missed out on education when it was dependent on technology were less likely than their peers to return to school, even when schools reopened. Thus, while millions of children and youth navigated the complexity of accessing education and schooling via technology, millions more were excluded and at increased risk of never joining their peers in a classroom again.[1274]

As evidence mounted that the right to education was indeed losing ground as dependence on ed-tech grew, an appropriate response would have been the prioritization of actions to buttress and defend schools and low-tech solutions that have proven to be effective at reaching the most marginalized learners, and to do so quickly to prevent any backsliding in educational participation from becoming permanent. In this context, the emphasis on online learning as a first-order solution to the challenges of the pandemic was – and remains – confounding.

<aside>Future ed-tech policies and initiatives must be built on an ethic of inclusion.</aside>

Future ed-tech policies and initiatives must be built on an ethic of inclusion. However alluring the idea may be that ed-tech can provide a shortcut to reach those who are excluded or underserved by education, the experience of the pandemic shows that this remains in the hazy horizon of 'potential', rather than in the earthier realm of what has actually been delivered. There is little concrete evidence that digital learning alone is capable of closing equity divides. In fact, the evidence presented in this publication overwhelmingly indicates that digital learning has more often reinforced and widened inequities. Ed-tech needs to be built on a foundation that prioritizes the educational needs of the most marginalized learners and recognizes the many limitations of technology. Awareness of the extensive evidence documenting the shortcomings of ed-tech is essential to understanding how digital education can be approached in deliberative, inclusive ways that centre educational ideals to help those most likely to be excluded from educational opportunities.

"The most vulnerable learners are also among those who have poor digital skills and the least access to the hardware and connectivity required for distance learning solutions implemented during school closures."

– United Nations[ccviii]

The limitations of ed-tech implementation during the pandemic should inform the ways in which governments and leaders deploy connectivity and digital capacity-building initiatives. When education starts and ends with those who already have access to devices, connectivity and digital skills, educational inequalities grow in severity, as the experiences of the pandemic have demonstrated. When learning moved online, ed-tech benefited learners and educators first in regions and populations that already had reliable access to education and had devices on hand to support online learning. Only later and often much later did strategies emerge to establish points of connectivity and device distribution to make digital education more inclusive and accessible to those who are disadvantaged.

Going forward, policies, actions and investments related to digital learning should be designed to benefit, as a guiding goal, those most at risk of educational exclusion and marginalization. If public models and investments in ed-tech can work for the most underprivileged learners as a first step, they will be easier to transfer to more privileged learners. Asking how approaches can work for refugees, students with disabilities, girls and women in remote areas and other marginalized learners needs

> While the number of learners benefiting from digital learning has been rising steadily upwards at the global level, this obscures the fact that many students who were accessing digital learning in the past are no longer able to do so.

to be a point of departure. This will help bridge inequalities, spark needed innovation and make solutions easier to scale out to wider groups. Yet to date, public financing to assure approaches to bring ed-tech to vulnerable populations, including initiatives to achieve universal connectivity, remain tepid. More robust, predictable and sustained investments are necessary to provide every person, regardless of gender or socio-economic status, with a reliable connection to digital learning resources. This will not be a one-time expenditure, and backsliding will remain a risk. While the number of learners benefiting from digital learning has been rising steadily upwards at the global level, this obscures the fact that many students who were accessing digital learning in the past are no longer able to do so. It is therefore vital that good-quality digital learning opportunities are not only established but sustained. There are early signs that efforts to make digital learning more equitable during the COVID-19 pandemic are likely to fade away as school-provisioned connectivity plans run out of credit, investments in public digital learning content are abandoned, and programmes to provision ed-tech hardware given to poor students are not maintained. For digital learning to function as a driver of educational equity, it must reach all students and continuously so. This will require concerted and ongoing public commitments.

> The gender divides in access and use of digital technology that contribute to education inequality are largely shaped by social and cultural norms and will, therefore, require solutions that include but extend well beyond educational interventions.

Centring the most marginalized learners also requires connectivity and digital education to be gender responsive. The pandemic illuminated the persistence of digital gender divides and, in many contexts, widened them further, in part because men and boys often did not share scarce technology resources with women and girls inside families. The heavy toll of care and domestic labour during extended lockdowns presented other obstacles to technology use and could foreclose opportunities for women and girls to build digital skills and competencies. The multifaceted gender divides in access and use of digital technology that contribute to educational inequality are largely shaped by social and cultural norms that understand connected technology as male and will, therefore, require solutions that include but extend well beyond educational interventions.

Multi-country studies have established that boys are 1.5 times more likely to have a mobile phone than girls[1275] and that in some countries, internet use is four times greater for boys than for girls.[1276] Female teachers also consistently report higher levels of stress using digital technology for instructional purposes[1277] and lower self-perception of their digital competencies compared to male teachers.[1278] This troubling reality indicates that gender-blind or gender-neutral approaches to digital learning will not reconcile the deficits in technology access, skills, confidence and comfort for girls and women. How can education become a field where the biases and exclusions that are root causes of gender divides – including but not limited to digital gender divides – can start being dismantled? How can social norms be shifted to recognize that women and girls have the same right to use technology as men and boys, and that they can be equally or more skilled technology users? UNESCO advanced many concrete ideas and recommendations on this topic in its 2019 report *I'd Blush if I Could* that remain salient. It proposed using formal education and other sites of socialization and learning, such as community centres, libraries and museums, as vehicles to de-gender technology as male. Specific suggestions included: highlighting the contributions of female technology innovators and leaders; having women model new ways of working with technology for educational and other empowering purposes; and making technology classes such as computer science obligatory in secondary school, the level when girls tend to back away from early interest in technology subjects and fields.[1279]

Boys' disengagement from remote learning is also a significant concern. For example, a 2021 survey of students in five southern African countries (Lesotho, Malawi, Madagascar, Zambia and Zimbabwe) indicates that despite having generally more access to online devices than girls, a lower proportion of boys continued with their online studies during the pandemic.[1280] UNESCO further found that in regions such as Latin America, Africa and northern Europe, switching learning to remote and virtual modalities had an especially damaging effect on technical and vocational education, training and apprenticeships, which often provide educational trajectories for young men as well as growing cohorts of young women.[1281]

Efforts to centre the most marginalized in ed-tech planning and deployment means paying careful attention to the often unique needs of women and girls as well as men and boys to ensure technology facilitates education. It also entails paying closer attention to the limitations of technology-only interventions to bridge digital gender divides – much of this work will begin in schools and as part of in-person exchanges, away from screens rather than inside them.

CHAMPION SCHOOL-FIRST AND PUBLIC CONNECTIVITY AS A STEP TOWARDS ED-TECH INCLUSION

The right to education and a burgeoning right to connectivity are far from synonymous, but they can be mutually reinforcing, supporting the public wealth of resources that a community can rely on.

Despite the efforts of ed-tech advocates to equate ed-tech and online learning with uninterrupted, unencumbered education for anyone, anytime and anywhere, real-world experience has demonstrated that this is far from the case. Certain measures, such as making connectivity more of a public good and shared utility, could have mitigated some of the most obvious technical barriers that many students and teachers faced during the pandemic. The right to education and a burgeoning right to connectivity are far from synonymous, but they can be mutually reinforcing, supporting the public wealth of resources that a community can rely on, both in times of crisis and in times of stability. Policies should be developed to incentivize and steer greater investment into the equitable extension of connectivity to render it useful for education and other purposes. Focusing on school-first connectivity, as some countries and donor organizations have done, promises to help to ensure that in-person schooling remains central and well supported, while helping education systems experiment with digital learning pedagogies without turning educational experiences inside out by moving them fully into digital spaces. The ability to offer shared and networked connectivity of equal quality at a school expands the pedagogical possibilities for digital learning beyond what might be possible with limited and varied individual data plans. There are good reasons why businesses and other enterprises provide connectivity for all on-site employees and users and sometimes off-site employees as well. Schools and other educational institutions should be no different in this regard.

Making schools centres of internet connectivity helps turn connectivity into a public good.

School-first connectivity avoids excluding students who cannot make the jump to digital learning at home, whether due to device affordability, connectivity limitations, parental restrictions or other factors. Making schools centres of internet connectivity also helps turn connectivity into something more akin to a public good than private good and lifts financial burdens on students and families. When schools, libraries and other public institutions offer reliable and free internet connections, they are better able to help youth and adults pursue lifelong learning and develop digital skills. The closure of these spaces during the pandemic revealed how a reduction in public connectivity options tended to hurt marginalized groups the most because they did not have alternative options. Additionally, digital education that occurs in school contexts can be more easily complemented with the in-person care and guidance needed to help learners become familiar with digital tools and experiences. Public connectivity provisioned at schools can further fortify the right to education by allowing educational institutions to serve more students and better meet student needs, while helping learners take advantage of possibilities presented by digital innovations.

"Over a long period of time, the main force in favour of greater equality has been the diffusion of knowledge and skills."

– Thomas Piketty, economist[ccix]

> The Giga initiative is rightly using education as a cause and a means to move the world closer to universal connectivity.

The Giga initiative, led by UNICEF and the ITU, aims to boost national efforts to expand and improve school connectivity, with the goal of connecting all schools to the internet through mapping, innovative financing, procurement support to governments and partnerships with telecommunications companies. This and other initiatives are rightly using education as a cause and a means to move the world closer to universal connectivity. While it is undoubtedly important for students and educators to access the internet outside of schools to achieve digital equity and support out-of-school learning in ways that enrich and improve formal education conducted in schools, universal school connectivity is a realistic intermediate goal. Governments should set short, medium and long-term targets for connecting all schools and achieving target bandwidth objectives. A connected school provides an 'anchor' internet connection in a community and facilitates efforts to extend connectivity into communities more widely.

All connectivity efforts should include implementation plans to reach the most marginalized, including learners with disabilities and people on the move. This process will be facilitated by stripping commercial connectivity plans of unnecessary complexity. People should not need to wade through pages and pages of small print to determine which connectivity offers are sufficient to empower learning and education. Endless promotions and advertisements often confuse and frustrate people who simply want to link to the internet for educational purposes. Governments should consider mandating that internet and mobile service providers offer basic and easy-to-understand connectivity for education plans or credits at fixed or subsidized rates. Such requirements will help people find basic connectivity options to support their educational pursuits with minimal effort and at affordable costs.

Finally, connectivity efforts, including school connectivity efforts, should be steered by ministries of technology and telecom regulators, in close cooperation with network providers. Funding for this endeavour should come from budgets either beyond the education sector or in addition to existing allocations to education. Connecting schools should not entail divestments from the non-digital infrastructure of education – the rooms, desks, chairs, tables, roofs, windows, toilets, cafeterias, pencils, paper, books and playgrounds that remain vital to place-based education, no matter the sophistication of digital integration. The primary role of ministries of education and the wider education community is to ensure that the connectivity reaching schools and learners is leveraged to strengthen, expand and enrich learning and student well-being. Responsibility for assuring connectivity – a technical service that can facilitate education and much more – falls elsewhere.

SUPPORT THE DEVELOPMENT OF FREE, HIGH-QUALITY DIGITAL CONTENT AND PLATFORMS

> The rush to get learners connected often sucked up more energy than questions about what, exactly, learners would do with this connectivity.

Connectivity is valuable for educational purposes to the extent that it opens doors to high-quality educational content that facilitates learning and development. Too often, technology initiatives start and end with the provision of internet-connected devices and infrastructure. An over-emphasis on connectivity and hardware commonly eclipses attention paid to digital learning content, and this was frequently the case during the pandemic. The rush to get learners connected often sucked up more energy than questions about what, exactly, learners would do with this connectivity to continue their education when (or if) it arrived. In the future, content should be a starting point for investments in digital learning. Ideally, high-quality digital learning platforms and resources will be in place the moment students and teachers first acquire connected technology and as they develop digital skills and competencies to use this technology skilfully. If there is a sequence to the three 'keys' of digital learning mentioned as part of the Transforming Education Summit – content, capacity and connectivity – content should be first key, even though it is widely understood as the final one.[1282]

Dispiritingly and despite the intensive reliance on technology for education during the COVID-19 pandemic, there remain, in many countries, no public content options for public education on the internet. And even in places where free, open, curriculum-aligned, quality-controlled and government-assured content was established – due to the pressures of the pandemic and the imperative to support remote education – efforts to sustain and reinforce many of these investments stalled or backtracked when the pandemic abated and schools reopened. According to analysis by UNICEF, by September 2022, over one-third of national digital learning platforms built during the pandemic were no longer functional or maintained.[1283]

> Public options for public education in online as well as offline spaces are necessary. Public education does not – and cannot – stop where digitalization begins.

Presently, students and educators trying to use digital spaces for education continue to face a confusing array of heavily marketed apps and proprietary platforms controlled by organizations outside of public oversight. Many of the best digital learning resources continue to sit behind paywalls or require a subscription or a specific type of hardware or operating system to access. This needs to change. The virtual spaces of education that are increasingly central to teaching and learning must be developed and, if necessary, re-engineered to support education as a public good and a human right. Public options for public education in online as well as offline spaces are necessary. Public education does not – and cannot – stop where digitalization begins, as was so often the experience of families during the pandemic.

A movement to assert digital spaces as vibrant locations for public education should draw inspiration from national and international efforts to harness the power of radio and television for the public good. The internet is hardly the first technology that societies have moulded to ensure it strengthens shared aims like education, nor will it be the last. Almost exactly a century before the COVID-19 pandemic, the BBC was established in the UK and gradually became one of the earliest publicly funded efforts to direct the power of a novel communication technology to inform, educate and entertain. The BBC and other public broadcasters have provided models – applied first to radio and later to television – that have been emulated around the world. Collectively, they have helped establish a precedent for funding the creation of high-quality content that is widely accessible, advances public aims and can support and promote human rights. A similar effort is needed to support public education via the internet. Countries should look back to the ways that they created and sustained public broadcasting as they develop strategies to make connected digital technologies reliable engines to improve, strengthen and accelerate public education.

"States should invest in free and public digital platforms and infrastructure for education, grant adequate funding to public institutions to develop alternative free digital solutions and tools that do not involve the private personal data market, and support the development of non-proprietary data tools, platforms and services that are based around values of openness, transparency and common stewardship (rather than individual ownership) of data."

– Koumbou Boly Barry, UN Special Rapporteur on the right to education[ccx]

> Digital learning content will require fast, but still rigorous, quality control checks to keep material up-to-date and accommodate new innovations.

While the OER (open educational resources) movement has called necessary attention to the importance of freely and openly accessible content,[1284] what is often missing are platforms that make this content accessible to teachers and learners. High-quality platforms assure that there are front doors for public education on the internet – trusted and reliable first ports of call for connected learning that do not rely on advertising, data mining or monthly subscription fees. Free public digital learning platforms should be aligned with national curricula and offer engaging, accredited, well-organized and easy-to-find educational content that can be accessed from a wide range of internet-connected devices, including widely owned mobile phones. Efforts should also be made to consolidate this state-provisioned educational content under a single roof (rather than scattered across various sites and locations) and, when possible, include functionality to recognize and validate learning. This will help improve recognition of public digital learning resources and aid the findability of relevant content that is often peppered across a multitude of platforms. Governments that can figure out ways to quality control and align new digital content with national curricula at rapid speeds will be able to provision a far wider range of learning resources than printed textbooks. This does not mean printed textbooks will suddenly become irrelevant – digital resources will expand, enrich and complement paper-based learning material in addition to replacing some of it. But educational content in public digital learning spaces should be more plentiful, more varied and more interactive and media-rich than paper-based learning resources. This will require fast, but still rigorous, quality control checks to keep material up-to-date and accommodate new innovations. The often glacial approval processes applied to printed textbooks will need to be rethought and expedited for digital content.

Some countries have already taken action to build, sustain and improve public digital learning platforms, and others are planning to do so. While each country, and regions within countries, will have unique needs and require customization, the creation and curation of public digital learning platforms populated with high-quality learning content have enormous potential to strengthen education across dimensions of inclusion, accessibility, equity and quality. This effort will also open opportunities for expanded cross-country collaboration, such as the sharing of digital education resources in particular languages and coordination to ensure the technical interoperability of public learning platforms.

Schools and their resources have long been treated as public goods, with corresponding public support, oversight and governance. The same should be true for the digital spaces and infrastructures of learning.

To support this endeavour, UNESCO and UNICEF launched the Gateways to Public Digital Learning Initiative in late 2022 to help assert digital environments as locations for public education. Gateways is a global effort to ensure that every learner, teacher and family can easily find, access and use high-quality and curriculum-aligned digital education content to advance their learning. The initiative will map, describe and analyse existing public platforms and content, help countries create and strengthen platforms, identify and share best practices, and establish international norms and standards to guide the development of platforms in ways that advance national and international goals for education.[1285] Schools and their resources have long been treated as public goods, and rightly so. They benefit everyone and, as such, demand public support, oversight and governance. The same must hold true for the digital spaces and infrastructures of learning. The UNESCO-UNICEF initiative is notable in the way it is taking a major lesson from the pandemic – the dearth of public digital learning content – and working to take concrete steps in close partnership with countries to close the gap.

A global movement to establish and strengthen public digital learning platforms will also directly complement and reinforce wider efforts to expand digital connectivity and capacities for education. Building digital platforms and content requires relatively modest investments and limited dependence on sectors and government ministries outside education. Put simply, it is easier and cheaper to create digital learning platforms populated with excellent educational content than it is to connect all learners and their families to the internet and to ensure they have the requisite skills to use this connection for learning and other empowering purposes. The availability of free, high-quality digital learning content and platforms will, in turn, help increase demand for connectivity and provide greater incentives to develop digital capacities. Investments in digital learning content, therefore, help countries move closer towards the goal of full digital inclusion.

BUILD DIGITAL CAPACITIES AND FOSTER PEDAGOGICAL INNOVATION

In addition to highlighting the lack of relevant, findable and high-quality digital content, educational reliance on technology during the pandemic revealed that capacity gaps remain a major and persistent obstacle to connected learning. Inadequate digital skills and competencies consistently rank as the single greatest barrier to technology use for education, regardless of a country's development status.[1286] Digital skills gaps tend to be most pronounced for parents, followed by teachers, followed by students. Ultimately, connected education is dependent on digitally literate societies.

Countries must continue to work towards achieving universal digital literacy for education and other empowering purposes, with a special focus on women and girls in order to close long-standing digital skills gender divides. Much has been written on this important topic, and UNESCO has advanced specific ideas to help low-skilled and low-literate youth and adults develop digital skills as part of its initiatives on digital inclusion.[1287] Beyond knowledge work and guidelines, several international coalitions, such as EQUALS and the Broadband Commission, have launched efforts to help young people, and women and girls in particular, build strong digital skills.[1288] As this work proceeds, investments in digital learning should be complemented by teacher training for ed-tech and in-service support, using evidence-based approaches and leveraging existing tools and alliances such as the *UNESCO ICT Competency Framework for Teachers* and the Global Education Coalition founded by UNESCO.[1289] Teachers and education leaders must receive adequate training to ensure they can integrate technology into their practice and help their students gain digital skills. When learners, teachers and families have strong digital competencies, connected technologies become more versatile tools for education.

Online and virtual environments demand new types of learning content and new pedagogies that are less reliant on the proprietary and closed systems of many private sector digital providers.

Beyond building digital competencies, educators must be empowered to leverage technology for pedagogical innovation and change, and digital tools for teaching and learning should be responsive to the needs and expertise of those who will be using them. Online and virtual environments demand new types of learning content and new pedagogies. Time and again during the pandemic, experienced educators reported feeling out of their depth in the new digital spaces of education. The teaching approaches and strategies are not the same online and offline – even if there is some crossover. Innovation is needed to develop and test digital as well as hybrid learning models that are less reliant on the proprietary and closed systems of many private sector digital providers that enjoyed wide uptake during periods of school closures. New platforms and tools should be designed to support rather than replace teachers, and technology and technology-enabled pedagogies should be integrated in pre- and in-service teacher training. Teachers as well as families need to be involved in the development of digitally supported education and receive training to maximize the unique educational affordances of connected technologies while also being made aware of the many limitations of these tools. Training of this sort should be device and platform agnostic, rather than outsourced to private sector technology corporations that tend to provide training only in the use of their own proprietary tools and services.

At their best, digital spaces can foster new and effective pedagogies that increase educational equity, expand knowledge and skills, nurture creativity and foster responsible digital citizenship. Transitions between digital and non-digital modes of learning can be made more seamless and placed in the capable hands of skilled educators, rather than systems driven by unseeing algorithms and other forms of automation. Digital tools should respond to the needs of teachers, support their work in classrooms and help ease demanding job obligations. Too often, they present additional burdens.

"A Critical Digital Pedagogy demands that open and networked educational environments must not be merely repositories of content. They must be platforms for engaging students and teachers as full agents of their own learning."

– Jesse Stommel, co-founder of the Digital Pedagogy Lab[ccxi]

Digital learning investments with the most potential for impact are those that align with the robust evidence base on effective instructional practice, including, for example, mother-tongue instruction, teacher coaching, formative assessment, structured pedagogy and teacher reflection. These practices are possible without the use of technology, but technology can help facilitate them and widen their implementation. Digital learning can also enable a rich array of instructional approaches not possible without technology. For example, ed-tech can help students learn fundamental concepts through dynamic multimedia digital content and then apply these concepts practically and collaboratively at school. It can help reinvent assessment, moving it away from merely ranking and sorting and towards formative evaluations that can identify and fill knowledge and skills gaps in ways that strengthen educational progression. Similarly, blended and hybrid learning models have demonstrated some encouraging benefits, including enhancing social and collaborative skills while enabling access to learning experiences from locations beyond schools. Meanwhile, digital-only provision can be beneficial in certain situations, especially for adult learners balancing education with work and family obligations. As research continues to clarify the distinct advantages and disadvantages of physical, virtual and hybrid learning environments, efforts should be made to place them in more harmonious balance. An intervention portfolio approach that aligns context-specific needs with appropriate pedagogical approaches – with varying reliance on ed-tech – can help education systems provide holistic, human-centred educational experiences.

> Societies cannot continue to let a set of tools – however novel and powerful – dictate educational agendas.

For ed-tech to become better aligned with the aims of inclusion, equity and quality in education, teachers need to be given the space and autonomy to reflect with colleagues on how to best incorporate digital learning into their practice to take advantage of its unique affordances. This will require moving away from the regimes of automation and assessment proposed by many ed-tech companies. Instead, a new generation of ed-tech tools and services will need to consider the needs expressed by teachers working in contexts that can vary enormously, even within countries. Future ed-tech will require greater reflexivity in its designs, settings and environments, drawn from the perspectives and interests of those teaching and learning within them. Ed-tech will also need to support a much wider range of educational aims and objectives, including, for instance, increasing equity in and access to learning, and fostering collaboration to achieve more sustainable futures. Whittling educational objectives down to easily quantifiable indicators of progress in isolated subject areas can make technology-first means of education look highly attractive. But when digital learning is held to the more expansive objectives that communities usually expect from formal education, the limitations of ed-tech and excessive automation become more apparent. A lesson from the pandemic is that setting overly narrow objectives for education tends to result in practices that do not adequately support a holistic and human-centred learning experience. Only through pedagogical innovation will ed-tech come to better support these more expansive aims of education. Societies cannot continue to let a set of tools – however novel and powerful – dictate educational agendas.

Protect the right to education from shrinking ground

A particularly important lesson to draw from the technology-first educational experiences of the pandemic is an appreciation for the ways ed-tech is undermining decades-old understandings of the right to education and showing gaps in the legal architecture that has been constructed to assure it. In 1948, member states of the United Nations adopted the Declaration of Human Rights, which, in Article 26.1, asserts that "everyone has the right to education" and that, "at least in the elementary and fundamental stages", education shall be free and compulsory.[1290] This right was universally understood as a state obligation to ensure that all students have access to physical and in-person learning environments in a community of peers and educators. Education was also considered a "multiplier" right that is "an indispensable means of realizing other human rights", a designation that underscored the special importance of the right to education.[1291] The spectacular rise in school infrastructure, qualified teachers, community and family support for schooling, and student participation that followed reflected state commitments to realize this right to education for all students within and across countries. The second half of the 20th century saw an unprecedented expansion of mass education.[1292] By the century's end, schooling for children had become a global norm, and by 2015, more than 90 per cent of the world's children attended primary school.[1293]

"The spread of schooling around the globe remains one of the most widely successful 'going to scale' stories to date. Two hundred years ago, it would have been inconceivable in any country or cultural context that a central feature in a child's upbringing and preparation for adulthood would be his or her regular participation in classroom lessons and school life."

– Rebecca Winthrop and Eileen McGivney, Center for Universal Education[ccxii]

> The move from schools to ed-tech during COVID-19 disruptions replaced most of the tangible indicators of the right to education with virtual proxies.

Throughout this 75-year history, the extent to which the right to education could be considered fulfilled or neglected has depended largely on the presence of in-person school environments and human relationships dedicated to education. Legal apparatuses monitoring the right to education measure the existence of school buildings, enrolments, attendance, absences and completion. Over time, ensuring the right to education has come to encompass guarantees of transportation, learning progression, inclusion for students with disabilities, and face-to-face teaching and learning provided to all primary and secondary school-age children. The move from schools to ed-tech during COVID-19 disruptions, however, replaced most of these tangible indicators with virtual proxies. For example, online log-ins from students were counted as interchangeable with in-person attendance at a time when lockdowns and quarantines were at their most restrictive. This practice raised a question that had seemed far-fetched prior to 2020: Is access to virtual instruction and content an acceptable interpretation of state duties to assure the right to education?

This section examines the wide-scale pivot to ed-tech and remote learning during the pandemic in light of its impact on general understandings, commitments and shared resolve to assure the right to education for all. It considers how this right should be understood going forward – particularly in contexts where remote learning is now being proposed as a non-temporary substitute to in-person schooling – and raises questions about how to fulfil education's protective and humanistic aims when learning moves into digital spaces.

"States must ensure that digital technologies do not impair universal access to education or equality of opportunity in education. Nor should they be allowed to erode the concept of education as a public good."

– Kishore Singh, UN Special Rapporteur on the right to education[ccxiii]

ANCHOR THE RIGHT TO EDUCATION IN STANDARDS AND DEFINITIONS THAT PRIORITIZE IN-PERSON LEARNING

According to international human rights law, even in crisis situations when certain civic rights might be temporarily curtailed, the right to education should always be upheld. This position was expounded in a mid-2020 report from the UN Special Rapporteur on the right to education in the context of COVID-19. The Special Rapporteur at the time, Koumbou Boly Barry, wrote: "During crises, States parties to the International Covenant on Economic, Social and Cultural Rights must continue to ensure the right to education." She also cited the Committee on the Rights of the Child to affirm that "restrictions imposed on children's rights in order to protect public health must be imposed only when necessary, be proportionate and kept to an absolute minimum".[1294] This, of course, included the right to education, which is of particular importance to children.

"Extended school closures during the coronavirus pandemic effectively broke the social compact of universal, compulsory schooling."

– Anya Kamenetz, education reporter[ccxiv]

> Prolonged reliance on remote learning with ed-tech during the pandemic has muddied understandings of the right to education. In the new technology-first context, the 'free', 'compulsory', 'accessible' and 'available' tenets that give substance to this right were all degraded.

Yet the prolonged reliance on remote learning with ed-tech during the pandemic has muddied understandings of the right to education and undermined its main pillars: that education should be free, compulsory, accessible and available. Ed-tech modes of learning were almost never free for families or were, in many instances, significantly less free than in-person schooling had been. Families were regularly forced to pay for devices, connectivity, software, applications and subscriptions as they did their best to work with schools and teachers to maintain educational continuity. The compulsory aspect of schooling also became difficult to enforce or even define. The age-old act of logging attendance based on the physical presence of a student was often reduced to seeing a digital trace of a student in a virtual environment. The platforms used or repurposed for virtual schooling tended to provide teachers with limited means to ensure that students were indeed present after an initial log-in or a verification process involving a camera. And even when teachers could see signs that their students were logged in, they often had no way of knowing whether students were engaged in lessons or immersed in other virtual spaces, such as those dedicated to entertainment. Finally, and most concerningly, commitments to ensure access to education broke down entirely for many students when learning became wholly reliant on technology. Millions of families did not have the devices and connectivity they needed to exercise their right to education. Others had poor-quality devices or unreliable

connections that blocked their ability to access education. Still others did not have the digital skills and supports needed to use available devices for educational purposes. In the new technology-first context, the 'free', 'compulsory', 'accessible' and 'available' tenets that give substance to the right to education were all degraded.

> Human rights advocates argued that the durations of school closures were often unnecessarily prolonged and that authorities did not move quickly enough to develop plans to keep them to a minimum.

As these fissures grew more and more apparent, recommendations to uphold the right to education in the context of the pandemic became more forceful, as did clarifications that education should be defined as in-person schooling. The 2020 report of the Special Rapporteur on the right to education stressed that "the deployment of online distance learning (together with radio and TV), should be seen only as a temporary solution aimed at addressing a crisis. The digitalization of education should never replace on-site schooling with teachers".[1295] UNESCO has also been clear that digital-only approaches do not fulfil a state's obligation to provide quality education with its associated services that help assure protection, health and well-being. Yet despite this guidance, many school closures were extended even after the most deadly and disruptive waves of the pandemic had subsided and in spite of a preponderance of evidence that such measures seemed to do very little to slow the spread of the disease. Human rights advocates regularly expressed frustration that the durations of school closures were unnecessarily prolonged and that authorities did not move quickly enough to develop plans to keep closures to a minimum or as a measure of last resort.[1296]

It remains unclear how feasible, advisable or even legal it is to equate providing access to an online class with fulfilling the right to education. An alarming consequence of the COVID-19 education disruption is the way prolonged dependence on ed-tech options has established foundations for new policies that move education further from schools and closer to home-based modes of distance learning with technology. Since the initial

The pandemic ushered in a new reality, unimaginable to many prior to 2020, in which many families were able to select between technology-only modes of education or school-based education for their children.

upheavals of 2020, there have been policy proposals to make public online learning systems permanent alternatives to schools;[1297] to truncate in-person school weeks whereby students attend school for, say, three days in-person and two days online;[1298] and to establish dedicated government departments for ed-tech and digital schools, which may risk further entrenching technology-only modes of learning as mainstream alternatives to schools.[1299] In some countries and communities, the pandemic ushered in a new reality, unimaginable to many prior to 2020, in which many families were given an option to select between technology-only modes of education or school-based education for their children. It appears that this choice may, in some contexts, be offered indefinitely, despite overwhelming evidence of the superiority of school-based education.[1300]

"A thorough debate needs to take place on the place [of distance learning with technology] in the future, keeping in mind not only possible opportunities but also the deleterious effect screens have on children and youth, including their right to health and education."

– Koumbou Boly Barry, UN Special Rapporteur on the right to education[ccxv]

Students and families around the world have challenged notions that technology-mediated distance learning fulfils state obligations under the right to education, sometimes with lawsuits.[1301] In the USA, many of these legal challenges were brought by students with disabilities who were unable to benefit from ed-tech modes of education provisioned at a distance.[1302] Similarly, some countries and jurisdictions are now questioning whether online learning in fact meets the criteria of education as a human right. Leaders of the New York City School District in the USA, for example, found that the outcomes of remote online learning were so inequitable and so far below acceptable standards that the city stopped offering online options. Officials moved instead to make attendance at in-person schools mandatory, regardless of parental preference.[1303] The city effectively sent a message that ed-tech only modes of education were not acceptable choices and could not fulfil students' right to education. Several countries in Europe and other continents were also quick to resume and mandate in-person schooling across the board, seeing online options as falling too far short of acceptable standards to warrant maintaining them, even if some families voiced support for keeping this option.

The language and definitions that anchor and give substance to the right to education almost uniformly reflect tacit understandings that education will be an in-person and school-based experience. What constitutes school attendance, completion, entrance, exit, retention, enrolment, progression, suspension, expulsion, breaks and so forth generally have well-defined meanings when applied to school-based education. In almost all countries,

The hard edges of education – the spaces, times and schedules that clarify and define educational participation – are easily blurred in digital realms.

the legal architecture that helps assure and protect the right to education rests, to a considerable extent, on understandings that education will be conducted in physical spaces and, very often, according to fixed times and schedules. Yet these spaces, times and schedules – the hard edges of education – are easily blurred in digital realms. The terms and definitions connected to a state's obligation to fulfil the right to education become hard to define when teaching and learning is conducted exclusively through ed-tech. For example, does attendance in an online class equate to a student's name appearing in a digital list of participants, or must a teacher verify identity through a video and audio check? How might retention be measured if a student is jumping virtually from one online school to another with a few clicks and keystrokes? The experiences of the pandemic rarely answered these questions conclusively, even if they did bring them into sharp relief.

The ed-tech responses to the pandemic have scrambled norms surrounding the right to education and, in some instances, placed digital-only learning on the same plane as in-person, school-based and hybrid learning in ways that, without government intervention, might prove permanent. Scholars as well as human rights advocates have argued that this new equivalency is deeply flawed and should be unwound or, at the very least, interrogated.[1304] Moving forward, governments and other education stakeholders, must take steps to clearly define what it means to fulfil the right to education in a digital age with technology alternatives to school-based education. For the time being and given the disappointing results of fully remote online learning during the pandemic, in-person schooling must remain the cornerstone of the right to education. The context of digital learning. As the world emerges from the pandemic and reassesses education's relationship with ed-tech, it is imperative that the legal and practical standards around schooling be firmly anchored in education as a human right. Governments should pass laws and statutes to clarify that online-only modes of education are not equivalent to in-person and school-based modes of education, and that, with rare exception, only the latter successfully fulfils state obligations to assure the right to education. Laws to guarantee school-based education are most vital at the earliest grades, but are also warranted through the completion of upper secondary school. At age and grade levels where education is compulsory, school-based options should be available and mandatory.

ENSURE CHILDREN'S SAFETY AND WELL-BEING IN PHYSICAL AND DIGITAL LEARNING SPACES

Online education has emerged as a workaround to avoid larger structural overhauls needed to ensure student safety, health and well-being in schools.

It is clear that technology-dependent remote learning failed to fulfil the right to education for hundreds of millions of children and young people during the pandemic. Despite this, many school systems are positioning this mode of learning as an acceptable alternative to school-based education. This partly reflects the major investments governments made in ed-tech to support distance learning. Schools today have expanded options to allow or encourage remote learning and, in some instances, are under pressure to do so. COVID-19 also helped cement a narrative that schools – along with other important public spaces – can be unsafe for prolonged periods of time and 'replaced' with digital solutions. Such understandings can normalize decisions to suspend in-person learning. Deploying online learning as a safety measure, risks positioning it as an antidote to various challenges confronted by schools, including extreme weather events and security concerns in addition to pandemics. At the level of households, families have sought online alternatives to in-person learning to avoid bullying, substance abuse, violence and other threats present in some schools rather than mobilizing efforts to reconcile these problems directly and ensure that schools protect students in addition to educating them. Likewise, hazards posed by ageing physical educational infrastructure, such as deteriorating buildings, poor sanitation or inadequate heating or cooling capacity – a deficit set to present increased risk due to the punishing effects of climate change – can present further risks to the health and safety of students and tempt local authorities to resort to online classes rather than undergo expensive repairs.[1305] While many in education have long advocated for more public investment in schools and communities to better assure school safety and security, online education has emerged as a workaround to avoid larger structural overhauls.

"In the past, schools were closed due to pandemic induced lockdown for a long time. Efforts made to impart education through online classes have proved useless. This had an adverse impact on reading interests of children. Now again, by reducing regular classes [because of a heat wave], studies will be hit badly."

– Leaders of the Democratic Teachers Front, India[ccxvi]

Reinforcing the quality, safety and protection provided by schools has been an ongoing part of advancing the right to education over its 75-year history. These efforts built the trust needed to recognize and legitimize education's compulsory nature and assure confidence and buy-in from a wide range of stakeholders. Such an endeavour has high stakes. Requiring young people to exercise their right to education by participating in the

Requiring young people to exercise their right to education by participating in the social space of a school provides an impetus to make communities safe and welcoming for children.

social space of a school provides impetus to make communities safe and welcoming for children. Unfortunately, pandemic restrictions may have conditioned many families to understand school-based education as inherently dangerous and to see technology-reliant remote learning as a safer alternative. A mass retreat to remote learning conducted from the home might function to lower the prioritization of actions to ensure that public spaces are accommodating to children as well as adults. Dialling back the impulse to see remote digital learning as an adequate solution to perceived challenges of safety will require rebuilding trust and confidence in school and communities. Government leadership, in parallel with grassroots community efforts, are needed to create and fund actions to rectify safety risks and prioritize children's physical and psychological well-being in brick-and-mortar schools.[1306]

Important rights-based questions also need to be examined regarding how to extend the protective function of education to digital spaces. In the frenzied rush to connect students to online learning opportunities, millions of student accounts were created on behalf of minors without their explicit consent or the consent of their caregivers. These accounts contained personal information, including names, genders, birthdates, photographs, teacher notes, grades and geographical locations, information that was often held by and accessible to private corporations. In online environments, students were exposed to new and sometimes highly invasive forms of surveillance that were implemented with limited discussion or consensus and in ways that made agreement more or less obligatory.[1307] Around the world families were told, either explicitly or implicitly, that withdrawing their child's profile from an online platform – or failing to establish one – was tantamount to withdrawing their child from school and was not, therefore, a viable choice. Countries need to take bolder action to ensure that exercising the right to education does not require relinquishing the right to data privacy or online security.

Governments should consider the need for student rights and permissions to disconnect.

Finally, in situations where connected learning is a major component of education and at a moment when young people are spending more of their waking lives navigating digital worlds than ever before, governments should consider the need for rights and permissions to disconnect. While school-based education is and should remain compulsory, it is less clear if calls to use digital technologies for learning purposes, especially for long and uninterrupted periods of time, should also be compulsory. Just as there might be the beginnings of a right to connectivity under the right to education, there might also be the need for a right to unconnected education.[1308] Countries should work to assure learners opportunities and flexibility to opt-in and opt-out of screen-based learning according to their needs and to help prevent education from becoming an excessively digital and virtual undertaking.

RECONSTRUCT ED-TECH TO SUPPORT HOLISTIC EDUCATION AND ACCOMMODATE EDUCATIONAL DIVERSITY

With learning reduced to the proxy of an active log-in status and performance measured through the metrics of clicks, education is often narrowed to content consumption and task completion.

Education as a human right not only relates to access but also extends to the purpose, objectives and cultural rights of education. For example, Article 26.2 of the Universal Declaration of Human Rights states: "Education shall be directed to the full development of the human personality and to the strengthening of respect for human rights and fundamental freedoms. It shall promote understanding, tolerance, and friendship among all nations, racial or religious groups, and shall further the activities of the United Nations for the maintenance of peace."[1309] Digital solutions have demonstrated a poor track record in fulfilling or promoting these broader aspects of the right to education. Outside of the conducive environment of in-school learning with a community of peers and teachers, educators often had to winnow and condense the range of subjects, experiences, interactions and relationships to meet the instructional constraints of online learning. The back-to-basics approaches to learning with ed-tech were often thinly veiled actions to distil education down to academic learning, with an almost singular emphasis on building reading and mathematics skills. With learning reduced to the proxy of an active log-in status and performance measured through the metrics of clicks, education often narrowed to content consumption and task completion exclusively. This was a perversion of the broader social purposes of education enshrined in the Universal Declaration of Human Rights.

Also significant is Article 14 of the United Nations Declaration on the Rights of Indigenous Peoples (UNDRIP), adopted in 2007. This article asserts the rights of indigenous people to "establish and control their own educational systems and institutions" and to provide "education in their own languages, in a manner appropriate to their cultural methods of teaching and learning".[1310] The UNDRIP requires states to ensure both the protection of these rights as well as full consultation and cooperation with indigenous communities on the manner of educational provision. In the context of the pandemic, however, corporate entities overwhelmingly determined how education was applied. The manner of provision was set not by local communities but by Google, Microsoft, Tencent and other multinational technology companies. While many governments had not met UNDRIP obligations prior to the pandemic, the shift of education from schools embedded in local communities to technology platforms controlled by sprawling corporations struck many as a particular affront to the spirit of the declaration.

The de-territorialized and placeless nature of many online learning platforms unmoored education from geographic locations.

Indigenous scholars also argue for the inherently place-centric nature of indigenous culture and knowledge and the importance of territory in relationship to learning and education. The de-territorialized and placeless nature of many online learning platforms unmoored education from geographic locations that were anchored within corresponding webs of people, knowledge and culture. In technology spaces, the language of instruction also tended to be restricted to dominant and international languages, prioritizing written and scripted languages above oral language, intergenerational oral teachings, embodied knowledge and place-based learning. In addition to the UNDRIP, there are numerous regional human rights frameworks and instruments meant to uphold the cultural and linguistic self-determination of indigenous and minority groups through education that were restricted when education jumped from schools to ed-tech.[1311]

Technology-facilitated education can be reimagined to strengthen community ownership and stewardship of education.

Going forward, ed-tech needs to be reconceived so that it helps widen the aims and purposes of education beyond back-to-basics approaches and academic curricular learning exclusively. As affirmed in the Universal Declaration of Human Rights, education must be concerned with the full development of the human personality. Currently, online-only modes of learning cannot facilitate this holistic development in the same way that school- and place-based learning can. And although ed-tech modes of learning rolled out during the pandemic usually undermined community control over education, handing unprecedented influence to huge technology corporations, there was nothing inevitable about this process. Technology-facilitated education can be reimagined to strengthen community ownership and stewardship of education. It can resist the homogenization of learning experiences and accommodate greater diversity such that it complements and reinforces local and indigenous ways of knowing and being. In doing this, ed-tech can help preserve and strengthen the multiplicity of thought systems and education traditions that enrich the world.

While this task may seem daunting today, it is useful to remember that it was once understood as likely. When the internet was new and reaching large numbers of people in the 1990s, hopes were high that it would fuel an outpouring of diversity, particularly as it concerned knowledge and learning. People in different countries and communities would, it was assumed, find novel uses for this remarkable new tool – both in education and beyond it. Teaching and learning would become more varied, not less. This remains a distinct possibility but will require thinking beyond the automation and generic educational solutions that characterized many of the ed-tech experiences of the pandemic. There is nothing preordained about a continuation of the consolidation and regularization of online educational experiences. Ed-tech can still be reconfigured to support the diverse, holistic and community-anchored purposes societies ascribe to education.

CONCLUSION

Digital technologies have long promised to propel giant leaps forward for humanity, offering visions of more open, efficient, equitable, democratic, sustainable and data-driven futures unencumbered by outdated physical and analogue processes.

The hopes and expectations for educational technologies were the same: they would unlock previously intractable problems, both technical and social, and open up new and advanced possibilities for learning and development.

When the pandemic triggered a shift from physical classrooms to online user interfaces, from human instruction to algorithmic prompts, from paper textbooks to digital content, and from localized classrooms to globally connected networks, these shifts were widely assumed to signal progress – indicators of advances that would pave the way to more effective teaching, learning and assessment and, ultimately, to improved educational outcomes. Education was widely understood to be evolving in overdrive due to the technology-first innovations that arrived with the disruptions caused by the health emergency. As school closures became global, expanded and deepened technology reliance was, especially at the outset, framed as a natural, desirable and even inevitable breakthrough for education, even if it involved some bumps, as large transitions commonly do.

Yet the dramatic changes instigated between 2020 to early 2023 revealed an often-forgotten reality of technology implementations: in addition to solving problems, they create new ones, many of them not well anticipated. These new problems, detailed throughout this publication, came to light when digital technology became the main interface for educational participation and interaction during periods of school closures.

This publication has traced how a hurried and uncritical embrace of technology-centric approaches to formal learning during the pandemic placed education on a dangerous trajectory at odds with social expectations that it facilitate holistic human development in inclusive and equitable ways. In detailing the myriad problems that surfaced when ed-tech was deployed at scale with few regulatory guardrails and by offering in-depth analysis and recommendations, *An Ed-Tech Tragedy?* has proposed new and more desirable pathways to guide the digital changes reshaping education.

REMEMBERING THE ED-TECH EXPERIENCES OF THE PANDEMIC

COVID-19 has been labelled the most severe shock dealt to education in generations. Viewed from the global level, it is hard to argue with this assessment. No previous crisis disrupted education for so many and for so long.

How schools, communities and countries choose to remember this experience matters, because the memory will orient future actions, particularly as they relate to ed-tech. In many instances, recollections about technology-first responses to school closures have become detached from the global evidence about this chaotic period and the lived realities of learners, teachers and families. A prevailing narrative has taken hold that technology fell short of its considerable potential simply because there was not enough of it. Under this logic, faster and larger investments in technology-reliant solutions would have more successfully 'saved the day' and will be needed in the future to assure educational resilience. In this assessment, ed-tech's promise remains both unrealized and undiminished. Other narratives drive an argument that actions to construct education around connected technology as a response to COVID-19 disruptions provided a much-needed jolt to traditional practices in schools and universities. Forced ed-tech adoption was, in this perspective, a positive shock because it opened doors to technology-centric approaches to learning that will prove to be more effective, more personalized and of higher quality than pre-pandemic approaches. Remembering school closures in this way buttresses beliefs that technology offers a first-order remedy to the many challenges facing education and reflects an openness to approaches that often circumnavigate physical schools and human teachers.

Digital technology is an insufficient and brittle backbone for education.

A rarer takeaway is sober admission that massive and prolonged attempts to support the full weight of education with connected technology did not work out as planned or hoped. A reasoned analysis of the evidence about the ed-tech experiences of the pandemic indicates that digital technology is an insufficient and brittle backbone for education.

In documenting what occurred when education pivoted from schools to ed-tech, this publication has proposed that the techno-centric response to the educational disruptions of the pandemic and the spiralling consequences of this response are best framed as a tragedy – a regression instead of a progression and a period in which initial and often grand ambitions for technology-first approaches did not yield desired outcomes and instead often caused harm.

> The shortcomings of ed-tech implementations in response to school closures should increase receptivity to the possibility of education futures less constructed around technology.

Understanding the educational experience of the pandemic this way will help communities approach ed-tech with a more critical lens and enable more informed, humble and balanced decision-making around future implementations of technology-mediated education. The pandemic experience and its aftermath also provide a timely reminder that technology is not always a necessary component of educational improvement. The shortcomings of ed-tech implementations in response to school closures should increase receptivity to the possibility and desirability of education futures less constructed around screens, algorithmic pathways and AI automation.

THE ARC OF TRAGEDY

Aristotle, the Greek philosopher who is credited with putting forward the first formal definition of tragedy as a type of drama, insisted that the suffering, misfortune and reversal of intention that distinguish a tragedy should lead to revelation – lessons and wisdom that the audience as well as the protagonists in the story come to recognize.

This publication used tragedy as a metaphor to reveal how the hardships and unintended consequences that attended the ed-tech deployments during the COVID-19 health crisis also contain lessons and perhaps even revelation.

Act 1 recounted the high hopes – and, arguably, hubris – circulating among proponents of ed-tech ahead of the pandemic, alongside assurances emanating from various thought leaders and organizations that digital transformations would vault education forward. These voices presented ed-tech as a remedy to many problems facing education – from expanding access to those still out of school to improving the quality and relevance of learning. When the pandemic began, there was considerable optimism that technology would assure the continuity of learning and, beyond this, pull education out of 20th century 'factory models' of schooling and move it into a future of digital and personalized learning.

Act 2 juxtaposed the promises this discourse held for ed-tech against the realities of what ed-tech delivered as a response to COVID-19 school closures. It explained how gaping digital divides prevented most young people from accessing remote learning and documented how those who were reached generally found that their education was diminished. Globally, poor learning outcomes; curtailed development of social, emotional and motor skills; and diminished physical and mental health tended to characterize the pivot from schools to exclusive reliance on ed-tech. These educational declines played out against a backdrop of other adverse effects – a sharp swing towards an increased reliance on commercial learning solutions provisioned by for-profit corporations, heightened privacy and surveillance risks as student data were tracked and harvested by ed-tech companies, and the ecological tolls of the heavy extractive industries needed to manufacture ed-tech and the resulting e-waste pollution.

The Inter-Act examined various alternative scenarios to challenge the assumption that reliance on ed-tech was the only option for responding to the educational disruptions of the pandemic. These scenarios interrogated whether overconfidence in ed-tech's potential might have prolonged school closures in some contexts. They showed how views regarding the effectiveness of prolonged school closures as a measure to protect public

health evolved over time, weakening the rationale for full reliance on remote learning. The Inter-Act further considered how the notion of 'crisis' framed the educational challenges to be addressed by ed-tech and questioned whether ed-tech is indeed, as it is often described, a pillar of educational resilience.

Act 3 returned to the experiences of ed-tech during the pandemic to identify lessons for achieving more equitable, effective and beneficial results from ed-tech. It explained the hazards of looking to technology for quick fixes to problems with deep social roots and proposed instead pursuing solutions that make richer use of the social space of schools, solutions that involve technology but are not fully reliant on or constructed around it. Various subsections clarified the importance of what is at stake in debates about heavy ed-tech reliance – from the well-being, protection and care of the youngest members of society, to the safeguarding of education as a human right, now and for generations to come. Finally, Act 3 proposed recommendations and principles to chart a new course for technology integration in education in a digital age.

REORIENTING AND STEERING THE DIGITAL TRANSFORMATION OF EDUCATION

Societies should be vigilant about the ways digital tools are reshaping education. The mobilization and application of ed-tech as a response to school closures during the COVID-19 pandemic cemented processes and logics in education that risk subverting its unique status as a human right and public good.

As this review has shown, learning that was fully or heavily reliant on digital technology often looked alarmingly dystopic: inert children staring at screens in isolation for six or more hours a day to complete compulsory education, the proliferation of corporately managed teaching and learning systems that homogenize and automate education, and flawed computer assessments of learning that influence students' future opportunities.

The education community must not merely react to technological change but seek to steer it towards desired objectives.

Going forward, the education community must not merely react to technological change but seek to steer it towards desired objectives. It is necessary to interrogate the parties and interests that benefit from different models of technology integration. Technology is a tool, but how it is used and towards what ends can vary widely. As advised by UNESCO's 2023

Global Education Monitoring Report, a crucial question to ask of ed-tech is "A tool on whose terms?"[1312]

Questions about ed-tech – its uses, misuses and non-uses – stand at the very centre of contemporary debates about education. Technology can be a powerful enabler of inclusive, equitable and high-quality education that balances the multifaceted needs of students, but it needs to be directed and integrated by teachers and others with deep knowledge of pedagogy. Determining the role ed-tech will play in education requires broad consultation and deliberation. The top-down and unilateral decisions taken at the outset of the pandemic should give way to more open decision-making processes that invite ideas from parents, school leaders and, of course, learners themselves.

> Technology does not have a monopoly on educational innovation, nor on the future of education.

While this publication calls critical attention to ed-tech, it is simultaneously a call to infuse more ambition and imagination into questions about what humans can do to strengthen and revitalize the essential aims of education. Technology does not have a monopoly on educational innovation, nor on the future of education. Teaching and learning can and often do advance without moving digital technology to the core of these vital enterprises.

Moderating expectations for what is achievable with ed-tech invites people to look away from screens and towards each other, reasserting their human agency to improve education both with and without technology.

WORKS CITED

This publication contains three lists of works cited.

The first list provides sources for information contained in the narrative text of the publication. It includes over 1,300 sources and uses a standard numerical system of citation.

The second list provides the sources for the 'voices from the ground' — quotes from people who directly experienced ed-tech modes of teaching and learning, as well as from various experts, leaders, thinkers and other individuals. These quotes, numbering over 200, are peppered throughout the publication and use a Roman numeral system of citation.

The third list provides sources for the data used to create the 26 figures contained in the publication. The cited sources correspond directly to the figure numbers.

WORKS CITED

Narrative text

1. Tawil, S. & West, M. 2020. February 28. The world has been moving learning to digital portals for decades. The coronavirus just turned it into a sprint. UNESCO. https://en.unesco.org/futuresofeducation/ideas-lab/moving-learning-digital-portals.

2. *EdTech: Focus on Higher Education*. 2022. About us. https://edtechmagazine.com/higher/about-us. (Accessed 30 November 2022.)

3. Torchia, R. 2022, January 20. New Adobe product simplifies digital design. *EdTech: Focus on Higher Education*. https://edtechmagazine.com/k12/article/2022/01/new-adobe-product-simplifies-digital-design.

4. Stone, A. 2022, March 15. Is dated technology contributing to the great teacher resignation? *EdTech: Focus on Higher Education*. https://edtechmagazine.com/k12/article/2022/03/dated-technology-contributing-great-teacher-resignation.

5. CDW. 2022. About CDW. https://www.cdw.com/content/cdw/en/about/overview.html. (Accessed 30 November 2022.)

6. The EdTech Fund. 2022. About. http://www.theedtechfund.com/about/. (Accessed 30 November 2022.)

7. Williamson, B. 2020, September 15. Edtech index investing. *Code Acts in Education*. https://codeactsineducation.wordpress.com/2020/09/15/edtech-index-investing/.

8. Frankenfield, J. 2022, September 28. What Is EdTech? Definition, example, pros & cons. *Investopedia*. https://www.investopedia.com/terms/e/edtech.asp.

9. Weller, M. 2018, July 2. Twenty years of Edtech. *EDUCAUSE Review*. https://er.educause.edu/articles/2018/7/twenty-years-of-edtech.

10. See *Educational Technology and Society*. https://www.j-ets.net/; *Educational Technology Research and Development*. https://www.springer.com/journal/11423/aims-and-scope; *British Journal of Educational Technology*. https://bera-journals.onlinelibrary.wiley.com/journal/14678535.

11. See *Learning, Media and Technology*. https://www.tandfonline.com/toc/cjem20/current; *Computers and Education*. https://www.sciencedirect.com/journal/computers-and-education.

12. Nicolai, S. 2019, October 9. Introducing the EdTech Hub. EdTech Hub. https://edtechhub.org/2019/10/09/introducing-the-edtech-hub/.

13. Edwards, S. 2019, June 19. Ed tech research hub launched. Devex. https://www.devex.com/news/sponsored/ed-tech-research-hub-launched-95129.

14. Kennedy, K. 2019, June 25. UK government launches global Edtech Hub. The Pie News. https://thepienews.com/news/118082/.

15. EdTech Hub. 2022. Our team. https://edtechhub.org/our-team/. (Accessed 2 September 2022.)

16. Kay, S. 2020, October 10. New report calls for dedicated 'Office for Edtech' to drive change. *Schools Week*. https://schoolsweek.co.uk/new-report-calls-for-dedicated-office-for-edtech-to-drive-change/.

17. Office of Educational Technology. 2022. Meet the OET team. https://tech.ed.gov/team/. (Accessed 2 September 2022.)

18. Ministry of Education Singapore. 2022. Educational technology plan. http://www.moe.gov.sg/education-in-sg/educational-technology-journey/edtech-plan. (Accessed 2 September 2022.)

19. See, for example, the website of the Federal Ministry of Education, Nigeria. https://education.gov.ng/. (Accessed 2 September 2022.)

20. UNICEF. 2022, March 1. UNICEF and Extreme Tech Challenge announce strategic partnership to advance the future of learning. Press release. https://www.unicef.org/innovation/press-releases/unicef-and-extreme-tech-challenge-announce-strategic-partnership-advance-future.

21. Muster, H. 2017, September 13. Was ist EdTech (Educational Technology) und wie kommt sie zum Einsatz? [What is EdTech (Educational Technology) and how is it used?]. PINKTUM. https://www.pinktum.com/de/blog/edtech-educational-technology-und-was-dahinter-steckt/.

22. Morozov, E. 2014. *To Save Everything, Click Here: The Folly of Technological Solutionism*. New York: Public Affairs.

23. UNESCO. 2022. COVID-19 Recovery. Education: From school closure to recovery. Monitoring of school closures https://en.unesco.org/covid19/educationresponse. (Accessed 29 June 2022.)

24. UNESCO. 2021, March 19. One year into COVID-19 education disruption: Where do we stand? https://en.unesco.org/news/one-year-covid-19-education-disruption-where-do-we-stand.

25. UNICEF. 2021, September 16. Around 2 in 3 children are still out of the classroom in Latin America and the Caribbean. Press release. https://www.unicef.org/press-releases/around-2-3-children-are-still-out-classroom-latin-america-and-caribbean.

26. World Health Organization. 2030, May 5. WHO Director-General's opening remarks at the media briefing – 5 May 2023. https://www.who.int/news-room/speeches/item/who-director-general-s-opening-remarks-at-the-media-briefing---5-may-2023.

27. UNESCO. 2022. Global monitoring of school closures caused by COVID-19 pandemic. https://covid19.uis.unesco.org/global-monitoring-school-closures-covid19/.

28. Evans, D., Hares, S., Mendez Acosta, A. & Saintis, C. 2021, February 10. It's been a year since schools started to close due to COVID-19. Center for Global Development. Blog post. https://www.cgdev.org/blog/its-been-year-schools-started-close-due-covid-19.

29. World Bank. 2020, December 6. Learning losses from COVID-19 could cost this generation of students close to $17 trillion in lifetime earnings. Press release. https://www.worldbank.org/en/news/press-release/2021/12/06/learning-losses-from-covid-19-could-cost-this-generation-of-students-close-to-17-trillion-in-lifetime-earnings.

30. World Bank, UNESCO, UNICEF, USAID, FCDO, & Bill & Melinda Gates Foundation. 2022. *The State of Global Learning Poverty*. https://www.unicef.org/media/122921/file/State%20of%20Learning%20Poverty%202022.pdf.

31. World Health Organization. 2022, July 23. WHO Director-General declares the ongoing monkeypox outbreak a Public Health Emergency of International Concern. Press release. https://www.who.int/europe/news/item/23-07-2022-who-director-general-declares-the-ongoing-monkeypox-outbreak-a-public-health-event-of-international-concern.

32. Vartabedian, M. 2020, March 19. Ed-tech startups and investors shift into overdrive amid coronavirus crisis. *Wall Street Journal*. https://www.wsj.com/articles/ed-tech-startups-and-investors-shift-into-overdrive-amid-coronavirus-crisis-11584615601.

33. Credit Suisse in partnership with the Financial Times Commercial department. 2020. Education is having its 'Netflix' moment as a result of the coronavirus pandemic. *Financial Times*. https://www.ft.com/partnercontent/credit-suisse/education-is-having-its-netflix-moment-as-a-result-of-the-coronavirus-pandemic.html. (Accessed 30 November 2022.)

34. Ruehl, M., Jack, A. & Riordan, P. 2020, March 18. Coronavirus proves a bonanza for Asia edtech start-ups. *Financial Times*. https://www.ft.com/content/879ba44b-fa16-4a9d-afa4-f7f4e149edec.

35. Sydow, L. 2020. Mobile Minute: Global classrooms rely on education apps as remote learning accelerates. App Annie. Blog post. https://www.appannie.com/en/insights/mobile-minute/education-apps-grow-remote-learning-coronavirus/. (Accessed 30 November 2022.)

36. Li, C. & Lalani, F. 2020, April 29. The COVID-19 pandemic has changed education forever. This is how. World Economic Forum. https://www.weforum.org/agenda/2020/04/coronavirus-education-global-covid19-online-digital-learning/.

37. Lazare, M. 2021, February 17. A peek at what's next for Google Classroom. Google Education. Blog post. https://blog.google/outreach-initiatives/education/classroom-roadmap/.

38. *THE Journal*. 2021, September 9. Ed tech use continues growth beyond the peak of the pandemic. https://thejournal.com/articles/2021/09/09/ed-tech-use-accelerates-beyond-the-peak-of-the-pandemic.aspx.

39. Chandran, S. 2020, October 24. The surge of EdTech startups in the Middle East amidst a pandemic. Global EdTech. https://global-edtech.com/the-surge-of-edtech-startups-in-the-middle-east-amidst-a-pandemic/.

40. Giannini, S. 2020, May 15. Distance learning denied. Global Education Monitoring (GEM) Report. https://gemreportunesco.wordpress.com/2020/05/15/distance-learning-denied/.

41. Tyack, D.B. & Cuban, Larry. 1995. *Tinkering toward Utopia: A Century of Public School Reform*. Cambridge, MA: Harvard University Press.

42. Watters, A. 2021. *Teaching Machines: The History of Personalized Learning*. Cambridge, MA: MIT Press.

43. Smith, F.J. 1913, July 9. The evolution of the motion picture: VI – Looking into the future with Thomas A. Edison. *New York Dramatic Mirror*. New York (Old Fulton). http://www.laviemoderne.net/images/forum_pics/2017/20171116%20New%20York%20NY%20Dramatic%20Mirror%201913%20Mar-Apr%201914%20Grayscale%20-%200690.pdf.

44. Watters, A. 2021. *Teaching Machines: The History of Personalized Learning*. Cambridge, MA: MIT Press.

45. Ames, M.G. 2019. *The Charisma Machine: The Life, Death, and Legacy of One Laptop per Child*. Cambridge, MA: MIT Press.

46. Papert, S. 1981. *Mindstorms: Children, Computers and Powerful Ideas*. New York: Basic Books.

47. Ibid.

48. Christensen, C.M., Horn, M.B. & Johnson, C.W. 2008. *Disrupting Class: How Disruptive Innovation Will Change the Way the World Learns*. New York: McGraw-Hill.

49. Pappano, L. 2012, November 2. The year of the MOOC. *New York Times*. https://www.nytimes.com/2012/11/04/education/edlife/massive-open-online-courses-are-multiplying-at-a-rapid-pace.html.

50. Tyack, D.B. & Cuban, Larry. 1995. *Tinkering toward Utopia: A Century of Public School Reform*. Cambridge, MA: Harvard University Press.

51. Mullaney, T.S., Peters, B., Hicks, M. & Philip, K. (eds). 2021. *Your Computer is on Fire*. Cambridge, MA: MIT Press.

52. UNESCO. 2018. *A Lifeline to Learning: Leveraging Mobile Technology to Support Education for Refugees*. UNESCO. https://unesdoc.unesco.org/ark:/48223/pf0000261278.

53. Davis, R.A., Conroy, J.C. & Clague, J. 2020. Schools as factories: The limits of a metaphor. *Journal of Philosophy of Education*, 54(5): 1471–1488. https://doi.org/10.1111/1467-9752.12525.

54. Tally, B. 2007. Digital technology and the end of social studies education. *Theory & Research in Social Education*, 35(2): 305–321. https://doi.org/10.1080/00933104.2007.10473337.

55. Mitra, S. & Rana, V. 2001. Children and the Internet: Experiments with minimally invasive education in India. *British Journal of Educational Technology*, 32: 221–232. https://doi.org/10.1111/1467-8535.00192.

56. Mitra, S. 2013. Build a school in the cloud. TED Talks. https://www.ted.com/talks/sugata_mitra_build_a_school_in_the_cloud.

57. Mitra, S. 2000. Minimally invasive education for mass computer literacy. Paper presented as the CRIDALA 2000 conference, Hong Kong, 21–25 June. https://www.researchgate.net/publication/228356449_Minimally_invasive_education_for_mass_computer_literacy.

58. Hole-in-the-Wall Education Ltd. About HiWEL: Beginnings. https://web.archive.org/web/20071013033113/http://www.hole-in-the-wall.com/Beginnings.html.

59. Reuters. 2009, February 17. Oscar favorite Slumdog Millionaire inspired by NIIT's 'Hole in the Wall' initiative. https://web.archive.org/web/20090301093437/http://www.reuters.com/article/pressRelease/idUS191330+17-Feb-2009+BW20090217.

60. Mitra, S. 2012. *Beyond the Hole in the Wall: Discover the Power of Self-Organized Learning*. Independently published.

61. *Economic Times*. 2009, February 18. Oscar favorite Slumdog Millionaire inspired by NIIT's 'Hole in the Wall' initiative. https://economictimes.indiatimes.com/oscar-favorite-slumdog-millionaire-inspired-by-niits-hole-in-the-wall-initiative/articleshow/4151133.cms.

62. Tobin, L. 2009, March 3. Slumdog professor. *The Guardian*. https://www.theguardian.com/education/2009/mar/03/professor-sugata-mitra.

63. Rajghatta, C. 2013, February 7. NRI education pioneer, Dr Sugata Mitra, wins $ 1 million TED prize. *Times of India*. https://timesofindia.indiatimes.com/nri/us-canada-news/nri-education-pioneer-dr-sugata-mitra-wins-1-million-ted-prize/articleshow/18705008.cms.

64. Mitra, S. 2013. Build a school in the cloud. TED Talks. https://www.ted.com/talks/sugata_mitra_build_a_school_in_the_cloud.

65. Mitra, S. 2009. Remote presence: Technologies for 'beaming' teachers where they cannot go. *Journal of Emerging Technologies in Web Intelligence*, 1(1): 55–59. https://www.researchgate.net/publication/42802925_Remote_Presence_Technologies_for_'Beaming'_Teachers_Where_They_Cannot_Go\.

66. Mitra, S. 2010. The child-driven education. TED Talks. https://www.ted.com/talks/sugata_mitra_the_child_driven_education.

67. TED. 2022. History of TED. https://www.ted.com/about/our-organization/history-of-ted. (Accessed 30 November 2022.)

68. Robinson, K. 2006. Do schools kill creativity? TED Talks. https://www.ted.com/talks/sir_ken_robinson_do_schools_kill_creativity.

69. Robinson, K. 2013. How to escape education's death valley. TED Talks. https://www.ted.com/talks/sir_ken_robinson_how_to_escape_education_s_death_valley.

70. TED. 2022. Sugata Mitra: Education researcher. https://www.ted.com/speakers/sugata_mitra. (Accessed 30 November 2022.)

71. See TED. Search results for 'education'. https://www.ted.com/search?q=education. (Accessed 30 November 2022.)

72. Mitra, S. 2013. Build a school in the cloud. TED Talks. https://www.ted.com/talks/sugata_mitra_build_a_school_in_the_cloud.

73. Wilson, J. 2013, June 11. Filmmaker to make documentary about TED Prize winner Sugata Mitra. TED. Blog post. https://blog.ted.com/filmmaker-to-make-documentary-about-ted-prize-winner-sugata-mitra/.

74. Jerry Rothwell. 2018, August 30. *The School in the Cloud (2018)*. https://jerryrothwell.com/2018/08/30/theschoolinthecloud/.

75. Mitra, S. 2019. *The School in the Cloud: The Emerging Future of Learning*. London: SAGE Publishing.

76. Davis, R.A., Conroy, J.C. & Clague, J. 2020. Schools as factories: The limits of a metaphor. *Journal of Philosophy of Education*, 54(5): 1471–1488. https://doi.org/10.1111/1467-9752.12525.

77. Arora, P. 2010, May. Hope-in-the-Wall? A digital promise for free learning. British Journal of Educational Technology, 41(5). https://www.researchgate.net/publication/229788949_Hope-in-the-Wall_A_digital_promise_for_free_learning.

78. Warschauer, M. 2002. Reconceptualizing the digital divide. *First Monday*, 7(7). https://journals.uic.edu/ojs/index.php/fm/article/download/967/888.

79. van Cappelle, F. 2003. The darker side of the digital divide – Inequalities of opportunities in public computer usage in rural India. Master's thesis. University of Amsterdam. https://www.academia.edu/s/af9b1d15c8.

80. van Cappelle, F. & Evers, V. 2005, January. Investigating the effects of unsupervised computer use on educationally disadvantaged children's knowledge and understanding of computers. *IEEE Transactions on Pattern Analysis and Machine Intelligence (PAMI)*. https://www.researchgate.net/publication/237134201_Investigating_the_effects_of_unsupervised_computer_use_on_educationally_disadvantaged_children's_knowledge_and_understanding_of_computers.

81. van Cappelle, F. 2003. The darker side of the digital divide – Inequalities of opportunities in public computer usage in rural India. Master's thesis. University of Amsterdam. https://www.academia.edu/s/af9b1d15c8.

82. Ibarrarán, P. 2012, March 6. And the jury is back: One Laptop per Child is not enough. Inter-American Development Bank. Blog post. https://blogs.iadb.org/efectividad-desarrollo/en/and-the-jury-is-back-one-laptop-per-child-is-not-enough/.

83. Ames, M.G. 2019. *The Charisma Machine: The Life, Death, and Legacy of One Laptop per Child*. Cambridge, MA: MIT Press.

84. Trucano, M. 2012, March 23. Evaluating one laptop per child (OLPC) in Peru. World Bank Blogs. https://blogs.worldbank.org/edutech/olpc-peru2.

85. Trucano, M. 2010, April 30. Worst practice in ICT use in education. World Bank Blogs. https://blogs.worldbank.org/edutech/worst-practice.

86. Cuban, L. 2013, March 18. No end to magical thinking when it comes to high-tech schooling. Larry Cuban on School Reform and Classroom Practice. Blog post. https://larrycuban.wordpress.com/2013/03/18/no-end-to-magical-thinking-when-it-comes-to-high-tech-schooling/.

87. UNESCO. 2020. *UNESCO COVID-19 Education Response: Education Sector Issue Notes*. Issue note no. 7.1–April 2020. https://unesdoc.unesco.org/ark:/48223/pf0000373275.

88. Anderson, J. 2020, March 29. The coronavirus pandemic is reshaping education. Quartz. https://qz.com/1826369/how-coronavirus-is-changing-education/.

89. Misk Foundation. 2020. *The Impact of COVID-19 on Saudi Youth*. https://misk.org.sa/wp-content/uploads/2021/12/Misk-covid-report.pdf.

90. Google for Education. 2018. *Future of the Classroom: Emerging trends in the K-12 Education*. https://services.google.com/fh/files/misc/future_of_the_classroom_emerging_trends_in_k12_education.pdf.

91. Lieberman, M. 2020, June 2. Like it or not, K-12 schools are doing a digital leapfrog during COVID-19. *Education Week*. https://www.edweek.org/technology/like-it-or-not-k-12-schools-are-doing-a-digital-leapfrog-during-covid-19/2020/06.

92. Fearn, N. 2021, March 8. Remote learning shows the power of the cloud to transform education. *Financial Times*. https://www.ft.com/content/3596847e-a981-42c0-8a6c-bc1c52d5cf04.

93. Pearson. 2020. *The Global Learner Survey: August 2020*. https://plc.pearson.com/sites/pearson-corp/files/Pearson_Global-Learners-Survey_2020_FINAL.pdf.

94. UNESCO. 2020. *UNESCO COVID-19 Education Response: Education Sector Issue Notes*. Issue note no. 2.5 - June 2020. https://unesdoc.unesco.org/ark:/48223/pf0000373815.

95. Mehmood, F. 2021. *Covid-19: Bridging the Digital Divide in Education*. Centre for Human Rights. https://cfhr.com.pk/wp-content/uploads/2022/01/Covid-19-Bridging-the-Digital-Divide-in-Education-CFHR-Report-2022.pdf.

96. ITU Publications. 2020. *Measuring Digital Development: Facts and Figures 2020*. https://www.itu.int/en/ITU-D/Statistics/Documents/facts/FactsFigures2020.pdf.

97. Mizunoya, S. et al. 2020. *How Many Children and Young People Have Internet Access at Home? Estimating Digital Connectivity During the COVID-19 Pandemic*. UNICEF & ITU. https://data.unicef.org/resources/children-and-young-people-internet-access-at-home-during-covid19/.

98. UNESCO. 2021. *When Schools Shut: Gendered Impacts of COVID-19 School Closures*. https://unesdoc.unesco.org/ark:/48223/pf0000379270.

99. Crawfurd, L. 2020, May 18. Why the COVID crisis is not edtech's moment in Africa. Center for Global Development. Blog post. https://www.cgdev.org/blog/why-covid-crisis-not-edtechs-moment-africa.

100. Uwezo. 2020. *Are Our Children Learning? The Status of Remote-Learning among School-Going Children in Kenya During the Covid-19 Crisis*. Usawa Agenda. https://www.humanitarianresponse.info/sites/www.humanitarianresponse.info/files/documents/files/are_our_children_learning_-_remote_learning_-_uwezo_usawa-agenda-2020-report_1.pdf.

101. ITU Publications. 2021. *Digital Trends in Africa 2021: Information and Communication Technology Trends and Developments in the Africa Region, 2017-2020*. https://www.itu.int/dms_pub/itu-d/opb/ind/D-IND-DIG_TRENDS_AFR.01-2021-PDF-E.pdf.

102. Le Nestour, A., Mbaye, S. & Moscoviz, L. 2020, *Phone survey on the COVID crisis in Senegal*. Harvard Dataverse. https://doi.org/10.7910/DVN/9XE95F/95RW9C.

103. Le Nestour, A. & Moscoviz, L. 2020, April 24. Five findings from a new phone survey in Senegal. Center for Global Development. Blog post. https://www.cgdev.org/blog/five-findings-new-phone-survey-senegal.

104. Human Rights Watch. 2020, August 26. Impact of Covid-19 on children's education in Africa. 35th ordinary session. https://www.hrw.org/news/2020/08/26/impact-covid-19-childrens-education-africa#_edn6.

105. del Ninno, C. & Mills, B. 2015. *Safety Nets in Africa: Effective Mechanisms to Reach the Poor and Most Vulnerable*. Washington, DC: World Bank. https://elibrary.worldbank.org/doi/abs/10.1596/978-1-4648-0435-9.

106. Sarangapani, P., Thirumalai, B., Ramanathan, A., Kumar, R. & Ramchand, M. 2021. *No Teacher, No Class: State of the Education Report for India, 2021*. UNESCO Office in New Delhi. https://unesdoc.unesco.org/ark:/48223/pf0000379115.

107. von Lautz-Cauzanet, E. 2022. EdTech: Why the project-based approach must change in order to contribute to system resilience. *PROSPECTS*, 51: 573–581. https://doi.org/10.1007/s11125-021-09580-8.

108. World Bank. 2020, December 2. COVID-19 prompts urgency of bridging digital divide in Central Asia. Press release. https://www.worldbank.org/en/news/press-release/2020/12/02/urgency-of-bridging-digital-divide-in-central-asia-increases-as-a-result-of-the-covid-19-pandemic.

109. Low, J., Dujacquier, D. & Kaur, S. 2021, February. *Bridging the Digital Divide: Improving Digital Inclusion in Southeast Asia*. Roland Berger. https://www.rolandberger.com/en/Insights/Publications/Bridging-the-digital-divide.html.

110. Mizunoya, S. et al. 2020. *How Many Children and Young People Have Internet Access at Home? Estimating Digital Connectivity During the COVID-19 Pandemic*. UNICEF and ITU. https://data.unicef.org/resources/children-and-young-people-internet-access-at-home-during-covid19/.

111. Figure calculated by UNESCO based on ITU data. See Giannini, S. 2020, May 15. Distance learning denied. Global Education Monitoring (GEM) Report. https://gemreportunesco.wordpress.com/2020/05/15/distance-learning-denied/.

112. Chandra, S. et al. 2020. *Closing the K–12 Digital Divide in the Age of Distance Learning*. Common Sense & Boston Consulting Group. https://www.commonsensemedia.org/sites/default/files/featured-content/files/common_sense_media_report_final_7_1_3pm_web.pdf.

113. Montacute, R. & Cullinane, C. 2021, January 21. *Learning in Lockdown*. The Sutton Trust. https://www.suttontrust.com/our-research/learning-in-lockdown/.

114. UNESCO. 2020, October 16. Why the world must urgently strengthen learning and protect finance for education. https://en.unesco.org/news/why-world-must-urgently-strengthen-learning-and-protect-finance-education.

115. Human Rights Watch. 2021, May 17. "Years Don't Wait for Them": Increased Inequalities in Children's Right to Education Due to the Covid-19 Pandemic. https://www.hrw.org/report/2021/05/17/years-dont-wait-them/increased-inequalities-childrens-right-education-due-covid.

116. Langthaler, M. 2021, March. Lessons from COVID 19: Digitalization calls for strong public education systems. NORRAG. https://resources.norrag.org/resource/638/lessons-from-covid-19-digitalization-calls-for-strong-public-education-systems-by-margarita-langthaler.

117. Giannini, S. 2020, May 15. Distance learning denied. Global Education Monitoring (GEM) Report. https://gemreportunesco.wordpress.com/2020/05/15/distance-learning-denied/.

118. Aedo, C., Nahata, V. & Sabarwal, S. 2020, November 10. The remote learning paradox: How governments can truly minimize COVID-related learning losses. World Bank Blogs. https://blogs.worldbank.org/education/remote-learning-paradox-how-governments-can-truly-minimize-covid-related-learning-losses.

119. Chang, V. 2020, August 25. Tablet sales boosted by Covid-19 pandemic lockdown measures. *Straits Times*. https://www.straitstimes.com/tech/tablets/tablet-sales-boosted-by-pandemic-lockdown-measures.

120. Alliance for Affordable Internet. 2020. *From Luxury to Lifeline: Reducing the Cost of Mobile Devices to Reach Universal Internet Access*. World Wide Web Foundation. https://webfoundation.org/research/from-luxury-to-lifeline-reducing-the-cost-of-mobile-devices-to-reach-universal-internet-access/.

121. Ofman, D. 2020, November 19. Siberian student scales birch tree for internet access as classes move online. The World. https://theworld.org/stories/2020-11-19/siberian-student-scales-birch-tree-internet-access-classes-move-online.

122. Dvorak, P. 2020, August 27. When 'back to school' means a parking lot and the hunt for a WiFi signal. *Washington Post*. https://www.washingtonpost.com/local/when-back-to-school-means-a-parking-lot-and-the-hunt-for-a-wifi-signal/2020/08/27/0f785d5a-e873-11ea-970a-64c73a1c2392_story.html.

123. Brown, M. 2020, September 1. Photo of kids forced to use Taco Bell WiFi for homework is startling reminder that many families have no internet. Parents. https://www.parents.com/news/photo-of-kids-using-taco-bell-wifi-is-a-startling-reminder-of-the-digital-divide/.

124. Reneau, A. 2020, April 15. School districts are transforming buses into WiFi hotspots for students without internet. Upworthy. https://www.upworthy.com/school-buses-become-wifi-hotspots-for-students.

125. UNICEF. 2020. COVID-19: Are children able to continue learning during school closures? Factsheet. https://data.unicef.org/resources/remote-learning-reachability-factsheet/.

126. Reynard, M. 2020, November 4. L'éducation en situations de crise: Rapport de la délégation suisse présenté par le conseiller national Mathias Reynard [Education in crisis situations: Report of the Swiss delegation presented by national councillor Mathias Reynard]. Committee on Education, Communication and Cultural Affairs and Network of Young Parliamentarians. http://apf.francophonie.org/IMG/pdf/rapport_sur_l_education_en_situations_de_crise.pdf.

127. Esquivel, P., Blume, H., Poston, B. & Barajas, J. 2020, August 13. A generation left behind? Online learning cheats poor students, Times survey finds. *Los Angeles Times*. https://www.latimes.com/california/story/2020-08-13/online-learning-fails-low-income-students-covid-19-left-behind-project.

128. USA Facts. 2020, June 4. 4.4 million households with children don't have consistent access to computers for online learning during the pandemic. https://usafacts.org/articles/internet-access-students-at-home/#.

129. Villamil, S. et al. 2021, June 26. 1+1=4? Latin America confronts a pandemic education crisis. *New York Times*. https://www.nytimes.com/2021/06/26/world/americas/latin-america-pandemic-education.html.

130. Trucano, M. 2020, April 2. How ministries of education work with mobile operators, telecom providers, ISPs and others to increase access to digital resources during COVID19-driven school closures (Coronavirus). World Bank Blogs. https://blogs.worldbank.org/education/how-ministries-education-work-mobile-operators-telecom-providers-isps-and-others-increase.

131. Telecom Regulatory Authority of India. 2020, March 29. Subject: Measures regarding ensuring availability of recharge vouchers and payment options for prepaid services. Letter. https://www.medianama.com/wp-content/uploads/TRAI-Prepaid-Letter.pdf.

132. Bhandari, V. 2020, August. *Improving Internet Connectivity during Covid-19*. Digital Pathways at Oxford. Paper series 4. https://pathwayscommission.bsg.ox.ac.uk/sites/default/files/2020-09/improving_internet_connectivity_during_covid-19_0.pdf.

133. Cellular Operators Association of India. 2020, April 9. Subject: Measures regarding ensuring availability of recharge vouchers and payment options for prepaid services. Letter. https://www.medianama.com/wp-content/uploads/Ltr-to-TRAI-on-Connectivity-to-Prepaid-susbcribers-Final.pdf.pdf.

134. Bhandari, V. 2020, August. *Improving Internet Connectivity during Covid-19*. Digital Pathways at Oxford. Paper series 4. https://pathwayscommission.bsg.ox.ac.uk/sites/default/files/2020-09/improving_internet_connectivity_during_covid-19_0.pdf.

135. ITU Publications. 2020. *Measuring Digital Development: Facts and Figures 2020*. https://www.itu.int/en/ITU-D/Statistics/Documents/facts/FactsFigures2020.pdf.

136. Broadband Commission for Sustainable Development. 2025 targets: "Connecting the other half". ITU & UNESCO. https://broadbandcommission.org/Documents/publications/wef2018.pdf.

137. Cable.co.uk. 2022. Worldwide mobile data pricing 2022: The cost of 1GB of mobile data in 230 countries. https://www.cable.co.uk/mobiles/worldwide-data-pricing/#highlights. (Accessed 30 November 2022.)

138. Ibid.

139. Carter, S. & Moncrieff, I. 2021, May. *COVID-19 School Closures in the DRC: Impact on the Health, Protection and Education of Children and Youth*. Social Sciences Analytics Cell. https://www.unicef.org/drcongo/media/5716/file/COD-CASS-school-closures-impacts.pdf.

140. Foster, V., Comini, N. & Srinivasan, S. 2021, May 6. Improving data infrastructure helps ensure equitable access for poor people in poor countries. World Bank Blogs. https://blogs.worldbank.org/opendata/improving-data-infrastructure-helps-ensure-equitable-access-poor-people-poor-countries.

141. UNESCO. 2023. Global Education Monitoring Report 2023. Technology in Education: A Tool on Whose Terms? https://unesdoc.unesco.org/ark:/48223/pf0000385723.locale=en

142. Ibid.

143. UNESCO. 2018. *Global Education Monitoring Report 2017/8. Accountability in Education: Meeting Our Commitments*. https://en.unesco.org/gem-report/report/2017/accountability-education.

144. Amaro, D., Pandolfelli, L., Sanchez-Tapia, I. & Brossard, M. 2020, August 4. COVID-19 and education: The digital gender divide among adolescents in sub-Saharan Africa. UNICEF. https://data.unicef.org/data-for-action/covid-19-and-education-the-digital-gender-divide-among-adolescents-in-sub-saharan-africa/.

145. UNICEF. 2021. *What We Know about the Gender Digital Divide for Girls: A Literature Review*. https://www.unicef.org/eap/media/8311/file/What we know about the gender digital divide for girls: A literature review.pdf.

146. Ford, K. 2021, October 11. Addressing the gender digital divide is critical to ensure no one is left behind from COVID-19. Young Lives. https://www.younglives.org.uk/news/addressing-gender-digital-divide-critical-ensure-no-one-left-behind-covid-19.

147. Ibid.

148. Girl Effect & Vodafone Foundation. 2018. *Real Girls, Real Lives, Connected*. https://www.global.girleffect.org/stories/real-girls-real-lives-connected/.

149. UNESCO. 2021. *When Schools Shut: Gendered Impacts of COVID-19 School Closures*. https://unesdoc.unesco.org/ark:/48223/pf0000379270.

150. Organisation for Economic Co-operation and Development. 2020. *PISA 2018 Results (Volume V): Effective Policies, Successful Schools*. https://www.oecd.org/education/pisa-2018-results-volume-v-ca768d40-en.htm.

151. Munoz-Najar, A. et al. 2021. *Remote Learning During COVID-19: Lessons from Today, Principles for Tomorrow*. World Bank Group. https://documents1.worldbank.org/curated/en/160271637074230077/pdf/Remote-Learning-During-COVID-19-Lessons-from-Today-Principles-for-Tomorrow.pdf.

152. Organisation for Economic Co-operation and Development. 2020. New OECD PISA report reveals challenge of online learning for many students and schools. https://www.oecd.org/education/new-oecd-pisa-report-reveals-challenge-of-online-learning-for-many-students-and-schools.htm.

153. Organisation for Economic Co-operation and Development. 2021, June. *What's Next? Lessons on Education Recovery: Findings from a Survey of Ministries of Education amid the COVID-19 Pandemic*. https://www.oecd-ilibrary.org/docserver/697bc36e-en.pdf.

154. UNESCO. 2022. *National Distance Learning Programmes in Response to the COVID-19 Education Disruption: Case Study of the Kingdom of Saudi Arabia*. https://unesdoc.unesco.org/ark:/48223/pf0000381533.

155. Colclough, C. 2020, September. *Teaching with Tech: The Role of Education Unions in Shaping the Future*. Education International. https://issuu.com/educationinternational/docs/2020_ei_research_teachingwithtech_eng.

156. Barron, M., Cobo, C., Munoz-Najar, A. & Ciarrusta, I.S. 2021, February 18. The changing role of teachers and technologies amidst the COVID 19 pandemic: Key findings from a cross-country study. World Bank Blogs. https://blogs.worldbank.org/education/changing-role-teachers-and-technologies-amidst-covid-19-pandemic-key-findings-cross.

157. Pota, V. et al. 2021, September. *Turning to Technology: A Global Survey of Teachers' Responses to the Covid-19 Pandemic*. T4 and EdTech Hub. https://t4.education/t4-insights/reports/turning-to-technology.

158. Mehmood, F. 2021. *Covid-19: Bridging the Digital Divide in Education*. Centre for Human Rights. https://cfhr.com.pk/wp-content/uploads/2022/01/Covid-19-Bridging-the-Digital-Divide-in-Education-CFHR-Report-2022.pdf.

159. Ballotpedia. 2022. Lawsuits about state actions and policies in response to the coronavirus (COVID-19) pandemic. https://ballotpedia.org/Lawsuits_about_state_actions_and_policies_in_response_to_the_coronavirus_(COVID-19)_pandemic.

160. Vegas, E. 2020, April 14. School closures, government responses, and learning inequality around the world during COVID-19. Brookings. https://www.brookings.edu/research/school-closures-government-responses-and-learning-inequality-around-the-world-during-covid-19/.

161. Giannini, S. 2020, May 15. Distance learning denied. Global Education Monitoring GEM) Report. https://gemreportunesco.wordpress.com/2020/05/15/distance-learning-denied/.

162. Ibid.

163. Rivers, M., Suarez, K. & Gallón, N. 2020, August 27. Mexico's solution to the Covid-19 educational crisis: Put school on television. CNN. https://edition.cnn.com/2020/08/22/americas/mexico-covid-19-classes-on-tv-intl/index.html; World Bank. 2021, May 19. Thinking inside the 'box': Pakistan turns to education TV during COVID-19. https://www.worldbank.org/en/news/feature/2021/05/19/pakistan-turns-to-education-tv.

164. UNESCO, UNICEF & World Bank. 2020, October. *What Have We Learnt? Overview of Findings from a Survey of Ministries of Education on National Responses to COVID-19*. https://tcg.uis.unesco.org/wp-content/uploads/sites/4/2020/10/National-Education-Responses-to-COVID-19-WEB-final_EN.pdf.

165. Brookings. 2020, September 14. Beyond reopening: A leapfrog moment to transform education? https://www.brookings.edu/events/beyond-reopening-a-leapfrog-moment-to-transform-education/.

166. Transcript of Brookings webinar. 2020, September 14. Beyond reopening: A leapfrog moment to transform education? Available at https://www.brookings.edu/wp-content/uploads/2020/09/global_20200914_reopening_education_transcript.pdf.

167. Mullan, J. & Taddese, A. 2020. *Edtech in Sierra Leone: A Rapid Scan*. EdTech Hub. https://docs.edtechhub.org/lib/C5MWWQI2/download/SL8ULFEM/Mullan_Taddese_2020_EdTech%20in%20Sierra%20Leone.pdf.

168. Rauf, D. 2020, April 16. Coronavirus squeezes supply of Chromebooks, iPads, and other digital learning devices. *Education Week*. https://www.edweek.org/education-industry/coronavirus-squeezes-supply-of-chromebooks-ipads-and-other-digital-learning-devices/2020/04.

169. Ericsson. 2021. *This is 5G*. https://www.ericsson.com/49f1c9/assets/local/5g/documents/07052021-ericsson-this-is-5g.pdf.

170. Thales Group. 2021, April 5. 5G technology and networks (speed, use cases, rollout). https://www.thalesgroup.com/en/markets/digital-identity-and-security/mobile/inspired/5G.

171. Calculations enabled by https://www.broadbandgenie.co.uk/broadband/help/broadband-download-time-speed-calculator. These results are theoretical and do not take into account a variety of factors that influence actual download speeds, such as network location, the distance to nearby masts, the amount of congestion, and so on.

172. Kirkpatrick, D. 2016, September 12. Google: 53% of mobile users abandon sites that take over 3 seconds to load. *Marketing Dive*. https://www.marketingdive.com/news/google-53-of-mobile-users-abandon-sites-that-take-over-3-seconds-to-load/426070/.

173. ITU Publications. 2021. *Measuring Digital Development: Facts and Figures 2021*. https://www.itu.int/en/ITU-D/Statistics/Documents/facts/FactsFigures2021.pdf.

174. Ericsson. 2020. *Ericsson Mobility Report*. https://www.ericsson.com/4adc87/assets/local/reports-papers/mobility-report/documents/2020/november-2020-ericsson-mobility-report.pdf.

175. CBC Radio. 2018, November 2. Bad algorithms are making racist decisions. https://www.cbc.ca/radio/spark/412-1.4887497/bad-algorithms-are-making-racist-decisions-1.4887504.

176. Gilliard, C. 2017. Pedagogy and the logic of platforms. *EDUCAUSE Review*, 52(4): 64–65. https://er.educause.edu/articles/2017/7/pedagogy-and-the-logic-of-platforms.

177. Tibken, S. 2021, June 28. The broadband gap's dirty secret: Redlining still exists in digital form. CNET. https://www.cnet.com/features/the-broadband-gaps-dirty-secret-redlining-still-exists-in-digital-form/.

178. CBC Radio. 2018, November 2. Bad algorithms are making racist decisions. https://www.cbc.ca/radio/spark/412-1.4887497/bad-algorithms-are-making-racist-decisions-1.4887504.

179. Access Now. 2021. #KeepItOn: Fighting internet shutdowns around the world. https://www.accessnow.org/keepiton/. (Accessed 30 November 2022.)

180. Kumar, A. 2019, December 19. Shutting down the Internet to shut up critics. Human Rights Watch. https://www.hrw.org/news/2019/12/19/shutting-down-internet-shut-critics.

181. Nadaf, A.H. 2021. 'Lockdown within a lockdown': The 'digital redlining' and paralyzed online teaching during COVID-19 in Kashmir, a conflict territory. *Communication, Culture and Critique*, 14(2): 343–346. https://doi.org/10.1093/ccc/tcab019.

182. Global Coalition to Protect Education from Attack. 2022. The Safe Schools Declaration. https://ssd.protectingeducation.org/safe-schools-declaration-and-guidelines-on-military-use/.

183. Estes, A.C. 2020, March 25. Why the internet (probably) won't break during the coronavirus pandemic. Vox. https://www.vox.com/recode/2020/3/25/21188391/internet-surge-traffic-coronavirus-pandemic.

184. ITU Publications. 2021, October. *Connect2Recover: A methodology for identifying Connectivity Gaps and Strengthening Resilience in the New Normal.* https://www.itu.int/dms_pub/itu-d/opb/tnd/D-TND-04-2021-PDF-E.pdf.

185. British Telecommunications. 2020, March 20. The facts about our network and Coronavirus. https://newsroom.bt.com/the-facts-about-our-network-and-coronavirus/.

186. Telefonica. 2021, July 7. The value of connectivity and open internet. https://www.telefonica.com/en/communication-room/blog/the-value-of-connectivity-and-open-internet/.

187. Kang, C., Alba, D. & Satariano, A. 2020, March 26. Surging traffic is slowing down our internet. *New York Times*. https://www.nytimes.com/2020/03/26/business/coronavirus-internet-traffic-speed.html.

188. Ibid.

189. Organisation for Economic Co-operation and Development. 2020, May 4. Keeping the internet up and running in times of crisis. https://www.oecd.org/coronavirus/policy-responses/keeping-the-internet-up-and-running-in-times-of-crisis-4017c4c9/.

190. Kang, C., Alba, D. & Satariano, A. 2020, March 26. Surging traffic is slowing down our internet. *New York Times*. https://www.nytimes.com/2020/03/26/business/coronavirus-internet-traffic-speed.html.

191. Orange. 2021, January 19. Orange takes a leading role in the US to Europe route with two new generation submarine cables linking the East Coast to France. https://internationalcarriers.orange.com/en/news/orange-takes-a-leading-role-in-the-us-to-europe-route-with-two-new-generation-submarine-cables-linking-the-east-coast-to-france.html.

192. Federal Communications Commission. 2020, March 15. FCC grants T-Mobile temporary spectrum access during coronavirus. Press release. https://www.fcc.gov/document/fcc-grants-t-mobile-temporary-spectrum-access-during-coronavirus.

193. ITU & UNESCO. 2020, September. *The State of Broadband 2020: Tackling Digital Inequalities – A Decade for Action.* https://www.itu.int/hub/publication/s-pol-broadband-21-2020/.

194. Gallup Pakistan. 2020. National opinion poll on support and opposition for remote (online) education. https://gallup.com.pk/post/29335.

195. Malhotra, S. 2020, May 15. DU exams 2020: Our survey finds 85% students against online exams, 76% don't have study material in Delhi University. DU EXPRESS. https://duexpress.in/du-exams-2020-our-survey-finds-85-students-against-online-exams-76-dont-have-study-material-in-delhi-university/.

196. TEQSA. 2020. *Foundations for Good Practice: The Student Experience of Online Learning in Australian Higher Education During the COVID-19 Pandemic.* Australian Government. Tertiary Education Quality and Standards Agency. https://www.teqsa.gov.au/sites/default/files/student-experience-of-online-learning-in-australian-he-during-covid-19.pdf.

197. DeSantis, R. 2020, September 3. 2 Calif. students get internet hotspot after viral tweet showed them using Taco Bell's free WiFi. *People*. https://people.com/human-interest/calif-students-internet-hotspot-taco-bells-wifi/.

198. Hannon, T. 2021, May 19. FCC approves school bus Wi-Fi hotspots under COVID-19 emergency connectivity fund. *School Transportation News*. https://stnonline.com/news/fcc-approves-school-bus-wi-fi-hotspots-under-covid-19-emergency-connectivity-fund/.

199. Oxford University Press. 2021. *Addressing the Deepening Digital Divide*. https://oup.foleon.com/report/digital-divide/cover/.

200. Ibid.

201. Russell, N. 2020, July 27. I can't keep doing this. Please open the schools. *The Atlantic*. https://www.theatlantic.com/ideas/archive/2020/07/please-open-schools/614605/; Harris, E.A. 2020, April 27. 'It was just too much': How remote learning is breaking parents. *New York Times*. https://www.nytimes.com/2020/04/27/nyregion/coronavirus-homeschooling-parents.html; Moscardino, U., Dicataldo, R., Roch, M., Carbone, M. & Mammarella, I.C. 2021. Parental stress during COVID-19: A brief report on the role of distance education and family resources in an Italian sample. *Current Psychology*, 40(11). https://link.springer.com/article/10.1007/s12144-021-01454-8; Calvano, C., Engelke, L., Di Bella, J., Kindermann, J., Renneberg, B. & Winter S.M.2022. Families in the COVID-19 pandemic: Parental stress, parent mental health and the occurrence of adverse childhood experiences-results of a representative survey in Germany. *European Child & Adolescent Psychiatry*. 31(7). https://link.springer.com/article/10.1007/s00787-021-01739-0.

202. Li, G. et al. 2020, August. Education and EdTech during COVID-19: Evidence from a large-scale survey during school closures in China. Rural Education Action Program. Working paper. https://fsi-live.s3.us-west-1.amazonaws.com/s3fs-public/education_and_edtech_during_covid-19-final-08032020.pdf.

203. Rozelle, S., Rahimi, H., Wang, H. & Dill, E. 2020, March 30. Lockdowns are protecting China's rural families from COVID-19, but the economic burden is heavy. International Food Policy Research Institute. Blog post. https://www.ifpri.org/blog/lockdowns-are-protecting-chinas-rural-families-covid-19-economic-burden-heavy.

204. Gao, N., Lafortune, J. & Hill, L. 2020, October. *Who is Losing Ground with Distance Learning in California?* Public Policy Institute of California. https://www.ppic.org/wp-content/uploads/who-is-losing-ground-with-distance-learning-in-california-october-2020.pdf.

205. Moyer, M.W. 2020, July 22. Pods, microschools and tutors: Can parents solve the education crisis on their own? *New York Times*. https://www.nytimes.com/2020/07/22/parenting/school-pods-coronavirus.html.

206. Zweig, D. 2020, July 30. $25,000 pod schools: How well-to-do children will weather the pandemic. *New York Times*. https://www.nytimes.com/2020/07/30/nyregion/pod-schools-hastings-on-hudson.html.

207. Tysons Reporter. 2020, August 19. Poll: What do you think of 'learning pods' for kids? https://www.tysonsreporter.com/2020/08/19/poll-what-do-you-think-of-learning-pods-for-kids/.

208. Goodnough, A. 2020, August 14. Families priced out of 'learning pods' seek alternatives. *New York Times*. https://www.nytimes.com/2020/08/14/us/covid-schools-learning-pods.html.

209. *India Today*. 2021, October 8. Why are students moving from private schools to government schools amidst Covid-19? https://www.indiatoday.in/education-today/news/story/students-moving-from-private-schools-to-government-schools-1858123-2021-10-08.

210. Cukier, A. 2021, October 1. Families continue to jump to private school amid the pandemic. *Globe and Mail*. https://www.theglobeandmail.com/featured-reports/article-families-continue-to-jump-to-private-school-amid-the-pandemic/.

211. Musaddiq, T., Stange, K., Bacher-Hicks, A. & Goodman, J. 2021, September. The pandemic's effect on demand for public schools, homeschooling, and private schools. Working paper. Education Policy Initiative and Wheelock Education Policy Center. https://edpolicy.umich.edu/sites/epi/files/2021-09/Pandemics%20Effect%20Demand%20Public%20Schools%20Working%20Paper%20Final%20%281%29.pdf.

212. Associated Press. 2020, October 20. Coronavirus pandemic widens learning gap in education-obsessed South Korea. CNBC. https://www.cnbc.com/2020/10/21/pandemic-widens-learning-gap-in-education-obsessed-south-korea.html.

213. Dudley, T. 2020, August 18. *College Marketing in the COVID-19 Economy*. The Century Foundation. https://tcf.org/content/report/college-marketing-covid-19-economy/.

214. North Star Marketing. 2021. Stories of recruitment success during the pandemic. https://www.northstarmarketing.com/how-to-pivot-your-private-school-marketing-strategy-during-crisis/. (Accessed 1 December 2022.)

215. Chen, L., Dorn, E., Sarakatsannis, J. & Wiesinger, A. 2021, March 1. Teacher survey: Learning loss is global—and significant. McKinsey & Company. https://www.mckinsey.com/industries/education/our-insights/teacher-survey-learning-loss-is-global-and-significant.

216. Sullivan, P. 2020, October 9. Private schools hold new attraction for rich parents. *New York Times*. https://www.nytimes.com/2020/10/09/your-money/private-schools-wealthy-parents.html.

217. Dickler, J. 2020, November 8. Families jump to private schools as coronavirus drags on. CNBC. https://www.cnbc.com/2020/11/08/coronavirus-why-families-are-jumping-to-private-schools.html.

218. Graham, R. 2021, October 19. Christian schools boom in a revolt against curriculum and pandemic rules. *New York Times*. https://www.nytimes.com/2021/10/19/us/christian-schools-growth.html.

219. Goudeau, S., Sanrey, C., Stanczak, A., Manstead, A. & Darnon, C. 2021. Why lockdown and distance learning during the COVID-19 pandemic are likely to increase the social class achievement gap. *Nature Human Behaviour*, 5(10): 1273–1281. https://doi.org/10.1038/s41562-021-01212-7.

220. Andrew, A. et al. 2020. Inequalities in children's experiences of home learning during the COVID-19 lockdown in England. *Fiscal Studies*, 41(3). https://onlinelibrary.wiley.com/doi/10.1111/1475-5890.12240; Pota, V. et al. 2021, September. *Turning to Technology: A Global Survey of Teachers' Responses to the Covid-19 Pandemic*. T4 and EdTech Hub. https://t4.education/t4-insights/reports/turning-to-technology.

221. Lareau, A. 1989. *Home Advantage: Social Class and Parental Intervention in Elementary Education*. Philadelphia, PA: Falmer Press.

222. Brady, L. et al. 2020, December 31. 7 ways for teachers to truly connect with parents. *Education Week*. https://www.edweek.org/leadership/opinion-7-ways-for-teachers-to-truly-connect-with-parents/2020/12.

223. Ahmed, Q.W., Rönkä, A. & Perälä-Littunen, S. 2021. Parental involvement or interference? Rural teachers' perceptions. *Education Research International*, 2021. https://doi.org/10.1155/2021/3182822.

224. Maldonado, J. & De Witte, K. 2021. The effect of school closures on standardised student test. *British Educational Research Journal*, 48(1): 49–94. https://doi.org/10.1002/berj.3754.

225. Andreu, S. et al. 2020, November. *Évaluations 2020 Repères CP, CE1 : premiers résultats, Document de travail [2020 assessments CP, CE1 benchmarks: First results]*. Ministère de l'éducation nationale et de la jeunesse. https://www.education.gouv.fr/evaluations-2020-reperes-cp-ce1-premiers-resultats-307122.

226. Engzell, P., Frey, A. & Verhagen, M. 2020, October 29. Learning loss due to school closures during the COVID-19 pandemic. *PNAS*, 118(17). https://doi.org/10.1073/pnas.2022376118.

227. Reddy, V., Soudien, C. & Winnaar, L. 2020, May 5. Impact of school closures on education outcomes in South Africa. The Conversation. https://theconversation.com/impact-of-school-closures-on-education-outcomes-in-south-africa-136889.

228. Domingue, B., Hough, H., Lang, D. & Yeatman, J. 2021, March. Changing patterns of growth in oral reading fluency during the COVID-19 pandemic. Policy Analysis for California Education. https://edpolicyinca.org/publications/changing-patterns-growth-oral-reading-fluency-during-covid-19-pandemic.

229. Andrew, A. et al. 2020. Inequalities in children's experiences of home learning during the COVID-19 lockdown in England. *Fiscal Studies*, 41(3). https://onlinelibrary.wiley.com/doi/10.1111/1475-5890.12240.

230. Montacute, R. 2020, April. *Social Mobility and Covid-19: Implications of the Covid-19 Crisis for Educational Inequality*. The Sutton Trust. https://dera.ioe.ac.uk/35323/2/COVID-19-and-Social-Mobility-1.pdf.

231. Dorn, E., Hancock, B., Sarakatsannis, J. & Viruleg, E. 2020, June 1. COVID-19 and student learning in the United States: The hurt could last a lifetime. McKinsey & Company. https://www.mckinsey.com/industries/education/our-insights/covid-19-and-student-learning-in-the-united-states-the-hurt-could-last-a-lifetime.

232. Tobisch, A. & Dresel, M. 2017. Negatively or positively biased? Dependencies of teachers' judgments and expectations based on students' ethnic and social backgrounds. *Social Psychology of Education*, 20(4): 731–752. https://doi.org/10.1007/s11218-017-9392-z.

233. Goudeau, S., Sanrey, C., Stanczak, A., Manstead, A. & Darnon, C. 2021. Why lockdown and distance learning during the COVID-19 pandemic are likely to increase the social class achievement gap. *Nature Human Behaviour*, 5(10): 1273–1281. https://doi.org/10.1038/s41562-021-01212-7.

234. Diliberti, M. & Kaufman, J. 2020. *Will this School Year Be Another Casualty of the Pandemic? Key Findings from the American Educator Panels Fall 2020 COVID-19 Surveys*. RAND Corporation. https://www.rand.org/pubs/research_reports/RRA168-4.html.

235. Bol, T. 2020, April 30. Inequality in homeschooling during the Corona crisis in the Netherlands. First results from the LISS Panel. *SocArXiv*. https://doi.org/10.31235/osf.io/hf32q.

236. Barrot, J.S., Llenares, I.I. & Del Rosario, L.S. 2021. Students' online learning challenges during the pandemic and how they cope with them: The case of the Philippines. *Education and Information Technologies*, 26(6): 1–18. https://pubmed.ncbi.nlm.nih.gov/34075300.

237. Blaskó, Z. & Schnepf, S. 2021. Educational inequalities in Europe and physical school closures during Covid-19. *European Commission* Knowledge for Policy. https://knowledge4policy.ec.europa.eu/publication/educational-inequalities-europe-physical-school-closures-during-covid-19_en.

238. Mervosh, S. & Wu, A. 2022, October 24. Math scores fell in nearly every state, and reading dipped on national exam. *New York Times*. https://www.nytimes.com/2022/10/24/us/math-reading-scores-pandemic.html.

239. Li, G. et al. 2020, August. Education and EdTech during COVID-19: Evidence from a large-scale survey during school closures in China. Rural Education Action Program. Working paper. https://fsi-live.s3.us-west-1.amazonaws.com/s3fs-public/education_and_edtech_during_covid-19-final-08032020.pdf.

240. Crew, M. 2021. *Literature Review on the Impact of COVID-19 on Families, and Implications for the Home Learning Environment*. National Literacy Trust. https://cdn.literacytrust.org.uk/media/documents/Updated_COVID-19_Literature_Review.pdf.

241. Brown, N., Riele, K., Shelley, B. & Woodroffe, J. 2020, April. *Learning at Home during COVID-19: Effects on Vulnerable Young Australians: Independent Rapid Response Report*. Peter Underwood Centre for Educational Attainment, University of Tasmania. https://www.utas.edu.au/__data/assets/pdf_file/0008/1324268/Learning-at-home-during-COVID-19-updated.pdf.

242. Baltimore City Public Schools. 2020, November 2. City Schools announces list of additional small group in-person learning sites. Press release. https://www.baltimorecityschools.org/node/1339.

243. Tamez-Robledo, N. 2021, January 11. Schools are a lifeline for homeless students. COVID-19 is severing the connection. EdSurge. https://www.edsurge.com/news/2021-01-11-schools-are-a-lifeline-for-homeless-students-covid-19-is-severing-the-connection.

244. Racheva, V. 2018, December. Social aspects of synchronous virtual learning environments. *AIP Conference Proceedings*, 2048 (1). https://doi.org/10.1063/1.5082050.

245. Lin, X. & Gao, L. 2020. Students' sense of community and perspectives of taking synchronous and asynchronous online courses. *Asian Journal of Distance Education*, 15(1): 169–179. https://eric.ed.gov/?id=EJ1289947.

246. Cacioppo, J.T. & Hawkley, L.C. 2009. Perceived social isolation and cognition. *Trends in Cognitive Sciences*, 13(10): 447–454. https://www.sciencedirect.com/science/article/pii/S1364661309001478.

247. Wong, B. 2020, September 17. How remote learning has changed the nature of school bullying. HuffPost. https://www.huffpost.com/entry/bullying-problem-remote-learning_l_5f61214fc5b68d1b09c8dc16.

248. Wohlheiter, K. 2020, November 11. Online school and bullying – Know the signs and how to prevent it. Nemours Children's Health. Blog post. https://blog.nemours.org/2020/11/online-school-and-bullying-know-the-signs-and-how-to-prevent-it/.

249. Yasar, K. 2021, March 26. Does Zoom notify me if someone takes a screenshot? MUO. https://www.makeuseof.com/does-zoom-notify-screenshot/.

250. Help Your Teen Now. 2021, March 24. Recognizing if cyberbullying is happening over Zoom classes. Blog post. https://helpyourteennow.com/cyberbullying-in-online-zoom-classes/.

251. Ghallager, R. 2020, December 17. Best practices for securing your virtual classroom. Zoom. Blog post. https://blog.zoom.us/best-practices-for-securing-your-virtual-classroom/.

252. Zhou, N. 2020, December 2. Up to 50% of university students unhappy with online learning, regulator finds. *The Guardian*. https://www.theguardian.com/australia-news/2020/dec/02/up-to-50-of-university-students-unhappy-with-online-learning-regulator-finds.

253. Thai PBS World. 2021, June 5. School uniform filters created to help students in online class. https://www.thaipbsworld.com/school-uniform-filters-created-to-help-students-in-online-class/.

254. Iran International. 2020, September 27. Iranian parents say schools pressuring girls to wear hijab in online classes. https://old.iranintl.com/en/iran-in-brief/iranian-parents-say-schools-pressuring-girls-wear-hijab-online-classes.

255. Will, M. 2020, October 20. Most educators require kids to turn cameras on in virtual class, despite equity concerns. *Education Week*. https://www.edweek.org/teaching-learning/most-educators-require-kids-to-turn-cameras-on-in-virtual-class-despite-equity-concerns/2020/10.

256. Ibid.

257. Nicandro, V., Khandelwal, A. & Weitzman, A. 2020, June 1. Please, let students turn their videos off in class. *Stanford Daily*. https://www.stanforddaily.com/2020/06/01/please-let-students-turn-their-videos-off-in-class/.

258. Castelli, F.R. & Sarvary, M.A. 2021. Why students do not turn on their video cameras during online classes and an equitable and inclusive plan to encourage them to do so. *Ecology and Evolution, 11(8): 3565–3576*. https://www.ncbi.nlm.nih.gov/pmc/articles/PMC8057329/.

259. Cornell University. Detailed breakdown of 2021-2022 estimated cost of attendance. Financial Aid. https://finaid.cornell.edu/detailed-breakdown-of-estimated-cost-attendance.

260. World Health Organization. 2011. *World Report on Disability*. https://www.who.int/publications/i/item/9789241564182.

261. United Nations. 2022. Factsheet on persons with disabilities. Department of Economic and Social Affairs. https://www.un.org/development/desa/disabilities/resources/factsheet-on-persons-with-disabilities.html. (Accessed 1 December 2022.)

262. UNESCO. 2020, June 23. UNESCO report on inclusion in education shows 40% of poorest countries did not provide specific support to disadvantaged learners during COVID-19 crisis. Press release. https://en.unesco.org/news/unesco-report-inclusion-education-shows-40-poorest-countries-did-not-provide-specific-support.

263. National School Boards Association. 2019, April 1. Data on disabilities. https://www.nsba.org:443/ASBJ/2019/April/Graduation-Rates-Students-Disabilities.

264. Richler, D. 2004. *Quality Education for Persons with Disabilities*. UNESCO. https://unesdoc.unesco.org/ark:/48223/pf0000146694.

265. World Bank. 2017. Education: Children with disabilities are being left behind, says World Bank/GPE report. Press release. https://www.worldbank.org/en/news/press-release/2017/12/01/children-with-disabilities-are-being-left-behind.

266. Collins, B. 2018, August 29. Online education is a disability rights issue. *Inside Higher Ed*. https://www.insidehighered.com/digital-learning/views/2018/08/29/online-education-disability-rights-issue-lets-treat-it-way-opinion.

267. World Health Organization 2021, November 24. Disability and health. Press release. https://www.who.int/news-room/fact-sheets/detail/disability-and-health.

268. Morris, A. & Anthes, E. 2021, August 23. For some college students, remote learning is a game changer. *New York Times*. https://www.nytimes.com/2021/08/23/health/covid-college-disabilities-students.html.

269. United Nations. 2020, May. *Policy Brief: A Disability-Inclusive Response to COVID-19*. https://unsdg.un.org/sites/default/files/2020-05/Policy-Brief-A-Disability-Inclusive-Response-to-COVID-19.pdf.

270. UNICEF. 2020, December. *Children with Disabilities: Ensuring Their Inclusion in COVID-19 Response Strategies and Evidence Generation*. https://data.unicef.org/resources/children-with-disabilities-ensuring-inclusion-in-covid-19-response/.

271. Ibid.

272. Nowicki, J. 2020, November 19. *Distance Learning: Challenges Providing Services to K-12 English Learners and Students with Disabilities During COVID-19*. United States Government Accountability Office. https://www.gao.gov/products/gao-21-43.

273. Department of Education. 2021, June. *Education in a Pandemic: The Disparate Impacts of COVID-19 on America's Students*. Office for Civil Rights. https://www2.ed.gov/about/offices/list/ocr/docs/20210608-impacts-of-covid19.pdf.

274. UK Government. 2021, August 24. [Withdrawn] Coronavirus (COVID-19): guidance for care staff supporting adults with learning disabilities and autistic adults. https://www.gov.uk/government/publications/covid-19-supporting-adults-with-learning-disabilities-and-autistic-adults/coronavirus-covid-19-guidance-for-care-staff-supporting-adults-with-learning-disabilities-and-autistic-adults.

275. Tokatly Latzer, I., Leitner, Y. & Karnieli-Miller, O. 2021. Core experiences of parents of children with autism during the COVID-19 pandemic lockdown. *Autism*, 25(4): 1047–1059. https://journals.sagepub.com/doi/full/10.1177/1362361320984317.

276. Mbukwa-Ngwira, J. et al. 2021, March 19. Impact of COVID-19 on the education of children with disabilities in Malawi: Results from a survey with parents. Education and Development Forum. https://www.ukfiet.org/2021/impact-of-covid-19-on-the-education-of-children-with-disabilities-in-malawi-results-from-a-survey-with-parents/.

277. Tancredi, H. 2020. Consulting Students with Disability: A Practice Guide for Educators and Other Professionals. Queensland University of Technology Centre for Inclusive Education. https://research.qut.edu.au/c4ie/wp-content/uploads/sites/281/2022/02/Practice_Guides_Student_Consultation.pdf.

278. UNICEF. 2020, December. *Children with Disabilities: Ensuring Their Inclusion in COVID-19 Response Strategies and Evidence Generation*. https://data.unicef.org/resources/children-with-disabilities-ensuring-inclusion-in-covid-19-response/.

279. McClain-Nhlapo, C. 2020, May 11. An inclusive response to COVID-19: Education for children with disabilities. Global Partnership for Education. https://www.globalpartnership.org/blog/inclusive-response-covid-19-education-children-disabilities.

280. UNICEF. 2020, December 3. UNICEF calls for inclusion of children and young persons with disabilities. Press release. https://uzbekistan.un.org/en/104300-unicef-calls-inclusion-children-and-young-persons-disabilities.

281. West, M., Kraut, R. & Chew, H.E. 2019. *I'd Blush if I Could: Closing Gender Divides in Digital Skills through Education*. EQUALS Skills Coalition & UNESCO. https://unesdoc.unesco.org/ark:/48223/pf0000367416.

282. ITU Publications. 2021, July. Bridging the gender divide. https://www.itu.int/en/mediacentre/backgrounders/Pages/bridging-the-gender-divide.aspx.

283. West, M., Kraut, R. & Chew, H.E. 2019. *I'd Blush if I Could: Closing Gender Divides in Digital Skills through Education*. EQUALS Skills Coalition & UNESCO. https://unesdoc.unesco.org/ark:/48223/pf0000367416; Webb, D., Barringer, K., Torrance, R. & Mitchell, J. 2020. *Girls' Education and EdTech: A Rapid Evidence Review*. EdTech Hub. https://docs.edtechhub.org/lib/CZBRW85R.

284. West, M., Kraut, R. & Chew, H.E. 2019. *I'd Blush if I Could: Closing Gender Divides in Digital Skills through Education*. EQUALS Skills Coalition & UNESCO. https://unesdoc.unesco.org/ark:/48223/pf0000367416.

285. Portillo, J., Garay, U., Tejada, E. & Bilbao, N. 2020. Self-perception of the digital competence of educators during the COVID-19 Pandemic: A cross-analysis of different educational stages. *Sustainability*, 12(23): 101–128. https://doi.org/10.3390/su122310128; Loziak, A., Fedaková, D. & Čopková, R. 2020. Work-related stressors of female teachers during Covid-19 school closure. *Journal of Women's Entrepreneurship and Education*, 3–4: 59–78. https://www.library.ien.bg.ac.rs/index.php/jwee/article/view/1304.

286. World Wide Web Foundation. 2015. *Women's Rights Online: Translating Access into Empowerment*. https://webfoundation.org/research/womens-rights-online-2015/.

287. West, M., Kraut, R. & Chew, H.E. 2019. *I'd Blush if I Could: Closing Gender Divides in Digital Skills through Education*. EQUALS Skills Coalition & UNESCO. https://unesdoc.unesco.org/ark:/48223/pf0000367416.

288. Accenture. 2016. *Cracking the Gender Code: Get 3x More Women in Computing*. https://www.accenture.com/_acnmedia/PDF-150/Accenture-Cracking-The-Gender-Code-Report.pdf.

289. West, M., Kraut, R. & Chew, H.E. 2019. *I'd Blush if I Could: Closing Gender Divides in Digital Skills through Education*. EQUALS Skills Coalition & UNESCO. https://unesdoc.unesco.org/ark:/48223/pf0000367416.

290. UNESCO Institute for Lifelong Learning. 2015, September 16. Pink phone, Cambodia. https://uil.unesco.org/case-study/effective-practices-database-litbase-0/pink-phone-cambodia.

291. West, M., Kraut, R. & Chew, H.E. 2019. *I'd Blush If I Could: Closing Gender Divides in Digital Skills through Education*. EQUALS Skills Coalition & UNESCO. https://unesdoc.unesco.org/ark:/48223/pf0000367416.

292. Fisher, A. & Margolis, J. 2002. Unlocking the clubhouse: the Carnegie Mellon experience. *Inroads SIGCSE Bulletin*, 34(2): 79–83. https://dl.acm.org/doi/10.1145/543812.543836.

293. Girl Effect & Vodafone Foundation. 2018. *Real Girls, Real Lives, Connected*. https://www.global.girleffect.org/stories/real-girls-real-lives-connected/.

294. UNICEF. 2021. *What We Know about the Gender Digital Divide for Girls: A Literature Review*. https://www.unicef.org/eap/media/8311/file/What we know about the gender digital divide for girls: A literature review.pdf.

295. Ibid.

296. Girl Effect & Vodafone Foundation. 2018. *Real Girls, Real Lives, Connected*. https://www.global.girleffect.org/stories/real-girls-real-lives-connected/.

297. Challenge Success & NBC News. 2021, February. *Kids under Pressure: A Look at Student Well-Being and Engagement during the Pandemic*. https://challengesuccess.org/wp-content/uploads/2021/02/CS-NBC-Study-Kids-Under-Pressure-PUBLISHED.pdf.

298. ITU Publications. 2022. November 15. *ITU Facts and Figures 2022*. The gender digital divide. https://www.itu.int/itu-d/reports/statistics/2022/11/24/ff22-the-gender-digital-divide/.

299. Bluedorn, J.C., Caselli, F.G., Hansen, N.-J.H., Shibata, I. & Mendes Tavares, M. 2021, March 31. Gender and employment in the COVID-19 recession: Evidence on "she-cessions". Working paper no. 2021/095. International Monetary Fund. https://www.imf.org/en/Publications/WP/Issues/2021/03/31/Gender-and-Employment-in-the-COVID-19-Recession-Evidence-on-She-cessions-50316.

300. Tedeschi, E. 2020, October 29. The mystery of how many mothers have left work because of school closings. *New York Times*. https://www.nytimes.com/2020/10/29/upshot/mothers-leaving-jobs-pandemic.html.

301. Marte, J. 2021, October 9. Women left U.S. workforce last month, but in fewer numbers than a year ago. Reuters. https://www.reuters.com/business/women-left-us-workforce-last-month-fewer-numbers-than-year-ago-2021-10-08/.

302. Djankov, S., Zhang, Y. 2020, December 15. COVID-19 widens gender gap in labor force participation in some but not other advanced economies. Peterson Institute for International Economics. https://www.piie.com/blogs/realtime-economic-issues-watch/covid-19-widens-gender-gap-labor-force-participation-some-not.

303. International Labour Organization. 2020, November 27. Fallout of COVID-19: Working moms are being squeezed out of the labour force. https://ilostat.ilo.org/fallout-of-covid-19-working-moms-are-being-squeezed-out-of-the-labour-force/.

304. International Labour Organization. 2022, March 8. Over 2 million moms left the labour force in 2020 according to new global estimates. https://ilostat.ilo.org/over-2-million-moms-left-the-labour-force-in-2020-according-to-new-global-estimates/.

305. International Labour Organization & UNICEF. 2021. *Child Labour: Global Estimates 2020, Trends and the Road Forward*. https://www.ilo.org/wcmsp5/groups/public/---ed_norm/---ipec/documents/publication/wcms_797515.pdf.

306. International Labour Organization. 2021, June 12. How COVID-19 has accelerated child labour in the construction sector. https://www.ilo.org/africa/technical-cooperation/accel-africa/WCMS_801839/lang--en/index.htm.

307. UNESCO. 2021. *When Schools Shut: Gendered Impacts of COVID-19 School Closures*. https://unesdoc.unesco.org/ark:/48223/pf0000379270; UNICEF. 2021, June 9. Child labour rises to 160 million – first increase in two decades. Press release. https://www.unicef.org/press-releases/child-labour-rises-160-million-first-increase-two-decades.

308. Bernheim, R. & Padilla, K. 2020. *Act Now: Experiences and Recommendations of Girls and Boys in West Africa during COVID-19*. World Vision International. https://www.wvi.org/sites/default/files/2020-11/5-WV-WARO-Report-29-10-20.pdf.

309. Franceinfo Afrique. 2020, June 29. Burkina Faso: malgré le coronavirus, les enfants travaillent toujours dans la carrière de Pissy [Burkina Faso: Despite the coronavirus, children are still working in Pissy's quarry]. https://www.francetvinfo.fr/monde/afrique/burkina-faso/burkina-faso-malgre-le-coronavirus-les-enfants-travaillent-toujours-dans-la-carriere-de-pissy_4023037.html.

310. UNESCO. 2021. *When Schools Shut: Gendered Impacts of COVID-19 School Closures.* https://unesdoc.unesco.org/ark:/48223/pf0000379270.

311. International Labour Organization & UNICEF. 2021. *Child Labour: Global Estimates 2020, Trends and the Road Forward.* https://www.ilo.org/wcmsp5/groups/public/---ed_norm/---ipec/documents/publication/wcms_797515.pdf.

312. Green, F. 2020. *Schoolwork in Lockdown: New Evidence on the Epidemic of Educational Poverty. LLAKES Research Paper 67.* UCL Institute of Education and Centre for Learning and Life Chances in Knowledge Economies and Societies. https://www.llakes.ac.uk/wp-content/uploads/2021/01/67-Francis-Green-Research-Paper-combined-file.pdf.

313. Asanov, I., Flores, F., McKenzie, D., Mensmann, M. & Schulte, M. 2020, May. Remote-learning, time-use, and mental health of Ecuadorian high-school students during the COVID-19 quarantine. Working paper 9252. World Bank Group. http://documents1.worldbank.org/curated/en/328261589899308503/pdf/Remote-learning-Time-Use-and-Mental-Health-of-Ecuadorian-High-School-Studentsduring-the-COVID-19-Quarantine.pdf.

314. Asadullah, N. 2020, June 25. *COVID-19, Schooling and Learning.* BRAC Institute of Governance and Development. https://bigd.bracu.ac.bd/wp-content/uploads/2020/06/COVID-19-Schooling-and-Learning_June-25-2020.pdf.

315. Bosumtwi-Sam, C. & Kabay, S. 2020, August 19. Using data and evidence to inform school reopening in Ghana. Innovation for Poverty Action. https://www.poverty-action.org/blog/using-data-and-evidence-inform-school-reopening-ghana.

316. Gao, N., Lafortune, J. & Hill, L. 2020, October. *Who is Losing Ground with Distance Learning in California?* Public Policy Institute of California. https://www.ppic.org/wp-content/uploads/who-is-losing-ground-with-distance-learning-in-california-october-2020.pdf.

317. Cattan, S. et al. 2021, February 19. Inequalities in responses to school closures over the course of the first COVID-19 lockdown. Institute for Fiscal Studies. Working paper. https://ifs.org.uk/publications/inequalities-responses-school-closures-over-course-first-covid-19-lockdown.

318. Wößmann, L. et al. 2020. Education in the coronavirus crisis: How did schoolchildren spend their time when schools were closed, and what educational measures do the Germans advocate? *ifo Schnelldienst*, 73(9): 25–39. https://www.ifo.de/en/publikationen/2020/article-journal/education-coronavirus-crisis-how-did-schoolchildren-spend-their.

319. *The Economist*. 2020, November 24. People are working longer hours during the pandemic. https://www.economist.com/graphic-detail/2020/11/24/people-are-working-longer-hours-during-the-pandemic.

320. Andersen, S.K., Humlum, M.K. & Nandrup, A.B. 2016, June 20. Increasing instruction time in school does increase learning. *PNAS*, 113(27). https://www.pnas.org/doi/10.1073/pnas.1516686113.

321. Goldhaber, D. et al. 2022, May. *The Consequences of Remote and Hybrid Instruction During the Pandemic.* Center for Education Policy Research, Harvard University. https://cepr.harvard.edu/files/cepr/files/5-4.pdf.

322. Fitzpatrick, B.R., Berends, M., Ferrare, J.J. & Waddington, R.J. 2020. Virtual illusion: Comparing student achievement and teacher and classroom characteristics in online and brick-and-mortar charter schools. *Educational Researcher*, 49(3): 161–175. https://doi.org/10.3102/0013189X20909814; Bettinger, E. & Loeb, S. 2017, June 9. Promises and pitfalls of online education. Brookings. https://www.brookings.edu/research/promises-and-pitfalls-of-online-education/.

323. Chetty, R., Friedman, J.N., Hendren, N., Stepner, M. & The Opportunity Insights Team. 2020, June. How did Covid-19 and stabilization policies affect spending and employment? A new real-time economic tracker based on private sector data. Working paper 27431. National Bureau of Economic Research. http://www.nber.org/papers/w27431.

324. Schult, J., Mahler, M., Faut, B. & Lindner, M.A. 2021. Did students learn less during the COVID-19 pandemic? Reading and mathematics competencies before and after the first pandemic wave. *School Effectiveness and School Improvement*, 33(4): 544–563. https://doi.org/10.1080/09243453.2022.2061014.

325. Coskun, K. & Kara, C. 2022, June. The impact of the COVID-19 pandemic on primary school students' mathematical reasoning skills: A mediation analysis. *London Review of Education*, 20(1): 1–16. https://uclpress.scienceopen.com/hosted-document?doi=10.14324/LRE.20.1.19; Pier, L., Christian, M., Tymeson, H. & Meyer, R.H. 2021, June. *COVID-19 Impacts on Student Learning: Evidence from Interim Assessments in California*. Policy Analysis for California Education. https://edpolicyinca.org/publications/covid-19-impacts-student-learning.

326. Montgomery, M. 2019, September 3. This math EdTech startup says it's found a winning formula with on-demand tutoring. Forbes. https://www.forbes.com/sites/mikemontgomery/2019/09/03/this-math-edtech-says-its-found-a-winning-formula-with-on-demand-tutoring/.

327. Sawchuck, S. & Sparks, S. 2020, December 2. Kids are behind in math because of COVID-19. Here's what research says could help. *Education Week*. https://www.edweek.org/teaching-learning/kids-are-behind-in-math-because-of-covid-19-heres-what-research-says-could-help/2020/12.

328. Aldon, G., Cusi, A., Schacht, F. & Swidan, O. 2021. Teaching mathematics in a context of lockdown: A study focused on teachers' praxeologies. *Education Sciences*, 11(2). https://doi.org/10.3390/educsci11020038.

329. Ibid.

330. Engzell, P., Frey, A. & Verhagen, M. 2020, October 29. Learning loss due to school closures during the COVID-19 pandemic. *PNAS*, 118(17). https://doi.org/10.1073/pnas.2022376118.

331. Azim Premji University. 2021, February. *Loss of Learning during the Pandemic*. Field Studies in Education. https://cdn.azimpremjiuniversity.edu.in/apuc3/media/publications/downloads/Learning-Loss-during-pandemicc.f1660288401.pdf.

332. Dorn, E., Hancock, B., Sarakatsannis, J. & Viruleg, E. 2020, June 1. COVID-19 and student learning in the United States: The hurt could last a lifetime. McKinsey & Company. https://www.mckinsey.com/industries/education/our-insights/covid-19-and-student-learning-in-the-united-states-the-hurt-could-last-a-lifetime.

333. Curriculum Associates. 2020, October 5. New data from Curriculum Associates quantifies impact of COVID learning loss; raises questions about at-home testing. Press release. https://www.curriculumassociates.com/about/press-releases/2020/10/covid-learning-loss.

334. iReady & Curriculum Associates. 2021. *Academic Achievement at the End of the 2020–2021 School Year*. https://www.curriculumassociates.com/-/media/mainsite/files/i-ready/iready-understanding-student-needs-paper-spring-results-2021.pdf.

335. National Assessment of Educational Progress. 2022, November 8. Reading and mathematics scores decline during COVID-19 pandemic. https://www.nationsreportcard.gov/highlights/ltt/2022/.

336. Mervosh, S. & Wu, A. 2022, October 24. Math scores fell in nearly every state, and reading dipped on national exam. *New York Times*. https://www.nytimes.com/2022/10/24/us/math-reading-scores-pandemic.html.

337. Kamenetz, A. 2022, September 1. School is for everyone. *New York Times*. https://www.nytimes.com/2022/09/01/opinion/us-school-history.html.

338. St. George, D. 2022, September 1. American students' test scores plunge to levels unseen for decades. *Washington Post*. https://www.washingtonpost.com/education/2022/09/01/student-test-scores-plunged-pandemic/.

339. Mervosh, S. & Wu, A. 2022, October 24. Math scores fell in nearly every state, and reading dipped on national exam. *New York Times*. https://www.nytimes.com/2022/10/24/us/math-reading-scores-pandemic.html.

340. Goldhaber, D. et al. 2022, May. *The Consequences of Remote and Hybrid Instruction During the Pandemic*. Center for Education Policy Research, Harvard University. https://cepr.harvard.edu/files/cepr/files/5-4.pdf.

341. Khullar, D. 2022, September 26. Living with our pandemic trade-offs. *New Yorker*. https://www.newyorker.com/magazine/2022/09/26/living-with-our-pandemic-trade-offs.

342. Kane, T. 2022, May 22. Kids are far, far behind in school. *The Atlantic*. https://www.theatlantic.com/ideas/archive/2022/05/schools-learning-loss-remote-covid-education/629938/.

343. BusinessTech. 2021, February 22. Here are South Africa's matric results for 2020. https://businesstech.co.za/news/government/470012/here-are-south-africas-matric-results-for-2020/.

344. Vegas, E. 2022, April. *COVID-19's Impact on Learning Losses and Learning Inequality in Colombia*. Center for Universal Education at Brookings. https://www.brookings.edu/wp-content/uploads/2022/04/COVID-19s-impact-on-learning-losses_Final.pdf.

345. Ministry of Education. 2021, May 26. Estudiantes de enseñanza media no alcanzaron el 60% de los aprendizajes necesarios en 2020 [High school students did not reach 60% of the necessary learning in 2020]. https://www.mineduc.cl/en-ensenanza-media-no-se-alcanzo-el-60-de-los-aprendizajes-minimos/.

346. Hevia, F.J., Vergara-Lope, S., Velásquez-Durán, A. & Calderón, D. 2022. Estimation of the fundamental learning loss and learning poverty related to COVID-19 pandemic in Mexico. *International Journal of Educational Development*, 88. https://doi.org/10.1016/j.ijedudev.2021.102515.

347. Lichand, G., Dória, C.A., Neto, O.L. & Cossi Fernandes, J.P. 2022, May. The impacts of remote learning in secondary education: evidence from Brazil during the pandemic. *Nature Human Behaviour*, 6: 1079–1086. https://www.nature.com/articles/s41562-022-01350-6.

348. Borgonovi, F. & Ferrara, A. 2022, July 26. The effects of COVID-19 on inequalities in educational achievement in Italy. https://ssrn.com/abstract=4171968.

349. Jack, A. 2021, April 6. Invest now to repair 'huge' learning loss, educators urge. *Financial Times*. https://www.ft.com/content/b3d0cc12-61de-4143-91a6-ab9f98bbc7a9.

350. Chen, L., Dorn, E., Sarakatsannis, J. & Wiesinger, A. 2021, March 1. Teacher survey: Learning loss is global—and significant. McKinsey & Company. https://www.mckinsey.com/industries/education/our-insights/teacher-survey-learning-loss-is-global-and-significant.

351. Azevedo, J. et al. 2021. *The State of the Global Education Crisis: A Path to Recovery (Vol. 2): Executive Summary* (English). World Bank Group. http://documents.worldbank.org/curated/en/184161638768635066/Executive-Summary.

352. World Bank. 2022, June 23. *The State of Global Learning Poverty: 2022 Update*. Conference edition. https://thedocs.worldbank.org/en/doc/e52f55322528903b27f1b7e61238e416-0200022022/original/Learning-poverty-report-2022-06-21-final-V7-0-conferenceEdition.pdf.

353. McKinsey & Company. 2022, April 4. How COVID-19 caused a global learning crisis. https://www.mckinsey.com/industries/education/our-insights/how-covid-19-caused-a-global-learning-crisis.

354. Betthäuser, B.A., Bach-Mortensen, A.M. & Engzell, P. 2023, January 30. A systematic review and meta-analysis of the evidence on learning during the COVID-19 pandemic. *Nature Human Behaviour*, 7. https://doi.org/10.1038/s41562-022-01506-4.

355. Cappa, C. & Murray, C. 2021. *COVID-19: A Threat to Progress against Child Marriage*. UNICEF. https://data.unicef.org/resources/covid-19-a-threat-to-progress-against-child-marriage/.

356. International Labour Organization. 2021, June 2. An update on the youth labour market impact of the COVID-19 crisis. Briefing note. https://www.ilo.org/emppolicy/pubs/WCMS_795479/lang--en/index.htm.

357. Prothero, A. & Harwin, A. 2019, April 18. Many online charter schools fail to graduate even half of their students on time. *Education Week*. https://www.edweek.org/teaching-learning/many-online-charter-schools-fail-to-graduate-even-half-of-their-students-on-time/2019/04.

358. Hew, K.F. & Cheung, W.S. 2014. Students' and instructors' use of massive open online courses (MOOCs): Motivations and challenges. *Educational Research Review*, 12: 45–58. https://doi.org/10.1016/j.edurev.2014.05.001.

359. Reich, J. 2020. *Failure to Disrupt: Why Technology Alone Can't Transform Education*. Cambridge, MA: Harvard University Press.

360. Barbour, M.K. 2018. The landscape of K-12 online learning: Examining what is known. In Moore M.G. & Diehl, W.C. (eds). *Handbook of Distance Education*. 4th ed. New York: Routledge.

361. Escueta, M., Quan, V., Nickow, A.J. & Oreopoulos, P. 2017, August. Education technology: An evidence-based review. Working paper 23744. National Bureau of Economic Research. https://www.nber.org/papers/w23744.

362. Barbour, M.K. 2018. The landscape of K-12 online learning: Examining what is known. In Moore M.G. & Diehl, W.C. (eds). *Handbook of Distance Education*. 4th ed. New York: Routledge.

363. Mosher, R., Hartwell, A. & Brown, B. 2021, May 6. 5 factors that contribute to students finishing high school. The Conversation. https://theconversation.com/5-factors-that-contribute-to-students-finishing-high-school-155282.

364. Three Amigos. 2020, August 3. Eve Project: Excellence in virtual teaching - Results V1. https://amigos-3.com/eve-project.

365. Challenge Success & NBC News. 2021, February. *Kids under Pressure: A Look at Student Well-Being and Engagement during the Pandemic*. https://challengesuccess.org/wp-content/uploads/2021/02/CS-NBC-Study-Kids-Under-Pressure-PUBLISHED.pdf.

366. ABC News. 2021, August 13. Mexico says 5.2 million dropped out of school in pandemic. https://abcnews.go.com/International/wireStory/mexico-52-million-dropped-school-pandemic-79447998.

367. Cárdenas, S., Lomelí, D. & Ruelas, I. 2021. COVID-19 and post-pandemic educational policies in Mexico. What is at stake? In Reimers, F.M. (ed). *Primary and Secondary Education during Covid-19: Disruptions to Educational Opportunity During a Pandemic.* New York: Springer.

368. Valencia, J. 2020, October 8. Mexico City tortilla shop provides free Wi-Fi for kids to access virtual school. The World. https://theworld.org/stories/2020-10-08/mexico-city-tortilla-shop-provides-free-wi-fi-kids-access-virtual-school; Abi-Habib, M. & Lopez, O. 2022, July 18. Mexico's leader says poverty is his priority. But his policies hurt the poor. *New York Times*. https://www.nytimes.com/2022/07/18/world/americas/mexico-economy-poverty.html.

369. Cheney, C. 2021, November 1. Ed tech, long overhyped, missed its moment amid COVID-19. What now? Devex. https://www.devex.com/news/ed-tech-long-overhyped-missed-its-moment-amid-covid-19-what-now-101835.

370. Mamun, S. 2020, August 7. Covid-19: Over 45% secondary school students may drop out. *Dhaka Tribune*. https://www.dhakatribune.com/bangladesh/2020/08/07/covid-19-over-45-secondary-school-students-may-drop-out.

371. Subramanian, S. 2021, July 4. The lost year in education. Maclean's. https://www.macleans.ca/longforms/covid-19-pandemic-disrupted-schooling-impact/.

372. Ecolhuma. 2020, May. Enquête – Confinement et décrochage scolaire [Survey – Confinement and dropping out of school]. https://ecolhuma.fr/communiques/enquete-confinement-et-decrochage-scolaire/.

373. Zavala, F. et al. 2020, July 24. *Impactos de la crisis del COVID-19 en la educación y respuesta de política en Colombia [Impacts of the COVID-19 crisis on education and policy response in Colombia]*. World Bank. http://documents1.worldbank.org/curated/en/461641598291954248/pdf/Impactos-de-la-Crisis-del-Covid-19-en-la-Educacion-y-Respuestas-de-Politica-en-Colombia.pdf.

374. Inotai, E. 2021, January 19. Learning losses may lead to earning losses. Visegrad / Insight. https://visegradinsight.eu/learning-losses-may-lead-to-earning-losses/.

375. McBride, M. 2021, February 16. Sign on, Zoom in, drop out: Covid-19 sparks fears over early school leaving. *Irish Times*. https://www.irishtimes.com/news/education/sign-on-zoom-in-drop-out-covid-19-sparks-fears-over-early-school-leaving-1.4480245.

376. Chauvin, L.O. & Faiola, A. 2020, October 16. Remote learning is deepening the divide between rich and poor. *Washington Post*. https://www.washingtonpost.com/world/2020/10/16/coronavirus-peru-remote-learning-inequality/.

377. Nortajuddin, A. 2020, November 3. More school dropouts in a pandemic? *Asean Post*. https://theaseanpost.com/article/more-school-dropouts-pandemic.

378. Mlaba, K. 2020, November 25. Over 300,000 South African children may have dropped out of primary school during COVID-19. *Global Citizen*. https://www.globalcitizen.org/en/content/south-africa-children-school-drop-out-covid-19/.

379. Dowsett, S. 2020, June 23. Generation COVID: The Spanish learners lost to lockdown. Reuters. https://www.reuters.com/article/us-health-coronavirus-spain-education-in-idUSKBN23U1EP.

380. ABC7 Eyewitness News. 2022, August 16. Nearly 50,000 LAUSD students reported absent on first day of new school year. https://abc7.com/lausd-los-angeles-unified-school-district-students-superintendent/12131247/.

381. UNESCO. 2021, March 19. One year into COVID-19 education disruption: Where do we stand? https://en.unesco.org/news/one-year-covid-19-education-disruption-where-do-we-stand.

382. Center on Reinventing Public Education. 2021, July. *How Much Have Students Missed Academically Because of the Pandemic? A Review of the Evidence to Date*. University of Washington Bothell. https://crpe.org/wp-content/uploads/8_5_final_academic_impacts_report_2021.pdf.

383. Carminucci, J., Hodgman, S., Rickles, J. & Garet, M. 2021, June. *Research Brief: Student Attendance and Enrollment Loss in 2020–21*. American Institutes for Research. https://www.air.org/sites/default/files/2021-07/research-brief-covid-survey-student-attendance-june-2021_0.pdf.

384. Attendance Works & Everyone Graduates Center. 2021, February. *Using Chronic Absence to Map Interrupted Schooling, Instructional Loss and Educational Inequity*. https://www.attendanceworks.org/wp-content/uploads/2019/06/Attendance-Works-Using-Chronic-Absence-to-Map_020221.pdf.

385. National Center for Education Statistics. 2022, July 6. More than 80 percent of U.S. Public schools report pandemic has negatively impacted student behavior and socio-emotional development. Press release. https://nces.ed.gov/whatsnew/press_releases/07_06_2022.asp.

386. Ibid.

387. Malkus, N. 2022, July. *Pandemic Enrollment Fallout: School District Enrollment Changes Across COVID-19 Response*. American Enterprise Institute. https://www.aei.org/wp-content/uploads/2022/07/Pandemic-Enrollment-Fallout.pdf.

388. BR24. 2022, January 30. Schulschwänzen wegen Corona: Hunderte Bußgeldverfahren in Bayern [Truancy because of Corona: Hundreds of fines in Bavaria]. https://www.br.de/nachrichten/bayern/schulschwaenzen-wegen-corona-hunderte-bussgeldverfahren-in-bayern,SvyrF9F.

389. Sedmark, T. 2020, October 15. Fall 2020 undergraduate enrollment down 4% compared to same time last year. National Student Clearinghouse. Press release. https://www.studentclearinghouse.org/blog/fall-2020-undergraduate-enrollment-down-4-compared-to-same-time-last-year/.

390. National Student Clearinghouse Research Center. 2021, June 10. Spring 2021: Current term enrollment estimates. https://nscresearchcenter.org/current-term-enrollment-estimates/; Nietzel, N. 2021, June 10. Latest numbers show largest college enrollment decline in a decade. Forbes. https://www.forbes.com/sites/michaeltnietzel/2021/06/10/updated-numbers-show-largest-college-enrollment-decline-in-a-decade/.

391. OneClass. 2020, April 1. 75% of college students unhappy with quality of e-learning during Covid-19. Blog post. https://oneclass.com/blog/featured/177356-7525-of-college-students-unhappy-with-quality-of-elearning-during-covid-19.en.html.

392. OneClass. 2020, May 1. Will you withdraw if your current school only offers remote / e-learning option for Fall 2020. Blog post. https://oneclass.com/blog/featured/178552-will-you-withdraw-if-your-current-school-only-offers-remote-2F-e-learning-option-for-fall-2020.en.html.

393. *Japan Times*. 2022, March 20. Pandemic-related college dropouts up 40% in Japan. https://www.japantimes.co.jp/news/2022/03/02/national/pandemic-college-dropouts-2021/.

394. Rimmer, S., McGuire, K. & Gill, N. 2020, December 16. Stressed out, dropping out: COVID has taken its toll on uni students. The Conversation. https://theconversation.com/stressed-out-dropping-out-covid-has-taken-its-toll-on-uni-students-152004.

395. Vieyra Molina, A., Belden, M., de la Calle, J.R. & Martinezparente, A. 2020, July. *The Impact of the COVID-19 Pandemic on Higher Education in Mexico, Colombia and Peru*. EY-Parthenon Education. https://assets.ey.com/content/dam/ey-sites/ey-com/es_mx/topics/covid-19/ey-parthenon-educacion.pdf.

396. Hershberg, E., Flinn-Palcic, A. & Kambhu, C. 2020, June 2. *The COVID-19 Pandemic and Latin American Universities*. Center for Latin American & Latino Studies at American University. https://www.american.edu/centers/latin-american-latino-studies/upload/la-higher-ed-covid-final.pdf.

397. Vieyra Molina, A., Belden, M., de la Calle, J.R. & Martinezparente, A. 2020, July. *The Impact of the COVID-19 Pandemic on Higher Education in Mexico, Colombia and Peru*. EY-Parthenon Education. https://assets.ey.com/content/dam/ey-sites/ey-com/es_mx/topics/covid-19/ey-parthenon-educacion.pdf.

398. World Bank. 2021. *Acting Now to Protect the Human Capital of Our Children: The Costs of and Response to COVID-19 Pandemic's Impact on the Education Sector in Latin America and the Caribbean*. https://openknowledge.worldbank.org/handle/10986/35276.

399. Joung, M. 2020, August 17. Students protest tuition hikes as universities continue online. VOA News. https://www.voanews.com/a/covid-19-pandemic_students-protest-tuition-hikes-universities-continue-online/6194550.html.

400. Woo, J. 2020, July 1. Students file suit for tuition cuts as pandemic disrupts learning. Yonhap News Agency. https://en.yna.co.kr/view/AEN20200701008900315.

401. Stempel, J. 2021, June 21. Harvard defeats students' lawsuit over lack of COVID-19 tuition refunds. Reuters. https://www.reuters.com/legal/government/harvard-defeats-students-lawsuit-over-lack-covid-19-tuition-refunds-2021-06-21/.

402. Joung, M. 2020, August 17. Students protest tuition hikes as universities continue online. VOA News. https://www.voanews.com/a/covid-19-pandemic_students-protest-tuition-hikes-universities-continue-online/6194550.html.

403. House of Commons Education Committee. 2021, July 21. Strengthening Home Education: Third Report of Session 2021–22. https://committees.parliament.uk/publications/6974/documents/72808/default/.

404. *The Economist*. 2021, February 22. Covid-19 has persuaded some parents that home-schooling is better. https://www.economist.com/international/2021/02/22/covid-19-has-persuaded-some-parents-that-home-schooling-is-better.

405. Wright, A. 2022, March 3. Home schooling: A growing trend. School Governance. https://www.schoolgovernance.net.au/news/home-schooling-a-growing-trend.

406. Fitzsimmons, C. 2022, January 23. 'Sick of the disruption': Dramatic rise in children registered for home schooling. *Sydney Morning Herald*. https://www.smh.com.au/national/nsw/sick-of-the-disruption-dramatic-rise-in-children-registered-for-home-schooling-20220119-p59pfc.html.

407. Kadari-Ovadia, S. 2022, January 26. Israel sees fivefold increase in homeschooling requests over last decade. Haaretz. https://www.haaretz.com/israel-news/2022-01-26/ty-article/.premium/israel-sees-fivefold-increase-in-homeschooling-requests-over-last-decade/0000017f-db62-df9c-a17f-ff7acc870000.

408. Borthakur, P. 2020, September 2. COVID-19 pandemic ushers confidence in homeschooling culture in India. EastMojo. http://www.eastmojo.com/news/2020/09/02/covid-19-pandemic-ushers-confidence-in-homeschooling-culture-in-india/.

409. Agarwal, S. 2022, May 26. Why homeschooling is a rising trend among many parents? Issuu. https://issuu.com/agarwalsuresh/docs/1st_blog_why_homeschooling_is_a_rising_trend_among.

410. *The Economist*. 2021, February 22. Covid-19 has persuaded some parents that home-schooling is better. https://www.economist.com/international/2021/02/22/covid-19-has-persuaded-some-parents-that-home-schooling-is-better.

411. Eggleston, C. & Fields, J. 2021, March 21. Census bureau's household pulse survey shows significant increase in homeschooling rates in fall 2020. United States Census Bureau. https://www.census.gov/library/stories/2021/03/homeschooling-on-the-rise-during-covid-19-pandemic.html.

412. Ray, B.D. 2021, September 9. How many homeschool students are there in the United States? Pre-Covid-19 and post-Covid-19: New data. National Home Education Research Institute. https://www.nheri.org/how-many-homeschool-students-are-there-in-the-united-states-pre-covid-19-and-post-covid-19/.

413. ABC7 News. 2021, July 28. More parents now opting to homeschool their children. https://abc-7.com/news/national-world/2021/07/26/more-parents-now-opting-to-homeschool-their-children/.

414. Thürmann, E., Vollmer, H. & Pieper, I. 2010, November. Language(s) of schooling: Focusing on vulnerable learners. The Linguistic and Educational Integration of Children And Adolescents from Migrant Backgrounds. Language Policy Division, Council of Europe. https://rm.coe.int/16805a1caf.

415. Richards, E. 2020, May 24. Coronavirus' online school is hard enough. What if you're still learning to speak English? *USA Today*. https://eu.usatoday.com/in-depth/news/education/2020/05/14/coronavirus-online-classes-school-closures-esl-students-learn-english/5178145002/; Villegas, L. & Garcia, A. 2022, April. Educating English learners during the pandemic: Insights from experts, advocates, and practitioners. New America. https://files.eric.ed.gov/fulltext/ED619505.pdf.

416. Hearne, B. & Rodrigues, P. 2021, November. *The International Student Experience: Impact of the Covid-19 Pandemic on International Students in Ireland*. Next Steps for Teaching and Learning. https://www.researchgate.net/publication/356148792_The_International_Student_Experience_Impact_of_the_Covid-19_Pandemic_on_International_Students_in_Ireland.

417. Kim, J. 2020, December 29. Remote schooling brings bigger losses for children still learning to speak English. *New York Times*. https://www.nytimes.com/2020/12/29/world/remote-schooling-brings-bigger-losses-for-children-still-learning-to-speak-english.html.

418. Almeida, M., Challa, M., Ribeiro, M., Harrison, A.M. & Castro, M.C. 2022, May. Editorial perspective: The mental health impact of school closures during the COVID-19 pandemic. *Journal of Child Psychology and Psychiatry*, 63(5). https://www.ncbi.nlm.nih.gov/pmc/articles/PMC8657359/; Chavez Villegas, C., Peirolo, S., Rocca, M., Ipince, A. & Bakrania, S. 2021, July. Impacts of health-related school closures on child protection outcomes: A review of evidence from past pandemics and epidemics and lessons learned for COVID-19. *International Journal of Educational Development*, 84. https://www.ncbi.nlm.nih.gov/pmc/articles/PMC8132744/; Werber, C. 2015, November 6. How Ebola led to more teenage pregnancy in West Africa. Quartz. https://qz.com/africa/543354/how-ebola-led-to-more-teenage-pregnancy-in-west-africa; Rohwerder, S. 2020, February 21. Secondary impacts of major disease outbreaks in low- and middle-income countries. K4D Helpdesk Report 756. Institute of Development Studies. https://opendocs.ids.ac.uk/opendocs/bitstream/handle/20.500.12413/15129/756_Secondary_impacts_of_major_disease_outbreak_%20in_low_income_countries.pdf; Baytiyeh, H. 2018, January 29. Online learning during post-earthquake school closures. *Disaster Prevention and Management*, 27(2). https://doi.org/10.1108/DPM-07-2017-0173.

419. Madhav, N. et al. 2007. Pandemics: Risks, impacts, and mitigation. In Jameson D.T. et al. (eds). *Disease Control Priorities, Third Edition (Volume 9): Improving Health and Reducing Poverty*. World Bank Publications. Available at http://dcp-3.org/sites/default/files/chapters/DCP3%20Volume%209_Ch%2017.pdf.

420. UNICEF. 2021, January 27. Nutrition crisis looms as more than 39 billion in-school meals missed since start of pandemic – UNICEF & World Food Programme. Press release. https://www.unicef.org/press-releases/nutrition-crisis-looms-more-39-billion-school-meals-missed-start-pandemic-unicef-and.

421. Borkowski, A. et al. 2021. *COVID-19: Missing More Than a Classroom. The Impact of School Closures on Children's Nutrition*. UNICEF & World Food Programme. https://www.unicef-irc.org/publications/pdf/COVID-19_Missing_More_Than_a_Classroom_The_impact_of_school_closures_on_childrens_nutrition.pdf.

422. Bundy, D., de Silva, N., Horton, S., Jamison, D. & Patton, G. 2018. *Re-Imagining School Feeding: A High-Return Investment in Human Capital and Local Economy*. World Bank. https://docs.wfp.org/api/documents/WFP-0000116138/download/.

423. Yorke, L., Rose, P., Bayley, S., Meshesha, D.W. & Ramchandani, P. 2021. *The Importance of Students' Socio-Emotional Learning, Mental Health, and Wellbeing in the Time of COVID-19*. RISE. https://doi.org/10.35489/BSG-RISE-RI_2021/025.

424. World Health Organization. 2020, October 5. COVID-19 disrupting mental health services in most countries, WHO survey. Press release. https://www.who.int/news/item/05-10-2020-covid-19-disrupting-mental-health-services-in-most-countries-who-survey.

425. Stanistreet, P., Elfert, M. & Atchoarena, D. 2021, April. Education in the age of COVID-19: Implications for the future. *International Review of Education*, 67(1–2). https://link.springer.com/journal/11159/volumes-and-issues/67-1.

426. UNESCO, UNICEF, & World Bank. 2022. *Where Are We on Education Recovery?* https://unesdoc.unesco.org/ark:/48223/pf0000381091.

427. Ferlazzo, L. 2021, March 9. 'There is no playbook' for how to do hybrid teaching. *Education Week*. https://www.edweek.org/teaching-learning/opinion-there-is-no-playbook-for-how-to-do-hybrid-teaching/2021/03.

428. Schmidt, S. 2020, August 19. The centers helping child abuse victims have seen 40,000 fewer kids amid the pandemic. *Washington Post*. https://www.washingtonpost.com/dc-md-va/2020/08/19/child-abuse-victims-plunge-pandemic/.

429. Centers for Disease Control and Prevention. 2022, March 31. Adolescent behaviors and experiences survey (ABES). https://www.cdc.gov/healthyyouth/data/abes.htm.

430. Finkelhor, D., Turner, H.A., Shattuck, A. & Hamby, S.L. 2013. Violence, crime, and abuse exposure in a national sample of children and youth: An update. *JAMA Pediatrics*, 167(7): 614–621. https://jamanetwork.com/journals/jamapediatrics/fullarticle/1686983.

431. Barry, E. 2022, March 31. Many teens report emotional and physical abuse by parents during lockdown. *New York Times*. https://www.nytimes.com/2022/03/31/health/covid-mental-health-teens.html.

432. Pereda, N. & Díaz-Faes, D.A. 2020. Family violence against children in the wake of COVID-19 pandemic: A review of current perspectives and risk factors. *Child and Adolescent Psychiatry and Mental Health*, 14(1): 40. https://capmh.biomedcentral.com/articles/10.1186/s13034-020-00347-1.

433. Cappa, C. & Hereward, M. 2019, December 11. Fulfilling the right of street children to be counted. UNICEF Data & Analytics Section. https://data.unicef.org/data-for-action/fulfilling-the-right-of-street-children-to-be-counted/.

434. SchoolHouse Connection & Poverty Solutions at the University of Michigan. 2020. *Lost in the Masked Shuffle & Virtual Void: Children and Youth Experiencing Homelessness amidst the Pandemic*. https://schoolhouseconnection.org/wp-content/uploads/2020/11/Lost-in-the-Masked-Shuffle-and-Virtual-Void.pdf.

435. Turner, C. 2020, October 7. Homeless families struggle with impossible choices as school closures continue. NPR. https://www.npr.org/2020/10/07/920320592/an-impossible-choice-for-homeless-parents-a-job-or-their-childs-education.

436. Miao, F., Huang, R., Liu, D. & Zhuang, R. 2020. *Ensuring Effective Distance Learning during COVID-19 Disruption: Guidance for Teachers*. UNESCO. https://unesdoc.unesco.org/ark:/48223/pf0000375116.

437. Hillis, S.D. et al. 2021, July 20. Global minimum estimates of children affected by COVID-19-associated orphanhood and deaths of caregivers: a modelling study. *The Lancet*, 398(10298): 391–402. https://doi.org/10.1016/S0140-6736(21)01253-8.

438. Treglia, D. et al. 2021. *Hidden Pain: Children Who Lost a Parent or Caregiver to COVID-19 and What the Nation Can Do to Help Them*. COVID Collaborative and Social Policy Analytics. https://www.covidcollaborative.us/assets/uploads/img/HIDDEN-PAIN-FINAL.pdf.

439. Edwards, D. 2022, January 12. On Edtech, the public good, and democracy. Worlds of Education. https://www.ei-ie.org/en/item/24809:on-edtech-the-public-good-and-democracy.

440. Colclough, C. 2020, September. *Teaching with Tech: The Role of Education Unions in Shaping the Future*. Education International. https://issuu.com/educationinternational/docs/2020_ei_research_teachingwithtech_eng.

441. Human Rights Watch. 2022, May 25. *"How Dare They Peep into My Private Life?": Children's rights violations by governments that endorsed online learning during the COVID-19 pandemic*. https://www.hrw.org/report/2022/05/25/how-dare-they-peep-my-private-life/childrens-rights-violations-governments; Hooper, L., Livingstone, S. & Pothong, K. 2022. *Problems with Data Governance in UK Schools: The Cases of Google Classroom and ClassDojo*. Digital Futures Commission & 5Rights Foundation. https://digitalfuturescommission.org.uk/wp-content/uploads/2022/08/Problems-with-data-governance-in-UK-schools.pdf.

442. Rodriguez, M., Cobo, C., Muñoz-Najar, A. & Ciarrusta, I. 2021. *Remote Learning during the Global School Lockdown: Multi Country Lessons*. World Bank Group. https://documents1.worldbank.org/curated/en/668741627975171644/pdf/Remote-Learning-During-the-Global-School-Lockdown-Multi-Country-Lessons.pdf.

443. Pota, V. et al. 2021, September. *Turning to Technology: A Global Survey of Teachers' Responses to the Covid-19 Pandemic*. T4 and EdTech Hub. https://t4.education/t4-insights/reports/turning-to-technology.

444. Stanford Graduate School of Education. 2022. Learning, design and technology (LDT) MS degree. https://online.stanford.edu/programs/learning-design-and-technology-ldt-ms-degree. (Accessed 1 December 2022.)

445. Organisation for Economic Co-operation and Development. 2021. *OECD Digital Education Outlook 2021: Pushing the Frontiers with Artificial Intelligence, Blockchain and Robots*. https://doi.org/10.1787/589b283f-en.

446. De Vynck, G. 2020, April 9. Google Classroom users doubled as quarantines spread. Bloomberg. https://www.bloomberg.com/news/articles/2020-04-09/google-widens-lead-in-education-market-as-students-rush-online.

447. Mullaney, T.S., Peters, B., Hicks, M. & Philip, K. (eds). 2021. *Your Computer is on Fire*. Cambridge, MA: MIT Press.

448. Pellini, A. 2021, February 19. EdTech and Covid-19: Lessons from around the world. EdTech Hub. https://edexec.co.uk/edtech-lessons-from-around-the-world-part-two/.

449. Sil, D. 2020, August 14. Online learning platform Adda247 registers 5X revenue growth in vernacular business amid COVID-19 lockdown. *Entrepreneur India*. https://www.entrepreneur.com/article/354777.

450. Williams, S. 2020, September 30. Edtech case study: Using technology to enhance the teaching of Arabic. *New Statesman*. https://www.newstatesman.com/edtech-startup-focus/2020/09/edtech-case-study-using-technology-enhance-teaching-arabic-0.

451. Fakiya, V. 2021, August 10. How South African edtech startup, FoondaMate, is helping students study with WhatsApp. TechPoint Africa. https://techpoint.africa/2021/08/10/south-african-edtech-foondamate-whatsapp/.

452. Koenig, R. 2020, June 11. The post-pandemic outlook for edtech. EdSurge. https://www.edsurge.com/news/2020-06-11-the-post-pandemic-outlook-for-edtech.

453. LaBarre, S. 2020, September 3. Zoom is failing teachers. Here's how they would redesign it. Fast Company. https://www.fastcompany.com/90542917/zoom-is-failing-teachers-heres-how-they-would-redesign-it.

454. Zimmerman, A. & Veiga, C. 2020, May 7. NYC allows Zoom (once again) for remote learning. Chalkbeat. https://ny.chalkbeat.org/2020/5/6/21249689/nyc-schools-education-zoom-ban-reversed.

455. Yuan, E.S. 2020, April 1. A message to our users. Zoom. Blog post. https://blog.zoom.us/a-message-to-our-users/.

456. Reuters. 2020, April 30. Zoom says it has 300 million daily meeting participants, not users. https://www.reuters.com/article/us-zoom-video-commn-encryption/zoom-says-it-has-300-million-daily-meeting-participants-not-users-idUSKBN22C1T4.

457. Yuan, E.S. 2020, April 1. A message to our users. Zoom. Blog post. https://blog.zoom.us/a-message-to-our-users/.

458. Frank, R.H. 2020, June 5. Don't kid yourself: Online lectures are here to stay. *New York Times*. https://www.nytimes.com/2020/06/05/business/online-learning-winner-coronavirus.html.

459. The Learning Network. 2020, April 9. What students are saying about remote learning. *New York Times*. https://www.nytimes.com/2020/04/09/learning/what-students-are-saying-about-remote-learning.html; Sharma, K. 2020, November 12. As online classes drag on, fatigued students 'losing interest, becoming asocial', say parents. The Print. https://theprint.in/india/education/as-online-classes-drag-on-fatigued-students-losing-interest-becoming-asocial-say-parents/542253/.

460. Colclough, C. 2020, September. Teaching with Tech: *The Role of Education Unions in Shaping the Future*. Education International. https://issuu.com/educationinternational/docs/2020_ei_research_teachingwithtech_eng.

461. Mueed, A. et al. 2022. School closures help reduce the spread of COVID-19: A pre- and post-intervention analysis in Pakistan. *PLOS Global Public Health*, 2(4): e0000266. https://journals.plos.org/globalpublichealth/article?id=10.1371/journal.pgph.0000266; Liyaghatdar, Z., Pezeshkian, Z., Mohammadi-Dehcheshmeh, M. & Ebrahimie, E. 2021. Fast school closures correspond with a lower rate of COVID-19 incidence and deaths in most countries. *Informatics in Medicine Unlocked*, 27: 100805. https://www.sciencedirect.com/science/article/pii/S2352914821002720.

462. Nagata, J.M. et al. 2021. Screen time use among US adolescents during the COVID-19 pandemic: Findings from the Adolescent Brain Cognitive Development (ABCD) study. *JAMA Pediatrics*. https://jamanetwork.com/journals/jamapediatrics/fullarticle/2785686.

463. Winther, D. 2017. *How Does the Time Children Spend Using Digital Technology Impact Their Mental Well-being, Social Relationships and Physical Activity? An Evidence-focused Literature Review*. UNICEF Office of Research. https://www.unicef-irc.org/publications/925-how-does-the-time-children-spend-using-digital-technology-impact-their-mental-well.html.

464. Pandya, A. & Lodha, P. 2021. Social connectedness, excessive screen time during COVID-19 and mental health: A review of current evidence. *Frontiers in Human Dynamics*, 3: 45. https://www.frontiersin.org/article/10.3389/fhumd.2021.684137; Orben, A. & Przybylski, A.K. 2019. The association between adolescent well-being and digital technology use. *Nature Human Behaviour*, 3(2): 173–182. https://doi.org/10.1038/s41562-018-0506-1; Paulich, K.N., Ross, J., Lessem, J. & Hewitt, J. 2021. Screen time and early adolescent mental health, academic, and social outcomes in 9- and 10-year-old children: Utilizing the Adolescent Brain Cognitive Development (ABCD) study. *PLOS ONE*, 16(9). https://doi.org/10.1371/journal.pone.0256591.

465. Pandya, A. & Lodha, P. 2021. Social connectedness, excessive screen time during COVID-19 and mental health: A review of current evidence. *Frontiers in Human Dynamics*, 3. https://www.frontiersin.org/article/10.3389/fhumd.2021.684137.

466. Ibid.

467. Nagata, J.M. et al. 2021. Screen time use among US adolescents during the COVID-19 pandemic: Findings from the Adolescent Brain Cognitive Development (ABCD) study. *JAMA Pediatrics*. https://jamanetwork.com/journals/jamapediatrics/fullarticle/2785686.

468. Williams, A. 2015, September 19. Meet Alpha: The next 'next generation'. *New York Times*. https://www.nytimes.com/2015/09/19/fashion/meet-alpha-the-next-next-generation.html.

469. Bologna, C. 2019, November 8. What's the deal with Generation Alpha? Huffpost. https://www.huffpost.com/entry/generation-alpha-after-gen-z_l_5d420ef4e4b0aca341181574.

470. Qustodio. 2021, April. *Screen Time All the Time: Apps and Kids, a Year Trapped behind Screens*. https://qweb.cdn.prismic.io/qweb/da3cbc01-68b0-4e50-a18f-a9a3a0c74a72_EN_Kids+and+Apps+annual+report_20210408.pdf.

471. Ribner, A.D. et al. 2021. Screen time in the Coronavirus 2019 era: International trends of increasing use among 3- to 7-year-old children. *The Journal of Pediatrics*, 239: 59-66.e1. https://doi.org/10.1016/j.jpeds.2021.08.068.

472. Steiner-Adair, C. & Barker, T. 2014. *The Big Disconnect: Protecting Childhood and Family Relationships in the Digital Age*. New York: Harper.

473. Common Sense. 2019, October 28. The Common Sense census: Media use by tweens and teens, 2019. https://www.commonsensemedia.org/research/the-common-sense-census-media-use-by-tweens-and-teens-2019.

474. Bergmann, C. et al. 2021, May 31. Young children's screen time during the first COVID-19 lockdown in 12 countries. OSF Preprints. https://doi.org/10.31219/osf.io/p5gm4.

475. Chen, W. & Adler, J.L. 2019. Assessment of screen exposure in young children, 1997 to 2014. *JAMA Pediatrics*, 173(4): 391–393. https://doi.org/10.1001/jamapediatrics.2018.5546; Tooth, L., Moss, K., Hockey, R. & Mishra, G. 2019. Adherence to screen time recommendations for Australian children aged 0–12 years. *Medical Journal of Australia*, 211(4): 181–182. https://www.mja.com.au/journal/2019/211/4/adherence-screen-time-recommendations-australian-children-aged-0-12-years.

476. World Health Organization. 2019. *Guidelines on Physical Activity, Sedentary Behaviour and Sleep for Children under 5 Years of Age*. https://apps.who.int/iris/bitstream/handle/10665/311664/9789241550536-eng.pdf.

477. Ribner, A.D. et al. 2021. Screen time in the Coronavirus 2019 era: International trends of increasing use among 3- to 7-year-old children. *The Journal of Pediatrics*, 239: 59–66. E1. https://doi.org/10.1016/j.jpeds.2021.08.068.

478. Susilowati, I.H., Nugraha, S., Alimoeso, S. & Hasiholan, B.P. 2021. Screen time for preschool children: Learning from home during the COVID-19 pandemic. *Global Pediatric Health*, 8. https://doi.org/10.1177/2333794X211017836.

479. Seguin, D., Kuenzel, E., Morton, J.B. & Duerden, E.G. 2021. School's out: Parenting stress and screen time use in school-age children during the COVID-19 pandemic. *Journal of Affective Disorders Reports*, 6: 100217. https://www.sciencedirect.com/science/article/pii/S2666915321001438.

480. Pandya, A. & Lodha, P. 2021. Social connectedness, excessive screen time during COVID-19 and mental health: A review of current evidence. *Frontiers in Human Dynamics*, 3: 45. https://www.frontiersin.org/article/10.3389/fhumd.2021.684137.

481. Karingada, K.T. & Sony, M. 2021. Demonstration of the relationship between MSD and online learning during the COVID-19 pandemic. *Journal of Applied Research in Higher Education*. https://doi.org/10.1108/JARHE-08-2020-0269.

482. Cimberle, M. 2020, October 20. Increased digital screen time during COVID-19 may accelerate myopia epidemic. *Healio, Ophthalmology*. https://www.healio.com/news/ophthalmology/20201014/increased-digital-screen-time-during-covid19-may-accelerate-myopia-epidemic.

483. Wang, J. et al. 2021. Progression of myopia in school-aged children after COVID-19 home confinement. *JAMA Ophthalmic* 139(3):293-300. https://jamanetwork.com/journals/jamaophthalmology/fullarticle/2774808.

484. Robinson, T.N. et al. 2017. Screen media exposure and obesity in children and adolescents. *Pediatrics*, 140(2): 97–101. https://doi.org/10.1542/peds.2016-1758K.

485. King, K. 2021, February 14. Remote learning during Covid-19 is causing children to gain weight, doctors warn. *Wall Street Journal*. https://www.wsj.com/articles/remote-learning-during-covid-19-is-causing-children-to-gain-weight-doctors-warn-11613298602.

486. Mascarenhas, L. 2021, June 28. Cases of type 2 diabetes among children more than doubled during the coronavirus pandemic, research finds. CNN. https://edition.cnn.com/2021/06/25/health/diabetes-children-pandemic-wellness/index.html.

487. Stavridou, A. et al. 2021. Obesity in children and adolescents during COVID-19 pandemic. *Children*, 8(2). https://pubmed.ncbi.nlm.nih.gov/33673078/.

488. Cuschieri, S. & Grech, S. 2020. COVID-19: A one-way ticket to a global childhood obesity crisis? *Journal of diabetes and metabolic disorders*, 19(2): 1–4. https://doi.org/10.1007/s40200-020-00682-2.

489. Chaabane, S., Doraiswamy, S., Chaabna, K., Mamtani, R. & Cheema, S. 2021. The impact of COVID-19 school closure on child and adolescent health: A rapid systematic review. *Children*, 8(5). https://www.mdpi.com/2227-9067/8/5/415.

490. Schanzenbach, D. & Pitts, A. 2020, May 13. *Estimates of Food Insecurity during the COVID-19 Crisis: Results from the COVID Impact Survey, Week 1 (April 20-26, 2020)*. Institute for Policy Research Rapid Research Report. https://www.ipr.northwestern.edu/documents/reports/food-insecurity-covid_week1_report-13-may-2020.pdf.

491. Rezaeipour, M. 2020. COVID-19-related weight gain in school-aged children. Letter to the editor. *International Journal of Endocrinology and Metabolism*, 19(1). https://www.ncbi.nlm.nih.gov/pmc/articles/PMC8010564/.

492. Varea, V. & González-Calvo, G. 2020. Touchless classes and absent bodies: Reaching physical education in times of Covid-19. *Sport, Education and Society*, 26(8): 831–845. https://doi.org/10.1080/13573322.2020.1791814.

493. Piper, H., Garratt, D. & Taylor, B. 2013. Child abuse, child protection and defensive 'touch' in PE teaching and sports coaching. *Sport, Education and Society*, 18(5): 583–598. https://doi.org/10.1080/13573322.2012.735653.

494. Pierce, S. 2020, May 15. Touch starvation is a consequence of COVID-19's physical distancing. Texas Medical Center. https://www.tmc.edu/news/2020/05/touch-starvation/.

495. Kearney, R. 2021. *Touch: Recovering Our Most Vital Sense*. New York: Columbia University Press.

496. Pierce, S. 2020, May 15. Touch starvation is a consequence of COVID-19's physical distancing. Texas Medical Center. https://www.tmc.edu/news/2020/05/touch-starvation/.

497. Kearney, R. 2021. *Touch: Recovering Our Most Vital Sense*. New York: Columbia University Press.

498. Cox, S. 2020, October 6. Global study links positivity about touch to lower loneliness. Goldsmiths, University of London. https://www.gold.ac.uk/news/the-touch-test-results/.

499. Field, T. et al. 1996. Massage therapy reduces anxiety and enhances eeg pattern of alertness and math computations. *International Journal of Neuroscience*, 86(3–4): 197–205. https://doi.org/10.3109/00207459608986710.

500. Subramanian, S. 2021. *How to Feel: The Science and Meaning of Touch*. New York: Columbia University Press.

501. Ibid.

502. Akpinar, B. 2005. The effects of olfactory stimuli on scholastic performance. *The Irish Journal of Education / Iris Eireannach an Oideachais*, 36: 86–90. https://www.jstor.org/stable/30077505.

503. Kelly, C. 2021, April 27. Gaming: The next super platform. Accenture. https://www.accenture.com/us-en/insights/software-platforms/gaming-the-next-super-platform.

504. Clement, J. 2021, October 18. COVID-19 impact on the gaming industry worldwide - statistics & facts. Statista. https://www.statista.com/topics/8016/covid-19-impact-on-the-gaming-industry-worldwide/.

505. Kelly, C. 2021, April 27. Gaming: The next super platform. Accenture. https://www.accenture.com/us-en/insights/software-platforms/gaming-the-next-super-platform.

506. Ibid.

507. Ibid.

508. Drape, J. 2021, December 19. Step Aside, LeBron and Dak, and make room for Banjo and Kazooie. *New York Times*. https://www.nytimes.com/2021/12/19/sports/esports-fans-leagues-games.html.

509. Verdoodt, V., Fordyce, R., Archbold, L., Gordon, F. & Clifford, D. 2021. Esports and the platforming of child's play during covid-19. *International Journal of Children's Rights*, 29(2): 496–520. https://brill.com/view/journals/chil/29/2/article-p496_496.xml.

510. Aspen Institute. 2019, September 3. *State of Play 2019: Trends and Developments*. https://www.aspeninstitute.org/publications/state-of-play-2019-trends-and-developments/.

511. Solomon, J. 2019, August 9. Survey: Kids quit most sports by age 11. Aspen Institute Project Play. https://www.aspenprojectplay.org/national-youth-sport-survey/kids-quit-most-sports-by-age-11.

512. Baraniuk, C. 2020, October 27. They dreamed of esports glory. Then their bodies broke down. Wired. https://www.wired.co.uk/article/esports-injuries-mental-health.

513. World Health Organization. 2020, October 22. Addictive behaviours: Gaming disorder. https://www.who.int/news-room/questions-and-answers/item/addictive-behaviours-gaming-disorder.

514. Aspen Institute. 2021, October 12. Aspen Institute's Project Play report shows kids are losing programs to play sports during pandemic. https://www.aspeninstitute.org/news/press-release/state-of-play-2021/.

515. Buckley, C. 2021, August 30. China tightens limits for young online gamers and bans school night play. *New York Times*. https://www.nytimes.com/2021/08/30/business/media/china-online-games.html.

516. Ministry of Education of the People's Republic of China. 2021, March 31. 教育部办公厅关于进一步加强中小学生睡眠管理工作的通知 [Notice of the general office of the ministry of education on further strengthening the sleep management of primary and middle school students]. http://www.moe.gov.cn/srcsite/A06/s3321/202104/t20210401_523901.html; Buckley, C. 2021, August 30. China tightens limits for young online gamers and bans school night play. *New York Times*. https://www.nytimes.com/2021/08/30/business/media/china-online-games.html; Cyberspace Administration of China. 2021, August 27. 关于进一步加强"饭圈"乱象治理的通知-中共中央网络安全和信息化委员会办公室. 国家互联网信息办公室 [Notice on further strengthening the governance of chaos in the 'fan circle']. http://www.cac.gov.cn/2021-08/26/c_1631563902354584.htm; Stevenson, A., Chien, A.C. & Li, C. 2021, August 27. China's celebrity culture is raucous. The authorities want to change that. *New York Times*. https://www.nytimes.com/2021/08/27/business/media/china-celebrity-culture.html.

517. Verdoodt, V., Fordyce, R., Archbold, L., Gordon, F. & Clifford, D. 2021. Esports and the platforming of child's play during covid-19. *International Journal of Children's Rights*, 29(2): 496–520. https://brill.com/view/journals/chil/29/2/article-p496_496.xml.

518. Statista. 2022. Number of monthly active Facebook users worldwide as of 4th quarter 2021. https://www.statista.com/statistics/264810/number-of-monthly-active-facebook-users-worldwide/. (Accessed 1 December 2022.)

519. Frenkel, S., Mac, R. & Isaac, M. 2021, October 16. Instagram struggles with fears of losing its 'pipeline': Young users. *New York Times*. https://www.nytimes.com/2021/10/16/technology/instagram-teens.html.

520. Park, G. 2021, July 1. The 'metaverse' is growing. And now you can directly invest in it. *Washington Post*. https://www.washingtonpost.com/video-games/2021/07/01/metaverse-investments/.

521. Deyan, G. 2021, December 7. 21+ exciting WeChat statistics [2021 edition]. Tech Jury. Blog post. https://techjury.net/blog/wechat-statistics/#gref.

522. Ball, M. 2021, June 29. Payments, payment rails, and blockchains, and the metaverse. MatthewBall.vc. https://www.matthewball.vc/all/metaversepayments.

523. Qustodio. 2021, April. *Screen Time All the Time: Apps and Kids, a Year Trapped behind Screens*. https://qweb.cdn.prismic.io/qweb/da3cbc01-68b0-4e50-a18f-a9a3a0c74a72_EN_Kids+and+Apps+annual+report_20210408.pdf.

524. Ibid.

525. Dean, B. 2021, October 10. Roblox user and growth stats 2022. Backlinko. https://backlinko.com/roblox-users.

526. Dailey, N. 2021, December 7. Roblox has added nearly $26 billion to its market cap as metaverse mania pushes its value past brands like FedEx and Ferrari. Markets Insider. https://markets.businessinsider.com/news/stocks/roblox-more-valuable-than-fedex-ferrari-amid-metaverse-mania-2021-12.

527. Qustodio. 2021, April. *Screen Time All the Time: Apps and Kids, a Year Trapped behind Screens*. https://qweb.cdn.prismic.io/qweb/da3cbc01-68b0-4e50-a18f-a9a3a0c74a72_EN_Kids+and+Apps+annual+report_20210408.pdf.

528. Richtel, M. 2021, January 16. Children's screen time has soared in the pandemic, alarming parents and researchers. *New York Times*. https://www.nytimes.com/2021/01/16/health/covid-kids-tech-use.html.

529. Qustodio. 2021, April. *Screen Time All the Time: Apps and Kids, a Year Trapped behind Screens*. https://qweb.cdn.prismic.io/qweb/da3cbc01-68b0-4e50-a18f-a9a3a0c74a72_EN_Kids+and+Apps+annual+report_20210408.pdf.

530. Richtel, M. 2021, January 16. Children's screen time has soared in the pandemic, alarming parents and researchers. *New York Times*. https://www.nytimes.com/2021/01/16/health/covid-kids-tech-use.html.

531. Qustodio. 2021, April. *Screen Time All the Time: Apps and Kids, a Year Trapped behind Screens*. https://qweb.cdn.prismic.io/qweb/da3cbc01-68b0-4e50-a18f-a9a3a0c74a72_EN_Kids+and+Apps+annual+report_20210408.pdf.

532. Mayer, R.E. 2019, January 4. Computer games in education. *Annual Review of Psychology*, 70(1): 531–549. https://doi.org/10.1146/annurev-psych-010418-102744.

533. Schwartz, S. 2018, May 10. Decoding Fortnite: 5 things educators need to know about the hit video game. *Education Week*. https://www.edweek.org/technology/decoding-fortnite-5-things-educators-need-to-know-about-the-hit-video-game/2018/05.

534. Schwartz, S. 2018, May 31. Fortnite may be addictive, but could also promote learning, say Stanford experts. *Education Week*. https://www.edweek.org/technology/fortnite-may-be-addictive-but-could-also-promote-learning-say-stanford-experts/2018/05.

535. Haidt, J. 2022, April 11. Why the past 10 years of American life have been uniquely stupid. *The Atlantic*. https://www.theatlantic.com/magazine/archive/2022/05/social-media-democracy-trust-babel/629369/.

536. Zuboff, S. 2021, November 12. You are the object of a secret extraction operation. *New York Times*. https://www.nytimes.com/2021/11/12/opinion/facebook-privacy.html.

537. Akhtar, A. 2021, November 5. The singularity is here. *The Atlantic*. https://www.theatlantic.com/magazine/archive/2021/12/ai-ad-technology-singularity/620521/.

538. Ibid.

539. Qustodio. 2021, April. *Screen Time All the Time: Apps and Kids, a Year Trapped behind Screens*. https://qweb.cdn.prismic.io/qweb/da3cbc01-68b0-4e50-a18f-a9a3a0c74a72_EN_Kids+and+Apps+annual+report_20210408.pdf.

540. Ao, B. 2020, October 28. 'I felt like trash': How COVID-19 has affected body image in young people. *Philadelphia Inquirer*. https://www.inquirer.com/health/coronavirus/body-image-pandemic-quarantine-zoom-weight-gain-loss-20201028.html.

541. Bankhead, C. 2021, May 6. Another COVID-19 side effect: 'Zoom dysmorphia'. MedPage Today. https://www.medpagetoday.com/dermatology/generaldermatology/92463.

542. House of Commons Women and Equalities Committee. 2020. Body Image Survey Results. First Special Report of Session 2019–21. https://committees.parliament.uk/publications/2691/documents/26657/default/.

543. Czepczor-Bernat, K., Swami, V., Modrzejewska, A. & Modrzejewska, J. 2021. COVID-19-related stress and anxiety, body mass index, eating disorder symptomatology, and body image in women from Poland: A cluster analysis approach. *Nutrients*, 13(4). http://doi.org/10.3390/nu13041384.

544. Vall-Roqué, H., Andrés, A. & Saldaña, C. 2021. The impact of COVID-19 lockdown on social network sites use, body image disturbances and self-esteem among adolescent and young women. *Progress in Neuro-Psychopharmacology and Biological Psychiatry*, 110: 110293. https://www.sciencedirect.com/science/article/pii/S027858462100052X.

545. Pikoos, T.D., Buzwell, S., Sharp, G. & Rossell, S.L. 2021, December. The Zoom effect: Exploring the impact of video calling on appearance dissatisfaction and interest in aesthetic treatment during the COVID-19 pandemic. *Aesthetic Surgery Journal*, 41(12). https://doi.org/10.1093/asj/sjab257.

546. O'Sullivan, D., Duffy, C. & Jorgensen, S. 2021, October 4. Instagram promoted pages glorifying eating disorders to teen accounts. CNN. https://edition.cnn.com/2021/10/04/tech/instagram-facebook-eating-disorders/index.html.

547. Pelly, S. 2021, October 1. Whistleblower: Facebook is misleading the public on progress against hate speech, violence, misinformation. 60-minutes. CBS News. https://www.cbsnews.com/news/facebook-whistleblower-frances-haugen-misinformation-public-60-minutes-2021-10-03/.

548. Crouse, L. 2021, October 8. For teen girls, Instagram is a cesspool. *New York Times*. https://www.nytimes.com/2021/10/08/opinion/instagram-teen-girls-mental-health.html.

549. Satariano, A. & Mac, R. 2021, September 27. Facebook delays Instagram app for users 13 and younger. *New York Times*. https://www.nytimes.com/2021/09/27/technology/facebook-instagram-for-kids.html.

550. Dane, A. & Bhatia, K. 2023, March 22. The social media diet: A scoping review to investigate the association between social media, body image and eating disorders amongst young people. *PLOS Global Public Health*. https://doi.org/10.1371/journal.pgph.0001091.

551. Wolf. N. 1991. *The Beauty Myth: How Images of Female Beauty Are Used Against Women*. New York: William Morrow & Co.

552. Kearney, R. 2021. *Touch: Recovering Our Most Vital Sense*. New York: Columbia University Press.

553. Awan, H.A. et al. 2021. Internet and pornography use during the COVID-19 pandemic: Presumed impact and what can be done. *Frontiers in Psychiatry*, 12. https://www.frontiersin.org/article/10.3389/fpsyt.2021.623508.

554. Klemp, N. & Kemp, K. 2022, January 31. Decoding the so-called 'sex recession': How a partnership mindset shift may be the secret to restoring intimacy. Parent Map. https://www.parentmap.com/article/decoding-so-called-sex-recession.

555. Caltabiano, M., Castiglioni, M. & De-Rose, A. 2020. Changes in the sexual behaviour of young people: Introduction. *Genus*, 76(1): 38. https://doi.org/10.1186/s41118-020-00107-1.

556. BBC. 2020, November 9. Coronavirus: Will our day-to-day ever be the same? https://www.bbc.com/worklife/article/20201109-coronavirus-how-cities-travel-and-family-life-will-change.

557. United Nations. 2021, March 4. Mental health alert for 332 million children linked to COVID-19 lockdown policies: UNICEF. https://news.un.org/en/story/2021/03/1086372.

558. Blanshe, M. & Dahir, A.L. 2022, January 10. Uganda reopens schools after world's longest Covid shutdown. *New York Times*. https://www.nytimes.com/2022/01/10/world/africa/uganda-schools-reopen.html.

559. BR24. 2022, January 30. Schulschwänzen wegen Corona: Hunderte Bußgeldverfahren in Bayern. [Truancy because of corona: Hundreds of fines in Bavaria]. https://www.br.de/nachrichten/bayern/schulschwaenzen-wegen-corona-hunderte-bussgeldverfahren-in-bayern,SvyrF9F.

560. Biryabarema, E. 2022, January 10. Student joy, dropout heartache as Uganda reopens schools after long COVID-19 shutdown. Reuters. https://www.reuters.com/world/africa/student-joy-dropout-heartache-uganda-reopens-schools-after-long-covid-19-2022-01-10/.

561. Kakuchi, S. 2021, November 26. Student dropout rate due to COVID-19 is still rising. *University World News*. https://www.universityworldnews.com/post.php?story=202111261339042; Krishnan, M. 2022, January 8. Covid setback for schoolchildren in India as dropout rate surges. RFI. https://www.rfi.fr/en/international/20220108-covid-setback-for-schoolchildren-in-india-as-dropout-rate-surges.

562. Johnson, S. 2021, October 5. One in five 15- to 24-year-olds globally 'often feel depressed', finds Unicef. *The Guardian*. https://www.theguardian.com/global-development/2021/oct/05/one-in-five-15-to-24-year-olds-globally-often-feel-depressed-finds-unicef.

563. UNICEF. 2021. *The State of the World's Children 2021: On My Mind – Promoting, Protecting and Caring for Children's Mental Health*. https://www.unicef.org/media/114636/file/SOWC-2021-full-report-English.pdf.

564. Stiglic, N. & Viner, R.M. 2019. Effects of screentime on the health and well-being of children and adolescents: A systematic review of reviews. *BMJ Open*, 9(1). http://bmjopen.bmj.com/content/9/1/e023191.abstract.

565. Haidt, J. 2021, November 21. The dangerous experiment on teen girls. *The Atlantic*. https://www.theatlantic.com/ideas/archive/2021/11/facebooks-dangerous-experiment-teen-girls/620767/.

566. Twenge, J.M. et al. 2021. Worldwide increases in adolescent loneliness. *Journal of Adolescence*, 93: 257–269. https://pubmed.ncbi.nlm.nih.gov/34294429/.

567. Haidt, J. & Twenge, J.M. 2021, July 31. This is our chance to pull teenagers out of the smartphone trap. *New York Times*. https://www.nytimes.com/2021/07/31/opinion/smartphone-iphone-social-media-isolation.html.

568. World Health Organization. 2019, September 9. Suicide: One person dies every 40 seconds. Press release. https://www.who.int/news/item/09-09-2019-suicide-one-person-dies-every-40-seconds.

569. Kyodo News. 2021. Suicides among Japanese students hit record high in 2020. https://english.kyodonews.net/news/2021/03/a5e87a264301-suicides-among-japanese-students-hit-record-high-in-2020.html.

570. Japan Data. 2020, November 17. Suicide rate for minors highest ever in Japan. Nippon.com. https://www.nippon.com/en/japan-data/h00857/.

571. Yard, E. et al. 2021, June 11. Emergency department visits for suspected suicide attempts among persons aged 12–25 years before and during the COVID-19 pandemic — United States, January 2019–May 2021. *Morbidity and Mortality Weekly Report*, 70(24). https://stacks.cdc.gov/view/cdc/107051.

572. Wasserman, D., Iosue, M., Wuestefeld, A. & Carli V. 2020, October. Adaptation of evidence-based suicide prevention strategies during and after the COVID-19 pandemic. *World Psychiatry*, 19(3). https://onlinelibrary.wiley.com/doi/10.1002/wps.20801.

573. Bridge, J.A. 2023, February. Youth suicide during the first year of the COVID-19 pandemic. *Pediatrics*, 151(3). https://doi.org/10.1542/peds.2022-058375.

574. Ibid.

575. Centers for Disease Control and Prevention. 2022. Provisional COVID-19 deaths: Focus on ages 0-18 years. https://data.cdc.gov/NCHS/Provisional-COVID-19-Deaths-Focus-on-Ages-0-18-Yea/nr4s-juj3/data. (Accessed 12 November 2022.)

576. Cunningham, R., Walton, M., & Carter, P. 2018, December 20. The major causes of death in children and adolescents in the United States. *New England Journal of Medicine*, 369. https://www.nejm.org/doi/full/10.1056/NEJMsr1804754.

577. World Health Organization. 2020, October 23. Update 39 – What we know about COVID-19 transmission in schools. https://www.who.int/publications/m/item/update-39-what-we-know-about-covid-19-transmission-in-schools.

578. Camera, L. 2020, June 29. Pediatric group calls for children to return to schools despite Coronavirus. US News. https://www.usnews.com/news/education-news/articles/2020-06-29/pediatric-group-calls-for-children-to-return-to-schools-despite-coronavirus.

579. Racine, N. et al. 2021. Global prevalence of depressive and anxiety symptoms in children and adolescents during COVID-19: A meta-analysis. *JAMA Pediatrics*, 175(11): 1142–1150. https://doi.org/10.1001/jamapediatrics.2021.2482.

580. Luijten, M.A.J. et al. 2020. The impact of lockdown during the COVID-19 pandemic on mental and social health of children and adolescents. *Quality of Life Research*, 30: 2795–2804. https://doi.org/10.1007/s11136-021-02861-x.

581. NHS Digital. 2020, October 22. Mental health of children and young people in England, 2020: Wave 1 follow up to the 2017 survey. https://digital.nhs.uk/data-and-information/publications/statistical/mental-health-of-children-and-young-people-in-england/2020-wave-1-follow-up.

582. UNICEF. 2021, December 9. COVID-19 'biggest global crisis for children in our 75-year history' – UNICEF. Press release. https://www.unicef.org/yemen/press-releases/covid-19-biggest-global-crisis-children-our-75-year-history-unicef.

583. Twenge, J.M., Joiner, T.E., Rogers, M.L. & Martin, G.N. 2018. Increases in depressive symptoms, suicide-related outcomes, and suicide rates among U.S. adolescents after 2010 and links to increased new media screen time. *Clinical Psychological Science*, 6(1): 3–17. https://doi.org/10.1177/2167702617723376.

584. Madhav, K.C., Sherchand, S.P. & Sherchan, S. 2017. Association between screen time and depression among US adults. *Preventive medicine reports*, 8: 67–71. https://pubmed.ncbi.nlm.nih.gov/28879072.

585. Pappas, S. 2020, April 1. What do we really know about kids and screens? *Monitor on Psychology*, 51(3). https://www.apa.org/monitor/2020/04/cover-kids-screens.

586. Coyne, S.M. et al. 2021. Suicide risk in emerging adulthood: Associations with screen time over 10 years. *Journal of Youth and Adolescence*, 50(12): 2324–2338. https://doi.org/10.1007/s10964-020-01389-6; Twenge, J.M., Cooper, A.B., Joiner, T., Duffy, M. & Binau, S. 2019. Age, period, and cohort trends in mood disorder indicators and suicide-related outcomes in a nationally representative dataset, 2005–2017. *Journal of Abnormal Psychology*, 128(3): 185–199. https://doi.org/10.1037/abn0000410.

587. UNICEF. 2021. *The State of the World's Children 2021: On My Mind – Promoting, Protecting and Caring for Children's Mental Health*. https://www.unicef.org/media/114636/file/SOWC-2021-full-report-English.pdf.

588. Education Development Center. 2021, January 6. Interactive audio instruction makes a comeback. https://www.edc.org/interactive-audio-instruction-makes-comeback.

589. Teach For All. 2020, May 12. Radio lessons help keep teachers and students connected during lockdown. https://teachforall.org/news/radio-lessons-help-keep-teachers-and-students-connected-during-lockdown.

590. Miao, F., Holmes, W., Huang, R. & Zhang, H. 2021. *AI and Education: Guidance for Policymakers*. UNESCO. https://unesdoc.unesco.org/ark:/48223/pf0000376709.

591. Blanco, C. 2020, April 8. Changes in Duolingo usage during the COVID-19 pandemic. Duolingo. Blog post. https://blog.duolingo.com/changes-in-duolingo-usage-during-the-covid-19-pandemic/.

592. Alexander, J. 2020, March 27. 'With me' videos on YouTube are seeing huge spikes in viewership as people stay home. The Verge. https://www.theverge.com/2020/3/27/21197642/youtube-with-me-style-videos-views-coronavirus-cook-workout-study-home-beauty.

593. TheStrive Studies. 2017, October 15. Study with me (with music) 2.5 hours Pomodoro session! YouTube video. https://www.youtube.com/watch?v=dmDbesougG0.

594. Collins, B. 2020, March 3. The Pomodoro Technique explained. Forbes. https://www.forbes.com/sites/bryancollinseurope/2020/03/03/the-pomodoro-technique/.

595. Organisation for Economic Co-operation and Development. 2021. *OECD Digital Education Outlook 2021: Pushing the Frontiers with Artificial Intelligence, Blockchain and Robots*. https://doi.org/10.1787/589b283f-en.

596. Miller, C.C. & Sanger-Katz, M. 2022, February 28. School is back in person, but the five-day school week often isn't. *New York Times*. https://www.nytimes.com/2022/02/28/upshot/schools-covid-closings.html; Gassman-Pines, A., Ananat, E., Fitz-Henley, J. & Leer, J. 2022, January. Effects of daily school and care disruptions during the covid-19 pandemic on child mental health. National Bureau of Economic Research. Working paper 29659. https://www.nber.org/papers/w29659.

597. Krause, J. 2020, April 8. F*** COVID SCHOOL. Jill Krause. Blog post. https://jillkrause.com/f-covid-school/.

598. Operation Enduring Clusterfuck Teacher Gift Idea Funny Coffee Ceramic Mug,11 oz and 15 oz. Available on amazon.co.uk. https://www.amazon.co.uk/Operation-Enduring-Clusterfuck-Teacher-Ceramic/dp/B08S6MK3J3.

599. Abrahamson, R.P. 2020, April 10. As frustration grows, some parents are giving up on home schooling. Today. https://www.today.com/parents/some-parents-refuse-remote-learning-will-there-be-consequences-t178188 https://www.fox32chicago.com/news/some-parents-giving-up-on-distance-learning.

600. UNICEF et al. 2020, April. *COVID-19 and Its Implications for Protecting Children Online*. https://www.unicef.org/media/67396/file/COVID-19%20and%20Its%20Implications%20for%20Protecting%20Children%20Online.pdf.

601. National Crime Agency. 2020, April 4. Law enforcement in coronavirus online safety push as National Crime Agency reveals 300,000 in UK pose sexual threat to children. https://www.nationalcrimeagency.gov.uk/news/onlinesafetyathome.

602. *Times of India*. 2020, November 26. The Times of India & BYJU's kickstart #KeepLearning initiative to empower parents, students and teachers overcome e-learning challenges. https://timesofindia.indiatimes.com/spotlight/toi-byjus-kickstart-keeplearning-initiative-to-empower-parents-students-and-teachers-overcome-e-learning-challenges/articleshow/79367891.cms.

603. Welsh Government (Hwb). 2020, April 3. Online safety at home - Support and resources for parents and carers. https://hwb.gov.wales/zones/keeping-safe-online/news/articles/b8862e72-5d6a-4022-938d-8f37977dc34c.

604. Radesky, J.S. et al. 2020, July. Young children's use of smartphones and tablets. *Pediatrics*, 146(1). http://pediatrics.aappublications.org/content/146/1/e20193518.abstract.

605. Advertising Standards Authority. 2019. *Children's Exposure to Age-Restricted TV Ads: 2019 Update*. https://www.asa.org.uk/static/729cae41-cac1-4920-8e536bfb0b503253/ASA-TV-Ad-Exposure-Report-2019-Update.pdf; Dittmann, M. 2004, June. Protecting children from advertising. *American Psychological Association*, 35(6). https://www.apa.org/monitor/jun04/protecting.

606. Coupal, S. 2017, April 28. Younger children and recognition of online advertising. Advertising Standards Authority. https://www.asa.org.uk/news/younger-children-and-recognition-of-online-advertising.html.

607. Moondore, A., Blades, M., Oates, C. & Blumberg, F. 2009. Young children's ability to recognize advertisements in web page designs. *British Journal of Developmental Psychology*, 27. https://www.researchgate.net/publication/40459548_Young_children%27s_ability_to_recognize_advertisements_in_Web_page_designs.

608. Turkle, S. 2017. *Alone Together: Why We Expect More from Technology and Less from Each Other*. New York: Basic Books.

609. Ibid.

610. Ibid.

611. Willadsen, H. & Hornstrup Jespersen, M. 2021, April 6. Blogpost on student attention in the online school. Copenhagen Center for Social Data Science. https://sodas.ku.dk/projects/distract/distract-news/blogpost-on-student-attention-in-the-online-school/.

612. New York Times. 2020, April 23. Teachers and students describe a remote-learning life. https://www.nytimes.com/2020/04/23/education/learning/coronavirus-teachers-students-remote-learning.html.

613. Reich, J. et al. 2020, July. *What's Lost, What's Left, What's Next: Lessons Learned from the Lived Experiences of Teachers during the Pandemic*. Teaching Systems Lab. https://edarxiv.org/8exp9.

614. Sky News. 2018, April 18. Emoji leading to 'serious decline' in English skills. https://news.sky.com/story/emoji-leading-to-serious-decline-in-english-skills-11336247.

615. Klass, P. 2019, May 20. Is 'digital addiction' a real threat to kids? *New York Times*. https://www.nytimes.com/2019/05/20/well/family/is-digital-addiction-a-real-threat-to-kids.html; Konnikova, M. 2014, November 26. Is internet addiction a real thing? *New Yorker*. http://www.newyorker.com/science/maria-konnikova/internet-addiction-real-thing.

616. Zahariades, D. 2017. *Digital Detox: Unplug to Reclaim Your Life*. Independently published; Price, C. 2018. *How to Break Up with Your Phone: The 30-Day Plan to Take Back Your Life*. Berkeley, CA: Ten Speed Press; Ninkovic, S. 2021. *Untethered: Overcome Distraction, Build Healthy Digital Habits, and Use Tech to Create a Life You Love*. Independently published; Williams, J.W. & White, A. 2021. *Digital Minimalism in Everyday Life: Overcome Technology Addiction, Declutter Your Mind, and Reclaim Your Freedom*. Orlando, FL: Alakai Publishing; Burke, H. 2019. *The Phone Addiction Workbook: How to Identify Smartphone Dependency, Stop Compulsive Behavior and Develop a Healthy Relationship with Your Devices*. Berkeley, CA: Ulysses Press.

617. Jiang, J. 2018, August 22. How teens and parents navigate screen time and device distractions. *Pew Research Center*. https://www.pewresearch.org/internet/2018/08/22/how-teens-and-parents-navigate-screen-time-and-device-distractions/.

618. Ibid.

619. Robb, M.B., Bay, W. & Vennegaard, T. 2017. *The New Normal: Parents, Teens, and Digital Devices in Japan*. USC Annenberg & Common Sense. https://assets.uscannenberg.org/docs/CS_DigitalDevicesJapan_v8_press.pdf; Robb, M.B., Bay, W. & Vennegaard, T. 2019. *The New Normal: Parents, Teens, and Mobile Devices in Mexico*. USC Annenberg & Common Sense. https://www.commonsensemedia.org/sites/default/files/research/report/2019_thenewnormalmexico-final-release_eng-092519_web.pdf.

620. Newberry L. 021, October 25. 8 to 3: Why friendship is hard for many teens right now. *Los Angeles Times*. https://www.latimes.com/california/newsletter/2021-10-25/8-to-3-how-to-help-struggling-teens-8-to-3; The Learning Network. 2020, October 8. What students are saying about socially-distant friendships, school accountability and lessons from animals. *New York Times*. https://www.nytimes.com/2020/10/08/learning/what-students-are-saying-about-socially-distant-friendships-school-accountability-and-lessons-from-animals.html.

621. Naslund, J.A., Bondre, A., Torous, J. & Aschbrenner, K.A. 2020. Social media and mental health: benefits, risks, and opportunities for research and practice. *Journal of Technology in Behavioral Science*, 5(3): 245–257. https://link.springer.com/article/10.1007/s41347-020-00134-x.

622. World Economic Forum. 2016, January 20. *Digital Media and Society: Implications in a Hyperconnected Era*. https://www.weforum.org/reports/digital-media-and-society-implications-in-a-hyperconnected-era/.

623. Hobbs, C.N., Kreiner, D.S., Honeycutt, M.W., Hinds, R.M. & Brockman, C.J. 2010. The illusion of control in a virtual reality setting. *North American Journal of Psychology*, 12(3). https://www.proquest.com/docview/821544774.

624. Alter, A. 2017. *Irresistible: The Rise of Addictive Technology and the Business of Keeping Us Hooked*. New York: Penguin Books.

625. Nelson, C. 2022. Babies need humans, not screens. UNICEF. https://www.unicef.org/parenting/child-development/babies-screen-time.

626. Madigan, S., Browne, D., Racine, N., Mori, C. & Tough, S. 2019. Association between screen time and children's performance on a developmental screening test. *JAMA Pediatrics*, 173(3): 244–250. https://pubmed.ncbi.nlm.nih.gov/30688984/.

627. Troseth, G.L., Strouse, G.A., Verdine, B.N. & Saylor, M.M. 2018. Let's chat: On-screen social responsiveness is not sufficient to support toddlers' word learning from video. *Frontiers in Psychology*, 9. https://www.frontiersin.org/article/10.3389/fpsyg.2018.02195.

628. Pappas, S. 2020. What do we really know about kids and screens? *Monitor on Psychology*, 51(3). https://www.apa.org/monitor/2020/04/cover-kids-screens.

629. Orlando, A. 2020, April 13. Kids are growing up wired — and that's changing their brains. *Discover*. https://www.discovermagazine.com/mind/screen-time-is-replacing-playtime-and-thats-changing-kids-brains.

630. Hutton, J.S., Dudley, J., Horowitz-Kraus, T., DeWitt, T. & Holland, S.K. 2020. Associations between screen-based media use and brain white matter integrity in preschool-aged children. *JAMA Pediatrics*, 174(1): e193869. https://pubmed.ncbi.nlm.nih.gov/31682712/.

631. Klass, P. 2021, March 16. How children read differently from books vs. screens. *New York Times*. https://www.nytimes.com/2021/03/16/well/family/children-reading-screens-books.html.

632. Durant, D.M. 2017. *Reading in a Digital Age*. Charleston, VA: Against the Grain; Baron, N.S. 2015. *Words Onscreen: The Fate of Reading in a Digital World*. Oxford: Oxford University Press.

633. Carr, N. 2011. *The Shallows: What the Internet Is Doing to Our Brains*. New York: W.W. Norton.

634. Baron, N.S. 2015. *Words Onscreen: The Fate of Reading in a Digital World*. Oxford: Oxford University Press.

635. Association for Supervision and Curriculum Development. 2009, March 1. The importance of deep reading. *Educational Leadership*, 66(6). https://www.ascd.org/el/articles/the-importance-of-deep-reading.

636. Wolf, M. 2018. *Reader, Come Home: The Reading Brain in a Digital World*. New York: Harper.

637. Ginsburg, K.R., Committee on Communications & Committee on Psychosocial Aspects of Child and Family Health. 2007, January. The importance of play in promoting healthy child development and maintaining strong parent-child bonds. *Pediatrics*, 119(1): 182–191. https://pubmed.ncbi.nlm.nih.gov/17200287/.

638. Gray, P. 2011. The decline of play and the rise of psychopathology in children and adolescents. *American Journal of Play*, 3(4): 443–463. https://www.researchgate.net/publication/265449180_The_Decline_of_Play_and_the_Rise_of_Psychopathology_in_Children_and_Adolescents.

639. Horwitz, S. 2015, June 22. Cooperation over coercion: The importance of unsupervised childhood play for democracy and liberalism. SSRN. http://dx.doi.org/10.2139/ssrn.2621848.

640. United Nations. 1989. Convention on the Rights of the Child. https://www.ohchr.org/en/instruments-mechanisms/instruments/convention-rights-child.

641. Clements, R. 2004. An investigation of the status of outdoor play. *Contemporary Issues in Early Childhood*, 5(1): 68–80. https://www.researchgate.net/publication/250151481_An_Investigation_of_the_Status_of_Outdoor_Play.

642. Bergmann, C. et al. 2021, May 31. Young children's screen time during the first COVID-19 lockdown in 12 countries. OSF Preprints. https://doi.org/10.31219/osf.io/p5gm4.

643. Nabi, R.L. & Krcmar, M. 2016. It takes two: The effect of child characteristics on U.S. parents' motivations for allowing electronic media use. *Journal of Children and Media*, 10(3): 285–303. https://www.tandfonline.com/doi/abs/10.1080/17482798.2016.1162185.

644. Uhls, Y.T. & Robb, M.B. 2017. How parents mediate children's media consumption. In Blumberg, F.C. & Brooks, P.J. (eds). *Cognitive Development in Digital Contexts*. Cambridge, MA: Academic Press.

645. Walsh, J.J. et al. 2018. Associations between 24 hour movement behaviours and global cognition in US children: A cross-sectional observational study. *Lancet Child & Adolescent Health*, 2(11): 783–791. https://pubmed.ncbi.nlm.nih.gov/30268792/.

646. Organisation for Economic Co-operation and Development. 2021, June. *What's Next? Lessons on Education Recovery: Findings from a Survey of Ministries of Education amid the COVID-19 Pandemic*. https://read.oecd-ilibrary.org/education/what-s-next-lessons-on-education-recovery_697bc36e-en.

647. Organisation for Economic Co-operation and Development. 2021. *Using Digital Technologies for Early Education during COVID-19: OECD Report for the G20 2020 Education Working Group*. https://doi.org/10.1787/fe8d68ad-en.

648. Goldstein, D. & Parlapiano, A. 2021, August 7. The kindergarten exodus. *New York Times*. https://www.nytimes.com/2021/08/07/us/covid-kindergarten-enrollment.html.

649. Vernekar, N., Pandey, P., Rai, A.N., Pichhili, A.R. & Singhal, K. 2021, September. *Starting from Scratch: The Role of Parents, Teachers, and Tech in Early Childhood Education during COVID-19*. Vidhi Centre for Legal Policy. https://vidhilegalpolicy.in/research/starting-from-scratch-the-role-of-parents-teachers-and-tech-in-early-childhood-education-during-covid-19/.

650. Rosenberg, N.Y. 2017, April 28. 'Green schools' use EdTech to save the environment. EdTechReview. https://edtechreview.in/trends-insights/trends/2762-green-schools-use-tech.

651. Selwyn, N. 2018, October 22. EdTech is killing us all: Facing up to the environmental consequences of digital education. EduResearch Matters. https://www.aare.edu.au/blog/?p=3293.

652. Herold, B. 2020, July 23. Schools handed out millions of digital devices under COVID-19. Now, thousands are missing. *Education Week*. https://www.edweek.org/technology/schools-handed-out-millions-of-digital-devices-under-covid-19-now-thousands-are-missing/2020/07.

653. International Data Corporation. 2022, January 2022. Tablet and Chromebook shipments slowed in the fourth quarter but saw solid growth for 2021, according to IDC. https://www.idc.com/getdoc.jsp?containerId=prUS48826122.

654. Costello, K. & Rimol, M. 2020, October 12. Gartner says worldwide PC shipments grew 3.6% in third quarter of 2020. Gartner. https://www.gartner.com/en/newsroom/press-releases/2020-10-12-gartner-says-worldwide-pc-shipments-grew-3-point-six-percent-in-the-third-quarter-of-2020.

655. Statista. 2022, January. Chromebook unit shipments worldwide from 2019 to 2022. https://www.statista.com/statistics/749890/worldwide-chromebook-unit-shipments/.

656. Fowler, G. 2020, August 10. Back-to-school laptop guide: Pandemic survival edition. *Washington Post*. https://www.washingtonpost.com/technology/2020/08/10/laptop-buyers-guide-distance-learning/.

657. Rauf, D. 2020, April 16. Coronavirus squeezes supply of Chromebooks, iPads, and other digital learning devices. *Education Week*. https://www.edweek.org/education-industry/coronavirus-squeezes-supply-of-chromebooks-ipads-and-other-digital-learning-devices/2020/04.

658. Towler, B. 2022, May 31. E-readers vs books: Which are better for the environment? Commercial Waste. https://commercialwaste.trade/e-readers-vs-books-better-environment/; Goleman, D. & Norris, G. 2010, April 4. How green is my iPad? *New York Times*. https://archive.nytimes.com/www.nytimes.com/interactive/2010/04/04/opinion/04opchart.html.

659. The Restart Project. 2018. Mobiles: the global carbon footprint. https://therestartproject.org/the-global-footprint-of-mobiles/. (Accessed 28 November 2022.)

660. Towler, B. 2022, May 31. E-readers vs books: Which are better for the environment? Commercial Waste. https://commercialwaste.trade/e-readers-vs-books-better-environment/.

661. Hodgson, D. & Papadimoulis, F. 2022, September. *Pulp and Paper*. International Energy Agency. https://www.iea.org/reports/pulp-and-paper; Summanen, M. 2021, December 28. Pulp and paper industry trends to watch in 2022. Forest2Market. https://www.forest2market.com/blog/pulp-paper-industry-trends-to-watch-in-2022.

662. Shaer, M. 2022, November 28. Where does all the cardboard come from? I had to know. *New York Times*. https://www.nytimes.com/2022/11/28/magazine/cardboard-international-paper.html.

663. Masanet, E., Shehabi, A., Lei, N., Smith, S. & Koomey, J. 2020. Recalibrating global data center energy-use estimates. *Science*, 367(6481): 984–986. https://www.science.org/doi/10.1126/science.aba3758; Kamiya, G. 2020, December 11. The carbon footprint of streaming video: fact-checking the headlines. International Energy Agency. https://www.iea.org/commentaries/the-carbon-footprint-of-streaming-video-fact-checking-the-headlines.

664. Mullaney, T.S., Peters, B., Hicks, M. & Philip, K. (eds). 2021. *Your Computer is on Fire*. Cambridge, MA: MIT Press.

665. Carter, N. 2021, May 5. How much energy does Bitcoin actually consume? *Harvard Business Review*. https://hbr.org/2021/05/how-much-energy-does-bitcoin-actually-consume.

666. Stokel-Walker, C. 2023, February 10. The generative AI race has a dirty secret. Wired. https://www.wired.com/story/the-generative-ai-search-race-has-a-dirty-secret/.

667. Maslej, N. et al. 2023, April. *The AI Index 2023 Annual Report*. AI Index Steering Committee, Institute for Human-Centered AI, Stanford University. https://aiindex.stanford.edu/wp-content/uploads/2023/04/HAI_AI-Index-Report_2023.pdf.

668. Ludvigsen, K. 2023, March 1. ChatGPT's electricity consumption. Towards Data Science. https://towardsdatascience.com/chatgpts-electricity-consumption-7873483feac4.

669. DeGeurin, M. 2023, May 10. 'Thirsty' AI: Training ChatGPT required enough water to fill a nuclear reactor's cooling tower, study finds. Gizmodo. https://gizmodo.com/chatgpt-ai-water-185000-gallons-training-nuclear-1850324249.

670. Belkhir, L. & Elmeligi, A. 2018. Assessing ICT global emissions footprint: Trends to 2040 and recommendations. *Journal of Cleaner Production*, 177: 448–463. https://www.sciencedirect.com/science/article/pii/S095965261733233X.

671. Larmer, B. 2018, July 5. E-waste offers an economic opportunity as well as toxicity. *New York Times*. https://www.nytimes.com/2018/07/05/magazine/e-waste-offers-an-economic-opportunity-as-well-as-toxicity.html.

672. Forti, V., Balde, C., Kuehr, R. & Bel, G. 2020, July. *The Global E-Waste Monitor 2020: Quantities, Flows and the Circular Economy Potential*. United Nations University/ United Nations Institute for Training, International Telecommunication Union, and Research and International Solid Waste Association. https://collections.unu.edu/view/UNU:7737.

673. UNEP. N.d. E-Waste 2.0. https://wedocs.unep.org/bitstream/handle/20.500.11822/7587/e_waste_infog_en.pdf; Chadwick, J. 2020, July 2. Shocking 52.7 MILLION tons of electronic waste made up of phones, TVs and other gadgets was produced worldwide in 2019 – weighing the equivalent of 350 cruise ships. *Daily Mail*. https://www.dailymail.co.uk/sciencetech/article-8483361/56-3-megatonnes-e-waste-produced-2019-says.html.

674. Chatterji, M. 2021, July 9. Repairing – not recycling – is the first step to tackling e-waste from smartphones. Here's why. World Economic Forum. https://www.weforum.org/agenda/2021/07/repair-not-recycle-tackle-ewaste-circular-economy-smartphones/.

675. Apple. 2021, November 17. Apple announces Self Service Repair. Press release. https://www.apple.com/newsroom/2021/11/apple-announces-self-service-repair/.

676. Sajn, N. 2022, January 12. Right to repair. Briefing paper. European Parliament. https://www.europarl.europa.eu/thinktank/en/document/EPRS_BRI(2022)698869; Ministry of Ecological Transition and Territorial Cohesion. 2021, December 1. Indice de réparabilité [Reparability index]. Government of France. https://www.ecologie.gouv.fr/indice-reparabilite.

677. See Fairphone. https://www.fairphone.com/en/.

678. Bang & Olufsen's. 2022. The future is circular. https://www.bang-olufsen.com/en/dk/story/cradle-to-cradle-certification. (Accessed 28 November 2022.)

679. Cradle to Cradle Products Innovation Institute. 2022. What is Cradle to Cradle Certified? https://www.c2ccertified.org/get-certified/product-certification. (Accessed 28 November 2022.)

680. Gill, V. 2022, October 14. E-waste: Five billion phones to be thrown away in 2022. BBC News. https://www.bbc.com/news/science-environment-63245150.

681. United Nations University. 2020, July 2. Global e-waste surging: Up 21% in 5 years. https://unu.edu/media-relations/releases/global-e-waste-surging-up-21-in-5-years.html.

682. State of California. 2003. Electronic Waste Recycling Act of 2003. *CalRecycle*. https://calrecycle.ca.gov/electronics/act2003/.

683. European Union. 2012, July 4. Directive 2012/19/EU of the European Parliament and of the Council of 4 July 2012 on waste electrical and electronic equipment (WEEE). https://eur-lex.europa.eu/eli/dir/2012/19/2018-07-04.

684. Selwyn, N. 2018, October 22. EdTech is killing us all: Facing up to the environmental consequences of digital education. EduResearch Matters. https://www.aare.edu.au/blog/?p=3293.

685. World Health Organization. 2021, June 15. Facts in pictures: E-waste and child health. https://www.who.int/news-room/facts-in-pictures/detail/e-waste-and-child-health.

686. World Health Organization. 2021, June. *Children and Digital Dumpsites: E-Waste Exposure and Child Health*. https://www.who.int/publications/i/item/9789240023901.

687. World Health Organization. 2021, June 15. Facts in pictures: E-waste and child health. https://www.who.int/news-room/facts-in-pictures/detail/e-waste-and-child-health.

688. Michele Fabiola Lawson. 2021, September 1. The DRC mining industry: Child labor and formalization of small-scale mining. Wilson Center. https://www.wilsoncenter.org/blog-post/drc-mining-industry-child-labor-and-formalization-small-scale-mining.

689. Tria, E. 2021, May 4. The impact of Covid-19 on child labour in cobalt mines in the DRC. Humanium. https://www.humanium.org/en/the-impact-of-covid-19-on-child-labour-in-cobalt-mines-in-the-drc/; Amnesty International. 2020, May 6. DRC: Alarming research shows long lasting harm from cobalt mine abuses. https://www.amnesty.org/en/latest/news/2020/05/drc-alarming-research-harm-from-cobalt-mine-abuses/.

690. Michele Fabiola Lawson. 2021, September 1. The DRC mining industry: Child labor and formalization of small-scale mining. Wilson Center. https://www.wilsoncenter.org/blog-post/drc-mining-industry-child-labor-and-formalization-small-scale-mining.

691. See DW News. 2020, February 22. The deadly cost of cobalt or smartphones | DW Stories. YouTube video. https://www.youtube.com/watch?v=LJjH4EQcayk.

692. Kelly, A. 2019, December 16. Apple and Google named in US lawsuit over Congolese child cobalt mining deaths. *The Guardian*. https://www.theguardian.com/global-development/2019/dec/16/apple-and-google-named-in-us-lawsuit-over-congolese-child-cobalt-mining-deaths.

693. Simpson, D. 2021. Apple, Google, Tesla, Microsoft beat child labor mine suit. Law360. https://www.law360.com/articles/1437141/apple-google-tesla-microsoft-beat-child-labor-mine-suit.

694. International Rights Advocates. 2022. Multinational companies are liable for human rights abuses within their supply chains. https://www.internationalrightsadvocates.org/cases/cobalt. (Accessed 28 November 2022.)

695. Azevedo, M., Campagnol, N., Hagenbruch, T., Hoffman, K., Lala, A. & Ramsbottom, O. 2018. Lithium and cobalt: A tale of two commodities. McKinsey & Company. https://www.mckinsey.com/industries/metals-and-mining/our-insights/lithium-and-cobalt-a-tale-of-two-commodities.

696. Tria, E. 2021, May 4. The impact of Covid-19 on child labour in cobalt mines in the DRC. Humanium. https://www.humanium.org/en/the-impact-of-covid-19-on-child-labour-in-cobalt-mines-in-the-drc/.

697. Ladd, J.M., Tucker, J.A. & Kates, S. 2018. *2018 American Institutional Confidence Poll: The Health of American Democracy in an Era of Hyper Polarization*. Report by the Baker Center for Leadership & Governance, Georgetown University, & the John S. and James L. Knight Foundation. https://www.aicpoll.org/uploads/5/3/6/6/5366295/2018-american-institutional-confidence-poll-1.pdf; Tiffany, K. 2018, October 25. In Amazon we trust — but why? Vox. https://www.vox.com/the-goods/2018/10/25/18022956/amazon-trust-survey-american-institutions-ranked-georgetown.

698. Morning Consult. 2020. *Special Report: The State of Consumer Trust*. https://morningconsult.com/wp-content/uploads/2020/01/Morning-Consult-The-State-of-Consumer-Trust.pdf; Pesce, N.L. 2020, January 18. Americans trust Amazon and Google more than the police or the government. Market Watch. https://www.marketwatch.com/story/people-trust-amazon-and-google-more-than-the-police-or-the-government-2020-01-14.

699. Bamberger, M. 2020, June 1. Why is Amazon, by far, the most trusted brand during the pandemic? Tetra Insights. https://www.tetrainsights.com/why-is-amazon-by-far-the-most-trusted-brand-during-the-pandemic/.

700. Ipsos. 2022, January 17. Pharmaceutical and banking companies and governments are now seen as more trustworthy. Ipsos. https://www.ipsos.com/en/global-trustworthiness-monitor-2021.

701. Ibid.

702. Fleming, N. 2021, January 23. After Covid, will digital learning be the new normal? *The Guardian*. https://www.theguardian.com/education/2021/jan/23/after-covid-will-digital-learning-be-the-new-normal.

703. HolonIQ. 2022, January 2. Global EdTech venture capital report: Full year 2021. https://www.holoniq.com/notes/global-edtech-venture-capital-report-full-year-2021.

704. HolonIQ. 2020, October 15. EdTech unicorn mega-funding evolution. https://www.holoniq.com/notes/edtech-unicorn-mega-funding-evolution; HolonIQ. 2022. Global EdTech unicorns: The complete list of global EdTech unicorns. https://www.holoniq.com/edtech-unicorns. (Accessed 7 December 2022.)

705. HolonIQ. 2020, August 6. Global EdTech market to reach $404B by 2025 – 16.3% CAGR. https://www.holoniq.com/notes/global-education-technology-market-to-reach-404b-by-2025/.

706. Chebib, K. 2020. *Education For All in the Time of COVID-19: How EdTech can be Part of the Solution*. GSMA. https://www.gsma.com/mobilefordevelopment/wp-content/uploads/2020/09/EdTech-Final-WEB.pdf.

707. Terrisse, A. 2020, September 28. How has the pandemic changed the face of edtech? EU-Startups. https://www.eu-startups.com/2020/09/how-has-the-pandemic-changed-the-face-of-edtech/.

708. HolonIQ. 2020, May 21. Prototyping global education stock indices. https://www.holoniq.com/notes/prototyping-global-education-stock-indices/.

709. UN General Assembly Human Rights Council. 2022, April 19. Impact of the digitalization of education on the right to education. Report of the Special Rapporteur on the right to education. https://documents-dds-ny.un.org/doc/UNDOC/GEN/G22/322/37/PDF/G2232237.pdf.

710. Lazare, M. 2021, February 17. A peek at what's next for Google Classroom. Google Education. Blog post. https://blog.google/outreach-initiatives/education/classroom-roadmap/.

711. Eurostat. 2021, April 27. Almost 76 million pupils and students enrolled in the EU. https://ec.europa.eu/eurostat/web/products-eurostat-news/-/ddn-20210427-1.

712. Lazare, M. 2021, February 17. A peek at what's next for Google Classroom. Google Education. Blog post. https://blog.google/outreach-initiatives/education/classroom-roadmap/.

713. Singer, N. 2017, May 13. How Google took over the classroom. *New York Times*. https://www.nytimes.com/2017/05/13/technology/google-education-chromebooks-schools.html.

714. Ibid.

715. Google Play. 2022. Google Classroom. https://play.google.com/store/apps/details?id=com.google.android.apps.classroom. (Accessed 30 August 2022.); App Store Preview. Google Classroom. Apple. https://apps.apple.com/us/app/google-classroom/id924620788. (Accessed 30 August 2022.)

716. Spillane, J. 2022, April 6. App ratings and reviews: 2021 benchmarks. Business 2 Community. https://www.business2community.com/mobile-apps/app-ratings-and-reviews-2021-benchmarks-02396808.

717. Meisenzahl, M. 2020, April 15. Students bored of homeschooling spam Google Classroom app with one-star reviews thanks to a TikTok meme. Business Insider. https://www.businessinsider.com/google-classroom-app-spammed-with-one-star-reviews-by-students-2020-4.

718. Wang, X. 2020, March 5. The word from Wuhan. *London Review of Books*, 42(5). https://www.lrb.co.uk/the-paper/v42/n05/wang-xiuying/the-word-from-wuhan.

719. Whalen, A. 2020, March 19. Students are targeting Zoom and Classroom with bad reviews to end homework during coronavirus outbreak. *Newsweek*. https://www.newsweek.com/google-zoom-classroom-students-schools-closed-coronavirus-china-1493309.

720. Wang, X. 2020, March 5. The word from Wuhan. *London Review of Books*, 42(5). https://www.lrb.co.uk/the-paper/v42/n05/wang-xiuying/the-word-from-wuhan.

721. See, for example, Bushner, B. 2020, September 18. A list of things I hate about Google Classroom. Google Classroom Help. https://support.google.com/edu/classroom/thread/71858073/a-list-of-things-i-hate-about-google-classroom.

722. Impey, C. 2020, July 23. Massive online open courses see exponential growth during COVID-19 pandemic. The Conversation. http://theconversation.com/massive-online-open-courses-see-exponential-growth-during-covid-19-pandemic-141859.

723. Tse, C. & Roof, K. 2021, March 30. Coursera prices IPO at top of range to raise $519 million. Bloomberg. https://www.bloomberg.com/news/articles/2021-03-31/online-educator-coursera-s-top-of-range-ipo-raises-519-million.

724. McKenzie, L. 2021, April 9. Coursera IPO 'seized on the right moment'. *Inside Higher Ed*. https://www.insidehighered.com/news/2021/04/09/coursera-valuation-exceeds-expectations.

725. World Bank. 2022. Data: World Bank country and lending groups. https://datahelpdesk.worldbank.org/knowledgebase/articles/906519-world-bank-country-and-lending-groups. (Accessed 7 December 2022.)

726. World Bank. 2022. Data: Population, total – Low income. https://data.worldbank.org/indicator/SP.POP.TOTL?locations=XM. (Accessed 7 December 2022.)

727. World Bank. 2021, February 22. *Education Finance Watch 2021*. World Bank Group. https://www.worldbank.org/en/topic/education/publication/education-finance-watch-2021.

728. Majumdar, D. 2021, June 9. Coursera's IPO windfall: the takeaways for Indian ed-tech companies that plan to get listed. *Economic Times*. https://economictimes.indiatimes.com/prime/technology-and-startups/courseras-ipo-windfall-the-takeaways-for-indian-ed-tech-companies-that-plan-to-get-listed/primearticleshow/83346852.cms.

729. UNESCO. 2021, February 2022. COVID-19: Two-thirds of poorer countries are cutting their education budgets at a time when they can least afford to. https://en.unesco.org/gem-report/sites/default/files/Education_Finance_Watch_PR_Eng_0.pdf.

730. Roy, S. 2022, May 18. How pandemic has brought changes in edtech sector. *Business Standard*. https://www.business-standard.com/podcast/education/how-pandemic-has-brought-changes-in-edtech-sector-120091600700_1.html.

731. Dentsu. 2021. https://www.dentsu.com/id/en/our-work/case-study-dentsu-ruangguru-belajar-di-rumah-aja. (Accessed 7 December 2022.)

732. Ibid.

733. Ruangguru. 2021, April 19. Ruangguru secures USD 55 million new investment led by Tiger Global Management. https://www.ruangguru.com/blog/ruangguru-secures-usd-55-million-new-investment-led-by-tiger-global-management.

734. Ibanez, J. 2022, July 5. Indonesia's Ruangguru acquires two edtech startups. *Tech in Asia*. https://www.techinasia.com/indonesias-ruangguru-acquires-edtech-startups.

735. Forbes Kazakhstan. 2020, April 5. Казахстанский стартап предоставил всем желающим бесплатный доступ к онлайн-урокам [Kazakh startup provides everyone with free access to online lessons]. https://forbes.kz/process/kazahstanskiy_startap_predostavil_vsem_besplatnyiy_dostup_k_onlayn-urokam/.

736. Human Rights Watch. 2022, May 25. *"How Dare They Peep into My Private Life?": Children's rights violations by governments that endorsed online learning during the COVID-19 pandemic*. https://www.hrw.org/report/2022/05/25/how-dare-they-peep-my-private-life/childrens-rights-violations-governments.

737. Forbes Kazakhstan. 2020, April 5. Казахстанский стартап предоставил всем желающим бесплатный доступ к онлайн-урокам [Kazakh startup provides everyone with free access to online lessons]. https://forbes.kz/process/kazahstanskiy_startap_predostavil_vsem_besplatnyiy_dostup_k_onlayn-urokam/.

738. Forbes Kazakhstan. 2021, April 16. Как выходец из аула создал одну из крупнейших образовательных платформ в Казахстане [How a native of the village created one of the largest educational platforms in Kazakhstan]. https://forbes.kz/process/education/millionyi_besplatno_1618536199/.

739. Human Rights Watch. 2022, May 25. *"How Dare They Peep into My Private Life?": Children's rights violations by governments that endorsed online learning during the COVID-19 pandemic*. https://www.hrw.org/report/2022/05/25/how-dare-they-peep-my-private-life/childrens-rights-violations-governments.

740. Zahra-Malik, M. 2020, May 14. The coronavirus effect on Pakistan's digital divide. BBC. https://www.bbc.com/worklife/article/20200713-the-coronavirus-effect-on-pakistans-digital-divide.

741. Human Rights Watch. 2022, May 25. *"How Dare They Peep into My Private Life?": Children's rights violations by governments that endorsed online learning during the COVID-19 pandemic*. https://www.hrw.org/report/2022/05/25/how-dare-they-peep-my-private-life/childrens-rights-violations-governments.

742. World Bank. 2021, May 19. Thinking inside the 'box': Pakistan turns to education TV during COVID-19. https://www.worldbank.org/en/news/feature/2021/05/19/pakistan-turns-to-education-tv.

743. Zahra-Malik, M. 2020, May 14. The coronavirus effect on Pakistan's digital divide. BBC. https://www.bbc.com/worklife/article/20200713-the-coronavirus-effect-on-pakistans-digital-divide.

744. Chegg Investor Relations. 2021, February 8. Chegg reports 2020 financial results and raises 2021 guidance. Press release. https://investor.chegg.com/Press-Releases/press-release-details/2021/Chegg-Reports-2020-Financial-Results-and-Raises-2021-Guidance/default.aspx.

745. Ibid.

746. Companies Market Cap. 2022. Chegg: Market capitalization of Chegg (CHGG). https://companiesmarketcap.com/chegg/marketcap/. (Accessed November 25, 2022.)

747. Chegg Investor relations. 2022, February 7. Chegg reports 2021 financial results and gives 2022 guidance. Press release. https://investor.chegg.com/Press-Releases/press-release-details/2022/Chegg-Reports-2021-Financial-Results-and-Gives-2022-Guidance/default.aspx.

748. McKinsey & Company. 2022. May 2. Educational technology in the age of COVID-19. Podcast. https://www.mckinsey.com/il/podcast/educational-technology-in-the-age-of-covid.

749. Chegg Investor Relations. 2021, February 8. Chegg reports 2020 financial results and raises 2021 guidance. Press release. https://investor.chegg.com/Press-Releases/press-release-details/2021/Chegg-Reports-2020-Financial-Results-and-Raises-2021-Guidance/default.aspx.

750. UNESCO. 2022. UNESCO Map on School Closures: COVID-19 educational response: Country dashboard. https://covid19.uis.unesco.org/global-monitoring-school-closures-covid19/country-dashboard/. (Accessed 7 December 2022.)

751. Shleifer, E. & Kologrivaya, K. 2021, June 29. Out of lockdown: China's edtech market confronts the post-pandemic world. *South China Morning Post*. https://www.scmp.com/tech/tech-trends/article/3139056/out-lockdown-chinas-edtech-market-confronts-post-pandemic-world.

752. Chen, T.M. 2020, October 27. Edtech and Covid-19: It's complicated. TechNode. http://technode.com/2020/10/27/edtech-in-china-and-covid-19-its-complicated/.

753. Shu, C. 2020, December 28. Chinese online education app Zuoyebang raises $1.6 billion from investors including Alibaba. TechCrunch. https://techcrunch.com/2020/12/28/chinese-online-education-app-zuoyebang-raises-1-6-billion-from-investors-including-alibaba/; Wang, X. 2021, January 20. After a Covid-led boom in 2020, what next for China's K-12 edtech? CompassList. https://www.compasslist.com/research-analysis/after-a-covid-led-boom-in-2020-what-next-for-chinas-k-12-edtech; Reuters. 2020, June 28. Chinese online tutor Zuoyebang raises $750 million in fresh round. https://www.reuters.com/article/us-zuoyebang-fundraiisng-idINKBN240093.

754. Wang, X. 2021, January 20. After a Covid-led boom in 2020, what next for China's K-12 edtech? CompassList. https://www.compasslist.com/research-analysis/after-a-covid-led-boom-in-2020-what-next-for-chinas-k-12-edtech.

755. Lee, E. 2021, January 25. Edtech firm Huohua Siwei valued at $1.5 billion. TechNode. http://technode.com/2021/01/25/edtech-firm-huohua-siwei-valued-at-1-5-billion/.

756. Wang, X. 2021, January 20. After a Covid-led boom in 2020, what next for China's K-12 edtech? CompassList. https://www.compasslist.com/research-analysis/after-a-covid-led-boom-in-2020-what-next-for-chinas-k-12-edtech.

757. Mascarenhas, N. 2020, October 22. Chinese live tutoring app Yuanfudao is now worth $15.5 billion. TechCrunch. https://techcrunch.com/2020/10/22/chinese-live-tutoring-app-yuanfudao-is-now-worth-15-5-billion/.

758. Mathur, P. 2020, October 22. China's Yuanfudao claims global edtech valuation crown. PitchBook. https://pitchbook.com/news/articles/yuanfudao-edtech-valuation-china.

759. Shu, C. 2020, December 28. Chinese online education app Zuoyebang raises $1.6 billion from investors including Alibaba. TechCrunch. https://techcrunch.com/2020/12/28/chinese-online-education-app-zuoyebang-raises-1-6-billion-from-investors-including-alibaba/.

760. Mathur, P. 2020, October 22. China's Yuanfudao claims global edtech valuation crown. PitchBook. https://pitchbook.com/news/articles/yuanfudao-edtech-valuation-china.

761. Wang, X. 2021, January 20. After a Covid-led boom in 2020, what next for China's K-12 edtech? CompassList. https://www.compasslist.com/research-analysis/after-a-covid-led-boom-in-2020-what-next-for-chinas-k-12-edtech.

762. Ibid.

763. Ibid.

764. GlobalData Thematic Research. 2021, August 2. China's edtech companies face an uncertain financial future. Verdict. https://www.verdict.co.uk/chinas-edtech-companies-face-an-uncertain-financial-future/.

765. Chen, L. 2018, December 4. Chinese parents spend up to US$43,500 a year on after-school classes for their children. *South China Morning Post*. https://www.scmp.com/news/china/society/article/2176377/chinese-parents-spend-us43500-year-after-school-classes-their.

766. Lu, S. 2021, July 31. China's edtech crackdown isn't what you think. Here's why. Protocol. https://www.protocol.com/china/china-edtech-crackdown-education-inequality.

767. Lee, E. & Sheng, W. 2021, July 26. Chinese edtech upended by sweeping regulations. TechNode. http://technode.com/2021/07/26/chinese-edtech-upended-by-sweeping-regulations/.

768. Miao, T. 2022, January 21. Can EdTech be the path forward for China's education industry? GRC Insights. https://insights.grcglobalgroup.com/can-edtech-be-the-path-forward-for-chinas-education-industry/.

769. Lee, E. & Sheng, W. 2021, July 26. Chinese edtech upended by sweeping regulations. TechNode. http://technode.com/2021/07/26/chinese-edtech-upended-by-sweeping-regulations/.

770. *Business Standard*. 2021, July 26. China outlaws for-profit school tutoring in a sweeping overhaul. https://www.business-standard.com/article/international/china-outlaws-for-profit-school-tutoring-in-a-sweeping-overhaul-121072600032_1.html.

771. Lu, S. 2021, July 31. China's edtech crackdown isn't what you think. Here's why. Protocol. https://www.protocol.com/china/china-edtech-crackdown-education-inequality.

772. Ibid.

773. Sovereign. 2021, September 16. China makes sweeping reforms to 'edtech' sector. https://www.sovereigngroup.com/news/news-and-views/china-makes-sweeping-reforms-to-edtech-sector/.

774. Stevenson, A. 2021, July 26. China moves against private tutoring companies, causing shares to plunge. *New York Times*. https://www.nytimes.com/2021/07/26/business/china-private-education.html.

775. Spilka, D. 2021, April 18. Duolingo's IPO is a roaring success for retail investors. Investing.com. https://uk.investing.com/analysis/duolingos-ipo-is-a-roaring-success-for-retail-investors-200493881.

776. Young, J. 2021, July 28. Early edtech giant PowerSchool goes public. EdSurge. https://www.edsurge.com/news/2021-07-28-early-edtech-giant-powerschool-goes-public.

777. Temkin, M. 2021, November 1. Edtech backers rewarded as IPO pipeline heats up. PitchBook. https://pitchbook.com/news/articles/edtech-online-learning-pandemic-ipos.

778. Rauf, D. 2021, July 26. Another education company goes public: Instructure IPO gives ed-tech firm $2.9 billion valuation. EdWeek Market Brief. https://marketbrief.edweek.org/marketplace-k-12/another-education-company-goes-public-instructure-ipo-gives-ed-tech-firm-2-9-billion-valuation/.

779. Temkin, M. 2021, November 1. Edtech backers rewarded as IPO pipeline heats up. PitchBook. https://pitchbook.com/news/articles/edtech-online-learning-pandemic-ipos.

780. Zoom. 2021. Annual Report: Fiscal 2021. https://investors.zoom.us/static-files/a17fd391-13ae-429b-8cb3-bfd95b61b007.

781. Impey, C. 2020, July 23. Massive online open courses see exponential growth during COVID-19 pandemic. The Conversation. https://theconversation.com/massive-online-open-courses-see-exponential-growth-during-covid-19-pandemic-141859.

782. Shah, D. 2020, May 2. How different MOOC providers are responding to the pandemic (updated). Class Central. https://www.classcentral.com/report/mooc-providers-response-to-the-pandemic/.

783. Udemy. 2020. *Online Education Steps Up: What the World Is Learning (From Home)*. Special Report. https://research.udemy.com/wp-content/uploads/2020/04/Online-Education-Steps-Up-2020-2021-Rebrand-v2-gs.pdf.

784. Ederle, R. 2020. New Udemy report shows surge in global online education in response to COVID-19. Udemy. Press release. https://about.udemy.com/press-releases/new-udemy-report-shows-surge-in-global-online-education-in-response-to-covid-19/.

785. Roof, K. & Tse, C. 2021, October 28. Udemy raising $421 million in top-of-range IPO. Bloomberg. https://www.bloomberg.com/news/articles/2021-10-28/udemy-is-said-to-raise-421-million-in-top-of-range-ipo.

786. VOA News. 2021, July 29. World leaders pledge $4 billion to public education affected by pandemic. https://www.voanews.com/a/europe_world-leaders-pledge-4-billion-public-education-affected-pandemic/6208915.html.

787. ETF Express. 2020. September 20. Specialist Thematic ETF pioneer RIZE ETF launches sustainable food and edtech ETFs on SIX. Press release. https://rizeetf.com/wp-content/uploads/2020/09/03Sep20_Press_Release_Rize-launches-two-new-ETFs.pdf.

788. Swiss Fund Data. 2022. Credit Suisse (Lux) Edutainment Equity Fund B USD. https://www.swissfunddata.ch/sfdpub/en/funds/chart/114188#tab-content. (Accessed 25 November 2022.)

789. Palandrani, P. 2020, July 14. Introducing the Global X Education ETF (EDUT). Global X. https://www.globalxetfs.com/introducing-the-global-x-education-etf-edut/.

790. Williamson, B. 2020, September 15. Edtech index investing. *Code Acts in Education*. https://codeactsineducation.wordpress.com/2020/09/15/edtech-index-investing/.

791. UNESCO. 2021. Paris Declaration: A Global Call for Investing in the Futures of Education. https://unesdoc.unesco.org/ark:/48223/pf0000380116.

792. Balu, N. & Randewich, N. 2022, January 4. Apple becomes first company to hit $3 trillion market value, then slips. Reuters. https://www.reuters.com/markets/europe/apple-gets-closer-3-trillion-market-value-2022-01-03/.

793. Sharma, R. 2022, January 3. Apple (AAPL) Becomes world's first $3 trillion company. Investopedia. https://www.investopedia.com/apple-becomes-first-3-trillion-dollar-company-5214650.

794. World Bank. 2022. GDP (current US$). https://data.worldbank.org/indicator/NY.GDP.MKTP.CD. (Accessed 25 November 2022.)

795. UN General Assembly Human Rights Council. 2016, April 6. Report of the Special Rapporteur on the right to education. https://documents-dds-ny.un.org/doc/UNDOC/GEN/G16/070/33/PDF/G1607033.pdf.

796. UN General Assembly Human Rights Council. 2020, June 30. Right to education: impact of the coronavirus disease crisis on the right to education—concerns, challenges and opportunities. Report of the Special Rapporteur on the right to education. https://documents-dds-ny.un.org/doc/UNDOC/GEN/G20/158/03/PDF/G2015803.pdf.

797. UN General Assembly Human Rights Council. 2022, April 19. Impact of the digitalization of education on the right to education. Report of the Special Rapporteur on the right to education. https://documents-dds-ny.un.org/doc/UNDOC/GEN/G22/322/37/PDF/G2232237.pdf.

798. Norris, T. 2021, March 10. Tax 'pandemic profiteering' by tech companies to help fund public education. The Conversation. https://theconversation.com/tax-pandemic-profiteering-by-tech-companies-to-help-fund-public-education-155705.

799. Williamson, B. 2020, March 17. Emergency edtech. *Code Acts in Education*. https://codeactsineducation.wordpress.com/2020/03/17/emergency-edtech/.

800. Nayar, V. 2021, February 21. Misplaced celebrations: How edtech changed education from necessity to privilege. *Economic Times*. https://economictimes.indiatimes.com/small-biz/security-tech/technology/misplaced-celebrations-how-edtech-changed-education-from-necessity-to-privilege/articleshow/81121682.cms.

801. Human Rights Watch. 2022, May 25. *"How Dare They Peep into My Private Life?": Children's rights violations by governments that endorsed online learning during the COVID-19 pandemic*. https://www.hrw.org/report/2022/05/25/how-dare-they-peep-my-private-life/childrens-rights-violations-governments.

802. Yuhas, A. 2020, August 24. Partial Zoom outage is fixed after school disruptions. *New York Times*. https://www.nytimes.com/2020/08/24/business/zoom-down.html.

803. Hooper, L., Livingstone, S. & Pothong, K. 2022. *Problems with Data Governance in UK Schools: The Cases of Google Classroom and ClassDojo*. Digital Futures Commission & 5Rights Foundation. https://digitalfuturescommission.org.uk/wp-content/uploads/2022/08/Problems-with-data-governance-in-UK-schools.pdf.

804. Sawers, P. 2022, July 18. Denmark bans Chromebooks and Google Workspace in schools over data transfer risks. TechCrunch. https://techcrunch.com/2022/07/18/denmark-bans-chromebooks-and-google-workspace-in-schools-over-gdpr/.

805. Lorenz, T. 2020, March 20. 'Zoombombing': When video conferences go wrong. *New York Times*. https://www.nytimes.com/2020/03/20/style/zoombombing-zoom-trolling.html.

806. LaBarre, S. 2020, September 3. Zoom is failing teachers. Here's how they would redesign it. Fast Company. https://www.fastcompany.com/90542917/zoom-is-failing-teachers-heres-how-they-would-redesign-it.

807. Ibid.

808. Martins, D. 2021, June 30. Amazon is still the undisputed king of cloud. The Street. https://www.thestreet.com/amazon/aws/amazon-is-still-the-undisputed-king-of-cloud.

809. Williamson, B., Gulson, K.N., Perrotta, C. & Witzenberger, K. 2022, July 11. Amazon and the new global connective architectures of education governance. *Harvard Educational Review*, 92(2): 231–256. https://doi.org/10.17763/1943-5045-92.2.231.

810. Williamson, B., Gulson, K.N., Perrotta, C. & Witzenberger, K. 2022, July 12. How Amazon operates in education. *Code Acts in Education*. https://codeactsineducation.wordpress.com/2022/07/12/how-amazon-operates-in-education/.

811. Williamson, B., Gulson, K.N., Perrotta, C. & Witzenberger, K. 2022, July 11. Amazon and the new global connective architectures of education governance. *Harvard Educational Review*, 92(2): 231–256. https://doi.org/10.17763/1943-5045-92.2.231.

812. Williamson, B., Gulson, K.N., Perrotta, C. & Witzenberger, K. 2022, July 12. How Amazon operates in education. *Code Acts in Education*. https://codeactsineducation.wordpress.com/2022/07/12/how-amazon-operates-in-education/.

813. Human Rights Watch. 2022, May 25. *"How Dare They Peep into My Private Life?": Children's rights violations by governments that endorsed online learning during the COVID-19 pandemic*. https://www.hrw.org/report/2022/05/25/how-dare-they-peep-my-private-life/childrens-rights-violations-governments.

814. High, P. 2018, August 20. How 174-year-old Pearson is developing the Netflix of education. Forbes. https://www.forbes.com/sites/peterhigh/2018/08/20/how-174-year-old-pearson-is-developing-the-netflix-of-education/.

815. UN General Assembly Human Rights Council. 2016, April 6. Report of the Special Rapporteur on the right to education. https://documents-dds-ny.un.org/doc/UNDOC/GEN/G16/070/33/PDF/G1607033.pdf.

816. UN General Assembly Human Rights Council. 2022, April 19. Impact of the digitalization of education on the right to education. Report of the Special Rapporteur on the right to education. https://documents-dds-ny.un.org/doc/UNDOC/GEN/G22/322/37/PDF/G2232237.pdf.

817. Cramer-Flood, E. 2021, April 29. Worldwide digital ad spending 2021: Surprisingly resilient 2020 presages another surge. *Insider Intelligence*. https://www.insiderintelligence.com/content/worldwide-digital-ad-spending-2021.

818. Danner, J. 2018, May 14. 5 differences between consumer and institutional edtech. Medium. https://medium.com/beyond-schools/5-differences-between-consumer-and-institutional-edtech-23de38a27ace.

819. Williamson, B. 2020, July 10. "The edtech pandemic shock", by Ben Williamson & Anna Hogan. *Education International*. https://www.ei-ie.org/en/item/23423:the-edtech-pandemic-shock-by-ben-williamson-anna-hogan.

820. Defend Digital Me et al. 2020, April 16. An open letter to policy makers, data protection authorities, and providers worldwide, regarding rapid technology adoption for educational aims. Available at https://consumerfed.org/testimonial/childrens-rights-must-be-protected-in-remote-learning/.

821. The Abidjan Principles. 2019. *The Abidjan Principles: Guiding Principles on the Human Rights Obligations of States to Provide Public Education and to Regulate Private Involvement in Education*. https://static1.squarespace.com/static/5c2d081daf2096648cc801da/t/61484ef2125d785da37eb98d/1632128758265/ABIDJAN+PRINCIPLES_+ENGLISH_August2021.pdf.

822. Chawla, N. & Kumar, B. 2022, July 20. E-commerce and consumer protection in India: The emerging trend. *Journal of Business Ethics*, 180(2): 581–604. https://link.springer.com/article/10.1007/s10551-021-04884-3.

823. Singh, R. & Raj, Y. 2020, October 26. India: Ed-tech companies and the consumer protection act. Mondaq. https://www.mondaq.com/india/dodd-frank-consumer-protection-act/998116/ed-tech-companies-and-the-consumer-protection-act.

824. Bhat, A. 2022, August 3. "Hundreds of complaints": India's edtech startups are failing to regulate themselves. Rest of World. https://restofworld.org/2022/indias-edtech-startups-fail-to-regulate-themselves/.

825. Koenig, R. 2020, June 11. The post-pandemic outlook for edtech. EdSurge. https://www.edsurge.com/news/2020-06-11-the-post-pandemic-outlook-for-edtech.

826. Corcoran, B. 2021, July 30. The next wave of edtech will be very, very big — and global. EdSurge. https://www.edsurge.com/news/2021-07-30-the-next-wave-of-edtech-will-be-very-very-big-and-global.

827. *BFM avec RMC*. 2021, April 6. "Bug"... ou "cyberattaque" ? L'école à la maison (re)commence avec des problèmes informatiques ["Bug"... or "cyberattack"? School at home (again) starts with computer problems]. https://rmc.bfmtv.com/emission/bug-ou-cyberattaque-l-ecole-a-la-maison-recommence-avec-des-problemes-informatiques-2040525.html.

828. *Le Parisien*. 2021, April 8. Nouveaux bugs du dispositif «Ma classe à la maison», victime de «cyberattaques» [New bugs in the "My class at home" device, victim of "cyberattacks"]. https://www.leparisien.fr/societe/nouveaux-bugs-du-dispositif-ma-classe-a-la-maison-victime-de-cyberattaques-08-04-2021-4YOFIJO5OZDGJG23X6NGGNMIZE.php.

829. Richardson, T. 2020, April 27. Online learning portal crashes as students return to school. InDaily. https://indaily.com.au/news/2020/04/27/online-learning-portal-crashes-as-students-return-to-school/.

830. UNICEF. 2022, December 12. 1 in 3 digital learning platforms developed during COVID-19 no longer functional. Press release. https://www.unicef.org/press-releases/1-3-digital-learning-platforms-developed-during-covid-19-no-longer-functional.

831. Kneese, T. 2021, January 27. How a dead professor is teaching a university art history class. Slate. https://slate.com/technology/2021/01/dead-professor-teaching-online-class.html.

832. Apple. 2022. Learn more about Apple Distinguished Educators. K-12 Education. https://www.apple.com/education/k12/apple-distinguished-educator/. (Accessed 28 November 2022.)

833. Google for Education. 2022. Distinguish yourself in your classroom and career with certifications from Google for Education. https://edu.google.com/intl/ALL_us/for-educators/certification-programs/product-expertise/. (Accessed 28 November 2022.)

834. Microsoft. 2022. Microsoft Learn Educator Center: Microsoft Educator program. https://learn.microsoft.com/en-us/training/educator-center/programs/microsoft-educator/. (Accessed 28 November 2022.)

835. Google. 2022. Giving teachers and families the tools and tips they need to help keep students learning. Teach from Anywhere. https://teachfromanywhere.google/intl/en/. (Accessed 28 November 2022.)

836. Spataro, J. 2020, March 11. Helping teachers and students make the switch to remote learning. Microsoft 365. https://www.microsoft.com/en-us/microsoft-365/blog/2020/03/11/helping-teachers-students-switch-remote-learning/.

837. Lewis, S. 2022, July 17. Why is tech giant Apple trying to teach our teachers? The Conversation. https://theconversation.com/why-is-tech-giant-apple-trying-to-teach-our-teachers-186752.

838. Pota, V. et al. 2021, September. *Turning to Technology: A Global Survey of Teachers' Responses to the Covid-19 Pandemic*. T4 and EdTech Hub. https://t4.education/t4-insights/reports/turning-to-technology.

839. UNESCO. 2022. *The RewirEd Global Declaration on Connectivity for Education: #ConnectivityDeclaration*. https://unesdoc.unesco.org/ark:/48223/pf0000381482.

840. UNESCO. 2018. *UNESCO ICT Competency Framework for Teachers*. Version 3. https://unesdoc.unesco.org/ark:/48223/pf0000265721.

841. Turner, S., Pothong, K. & Livingstone, S. 2022. *Education Data Reality: The Challenges for Schools in Managing Children's Education Data*. Digital Futures Commission, 5Rights Foundation. https://digitalfuturescommission.org.uk/wp-content/uploads/2022/06/Education-data-reality-report.pdf.

842. Fischer, C. et al. 2020. Mining big data in education: Affordances and challenges. *Review of Research in Education*, 44(1): 130–160. https://doi.org/10.3102/0091732X20903304.

843. Microsoft Security Intelligence. 2022. Cyberthreats, viruses, and malware. https://www.microsoft.com/en-us/wdsi/threats. (Accessed 2 December 2022.)

844. Klein, N. 2020, May 13. Naomi Klein: How big tech plans to profit from the pandemic. *The Guardian*. https://www.theguardian.com/news/2020/may/13/naomi-klein-how-big-tech-plans-to-profit-from-coronavirus-pandemic.

845. Human Rights Watch. 2022, May 25. *"How Dare They Peep into My Private Life?": Children's rights violations by governments that endorsed online learning during the COVID-19 pandemic*. https://www.hrw.org/report/2022/05/25/how-dare-they-peep-my-private-life/childrens-rights-violations-governments.

846. Turner, S., Pothong, K. & Livingstone, S. 2022. *Education Data Reality: The Challenges for Schools in Managing Children's Education Data*. Digital Futures Commission, 5Rights Foundation. https://digitalfuturescommission.org.uk/wp-content/uploads/2022/06/Education-data-reality-report.pdf.

847. Ibid.

848. Jarke, J. & Breiter, A. (eds). 2021. *The Datafication of Education*. Abingdon, Oxfordshire: Routledge; Parks, M.R. 2014. Big data in communication research: Its contents and discontents. *Journal of Communication*, 64(2). http://onlinelibrary.wiley.com/doi/abs/10.1111/jcom.12090.

849. Bulger, M., McCormick, P. & Pitcan, M. 2017, February 2. The legacy of inBloom. Data & Society. https://datasociety.net/library/the-legacy-of-inbloom/; Solove, D. 2014. Why did inBloom die? A hard lesson about education privacy. Teach Privacy. https://teachprivacy.com/inbloom-die-hard-lesson-education-privacy/; Balkam, S. 2014, April 24. Learning the lessons of the inBloom failure. HuffPost. https://www.huffpost.com/entry/learning-the-lessons-of-t_b_5208724.

850. Strauss, V. 2021. $100 million Gates-funded student data project ends in failure. *Washington Post*. https://www.washingtonpost.com/news/answer-sheet/wp/2014/04/21/100-million-gates-funded-student-data-project-ends-in-failure/.

851. Ravitch, D. 2013, May 31. How will inBloom help students and schools? Diane Ravitch's blog. https://dianeravitch.net/2013/05/31/how-will-inbloom-help-students-and-schools/; Bulger, M., McCormick, P. & Pitcan, M. 2017, February 2. The legacy of inBloom. Working paper. Data & Society. https://datasociety.net/pubs/ecl/InBloom_feb_2017.pdf.

852. Mead, R. 2016, February 28. Learn different: Silicon Valley disrupts education. *New Yorker*. https://www.newyorker.com/magazine/2016/03/07/altschools-disrupted-education.

853. Herold, B. 2016, January 11. The future of big data and analytics in K-12 education. *Education Week*. https://www.edweek.org/policy-politics/the-future-of-big-data-and-analytics-in-k-12-education/2016/01.

854. Harris, A. 2014, May 9. How this startup's "micro-school" network could change the way we educate now. Fast Company. https://www.fastcompany.com/3028073/how-this-startups-micro-school-network-could-change-the-way-we-educate-now.

855. Satariano, A. 2015, June 10. What happens when an ex-Google executive creates a school system? Bloomberg. https://www.bloomberg.com/news/features/2015-06-10/what-happens-when-an-ex-google-executive-creates-a-school-system-.

856. Herold, B. 2016, January 11. The future of big data and analytics in K-12 education. *Education Week*. https://www.edweek.org/policy-politics/the-future-of-big-data-and-analytics-in-k-12-education/2016/01.

857. Kibbe, K. 2019, July 2. Tech billionaires wasted millions on failed education startup AltSchool. InsideHook. https://www.insidehook.com/daily_brief/news-opinion/tech-billionaires-wasted-millions-on-failed-education-startup-altschool; Russell, M. 2019. AltSchool's out: Zuckerberg-backed startup that tried to rethink education calls it quits. *San Francisco Chronicle*. https://www.sfchronicle.com/business/article/AltSchool-s-out-Zuckerberg-backed-startup-that-14058785.php.

858. Lapowsky, I. 2015, May 4. Inside the school Silicon Valley thinks will save education. Wired. https://www.wired.com/2015/05/altschool/; Madda, M.J. 2015, July 15. A peek Into Silicon Valley's newest bet: AltSchool. Medium. https://brightthemag.com/a-peek-into-silicon-valley-s-latest-bet-altschool-abf6c6973ecd.

859. Alba, D. 2016. Silicon Valley's New-Age AltSchool Unleashes Its Secrets. Wired. https://www.wired.com/2016/10/altschool-shares-secrets-outside-educators/; Russell, M. 2019. AltSchool's out: Zuckerberg-backed startup that tried to rethink education calls it quits. *San Francisco Chronicle*. https://www.sfchronicle.com/business/article/AltSchool-s-out-Zuckerberg-backed-startup-that-14058785.php; Adams, S. 2019. Can AltSchool—The edtech startup with $174M from billionaires like Zuckerberg and Thiel—save itself from failure? Forbes. https://www.forbes.com/sites/susanadams/2019/01/30/can-altschoolthe-edtech-startup-with-174m-from-billionaires-like-zuckerberg-and-thielsave-itself-from-failure/.

860. Robinson, M. 2017, November 21. Tech billionaires spent $170 million on a new kind of school — now classrooms are shrinking and some parents say their kids are 'guinea pigs'. Business Insider. https://www.businessinsider.com/altschool-why-parents-leaving-2017-11.

861. Loizos, C. 2017, November 22. AltSchool wants to change how kids learn, but fears have surfaced that it's failing students. TechCrunch. https://techcrunch.com/2017/11/22/altschool-wants-to-change-how-kids-learn-but-fears-that-its-failing-students-are-surfacing/.

862. Wan, T. 2019, June 28. AltSchool gets an alt-name and new leadership. EdSurge. https://www.edsurge.com/news/2019-06-28-altschool-gets-an-alt-name-and-new-leadership; Loizos, C. 2017, November 22. AltSchool wants to change how kids learn, but fears have surfaced that it's failing students. TechCrunch. https://techcrunch.com/2017/11/22/altschool-wants-to-change-how-kids-learn-but-fears-that-its-failing-students-are-surfacing/.

863. Wan, T. 2021, January 15. The edtech company formerly known as AltSchool sold its tech. So what's left? EdSurge. https://www.edsurge.com/news/2021-01-15-the-edtech-company-formerly-known-as-altschool-sold-its-tech-so-what-s-left.

864. Gillespie, T. 2014. The relevance of algorithms. In T. Gillespie, P. J. Boczkowski, & K. A. Foot. (eds). *Media technologies: Essays on communication, materiality, and society*. London: MIT Press; Jurgenson, N. & Davis, J.L. 2014. Context collapse: Theorizing context collusions and collisions. *Information, Communication & Society*, 17(4). https://www.tandfonline.com/doi/abs/10.1080/1369118X.2014.888458.

865. Williamson, B. 2019. Datafication of education. In Beetham, H. & Sharpe, R. (eds). *Rethinking Pedagogy for a Digital Age*. London: Routledge.

866. Human Rights Watch. 2022, May 25. *"How Dare They Peep into My Private Life?": Children's rights violations by governments that endorsed online learning during the COVID-19 pandemic*. https://www.hrw.org/report/2022/05/25/how-dare-they-peep-my-private-life/childrens-rights-violations-governments.

867. Kelly, G., Graham, J., Bronfman, J. & Garton, S. 2019. *2019 State of Edtech Privacy Report*. Common Sense. https://privacy.commonsense.org/content/resource/state-of-edtech-2019/cs-2019-state-of-edtech-privacy-report.pdf; Palfrey, Q., Good, N., Ghamrawi, L., Monge, W. & Boag, W. 2020, September 1. Privacy considerations as schools and parents expand utilization of ed tech apps during the COVID-19 pandemic. International Digital Accountability Council. https://digitalwatchdog.org/wp-content/uploads/2020/09/IDAC-Ed-Tech-Report-912020.pdf; Hooper, L., Livingstone, S. & Pothong, K. 2022. *Problems with Data Governance in UK Schools: The Cases of Google Classroom and ClassDojo*. Digital Futures Commission & 5Rights Foundation. https://digitalfuturescommission.org.uk/wp-content/uploads/2022/08/Problems-with-data-governance-in-UK-schools.pdf.

868. Human Rights Watch. 2022, May 25. *"How Dare They Peep into My Private Life?": Children's rights violations by governments that endorsed online learning during the COVID-19 pandemic*. https://www.hrw.org/report/2022/05/25/how-dare-they-peep-my-private-life/childrens-rights-violations-governments.

869. Patterson, D. 2021, March 11. Schools have become the leading targets of ransomware attacks. CBS News. https://www.cbsnews.com/news/schools-popular-ransomware-targets/.

870. California Legislative Information. 2022, September 26. Assembly Bill No.2355: School cybersecurity. https://leginfo.legislature.ca.gov/faces/billTextClient.xhtml?bill_id=202120220AB2355.

871. Microsoft Security Intelligence. 2022. Cyberthreats, viruses, and malware. https://www.microsoft.com/en-us/wdsi/threats. (Accessed 2 December 2022.)

872. O'Leary, J. 2022, September 22. Reducing the cost of cyber-attacks in higher education. Global Education News. https://qs-gen.com/reducing-the-cost-of-cyber-attacks-in-higher-education/.

873. Chakroun, B., Daelman-Balepa, K. & Keevy, J. 2022. *Minding the Data: Protecting Learners' Privacy and Security*. UNESCO. https://unesdoc.unesco.org/ark:/48223/pf0000381494/PDF/381494eng.pdf.multi.

874. Human Rights Watch. 2022, May 25. *"How Dare They Peep into My Private Life?": Children's rights violations by governments that endorsed online learning during the COVID-19 pandemic*. https://www.hrw.org/report/2022/05/25/how-dare-they-peep-my-private-life/childrens-rights-violations-governments.

875. Google for Education. 2022. Google Workspace for Education Terms of Service. https://workspace.google.com/terms/education_terms.html.

876. Turner, S., Pothong, K. & Livingstone, S. 2022. *Education Data Reality: The Challenges for Schools in Managing Children's Education Data*. Digital Futures Commission, 5Rights Foundation. https://digitalfuturescommission.org.uk/wp-content/uploads/2022/06/Education-data-reality-report.pdf.

877. Cakebread, C. 2017, November 15. You're not alone, no one reads terms of service agreements. Business Insider. https://www.businessinsider.com/deloitte-study-91-percent-agree-terms-of-service-without-reading-2017-11; Auxier, B. et al. 2019, November 15. Americans' attitudes and experiences with privacy policies and laws. Pew Research Center. https://www.pewresearch.org/internet/2019/11/15/americans-attitudes-and-experiences-with-privacy-policies-and-laws/.

878. Sandle, T. 2020, January 29. Report finds only 1 percent reads 'Terms & Conditions'. Digital Journal. https://www.digitaljournal.com/business/report-finds-only-1-percent-reads-terms-conditions/article/566127.

879. Obar, J.A. & Oeldorf-Hirsch, A. 2018, June 1. The biggest lie on the internet: Ignoring the privacy policies and terms of service policies of social networking services. *Information, Communication & Society*. TPRC 44: The 44th Research Conference on Communication, Information and Internet Policy. https://papers.ssrn.com/abstract=2757465.

880. Malik, D. 2020, April 29. Terms of services - A section often ignored because of its length (infographic). Digital Information World. https://www.digitalinformationworld.com/2020/04/the-length-of-the-fine-print-for-popular-apps-facebook-microsoft-tiktok.html.

881. Cohen, J. 2020, December 4. It would take 17 hours to read the Terms & Conditions of the 13 most popular apps. *PC Magazine*. https://www.pcmag.com/news/it-would-take-17-hours-to-read-the-terms-conditions-of-the-13-most-popular.

882. Ibid.

883. Berreby, D. 2017, March 3. Click to agree with what? No one reads terms of service, studies confirm. *The Guardian*. https://www.theguardian.com/technology/2017/mar/03/terms-of-service-online-contracts-fine-print.

884. Reboot. 2023. The industries with the longest Terms and Conditions. https://www.rebootonline.com/digital-pr/assets/industries-with-longest-terms-and-conditions/. (Accessed 3 March 2023.)

885. Hooper, L., Livingstone, S. & Pothong, K. 2022. *Problems with Data Governance in UK Schools: The Cases of Google Classroom and ClassDojo*. Digital Futures Commission & 5Rights Foundation. https://digitalfuturescommission.org.uk/wp-content/uploads/2022/08/Problems-with-data-governance-in-UK-schools.pdf.

886. Human Rights Watch. 2022, May 25. *"How Dare They Peep into My Private Life?": Children's rights violations by governments that endorsed online learning during the COVID-19 pandemic*. https://www.hrw.org/report/2022/05/25/how-dare-they-peep-my-private-life/childrens-rights-violations-governments.

887. Turner, S., Pothong, K. & Livingstone, S. 2022. *Education Data Reality: The Challenges for Schools in Managing Children's Education Data*. Digital Futures Commission, 5Rights Foundation. https://digitalfuturescommission.org.uk/wp-content/uploads/2022/06/Education-data-reality-report.pdf.

888. Zoom. 2021, September. Primary and Secondary Schools Privacy Statement. https://explore.zoom.us/en/schools-privacy-statement/.

889. Hooper, L., Livingstone, S. & Pothong, K. 2022. *Problems with Data Governance in UK Schools: The Cases of Google Classroom and ClassDojo*. Digital Futures Commission & 5Rights Foundation. https://digitalfuturescommission.org.uk/wp-content/uploads/2022/08/Problems-with-data-governance-in-UK-schools.pdf.

890. Turner, S., Pothong, K. & Livingstone, S. 2022. *Education Data Reality: The Challenges for Schools in Managing Children's Education Data*. Digital Futures Commission, 5Rights Foundation. https://digitalfuturescommission.org.uk/wp-content/uploads/2022/06/Education-data-reality-report.pdf.

891. Hooper, L., Livingstone, S. & Pothong, K. 2022. *Problems with Data Governance in UK Schools: The Cases of Google Classroom and ClassDojo*. Digital Futures Commission & 5Rights Foundation. https://digitalfuturescommission.org.uk/wp-content/uploads/2022/08/Problems-with-data-governance-in-UK-schools.pdf.

892. Ibid.

893. Kelion, L. 2019, September 24. Google wins landmark right to be forgotten case. BBC News. https://www.bbc.com/news/technology-49808208.

894. Colclough, C. 2020, September. *Teaching with Tech: The Role of Education Unions in Shaping the Future*. Education International. https://issuu.com/educationinternational/docs/2020_ei_research_teachingwithtech_eng.

895. Lazare, M. 2021, February 17. A peek at what's next for Google Classroom. Google Education. Blog post. https://blog.google/outreach-initiatives/education/classroom-roadmap/.

896. Jerome, J. 2021, April 15. Privacy is key: Holding EdTech accountable. Heinrich-Böll-Stiftung. https://us.boell.org/en/2021/03/31/privacy-key-holding-edtech-accountable.

897. Ibid.

898. Satariano, A. 2020, April 27. Europe's privacy law hasn't shown its teeth, frustrating advocates. *New York Times*. https://www.nytimes.com/2020/04/27/technology/GDPR-privacy-law-europe.html.

899. European Data Protection Board. 2020. Contribution of the EDPB to the evaluation of the GDPR under Article 97. https://edpb.europa.eu/sites/default/files/files/file1/edpb_contributiongdprevaluation_20200218.pdf.

900. Satariano, A. 2022, November 28. Meta fined $275 million for breaking E.U. data privacy law. *New York Times*. https://www.nytimes.com/2022/11/28/business/meta-fine-eu-privacy.html.

901. Palfrey, Q., Good, N., Ghamrawi, L., Monge, W. & Boag, W. 2020, September 1. Privacy considerations as schools and parents expand utilization of ed tech apps during the COVID-19 pandemic. International Digital Accountability Council. https://digitalwatchdog.org/wp-content/uploads/2020/09/IDAC-Ed-Tech-Report-912020.pdf.

902. Human Rights Watch. 2022, May 25. *"How Dare They Peep into My Private Life?": Children's rights violations by governments that endorsed online learning during the COVID-19 pandemic*. https://www.hrw.org/report/2022/05/25/how-dare-they-peep-my-private-life/childrens-rights-violations-governments.

903. Jetha, N. 2022, August 31. New report finds digital classrooms flout data protection law to exploit children's data for commercial gain. Digital Futures Commission. https://digitalfuturescommission.org.uk/blog/new-report-finds-digital-classrooms-flout-data-protection-law-to-exploit-childrens-data-for-commercial-gain/.

904. Common Sense. 2021. *State of Kids' Privacy 2021: Key Findings*. https://www.commonsensemedia.org/sites/default/files/research/report/common-sense-2021-state-of-kids-privacy-key-findings.pdf.

905. Singer, N. 2022, July 31. A cyberattack illuminates the shaky state of student privacy. *New York Times*. https://www.nytimes.com/2022/07/31/business/student-privacy-illuminate-hack.html.

906. Ball, S.J. ed. 2018. *Governing by Numbers: Education, Governance, and the Tyranny of Numbers*. Abingdon, Oxfordshire: Routledge.

907. Gulson, K.N., Sellar, S. & Webb, P.T. 2022. *Algorithms of Education: How Datafication and Artificial Intelligence Shape Policy*. Minneapolis: University of Minnesota Press.

908. Ballhaus, B. 2021, June 8. Bringing personalized experiences to education with you. Blackboard. Blog post. https://blog.blackboard.com/bringing-personalized-experiences-to-education-with-you/.

909. Williamson, B. 2019. Datafication of education. In Beetham, H. & Sharpe, R. (eds) *Rethinking Pedagogy for a Digital Age*. London: Routledge. Available at https://www.researchgate.net/publication/334008102_Datafication_of_Education.

910. Ibid.

911. Gulson, K.N., Sellar, S. & Webb, P.T. 2022. *Algorithms of Education: How Datafication and Artificial Intelligence Shape Policy*. Minneapolis: University of Minnesota Press.

912. Anand, P. & Bergen, M. 2021, October 28. Big teacher is watching: How AI spyware took over schools. Bloomberg. https://www.bloomberg.com/news/features/2021-10-28/how-goguardian-ai-spyware-took-over-schools-student-devices-during-covid.

913. Hooper, L., Livingstone, S. & Pothong, K. 2022. *Problems with Data Governance in UK Schools: The Cases of Google Classroom and ClassDojo*. Digital Futures Commission & 5Rights Foundation. https://digitalfuturescommission.org.uk/wp-content/uploads/2022/08/Problems-with-data-governance-in-UK-schools.pdf.

914. Hillman, V., Noula, I. & Wagner, B. 2021, July 14. Big tech firms can't be trusted to decide children's futures. *Jacobin*. https://jacobin.com/2021/07/big-tech-children-future-covid-pandemic-education-privacy-data.

915. Jarke, J. & Breiter, A. (eds). 2021. *The Datafication of Education*. Abingdon, Oxfordshire: Routledge.

916. Jack, A. 2020, July 9. Students and teachers hit at International Baccalaureate grading. *Financial Times*. https://www.ft.com/content/ee0f4d97-4e0c-4bc3-8350-19855e70f0cf; Simonite, T. 2020, July 10. Meet the secret algorithm that's keeping students out of college. Wired. https://www.wired.com/story/algorithm-set-students-grades-altered-futures/.

917. Lamont, T. 2021, February 18. The student and the algorithm: How the exam results fiasco threatened one pupil's future. *The Guardian*. https://www.theguardian.com/education/2021/feb/18/the-student-and-the-algorithm-how-the-exam-results-fiasco-threatened-one-pupils-future.

918. Sean Coughlan, Katherine Sellgren, & Judith Burns. 2020. A-levels: Anger over 'unfair' results this year. BBC News. https://www.bbc.com/news/education-53759832.

919. Lamont, T. 2021, February 18. The student and the algorithm: How the exam results fiasco threatened one pupil's future. *The Guardian*. https://www.theguardian.com/education/2021/feb/18/the-student-and-the-algorithm-how-the-exam-results-fiasco-threatened-one-pupils-future.

920. Katzenbach, C. & Ulbricht, L. 2019. Algorithmic governance. *Internet Policy Review*, 8(4). https://policyreview.info/concepts/algorithmic-governance.

921. Crawford, K. 2021. *Atlas of AI: Power, Politics, and the Planetary Costs of Artificial Intelligence*. New Haven: Yale University Press.

922. UNESCO. 2022. Ethics of artificial intelligence. https://www.unesco.org/en/artificial-intelligence/recommendation-ethics; Miao, F., Holmes, W., Huang, R. & Zhang, H. 2021. *AI and Education: Guidance for Policymakers*. UNESCO. https://unesdoc.unesco.org/ark:/48223/pf0000376709; UNESCO. 2021. Draft text of the recommendation on the ethics of artificial intelligence. https://unesdoc.unesco.org/ark:/48223/pf0000377897.

923. European Commission. 2021. Proposal for a regulation of the European Parliament and of the Council laying down harmonised rules on artificial intelligence (Artificial Intelligence Act) and amending certain union legislative acts. https://artificialintelligenceact.eu/the-act/.

924. Hillman, V., Noula, I. & Wagner, B. 2021, July 14. Big tech firms can't be trusted to decide children's futures. *Jacobin*. https://jacobinmag.com/2021/07/big-tech-children-future-covid-pandemic-education-privacy-data.

925. MIT Media Lab 2023. Project Overview - AttentivU. MIT Media Lab. https://www.media.mit.edu/projects/attentivu/overview/.

926. Williamson, B. 2021, September 8. New biological data and knowledge in education. *Code Acts in Education*. https://codeactsineducation.wordpress.com/2021/09/08/new-biological-data-knowledge-education/.

927. @PDChina. *People's Daily*. 2018, May 16. What else can surveillance cameras do in classroom other than exam supervision? High school in #Hangzhou uses camera to identify students' facial expression for class performance analysis and improvement. Twitter. https://twitter.com/PDChina/status/996755673093292032.

928. Li, P. & Jourdan, A. 2018, May 17. Sleepy pupils in the picture at high-tech Chinese school. Reuters. https://www.reuters.com/article/us-china-surveillance-education-idUSKCN1II123.

929. GETChina Insights. 2019, September 9. Schools using facial recognition system sparks privacy concerns in China. Medium. https://edtechchina.medium.com/schools-using-facial-recognition-system-sparks-privacy-concerns-in-china-d4f706e5cfd0.

930. Wanqing, Z. 2022, February 21. Chinese school faces backlash over use of facial recognition scanners. SixthTone. https://www.sixthtone.com/news/1009712.

931. BBC News. 2019, September 6. China to curb facial recognition and apps in schools. https://www.bbc.com/news/world-asia-49608459.

932. Cardinal, D. 2017, September 14. How Apple's iPhone X TrueDepth camera works. Extreme Tech. https://www.extremetech.com/mobile/255771-apple-iphone-x-truedepth-camera-works.

933. Pires, F. 2022, April 18. Intel develops controversial AI to detect emotional states of students. Tom's Hardware. https://www.tomshardware.com/news/intel-students-ai-controversy.

934. Chan, M. 2021, February 17. This AI reads children's emotions as they learn. CNN. https://edition.cnn.com/2021/02/16/tech/emotion-recognition-ai-education-spc-intl-hnk/index.html.

935. Find Solution Ai. 2023. Product features. https://www.findsolutionai.com. (Accessed 4 March 2023.)

936. Ibid.

937. Chan, M. 2021, February 17. This AI reads children's emotions as they learn. CNN. https://edition.cnn.com/2021/02/16/tech/emotion-recognition-ai-education-spc-intl-hnk/index.html.

938. Heaven, D. 2020, February 26. Why faces don't always tell the truth about feelings. *Nature*. https://www.nature.com/articles/d41586-020-00507-5; Russell, J.A. & Dols, J.M.F. (eds) 2017. *The Science of Facial Expression*. Oxford: Oxford University Press; Izard, C.E. 2010. The many meanings/aspects of emotion: Definitions, functions, activation, and regulation. *Emotion Review*, 2(4). https://journals.sagepub.com/doi/10.1177/1754073910374661; Crawford, K. 2021, April 27. Artificial intelligence is misreading human emotion. *The Atlantic*. https://www.theatlantic.com/technology/archive/2021/04/artificial-intelligence-misreading-human-emotion/618696/.

939. Barrett, L.F., Adolphs, R., Marsella, S., Martinez, A.M. & Pollak, S.D. 2019. Emotional expressions reconsidered: Challenges to inferring emotion from human facial movements. *Psychological Science in the Public Interest*, 20(1). https://journals.sagepub.com/eprint/SAUES8UM69EN8TSMUGF9/full; Gunes, H. & Pantic, M. 2010. Automatic, dimensional and continuous emotion recognition. *International Journal of Synthetic Emotions*, 1(1). https://ibug.doc.ic.ac.uk/media/uploads/documents/GunesPantic_IJSE_2010_camera.pdf; Crawford, K. 2021, April 6. Time to regulate AI that interprets human emotions. *Nature*. https://www.nature.com/articles/d41586-021-00868-5; Gershgorn, D. 2021, February 19. The shoddy science behind emotional recognition tech. OneZero. https://onezero.medium.com/the-shoddy-science-behind-emotional-recognition-tech-2e847fc526a0; Fedders, B. 2019. The constant and expanding classroom: Surveillance in K-12 public schools. *North Carolina Law Review*, 97(6). https://scholarship.law.unc.edu/nclr/vol97/iss6/4/.

940. Gunes, H. & Pantic, M. 2010. Automatic, dimensional and continuous emotion recognition. *International Journal of Synthetic Emotions*, 1(1). https://ibug.doc.ic.ac.uk/media/uploads/documents/GunesPantic_IJSE_2010_camera.pdf; Crawford, K. 2021, April 6. Time to regulate AI that interprets human emotions. *Nature*. https://www.nature.com/articles/d41586-021-00868-5; Gershgorn, D. 2021, February 19. The shoddy science behind emotional recognition tech. OneZero. https://onezero.medium.com/the-shoddy-science-behind-emotional-recognition-tech-2e847fc526a0; Barrett, L.F., Adolphs, R., Marsella, S., Martinez, A.M. & Pollak, S.D. 2019. Emotional expressions reconsidered: Challenges to inferring emotion from human facial movements. *Psychological Science in the Public Interest*, 20(1). https://journals.sagepub.com/eprint/SAUES8UM69EN8TSMUGF9/full; Barrett, L.F. 2014, February 28. What faces can't tell us. *New York Times*. https://www.nytimes.com/2014/03/02/opinion/sunday/what-faces-cant-tell-us.html; Fedders, B. 2019. The constant and expanding classroom: Surveillance in K-12 public schools. *North Carolina Law Review*, 97(6). https://scholarship.law.unc.edu/nclr/vol97/iss6/4/.

941. Barrett, L.F., Adolphs, R., Marsella, S., Martinez, A.M. & Pollak, S.D. 2019. Emotional expressions reconsidered: Challenges to inferring emotion from human facial movements. *Psychological Science in the Public Interest*, 20(1). https://journals.sagepub.com/eprint/SAUES8UM69EN8TSMUGF9/full.

942. Crawford, K., et al. 2019. *AI Now 2019 Report*. https://ainowinstitute.org/reports.html.

943. Bird, S. 2022, June 21. Responsible AI investments and safeguards for facial recognition. Azure. https://azure.microsoft.com/en-us/blog/responsible-ai-investments-and-safeguards-for-facial-recognition/.

944. Markets and Markets. 2022. Emotion detection and recognition (EDR) market. https://www.marketsandmarkets.com/Market-Reports/emotion-detection-recognition-market-23376176.html. (Accessed 28 November 2022.)

945. Hume AI. 2023. Expressive language. Hume AI. https://hume.ai/; Empath. 2023. Empath. https://www.webempath.com/.

946. Hume AI. 2023. Expressive language. Hume AI. https://hume.ai/.

947. Gillum, J. & Kao, J. 2019, June 25. Aggression detectors: The unproven, invasive surveillance technology schools are using to monitor students. ProPublica. https://features.propublica.org/aggression-detector/the-unproven-invasive-surveillance-technology-schools-are-using-to-monitor-students/.

948. Barrett, L.F., Adolphs, R., Marsella, S., Martinez, A.M. & Pollak, S.D. 2019. Emotional expressions reconsidered: Challenges to inferring emotion from human facial movements. *Psychological Science in the Public Interest*, 20(1). https://journals.sagepub.com/eprint/SAUES8UM69EN8TSMUGF9/full; Vincent, J. 2019, July 25. AI 'emotion recognition' can't be trusted. The Verge. https://www.theverge.com/2019/7/25/8929793/emotion-recognition-analysis-ai-machine-learning-facial-expression-review.

949. Gendron, M., Lindquist, K.A., Barsalou, L. & Barrett, L.F. 2012. Emotion words shape emotion percepts. *Emotion* 12(2). https://psycnet.apa.org/record/2012-03012-001; Lindquist, K.A., Barrett, L.F., Bliss-Moreau, E. & Russell, J.A. 2006. Language and the perception of emotion. *Emotion* 6(1). https://psycnet.apa.org/record/2006-04603-012.

950. Gendron, M., Roberson, D., van der Vyver, J.M. & Barrett, L.F. 2014. Perceptions of emotion from facial expressions are not culturally universal: Evidence from a remote culture. *Emotion* 14(2). https://pubmed.ncbi.nlm.nih.gov/24708506/.

951. *The Economist*. 2020, March 26. Countries are using apps and data networks to keep tabs on the pandemic. https://www.economist.com/briefing/2020/03/26/countries-are-using-apps-and-data-networks-to-keep-tabs-on-the-pandemic.

952. Foucault, M. 1975. *Discipline and Punish: The Birth of the Prison*. New York: Pantheon.

953. Grant-Chapman, H., Laird, E. & Venzke, C. 2021, September 21. Student activity monitoring software: Research insights and recommendations. Center for Democracy and Technology. https://cdt.org/insights/student-activity-monitoring-software-research-insights-and-recommendations/.

954. Li, H., Arnsperger, L. & Cerny, M. 2020, June 30. Censorship fears and vampire hours. The China Project. https://thechinaproject.com/2020/06/30/chinese-international-students-zoom-and-remote-learning/.

955. McNeill, S. 2021, June 30. "They don't understand the fear we have": How China's long reach of repression undermines academic freedom at Australia's universities. Human Rights Watch. https://www.hrw.org/report/2021/06/30/they-dont-understand-fear-we-have/how-chinas-long-reach-repression-undermines.

956. Faek, R. 2021, April 18. Self-censorship in Arab higher education: An untold problem. Al-Fanar Media. https://www.al-fanarmedia.org/2021/04/self-censorship-in-arab-higher-education-an-untold-problem/.

957. Hamamra, B., Qabaha, A. & Daragmeh, A. 2022. Online education and surveillance during COVID-19 pandemic in Palestinian universities. *International Studies in Sociology of Education*, 31(4): 446–466. https://www.tandfonline.com/doi/full/10.1080/09620214.2021.2016473.

958. Qiang, X. 2019. The road to digital unfreedom. *Journal of Democracy*, 30(1). https://muse.jhu.edu/article/713722; Abdel-Baqui, O. & Calfas, J. 2022, January 26. New Virginia hotline lets parents report 'divisive teaching practices'. *Wall Street Journal*. https://www.wsj.com/articles/new-virginia-hotline-lets-parents-report-divisive-teaching-practices-11643236044.

959. Thorsten Benner. 2021, September 8. The 'Zoomification' of academia: Addressing risks to academic freedom. Global Public Policy Institute. https://gppi.net/2021/09/08/the-zoomification-of-academia-addressing-risks-to-academic-freedom.

960. Satariano, A. & Mozur, P. 2021, October 22. Russia is censoring the internet, with coercion and black boxes. *New York Times*. https://www.nytimes.com/2021/10/22/technology/russia-internet-censorship-putin.html.

961. Hernandez, M.D., Anthonio, F., Cheng, S. & Skok, A. 2022, April 28. Internet shutdowns in 2021: The return of digital authoritarianism. Access Now. https://www.accessnow.org/internet-shutdowns-2021/.

962. Fatafta, M., Mnejja, K. & Anthonio, F. 2021, July 7. Internet shutdowns during exams: When MENA governments fail the test. Access Now. https://www.accessnow.org/mena-internet-shutdowns-during-exams/.

963. Yoo-Brannon, J. 2021, September 30. We need to make schools human again. That means treating teachers with respect. EdSurge. https://www.edsurge.com/news/2021-09-30-we-need-to-make-schools-human-again-that-means-treating-teachers-with-respect.

964. Walker, T. 2023, February 3. Cell phone bans in school are back. How far will they go? National Education Association. https://www.nea.org/advocating-for-change/new-from-nea/cellphone-bans-school-are-back-how-far-will-they-go.

965. Merikko, J. & Kivimäki, V. 2022, October 13. "Replacing teachers? Doubt it." Practitioners' views on adaptive learning technologies' impact on the teaching profession. *Frontiers in Education*, 7. https://www.frontiersin.org/articles/10.3389/feduc.2022.1010255.

966. Kneese, T. 2021, January 27. How a dead professor is teaching a university art history class. Slate. https://slate.com/technology/2021/01/dead-professor-teaching-online-class.html.

967. Zăvoianu, E.A. & Pânișoară, I.-O. 2021. Teachers' perception of the phenomenon of cyberbullying during the Covid-19 pandemic. *LUMEN Proceedings*, 17. https://proceedings.lumenpublishing.com/ojs/index.php/lumenproceedings/article/view/752; McMahon, S.D. et al. Violence against educators and school personnel: Crisis during COVID. American Psychological Association. https://www.apa.org/education-career/k12/violence-educators-technical-report.pdf.

968. O'Neil, C. 2016. *Weapons of Math Destruction: How Big Data Increases Inequality and Threatens Democracy*. New York: Crown.

969. Tiffany, G. 2020, August 12. Algorithmic grading is not an answer to the challenges of the pandemic. Algorithm Watch. https://algorithmwatch.org/en/uk-algorithmic-grading-gcse/.

970. Newton, D. 2021, April 26. From admissions to teaching to grading, AI is infiltrating higher education. The Hechinger Report. http://hechingerreport.org/from-admissions-to-teaching-to-grading-ai-is-infiltrating-higher-education/.

971. Swauger, S. 2021, November 12. The next normal: Algorithms will take over college, from admissions to advising. *Washington Post*. https://www.washingtonpost.com/outlook/next-normal-algorithms-college/2021/11/12/366fe8dc-4264-11ec-a3aa-0255edc02eb7_story.html.

972. Burke, L. 2020, December 14. The death and life of an admissions algorithm. *Inside Higher Ed*. https://www.insidehighered.com/admissions/article/2020/12/14/u-texas-will-stop-using-controversial-algorithm-evaluate-phd; Letters. 2020, August 17. Inbuilt biases and the problem of algorithms. *The Guardian*. https://www.theguardian.com/education/2020/aug/17/inbuilt-biases-and-the-problem-of-algorithms; Simonite, T. 2020, July 10. Meet the secret algorithm that's keeping students out of college. Wired. https://www.wired.com/story/algorithm-set-students-grades-altered-futures/.

973. Feathers, T. 2021, March 2. Major universities are using race as a "high impact predictor" of student success. The Markup. https://themarkup.org/machine-learning/2021/03/02/major-universities-are-using-race-as-a-high-impact-predictor-of-student-success.

974. Engler, A. 2021. Enrollment algorithms are contributing to the crises of higher education. Brookings. https://www.brookings.edu/research/enrollment-algorithms-are-contributing-to-the-crises-of-higher-education/.

975. International Baccalaureate. 2020. IB Assessment for May 2020 examination session during COVID-19 pandemic. https://www.ibo.org/globalassets/new-structure/covid-19/pdfs/assessment-model-letter-may-2020-en.pdf.

976. Zagmout, A. 2020. Justice for May 2020 IB Graduates - Build a Better Future! #IBSCANDAL. Change.org. https://www.change.org/p/international-baccalaureate-organisation-ibo-justice-for-may-2020-ib-graduates-build-a-better-future.

977. Kippin, S. & Cairney, P. 2022. The COVID-19 exams fiasco across the UK: Four nations and two windows of opportunity. *British Politics*, 17(1). https://doi.org/10.1057/s41293-021-00162-y.

978. Hern, A. 2020, August 21. Ofqual's A-level algorithm: Why did it fail to make the grade? *The Guardian*. https://www.theguardian.com/education/2020/aug/21/ofqual-exams-algorithm-why-did-it-fail-make-grade-a-levels.

979. Lamont, T. 2021, February 18. The student and the algorithm: How the exam results fiasco threatened one pupil's future. *The Guardian*. https://www.theguardian.com/education/2021/feb/18/the-student-and-the-algorithm-how-the-exam-results-fiasco-threatened-one-pupils-future.

980. Burgess, M. 2020, August 20. The lessons we all must learn from the A-levels algorithm debacle. Wired. https://www.wired.co.uk/article/gcse-results-alevels-algorithm-explained; Bewick, T. 2020, August 24. 'Results day 2020 was like the sinking of the Titanic'. *Tes Magazine*. https://www.tes.com/magazine/archive/results-day-2020-was-sinking-titanic; Malik, K. 2020, August 23. The cruel exams algorithm has laid bare the unfairness at the heart of our schools. *The Observer*. https://www.theguardian.com/commentisfree/2020/aug/23/the-cruel-exams-algorithm-has-laid-bare-the-unfairness-at-the-heart-of-our-schools; Letters. 2020, August 17. Inbuilt biases and the problem of algorithms. *The Guardian*. https://www.theguardian.com/education/2020/aug/17/inbuilt-biases-and-the-problem-of-algorithms; Harkness, T. 2020, August 18. How Ofqual failed the algorithm test. UnHerd. https://unherd.com/2020/08/how-ofqual-failed-the-algorithm-test/.

981. Adams, R., Weale, S. & Barr, C. 2020, August 13. A-level results: almost 40% of teacher assessments in England downgraded. *The Guardian*. https://www.theguardian.com/education/2020/aug/13/almost-40-of-english-students-have-a-level-results-downgraded.

982. Letters. 2020, August 17. Inbuilt biases and the problem of algorithms. *The Guardian*. https://www.theguardian.com/education/2020/aug/17/inbuilt-biases-and-the-problem-of-algorithms; Stewart, H. & Weale, S. 2020, August 17. Exam results: Gavin Williamson poised for algorithm climbdown. *The Guardian*. https://www.theguardian.com/education/2020/aug/17/no-10-hints-ministers-set-ditch-a-level-results-algorithm-england.

983. @HUCKmagazine. 2020, August 16. Chants of "fuck the algorithm" as a speaker talks of losing her place at medical school because she was downgraded. Twitter. https://twitter.com/HUCKmagazine/status/1294987261751234560.

984. Hern, A. 2020, August 21. Ofqual's A-level algorithm: Why did it fail to make the grade? *The Guardian*. https://www.theguardian.com/education/2020/aug/21/ofqual-exams-algorithm-why-did-it-fail-make-grade-a-levels.

985. Stewart, H. 2020, August 26. Boris Johnson blames 'mutant algorithm' for exams fiasco. *The Guardian*. https://www.theguardian.com/politics/2020/aug/26/boris-johnson-blames-mutant-algorithm-for-exams-fiasco.

986. Kippin, S. & Cairney, P. 2022. The COVID-19 exams fiasco across the UK: Four nations and two windows of opportunity. *British Politics*, 17(1). https://doi.org/10.1057/s41293-021-00162-y.

987. Lamont, T. 2021, February 18. The student and the algorithm: How the exam results fiasco threatened one pupil's future. *The Guardian*. https://www.theguardian.com/education/2021/feb/18/the-student-and-the-algorithm-how-the-exam-results-fiasco-threatened-one-pupils-future.

988. Parliamentlive.tv. 2020, September 2. The impact of COVID-19 on education and children's services. https://parliamentlive.tv/Event/Index/a3d523ca-09fc-49a5-84e3-d50c3a3bcbe3.

989. Lamont, T. 2021, February 18. The student and the algorithm: How the exam results fiasco threatened one pupil's future. *The Guardian*. https://www.theguardian.com/education/2021/feb/18/the-student-and-the-algorithm-how-the-exam-results-fiasco-threatened-one-pupils-future.

990. @yasmmeme. 2020, December 1. Tomorrow, the UMD physics department is hosting a very interesting colloquium talk on the use of machine-learning for graduate admissions. I'd like to take a second and explain why this talk is concerning. Twitter. https://twitter.com/yasmmeme/status/1333670480574771201.

991. Burke, L. 2020, December 14. The death and life of an admissions algorithm. *Inside Higher Ed*. https://www.insidehighered.com/admissions/article/2020/12/14/u-texas-will-stop-using-controversial-algorithm-evaluate-phd.

992. Waters, A. & Miikkulainen, R. 2013. GRADE: Machine learning support for graduate admissions. *AI Magazine*, 35(1). https://doi.org/10.1609/aimag.v35i1.2504; Burke, L. 2020, December 14. The death and life of an admissions algorithm. *Inside Higher Ed*. https://www.insidehighered.com/admissions/article/2020/12/14/u-texas-will-stop-using-controversial-algorithm-evaluate-phd.

993. Gulson, K.N., Sellar, S. & Webb, P.T. 2022. *Algorithms of Education: How Datafication and Artificial Intelligence Shape Policy*. Minneapolis: University of Minnesota Press; Vallee, H.Q. la & Duarte, N. 2019, August 12. Algorithmic systems in education: Incorporating equity and fairness when using student data. Center for Democracy and Technology. https://cdt.org/insights/algorithmic-systems-in-education-incorporating-equity-and-fairness-when-using-student-data/.

994. Gulson, K.N., Sellar, S. & Webb, P.T. 2022. *Algorithms of Education: How Datafication and Artificial Intelligence Shape Policy*. Minneapolis: University of Minnesota Press; Venkataramakrishnan, S. 2021, January 10. Algorithms and the coronavirus pandemic. *Financial Times*. https://www.ft.com/content/16f4ded0-e86b-4f77-8b05-67d555838941.

995. Feathers, T. 2019, August 20. Flawed algorithms are grading millions of students' essays. Vice. https://www.vice.com/en/article/pa7dj9/flawed-algorithms-are-grading-millions-of-students-essays.

996. Chin, M. 2020, September 3. These students figured out their tests were graded by AI — and the easy way to cheat. The Verge. https://www.theverge.com/2020/9/2/21419012/edgenuity-online-class-ai-grading-keyword-mashing-students-school-cheating-algorithm-glitch.

997. Hendry, J. 2018, January 30. Govts dump NAPLAN robo marking plans. iTnews. https://www.itnews.com.au/news/govts-dump-naplan-robo-marking-plans-482044.

998. The Wiley Network. 2020, September 21. How today's culture encourages student cheating (and what to do about it). https://www.wiley.com/en-us/network/education/instructors/teaching-strategies/how-todays-culture-encourages-student-cheating-and-what-to-do-about-it.

999. Fask, A., Englander, F. & Wang, Z. 2014. Do online exams facilitate cheating? An experiment designed to separate possible cheating from the effect of the online test taking environment. *Journal of Academic Ethics*, 12(2). https://doi.org/10.1007/s10805-014-9207-1.

1000. Watson, G.R. & Sottile, J. 2010. Cheating in the digital age: Do students cheat more in online courses? *Online Journal of Distance Learning Administration*, 13(1). https://eric.ed.gov/?id=EJ877536.

1001. McCabe, D.L., Trevino, L.K. & Butterfield, K.D. 2001. Cheating in academic institutions: A decade of research. *Ethics & Behavior*, 11(3). https://doi.org/10.1207/S15327019EB1103_2; Mazar, N., Amir, O. & Ariely, D. 2008. The dishonesty of honest people: A theory of self-concept maintenance. *Journal of Marketing Research*, 45(6). https://doi.org/10.1509/jmkr.45.6.633.

1002. Grajek, S. 2020, April 10. EDUCAUSE COVID-19 quickpoll results: Grading and proctoring. *EDUCAUSE Review*. https://er.educause.edu/blogs/2020/4/educause-covid-19-quickpoll-results-grading-and-proctoring.

1003. Kimmons, R. & Veletsianos, G. 2021, February 23. Proctoring software in higher ed: Prevalence and patterns. *EDUCAUSE Review*. https://er.educause.edu/articles/2021/2/proctoring-software-in-higher-ed-prevalence-and-patterns.

1004. Wan, T. 2020, March 23. A lockdown abroad disrupts testing at home. EdSurge. https://www.edsurge.com/news/2020-03-23-a-lockdown-abroad-disrupts-a-major-online-education-service-proctoring; Caplan-Bricker, N. 2021, May 27. Is online test-monitoring here to stay? *New Yorker*. https://www.newyorker.com/tech/annals-of-technology/is-online-test-monitoring-here-to-stay; Lu, C. & Darragh, E. 2021, November 5. Remote test proctoring apps are a form of mass surveillance. *Teen Vogue*. https://www.teenvogue.com/story/remote-proctoring-apps-tests.

1005. Proctorio. 2023. Our platform. https://proctorio.com/. (Accessed 4 March 2023.)

1006. Kelley, J. 2022, August 25. Federal judge: Invasive online proctoring 'room scans' are unconstitutional. Electronic Frontier Foundation. https://www.eff.org/deeplinks/2022/08/federal-judge-invasive-online-proctoring-room-scans-are-also-unconstitutional.

1007. Hill, K. 2022, May 27. Accused of cheating by an algorithm, and a professor she had never met. *New York Times*. https://www.nytimes.com/2022/05/27/technology/college-students-cheating-software-honorlock.html.

1008. ProctorU. 2020. ProctorU CCPA privacy policy. https://archive.md/FM8ba.

1009. Meazure Learning. 2023. Privacy Policy. https://www.meazurelearning.com/privacy-policy. (Accessed 23 March 2023.)

1010. Abrams, L. 2020, August 9. ProctorU confirms data breach after database leaked online. BleepingComputer. https://www.bleepingcomputer.com/news/security/proctoru-confirms-data-breach-after-database-leaked-online/.

1011. Britton, N.D. & Wang, C. 2020, August 5. Hackers publish Australian universities' ProctorU data. *Honi Soit*. http://honisoit.com/2020/08/hackers-publish-australian-universities-proctoru-data/.

1012. Source Forge. 2023. Online proctoring software: Compare the top online proctoring software of 2023. https://sourceforge.net/software/online-proctoring/.

[1013.] Kelley, J. 2021, June 22. A long overdue reckoning for online proctoring companies may finally be here. Electronic Frontier Foundation. https://www.eff.org/deeplinks/2021/06/long-overdue-reckoning-online-proctoring-companies-may-finally-be-here.

[1014.] Proctorio. 2023. Proctorio Gradebook in Canvas. http://www.fullerton.edu/it/services/software/proctorio/Canvas%20Proctorio%20Gradebook.pdf.

[1015.] Caines, A. & Silverman, S. 2021, December 10. Back doors, trap doors, and fourth-party deals: How you end up with harmful academic surveillance technology on your campus without even knowing. *Journal of Interactive Technology and Pedagogy*, 20. https://jitp.commons.gc.cuny.edu/back-doors-trap-doors-and-fourth-party-deals-how-you-end-up-with-harmful-academic-surveillance-technology-on-your-campus-without-even-knowing/.

[1016.] Kelley, J. 2021, June 22. A long overdue reckoning for online proctoring companies may finally be here. Electronic Frontier Foundation. https://www.eff.org/deeplinks/2021/06/long-overdue-reckoning-online-proctoring-companies-may-finally-be-here.

[1017.] Feathers, T. 2021, April 8. Proctorio is using racist algorithms to detect faces. Vice. https://www.vice.com/en/article/g5gxg3/proctorio-is-using-racist-algorithms-to-detect-faces.

[1018.] Perkowitz, S. 2021. The bias in the machine: Facial recognition technology and racial disparities. *MIT Case Studies in Social and Ethical Responsibilities of Computing* (Winter). https://mit-serc.pubpub.org/pub/bias-in-machine/release/1.

[1019.] Simonite, T. 2019, July 22. The best algorithms still struggle to recognize black faces. Wired. https://www.wired.com/story/best-algorithms-struggle-recognize-black-faces-equally/.

[1020.] Caplan-Bricker, N. 2021, May 27. Is online test-monitoring here to stay? *New Yorker*. https://www.newyorker.com/tech/annals-of-technology/is-online-test-monitoring-here-to-stay.

[1021.] @uhreeb [Alivardi Khan]. 2020, September 8. The @ExamSoft software can't "recognize" me due to "poor lighting" even though I'm sitting in a well lit room. Starting to think it has nothing to do with lighting. Pretty sure we all predicted their facial recognition software wouldn't work for people of color. Twitter. https://twitter.com/uhreeb/status/1303139738065481728; @futureesq1990. 2020, September 17. @ExamSoft I FINALLY figured out ON MY OWN 4 hours later (still on hold for an EXAM SOFT chat rep) HOW TO GET TO MY MOCK EXAM... ONLY TO BE TOLD THE SYSTEM CANT RECOGNIZE ME. I AM IN A BOARD ROOM WITH ALL OF THE LIGHTS TURNED ON AND THE SUN WAS STILL UP. MAKE IT MAKE SENSE. Twitter. https://twitter.com/futureesq1990/status/1306393725099278336.

[1022.] The Supreme Court of India Civil Appellate Jurisdiction. 2020. WRIT Petition (Civil) No. 1030 of 2020: Rakesh Kumar Agarwalla vs. National Law School of India University, Bengaluru. https://main.sci.gov.in/

[1023.] Shanahan, M. 2020, December 11. Students stranded after ProctorU crash. *Honi Soit*. https://honisoit.com/2020/12/students-stranded-after-proctoru-crash/.

[1024.] Brown, L.X.Z. 2020, November 16. How automated test proctoring software discriminates against disabled students. Center for Democracy and Technology. https://cdt.org/insights/how-automated-test-proctoring-software-discriminates-against-disabled-students/; Swauger, S. 2020, April 2. Our bodies encoded: Algorithmic test proctoring in higher education. *Hybrid Pedagogy*. https://hybridpedagogy.org/our-bodies-encoded-algorithmic-test-proctoring-in-higher-education/.

[1025.] Swauger, S. 2020, April 2. Our bodies encoded: Algorithmic test proctoring in higher education. *Hybrid Pedagogy*. https://hybridpedagogy.org/our-bodies-encoded-algorithmic-test-proctoring-in-higher-education/.

[1026.] Woldeab, D. & Brothen, T. 2019. 21st Century assessment: Online proctoring, test anxiety, and student performance. *International Journal of E-Learning & Distance Education*, 34(1). https://www.ijede.ca/index.php/jde/article/view/1106.

[1027.] Patil, A. & Bromwich, J.E. 2020, September 29. How it feels when software watches you take tests. *New York Times*. https://www.nytimes.com/2020/09/29/style/testing-schools-proctorio.html.

1028. Kharbat, F.F. & Abu Daabes, A.S. 2021. E-proctored exams during the COVID-19 pandemic: A close understanding. *Education and Information Technologies*, 26(6). https://doi.org/10.1007/s10639-021-10458-7; Ravi, V. 2020, April 22. Test anxiety and losing internet connection during online exams. Vijay Ravi. https://vijayravi.blog/blog/f/test-anxiety-and-losing-internet-connection-during-online-exams; Chin, M. 2020, April 29. Exam anxiety: How remote test-proctoring is creeping students out. The Verge. https://www.theverge.com/2020/4/29/21232777/examity-remote-test-proctoring-online-class-education.

1029. Legal Cheek. 2020, August 13. Proctoring problems: Bar students urinate in bottles and buckets over fears online exams will be terminated. https://www.legalcheek.com/2020/08/proctoring-problems-bar-students-urinate-in-bottles-and-buckets-over-fears-online-exams-will-be-terminated/.

1030. Harwell, D. 2020, April 1. Mass school closures in the wake of the coronavirus are driving a new wave of student surveillance. *Washington Post*. https://www.washingtonpost.com/technology/2020/04/01/online-proctoring-college-exams-coronavirus/.

1031. Murphy, H. 2020, October 13. She was going into labor. But she had a bar exam to finish. *New York Times*. https://www.nytimes.com/2020/10/13/us/bar-exam-labor.html.

1032. Assessment Systems. 2022, May 3. Remote proctoring: How examinees cheat and how to catch them. https://www.youtube.com/watch?v=AznXrUlmJXQ; EdTech Tools for Online Classes. 2022, March 19. Online proctoring, cheating methods, human, and AI-based proctoring tools. YouTube video. https://www.youtube.com/watch?v=pHg6aoywSQo.

1033. Assessment Systems. 2022, May 3. Remote proctoring: How examinees cheat and how to catch them. https://www.youtube.com/watch?v=AznXrUlmJXQ.

1034. Kelley, J. 2020, September 25. Students are pushing back against proctoring surveillance apps. Electronic Frontier Foundation. https://www.eff.org/deeplinks/2020/09/students-are-pushing-back-against-proctoring-surveillance-apps; Hancock, B. 2022, April 12. Open Letter to VC: Proctorio risks student privacy, mental health. https://tertangala.net/?p=596.

1035. J.S. 2020, August 31. Remove online proctoring methods from Auburn University. Change.org. https://www.change.org/p/auburn-university-remove-online-proctoring-methods-from-auburn-university; D. Anon. 2020, September 9. Stop CSUF from using Invasive programs like Proctorio. Change.org. https://www.change.org/p/california-state-university-fullerton-stop-csuf-from-using-invasive-programs-like-proctorio; Jazzi Brown. 2020. April 8. Request to ban FIU from forcing students to use Honorlock. Change.org. https://www.change.org/p/mark-b-rosenberg-request-to-ban-fiu-from-forcing-students-to-use-honorlock.

1036. Ontario Universities and Colleges Coalition. 2020, July 2. Letter to the Minister of Colleges and Universities. https://ocufa.on.ca/assets/OUCC-letter-to-MCU-on-ProctorTrack.pdf.

1037. Fight for the Future. Proctorio and its CEO are worse than a proctology exam. https://www.proctorioisworsethanaproctologyexam.com. (Accessed 3 March 2023.)

1038. Corbyn, Z. 2022, August 26. 'I'm afraid': Critics of anti-cheating technology for students hit by lawsuits. *The Guardian*. https://www.theguardian.com/us-news/2022/aug/26/anti-cheating-technology-students-tests-proctorio.

1039. Reichman, H. 2020. An egregious case of legal bullying. *Academe*. Blog post. https://academeblog.org/2020/03/27/an-egregious-case-of-legal-bullying/.

1040. University of California Santa Barbara Faculty Association. 2020, March 13. Letter to the chancellor and executive vice chancellor. https://pubcit.typepad.com/files/proctoru_2020-copy.pdf.

1041. Lucas, D.V. 2020, March 19. Letter from Bradley law firm to UCSB faculty association. https://pubcit.typepad.com/files/bradley-bullying-letter.pdf.

1042. Letter prepared by ProctorU attorneys. 2020, March 24. Re: Errors and misrepresentations regarding ProctorU on-line proctoring services. https://pubcit.typepad.com/files/demanded-apology-letter.pdf.

1043. Public Citizen. 2020, March 25. Can ProctorU be trusted with students' personal data? Consumer Law & Policy. Blog post. https://pubcit.typepad.com/clpblog/2020/03/can-proctoru-be-trusted-with-students-personal-data.html.

[1044.] Feathers, T. 2020, October 21. An exam surveillance company is trying to silence critics with lawsuits. Vice. https://www.vice.com/en/article/7k9zjy/an-exam-surveillance-company-is-trying-to-silence-critics-with-lawsuits; McKenzie, L. 2020, October 20. Ed-Tech specialist fights Proctorio lawsuit. *Inside Higher Ed*. https://www.insidehighered.com/quicktakes/2020/10/20/ed-tech-specialist-fights-proctorio-lawsuit.

[1045.] Corbyn, Z. 2022, August 26. 'I'm afraid': Critics of anti-cheating technology for students hit by lawsuits. *The Guardian*. https://www.theguardian.com/us-news/2022/aug/26/anti-cheating-technology-students-tests-proctorio.

[1046.] Linkletter, I. 2022, October 16. Stand against Proctorio's SLAPP. GoFundMe. https://www.gofundme.com/f/stand-against-proctorio.

[1047.] Proctorio. 2020, April 13. Letter to Shea Swauger and *Hybrid Pedagogy*. https://drive.google.com/file/d/1IYD1YIbSL-t8rWy70hyps8cV9IKigV0Y/view.

[1048.] Feathers, T. & Rose, J. 2020, September 24. Students are rebelling against eye-tracking exam surveillance tools. Vice. https://www.vice.com/en/article/n7wxvd/students-are-rebelling-against-eye-tracking-exam-surveillance-tools.

[1049.] Electronic Frontier Foundation. 2021, April 21. EFF sues Proctorio on behalf of student it falsely accused of copyright infringement to get critical tweets taken down. Press release. https://www.eff.org/press/releases/eff-sues-proctorio-behalf-student-it-falsely-accused-copyright-infringement-get.

[1050.] Rose, J. 2022, February 23. Proctorio is going after digital rights groups that bash their proctoring software. Vice. https://www.vice.com/en/article/epxqgw/proctorio-is-going-after-digital-rights-groups-that-bash-their-proctoring-software.

[1051.] Corbyn, Z. 2022, August 26. 'I'm afraid': Critics of anti-cheating technology for students hit by lawsuits. *The Guardian*. https://www.theguardian.com/us-news/2022/aug/26/anti-cheating-technology-students-tests-proctorio.

[1052.] Bergmans, L., Bouali, N., Luttikhuis, M. & Rensink, A. 2021. On the efficacy of online proctoring using Proctorio. In *Proceedings of the 13th International Conference on Computer Supported Education (CSEDU 2021) - Volume 1*. https://ris.utwente.nl/ws/portalfiles/

[1053.] Kelley, J. 2020, December 22. ExamSoft flags one-third of California Bar Exam test takers for cheating. Electronic Frontier Foundation. https://www.eff.org/deeplinks/2020/12/examsoft-flags-one-third-california-bar-exam-test-takers-cheating.

[1054.] Skolnik, S. 2020, December 30. Ninety percent of suspected cheaters cleared by California Bar. Bloomberg Law. https://news.bloomberglaw.com/business-and-practice/ninety-percent-of-suspected-cheaters-cleared-by-california-bar.

[1055.] Meazure Learning. 2021, May 24. ProctorU to discontinue exam integrity services that rely exclusively on AI. Press release. https://www.meazurelearning.com/resources/proctoru-to-discontinue-exam-integrity-services-that-rely-exclusively-on-ai.

[1056.] Miller, V. 2020, November 16. Iowa universities plugging holes in massive transition to online. *The Gazette*. https://www.thegazette.com/education/iowa-universities-plugging-holes-in-massive-transition-to-online/.

[1057.] Geiger, G. 2021, March 5. Students are easily cheating 'state-of-the-art' test proctoring tech. Vice. https://www.vice.com/en/article/3an98j/students-are-easily-cheating-state-of-the-art-test-proctoring-tech.

[1058.] UnethicalLifeProTips. 2019, February 22. ULPT: When taking an online proctored exam, write answers on your computer screen in expo marker or put post-it notes on it. https://www.reddit.com/r/UnethicalLifeProTips/comments/f7kly0/ulpt_when_taking_an_online_proctored_exam_write/.

[1059.] Chin, M. 2020, April 29. Exam anxiety: How remote test-proctoring is creeping students out. The Verge. https://www.theverge.com/2020/4/29/21232777/examity-remote-test-proctoring-online-class-education.

[1060.] Binstein, J. 2015, January. How to cheat with Proctortrack, Examity, and the rest. *Jake Binstein*. https://jakebinstein.com/blog/on-knuckle-scanners-and-cheating-how-to-bypass-proctortrack/.

[1061.] Chin, M. 2020, April 29. Exam anxiety: How remote test-proctoring is creeping students out. The Verge. https://www.theverge.com/2020/4/29/21232777/examity-remote-test-proctoring-online-class-education.

[1062.] Li, J. 2020, March 11. In China, quarantined students can pay $1.40 to cheat an online class. Quartz. https://qz.com/1816351/chinese-students-quarantined-from-coronavirus-can-pay-1-40-to-cheat-an-online-class.

1063. Harwell, D. 2020, November 12. Cheating-detection companies made millions during the pandemic. Now students are fighting back. *Washington Post*. https://www.washingtonpost.com/technology/2020/11/12/test-monitoring-student-revolt/.

1064. Hubler, S. 2020, May 10. Keeping online testing honest? Or an Orwellian overreach? *New York Times*. https://www.nytimes.com/2020/05/10/us/online-testing-cheating-universities-coronavirus.html.

1065. Caplan-Bricker, N. 2021, May 27. Is online test-monitoring here to stay? *New Yorker*. https://www.newyorker.com/tech/annals-of-technology/is-online-test-monitoring-here-to-stay.

1066. Ibid.

1067. Flaherty, C. 2020, May 11. Big proctor. *Inside Higher Ed*. https://www.insidehighered.com/news/2020/05/11/online-proctoring-surging-during-covid-19.

1068. Kelley, J. 2020, September 25. Students are pushing back against proctoring surveillance apps. Electronic Frontier Foundation. https://www.eff.org/deeplinks/2020/09/students-are-pushing-back-against-proctoring-surveillance-apps.

1069. Thompson, N. 2021. Types of remote proctoring: What's the best fit for me? Assessment Systems. https://assess.com/types-of-remote-proctoring/.

1070. Texas A&M International University. 2023. Instructional technology and distance education services: Proctorio. Texas A&M International University. https://www.tamiu.edu/distance/technology/proctorio.shtml.

1071. MarketWatch. 2022, December 26. Remote proctoring solutions market size was valued at USD 566.75 Million in 2021 and is expected to expand at a CAGR of 19.54% to 2027. Press release. https://www.marketwatch.com/press-release/remote-proctoring-solutions-market-size-was-valued-at-usd-56675-million-in-2021-and-is-expected-to-expand-at-a-cagr-of-1954-to-2027-2022-12-26.

1072. Newsmantraa. 2022, January 31. Online exam proctoring software market is going to boom with ProctorU, Pearson Vue, PSI Services, ExamSoft, Verificient. Digital Journal. https://www.digitaljournal.com/pr/online-exam-proctoring-software-market-is-going-to-boom-with-proctoru-pearson-vue-psi-services-examsoft-verificient.

1073. Feathers, T. 2021, February 26. Schools are abandoning invasive proctoring software after student backlash. Vice. https://www.vice.com/en/article/7k9ag4/schools-are-abandoning-invasive-proctoring-software-after-student-backlash; Flaherty, C. 2021, February 1. No more Proctorio. *Inside Higher Ed*. https://www.insidehighered.com/news/2021/02/01/u-illinois-says-goodbye-proctorio.

1074. MarketWatch. 2022, December 26. Remote proctoring solutions market size was valued at USD 566.75 Million in 2021 and is expected to expand at a CAGR of 19.54% to 2027. Press release.https://www.marketwatch.com/press-release/remote-proctoring-solutions-market-size-was-valued-at-usd-56675-million-in-2021-and-is-expected-to-expand-at-a-cagr-of-1954-to-2027-2022-12-26; MarketWatch. 2023, March 29. Remote proctoring solutions market share by 2031. Press release. https://www.marketwatch.com/press-release/remote-proctoring-solutions-market-share-by-2031-2023-03-29.

1075. Kimmons, R. & Veletsianos, G. 2021, February 23. Proctoring software in higher ed: Prevalence and patterns. *EDUCAUSE Review*. https://er.educause.edu/articles/2021/2/proctoring-software-in-higher-ed-prevalence-and-patterns.

1076. Caplan-Bricker, N. 2021, May 27. Is online test-monitoring here to stay? *New Yorker*. https://www.newyorker.com/tech/annals-of-technology/is-online-test-monitoring-here-to-stay; Young, J.R. 2021, November 29. Automated proctoring swept in during pandemic. It's likely to stick around, despite concerns. EdSurge. https://www.edsurge.com/news/2021-11-19-automated-proctoring-swept-in-during-pandemic-it-s-likely-to-stick-around-despite-concerns; Alemira. 2021, June 9. Is online proctoring here to stay? Alemira. https://alemira.com/blog/is-online-proctoring-here-to-stay/; Norris, S. 2022, December 7. Online proctored exams: Are they here to stay? *The Review*. https://udreview.com/online-proctored-exams-are-they-here-to-stay/.

1077. Martin Weller. 2020. *25 Years of Ed Tech*. Alberta: Athabasca University Press.

1078. Caplan-Bricker, N. 2021, May 27. Is online test-monitoring here to stay? *New Yorker*. https://www.newyorker.com/tech/annals-of-technology/is-online-test-monitoring-here-to-stay.

1079. O'Neil, C. 2016. *Weapons of Math Destruction: How Big Data Increases Inequality and Threatens Democracy* New York: Crown; Forrest, K.B. 2021. *When Machines Can Be Judge, Jury, and Executioner: Justice in the Age of Artificial Intelligence.* Hackensack, NJ: World Scientific Publishing Company.

1080. Burgess, M., Schot, E. & Geiger, G. 2023, March 6. This algorithm could ruin your life. Wired. https://www.wired.co.uk/article/welfare-algorithms-discrimination.

1081. Rakoff, J.S. 2021, June 10. Sentenced by algorithm. *New York Review of Books*. https://www.nybooks.com/articles/2021/06/10/prison-terms-sentenced-by-algorithm/.

1082. Geiger, G. et al. 2023, March 6. Suspicion machines. Lighthouse Reports. https://www.lighthousereports.com/investigation/suspicion-machines/.

1083. Maslej, N. et al. 2023, April. *The AI Index 2023 Annual Report*. AI Index Steering Committee, Institute for Human-Centered AI, Stanford University. https://aiindex.stanford.edu/wp-content/uploads/2023/04/HAI_AI-Index-Report_2023.pdf.

1084. Kelley, J. 2020, December 22. ExamSoft flags one-third of California Bar Exam test takers for cheating. Electronic Frontier Foundation. https://www.eff.org/deeplinks/2020/12/examsoft-flags-one-third-california-bar-exam-test-takers-cheating.

1085. Kelley, J., Budington, B. & Cope, S. 2021, April 15. Proctoring tools and dragnet investigations rob students of due process. Electronic Frontier Foundation. https://www.eff.org/deeplinks/2021/04/proctoring-tools-and-dragnet-investigations-rob-students-due-process.

1086. Singer, N. & Krolik, A. 2021, May 9. Online cheating charges upend Dartmouth medical school. *New York Times*. https://www.nytimes.com/2021/05/09/technology/dartmouth-geisel-medical-cheating.html.

1087. Ibid.

1088. Ibid.

1089. Das, B. 2021. Dartmouth drops online cheating charges against med students. *College Post*. https://thecollegepost.com/dartmouth-drops-online-cheating-charges/.

1090. Hill, K. 2022, May 27. Accused of cheating by an algorithm, and a professor she had never met. *New York Times*. https://www.nytimes.com/2022/05/27/technology/college-students-cheating-software-honorlock.html.

1091. Hawkins, S. 2022, March 15. Proctor360 faces class action for collecting student biometrics. Bloomberg Law. https://news.bloomberglaw.com/privacy-and-data-security/proctor360-faces-class-action-for-collecting-student-biometrics.

1092. Berens, M. 2021, September 17. One U.S. state stands out in restricting corporate use of biometrics: Illinois. Reuters. https://www.reuters.com/technology/one-us-state-stands-out-restricting-corporate-use-biometrics-illinois-2021-09-16/; Errick, K. 2021, March 15. Students sue online exam proctoring service ProctorU for biometrics violations following data breach. Law Street. https://lawstreetmedia.com/news/tech/students-sue-online-exam-proctoring-service-proctoru-for-biometrics-violations-following-data-breach/.

1093. Richard Blumenthal, Senator for Connecticut. 2020, December 3. Blumenthal leads call for virtual exam software companies to improve equity, accessibility & privacy for students amid troubling reports. Press release. https://www.blumenthal.senate.gov/newsroom/press/release/blumenthal-leads-call-for-virtual-exam-software-companies-to-improve-equity-accessibility-and-privacy-for-students-amid-troubling-reports.

1094. Electronic Frontier Foundation. 2021. Examsoft, Proctorio, ProctorU responses to Senate letter. https://www.eff.org/it/document/proctoring-companies-responses-senate-letter.

1095. Examsoft BIPA Settlement. 2022. Welcome to the Examsoft BIPA settlement. https://www.esbipasettlement.com/.

1096. United States District Court Northern District of Ohio Eastern Division. Case No. 1:21-cv-00500. Aaron M. Ogletree v. Cleveland State University. https://bbgohio.com/wp-content/uploads/2022/08/MSJ-decision.pdf.

1097. Tribunal administratif de Montreuil. 2022, December 14. No. 2216570. https://www.laquadrature.net/wp-content/uploads/sites/8/2022/12/1120693769_2216570P_ordo_anon.pdf.

1098. California Legislative Information. 2022, September 29. Senate Bill No. 1172. Student Test Taker Privacy Protection Act. https://leginfo.legislature.ca.gov/faces/billTextClient.xhtml?bill_id=202120220SB1172.

1099. Kelley, J. 2022, March 24. Stop invasive remote proctoring: Pass California's Student Test Taker Privacy Protection Act. Electronic Frontier Foundation. https://www.eff.org/deeplinks/2022/03/stop-invasive-remote-proctoring-pass-californias-student-test-taker-privacy.

1100. Ferguson, N. et al. 2006, April 26. Strategies for mitigating an influenza pandemic. *Nature*, 442: 448–452. https://www.nature.com/articles/nature04795.

1101. Auger, K.A. et al. 2020, July 29. Association between statewide school closure and COVID-19 incidence and mortality in the US. *JAMA*, 324(9): 859–870. https://jamanetwork.com/journals/jama/fullarticle/2769034; Consolazio, D., Sarti, S., Terraneo, M., Celata, C. & Russo, A.G. 2022, July 12. The impact of school closure intervention during the third wave of the COVID-19 pandemic in Italy: Evidence from the Milan area. *PLOS ONE*, 17(7): e0271404. https://doi.org/10.1371/journal.pone.0271404.

1102. Ferguson, N. et al. 2006, April 26. Strategies for mitigating an influenza pandemic. *Nature*, 442: 448–452. https://www.nature.com/articles/nature04795.

1103. Levinson, M., Cevik, M. & Lipsitch, M. 2020. Reopening primary schools during the pandemic. *New England Journal of Medicine*, 383(10): 981–985. https://www.nejm.org/doi/10.1056/NEJMms2024920; Fontanet, A., Grant, R., Greve-Isdahl, M. & Sridhar, D. 2021, February 24. Covid-19: Keeping schools as safe as possible. *BMJ*, 372. https://doi.org/10.1136/bmj.n524; Lewis, T. 2021, April 15. Schools can open safely during COVID, the latest evidence shows. *Scientific American*. https://www.scientificamerican.com/article/schools-can-open-safely-during-covid-the-latest-evidence-shows/.

1104. Lindblad, S. 2021, September 28. Only in Sweden primary school remained open. University of Gothenburg. https://www.gu.se/en/news/only-in-sweden-primary-school-remained-open.

1105. UNICEF. 2021, July 15. COVID-19 pandemic leads to major backsliding on childhood vaccinations, new WHO, UNICEF data shows. Press release. https://www.unicef.org/press-releases/covid-19-pandemic-leads-major-backsliding-childhood-vaccinations-new-who-unicef-data.

1106. WHO, UNICEF, & UNESCO. 2020, September 14. Considerations for school-related public health measures in the context of COVID-19. Annex to Considerations in adjusting public health and social measures in the context of COVID-19. https://www.who.int/publications/i/item/considerations-for-school-related-public-health-measures-in-the-context-of-covid-19.

1107. Levinson, M., Cevik, M. & Lipsitch, M. 2020. Reopening primary schools during the pandemic. *New England Journal of Medicine*, 383(10): 981–985. https://www.nejm.org/doi/10.1056/NEJMms2024920.

1108. World Health Organization. 2020, December 8. Schooling in the time of COVID-19: Opening statement at high-level meeting on keeping schools open and protecting all children amid surging COVID-19 cases. https://www.who.int/europe/news/item/08-12-2020-schooling-in-the-time-of-covid-19-opening-statement-at-high-level-meeting-on-keeping-schools-open-and-protecting-all-children-amid-surging-covid-19-cases.

1109. UNICEF. 2020, December 8. COVID-19: UNICEF warns of continued damage to learning and well-being as number of children affected by school closures soars again. Press release. https://www.unicef.org/turkey/en/press-releases/covid-19-unicef-warns-continued-damage-learning-and-well-being-number-children.

1110. European Centre for Disease Prevention and Control. 2020, December 23. COVID-19 in children and the role of school settings in transmission – first update. https://www.ecdc.europa.eu/sites/default/files/documents/COVID-19-in-children-and-the-role-of-school-settings-in-transmission-first-update_1.pdf.

1111. European Centre for Disease Prevention and Control. 2021, July 8. COVID-19 in children and the role of school settings in transmission – second update. https://www.ecdc.europa.eu/sites/default/files/documents/COVID-19-in-children-and-the-role-of-school-settings-in-transmission-second-update.pdf.

1112. Insights for Education. 2021, January 25. *One Year of School Disruption*. https://img1.wsimg.com/blobby/go/104fc727-3bad-4ff5-944f-c281d3ceda7f/20210125_One year of school disruption_Insight.pdf.

1113. Fontanet, A., Grant, R., Greve-Isdahl, M. & Sridhar, D. 2021, February 24. Covid-19: Keeping schools as safe as possible. *BMJ*, 372. https://doi.org/10.1136/bmj.n524.

1114. Vlachos, J., Hertegård, E. & B. Svaleryd, H. 2021, February 11. The effects of school closures on SARS-CoV-2 among parents and teachers. *Proceedings of the National Academy of Sciences*, 118(9). https://www.pnas.org/doi/full/10.1073/pnas.2020834118.

1115. Carter, S. & Moncrieff, I. 2021, May. *COVID-19 School Closures in the DRC: Impact on the Health, Protection and Education of Children and Youth*. Social Sciences Analytics Cell. https://www.unicef.org/drcongo/media/5716/file/COD-CASS-school-closures-impacts.pdf.

1116. Bismarck-Osten, C. von, Borusyak, K. & Schönberg, U. 2021, May 8. School closures did not contain the spread of the coronavirus in Germany. VoxEU. https://voxeu.org/article/school-closures-did-not-contribute-spread-coronavirus-germany.

1117. Oster, E. 2020, November 20. Schools are not spreading covid-19. This new data makes the case. *Washington Post*. https://www.washingtonpost.com/opinions/2020/11/20/covid-19-schools-data-reopening-safety/.

1118. Lewis, T. 2021, April 15. Schools can open safely during COVID, the latest evidence shows. *Scientific American*. https://www.scientificamerican.com/article/schools-can-open-safely-during-covid-the-latest-evidence-shows/.

1119. Fukumoto, K., McClean, C.T. & Nakagawa, K. 2021. No causal effect of school closures in Japan on the spread of COVID-19 in spring 2020. *Nature Medicine*, 27(12): 2111–2119. https://www.ncbi.nlm.nih.gov/pmc/articles/PMC8674136/.

1120. UNESCO. 2022. Global monitoring of school closures caused by COVID-19 pandemic. https://covid19.uis.unesco.org/global-monitoring-school-closures-covid19/.

1121. Wu, J.T. et al. 2021, November 22. A global assessment of the impact of school closure in reducing COVID-19 spread. *Philosophical Transactions of the Royal Society A: Mathematical, Physical and Engineering Sciences*, 380(2214): https://doi.org/10.1098/rsta.2021.0124; Brooks, S.K. et al. 2020, April 2. The impact of unplanned school closure on children's social contact: Rapid evidence review. *Eurosurveillance*, 25(13). https://www.eurosurveillance.org/content/10.2807/1560-7917.ES.2020.25.13.2000188; Head, J.R. et al. 2021, April 14. School closures reduced social mixing of children during COVID-19 with implications for transmission risk and school reopening policies. *Journal of the Royal Society Interface*, 18(177). https://royalsocietypublishing.org/doi/10.1098/rsif.2020.0970.

1122. Klein, N. 2020, May 13. Naomi Klein: How big tech plans to profit from the pandemic. *The Guardian*. https://www.theguardian.com/news/2020/may/13/naomi-klein-how-big-tech-plans-to-profit-from-coronavirus-pandemic.

1123. Shah, N. 2020, November 30. It's starting to sink in: Schools before bars. *POLITICO*. https://www.politico.com/news/2020/11/20/its-starting-to-sink-in-schools-before-bars-438555.

1124. @LizGoldbergMD. 2020, July 3. Thread about #SchoolReopening internationally showing the risks to kids (esp. if in elementary), parents, & teachers of #covid inf. is low. #closebarsopenschools. Twitter.https://twitter.com/LizGoldbergMD/status/1279001890496397312; @ DaveBrownToons. 2020, August 6. Tomorrow's @Independent cartoon... #SchoolsBeforePubs #ChildrensCommissioner #COVID19 #Coronavirus #LocalLockdown #2ndWave. Twitter. https://twitter.com/DaveBrownToons/status/1291067327300145152.

1125. Nuzzo, J.B. & Sharfstein, J.M. 2020, July 1. We have to focus on opening schools, not bars. *New York Times*. https://www.nytimes.com/2020/07/01/opinion/coronavirus-schools.html; Shah, N. 2020, November 30. It's starting to sink in: Schools before bars. *POLITICO*. https://www.politico.com/news/2020/11/20/its-starting-to-sink-in-schools-before-bars-438555.

1126. Ager, P., Eriksson, K., Karger, E., Nencka, P. & Thomasson, M.A. 2020, December. School closures during the 1918 flu pandemic. National Bureau of Economic Research. https://www.nber.org/system/files/working_papers/w28246/w28246.pdf.

1127. Markel, H. 2020, July 13. Analysis: Why some schools stayed open during the 1918 flu pandemic. PBS NewsHour. https://www.pbs.org/newshour/health/analysis-why-some-schools-stayed-open-during-the-1918-flu-pandemic.

1128. Levinson, M., Cevik, M. & Lipsitch, M. 2020. Reopening primary schools during the pandemic. *New England Journal of Medicine*, 383(10): 981–985. https://www.nejm.org/doi/10.1056/NEJMms2024920.

1129. UNESCO. 2020, May 5. New guidelines provide roadmap for safe reopening of schools. Press release. https://en.unesco.org/news/new-guidelines-provide-roadmap-safe-reopening-schools.

1130. UNICEF, WHO & IFRC. 2020, March. COVID-19: IFRC, UNICEF and WHO issue guidance to protect children and support safe school operations. Press release. https://www.unicef.org/pacificislands/press-releases/covid-19-ifrc-unicef-and-who-issue-guidance-protect-children-and-support-safe-school.

1131. UNESCO, UNICEF, World Bank & World Food Programme. 2020, June. *Framework for Reopening Schools*. https://unesdoc.unesco.org/ark:/48223/pf0000373348.

1132. Frieden, T.R., Duncan, A. & Spellings, M. 2020, July 9. These 8 basic steps will let us reopen schools. *The Atlantic*. https://www.theatlantic.com/ideas/archive/2020/07/eight-steps-reopen-schools/613939/.

1133. Kayyem, J. 2020, July 6. Reopening schools was just an afterthought. *The Atlantic*. https://www.theatlantic.com/ideas/archive/2020/07/reopening-bars-easy-schools-are-difficult/613861/.

1134. Yglesias, M. 2020, January 8. Installing air filters in classrooms has surprisingly large educational benefits. Vox. https://www.vox.com/2020/1/8/21051869/indoor-air-pollution-student-achievement.

1135. Gilraine, M. 2020. Air filters, pollution and student achievement. EdWorkingPaper 19-188. Retrieved from Annenberg Institute at Brown University. https://doi.org/10.26300/7mcr-8a10.

1136. Klein, N. 2020, May 13. Naomi Klein: How big tech plans to profit from the pandemic. *The Guardian*. https://www.theguardian.com/news/2020/may/13/naomi-klein-how-big-tech-plans-to-profit-from-coronavirus-pandemic.

1137. Carroll, A.E. 2020, August 28. When it comes to Covid-19, most of us have risk exactly backward. *New York Times*. https://www.nytimes.com/2020/08/28/opinion/coronavirus-schools-tradeoffs.html.

1138. Stern, A.M., Reilly, M.B., Cetron, M.S. & Markel, H. 2010, April 1. "Better off in school": School medical inspection as a public health strategy during the 1918–1919 influenza pandemic in the United States. *Public Health Reports*, 125(3): 63–70. https://journals.sagepub.com/doi/10.1177/00333549101250S309; Waldrop, T. 2020, August 19. Here's what happened when students went to school during the 1918 pandemic. CNN. https://www.cnn.com/2020/08/19/us/schools-flu-pandemic-1918-trnd/index.html.

1139. Battenfeld, M. 2020, June 16. 3 lessons from how schools responded to the 1918 pandemic worth heeding today. The Conversation. http://theconversation.com/3-lessons-from-how-schools-responded-to-the-1918-pandemic-worth-heeding-today-138403.

1140. Gilmore, N. 2020, August 14. America's school nursing crisis came at the worst time. *Saturday Evening Post*. https://www.saturdayeveningpost.com/2020/08/americas-school-nursing-crisis-came-at-the-worst-time/.

1141. Launder, M. 2021, October 27. Reverse 'devastating' public health cuts, school nurses tell government. *Nursing in Practice*. https://www.nursinginpractice.com/community-nursing/reverse-devastating-public-health-cuts-school-nurses-tell-government/; Buttner, A. 2021, January 5. Diagnosing the school nurse shortage. *Frontline Education*. https://www.frontlineeducation.com/blog/school-nurse-shortage/.

1142. UNESCO. 2022. Global monitoring of school closures caused by COVID-19 pandemic. https://covid19.uis.unesco.org/global-monitoring-school-closures-covid19/.

1143. Jabar, M.A. 2010, June 1. How do Japanese schools promote parental involvement? *International Journal of Social Sciences and Humanity Studies*, 2(1). https://dergipark.org.tr/en/pub/ijsshs/issue/26223/276230.

1144. Cheney, C. 2021, November 1. Ed tech, long overhyped, missed its moment amid COVID-19. What now? Devex. https://www.devex.com/news/sponsored/ed-tech-long-overhyped-missed-its-moment-amid-covid-19-what-now-101835.

1145. Dube, R. 2020, August 4. Bolivia decision to cancel school because of Covid-19 upsets parents. *Wall Street Journal*. https://www.wsj.com/articles/bolivia-decision-to-cancel-school-because-of-covid-19-upsets-parents-11596577822; Reuters. 2020, September 2. Virtual schooling in pandemic sharpens divide for Bolivia's poor. https://www.reuters.com/article/us-health-coronavirus-bolivia-education-idUSKBN25T20F.

1146. BBC News. 2020, July 7. Coronavirus: Kenyan schools to remain closed until 2021. https://www.bbc.com/news/world-africa-53325741.

1147. Ministry of Education, Republic of Kenya. 2020, May. *Kenya Basic Education Covid-19 Emergency Response Plan*. https://planipolis.iiep.unesco.org/sites/default/files/ressources/kenya_emergency_response_plan_4_may_2020.pdf.

1148. Dube, R. 2020, August 4. Bolivia decision to cancel school because of Covid-19 upsets parents. *Wall Street Journal*. https://www.wsj.com/articles/bolivia-decision-to-cancel-school-because-of-covid-19-upsets-parents-11596577822.

1149. Schleicher, A. 2021, April 19. Repeating the school year not the answer to COVID learning losses: Andreas Schleicher. *OECD Education and Skills Today*. https://oecdedutoday.com/repeating-school-year-not-the-answer-to-covid-learning-losses/.

1150. Antoninis, M. 2021, March 23. Opinion: How will countries make up for lost learning during the pandemic? Devex. https://www.devex.com/news/opinion-how-will-countries-make-up-for-lost-learning-during-the-pandemic-99453.

1151. CNN Philippines. 2020, May 10. DepEd sets guidelines for summer classes amid COVID-19 pandemic. https://www.cnnphilippines.com/news/2020/5/10/DepEd-sets-guidelines-for-summer-classes-amid-COVID-19-pandemic.html.

1152. Schleicher, A. 2021, April 19. Repeating the school year not the answer to COVID learning losses: Andreas Schleicher. *OECD Education and Skills Today*. https://oecdedutoday.com/repeating-school-year-not-the-answer-to-covid-learning-losses/.

1153. UNICEF. 2020, November 17. Nine million children in Ghana to benefit from learning programmes supported by UNICEF and Mastercard Foundation partnership. Press release. https://www.unicef.org/ghana/press-releases/nine-million-children-ghana-benefit-learning-programmes-supported-unicef-and.

1154. UK Government Department of Education. 2021, 27 April. Catch-up premium. https://www.gov.uk/government/publications/catch-up-premium-coronavirus-covid-19/catch-up-premium.

1155. UNESCO, in collaboration with McKinsey & Company. 2020, July. *COVID-19 Response - Remediation: Helping Students Catch Up on Lost Learning, with a Focus on Closing Equity Gaps*. Version 2. https://www.mckinsey.com/~/media/McKinsey/About Us/COVID Response Center/Overview/COVID-19 Education Response Toolkit/202010_UNESCO-McKinsey Response Toolkit_Remediation_VF.pdf.

1156. Population Council. 2021. *Promises to Keep: Impact of Covid-19 on Adolescents in Kenya*. https://www.popcouncil.org/uploads/pdfs/2021PGY_ImpactCovidAdolKenya.pdf.

1157. Gikandi, H. 2020, October 16. After months of closure, Kenya's schools adjust to sudden reopening. The World. https://theworld.org/stories/2020-10-16/after-months-closure-kenyas-schools-adjust-sudden-reopening.

1158. Yusuf, M. 2021, January 4. Kenyan schools reopen despite coronavirus concerns. VOA News. https://www.voanews.com/a/africa_kenyan-schools-reopen-despite-coronavirus-concerns/6200298.html.

1159. Mweyeri, M. & Gathuru, G. 2021, September 27. The impact of Covid-19 on education in Kenya. IEA Kenya. https://ieakenya.or.ke/blog/the-impact-of-covid-19-on-education-in-kenya/.

1160. Ibid.

1161. Dahir, A.L. 2020, August 5. Kenya's unusual solution to the school problem: Cancel the year and start over. *New York Times*. https://www.nytimes.com/2020/08/05/world/africa/Kenya-cancels-school-year-coronavirus.html.

1162. Dube, R. 2020, August 4. Bolivia decision to cancel school because of Covid-19 upsets parents. *Wall Street Journal*. https://www.wsj.com/articles/bolivia-decision-to-cancel-school-because-of-covid-19-upsets-parents-11596577822.

1163. Branswell, H. 2021, May 19. How the Covid pandemic ends: Scientists look to the past to see the future. *STAT*. https://www.statnews.com/2021/05/19/how-the-covid-pandemic-ends-scientists-look-to-the-past-to-see-the-future/.

1164. Schleicher, A. 2021, April 19. Repeating the school year not the answer to COVID learning losses: Andreas Schleicher. *OECD Education and Skills Today*. https://oecdedutoday.com/repeating-school-year-not-the-answer-to-covid-learning-losses/.

1165. Ager, P., Eriksson, K., Karger, E., Nencka, P. & Thomasson, M.A. 2020, December. School closures during the 1918 flu pandemic. National Bureau of Economic Research. https://www.nber.org/system/files/working_papers/w28246/w28246.pdf.

1166. Portuguese School of Luanda. 2022, January 15. Comunicado – Retoma das aulas na modalidade presencial [Announcement – Resumption of classes in face-to-face modality]. https://www.epluanda.pt/9315-comunicado-retoma-das-aulas-na-modalidade-presencial; Presidency of the Dominican Republic. 2022, January 7. Gobierno llama al reinicio de clases próximo martes 11 de enero de manera presencial y voluntaria [Government calls for the restart of classes next Tuesday, January 11 in person and voluntarily]. https://presidencia.gob.do/noticias/gobierno-llama-al-reinicio-de-clases-proximo-martes-11-de-enero-de-manera-presencial-y; Dyusengulova, R. 2022, January 17. Как будут учиться казахстанские школьники и студенты [How Kazakhstani schoolchildren and students will study]. Tengrinews. https://tengrinews.kz/kazakhstan_news/kak-budut-uchitsya-kazahstanskie-shkolniki-i-studentyi-459401/.

1167. Froehlich, M. 2021, July 27. Helping parents feel more comfortable with tech. Edutopia. https://www.edutopia.org/article/helping-parents-feel-more-comfortable-tech.

1168. Education and Early Childhood Development Executive Council. 2020, July 6. Provincial government announces $20 million for technology to support digital learning. Government of Newfoundland and Labrador. Press release. https://www.gov.nl.ca/releases/2020/eecd/0706n02/; Anderson, J. 2022, February 7. Government announces £1.3m fund for schools to purchase computers. Holyrood. https://www.holyrood.com/news/view,government-announces-13m-fund-for-schools-to-purchase-computers.

1169. Goodman, P.S. & Bradsher, K. 2021, August 30. The world is still short of everything. get used to it. *New York Times*. https://www.nytimes.com/2021/08/30/business/supply-chain-shortages.html.

1170. West, M. & Chew, H.E. 2014. *Reading in the Mobile Era: A Study of Mobile Reading in Developing Countries*. UNESCO. https://unesdoc.unesco.org/ark:/48223/pf0000227436.

1171. Neuman, S.B. 2007. The knowledge gap: Implications for early education. Dickinson, D.K. & Neuman, S.B. *Handbook of Early Literacy Research*. Vol. 2. New York: Guilford Press.

1172. Phair, R. 2020, April 3. During the coronavirus crisis, children need books more than ever! *OECD Education and Skills Today*. https://oecdedutoday.com/during-coronavirus-crisis-children-need-books/.

1173. Klass, P. 2021, March 16. How children read differently from books vs. screens. *New York Times*. https://www.nytimes.com/2021/03/16/well/family/children-reading-screens-books.html.

1174. Goudeau, S., Sanrey, C., Stanczak, A., Manstead, A. & Darnon, C. 2021. Why lockdown and distance learning during the COVID-19 pandemic are likely to increase the social class achievement gap. *Nature Human Behaviour*, 5(10): 1273–1281. https://doi.org/10.1038/s41562-021-01212-7.

1175. Moyer, M.W. 2020, July 22. Pods, microschools and tutors: Can parents solve the education crisis on their own? *New York Times*. https://www.nytimes.com/2020/07/22/parenting/school-pods-coronavirus.html.

1176. Mokolé, J. & Toukan, E. 2020, 21 July. Community schools continue teaching and learning during Covid-19 in the Central African Republic. REACH. Harvard Graduate School of Education. https://www.reach.gse.harvard.edu/blogs/covid-19/series/community-schools-continue-teaching-and-learning-during-covid-19-in-the-central-african-republic.

1177. Aboriginal Education Research Centre, Making the Shift Youth Homelessness Social Innovation Lab & Dechinta Centre for Research and Learning. 2021. *Indigenous Land-Based Education and the COVID-19 Pandemic*. https://aerc.usask.ca/documents/indigenous-land-based-education-and-the-covid-19-pandemic.pdf.

1178. Dickler, J. 2021, May 7. During Covid, more families switch to private school from public education. CNBC. https://www.cnbc.com/2021/05/07/during-covid-more-families-switch-to-private-school-from-public-.html.

1179. Bridge International. 2022. Teacher tools. https://bridgeschools.in/teaching/teacher-tools/. (Accessed 28 November 2022.)

1180. World Bank, UNESCO, UNICEF, USAID, FCDO, & Bill & Melinda Gates Foundation. 2022. *The State of Global Learning Poverty*. https://www.unicef.org/media/122921/file/State%20of%20Learning%20Poverty%202022.pdf.

1181. Ahlgren, E. et al. 2022, January 6. The global education crisis is even worse than we thought. Here's what needs to happen. World Economic Forum. https://www.weforum.org/agenda/2022/01/global-education-crisis-children-students-covid19/.

1182. Save our Future. 2020. *Averting an Education Catastrophe for the World's Children*. https://saveourfuture.world/white-paper/.

1183. UNESCO. 2020. *Education in a Post-COVID World: Nine Ideas for Public Action*. International Commission on the Futures of Education. https://en.unesco.org/news/education-post-covid-world-nine-ideas-public-action.

1184. UNICEF. 2022, January 23. COVID:19 Scale of education loss 'nearly insurmountable', warns UNICEF. Press release. https://www.unicef.org/press-releases/covid19-scale-education-loss-nearly-insurmountable-warns-unicef.

1185. Goldstein, D. 2022, January 21. Back to school, but still learning online. *New York Times*. https://www.nytimes.com/2022/01/21/us/online-tutoring-stimulus-funding.html; Suvarna, A. & Patwardhan, N. 2022, February 2. Edtech companies set to get a boost from government's digitization push. Mint. https://www.livemint.com/budget/edtech-companies-set-to-get-a-boost-from-government-s-digitization-push-11643742423720.html; Leprince-Ringuet, D. 2020, January 23. Government wants more tech in schools: Paying for it will be the first challenge. ZDNet. https://www.zdnet.com/article/government-wants-more-tech-in-schools-paying-for-it-will-be-the-first-challenge/.

1186. Verger, A., Fontdevila, C. & Zancajo, A. 2016. *The Privatization of Education: A Political Economy of Global Education Reform*. New York: Teachers College Press.

1187. Klein, N. 2008. *The Shock Doctrine: The Rise of Disaster Capitalism*. London: Penguin Books.

1188. Verger, A., Fontdevila, C. & Zancajo, A. 2017. Multiple paths towards education privatization in a globalizing world: A cultural political economy review. *Journal of Education Policy*, 32(6): 757–787. https://doi.org/10.1080/02680939.2017.1318453.

1189. Le, H.M. 2019. Private encroachment through crisis-making: The privatization of education for refugees. *Education Policy Analysis Archives*, 27(26): 126–126. https://doi.org/10.14507/epaa.27.4325.

1190. Noeth, R.J. & Volkov, B.B. 2004. *Evaluating the Effectiveness of Technology in Our Schools: ACT Policy Report*. https://www.act.org/content/dam/act/unsecured/documents/school_tech.pdf; Winters, M. 2017, May 8. The hard truths and false starts about edtech efficacy research. EdSurge. https://www.edsurge.com/news/2017-05-08-the-hard-truths-and-false-starts-about-edtech-efficacy-research.

1191. Organisation for Economic Co-operation and Development. 2015. *Students, Computers and Learning: Making the Connection*. https://www.oecd.org/publications/students-computers-and-learning-9789264239555-en.htm.

1192. Code.org. 2022. Why computer science? https://code.org/promote. (Accessed 2 December 2022.)

1193. Vu, B.T. & Savonitto, I.O. 2020, July 21. *Building Back Better: Education Systems for Resilience, Equity and Quality in the Age of COVID-19*. World Bank. http://documents1.worldbank.org/curated/en/497341595425543327/Building-Back-Better-Education-Systems-for-Resilience-Equity-and-Quality-in-the-Age-of-COVID-19.pdf.

1194. UNICEF. 2021. *Reopening with Resilience: Lessons from Remote Learning during COVID-19*. https://www.unicef-irc.org/publications/1220-reopening-with-resilience-lessons-from-remote-learning-during-covid19.html.

1195. Reich, J. 2021, April 15. Tinkering with tech: How the pandemic exposed the flaws of digital education. Heinrich-Böll-Stiftung. https://us.boell.org/en/2021/03/31/tinkering-tech-how-pandemic-exposed-flaws-digital-education.

1196. Al-Samarrai, S. et al. 2021. *Education Finance Watch 2021*. World Bank. https://thedocs.worldbank.org/en/doc/507681613998942297-0090022021/original/EFWReport2021219.pdf.

1197. Organisation for Economic Co-operation and Development. 2020, December. *Lessons for Education from COVID-19: A Policy Maker's Handbook for More Resilient Systems*. https://www.oecd-ilibrary.org/education/lessons-for-education-from-covid-19_0a530888-en.

1198. ITU Publications. 2020, August. *Connecting Humanity: Assessing Investment Needs of Connecting Humanity to the Internet by 2030*. https://www.itu.int/dms_pub/itu-d/opb/gen/D-GEN-INVEST.CON-2020-PDF-E.pdf.

1199. Padmanabhan, V. & Alexander, S. 2019, March 11. The curious case of electrification in India amid discom blackouts. Mint. https://www.livemint.com/elections/lok-sabha-elections/the-curious-case-of-electrification-in-india-amid-power-discom-blackouts-1552257301715.html.

1200. World Bank. 2020. Access to electricity (% of population) - Sub-Saharan Africa (excluding high income). https://data.worldbank.org/indicator/EG.ELC.ACCS.ZS?view=map&locations=ZF. (Accessed 2 December 2022.)

1201. Tyack, D.B. & Cuban, Larry. 1995. *Tinkering toward Utopia: A Century of Public School Reform*. Cambridge, MA: Harvard University Press; Ames, M.G. 2019. *The Charisma Machine: The Life, Death, and Legacy of One Laptop per Child*. Cambridge, MA: MIT Press.

1202. Ames, M.G. 2019. *The Charisma Machine: The Life, Death, and Legacy of One Laptop per Child*. Cambridge, MA: MIT Press.

1203. Cuban, L. 2003. *Oversold and Underused: Computers in the Classroom*. Cambridge, MA: Harvard University Press.

1204. Rauf, D. 2020, April 16. Coronavirus squeezes supply of Chromebooks, iPads, and other digital learning devices. *Education Week*. https://www.edweek.org/education-industry/coronavirus-squeezes-supply-of-chromebooks-ipads-and-other-digital-learning-devices/2020/04.

1205. Isaac, M. & Frenkel, S. 2021, October 4. Gone in minutes, out for hours: Outage shakes Facebook. *New York Times*. https://www.nytimes.com/2021/10/04/technology/facebook-down.html.

1206. Dewar, C. 2021, October 4. Users report Twitter outage hours after Facebook, WhatsApp and Instagram go down. *The Herald*. https://www.heraldscotland.com/news/19624807.twitter-users-report-outage-facebook-whatsapp-instagram-go/.

1207. Tung, L. 2019, June 25. Amazon, Facebook internet outage: Verizon blamed for 'cascading catastrophic failure'. ZDNet. https://www.zdnet.com/article/amazon-facebook-internet-outage-verizon-blamed-for-cascading-catastrophic-failure/.

1208. Baynes, C. 2018, April 11. Entire country taken offline for two days after undersea internet cable cut. *The Independent*. https://www.independent.co.uk/tech/mauritiana-internet-cut-underwater-cable-offline-days-west-africa-a8298551.html.

1209. NetBlocks. 2022, March 4. Widespread internet outage registered in Iran amid reports of fire at datacenter. https://netblocks.org/reports/widespread-internet-outage-registered-in-iran-amid-reports-of-fire-at-datacenter-eBOQzz8Z.

1210. Microsoft Security Intelligence. 2022. Cyberthreats, viruses, and malware. https://www.microsoft.com/en-us/wdsi/threats. (Accessed 2 December 2022.)

1211. Scholz, S., Hagen, W. & Lee, C. 2021, June 22. The increasing threat of ransomware in higher education. *EDUCAUSE Review*. https://er.educause.edu/articles/2021/6/the-increasing-threat-of-ransomware-in-higher-education.

1212. Freed, B. 2021, July 23. 44% of education institutions targeted by ransomware in 2020, survey finds. EDSCOOP. https://edscoop.com/ransomware-education-institutions-sophos/.

1213. Bischoff, P. 2021, June 23. Ransomware attacks on US schools and colleges cost $6.62bn in 2020. Comparitech. https://www.comparitech.com/blog/information-security/school-ransomware-attacks/.

1214. Levin, D.A. 2021. *The State of K-12 Cybersecurity: 2020 Year in Review*. EdTech Strategies/K-12 Cybersecurity Resource Center & K12 Security Information Exchange. https://static1.squarespace.com/static/5e441b46adfb340b05008fe7/t/620d58f6f14b822a371b8c7b/1645041911977/StateofK12Cybersecurity-2020.pdf.

1215. Lyngaas, S. 2022, January 7. Ransomware attack affects the websites of 5,000 schools. CNN. https://www.cnn.com/2022/01/07/politics/ransomware-schools-website/index.html.

1216. Klein, A. 2022, January 10. Thousands of school websites went down in a cyberattack. It'll happen again, experts say. *Education Week*. https://www.edweek.org/technology/thousands-of-school-websites-went-down-in-a-cyberattack-itll-happen-again-experts-say/2022/01.

1217. Querolo, N. & Singh, S. 2021, August 9. Schools brace for more cyberattacks after record in 2020. Bloomberg. https://www.bloomberg.com/news/features/2021-08-09/schools-brace-for-more-cyberattacks-after-record-2020.

1218. University of California San Francisco. 2020, June 26. Update on IT security incident at UCSF. https://www.ucsf.edu/news/2020/06/417911/update-it-security-incident-ucsf.

1219. Freed, B. 2021, August 6. Texas school district paid $547K ransomware demand. EDSCOOP. https://edscoop.com/texas-school-paid-547k-ransomware-jam/; Cerulus, L. 2021, September 1. Ransomware's next target: Schools. *POLITICO*. https://www.politico.eu/article/its-back-to-school-for-ransomware-criminals/.

1220. Collier, K. 2021, September 10. Hackers are leaking children's data — and there's little parents can do. NBC News. https://www.nbcnews.com/tech/security/hackers-are-leaking-childrens-data-s-little-parents-can-rcna1926.

1221. Singer, N. 2022. A cyberattack illuminates the shaky state of student privacy. *New York Times*. https://www.nytimes.com/2022/07/31/business/student-privacy-illuminate-hack.html.

1222. Check Point Research. 2021, August 23. 93% increase in cyberattacks targeting the UK's education sector. FE News. https://www.fenews.co.uk/skills/93-increase-in-cyberattacks-targeting-the-uk-s-education-sector/.

1223. Kshetri, N. 2021, September 15. Cybercriminals use pandemic to attack schools and colleges. The Conversation. http://theconversation.com/cybercriminals-use-pandemic-to-attack-schools-and-colleges-167619.

1224. Deutsche Welle. 2021, September 19. Nigerian kidnappers free 10 more students. https://www.dw.com/en/nigerian-kidnappers-free-10-more-students-after-collecting-ransom/a-59229911.

1225. White House Briefing Room. 2021, October 8. Statement of President Joe Biden on signing the K-12 Cybersecurity Act into law. https://www.whitehouse.gov/briefing-room/statements-releases/2021/10/08/statement-of-president-joe-biden-on-signing-the-k-12-cybersecurity-act-into-law/.

1226. Sharma, S. 2022, January 24. Education sector hounded by cyberattacks in 2021. CSO. https://www.csoonline.com/article/3647760/education-sector-hounded-by-cyberattacks-in-2021.html.

1227. Access Now. 2021. #KeepItOn: Fighting internet shutdowns around the world. https://www.accessnow.org/keepiton/. (Accessed 3 October 2022.)

1228. Human Rights Watch. 2020, June 19. Myanmar: End world's longest internet shutdown. https://www.hrw.org/news/2020/06/19/myanmar-end-worlds-longest-internet-shutdown.

1229. Dahir, A.L. 2018, August 6. This documentary tells the story of Africa's longest internet shutdown. Quartz. https://qz.com/africa/1349108/cameroons-internet-shutdown-in-blacked-out-documentary/.

1230. Sayadi, E. & Samaro, D. 2020, October 5. Internet shutdowns in Algeria and Sudan: Damaging practices during exceptional circumstances. Access Now. https://www.accessnow.org/internet-shutdowns-in-algeria-and-sudan-damaging-practices-during-exceptional-circumstances/.

1231. Access Now. 2021. #KeepItOn: Fighting internet shutdowns around the world. https://www.accessnow.org/keepiton/. (Accessed 3 October 2022.)

1232. West, M., Kraut, R. & Chew, H.E. 2019. *I'd Blush if I Could: Closing Gender Divides in Digital Skills through Education*. EQUALS Skills Coalition & UNESCO. https://unesdoc.unesco.org/ark:/48223/pf0000367416; Vosloo, S. 2018. *Guidelines: Designing Inclusive Digital Solutions and Developing Digital Skills*. UNESCO Education Sector. https://unesdoc.unesco.org/ark:/48223/pf0000265537.

1233. HolonIQ. 2021. Education technology in 10 charts: Everything you need to know about the global EdTech market in 10 charts. https://www.holoniq.com/edtech-in-10-charts.

1234. Ibid.

1235. Ibid.

1236. Ibid.

1237. World Bank. 2020, November 10. Ask why: Reimagining human connections technology and innovation in education at the World Bank. https://www.worldbank.org/en/topic/edutech/brief/ask-why-reimagining-human-connections-technology-and-innovation-in-education-at-the-world-bank.

1238. HolonIQ. 2021. Education technology in 10 charts: Everything you need to know about the global EdTech market in 10 charts. https://www.holoniq.com/edtech-in-10-charts.

1239. Markow, W. & Hughes, D. 2018. *The New Foundational Skills of the Digital Economy*. Business-Higher Education Forum & Burning Glass Technologies. https://www.burning-glass.com/wp-content/uploads/New_Foundational_Skills.pdf.

1240. Williamson, B. 2020, December 15. New financial actors and valuation platforms in education technology markets. *Code Acts in Education*. https://codeactsineducation.wordpress.com/2020/12/15/new-financial-platforms-education/.

1241. Anderson, J. & Rainie, L. 2018, April 17. The future of well-being in a tech-saturated world. Pew Research Center. https://www.pewresearch.org/internet/2018/04/17/the-future-of-well-being-in-a-tech-saturated-world/.

1242. Fortin, J. 2022, April 20. More pandemic fallout: The chronically absent student. *New York Times*. https://www.nytimes.com/2022/04/20/us/school-absence-attendance-rate-covid.html.

1243. Auxier, B., Anderson, M., Perrin, A. & Turner, E. 2020, July 28. Parental views about YouTube. Pew Research Center. https://www.pewresearch.org/internet/2020/07/28/parental-views-about-youtube/.

1244. Linn, S. 2005. *Consuming Kids: Protecting Our Children from the Onslaught of Marketing and Advertising*. New York: Anchor Books.

1245. Meinck, S., Fraillon, J. & Strietholt, R. 2022. *The Impact of the COVID-19 Pandemic on Education: International Evidence from the Responses to Educational Disruption Survey (REDS)*. UNESCO & International Association for the Evaluation of Educational Achievement. https://unesdoc.unesco.org/ark:/48223/pf0000380398.

1246. Klein, A. 2022, March 8. Tech fatigue is real for teachers and students. Here's how to ease the burden. *Education Week*. https://www.edweek.org/technology/tech-fatigue-is-real-for-teachers-and-students-heres-how-to-ease-the-burden/2022/03.

1247. International Commission on the Futures of Education. 2021. *Reimagining Our Futures Together: A New Social Contract for Education*. UNESCO. https://unesdoc.unesco.org/ark:/48223/pf0000379707.

1248. Hern, A. 2021, September 2. UK children's digital privacy code comes into effect. *The Guardian*. https://www.theguardian.com/technology/2021/sep/02/uk-childrens-digital-privacy-code-comes-into-effect.

1249. Information Commissioner's Office. 2023. Introduction to the Children's code. https://ico.org.uk/for-organisations/uk-gdpr-guidance-and-resources/childrens-information/childrens-code-guidance-and-resources/introduction-to-the-childrens-code/.

1250. Tait, A. 2021, September 19. Beeban Kidron v. Silicon Valley: One woman's fight to protect children online. *The Observer*. https://www.theguardian.com/film/2021/sep/19/beeban-kidron-v-silicon-valley-one-womans-fight-to-protect-children-online.

1251. Jargon, J. 2019, June 18. How 13 became the internet's age of adulthood. *Wall Street Journal*. https://www.wsj.com/articles/how-13-became-the-internets-age-of-adulthood-11560850201.

1252. Satariano, A. 2022, March 24. E.U. takes aim at big tech's power with landmark digital act. *New York Times*. https://www.nytimes.com/2022/03/24/technology/eu-regulation-apple-meta-google.html.

1253. Office of Governor Gavin Newsom. 2022, September 15. Governor Newsom signs first-in-nation bill protecting children's online data and privacy. https://www.gov.ca.gov/2022/09/15/governor-newsom-signs-first-in-nation-bill-protecting-childrens-online-data-and-privacy/.

1254. Satariano, A. 2020, April 27. Europe's privacy law hasn't shown its teeth, frustrating advocates. *New York Times*. https://www.nytimes.com/2020/04/27/technology/GDPR-privacy-law-europe.html; Scott, M., Cerulus, L. & Overly, S. 2019, May 25. How Silicon Valley gamed the world's toughest privacy rules. *POLITICO*. https://www.politico.com/story/2019/05/25/how-silicon-valley-gamed-the-worlds-toughest-privacy-rules-1466148.

1255. Data Protection Commission. 2022, September 15. Data Protection Commission announces decision in Instagram inquiry. Press release. https://www.dataprotection.ie/news-media/press-releases/data-protection-commission-announces-decision-instagram-inquiry.

1256. Satariano, A. 2022, September 5. Meta fined $400 million for treatment of children's data on Instagram. *New York Times*. https://www.nytimes.com/2022/09/05/business/meta-children-data-protection-europe.html.

1257. McMallum, S. & Gerken, T. 2022, September 5. Instagram fined €405m over children's data privacy. BBC News. https://www.bbc.com/news/technology-62800884.

1258. Satariano, A. 2022, November 28. Meta fined $275 million for breaking E.U. data privacy law. *New York Times*. https://www.nytimes.com/2022/11/28/business/meta-fine-eu-privacy.html.

1259. Yang, M. & Beardsley, E. 2023, May 22. European watchdog fines Meta $1.3 billion over privacy violations. NPR. https://www.npr.org/2023/05/22/1177472768/eu-europe-meta-facebook-instagram-record-fine-data-privacy.

1260. Commission nationale de l'informatique et des libertés. 2022, January 6. Cookies: The CNIL fines GOOGLE a total of 150 million euros and FACEBOOK 60 million euros for non-compliance with French legislation. https://www.cnil.fr/en/cookies-cnil-fines-google-total-150-million-euros-and-facebook-60-million-euros-non-compliance.

[1261.] UNICEF. 2021, July 15. COVID-19 pandemic leads to major backsliding on childhood vaccinations, new WHO, UNICEF data shows. Press release. https://www.unicef.org/press-releases/covid-19-pandemic-leads-major-backsliding-childhood-vaccinations-new-who-unicef-data.

[1262.] Williamson, B. 2021, May 28. Google's plans to bring AI to education make its dominance in classrooms more alarming. Fast Company. https://www.fastcompany.com/90641049/google-education-classroom-ai; Hao, K. 2020, December 4. We read the paper that forced Timnit Gebru out of Google. Here's what it says. *MIT Technology Review*. https://www.technologyreview.com/2020/12/04/1013294/google-ai-ethics-research-paper-forced-out-timnit-gebru/.

[1263.] Drape, J. 2021, December 19. Step aside, LeBron and Dak, and make room for Banjo and Kazooie. *New York Times*. https://www.nytimes.com/2021/12/19/sports/esports-fans-leagues-games.html.

[1264.] Vogels, E., Gelles-Watnick, R. & Massarat, N. 2022, August 10. *Teens, Social Media and Technology 2022*. Pew Research Center. https://www.pewresearch.org/internet/wp-content/uploads/sites/9/2022/08/PI_2022.08.10_Teens-and-Tech_FINAL.pdf; Press Association. 2022, February 14. Most 5-year-olds spend too much time online, survey shows. Bloomberg. https://www.bloomberg.com/news/articles/2022-02-14/most-5-year-olds-spend-too-much-time-online-survey-shows.

[1265.] Hallett, V. 2021, February 10. How the pandemic is changing children's friendships. *National Geographic*. https://www.nationalgeographic.co.uk/family/2021/02/how-the-pandemic-is-changing-childrens-friendships.

[1266.] Miao, F. et al. 2022. *Guidelines for ICT in Education Policies and Masterplans*. UNESCO. https://unesdoc.unesco.org/ark:/48223/pf0000380926.

[1267.] Mizunoya, S. et al. 2020. *How Many Children and Young People Have Internet Access at Home? Estimating Digital Connectivity During the COVID-19 Pandemic*. UNICEF & ITU. https://data.unicef.org/resources/children-and-young-people-internet-access-at-home-during-covid19/.

[1268.] ITU Publications. 2018. *Measuring the Information Society Report: Volume 1, 2008*. International Telecommunication Union. https://www.itu.int/en/ITU-D/Statistics/Documents/publications/misr2018/MISR-2018-Vol-1-E.pdf.

[1269.] United Nations. 2020, May 29. Road map for digital cooperation: Implementation of the recommendations of the High-level Panel on Digital Cooperation. Report of the Secretary-General. https://documents-dds-ny.un.org/doc/UNDOC/GEN/N20/102/51/PDF/N2010251.pdf.

[1270.] UNESCO. 2022. *The RewirEd Global Declaration on Connectivity for Education: #ConnectivityDeclaration*. https://unesdoc.unesco.org/ark:/48223/pf0000381482.

[1271.] UNESCO. 2022, July 15. Thematic action track 4 on digital learning and transformation. United Nations Transforming Education Summit. Discussion paper. https://transformingeducationsummit.sdg4education2030.org/system/files/2022-07/Digital%20AT4%20dicussion%20paper%20July%202022.pdf.

[1272.] United Nations. 2022. Assuring and improving quality public digital learning for all. United Nations Transforming Education Summit. https://www.un.org/en/transforming-education-summit/digital-learning-all.

[1273.] UNESCO Institute for Statistics. 2016. Out-of-school children and youth. http://uis.unesco.org/en/topic/out-school-children-and-youth; UNESCO. 2022, September. International Literacy Day: Transforming literacy learning spaces. https://en.unesco.org/sites/default/files/ild-2022-cn-en.pdf.

[1274.] McMorris-Santoro, E. 2021, March 8. Thousands of students have dropped out of school due to Covid-19. These are the educators trying to track them down. CNN. https://www.cnn.com/2021/03/06/us/covid-pandemic-high-school-dropout/index.html; Lichand, G., Dória, C.A., Neto, O.L. & Cossi Fernandes, J.P. 2022, May. The impacts of remote learning in secondary education: evidence from Brazil during the pandemic. *Nature Human Behaviour*, 6: 1079–1086. https://www.nature.com/articles/s41562-022-01350-6.

[1275.] Mlambo-Ngcuka, P. & Albrectsen, A. 2020, May 4. Opinion: We cannot allow COVID-19 to reinforce the digital gender divide. Devex. https://www.devex.com/news/opinion-we-cannot-allow-covid-19-to-reinforce-the-digital-gender-divide-97118.

[1276.] Tyers-Chowdhury, A. & Binder, G. 2021. *What We know about the Gender Digital Divide for Girls: A Literature Review*. UNICEF. https://www.unicef.org/eap/media/8311/file/What we know about the gender digital divide for girls: A literature review.pdf.

1277. Portillo, J., Garay, U., Tejada, E. & Bilbao, N. 2020. Self-perception of the digital competence of educators during the COVID-19 Pandemic: A cross-analysis of different educational stages. *Sustainability*, 12(23): 101–128. https://doi.org/10.3390/su122310128.

1278. Loziak, A., Fedakova, D. & Čopková, R. 2020. Work-related stressors of female teachers during Covid-19 school closure. *Journal of Women's Entrepreneurship and Education*, 3–4: 59–78. https://www.library.ien.bg.ac.rs/index.php/jwee/article/view/1304.

1279. West, M., Kraut, R. & Chew, H.E. 2019. *I'd Blush if I Could: Closing Gender Divides in Digital Skills through Education*. EQUALS Skills Coalition & UNESCO. https://unesdoc.unesco.org/ark:/48223/pf0000367416.

1280. MIET AFRICA. 2021, June. *The Impact of COVID-19 on Adolescents and Young People in the Southern African Development Community Region*. https://mietafrica.org/wp-content/uploads/2021/07/REPORT-Impact_COVID_19_AYP_SADCRegional.pdf.

1281. UNESCO. 2022. *Leave No Child Behind: Global Report on Boys' Disengagement from Education*. https://unesdoc.unesco.org/ark:/48223/pf0000381105.

1282. United Nations. 2022. Assuring and improving quality public digital learning for all. United Nations Transforming Education Summit. https://www.un.org/en/transforming-education-summit/digital-learning-all.

1283. United Nations. 2022, September 19. Gateways to public digital learning: A multi-partner initiative to create and strengthen inclusive digital learning platforms and content. United Nations Transforming Education Summit. Spotlight session. https://www.un.org/sites/un2.un.org/files/2022/09/gateways_to_public_digital_learning_long.pdf.

1284. UNESCO. 2019, November 25. Recommendation on Open Educational Resources (OER). https://www.unesco.org/en/legal-affairs/recommendation-open-educational-resources-oer.

1285. United Nations. 2022, September 19. Gateways to public digital learning: A multi-partner initiative to create and strengthen inclusive digital learning platforms and content. United Nations Transforming Education Summit. Spotlight session. https://www.un.org/sites/un2.un.org/files/2022/09/gateways_to_public_digital_learning_long.pdf.

1286. UNESCO. 2022. *The RewirEd Global Declaration on Connectivity for Education: #ConnectivityDeclaration*. https://unesdoc.unesco.org/ark:/48223/pf0000381482.

1287. UNESCO. 2017. *UNESCO-Pearson Initiative for Literacy: Improved Livelihoods in a Digital World*. https://unesdoc.unesco.org/ark:/48223/pf0000247599.

1288. EQUALS Global Partnership for Gender Equality in the Digital Age. 2022. We are EQUALS. https://www.equalsintech.org/about. (Accessed 15 December 2022.); Broadband Commission for Sustainable Development. 2022. About us: Bringing the goal of universal connectivity to the forefront of policy discussions. https://www.broadbandcommission.org/about-us/. (Accessed 15 December 2022.)

1289. UNESCO. 2018. *UNESCO ICT Competency Framework for Teachers: Version 3*. https://unesdoc.unesco.org/ark:/48223/pf0000265721; UNESCO. 2022. Global Education Coalition. https://globaleducationcoalition.unesco.org/. (Accessed 15 December 2022.)

1290. United Nations. 1948. Article 26. Universal Declaration of Human Rights. https://www.un.org/en/about-us/universal-declaration-of-human-rights.

1291. UNESCO. 2019. *Right to Education Handbook*. https://unesdoc.unesco.org/ark:/48223/pf0000366556.

1292. Meyer, J.W., Ramirez, F.O. & Soysal, Y.N. 1992. World Expansion of Mass Education, 1870–1980. *Sociology of Education*, 65(2): 128–149. https://www.jstor.org/stable/2112679.

1293. Winthrop, R. & McGivney, E. 2015, June 10. Why wait 100 years? Bridging the gap in global education. Brookings. https://www.brookings.edu/research/why-wait-100-years-bridging-the-gap-in-global-education/.

1294. UN General Assembly Human Rights Council. 2020, June 30. Right to education: Impact of the Coronavirus disease crisis on the Right to Education—concerns, challenges and opportunities. Report of the Special Rapporteur on the right to education. https://documents-dds-ny.un.org/doc/UNDOC/GEN/G20/158/03/PDF/G2015803.pdf.

1295. Ibid.

1296. Human Rights Watch. 2021, May 17. *"Years Don't Wait for Them": Increased Inequalities in Children's Right to Education Due to the Covid-19 Pandemic*. https://www.hrw.org/report/2021/05/17/years-dont-wait-them/increased-inequalities-childrens-right-education-due-covid.

1297. People for Education. 2022, February 14. Major changes coming to online learning in Ontario. https://peopleforeducation.ca/our-work/major-changes-coming-to-online-learning-in-ontario/.

1298. AP News. 2022, February 24. Schools in Eldon to move to 4-day school week next year. https://apnews.com/article/iowa-43729ed982f6486270585082bffcf64e.

1299. Kay, S. 2020, October 10. New report calls for dedicated 'Office for Edtech' to drive change. Schools Week. https://schoolsweek.co.uk/new-report-calls-for-dedicated-office-for-edtech-to-drive-change/.

1300. Lockee, B.B. 2021, January. Online education in the post-COVID era. *Nature Electronics*, 4(1): 5–6. https://www.nature.com/articles/s41928-020-00534-0.

1301. Krauth, O. & Kobin, B. 2021, February 2. New lawsuit seeks to force Kentucky public schools to reopen during the pandemic. *Louisville Courier Journal*. https://www.courier-journal.com/story/news/education/2021/02/02/covid-19-kentucky-lawsuit-seeks-force-reopening-public-schools/4364190001/; Roberto, M. 2020, June 30. 80 Law students sue University of Nairobi over online classes, exams. TUKO. https://www.tuko.co.ke/365407-80-law-students-sue-university-nairobi-online-classes-exams-citing-inequality.html; Legal Services NYC. 2022, January 7. Low-income families sue departments of education to force them to provide working devices, internet, and instruction for periods of remote learning. https://www.legalservicesnyc.org/news-and-events/press-room/1748-low-income-families-sue-departments-of-education-to-force-them-to-provide-working-devices-internet-and-instruction-for-periods-of-remote-learning; Wightwick, A. 2022, October 31. Students launch legal action against Cardiff and other universities for worse experience during Covid and staff strikes. Wales Online. https://www.walesonline.co.uk/news/education/students-launch-legal-action-against-25390845; Tadayon, A. 2020, November 30. California parents sue state alleging inequity in distance learning. EdSource. https://edsource.org/updates/california-parents-sue-state-alleging-inequity-in-distance-learning.

1302. Thompson, F. 2020, August 12. Lawsuit filed against Washington state for 'denying basic education' to special needs children amid COVID-19. FOX 13. https://www.q13fox.com/news/lawsuit-filed-against-washington-state-for-denying-basic-education-to-special-needs-children-amid-covid-19; Oriomoni, A. 2022, June 8. Tension between U of T law and disabled students raises a broader policy implication: lawyer. *Law Times*. https://www.lawtimesnews.com/resources/legal-education/tension-between-u-of-t-law-and-disabled-students-raises-a-broader-policy-implication-lawyer/367300; Henriques-Gomes, L. 2020, August 19. Australian children with disabilities excluded from online learning during pandemic, inquiry told. *The Guardian*. https://www.theguardian.com/australia-news/2020/aug/19/australian-children-with-disabilities-excluded-from-online-learning-during-pandemic-inquiry-told.

1303. Goldstein, J. & Otterman, S. 2022, March 17. What New York got wrong about the pandemic, and what it got right. *New York Times*. https://www.nytimes.com/2022/03/17/nyregion/new-york-pandemic-lessons.html.

1304. Ferguson, L. 2021. Vulnerable children's right to education, school exclusion, and pandemic law-making. *Emotional and Behavioural Difficulties*, 26(1): 101–115. https://www.tandfonline.com/doi/full/10.1080/13632752.2021.1913351; Fredman, S. 2021. A human rights approach: The right to education in the time of COVID-19. *Child Development*, 92(5): e900–e903. https://srcd.onlinelibrary.wiley.com/doi/10.1111/cdev.13654; UN General Assembly Human Rights Council. 2022, April 19. Impact of the digitalization of education on the right to education. Report of the Special Rapporteur on the right to education. https://documents-dds-ny.un.org/doc/UNDOC/GEN/G22/322/37/PDF/G2232237.pdf.

1305. *The Tribune*. 2022, May 3. Give priority to regular classes in Punjab: Democratic Teachers Front. https://www.tribuneindia.com/news/ludhiana/give-priority-to-regular-classes-democratic-teachers-front-391360.

1306. Woodland, L. et al. 2021. Why did some parents not send their children back to school following school closures during the COVID-19 pandemic: a cross-sectional survey. *BMJ Paediatrics Open*, 5(1): e001014. https://pubmed.ncbi.nlm.nih.gov/34611551/.

1307. Human Rights Watch. 2022, May 25. *"How Dare They Peep into My Private Life?": Children's rights violations by governments that endorsed online learning during the COVID-19 pandemic*. https://www.hrw.org/report/2022/05/25/how-dare-they-peep-my-private-life/childrens-rights-violations-governments.

1308. Centre for Human Rights, Pakistan. 2022, March 1. COVID-19 and the Digital Divide in Education. Webinar. Posted to YouTube 23 March 2022. CFHR talks: Bridging the digital divide in education during COVID-19. https://www.youtube.com/watch?v=f01vODlpDE8.

1309. United Nations. 1948. Article 26. Universal Declaration of Human Rights. https://www.un.org/en/about-us/universal-declaration-of-human-rights.

1310. United Nations. 2007. Article 14. United Nations Declaration on the Rights of Indigenous Peoples. https://www.un.org/development/desa/indigenouspeoples/wp-content/uploads/sites/19/2018/11/UNDRIP_E_web.pdf.

1311. Graham, L.M. & Van Zyl-Chavarro, A.B. 2018. Part III rights to culture: Ch. 13 Indigenous education and the UNDRIP: Article 14. In Hohmann, J. & Weller, M. (eds). *The UN Declaration on the Rights of Indigenous Peoples: A Commentary*. Oxford: Oxford University Press.

1312. UNESCO. 2023. *Global Education Monitoring Report 2023. Technology in Education: A Tool on Whose Terms?* https://unesdoc.unesco.org/ark:/48223/pf0000385723.locale=en

WORKS CITED
Voices from the ground

[i.] Williamson, B. 2021. Meta-edtech. *Learning, Media and Technology*, 46(1). https://doi.org/10.1080/17439884.2021.1876089.

[ii.] Chebib, K. 2020. *Education For All in the Time of COVID-19: How EdTech can be Part of the Solution*. GSMA. https://www.gsma.com/mobilefordevelopment/wp-content/uploads/2020/09/EdTech-Final-WEB.pdf.

[iii.] Wan, T. 2021, July 1. U.S Edtech roars with over $3.2 billion invested in first half of 2021. *Medium*. https://medium.com/reach-capital/u-s-edtech-roars-with-over-3-2-billion-invested-in-first-half-of-2021-d69049dbce30.

[iv.] Paquet, G. 2005. *The New Geo-Governance: A Baroque Approach (Governance Series)*. Ottawa: University of Ottawa Press.

[v.] Morozov, E. 2014. *To Save Everything, Click Here: The Folly of Technological Solutionism*. New York: Public Affairs.

[vi.] Postman, N. 1993. *Technopoly: The Surrender of Culture to Technology*. New York: Vintage Books.

[vii.] Culkin, J.M. 1967, March 18. A schoolman's guide to Marshall McLuhan. *Saturday Review*. https://www.unz.com/print/SaturdayRev-1967mar18-00051/.

[viii.] Gifford, J. & Pyshkin, K. 2020. *Education Technology. Coronavirus and Beyond*. Credit Suisse. https://www.credit-suisse.com/media/assets/microsite/docs/responsibleinvesting/cs-education-technology-spread.pdf.

[ix.] Smith, F.J. 1913, July 9. The evolution of the motion picture: VI – Looking into the future with Thomas A. Edison. *New York Dramatic Mirror*. New York (Old Fulton).

[x.] Watters, A. 2021. *Teaching Machines: The History of Personalized Learning*. Cambridge, MA: MIT Press.

[xi.] Seldon, A. & Abidoye, O. 2018. *The Fourth Education Revolution. Will Artificial Intelligence Liberate or Infantilise Humanity?* Buckingham, UK: University of Buckingham Press.

[xii.] Postman, N. 2005. *Amusing Ourselves to Death: Public Discourse In The Age Of Show Business*. New York: Penguin Books.

[xiii.] Arora, P. 2010, May. Hope-in-the-Wall? A digital promise for free learning. *British Journal of Educational Technology*, 41(5). https://www.researchgate.net/publication/229788949_Hope-in-the-Wall_A_digital_promise_for_free_learning.

[xiv.] Mitra, S. 2013. Build a school in the cloud. TED Talks. https://www.ted.com/talks/sugata_mitra_build_a_school_in_the_cloud.

[xv.] Rose, J. 2012, May 9. How to break free of our 19th-century factory-model education system. *The Atlantic*. https://www.theatlantic.com/business/archive/2012/05/how-to-break-free-of-our-19th-century-factory-model-education-system/256881/.

[xvi.] Keniston, K. 2002. Grassroots ICT projects in India: Some preliminary hypotheses. *ASCI Journal of Management*, 31(1&2). http://web.mit.edu/~kken/Public/PAPERS/ASCI_Journal_Intro__ASCI_version_.html.

[xvii.] Kirp, D., Wechsler, M., Gardner, M. & Tinubu Ali, T. 2022. *Disrupting Disruption: The Steady Work of Transforming Schools*. Oxford: Oxford University Press.

[xviii.] Friedman, M. 1962. *Capitalism and Freedom*. Chicago: University of Chicago Press.

[xix.] World Bank. 2020, December 2. COVID-19 prompts urgency of bridging digital divide in Central Asia. Press release. https://www.worldbank.org/en/news/press-release/2020/12/02/urgency-of-bridging-digital-divide-in-central-asia-increases-as-a-result-of-the-covid-19-pandemic.

[xx.] Human Rights Watch. 2021, May 17. "It feels like maybe I won't ever go to school again": Children, parents, and teachers describe the impact of Covid school closures. https://www.hrw.org/video-photos/interactive/2021/05/17/it-feels-maybe-i-wont-ever-go-school-again.

xxi. Ibid.

xxii. Ibid.

xxiii. UNICEF. 2020, June 4. Unequal access to remote schooling amid COVID-19 threatens to deepen global learning crisis. Press release. https://www.unicef.org/press-releases/unequal-access-remote-schooling-amid-covid-19-threatens-deepen-global-learning.

xxiv. Schmall, E. & Yasir, S. 2022, January 27. India schools stay closed, and hopes fade for a lost generation. *New York Times*. https://www.nytimes.com/2022/01/27/world/asia/india-schools.html.

xxv. Human Rights Watch. 2021, May 17. "It feels like maybe I won't ever go to school again": Children, parents, and teachers describe the impact of Covid school closures. https://www.hrw.org/video-photos/interactive/2021/05/17/it-feels-maybe-i-wont-ever-go-school-again.

xxvi. Ibid.

xxvii. Carter, S. & Moncrieff, I. 2021, May. *COVID-19 School Closures in the DRC: Impact on the Health, Protection and Education of Children and Youth*. Social Sciences Analytics Cell. https://www.unicef.org/drcongo/media/5716/file/COD-CASS-school-closures-impacts.pdf.

xxviii. Human Rights Watch. 2021, May 17. "It feels like maybe I won't ever go to school again": Children, parents, and teachers describe the impact of Covid school closures. https://www.hrw.org/video-photos/interactive/2021/05/17/it-feels-maybe-i-wont-ever-go-school-again.

xxix. Girl Effect & Vodafone Foundation. 2018. *Real Girls, Real Lives, Connected*. https://www.global.girleffect.org/stories/real-girls-real-lives-connected/.

xxx. Human Rights Watch. 2021, May 17. *"Years Don't Wait for Them": Increased Inequalities in Children's Right to Education Due to the Covid-19 Pandemic*. https://www.hrw.org/report/2021/05/17/years-dont-wait-them/increased-inequalities-childrens-right-education-due-covid.

xxxi. Human Rights Watch. 2021, May 17. "It feels like maybe I won't ever go to school again": Children, parents, and teachers describe the impact of Covid school closures. https://www.hrw.org/video-photos/interactive/2021/05/17/it-feels-maybe-i-wont-ever-go-school-again.

xxxii. Greene, D. 2021. *The Promise of Access: Technology, Inequality, and the Political Economy of Hope*. Cambridge, MA: MIT Press.

xxxiii. *The Economist*. 2016, August 4. Look before you leap. https://www.economist.com/business/2016/08/04/look-before-you-leap.

xxxiv. Gupta, R. 2020, May 15. No internet, no electricity: Online education a struggle for rural students. *SheThePeople*. https://www.shethepeople.tv/home-top-video/online-eduction-rural-students-india.

xxxv. Nadaf, A.H. 2021, June. "Lockdown within a lockdown": The "digital redlining" and paralyzed online teaching during COVID-19 in Kashmir, a conflict territory. *Communication, Culture and Critique*, 14(2). https://doi.org/10.1093/ccc/tcab019.

xxxvi. Turner, C. 2020, October 7. Homeless families struggle with impossible choices as school closures continue. NPR. https://www.npr.org/2020/10/07/920320592/an-impossible-choice-for-homeless-parents-a-job-or-their-childs-education.

xxxvii. Russell, N. 2020, July 27. I can't keep doing this. Please open the schools. *The Atlantic*. https://www.theatlantic.com/ideas/archive/2020/07/please-open-schools/614605/.

xxxviii. Strauss, V. 2020, July 20. The huge problem with education 'pandemic pods' suddenly popping up. *Washington Post*. https://www.washingtonpost.com/education/2020/07/22/huge-problem-with-education-pandemic-pods-suddenly-popping-up/.

xxxix. Human Rights Watch. 2021, May 17. "It feels like maybe I won't ever go to school again": Children, parents, and teachers describe the impact of Covid school closures. https://www.hrw.org/video-photos/interactive/2021/05/17/it-feels-maybe-i-wont-ever-go-school-again.

xl. Goudeau, S., Sanrey, C., Stanczak, A., Manstead, A. & Darnon, C. 2021. Why lockdown and distance learning during the COVID-19 pandemic are likely to increase the social class achievement gap. *Nature Human Behaviour*, 5(10): 1273–1281. https://doi.org/10.1038/s41562-021-01212-7.

xli. Andrew, A. et al. 2020. Inequalities in children's experiences of home learning during the COVID-19 lockdown in England. *Fiscal Studies*, 41(3). https://onlinelibrary.wiley.com/doi/10.1111/1475-5890.12240.

xlii. Rafalow, M.H. 2020. *Digital Divisions: How Schools Create Inequality in the Tech Era*. Chicago: University of Chicago Press.

xliii. Human Rights Watch. 2021, May 17. "It feels like maybe I won't ever go to school again": Children, parents, and teachers describe the impact of Covid school closures. https://www.hrw.org/video-photos/interactive/2021/05/17/it-feels-maybe-i-wont-ever-go-school-again.

xliv. Ibid.

xlv. Human Rights Watch. 2021, May 27. *"Years Don't Wait for Them": Increased Inequalities in Children's Right to Education Due to the Covid-19 Pandemic*. https://www.hrw.org/report/2021/05/17/years-dont-wait-them/increased-inequalities-childrens-right-education-due-covid.

xlvi. Literat, I. 2021, February 25. "Teachers act like we're robots": TikTok as a window into youth experiences of online learning during COVID-19. *AERA Open, 7*. https://doi.org/10.1177/2332858421995537.

xlvii. Nicandro, V., Khandelwal, A. & Weitzman, A. 2020, June 1. Please, let students turn their videos off in class. *Stanford Daily*. https://www.stanforddaily.com/2020/06/01/please-let-students-turn-their-videos-off-in-class/.

xlviii. Ibid.

xlix. Klass, P. 2020, July 27. The pandemic's toll on children with special needs and their parents. *New York Times*. https://www.nytimes.com/2020/07/27/well/family/children-special-needs-pandemic.html.

l. Luterman, S. 2022, February 1. 'We feel like we lost two years of education': School closings are more complicated for parents of children with disabilities. *The 19th*. https://19thnews.org/2022/02/covid-school-closures-remote-learning-complicated-students-disabilities/.

li. Mbukwa-Ngwira, J. et al. 2021, March 19. Impact of COVID-19 on the education of children with disabilities in Malawi: Results from a survey with parents. Education and Development Forum. https://www.ukfiet.org/2021/impact-of-covid-19-on-the-education-of-children-with-disabilities-in-malawi-results-from-a-survey-with-parents/.

lii. Girl Effect & Vodafone Foundation. 2018. *Real Girls, Real Lives, Connected*. https://www.global.girleffect.org/stories/real-girls-real-lives-connected/.

liii. Ibid.

liv. Human Rights Watch. 2021, May 17. *"Years Don't Wait for Them": Increased Inequalities in Children's Right to Education Due to the Covid-19 Pandemic*. https://www.hrw.org/report/2021/05/17/years-dont-wait-them/increased-inequalities-childrens-right-education-due-covid.

lv. Turner, C. 2020, October 7. Homeless families struggle with impossible choices as school closures continue. NPR. https://www.npr.org/2020/10/07/920320592/an-impossible-choice-for-homeless-parents-a-job-or-their-childs-education.

lvi. UNESCO. 2021. *When Schools Shut: Gendered Impacts of COVID-19 School Closures*. https://unesdoc.unesco.org/ark:/48223/pf0000379270.

lvii. Bernheim, R. & Padilla, K. 2020. *Act Now: Experiences and Recommendations of Girls and Boys in West Africa during COVID-19*. World Vision International. https://www.wvi.org/sites/default/files/2020-11/5-WV-WARO-Report-29-10-20.pdf.

lviii. Quintanilla, D. 2021, July 29. Latino college enrollment was rising before Covid, but the pandemic has taken a toll. CNBC. https://www.cnbc.com/2021/07/29/latinx-college-enrollment-was-rising-before-covid-but-the-pandemic-has-taken-a-toll.html.

lix. Kane, T. 2022, May 22. Kids are far, far behind in school. *The Atlantic*. https://www.theatlantic.com/ideas/archive/2022/05/schools-learning-loss-remote-covid-education/629938/.

lx. Betthäuser, B.A., Bach-Mortensen, A.M. & Engzell, P. 2023, January 30. A systematic review and meta-analysis of the evidence on learning during the COVID-19 pandemic. *Nature Human Behaviour, 7*. https://doi.org/10.1038/s41562-022-01506-4.

lxi. Jacobson, L. 2021, March 16. The teens who clean homes during Zoom classes: Juggling work and school in the pandemic. *The Guardian*. https://www.theguardian.com/us-news/2021/mar/16/us-teens-school-work-keep-families-afloat-recession.

lxii. Grant, H., Hayden, S., Kumar, R. & Taylor, L. 2021, April 5. 'I miss school': 800m children still not fully back in classes. *The Guardian*. https://www.theguardian.com/global-development/2021/apr/05/schools-800-million-children-education-disrupted.

lxiii. Singha, M. 2022, December 17. Don't want online classes, say students. *Times of India*. http://timesofindia.indiatimes.com/articleshow/96532448.cms.

lxiv. Malkus, N. 2022, July. *Pandemic Enrollment Fallout: School District Enrollment Changes Across COVID-19 Response*. American Enterprise Institute. https://www.aei.org/wp-content/uploads/2022/07/Pandemic-Enrollment-Fallout.pdf.

lxv. Joung, M. 2020, August 17. Students protest tuition hikes as universities continue online. VOA News. https://www.voanews.com/a/covid-19-pandemic_students-protest-tuition-hikes-universities-continue-online/6194550.html.

lxvi. Tufekci, Z. 2021, September 20. The pandemic is no excuse to surveil students. *The Atlantic*. https://www.theatlantic.com/technology/archive/2020/09/pandemic-no-excuse-colleges-surveil-students/616015/.

lxvii. Kim, J. 2020, December 29. Remote schooling brings bigger losses for children still learning to speak English. *New York Times*. https://www.nytimes.com/2020/12/29/world/remote-schooling-brings-bigger-losses-for-children-still-learning-to-speak-english.html.

lxviii. UNICEF. 2021, September 16. Around 2 in 3 children are still out of the classroom in Latin America and the Caribbean. Press release. https://www.unicef.org/press-releases/around-2-3-children-are-still-out-classroom-latin-america-and-caribbean.

lxix. Human Rights Watch. 2021, May 17. *"Years Don't Wait for Them": Increased Inequalities in Children's Right to Education Due to the Covid-19 Pandemic*. https://www.hrw.org/report/2021/05/17/years-dont-wait-them/increased-inequalities-childrens-right-education-due-covid.

lxx. Grose, J. 2022, September 1. School is for care. *New York Times*. https://www.nytimes.com/2022/09/01/opinion/us-school-care.html.

lxxi. SchoolHouse Connection & Poverty Solutions at the University of Michigan. 2020, November. *Lost in the Masked Shuffle and Virtual Void: Children and Youth Experiencing Homelessness amidst the Pandemic*. https://schoolhouseconnection.org/wp-content/uploads/2020/11/Lost-in-the-Masked-Shuffle-and-Virtual-Void.pdf.

lxxii. Literat, I. 2021. February 25. "Teachers act like we're robots": TikTok as a window into youth experiences of online learning during COVID-19. *AERA Open, 7*. https://doi.org/10.1177/2332858421995537.

lxxiii. Lynch, M. 2019, January 15. Edtech should complement good pedagogy, not attempt to replace it. The Tech Advocate. https://www.thetechedvocate.org/edtech-should-complement-good-pedagogy-not-attempt-to-replace-it/.

lxxiv. Vera, K. & Ellis, B. 2020, October 15. Virtual learning: A teacher's perspective. *The Lion's Roar*. https://mhslionsroar.com/15991/features/virtual-learning-a-teachers-perspective/.

lxxv. Hirsh-Pasek, K. et al. 2015. Putting education in 'educational' apps: Lessons from the science of learning. *Psychological Science in the Public Interest,* 16(1): 3–34. https://doi.org/10.1177/1529100615569721.

lxxvi. Almagor, L. 2021, June 16. I taught online school this year. It was a disgrace. *New York Times*. https://www.nytimes.com/2021/06/16/opinion/remote-learning-failure.html.

lxxvii. Kumar, J.A., Bervell, B. & Osman, S. 2020. Google classroom: Insights from Malaysian higher education students' and instructors' experiences. *Education and Information Technologies*, 25(5): 4175–4195. https://link.springer.com/article/10.1007/s10639-020-10163-x.

lxxviii. Harris, B. 2021, April 3. Tears, sleepless nights and small victories: How first-year teachers are weathering the crisis. *Southern Maryland Chronicle*. https://southernmarylandchronicle.com/2021/04/03/tears-sleepless-nights-and-small-victories-how-first-year-teachers-are-weathering-the-crisis/.

lxxix. Webster, N. 1787, December. On the education of youth in America. *American Magazine*. Available at https://americainclass.org/sources/makingrevolution/independence/text3/websteramericanidentity.pdf.

[lxxx.] Robles, Y. 2020, April 14. In Aurora online learning, students and parents are missing the teacher connection and support. Chalkbeat. https://co.chalkbeat.org/2020/4/13/21225487/in-aurora-online-learning-students-and-parents-are-missing-the-teacher-connection-and-support.

[lxxxi.] Hansen, M. & Komljenovic, J. 2022. Automating Learning Situations in EdTech: Techno-Commercial Logic of Assetisation. *Postdigital Science and Education*, 5. https://doi.org/10.1007/s42438-022-00359-4.

[lxxxii.] Rodriguez, A. 2021, November 1. Screen time among teenagers during COVID more than doubled outside of virtual school, study finds. *USA Today*. https://eu.usatoday.com/story/news/health/2021/11/01/covid-screen-time-among-teens-doubles-during-pandemic-study-finds/6230769001/.

[lxxxiii.] Mackee, N. 2019, August 19. Screen time in under 2s "breathtaking". *InSight+*. https://insightplus.mja.com.au/2019/32/screen-time-in-under-2s-breathtaking/.

[lxxxiv.] Klass, P. 2020, August 17. How children's sleep habits have changed in the pandemic. *New York Times*. https://www.nytimes.com/2020/08/17/well/family/children-sleep-pandemic.html.

[lxxxv.] Berthold, J. 2021, November 1. Adolescents' recreational screen time doubled during pandemic, affecting mental health. University of California San Francisco, Department of Epidemiology and Biostatistics. https://epibiostat.ucsf.edu/news/adolescents%E2%80%99-recreational-screen-time-doubled-during-pandemic-affecting-mental-health.

[lxxxvi.] Kearney, R. 2021. *Touch: Recovering Our Most Vital Sense*. New York: Columbia University Press.

[lxxxvii.] Warren, T.H. 2022, January 30. Why churches should drop their online services. *New York Times*. https://www.nytimes.com/2022/01/30/opinion/church-online-services-covid.html.

[lxxxviii.] Novak, J. 2021, November 26. We're longing for the one thing the metaverse can't give us. *New York Times*. https://www.nytimes.com/2021/11/26/opinion/touch-starvation-metaverse-virtual-worlds.html.

[lxxxix.] Siu, W. 2022, November 26. I make video games. I won't let my daughters play them. *New York Times*. https://www.nytimes.com/2022/10/02/opinion/video-game-addiction.html.

[xc.] Lockett, H., McMorrow, R. & Yu, S. 2021, August 3. China's Tencent imposes controls to tackle gaming addiction among children. *Financial Times*. https://www.ft.com/content/1ee4f40b-cad8-45f7-b8dd-de25b89736d3.

[xci.] Lightman, A. 2022, January 15. This is no way to be human. *The Atlantic*. https://www.theatlantic.com/technology/archive/2022/01/machine-garden-natureless-world/621268/.

[xcii.] Alter, A. 2017. *Irresistible: The Rise of Addictive Technology and the Business of Keeping Us Hooked*. London: Penguin Books.

[xciii.] Haidt, J. 2022, April 11. Why the past 10 years of American life have been uniquely stupid. *The Atlantic*. https://www.theatlantic.com/magazine/archive/2022/05/social-media-democracy-trust-babel/629369/.

[xciv.] Applebaum, A. & Pomerantsev, P. 2021, April. How to put out democracy's dumpster fire. *The Atlantic*. https://www.theatlantic.com/magazine/archive/2021/04/the-internet-doesnt-have-to-be-awful/618079/.

[xcv.] Precarity Lab. 2020. *Technoprecarious*. London: Goldsmiths Press.

[xcvi.] Abramson, A. 2021, October 3. From a pandemic to plastic surgery: How Covid changed the way we see our faces. *The Guardian*. https://www.theguardian.com/us-news/2021/oct/03/zoom-dysmorphia-covid-coronavirus-anxiety.

[xcvii.] Klein, E. 2022, August 7. I didn't want it to be true, but the medium really is the message. *New York Times*. https://www.nytimes.com/2022/08/07/opinion/media-message-twitter-instagram.html.

[xcviii.] Tuohy, W. 2021, November 1. "Like the worst kind of bully": Spike in video calls leads to image problems. *Sydney Morning Herald*. https://www.smh.com.au/national/like-the-worst-kind-of-bully-spike-in-video-calls-leads-image-problems-20211031-p594ok.html.

[xcix.] Human Rights Watch. 2021, May 17. *"Years Don't Wait for Them": Increased Inequalities in Children's Right to Education Due to the Covid-19 Pandemic*. https://www.hrw.org/report/2021/05/17/years-dont-wait-them/increased-inequalities-childrens-right-education-due-covid.

c. Kearney, R. 2021. *Touch: Recovering Our Most Vital Sense*. New York: Columbia University Press.

ci. Carr, S. 2021, May 18. As a district re-opens, one middle schooler returned to school and another remained home. The *Hechinger Report*. https://hechingerreport.org/as-a-district-re-opens-one-middle-schooler-returned-to-school-and-another-remained-home/.

cii. Twenge, J.M., Martin, G.N. & Campbell, W.K. 2018, September 18. Decreases in psychological well-being among American adolescents after 2012 and links to screen time during the rise of smartphone technology. *Emotion*, 18(6): 765–780. https://doi.org/10.1037/emo0000403.

ciii. World Health Organization. 2020, October 5. COVID-19 disrupting mental health services in most countries, WHO survey. Press release. https://www.who.int/news/item/05-10-2020-covid-19-disrupting-mental-health-services-in-most-countries-who-survey.

civ. Reich, J. 2020. *Failure to Disrupt: Why Technology Alone Can't Transform Education*. Cambridge, MA: Harvard University Press.

cv. France, P.E. 2020. *Reclaiming Personalized Learning: A Pedagogy for Restoring Equity and Humanity in Our Classrooms*. Thousand Oaks, CA: Corwin.

cvi. Simon, C. 2021, 9 July. How COVID taught America about inequity in education. The Harvard Gazette. https://news.harvard.edu/gazette/story/2021/07/how-covid-taught-america-about-inequity-in-education/.

cvii. Ewe, K. 2021, February 16. The wholesome appeal of watching people study on YouTube. Vice. https://www.vice.com/en/article/wx8yb9/study-with-me-gongbang-youtube-video-trend-asmr.

cviii. Miller, C.C. & Sanger-Katz, M. 2022, February 28. School is back in person, but the five-day school week often isn't. *New York Times*. https://www.nytimes.com/2022/02/28/upshot/schools-covid-closings.html.

cix. Human Rights Watch. 2021, May 17. *"Years Don't Wait for Them": Increased Inequalities in Children's Right to Education Due to the Covid-19 Pandemic*. https://www.hrw.org/report/2021/05/17/years-dont-wait-them/increased-inequalities-childrens-right-education-due-covid.

cx. Haidt, J. & Twenge, J.M. 2021, July 31. This is our chance to pull teenagers out of the smartphone trap. *New York Times*. https://www.nytimes.com/2021/07/31/opinion/smartphone-iphone-social-media-isolation.html.

cxi. Turkle, S. 2017. *Alone Together: Why We Expect More from Technology and Less from Each Other*. New York: Basic Books.

cxii. Reich, J. et al. 2020, July. *What's Lost, What's Left, What's Next: Lessons Learned from the Lived Experiences of Teachers during the Pandemic*. Teaching Systems Lab. https://edarxiv.org/8exp9.

cxiii. Sky News. 2018, April 18. Emoji leading to 'serious decline' in English skills. https://news.sky.com/story/emoji-leading-to-serious-decline-in-english-skills-11336247.

cxiv. Klass, P. 2019, May 20. Is 'digital addiction' a real threat to kids? *New York Times*. https://www.nytimes.com/2019/05/20/well/family/is-digital-addiction-a-real-threat-to-kids.html.

cxv. Turkle, S. 2015. *Reclaiming Conversation: The Power Of Talk in a Digital Age*. New York: Penguin Books.

cxvi. UCL News. 2021, May 10. Smartphones have led to the 'death of proximity'. https://www.ucl.ac.uk/news/2021/may/smartphones-have-led-death-proximity.

cxvii. Nelson, C. 2022. Babies need humans, not screens. UNICEF. https://www.unicef.org/parenting/child-development/babies-screen-time.

cxviii. Baron, N.S. 2015. *Words Onscreen: The Fate of Reading in a Digital World*. Oxford: Oxford University Press.

cxix. Gould, E. 2020, August 18. Remote learning is a bad joke. *The Atlantic*. https://www.theatlantic.com/ideas/archive/2020/08/kindergartener-virtual-education/615316/.

cxx. Pappas, S. 2020, April 1. What do we really know about kids and screens? *Monitor on Psychology*, 51(3). https://www.apa.org/monitor/2020/04/cover-kids-screens.

cxxi. Reich, J. 2020. *Failure to Disrupt: Why Technology Alone Can't Transform Education*. Cambridge, MA: Harvard University Press.

cxxii. Schmall, E. & Yasir, S. 2022, January 27. India schools stay closed, and hopes fade for a lost generation. *New York Times*. https://www.nytimes.com/2022/01/27/world/asia/india-schools.html.

cxxiii. Blum, A. 2012. *Tubes: A Journey to the Center of the Internet*. New York: Ecco.

cxxiv. Klein, A. 2021, April 20. During COVID-19, schools have made a mad dash to 1-to-1 computing. What happens next? *Education Week*. https://www.edweek.org/technology/during-covid-19-schools-have-made-a-mad-dash-to-1-to-1-computing-what-happens-next/2021/04.

cxxv. Selwyn, N. 2018, October 22. EdTech is killing us all: Facing up to the environmental consequences of digital education. EduResearch Matters. https://www.aare.edu.au/blog/?p=3293.

cxxvi. WEEE Forum. 2022, October 14. International E-waste Day: Of ~16 billion mobile phones possessed worldwide, ~5.3 billion will become waste in 2022. https://weee-forum.org/ws_news/of-16-billion-mobile-phones-possessed-worldwide-5-3-billion-will-become-waste-in-2022/.

cxxvii. Tria, E. 2021, May 4. The impact of Covid-19 on child labour in cobalt mines in the DRC. Humanium. https://www.humanium.org/en/the-impact-of-covid-19-on-child-labour-in-cobalt-mines-in-the-drc/.

cxxviii. Lohr, S. 2020, May 26. Remember the MOOCs? After near-death, they're booming. *New York Times*. https://www.nytimes.com/2020/05/26/technology/moocs-online-learning.html.

cxxix. UN General Assembly Human Rights Council. 2022, April 19. Impact of the digitalization of education on the right to education. Report of the Special Rapporteur on the right to education. https://documents-dds-ny.un.org/doc/UNDOC/GEN/G22/322/37/PDF/G2232237.pdf.

cxxx. Williamson, B. 2022, March 17. Google magic. *Code Acts in Education*. https://codeactsineducation.wordpress.com/2022/03/17/google-magic/.

cxxxi. User review. 2022, September 28. Unusable app. Google Classroom. Ratings and Reviews. https://apps.apple.com/us/app/google-classroom/id924620788.

cxxxii. McKenzie, L. 2021, April 9. Coursera IPO 'seized on the right moment'. *Inside Higher Ed*. https://www.insidehighered.com/news/2021/04/09/coursera-valuation-exceeds-expectations.

cxxxiii. Rize ETF. 2020, September 3. Specialist thematic ETF pioneer Rize ETF launches sustainable food and education ETFs. Press release. https://rizeetf.com/wp-content/uploads/2020/09/03Sep20_Press_Release_Rize-launches-two-new-ETFs.pdf.

cxxxiv. Palandrani, P. 2020, July 14. Introducing the Global X Education ETF (EDUT). Global X. https://www.globalxetfs.com/introducing-the-global-x-education-etf-edut/.

cxxxv. UN General Assembly Human Rights Council. 2022, April 19. Impact of the digitalization of education on the right to education. Report of the Special Rapporteur on the right to education. https://documents-dds-ny.un.org/doc/UNDOC/GEN/G22/322/37/PDF/G2232237.pdf.

cxxxvi. Molitorisz, S. 2020. *Net Privacy: How We Can Be Free in an Age of Surveillance*. Montreal: McGill-Queen's University Press.

cxxxvii. Williamson, B., Gulson, K.N., Perrotta, C. & Witzenberger, K. 2022, July 12. How Amazon operates in education. *Code Acts in Education*. https://codeactsineducation.wordpress.com/2022/07/12/how-amazon-operates-in-education/.

cxxxviii. Williamson, B. & Hogan, A. 2021, February 10. Pandemic privatization and digitalization in higher education. *Code Acts in Education*. https://codeactsineducation.wordpress.com/2021/02/10/pandemic-privatization-digitalization-higher-education/.

cxxxix. Ball, S.J. 2012. Show me the money! Neoliberalism at work in education. *FORUM*, 54(1). https://doi.org/10.2304/FORUM.2012.54.1.23.

cxl. Ravitch, D. 2016, February 23. Wendy Lecker: Why "personalized learning" is neither. Diane Ravitch's blog. https://dianeravitch.net/2016/02/23/wendy-lecker-why-personalized-learning-is-neither/.

cxli. Koenig, R. 2020, Jun 11. The post-pandemic outlook for edtech. EdSurge. https://www.edsurge.com/news/2020-06-11-the-post-pandemic-outlook-for-edtech.

cxlii. The Abidjan Principles. 2019. *The Abidjan Principles: Guiding Principles on the Human Rights Obligations of States to Provide Public Education and to Regulate Private Involvement in Education*. https://static1.squarespace.com/static/5c2d081daf2096648cc801da/t/61484ef2125d785da37eb98d/1632128758265/ABIDJAN+PRINCIPLES_+ENGLISH_August2021.pdf.

cxliii. Oremus, W. 2020, September 12. The privatized internet is failing our kids. OneZero. https://onezero.medium.com/the-travesty-of-remote-learning-is-unfolding-in-real-time-6307975560e8.

cxliv. Smith, M. 2020, December 6. A mom's view: online learning isn't working for students, parents or teachers. Here's what's happening in my home. The 74. https://www.the74million.org/article/a-moms-view-online-learning-isnt-working-for-students-parents-or-teachers-heres-whats-happening-in-my-home/.

cxlv. Kneese, T. 2021, January 27. How a dead professor is teaching a university art history class. Slate. https://slate.com/technology/2021/01/dead-professor-teaching-online-class.html.

cxlvi. Santhakumar, V. 2021, August 22. Will edtech devalue teachers? *University World News*. https://www.universityworldnews.com/post.php?story=202108171255039.

cxlvii. Google. 2022. Teach from Anywhere. https://teachfromanywhere.google/intl/en/.

cxlviii. Gulson, K.N., Sellar, S. & Webb, P.T. 2022. *Algorithms of Education: How Datafication and Artificial Intelligence Shape Policy*. Minneapolis: University of Minnesota Press.

cxlix. Pothong, K., Atabey, A., Turner, S. & Livingstone, S. 2022, June 19. The DFC to launch education data reality. Digital Futures Commission. https://digitalfuturescommission.org.uk/blog/the-dfc-to-launch-education-data-reality/.

cl. Teräs, M., Suoranta, J., Teräs, H. & Curcher, M. 2020. Post-Covid-19 education and education technology 'solutionism': A seller's market. *Postdigital Science and Education*, 2(3). https://www.ncbi.nlm.nih.gov/pmc/articles/PMC7355515/.

cli. Greene, P. 2019, July 15. What can we learn from an experimental high tech Wunderschool failure? Forbes. https://www.forbes.com/sites/petergreene/2019/07/15/what-can-we-learn-from-an-experimental-high-tech-charter-wunderschool-failure/.

clii. Battelle, J. 2016, July 13. Max Ventilla of AltSchool: The full shift dialogs transcript. Newco Shift. https://shift.newco.co/2016/07/13/max-ventilla-of-altschool-the-full-shift-dialogs-transcript/.

cliii. Human Rights Watch. 2022, May 25. Governments harm children's rights in online learning. https://www.hrw.org/news/2022/05/25/governments-harm-childrens-rights-online-learning.

cliv. Singer, N. 2022, July 31. A cyberattack illuminates the shaky state of student privacy. *New York Times*. https://www.nytimes.com/2022/07/31/business/student-privacy-illuminate-hack.html.

clv. Turner, S., Pothong, K. & Livingstone, S. 2022. *Education Data Reality: The Challenges for Schools in Managing Children's Education Data*. Digital Futures Commission, 5Rights Foundation. https://digitalfuturescommission.org.uk/wp-content/uploads/2022/06/Education-data-reality-report.pdf.

clvi. Jerome, J. 2021, April 15. Privacy is key: Holding edtech accountable. Heinrich-Böll-Stiftung. https://us.boell.org/en/2021/03/31/privacy-key-holding-edtech-accountable.

clvii. Ibid.

clviii. Igo, S.E. 2022, April 6. The price of privacy. *The Atlantic*. https://www.theatlantic.com/magazine/archive/2022/05/privacy-law-technology-california-gajda-seek-and-hide/629373/.

clix. Hooper, L., Livingstone, S. & Pothong, K. 2022. *Problems with Data Governance in UK Schools: The Cases of Google Classroom and ClassDojo*. Digital Futures Commission & 5Rights Foundation. https://digitalfuturescommission.org.uk/wp-content/uploads/2022/08/Problems-with-data-governance-in-UK-schools.pdf.

clx. Fairplay. 2020, April 16. An open letter to policy makers, data protection authorities, and providers worldwide, regarding rapid edtech adoption. https://fairplayforkids.org/edtech-letter-blog/.

clxi. Singer, N. 2022, July 31. A cyberattack illuminates the shaky state of student privacy. *New York Times*. https://www.nytimes.com/2022/07/31/business/student-privacy-illuminate-hack.html.

clxii. Pangrazi, L. & Sefton-Green, J. 2022. *Learning to Live with Datafication: Educational Case Studies and Initiatives from Across the World*. Abingdon, Oxfordshire: Routledge.

clxiii. Williamson, B. 2019. Datafication of education. In Beetham, H. & Sharpe, R. (eds) *Rethinking Pedagogy for a Digital Age*. London: Routledge. Available at https://www.researchgate.net/publication/334008102_Datafication_of_Education.

clxiv. Day, J. 2014, August 19. A transfigured faith. *Catholic Exchange*. https://catholicexchange.com/transfigured-faith/.

clxv. Wiggins, C. & Jones, M. 2023. *How Data Happened: A History from the Age of Reason to the Age of Algorithms*. New York: W. W. Norton & Company.

clxvi. Moon, L. 2018, May 16. Pay attention at the back: School uses facial scans to monitor pupils. *South China Morning Post*. https://www.scmp.com/news/china/society/article/2146387/pay-attention-back-chinese-school-installs-facial-recognition.

clxvii. Vincent, J. 2019, July 25. AI 'emotion recognition' can't be trusted. The Verge. https://www.theverge.com/2019/7/25/8929793/emotion-recognition-analysis-ai-machine-learning-facial-expression-review.

clxviii. Crawford, K. 2021, April 6. Time to regulate AI that interprets human emotions. *Nature*. https://www.nature.com/articles/d41586-021-00868-5.

clxix. Faek, R. 2021. April 18. Self-censorship in Arab higher education: An untold problem. Al-Fanar Media. https://www.al-fanarmedia.org/2021/04/self-censorship-in-arab-higher-education-an-untold-problem/.

clxx. Watermeyer, R., Crick, T., Knight, C. & Goodall, J. 2020, April 9. Forced shift to online teaching in pandemic unleashes educators' deepest job fears. Nature Index. https://www.nature.com/nature-index/news-blog/forceshift-to-online-teaching-in-coronavirus-pandemic-unleashes-educators-deepest-job-fears-.

clxxi. Anand, P. & Bergen, M. 2021, October 28. Big teacher is watching: How AI spyware took over schools. Bloomberg. https://www.bloomberg.com/news/features/2021-10-28/how-goguardian-ai-spyware-took-over-schools-student-devices-during-covid.

clxxii. Fischer, C. et al. 2020. Mining big data in education: Affordances and challenges. *Review of Research in Education*, 44(1): 130–160. https://doi.org/10.3102/0091732X20903304.

clxxiii. Donovan, J., Caplan, R., Matthews, J. & Hanson, L. 2018, April 18. Algorithmic accountability: A primer. Data & Society. https://datasociety.net/wp-content/uploads/2018/04/Data_Society_Algorithmic_Accountability_Primer_FINAL.pdf.

clxxiv. Zagmout, A. 2020. Justice for May 2020 IB Graduates - Build a Better Future! #IBSCANDAL. Change.org. https://www.change.org/p/international-baccalaureate-organisation-ibo-justice-for-may-2020-ib-graduates-build-a-better-future.

clxxv. Quinn, B. & Adams, R. 2020, August 20. England exams row timeline: Was Ofqual warned of algorithm bias? *The Guardian*. https://www.theguardian.com/education/2020/aug/20/england-exams-row-timeline-was-ofqual-warned-of-algorithm-bias.

clxxvi. Malik, K. 2020, August 23. The cruel exams algorithm has laid bare the unfairness at the heart of our schools. *The Observer*. https://www.theguardian.com/commentisfree/2020/aug/23/the-cruel-exams-algorithm-has-laid-bare-the-unfairness-at-the-heart-of-our-schools.

clxxvii. Harwell, D. 2020, April 1. Mass school closures in the wake of the coronavirus are driving a new wave of student surveillance. *Washington Post*. https://www.washingtonpost.com/technology/2020/04/01/online-proctoring-college-exams-coronavirus/.

clxxviii. Hill, K. 2022, May 27. Accused of cheating by an algorithm, and a professor she had never met. *New York Times*. https://www.nytimes.com/2022/05/27/technology/college-students-cheating-software-honorlock.html.

clxxix. Swauger, S. 2020, April 2. Our bodies encoded: Algorithmic test proctoring in higher education. *Hybrid Pedagogy*. https://hybridpedagogy.org/our-bodies-encoded-algorithmic-test-proctoring-in-higher-education/.

clxxx. @cham_omot. 2021, February 24. THIS! There's no reason I should have to collect all the light God has to offer, just for Proctorio to pretend my face is still undetectable. Twitter. https://twitter.com/cham_omot/status/1364376131516854275.

clxxxi. Hill, K. 2022, May 27. Accused of cheating by an algorithm, and a professor she had never met. *New York Times*. https://www.nytimes.com/2022/05/27/technology/college-students-cheating-software-honorlock.html.

clxxxii. *Daily Illini*. 2020, October 15. Virtual proctors worsen the overall academic environment. https://dailyillini.com/opinions/2020/10/15/editorial-virtual-proctors-worsen-the-overall-academic-environment/.

clxxxiii. Corbyn, Z. 2022, August 26. 'I'm afraid': Critics of anti-cheating technology for students hit by lawsuits. *The Guardian*. https://www.theguardian.com/us-news/2022/aug/26/anti-cheating-technology-students-tests-proctorio.

clxxxiv. Burgess, M., Schot, E. & Geiger, G. 2023, March 6. This algorithm could ruin your life. *Wired*. https://www.wired.co.uk/article/welfare-algorithms-discrimination.

clxxxv. Hill, K. 2022, May 27. Accused of cheating by an algorithm, and a professor she had never met. *New York Times*. https://www.nytimes.com/2022/05/27/technology/college-students-cheating-software-honorlock.html.

clxxxvi. Singer, N. & Krolik, A. 2021, May 9. Online cheating charges upend Dartmouth Medical School. *New York Times*. https://www.nytimes.com/2021/05/09/technology/dartmouth-geisel-medical-cheating.html.

clxxxvii. Foucault, M. 1975. *Discipline and Punish: The Birth of the Prison*. New York: Pantheon.

clxxxviii. World Health Organization. 2020, September 15. WHO Director-General's introductory remarks at the press briefing with UNESCO and UNICEF. https://www.who.int/director-general/speeches/detail/who-director-general-s-introductory-remarks-at-the-press-briefing-with-unesco-and-unicef.

clxxxix. World Health Organization. 2021, June 10. School reopening can't wait. https://www.who.int/westernpacific/news-room/commentaries/detail-hq/school-reopening-can-t-wait.

cxc. Klein, N. 2020, May 13. How big tech plans to profit from the pandemic. *The Guardian*. https://www.theguardian.com/news/2020/may/13/naomi-klein-how-big-tech-plans-to-profit-from-coronavirus-pandemic.

cxci. Wen, L.S. 2021, February 24. Both sides of the school reopening debate have it wrong. *Washington Post*. https://www.washingtonpost.com/opinions/2021/02/24/both-sides-school-reopening-debate-have-it-wrong/.

cxcii. Oster, E. 2020, October 9. Schools aren't super-spreaders. *The Atlantic*. https://www.theatlantic.com/ideas/archive/2020/10/schools-arent-superspreaders/616669/.

cxciii. BBC News. 2020, July 7. Coronavirus: Kenyan schools to remain closed until 2021. https://www.bbc.com/news/world-africa-53325741.

cxciv. da Silva, I.S. 2020, May 28. Covid-19 reveals digital divide as Africa struggles with distance learning. *TRT World*. https://www.trtworld.com/magazine/covid-19-reveals-digital-divide-as-africa-struggles-with-distance-learning-37299.

cxcv. Friedman, S.D. 2008, November 25. Do not waste this crisis. *Harvard Business Review*. https://hbr.org/2008/11/dont-waste-this-crisis.

cxcvi. Klein, N. 2008. *The Shock Doctrine: The Rise of Disaster Capitalism*. London: Penguin Books.

cxcvii. Saltman, K.J. 2007. *Schooling and the Politics of Disaster*. New York: Routledge.

cxcviii. UNICEF. 2021. *Reopening with Resilience: Lessons from Remote Learning during COVID-19*. https://www.unicef-irc.org/publications/1220-reopening-with-resilience-lessons-from-remote-learning-during-covid19.html.

cxcix. Castro, A.M. 2021, September 7. Teachers are key in protecting students' mental health during the COVID-19 Pandemic. UNICEF. https://www.unicef.org/lac/en/stories/teachers-are-key-in-protecting-students-mental-health-during-covid-19-pandemic.

cc. Singer, S. 2020, September 13. The everyday exhaustion of teaching during a global pandemic. *Gad Fly on the Wall*. Blog post. https://gadflyonthewallblog.com/2020/09/13/the-everyday-exhaustion-of-teaching-during-a-global-pandemic/.

cci. Hillman, V. & Esquivel, M. 2022, May 18. Algorithmic personalization is disrupting a healthy teaching environment. London School of Economics. https://blogs.lse.ac.uk/medialse/2022/05/18/algorithmic-personalization-is-disrupting-a-healthy-teaching-environment/.

ccii. Reich, J. 2021. Ed tech's failure during the pandemic, and what comes after. *Phi Delta Kappan*, 102(6): 20–24. https://journals.sagepub.com/doi/10.1177/0031721721998149.

ccii. Paul, K. 2022, August 30. First-of-its-kind legislation will keep California's children safer while online. *The Guardian*. https://www.theguardian.com/technology/2022/aug/30/california-protect-children-online-privacy.

cciv. Porter, H. 2014, January 18. The internet revolution versus the House of Lords. *The Observer*. https://www.theguardian.com/commentisfree/2014/jan/18/house-of-lords-debate-world-wide-web.

ccv. Garlen, J.C. 2021. The end of innocence: Childhood and schooling for a post-pandemic world. *Journal of Teaching and Learning*, 15(2): 21–39. https://jtl.uwindsor.ca/index.php/jtl/article/view/6724.

ccvi. Acemoglu, D. & Johnson, S. 2023, June 9. Big tech is bad. Big A.I. will be worse. *New York Times*. https://www.nytimes.com/2023/06/09/opinion/ai-big-tech-microsoft-google-duopoly.html.

ccvii. Pew Research Center. 2018, April 17. *The Expanded Edition: The Future of Well-Being in a Tech-Saturated World*. https://assets.pewresearch.org/wp-content/uploads/sites/14/2018/04/16140055/PI_2018.04.17_Future-of-Well-Being_EXPANDED.pdf.

ccviii. United Nations. 2020, August. Policy Brief: Education during COVID-19 and beyond. https://www.un.org/development/desa/dspd/wp-content/uploads/sites/22/2020/08/sg_policy_brief_covid-19_and_education_august_2020.pdf.

ccix. Piketty, T. 2014. *Capital in the Twenty-First Century*. Cambridge, MA: Belknap Press.

ccx. UN General Assembly Human Rights Council. 2022, April 19. Impact of the digitalization of education on the right to education. Report of the Special Rapporteur on the right to education. https://documents-dds-ny.un.org/doc/UNDOC/GEN/G22/322/37/PDF/G2232237.pdf.

ccxi. Stommel, J. 2014, November 17. Critical Digital Pedagogy: A definition. *Hybrid Pedagogy*. https://hybridpedagogy.org/critical-digital-pedagogy-definition/.

ccxii. Winthrop, R. & McGivney, E. 2015, June 10. Why wait 100 years? Bridging the gap in global education. Brookings. https://www.brookings.edu/research/why-wait-100-years-bridging-the-gap-in-global-education/.

ccxiii. UN General Assembly Human Rights Council. 2016, April 6. Report of the Special Rapporteur on the right to education. https://documents-dds-ny.un.org/doc/UNDOC/GEN/G16/070/33/PDF/G1607033.pdf.

ccxiv. Kamenetz, A. 2022, September 1. School is for everyone. *New York Times*. https://www.nytimes.com/2022/09/01/opinion/us-school-history.html.

ccxv. UN General Assembly Human Rights Council. 2020, June 30. Right to education: Impact of the Coronavirus disease crisis on the Right to Education—concerns, challenges and opportunities. Report of the Special Rapporteur on the right to education. https://documents-dds-ny.un.org/doc/UNDOC/GEN/G20/158/03/PDF/G2015803.pdf.

ccxvi. *The Tribune*. 2022, May 3. Give priority to regular classes in Punjab: Democratic Teachers Front. https://www.tribuneindia.com/news/ludhiana/give-priority-to-regular-classes-democratic-teachers-front-391360.

WORKS CITED

Figures

Figure 1 Alexander, M. 2019, March 7. Rwanda introduces new 500 and 1000 Franc banknotes. *CoinsWeekly*. https://coinsweekly.com/rwanda-introduces-new-500-and-1000-franc-banknotes/

Figure 2 Mizunoya, S. et al. 2020. *How Many Children and Young People Have Internet Access at Home? Estimating Digital Connectivity During the COVID-19 Pandemic*. UNICEF and ITU. https://data.unicef.org/resources/children-and-young-people-internet-access-at-home-during-covid19/.

Figure 3 Chandra, S. et al. 2020. *Closing the K–12 Digital Divide in the Age of Distance Learning*. Boston Consulting Group in partnership with Common Sense. https://www.commonsensemedia.org/sites/default/files/featured-content/files/common_sense_media_report_final_7_1_3pm_web.pdf.

Figure 4 Alliance for Affordable Internet. 2020. *From Luxury to Lifeline: Reducing the Cost of Mobile Devices to Reach Universal Internet Access*. World Wide Web Foundation. https://webfoundation.org/research/from-luxury-to-lifeline-reducing-the-cost-of-mobile-devices-to-reach-universal-internet-access/.

Figure 5 ITU Publications. 2020. *Measuring Digital Development: Facts and Figures 2020*. https://www.itu.int/en/ITU-D/Statistics/Documents/facts/FactsFigures2020.pdf.

Figure 6 World Bank. 2021. *World Development Report 2021: Data for Better Lives*. https://elibrary.worldbank.org/doi/epdf/10.1596/978-1-4648-1600-0

Figure 7 World Bank. 2021. *World Development Report 2021: Data for Better Lives*. https://elibrary.worldbank.org/doi/epdf/10.1596/978-1-4648-1600-0

Figure 8 UNESCO. 2023. Global Education Monitoring Report 2023. *Technology in Education: A Tool on Whose Terms?* https://unesdoc.unesco.org/ark:/48223/pf0000385723.locale=en

Figure 9 Ken's Tech Tips. 2018, November 3. *Download speeds: What do 2G, 3G, 4G & 5G actually mean?* https://kenstechtips.com/index.php/download-speeds-2g-3g-and-4g-actual-meaning

Figure 10 Blaskó, Z. & Schnepf, S. 2021. Educational inequalities in Europe and physical school closures during Covid-19. European Commission Knowledge for Policy. https://knowledge4policy.ec.europa.eu/publication/educational-inequalities-europe-physical-school-closures-during-covid-19_en.

Figure 11 Will, M. 2020, October 20. Most educators require kids to turn cameras on in virtual class, despite equity concerns. *Education Week*. https://www.edweek.org/teaching-learning/most-educators-require-kids-to-turn-cameras-on-in-virtual-class-despite-equity-concerns/2020/10.

Figure 12 Djankov, S., Zhang, Y. 2020, December 15. *COVID-19 widens gender gap in labor force participation in some but not other advanced economies*. Peterson Institute for International Economics. https://www.piie.com/blogs/realtime-economic-issues-watch/covid-19-widens-gender-gap-labor-force-participation-some-not

Figure 13 Chen, L.K., Dorn, E., Sarakatsannis, J., Wiesinger, A., 2021, March 1. *Teacher survey: Learning loss is global—and significant*. McKinsey & Company. https://www.mckinsey.com/industries/education/our-insights/teacher-survey-learning-loss-is-global-and-significant

Figure 14 Nagata, J.M. et al. 2021. Screen time use among US adolescents during the COVID-19 pandemic: Findings from the Adolescent Brain Cognitive Development (ABCD) study. *JAMA Pediatrics*. https://jamanetwork.com/journals/jamapediatrics/fullarticle/2785686.

Figure 15 Pikoos, T.D., Buzwell, S., Sharp, G. & Rossell, S.L. 2021, December. The Zoom effect: Exploring the impact of video calling on appearance dissatisfaction and interest in aesthetic treatment during the COVID-19 pandemic. *Aesthetic Surgery Journal*, 41(12). https://doi.org/10.1093/asj/sjab257.

Figure 16 Business Wire. 2021. *Tablet and Chromebook Shipments Continue to Surge During the First Quarter, According to IDC*. https://www.idc.com/getdoc.jsp?containerId=prUS47648021

Figure 17 Forti, V., Balde, C., Kuehr, R. & Bel, G. 2020, July. *The Global E-Waste Monitor 2020: Quantities, Flows and the Circular Economy Potential*. United Nations University/United Nations Institute for Training and Research and International Solid Waste Association. https://collections.unu.edu/view/UNU:7737.

Figure 18 Lazare, M. 2021, February 17. A peek at what's next for Google Classroom. Google Education. https://blog.google/outreach-initiatives/education/classroom-roadmap/.

Figure 19 Google. 2020. G Suite for Education (Online) Agreement. https://workspace.google.com/terms/2020/education_terms.html

Figure 20 Common Sense. 2021. State of kids' privacy report 2021: Key findings. https://www.commonsensemedia.org/sites/default/files/research/report/common-sense-2021-state-of-kids-privacy-key-findings.pdf.

Figure 21 Access Now, 2021. #Keep It On: Fighting internet shutdowns around the world. https://www.accessnow.org/keepiton/

Figure 22 Hern, A. 2020, August 21. Ofqual's A-level algorithm: Why did it fail to make the grade? *The Guardian*. https://www.theguardian.com/education/2020/aug/21/ofqual-exams-algorithm-why-did-it-fail-make-grade-a-levels.

Figure 23 Rankin, J. 2023. Exam Day: What to Expect. ProctorU. https://support.proctoru.com/hc/en-us/articles/360043565051-Exam-Day-What-to-Expect

Figure 24 Ager, P., Eriksson, K., Karger, E., Nencka, P. & Thomasson, M.A. 2020, December. School closures during the 1918 flu pandemic. National Bureau of Economic Research. https://www.nber.org/system/files/working_papers/w28246/w28246.pdf; UNESCO, 2021. UNESCO figures show two thirds of an academic year lost on average worldwide due to COVID-19 school closures. UNESCO. https://en.unesco.org/news/unesco-figures-show-two-thirds-academic-year-lost-average-worldwide-due-covid-19-school

Figure 25 UNESCO, 2022. UNESCO Map on School Closures: COVID-19 educational response: Country dashboard. https://covid19.uis.unesco.org/global-monitoring-school-closures-covid19/country-dashboard/

Figure 26 Microsoft Security Intelligence. 2022. Cyberthreats, viruses, and malware. https://www.microsoft.com/en-us/wdsi/threats.

Figure 27 HolonIQ. 2021. Education technology in 10 charts: Everything you need to know about the Global EdTech Market in 10 charts. https://www.holoniq.com/edtech-in-10-charts.

BIBLIOGRAPHY

@cham_omot. 2021, February 24. THIS! There's no reason I should have to collect all the light God has to offer, just for Proctorio to pretend my face is still undetectable. Twitter. https://twitter.com/cham_omot/status/1364376131516854275.

@DaveBrownToons. 2020, August 6. Tomorrow's @Independent cartoon... #SchoolsBeforePubs #ChildrensCommissioner #COVID19 #Coronavirus #LocalLockdown #2ndWave. Twitter. https://twitter.com/DaveBrownToons/status/1291067327300145152.

@futureesq1990. 2020, September 17. @ExamSoft I FINALLY figured out ON MY OWN 4 hours later (still on hold for an EXAM SOFT chat rep) HOW TO GET TO MY MOCK EXAM... ONLY TO BE TOLD THE SYSTEM CANT RECOGNIZE ME. I AM IN A BOARD ROOM WITH ALL OF THE LIGHTS TURNED ON AND THE SUN WAS STILL UP. MAKE IT MAKE SENSE. Twitter. https://twitter.com/futureesq1990/status/1306393725099278336.

@HUCKmagazine. 2020, August 16. Chants of "fuck the algorithm" as a speaker talks of losing her place at medical school because she was downgraded. Twitter. https://twitter.com/HUCKmagazine/status/1294987261751234560.

@LizGoldbergMD. 2020, July 3. Thread about #SchoolReopening internationally showing the risks to kids (esp. if in elementary), parents, & teachers of #covid inf. is low. #closebarsopenschools. Twitter. https://twitter.com/LizGoldbergMD/status/1279001890496397312.

@PDChina. *People's Daily*. 2018, May 16. What else can surveillance cameras do in classroom other than exam supervision? High school in #Hangzhou uses camera to identify students' facial expression for class performance analysis and improvement. Twitter. https://twitter.com/PDChina/status/996755673093292032.

@uhreeb [Alivardi Khan]. 2020, September 8. The @ ExamSoft software can't "recognize" me due to "poor lighting" even though I'm sitting in a well lit room. Starting to think it has nothing to do with lighting. Pretty sure we all predicted their facial recognition software wouldn't work for people of color. Twitter. https://twitter.com/uhreeb/status/1303139738065481728.

@yasmmeme. 2020, December 1. Tomorrow, the UMD physics department is hosting a very interesting colloquium talk on the use of machine-learning for graduate admissions. I'd like to take a second and explain why this talk is concerning. Twitter. https://twitter.com/yasmmeme/status/1333670480574771201.

ABC News. 2021, August 13. Mexico says 5.2 million dropped out of school in pandemic. https://abcnews.go.com/International/wireStory/mexico-52-million-dropped-school-pandemic-79447998.

ABC7 Eyewitness News. 2022, August 16. Nearly 50,000 LAUSD students reported absent on first day of new school year. https://abc7.com/lausd-los-angeles-unified-school-district-students-superintendent/12131247/.

ABC7 News. 2021, July 28. More parents now opting to homeschool their children. https://abc-7.com/news/national-world/2021/07/26/more-parents-now-opting-to-homeschool-their-children/.

Abdel-Baqui, O. & Calfas, J. 2022, January 26. New Virginia hotline lets parents report 'divisive teaching practices'. *Wall Street Journal*. https://www.wsj.com/articles/new-virginia-hotline-lets-parents-report-divisive-teaching-practices-11643236044.

Abidjan Principles. 2019. *The Abidjan Principles: Guiding Principles on the Human Rights Obligations of States to Provide Public Education and to Regulate Private Involvement in Education*. https://static1.squarespace.com/static/5c2d081daf2096648cc801da/t/61484ef2125d785da37eb98d/1632128758265/ABIDJAN+PRINCIPLES_+ENGLISH_August2021.pdf.

Abi-Habib, M. & Lopez, O. 2022, July 18. Mexico's leader says poverty is his priority. But his policies hurt the poor. *New York Times*. https://www.nytimes.com/2022/07/18/world/americas/mexico-economy-poverty.html.

Aboriginal Education Research Centre, Making the Shift Youth Homelessness Social Innovation Lab & Dechinta Centre for Research and Learning. 2021. *Indigenous Land-Based Education and the COVID-19 Pandemic*. https://aerc.usask.ca/documents/indigenous-land-based-education-and-the-covid-19-pandemic.pdf.

Abrahamson, R.P. 2020, April 10. As frustration grows, some parents are giving up on home schooling. Today. https://www.today.com/parents/some-parents-refuse-remote-learning-will-there-be-consequences-t178188 https://www.fox32chicago.com/news/some-parents-giving-up-on-distance-learning.

Abrams, L. 2020, August 9. ProctorU confirms data breach after database leaked online. BleepingComputer. https://www.bleepingcomputer.com/news/security/proctoru-confirms-data-breach-after-database-leaked-online/.

Abramson, A. 2021, October 3. From a pandemic to plastic surgery: How Covid changed the way we see our faces. *The Guardian*. https://www.theguardian.com/us-news/2021/oct/03/zoom-dysmorphia-covid-coronavirus-anxiety.

Accenture. 2016. *Cracking the Gender Code: Get 3x More Women in Computing*. https://www.accenture.com/_acnmedia/PDF-150/Accenture-Cracking-The-Gender-Code-Report.pdf.

Access Now. 2021. #KeepItOn: Fighting internet shutdowns around the world. https://www.accessnow.org/keepiton/.

Acemoglu, D. & Johnson, S. 2023, June 9. Big tech is bad. Big A.I. will be worse. *New York Times*. https://www.nytimes.com/2023/06/09/opinion/ai-big-tech-microsoft-google-duopoly.html.

Adams, R., Weale, S. & Barr, C. 2020, August 13. A-level results: almost 40% of teacher assessments in England downgraded. *The Guardian*. https://www.theguardian.com/education/2020/aug/13/almost-40-of-english-students-have-a-level-results-downgraded.

Adams, S. 2019. Can AltSchool—The edtech startup with $174M from billionaires like Zuckerberg and Thiel—save itself from failure? Forbes. https://www.forbes.com/sites/susanadams/2019/01/30/can-altschoolthe-edtech-startup-with-174m-from-billionaires-like-zuckerberg-and-thielsave-itself-from-failure/.

Advertising Standards Authority. 2019. *Children's Exposure to Age-Restricted TV Ads: 2019 Update*. https://www.asa.org.uk/static/729cae41-cac1-4920-8e536bfb0b503253/ASA-TV-Ad-Exposure-Report-2019-Update.pdf.

Aedo, C., Nahata, V. & Sabarwal, S. 2020, November 10. The remote learning paradox: How governments can truly minimize COVID-related learning losses. World Bank Blogs. https://blogs.worldbank.org/education/remote-learning-paradox-how-governments-can-truly-minimize-covid-related-learning-losses.

Agarwal, S. 2022, May 26. Why homeschooling is a rising trend among many parents? Issuu. https://issuu.com/agarwalsuresh/docs/1st_blog_why_homeschooling_is_a_rising_trend_among.

Ager, P., Eriksson, K., Karger, E., Nencka, P. & Thomasson, M.A. 2020, December. School closures during the 1918 flu pandemic. National Bureau of Economic Research. https://www.nber.org/system/files/working_papers/w28246/w28246.pdf.

Ahlgren, E. et al. 2022, January 6. The global education crisis is even worse than we thought. Here's what needs to happen. World Economic Forum. https://www.weforum.org/agenda/2022/01/global-education-crisis-children-students-covid19/.

Ahmed, Q.W., Rönkä, A. & Perälä-Littunen, S. 2021. Parental involvement or interference? Rural teachers' perceptions. *Education Research International*, 2021. https://doi.org/10.1155/2021/3182822.

Akhtar, A. 2021, November 5. The singularity is here. *The Atlantic*. https://www.theatlantic.com/magazine/archive/2021/12/ai-ad-technology-singularity/620521/.

Akpinar, B. 2005. The effects of olfactory stimuli on scholastic performance. *The Irish Journal of Education / Iris Eireannach an Oideachais*, 36: 86–90. https://www.jstor.org/stable/30077505.

Al-Samarrai, S. et al. 2021. *Education Finance Watch 2021*. World Bank. https://thedocs.worldbank.org/en/doc/507681613998942297-0090022021/original/EFWReport2021219.pdf.

Alba, D. 2016. Silicon Valley's New-Age AltSchool Unleashes Its Secrets. Wired. https://www.wired.com/2016/10/altschool-shares-secrets-outside-educators/.

Aldon, G., Cusi, A., Schacht, F. & Swidan, O. 2021. Teaching mathematics in a context of lockdown: A study focused on teachers' praxeologies. *Education Sciences*, 11(2). https://doi.org/10.3390/educsci11020038.

Alemira. 2021, June 9. Is online proctoring here to stay? Alemira. https://alemira.com/blog/is-online-proctoring-here-to-stay/.

Alexander, J. 2020, March 27. 'With me' videos on YouTube are seeing huge spikes in viewership as people stay home. The Verge. https://www.theverge.com/2020/3/27/21197642/youtube-with-me-style-videos-views-coronavirus-cook-workout-study-home-beauty.

Alexander, M. 2019, March 7. Rwanda introduces new 500 and 1000 franc banknotes. *CoinsWeekly*. https://coinsweekly.com/rwanda-introduces-new-500-and-1000-franc-banknotes/.

Alliance for Affordable Internet. 2020. *From Luxury to Lifeline: Reducing the Cost of Mobile Devices to Reach Universal Internet Access*. World Wide Web Foundation. https://webfoundation.org/research/from-luxury-to-lifeline-reducing-the-cost-of-mobile-devices-to-reach-universal-internet-access/.

Almagor, L. 2021, June 16. I taught online school this year. It was a disgrace. *New York Times*. https://www.nytimes.com/2021/06/16/opinion/remote-learning-failure.html.

Almeida, M., Challa, M., Ribeiro, M., Harrison, A.M. & Castro, M.C. 2022, May. Editorial perspective: The mental health impact of school closures during the COVID-19 pandemic. *Journal of Child Psychology and Psychiatry*, 63(5). https://www.ncbi.nlm.nih.gov/pmc/articles/PMC8657359/.

Alter, A. 2017. *Irresistible: The Rise of Addictive Technology and the Business of Keeping Us Hooked*. New York: Penguin Books.

Amaro, D., Pandolfelli, L., Sanchez-Tapia, I. & Brossard, M. 2020, August 4. COVID-19 and education: The digital gender divide among adolescents in sub-Saharan Africa. UNICEF. https://data.unicef.org/data-for-action/covid-19-and-education-the-digital-gender-divide-among-adolescents-in-sub-saharan-africa/.

Ames, M.G. 2019. *The Charisma Machine: The Life, Death, and Legacy of One Laptop per Child*. Cambridge, MA: MIT Press.

Amnesty International. 2020, May 6. DRC: Alarming research shows long lasting harm from cobalt mine abuses. https://www.amnesty.org/en/latest/news/2020/05/drc-alarming-research-harm-from-cobalt-mine-abuses/.

Anand, P. & Bergen, M. 2021, October 28. Big teacher is watching: How AI spyware took over schools. Bloomberg. https://www.bloomberg.com/news/features/2021-10-28/how-goguardian-ai-spyware-took-over-schools-student-devices-during-covid.

Andersen, S.K., Humlum, M.K. & Nandrup, A.B. 2016, June 20. Increasing instruction time in school does increase learning. *PNAS*, 113(27). https://www.pnas.org/doi/10.1073/pnas.1516686113.

Anderson, J. & Rainie, L. 2018, April 17. The future of well-being in a tech-saturated world. Pew Research Center. https://www.pewresearch.org/internet/2018/04/17/the-future-of-well-being-in-a-tech-saturated-world/.

Anderson, J. 2020, March 29. The coronavirus pandemic is reshaping education. Quartz. https://qz.com/1826369/how-coronavirus-is-changing-education/.

Anderson, J. 2022, February 7. Government announces £1.3m fund for schools to purchase computers. *Holyrood*. https://www.holyrood.com/news/view,government-announces-13m-fund-for-schools-to-purchase-computers.

Andreu, S. et al. 2020, November. *Évaluations 2020 Repères CP, CE1 : premiers résultats, Document de travail* [2020 assessments CP, CE1 benchmarks: First results]. Ministère de l'éducation nationale et de la jeunesse. https://www.education.gouv.fr/evaluations-2020-reperes-cp-ce1-premiers-resultats-307122.

Andrew, A. et al. 2020. Inequalities in children's experiences of home learning during the COVID-19 lockdown in England. *Fiscal Studies*, 41(3). https://onlinelibrary.wiley.com/doi/10.1111/1475-5890.12240.

Antoninis, M. 2021, March 23. Opinion: How will countries make up for lost learning during the pandemic? Devex. https://www.devex.com/news/opinion-how-will-countries-make-up-for-lost-learning-during-the-pandemic-99453.

Ao, B. 2020, October 28. 'I felt like trash': How COVID-19 has affected body image in young people. *Philadelphia Inquirer*. https://www.inquirer.com/health/coronavirus/body-image-pandemic-quarantine-zoom-weight-gain-loss-20201028.html.

AP News. 2022, February 24. Schools in Eldon to move to 4-day school week next year. https://apnews.com/article/iowa-43729ed982f6486270585082bffcf64e.

App Store Preview. Google Classroom. Apple. https://apps.apple.com/us/app/google-classroom/id924620788.

Apple. 2021, November 17. Apple announces Self Service Repair. Press release. https://www.apple.com/newsroom/2021/11/apple-announces-self-service-repair/.

Apple. 2022. Learn more about Apple Distinguished Educators. K-12 Education. https://www.apple.com/education/k12/apple-distinguished-educator/.

Applebaum, A. & Pomerantsev, P. 2021, April. How to put out democracy's dumpster fire. *The Atlantic*. https://www.theatlantic.com/magazine/archive/2021/04/the-internet-doesnt-have-to-be-awful/618079/.

Arora, P. 2010, May. Hope-in-the-Wall? A digital promise for free learning. *British Journal of Educational Technology*, 41(5). https://www.researchgate.net/publication/229788949_Hope-in-the-Wall_A_digital_promise_for_free_learning.

Asadullah, N. 2020, June 25. *COVID-19, Schooling and Learning*. BRAC Institute of Governance and Development. https://bigd.bracu.ac.bd/wp-content/uploads/2020/06/COVID-19-Schooling-and-Learning_June-25-2020.pdf.

Asanov, I., Flores, F., McKenzie, D., Mensmann, M. & Schulte, M. 2020, May. Remote-learning, time-use, and mental health of Ecuadorian high-school students during the COVID-19 quarantine. Working paper 9252. World Bank Group. http://documents1.worldbank.org/curated/en/328261589899308503/pdf/Remote-learning-Time-Use-and-Mental-Health-of-Ecuadorian-High-School-Studentsduring-the-COVID-19-Quarantine.pdf.

Asher-Schapiro, A. 2020, November 10. 'Unfair surveillance'? Online exam software sparks global student revolt. Reuters. https://www.reuters.com/article/global-tech-education-idUSL8N2HP5DS.

Aspen Institute. 2019, September 3. *State of Play 2019: Trends and Developments*. https://www.aspeninstitute.org/publications/state-of-play-2019-trends-and-developments/.

Aspen Institute. 2021, October 12. Aspen Institute's Project Play report shows kids are losing programs to play sports during pandemic. https://www.aspeninstitute.org/news/press-release/state-of-play-2021/.

Assessment Systems. 2022, May 3. Remote proctoring: How examinees cheat and how to catch them. https://www.youtube.com/watch?v=AznXrUImJXQ.

Associated Press. 2020, October 20. Coronavirus pandemic widens learning gap in education-obsessed South Korea. CNBC. https://www.cnbc.com/2020/10/21/pandemic-widens-learning-gap-in-education-obsessed-south-korea.html.

Association for Supervision and Curriculum Development. 2009, March 1. The importance of deep reading. *Educational Leadership*, 66(6). https://www.ascd.org/el/articles/the-importance-of-deep-reading.

Attendance Works & Everyone Graduates Center. 2021, February. *Using Chronic Absence to Map Interrupted Schooling, Instructional Loss and Educational Inequity*. https://www.attendanceworks.org/wp-content/uploads/2019/06/Attendance-Works-Using-Chronic-Absence-to-Map_020221.pdf.

Auger, K.A. et al. 2020, July 29. Association between statewide school closure and COVID-19 incidence and mortality in the US. *JAMA*, 324(9): 859–870. https://jamanetwork.com/journals/jama/fullarticle/2769034.

Auxier, B. et al. 2019, November 15. Americans' attitudes and experiences with privacy policies and laws. Pew Research Center. https://www.pewresearch.org/internet/2019/11/15/americans-attitudes-and-experiences-with-privacy-policies-and-laws/.

Auxier, B., Anderson, M., Perrin, A. & Turner, E. 2020, July 28. Parental views about YouTube. Pew Research Center. https://www.pewresearch.org/internet/2020/07/28/parental-views-about-youtube/.

Awan, H.A. et al. 2021. Internet and pornography use during the COVID-19 pandemic: Presumed impact and what can be done. *Frontiers in Psychiatry*, 12. https://www.frontiersin.org/article/10.3389/fpsyt.2021.623508.

Azevedo, J. et al. 2021. *The State of the Global Education Crisis: A Path to Recovery (Vol. 2): Executive Summary* (English). World Bank Group. http://documents.worldbank.org/curated/en/184161638768635066/Executive-Summary.

Azevedo, M., Campagnol, N., Hagenbruch, T., Hoffman, K., Lala, A. & Ramsbottom, O. 2018. Lithium and cobalt: A tale of two commodities. McKinsey & Company. https://www.mckinsey.com/industries/metals-and-mining/our-insights/lithium-and-cobalt-a-tale-of-two-commodities.

Azim Premji University. 2021, February. *Loss of Learning during the Pandemic*. Field Studies in Education. https://cdn.azimpremjiuniversity.edu.in/apuc3/media/publications/downloads/Learning-Loss-during-pandemicc.f1660288401.pdf.

Balkam, S. 2014, April 24. Learning the lessons of the inBloom failure. HuffPost. https://www.huffpost.com/entry/learning-the-lessons-of-t_b_5208724.

Ball, M. 2021, June 29. Payments, payment rails, and blockchains, and the metaverse. MatthewBall.vc. https://www.matthewball.vc/all/metaversepayments.

Ball, S.J. 2012. Show me the money! Neoliberalism at work in education. *FORUM*, 54(1). https://doi.org/10.2304/FORUM.2012.54.1.23.

Ball, S.J. ed. 2018. *Governing by Numbers: Education, Governance, and the Tyranny of Numbers*. Abingdon, Oxfordshire: Routledge.

Ballhaus, B. 2021, June 8. Bringing personalized experiences to education with you. Blackboard. Blog post. https://blog.blackboard.com/bringing-personalized-experiences-to-education-with-you/.

Ballotpedia. 2022. Lawsuits about state actions and policies in response to the coronavirus (COVID-19) pandemic. https://ballotpedia.org/Lawsuits_about_state_actions_and_policies_in_response_to_the_coronavirus_(COVID-19)_pandemic.

Baltimore City Public Schools. 2020, November 2. City Schools announces list of additional small group in-person learning sites. Press release. https://www.baltimorecityschools.org/node/1339.

Balu, N. & Randewich, N. 2022, January 4. Apple becomes first company to hit $3 trillion market value, then slips. Reuters. https://www.reuters.com/markets/europe/apple-gets-closer-3-trillion-market-value-2022-01-03/.

Bamberger, M. 2020, June 1. Why is Amazon, by far, the most trusted brand during the pandemic? Tetra Insights. https://www.tetrainsights.com/why-is-amazon-by-far-the-most-trusted-brand-during-the-pandemic/.

Bang & Olufsen's. 2022. The future is circular. https://www.bang-olufsen.com/en/dk/story/cradle-to-cradle-certification.

Bankhead, C. 2021, May 6. Another COVID-19 side effect: 'Zoom dysmorphia'. MedPage Today. https://www.medpagetoday.com/dermatology/generaldermatology/92463.

Baraniuk, C. 2020, October 27. They dreamed of esports glory. Then their bodies broke down. Wired. https://www.wired.co.uk/article/esports-injuries-mental-health.

Barbour, M.K. 2018. The landscape of K-12 online learning: Examining what is known. In Moore M.G. & Diehl, W.C. (eds). *Handbook of Distance Education*. 4th ed. New York: Routledge.

Baron, N.S. 2015. *Words Onscreen: The Fate of Reading in a Digital World*. Oxford: Oxford University Press.

Barrett, L.F. 2014, February 28. What faces can't tell us. *New York Times*. https://www.nytimes.com/2014/03/02/opinion/sunday/what-faces-cant-tell-us.html.

Barrett, L.F., Adolphs, R., Marsella, S., Martinez, A.M. & Pollak, S.D. 2019. Emotional expressions reconsidered: Challenges to inferring emotion from human facial movements. *Psychological Science in the Public Interest*, 20(1). https://journals.sagepub.com/eprint/SAUES8UM69EN8TSMUGF9/full.

Barron, M., Cobo, C., Munoz-Najar, A. & Ciarrusta, I.S. 2021, February 18. The changing role of teachers and technologies amidst the COVID 19 pandemic: Key findings from a cross-country study. World Bank Blogs. https://blogs.worldbank.org/education/changing-role-teachers-and-technologies-amidst-covid-19-pandemic-key-findings-cross.

Barrot, J.S., Llenares, I.I. & Del Rosario, L.S. 2021. Students' online learning challenges during the pandemic and how they cope with them: The case of the Philippines. *Education and Information Technologies*, 26(6): 1–18. https://pubmed.ncbi.nlm.nih.gov/34075300.

Barry, E. 2022, March 31. Many teens report emotional and physical abuse by parents during lockdown. *New York Times*. https://www.nytimes.com/2022/03/31/health/covid-mental-health-teens.html.

Battelle, J. 2016, July 13. Max Ventilla of AltSchool: The full shift dialogs transcript. Newco Shift. https://shift.newco.co/2016/07/13/max-ventilla-of-altschool-the-full-shift-dialogs-transcript/.

Battenfeld, M. 2020, June 16. 3 lessons from how schools responded to the 1918 pandemic worth heeding today. The Conversation. http://theconversation.com/3-lessons-from-how-schools-responded-to-the-1918-pandemic-worth-heeding-today-138403.

Baynes, C. 2018, April 11. Entire country taken offline for two days after undersea internet cable cut. *The Independent*. https://www.independent.co.uk/tech/mauritiana-internet-cut-underwater-cable-offline-days-west-africa-a8298551.html.

Baytiyeh, H. 2018, January 29. Online learning during post-earthquake school closures. *Disaster Prevention and Management*, 27(2). https://doi.org/10.1108/DPM-07-2017-0173.

BBC News. 2019, September 6. China to curb facial recognition and apps in schools. https://www.bbc.com/news/world-asia-49608459.

BBC News. 2020, July 7. Coronavirus: Kenyan schools to remain closed until 2021. https://www.bbc.com/news/world-africa-53325741.

BBC. 2020, November 9. Coronavirus: Will our day-to-day ever be the same? https://www.bbc.com/worklife/article/20201109-coronavirus-how-cities-travel-and-family-life-will-change.

Belkhir, L. & Elmeligi, A. 2018. Assessing ICT global emissions footprint: Trends to 2040 and recommendations. *Journal of Cleaner Production*, 177: 448–463. https://www.sciencedirect.com/science/article/pii/S095965261733233X.

Berens, M. 2021, September 17. One U.S. state stands out in restricting corporate use of biometrics: Illinois. Reuters. https://www.reuters.com/technology/one-us-state-stands-out-restricting-corporate-use-biometrics-illinois-2021-09-16/.

Bergmann, C. et al. 2021, May 31. Young children's screen time during the first COVID-19 lockdown in 12 countries. OSF Preprints. https://doi.org/10.31219/osf.io/p5gm4.

Bergmans, L., Bouali, N., Luttikhuis, M. & Rensink, A. 2021. On the efficacy of online proctoring using Proctorio. In *Proceedings of the 13th International Conference on Computer Supported Education (CSEDU 2021) - Volume 1*. https://ris.utwente.nl/ws/portalfiles/

Bernheim, R. & Padilla, K. 2020. *Act Now: Experiences and Recommendations of Girls and Boys in West Africa during COVID-19*. World Vision International. https://www.wvi.org/sites/default/files/2020-11/5-WV-WARO-Report-29-10-20.pdf.

Berreby, D. 2017, March 3. Click to agree with what? No one reads terms of service, studies confirm. *The Guardian*. https://www.theguardian.com/technology/2017/mar/03/terms-of-service-online-contracts-fine-print.

Berthold, J. 2021, November 1. Adolescents' recreational screen time doubled during pandemic, affecting mental health. University of California San Francisco, Department of Epidemiology and Biostatistics. https://epibiostat.ucsf.edu/news/adolescents%E2%80%99-recreational-screen-time-doubled-during-pandemic-affecting-mental-health.

Betthäuser, B.A., Bach-Mortensen, A.M. & Engzell, P. 2023, January 30. A systematic review and meta-analysis of the evidence on learning during the COVID-19 pandemic. *Nature Human Behaviour*, 7. https://doi.org/10.1038/s41562-022-01506-4.

Bettinger, E. & Loeb, S. 2017, June 9. Promises and pitfalls of online education. Brookings. https://www.brookings.edu/research/promises-and-pitfalls-of-online-education/.

Bewick, T. 2020, August 24. 'Results day 2020 was like the sinking of the Titanic'. *Tes Magazine*. https://www.tes.com/magazine/archive/results-day-2020-was-sinking-titanic.

BFM avec RMC. 2021, April 6. "Bug"... ou "cyberattaque" ? L'école à la maison (re)commence avec des problèmes informatiques ["Bug"... or "cyberattack"? School at home (again) starts with computer problems]. https://rmc.bfmtv.com/emission/bug-ou-cyberattaque-l-ecole-a-la-maison-recommence-avec-des-problemes-informatiques-2040525.html.

Bhandari, V. 2020, August. *Improving Internet Connectivity during Covid-19*. Digital Pathways at Oxford. Paper series 4. https://pathwayscommission.bsg.ox.ac.uk/sites/default/files/2020-09/improving_internet_connectivity_during_covid-19_0.pdf.

Bhat, A. 2022, August 3. "Hundreds of complaints": India's edtech startups are failing to regulate themselves. Rest of World. https://restofworld.org/2022/indias-edtech-startups-fail-to-regulate-themselves/.

Binstein, J. 2015, January. How to cheat with Proctortrack, Examity, and the rest. *Jake Binstein*. https://jakebinstein.com/blog/on-knuckle-scanners-and-cheating-how-to-bypass-proctortrack/.

Bird, S. 2022, June 21. Responsible AI investments and safeguards for facial recognition. Azure. https://azure.microsoft.com/en-us/blog/responsible-ai-investments-and-safeguards-for-facial-recognition/.

Biryabarema, E. 2022, January 10. Student joy, dropout heartache as Uganda reopens schools after long COVID-19 shutdown. Reuters. https://www.reuters.com/world/africa/student-joy-dropout-heartache-uganda-reopens-schools-after-long-covid-19-2022-01-10/.

Bischoff, P. 2021, June 23. Ransomware attacks on US schools and colleges cost $6.62bn in 2020. Comparitech. https://www.comparitech.com/blog/information-security/school-ransomware-attacks/.

Bismarck-Osten, C. von, Borusyak, K. & Schönberg, U. 2021, May 8. School closures did not contain the spread of the coronavirus in Germany. VoxEU. https://voxeu.org/article/school-closures-did-not-contribute-spread-coronavirus-germany.

Blanco, C. 2020, April 8. Changes in Duolingo usage during the COVID-19 pandemic. Duolingo. Blog post. https://blog.duolingo.com/changes-in-duolingo-usage-during-the-covid-19-pandemic/.

Blanshe, M. & Dahir, A.L. 2022, January 10. Uganda reopens schools after world's longest Covid shutdown. *New York Times*. https://www.nytimes.com/2022/01/10/world/africa/uganda-schools-reopen.html.

Blaskó, Z. & Schnepf, S. 2021. Educational inequalities in Europe and physical school closures during Covid-19. European Commission Knowledge for Policy. https://knowledge4policy.ec.europa.eu/publication/educational-inequalities-europe-physical-school-closures-during-covid-19_en.

Bluedorn, J.C., Caselli, F.G., Hansen, N.-J.H., Shibata, I. & Mendes Tavares, M. 2021, March 31. Gender and employment in the COVID-19 recession: Evidence on "she-cessions". Working paper no. 2021/095. International Monetary Fund. https://www.imf.org/en/Publications/WP/Issues/2021/03/31/Gender-and-Employment-in-the-COVID-19-Recession-Evidence-on-She-cessions-50316.

Blum, A. 2012. *Tubes: A Journey to the Center of the Internet*. New York: Ecco.

Bol, T. 2020, April 30. Inequality in homeschooling during the Corona crisis in the Netherlands. First results from the LISS Panel. *SocArXiv*. https://doi.org/10.31235/osf.io/hf32q.

Bologna, C. 2019, November 8. What's the deal with Generation Alpha? Huffpost. https://www.huffpost.com/entry/generation-alpha-after-gen-z_l_5d420ef4e4b0aca341181574.

Borgonovi, F. & Ferrara, A. 2022, July 26. The effects of COVID-19 on inequalities in educational achievement in Italy. https://ssrn.com/abstract=4171968.

Borkowski, A. et al. 2021. *COVID-19: Missing More Than a Classroom. The Impact of School Closures on Children's Nutrition*. UNICEF & World Food Programme. https://www.unicef-irc.org/publications/pdf/COVID-19_Missing_More_Than_a_Classroom_The_impact_of_school_closures_on_childrens_nutrition.pdf.

Borthakur, P. 2020, September 2. COVID-19 pandemic ushers confidence in homeschooling culture in India. EastMojo. http://www.eastmojo.com/news/2020/09/02/covid-19-pandemic-ushers-confidence-in-homeschooling-culture-in-india/.

Bosumtwi-Sam, C. & Kabay, S. 2020, August 19. Using data and evidence to inform school reopening in Ghana. Innovation for Poverty Action. https://www.poverty-action.org/blog/using-data-and-evidence-inform-school-reopening-ghana.

BR24. 2022, January 30. Schulschwänzen wegen Corona: Hunderte Bußgeldverfahren in Bayern [Truancy because of Corona: Hundreds of fines in Bavaria]. https://www.br.de/nachrichten/bayern/schulschwaenzen-wegen-corona-hunderte-bussgeldverfahren-in-bayern,SvyrF9F.

Brady, L. et al. 2020, December 31. 7 ways for teachers to truly connect with parents. *Education Week*. https://www.edweek.org/leadership/opinion-7-ways-for-teachers-to-truly-connect-with-parents/2020/12.

Branswell, H. 2021, May 19. How the Covid pandemic ends: Scientists look to the past to see the future. *STAT*. https://www.statnews.com/2021/05/19/how-the-covid-pandemic-ends-scientists-look-to-the-past-to-see-the-future/.

Bridge International. 2022. Teacher tools. https://bridgeschools.in/teaching/teacher-tools/.

Bridge, J.A. 2023, February. Youth suicide during the first year of the COVID-19 pandemic. *Pediatrics*, 151(3). https://doi.org/10.1542/peds.2022-058375.

British Journal of Educational Technology. https://bera-journals.onlinelibrary.wiley.com/journal/14678535.

British Telecommunications. 2020, March 20. The facts about our network and Coronavirus. https://newsroom.bt.com/the-facts-about-our-network-and-coronavirus/.

British Telecommunications. 2020, March 20. The facts about our network and Coronavirus. https://newsroom.bt.com/the-facts-about-our-network-and-coronavirus/.

Britton, N.D. & Wang, C. 2020, August 5. Hackers publish Australian universities' ProctorU data. *Honi Soit*. http://honisoit.com/2020/08/hackers-publish-australian-universities-proctoru-data/.

Broadband Commission for Sustainable Development. 2022. About us: Bringing the goal of universal connectivity to the forefront of policy discussions. https://www.broadbandcommission.org/about-us/.

Broadband Commission for Sustainable Development. 2025 targets: "Connecting the other half". ITU & UNESCO. https://broadbandcommission.org/Documents/publications/wef2018.pdf.

Brookings. 2020, September 14. Beyond reopening: A leapfrog moment to transform education? https://www.brookings.edu/events/beyond-reopening-a-leapfrog-moment-to-transform-education/.

Brooks, S.K. et al. 2020, April 2. The impact of unplanned school closure on children's social contact: Rapid evidence review. *Eurosurveillance*, 25(13). https://www.eurosurveillance.org/content/10.2807/1560-7917.ES.2020.25.13.2000188.

Brown, L.X.Z. 2020, November 16. How automated test proctoring software discriminates against disabled students. Center for Democracy and Technology. https://cdt.org/insights/how-automated-test-proctoring-software-discriminates-against-disabled-students/.

Brown, M. 2020, September 1. Photo of kids forced to use Taco Bell WiFi for homework is startling reminder that many families have no internet. Parents. https://www.parents.com/news/photo-of-kids-using-taco-bell-wifi-is-a-startling-reminder-of-the-digital-divide/.

Brown, N., Riele, K., Shelley, B. & Woodroffe, J. 2020, April. *Learning at Home during COVID-19: Effects on Vulnerable Young Australians: Independent Rapid Response Report*. Peter Underwood Centre for Educational Attainment, University of Tasmania. https://www.utas.edu.au/__data/assets/pdf_file/0008/1324268/Learning-at-home-during-COVID-19-updated.pdf.

Buckley, C. 2021, August 30. China tightens limits for young online gamers and bans school night play. *New York Times*. https://www.nytimes.com/2021/08/30/business/media/china-online-games.html.

Bulger, M., McCormick, P. & Pitcan, M. 2017, February 2. The legacy of inBloom. Data & Society. https://datasociety.net/library/the-legacy-of-inbloom/.

Bundy, D., de Silva, N., Horton, S., Jamison, D. & Patton, G. 2018. *Re-Imagining School Feeding: A High-Return Investment in Human Capital and Local Economy*. World Bank. https://docs.wfp.org/api/documents/WFP-0000116138/download/.

Burgess, M. 2020, August 20. The lessons we all must learn from the A-levels algorithm debacle. Wired. https://www.wired.co.uk/article/gcse-results-alevels-algorithm-explained.

Burgess, M., Schot, E. & Geiger, G. 2023, March 6. This algorithm could ruin your life. Wired. https://www.wired.co.uk/article/welfare-algorithms-discrimination.

Burke, H. 2019. *The Phone Addiction Workbook: How to Identify Smartphone Dependency, Stop Compulsive Behavior and Develop a Healthy Relationship with Your Devices*. Berkeley, CA: Ulysses Press.

Burke, L. 2020, December 14. The death and life of an admissions algorithm. *Inside Higher Ed*. https://www.insidehighered.com/admissions/article/2020/12/14/u-texas-will-stop-using-controversial-algorithm-evaluate-phd.

Bushner, B. 2020, September 18. A list of things I hate about Google Classroom. Google Classroom Help. https://support.google.com/edu/classroom/thread/71858073/a-list-of-things-i-hate-about-google-classroom.

Business Standard. 2021, July 26. China outlaws for-profit school tutoring in a sweeping overhaul. https://www.business-standard.com/article/international/china-outlaws-for-profit-school-tutoring-in-a-sweeping-overhaul-121072600032_1.html.

BusinessTech. 2021, February 22. Here are South Africa's matric results for 2020. https://businesstech.co.za/news/government/470012/here-are-south-africas-matric-results-for-2020/.

Buttner, A. 2021, January 5. Diagnosing the school nurse shortage. *Frontline Education*. https://www.frontlineeducation.com/blog/school-nurse-shortage/.

Cable.co.uk. 2022. Worldwide mobile data pricing 2022: The cost of 1GB of mobile data in 230 countries. https://www.cable.co.uk/mobiles/worldwide-data-pricing/#highlights.

Cacioppo, J.T. & Hawkley, L.C. 2009. Perceived social isolation and cognition. *Trends in Cognitive Sciences*, 13(10): 447–454. https://www.sciencedirect.com/science/article/pii/S1364661309001478.

Caines, A. & Silverman, S. 2021, December 10. Back doors, trap doors, and fourth-party deals: How you end up with harmful academic surveillance technology on your campus without even knowing. *Journal of Interactive*

Technology and Pedagogy, 20. https://jitp.commons.gc.cuny.edu/back-doors-trap-doors-and-fourth-party-deals-how-you-end-up-with-harmful-academic-surveillance-technology-on-your-campus-without-even-knowing/.

Cakebread, C. 2017, November 15. You're not alone, no one reads terms of service agreements. Business Insider. https://www.businessinsider.com/deloitte-study-91-percent-agree-terms-of-service-without-reading-2017-11.

California Legislative Information. 2022, September 26. Assembly Bill No.2355: School cybersecurity. https://leginfo.legislature.ca.gov/faces/billTextClient.xhtml?bill_id=202120220AB2355.

California Legislative Information. 2022, September 29. Senate Bill No. 1172. Student Test Taker Privacy Protection Act. https://leginfo.legislature.ca.gov/faces/billTextClient.xhtml?bill_id=202120220SB1172.

Caltabiano, M., Castiglioni, M. & De-Rose, A. 2020. Changes in the sexual behaviour of young people: Introduction. *Genus*, 76(1): 38. https://doi.org/10.1186/s41118-020-00107-1.

Calvano, C., Engelke, L., Di Bella, J., Kindermann, J., Renneberg, B. & Winter S.M.2022. Families in the COVID-19 pandemic: Parental stress, parent mental health and the occurrence of adverse childhood experiences-results of a representative survey in Germany. *European Child & Adolescent Psychiatry*. 31(7). https://link.springer.com/article/10.1007/s00787-021-01739-0.

Camera, L. 2020, June 29. Pediatric group calls for children to return to schools despite Coronavirus. US News. https://www.usnews.com/news/education-news/articles/2020-06-29/pediatric-group-calls-for-children-to-return-to-schools-despite-coronavirus.

Caplan-Bricker, N. 2021, May 27. Is online test-monitoring here to stay? *New Yorker*. https://www.newyorker.com/tech/annals-of-technology/is-online-test-monitoring-here-to-stay.

Cappa, C. & Hereward, M. 2019, December 11. Fulfilling the right of street children to be counted. UNICEF Data & Analytics Section. https://data.unicef.org/data-for-action/fulfilling-the-right-of-street-children-to-be-counted/.

Cappa, C. & Murray, C. 2021. *COVID-19: A Threat to Progress against Child Marriage*. UNICEF. https://data.unicef.org/resources/covid-19-a-threat-to-progress-against-child-marriage/.

Cárdenas, S., Lomelí, D. & Ruelas, I. 2021. COVID-19 and post-pandemic educational policies in Mexico. What is at stake? In Reimers, F.M. (ed). *Primary and Secondary Education during Covid-19: Disruptions to Educational Opportunity During a Pandemic*. New York: Springer.

Cardinal, D. 2017, September 14. How Apple's iPhone X TrueDepth camera works. Extreme Tech. https://www.extremetech.com/mobile/255771-apple-iphone-x-truedepth-camera-works.

Carminucci, J., Hodgman, S., Rickles, J. & Garet, M. 2021, June. *Research Brief: Student Attendance and Enrollment Loss in 2020–21*. American Institutes for Research. https://www.air.org/sites/default/files/2021-07/research-brief-covid-survey-student-attendance-june-2021_0.pdf.

Carr, N. 2011. *The Shallows: What the Internet Is Doing to Our Brains*. New York: W.W. Norton.

Carr, S. 2021, May 18. As a district re-opens, one middle schooler returned to school and another remained home. The Hechinger Report. https://hechingerreport.org/as-a-district-re-opens-one-middle-schooler-returned-to-school-and-another-remained-home/.

Carroll, A.E. 2020, August 28. When it comes to Covid-19, most of us have risk exactly backward. *New York Times*. https://www.nytimes.com/2020/08/28/opinion/coronavirus-schools-tradeoffs.html.

Carter, N. 2021, May 5. How much energy does Bitcoin actually consume? *Harvard Business Review*. https://hbr.org/2021/05/how-much-energy-does-bitcoin-actually-consume.

Carter, S. & Moncrieff, I. 2021, May. *COVID-19 School Closures in the DRC: Impact on the Health, Protection and Education of Children and Youth*. Social Sciences Analytics Cell. https://www.unicef.org/drcongo/media/5716/file/COD-CASS-school-closures-impacts.pdf.

Castelli, F.R. & Sarvary, M.A. 2021. Why students do not turn on their video cameras during online classes and an equitable and inclusive plan to encourage them to do so. *Ecology and Evolution, 11(8): 3565–3576*. https://www.ncbi.nlm.nih.gov/pmc/articles/PMC8057329/.

Castro, A.M. 2021, September 7. Teachers are key in protecting students' mental health during the COVID-19 Pandemic. UNICEF. https://www.unicef.org/lac/en/stories/teachers-are-key-in-protecting-students-mental-health-during-covid-19-pandemic.

Cattan, S. et al. 2021, February 19. Inequalities in responses to school closures over the course of the first COVID-19 lockdown. Institute for Fiscal Studies. Working paper. https://ifs.org.uk/publications/inequalities-responses-school-closures-over-course-first-covid-19-lockdown.

CBC Radio. 2018, November 2. Bad algorithms are making racist decisions. https://www.cbc.ca/radio/spark/412-1.4887497/bad-algorithms-are-making-racist-decisions-1.4887504.

CDW. 2022. About CDW. https://www.cdw.com/content/cdw/en/about/overview.html.

Cellular Operators Association of India. 2020, April 9. Subject: Measures regarding ensuring availability of recharge vouchers and payment options for prepaid services. Letter. https://www.medianama.com/wp-content/uploads/Ltr-to-TRAI-on-Connectivity-to-Prepaid-susbcribers-Final.pdf.pdf.

Center on Reinventing Public Education. 2021, July. *How Much Have Students Missed Academically Because of the Pandemic? A Review of the Evidence to Date.* University of Washington Bothell. https://crpe.org/wp-content/uploads/8_5_final_academic_impacts_report_2021.pdf.

Centers for Disease Control and Prevention. 2022, March 31. Adolescent behaviors and experiences survey (ABES). https://www.cdc.gov/healthyyouth/data/abes.htm.

Centers for Disease Control and Prevention. 2022. Provisional COVID-19 deaths: Focus on ages 0-18 years. https://data.cdc.gov/NCHS/Provisional-COVID-19-Deaths-Focus-on-Ages-0-18-Yea/nr4s-juj3/data.

Centre for Human Rights, Pakistan. 2022, March 1. COVID-19 and the Digital Divide in Education. Webinar. Posted to YouTube 23 March 2022. CFHR talks: Bridging the digital divide in education during COVID-19. https://www.youtube.com/watch?v=f01vODlpDE8.

Cerulus, L. 2021, September 1. Ransomware's next target: Schools. *POLITICO.* https://www.politico.eu/article/its-back-to-school-for-ransomware-criminals/.

Chaabane, S., Doraiswamy, S., Chaabna, K., Mamtani, R. & Cheema, S. 2021. The impact of COVID-19 school closure on child and adolescent health: A rapid systematic review. *Children*, 8(5). https://www.mdpi.com/2227-9067/8/5/415.

Chadwick, J. 2020, July 2. Shocking 52.7 MILLION tons of electronic waste made up of phones, TVs and other gadgets was produced worldwide in 2019 – weighing the equivalent of 350 cruise ships. *Daily Mail.* https://www.dailymail.co.uk/sciencetech/article-8483361/56-3-megatonnes-e-waste-produced-2019-says.html.

Chakroun, B., Daelman-Balepa, K. & Keevy, J. 2022. *Minding the Data: Protecting Learners' Privacy and Security.* UNESCO. https://unesdoc.unesco.org/ark:/48223/pf0000381494/PDF/381494eng.pdf.multi.

Challenge Success & NBC News. 2021, February. *Kids under Pressure: A Look at Student Well-Being and Engagement during the Pandemic.* https://challengesuccess.org/wp-content/uploads/2021/02/CS-NBC-Study-Kids-Under-Pressure-PUBLISHED.pdf.

Chan, M. 2021, February 17. This AI reads children's emotions as they learn. CNN. https://edition.cnn.com/2021/02/16/tech/emotion-recognition-ai-education-spc-intl-hnk/index.html.

Chandra, S. et al. 2020. *Closing the K–12 Digital Divide in the Age of Distance Learning.* Common Sense & Boston Consulting Group. https://www.commonsensemedia.org/sites/default/files/featured-content/files/common_sense_media_report_final_7_1_3pm_web.pdf.

Chandran, S. 2020, October 24. The surge of EdTech startups in the Middle East amidst a pandemic. Global EdTech. https://global-edtech.com/the-surge-of-edtech-startups-in-the-middle-east-amidst-a-pandemic/.

Chang, V. 2020, August 25. Tablet sales boosted by Covid-19 pandemic lockdown measures. *Straits Times.* https://www.straitstimes.com/tech/tablets/tablet-sales-boosted-by-pandemic-lockdown-measures.

Chatterji, M. 2021, July 9. Repairing – not recycling – is the first step to tackling e-waste from smartphones. Here's why. World Economic Forum. https://www.weforum.org/agenda/2021/07/repair-not-recycle-tackle-ewaste-circular-economy-smartphones/.

Chauvin, L.O. & Faiola, A. 2020, October 16. Remote learning is deepening the divide between rich and poor. *Washington Post*. https://www.washingtonpost.com/world/2020/10/16/coronavirus-peru-remote-learning-inequality/.

Chavez Villegas, C., Peirolo, S., Rocca, M., Ipince, A. & Bakrania, S. 2021, July. Impacts of health-related school closures on child protection outcomes: A review of evidence from past pandemics and epidemics and lessons learned for COVID-19. *International Journal of Educational Development*, 84. https://www.ncbi.nlm.nih.gov/pmc/articles/PMC8132744/.

Chawla, N. & Kumar, B. 2022, July 20. E-commerce and consumer protection in India: The emerging trend. *Journal of Business Ethics*, 180(2): 581–604. https://link.springer.com/article/10.1007/s10551-021-04884-3.

Chebib, K. 2020. *Education For All in the Time of COVID-19: How EdTech can be Part of the Solution*. GSMA. https://www.gsma.com/mobilefordevelopment/wp-content/uploads/2020/09/EdTech-Final-WEB.pdf.

Check Point Research. 2021, August 23. 93% increase in cyberattacks targeting the UK's education sector. FE News. https://www.fenews.co.uk/skills/93-increase-in-cyberattacks-targeting-the-uk-s-education-sector/.

Chegg Investor Relations. 2021, February 8. Chegg reports 2020 financial results and raises 2021 guidance. Press release. https://investor.chegg.com/Press-Releases/press-release-details/2021/Chegg-Reports-2020-Financial-Results-and-Raises-2021-Guidance/default.aspx.

Chegg Investor relations. 2022, February 7. Chegg reports 2021 financial results and gives 2022 guidance. Press release. https://investor.chegg.com/Press-Releases/press-release-details/2022/Chegg-Reports-2021-Financial-Results-and-Gives-2022-Guidance/default.aspx.

Chen, L. 2018, December 4. Chinese parents spend up to US$43,500 a year on after-school classes for their children. *South China Morning Post*. https://www.scmp.com/news/china/society/article/2176377/chinese-parents-spend-us43500-year-after-school-classes-their.

Chen, L., Dorn, E., Sarakatsannis, J. & Wiesinger, A. 2021, March 1. Teacher survey: Learning loss is global—and significant. McKinsey & Company. https://www.mckinsey.com/industries/education/our-insights/teacher-survey-learning-loss-is-global-and-significant.

Chen, T.M. 2020, October 27. Edtech and Covid-19: It's complicated. TechNode. http://technode.com/2020/10/27/edtech-in-china-and-covid-19-its-complicated/.

Chen, W. & Adler, J.L. 2019. Assessment of screen exposure in young children, 1997 to 2014. *JAMA Pediatrics*, 173(4): 391–393. https://doi.org/10.1001/jamapediatrics.2018.5546.

Cheney, C. 2021, November 1. Ed tech, long overhyped, missed its moment amid COVID-19. What now? Devex. https://www.devex.com/news/ed-tech-long-overhyped-missed-its-moment-amid-covid-19-what-now-101835.

Chetty, R., Friedman, J.N., Hendren, N., Stepner, M. & The Opportunity Insights Team. 2020, June. How did Covid-19 and stabilization policies affect spending and employment? A new real-time economic tracker based on private sector data. Working paper 27431. National Bureau of Economic Research. http://www.nber.org/papers/w27431.

Chin, M. 2020, April 29. Exam anxiety: How remote test-proctoring is creeping students out. The Verge. https://www.theverge.com/2020/4/29/21232777/examity-remote-test-proctoring-online-class-education.

Chin, M. 2020, September 3. These students figured out their tests were graded by AI — and the easy way to cheat. The Verge. https://www.theverge.com/2020/9/2/21419012/edgenuity-online-class-ai-grading-keyword-mashing-students-school-cheating-algorithm-glitch.

Christensen, C.M., Horn, M.B. & Johnson, C.W. 2008. *Disrupting Class: How Disruptive Innovation Will Change the Way the World Learns*. New York: McGraw-Hill.

Cimberle, M. 2020, October 20. Increased digital screen time during COVID-19 may accelerate myopia epidemic. *Healio, Ophthalmology*. https://www.healio.com/news/ophthalmology/20201014/increased-digital-screen-time-during-covid19-may-accelerate-myopia-epidemic.

Clement, J. 2021, October 18. COVID-19 impact on the gaming industry worldwide - statistics & facts. Statista. https://www.statista.com/topics/8016/covid-19-impact-on-the-gaming-industry-worldwide/.

Clements, R. 2004. An investigation of the status of outdoor play. *Contemporary Issues in Early Childhood*, 5(1): 68–80. https://www.researchgate.net/publication/250151481_An_Investigation_of_the_Status_of_Outdoor_Play.

CNN Philippines. 2020, May 10. DepEd sets guidelines for summer classes amid COVID-19 pandemic. https://www.cnnphilippines.com/news/2020/5/10/DepEd-sets-guidelines-for-summer-classes-amid-COVID-19-pandemic.html.

Code.org. 2022. Why computer science? https://code.org/promote.

Cohen, J. 2020, December 4. It would take 17 hours to read the Terms & Conditions of the 13 most popular apps. *PC Magazine*. https://www.pcmag.com/news/it-would-take-17-hours-to-read-the-terms-conditions-of-the-13-most-popular.

Colclough, C. 2020, September. *Teaching with Tech: The Role of Education Unions in Shaping the Future*. Education International. https://issuu.com/educationinternational/docs/2020_ei_research_teachingwithtech_eng.

Collier, K. 2021, September 10. Hackers are leaking children's data — and there's little parents can do. NBC News. https://www.nbcnews.com/tech/security/hackers-are-leaking-childrens-data-s-little-parents-can-rcna1926.

Collins, B. 2018, August 29. Online education is a disability rights issue. *Inside Higher Ed*. https://www.insidehighered.com/digital-learning/views/2018/08/29/online-education-disability-rights-issue-lets-treat-it-way-opinion.

Collins, B. 2020, March 3. The Pomodoro Technique explained. Forbes. https://www.forbes.com/sites/bryancollinseurope/2020/03/03/the-pomodoro-technique/.

Commission nationale de l'informatique et des libertés. 2022, January 6. Cookies: The CNIL fines GOOGLE a total of 150 million euros and FACEBOOK 60 million euros for non-compliance with French legislation. https://www.cnil.fr/en/cookies-cnil-fines-google-total-150-million-euros-and-facebook-60-million-euros-non-compliance.

Common Sense. 2019, October 28. The Common Sense census: Media use by tweens and teens, 2019. https://www.commonsensemedia.org/research/the-common-sense-census-media-use-by-tweens-and-teens-2019.

Common Sense. 2021. *State of Kids' Privacy 2021: Key Findings*. https://www.commonsensemedia.org/sites/default/files/research/report/common-sense-2021-state-of-kids-privacy-key-findings.pdf.

Companies Market Cap. 2022. Chegg: Market capitalization of Chegg (CHGG). https://companiesmarketcap.com/chegg/marketcap/.

Computers and Education. https://www.sciencedirect.com/journal/computers-and-education.

Consolazio, D., Sarti, S., Terraneo, M., Celata, C. & Russo, A.G. 2022, July 12. The impact of school closure intervention during the third wave of the COVID-19 pandemic in Italy: Evidence from the Milan area. *PLOS ONE*, 17(7): e0271404. https://doi.org/10.1371/journal.pone.0271404.

Corbyn, Z. 2022, August 26. 'I'm afraid': Critics of anti-cheating technology for students hit by lawsuits. *The Guardian*. https://www.theguardian.com/us-news/2022/aug/26/anti-cheating-technology-students-tests-proctorio.

Corcoran, B. 2021, July 30. The next wave of edtech will be very, very big — and global. EdSurge. https://www.edsurge.com/news/2021-07-30-the-next-wave-of-edtech-will-be-very-very-big-and-global.

Cornell University. Detailed breakdown of 2021-2022 estimated cost of attendance. Financial Aid. https://finaid.cornell.edu/detailed-breakdown-of-estimated-cost-attendance.

Coskun, K. & Kara, C. 2022, June. The impact of the COVID-19 pandemic on primary school students' mathematical reasoning skills: A mediation analysis. *London Review of Education*, 20(1): 1–16. https://uclpress.scienceopen.com/hosted-document?doi=10.14324/LRE.20.1.19.

Costello, K. & Rimol, M. 2020, October 12. Gartner says worldwide PC shipments grew 3.6% in third quarter of 2020. Gartner. https://www.gartner.com/en/newsroom/press-releases/2020-10-12-gartner-says-worldwide-pc-shipments-grew-3-point-six-percent-in-the-third-quarter-of-2020.

Coupal, S. 2017, April 28. Younger children and recognition of online advertising. Advertising Standards Authority. https://www.asa.org.uk/news/younger-children-and-recognition-of-online-advertising.html.

Cox, S. 2020, October 6. Global study links positivity about touch to lower loneliness. Goldsmiths, University of London. https://www.gold.ac.uk/news/the-touch-test-results/.

Coyne, S.M. et al. 2021. Suicide risk in emerging adulthood: Associations with screen time over 10 years. *Journal of Youth and Adolescence*, 50(12): 2324–2338. https://doi.org/10.1007/s10964-020-01389-6.

Cradle to Cradle Products Innovation Institute. 2022. What is Cradle to Cradle Certified? https://www.c2ccertified.org/get-certified/product-certification.

Cramer-Flood, E. 2021, April 29. Worldwide digital ad spending 2021: Surprisingly resilient 2020 presages another surge. *Insider Intelligence*. https://www.insiderintelligence.com/content/worldwide-digital-ad-spending-2021.

Crawford, K. 2021, April 27. Artificial intelligence is misreading human emotion. *The Atlantic*. https://www.theatlantic.com/technology/archive/2021/04/artificial-intelligence-misreading-human-emotion/618696/.

Crawford, K. 2021, April 6. Time to regulate AI that interprets human emotions. *Nature*. https://www.nature.com/articles/d41586-021-00868-5.

Crawford, K. 2021. *Atlas of AI: Power, Politics, and the Planetary Costs of Artificial Intelligence*. New Haven: Yale University Press.

Crawford, K., et al. 2019. *AI Now 2019 Report*. https://ainowinstitute.org/reports.html.

Crawfurd, L. 2020, May 18. Why the COVID crisis is not edtech's moment in Africa. Center for Global Development. Blog post. https://www.cgdev.org/blog/why-covid-crisis-not-edtechs-moment-africa.

Credit Suisse in partnership with the Financial Times Commercial department. 2020. Education is having its 'Netflix' moment as a result of the coronavirus pandemic. *Financial Times*. https://www.ft.com/partnercontent/credit-suisse/education-is-having-its-netflix-moment-as-a-result-of-the-coronavirus-pandemic.html.

Crew, M. 2021. *Literature Review on the Impact of COVID-19 on Families, and Implications for the Home Learning Environment*. National Literacy Trust. https://cdn.literacytrust.org.uk/media/documents/Updated_COVID-19_Literature_Review.pdf.

Crouse, L. 2021, October 8. For teen girls, Instagram is a cesspool. *New York Times*. https://www.nytimes.com/2021/10/08/opinion/instagram-teen-girls-mental-health.html.

Cuban, L. 2003. *Oversold and Underused: Computers in the Classroom*. Cambridge, MA: Harvard University Press.

Cuban, L. 2013, March 18. No end to magical thinking when it comes to high-tech schooling. Larry Cuban on School Reform and Classroom Practice. Blog post. https://larrycuban.wordpress.com/2013/03/18/no-end-to-magical-thinking-when-it-comes-to-high-tech-schooling/.

Cukier, A. 2021, October 1. Families continue to jump to private school amid the pandemic. *Globe and Mail*. https://www.theglobeandmail.com/featured-reports/article-families-continue-to-jump-to-private-school-amid-the-pandemic/.

Culkin, J.M. 1967, March 18. A schoolman's guide to Marshall McLuhan. *Saturday Review*. https://www.unz.com/print/SaturdayRev-1967mar18-00051/.

Cunningham, R., Walton, M., & Carter, P. 2018, December 20. The major causes of death in children and adolescents in the United States. *New England Journal of Medicine*, 369. https://www.nejm.org/doi/full/10.1056/NEJMsr1804754.

Curriculum Associates. 2020, October 5. New data from Curriculum Associates quantifies impact of COVID learning loss; raises questions about at-home testing. Press release. https://www.curriculumassociates.com/about/press-releases/2020/10/covid-learning-loss.

Cuschieri, S. & Grech, S. 2020. COVID-19: A one-way ticket to a global childhood obesity crisis? *Journal of diabetes and metabolic disorders*, 19(2): 1–4. https://doi.org/10.1007/s40200-020-00682-2.

Cyberspace Administration of China. 2021, August 27. 关于进一步加强"饭圈"乱象治理的通知-中共中央网络安全和信息化委员会办公室. 国家互联网信息办公室 [Notice on further strengthening the governance of chaos in the 'fan circle']. http://www.cac.gov.cn/2021-08/26/c_1631563902354584.htm.

Czepczor-Bernat, K., Swami, V., Modrzejewska, A. & Modrzejewska, J. 2021. COVID-19-related stress and anxiety, body mass index, eating disorder symptomatology, and body image in women from Poland: A cluster analysis approach. *Nutrients*, 13(4). http://doi.org/10.3390/nu13041384.

D. Anon. 2020, September 9. Stop CSUF from using Invasive programs like Proctorio. Change.org. https://www.change.org/p/california-state-university-fullerton-stop-csuf-from-using-invasive-programs-like-proctorio.

da Silva, I.S. 2020, May 28. Covid-19 reveals digital divide as Africa struggles with distance learning. *TRT World*. https://www.trtworld.com/magazine/covid-19-reveals-digital-divide-as-africa-struggles-with-distance-learning-37299.

Dahir, A.L. 2018, August 6. This documentary tells the story of Africa's longest internet shutdown. Quartz. https://qz.com/africa/1349108/cameroons-internet-shutdown-in-blacked-out-documentary/.

Dahir, A.L. 2020, August 5. Kenya's unusual solution to the school problem: Cancel the year and start over. *New York Times*. https://www.nytimes.com/2020/08/05/world/africa/Kenya-cancels-school-year-coronavirus.html.

Dailey, N. 2021, December 7. Roblox has added nearly $26 billion to its market cap as metaverse mania pushes its value past brands like FedEx and Ferrari. Markets Insider. https://markets.businessinsider.com/news/stocks/roblox-more-valuable-than-fedex-ferrari-amid-metaverse-mania-2021-12.

Daily Illini. 2020, October 15. Virtual proctors worsen the overall academic environment. https://dailyillini.com/opinions/2020/10/15/editorial-virtual-proctors-worsen-the-overall-academic-environment/.

Dane, A. & Bhatia, K. 2023, March 22. The social media diet: A scoping review to investigate the association between social media, body image and eating disorders amongst young people. *PLOS Global Public Health*. https://doi.org/10.1371/journal.pgph.0001091.

Danner, J. 2018, May 14. 5 differences between consumer and institutional edtech. Medium. https://medium.com/beyond-schools/5-differences-between-consumer-and-institutional-edtech-23de38a27ace.

Das, B. 2021. Dartmouth drops online cheating charges against med students. *College Post*. https://thecollegepost.com/dartmouth-drops-online-cheating-charges/.

Data Protection Commission. 2022, September 15. Data Protection Commission announces decision in Instagram inquiry. Press release. https://www.dataprotection.ie/news-media/press-releases/data-protection-commission-announces-decision-instagram-inquiry.

Davis, R.A., Conroy, J.C. & Clague, J. 2020. Schools as factories: The limits of a metaphor. *Journal of Philosophy of Education*, 54(5): 1471–1488. https://doi.org/10.1111/1467-9752.12525.

Davis, W. 2022, February 24. How many words does it take to make a mistake? *London Review of Books*, 44(4). https://www.lrb.co.uk/the-paper/v44/n04/william-davies/how-many-words-does-it-take-to-make-a-mistake.

Day, J. 2014, August 19. A transfigured faith. *Catholic Exchange*. https://catholicexchange.com/transfigured-faith/.

De Vynck, G. 2020, April 9. Google Classroom users doubled as quarantines spread. Bloomberg. https://www.bloomberg.com/news/articles/2020-04-09/google-widens-lead-in-education-market-as-students-rush-online.

Dean, B. 2021, October 10. Roblox user and growth stats 2022. Backlinko. https://backlinko.com/roblox-users.

Defend Digital Me et al. 2020, April 16. An open letter to policy makers, data protection authorities, and providers worldwide, regarding rapid technology adoption for educational aims. Available at https://consumerfed.org/testimonial/childrens-rights-must-be-protected-in-remote-learning/.

DeGeurin, M. 2023, May 10. 'Thirsty' AI: Training ChatGPT required enough water to fill a nuclear reactor's cooling tower, study finds. Gizmodo. https://gizmodo.com/chatgpt-ai-water-185000-gallons-training-nuclear-1850324249.

del Ninno, C. & Mills, B. 2015. *Safety Nets in Africa: Effective Mechanisms to Reach the Poor and Most Vulnerable*. Washington, DC: World Bank. https://elibrary.worldbank.org/doi/abs/10.1596/978-1-4648-0435-9.

Dentsu. 2021. https://www.dentsu.com/id/en/our-work/case-study-dentsu-ruangguru-belajar-di-rumah-aja.

Department of Education. 2021, June. *Education in a Pandemic: The Disparate Impacts of COVID-19 on America's Students*. Office for Civil Rights. https://www2.ed.gov/about/offices/list/ocr/docs/20210608-impacts-of-covid19.pdf.

DeSantis, R. 2020, September 3. 2 Calif. students get internet hotspot after viral tweet showed them using Taco Bell's free WiFi. *People*. https://people.com/human-interest/calif-students-internet-hotspot-taco-bells-wifi/.

Deutsche Welle. 2021, September 19. Nigerian kidnappers free 10 more students. https://www.dw.com/en/nigerian-kidnappers-free-10-more-students-after-collecting-ransom/a-59229911.

Dewar, C. 2021, October 4. Users report Twitter outage hours after Facebook, WhatsApp and Instagram go down. *The Herald*. https://www.heraldscotland.com/news/19624807.twitter-users-report-outage-facebook-whatsapp-instagram-go/.

Deyan, G. 2021, December 7. 21+ exciting WeChat statistics [2021 edition]. Tech Jury. Blog post. https://techjury.net/blog/wechat-statistics/#gref.

Dickler, J. 2020, November 8. Families jump to private schools as coronavirus drags on. CNBC. https://www.cnbc.com/2020/11/08/coronavirus-why-families-are-jumping-to-private-schools.html.

Dickler, J. 2021, May 7. During Covid, more families switch to private school from public education. CNBC. https://www.cnbc.com/2021/05/07/during-covid-more-families-switch-to-private-school-from-public-.html.

Diliberti, M. & Kaufman, J. 2020. *Will this School Year Be Another Casualty of the Pandemic? Key Findings from the American Educator Panels Fall 2020 COVID-19 Surveys*. RAND Corporation. https://www.rand.org/pubs/research_reports/RRA168-4.html.

Dittmann, M. 2004, June. Protecting children from advertising. *American Psychological Association*, 35(6). https://www.apa.org/monitor/jun04/protecting.

Djankov, S., Zhang, Y. 2020, December 15. COVID-19 widens gender gap in labor force participation in some but not other advanced economies. Peterson Institute for International Economics. https://www.piie.com/blogs/realtime-economic-issues-watch/covid-19-widens-gender-gap-labor-force-participation-some-not.

Domingue, B., Hough, H., Lang, D. & Yeatman, J. 2021, March. Changing patterns of growth in oral reading fluency during the COVID-19 pandemic. Policy Analysis for California Education. https://edpolicyinca.org/publications/changing-patterns-growth-oral-reading-fluency-during-covid-19-pandemic.

Donovan, J., Caplan, R., Matthews, J. & Hanson, L. 2018, April 18. Algorithmic accountability: A primer. Data & Society. https://datasociety.net/wp-content/uploads/2018/04/Data_Society_Algorithmic_Accountability_Primer_FINAL.pdf.

Dorn, E., Hancock, B., Sarakatsannis, J. & Viruleg, E. 2020, June 1. COVID-19 and student learning in the United States: The hurt could last a lifetime. McKinsey & Company. https://www.mckinsey.com/industries/education/our-insights/covid-19-and-student-learning-in-the-united-states-the-hurt-could-last-a-lifetime.

Dowsett, S. 2020, June 23. Generation COVID: The Spanish learners lost to lockdown. Reuters. https://www.reuters.com/article/us-health-coronavirus-spain-education-in-idUSKBN23U1EP.

Drape, J. 2021, December 19. Step Aside, LeBron and Dak, and make room for Banjo and Kazooie. *New York Times*. https://www.nytimes.com/2021/12/19/sports/esports-fans-leagues-games.html.

Dube, R. 2020, August 4. Bolivia decision to cancel school because of Covid-19 upsets parents. *Wall Street Journal*. https://www.wsj.com/articles/bolivia-decision-to-cancel-school-because-of-covid-19-upsets-parents-11596577822.

Dudley, T. 2020, August 18. *College Marketing in the COVID-19 Economy*. The Century Foundation. https://tcf.org/content/report/college-marketing-covid-19-economy/.

Durant, D.M. 2017. *Reading in a Digital Age*. Charleston, VA: Against the Grain.

Dvorak, P. 2020, August 27. When 'back to school' means a parking lot and the hunt for a WiFi signal. *Washington Post*. https://www.washingtonpost.com/local/when-back-to-school-means-a-parking-lot-and-the-hunt-for-a-wifi-signal/2020/08/27/0f785d5a-e873-11ea-970a-64c73a1c2392_story.html.

DW News. 2020, February 22. The deadly cost of cobalt or smartphones | DW Stories. YouTube video. https://www.youtube.com/watch?v=LJjH4EQcayk.

Dyusengulova, R. 2022, January 17. Как будут учиться казахстанские школьники и студенты [How Kazakhstani schoolchildren and students will study]. Tengrinews. https://tengrinews.kz/kazakhstan_news/kak-budut-uchitsya-kazahstanskie-shkolniki-i-studentyi-459401/.

Ecolhuma. 2020, May. Enquête – Confinement et décrochage scolaire [Survey – Confinement and dropping out of school]. https://ecolhuma.fr/communiques/enquete-confinement-et-decrochage-scolaire/.

Economic Times. 2009, February 18. Oscar favorite Slumdog Millionaire inspired by NIIT's 'Hole in the Wall' initiative. https://economictimes.indiatimes.com/oscar-favorite-slumdog-millionaire-inspired-by-niits-hole-in-the-wall-initiative/articleshow/4151133.cms.

Economist, The. 2016, August 4. Look before you leap. https://www.economist.com/business/2016/08/04/look-before-you-leap.

Economist, The. 2020, March 26. Countries are using apps and data networks to keep tabs on the pandemic. https://www.economist.com/briefing/2020/03/26/countries-are-using-apps-and-data-networks-to-keep-tabs-on-the-pandemic.

Economist, The. 2020, November 24. People are working longer hours during the pandemic. https://www.economist.com/graphic-detail/2020/11/24/people-are-working-longer-hours-during-the-pandemic.

Economist, The. 2021, February 22. Covid-19 has persuaded some parents that home-schooling is better. https://www.economist.com/international/2021/02/22/covid-19-has-persuaded-some-parents-that-home-schooling-is-better.

Ederle, R. 2020. New Udemy report shows surge in global online education in response to COVID-19. Udemy. Press release. https://about.udemy.com/press-releases/new-udemy-report-shows-surge-in-global-online-education-in-response-to-covid-19/.

EdTech Fund. 2022. About. http://www.theedtechfund.com/about/.

EdTech Hub. 2022. Our team. https://edtechhub.org/our-team/.

EdTech Tools for Online Classes. 2022, March 19. Online proctoring, cheating methods, human, and AI-based proctoring tools. YouTube video. https://www.youtube.com/watch?v=pHg6aoywSQo.

EdTech: Focus on Higher Education. 2022. About us. https://edtechmagazine.com/higher/about-us.

Education and Early Childhood Development Executive Council. Government of Newfoundland and Labrador. 2020, July 6. Provincial government announces $20 million for technology to support digital learning. Government of Newfoundland and Labrador. Press release. https://www.gov.nl.ca/releases/2020/eecd/0706n02/.

Education Development Center. 2021, January 6. Interactive audio instruction makes a comeback. https://www.edc.org/interactive-audio-instruction-makes-comeback.

Educational Technology and Society. https://www.j-ets.net/.

Educational Technology Research and Development. https://www.springer.com/journal/11423/aims-and-scope.

Edwards, D. 2022, January 12. On Edtech, the public good, and democracy. Worlds of Education. https://www.ei-ie.org/en/item/24809:on-edtech-the-public-good-and-democracy.

Edwards, S. 2019, June 19. Ed tech research hub launched. Devex. https://www.devex.com/news/sponsored/ed-tech-research-hub-launched-95129.

Eggleston, C. & Fields, J. 2021, March 21. Census bureau's household pulse survey shows significant increase in homeschooling rates in fall 2020. United States Census Bureau. https://www.census.gov/library/stories/2021/03/homeschooling-on-the-rise-during-covid-19-pandemic.html.

Electronic Frontier Foundation. 2021, April 21. EFF sues Proctorio on behalf of student it falsely accused of copyright infringement to get critical tweets taken down. Press release. https://www.eff.org/press/releases/eff-sues-proctorio-behalf-student-it-falsely-accused-copyright-infringement-get.

Electronic Frontier Foundation. 2021. Examsoft, Proctorio, ProctorU responses to Senate letter. https://www.eff.org/it/document/proctoring-companies-responses-senate-letter.

Empath. 2023. Empath. https://www.webempath.com/.

Engler, A. 2021. Enrollment algorithms are contributing to the crises of higher education. Brookings. https://www.brookings.edu/research/enrollment-algorithms-are-contributing-to-the-crises-of-higher-education/.

Engzell, P., Frey, A. & Verhagen, M. 2020, October 29. Learning loss due to school closures during the COVID-19 pandemic. *PNAS*, 118(17). https://doi.org/10.1073/pnas.2022376118.

EQUALS Global Partnership for Gender Equality in the Digital Age. 2022. We are EQUALS. https://www.equalsintech.org/about.

Ericsson. 2020. *Ericsson Mobility Report*. https://www.ericsson.com/4adc87/assets/local/reports-papers/mobility-report/documents/2020/november-2020-ericsson-mobility-report.pdf.

Ericsson. 2021. *This is 5G*. https://www.ericsson.com/49f1c9/assets/local/5g/documents/07052021-ericsson-this-is-5g.pdf.

Errick, K. 2021, March 15. Students sue online exam proctoring service ProctorU for biometrics violations following data breach. Law Street. https://lawstreetmedia.com/news/tech/students-sue-online-exam-proctoring-service-proctoru-for-biometrics-violations-following-data-breach/.

Escueta, M., Quan, V., Nickow, A.J. & Oreopoulos, P. 2017, August. Education technology: An evidence-based review. Working paper 23744. National Bureau of Economic Research. https://www.nber.org/papers/w23744.

Esquivel, P., Blume, H., Poston, B. & Barajas, J. 2020, August 13. A generation left behind? Online learning cheats poor students, Times survey finds. *Los Angeles Times*. https://www.latimes.com/california/story/2020-08-13/online-learning-fails-low-income-students-covid-19-left-behind-project.

Estes, A.C. 2020, March 25. Why the internet (probably) won't break during the coronavirus pandemic. Vox. https://www.vox.com/recode/2020/3/25/21188391/internet-surge-traffic-coronavirus-pandemic.

ETF Express. 2020. September 20. Specialist Thematic ETF pioneer RIZE ETF launches sustainable food and edtech ETFs on SIX. Press release. https://rizeetf.com/wp-content/uploads/2020/09/03Sep20_Press_Release_Rize-launches-two-new-ETFs.pdf.

European Centre for Disease Prevention and Control. 2020, December 23. COVID-19 in children and the role of school settings in transmission – first update. https://www.ecdc.europa.eu/sites/default/files/documents/COVID-19-in-children-and-the-role-of-school-settings-in-transmission-first-update_1.pdf.

European Centre for Disease Prevention and Control. 2021, July 8. COVID-19 in children and the role of school settings in transmission – second update. https://www.ecdc.europa.eu/sites/default/files/documents/COVID-19-in-children-and-the-role-of-school-settings-in-transmission-second-update.pdf.

European Commission. 2021. Proposal for a regulation of the European Parliament and of the Council laying down harmonised rules on artificial intelligence (Artificial Intelligence Act) and amending certain union legislative acts. https://artificialintelligenceact.eu/the-act/.

European Data Protection Board. 2020. Contribution of the EDPB to the evaluation of the GDPR under Article 97. https://edpb.europa.eu/sites/default/files/files/file1/edpb_contributiongdprevaluation_20200218.pdf.

European Union. 2012, July 4. Directive 2012/19/EU of the European Parliament and of the Council of 4 July 2012 on waste electrical and electronic equipment (WEEE). https://eur-lex.europa.eu/eli/dir/2012/19/2018-07-04.

Eurostat. 2021, April 27. Almost 76 million pupils and students enrolled in the EU. https://ec.europa.eu/eurostat/web/products-eurostat-news/-/ddn-20210427-1.

Evans, D., Hares, S., Mendez Acosta, A. & Saintis, C. 2021, February 10. It's been a year since schools started to close due to COVID-19. Center for Global Development. Blog post. https://www.cgdev.org/blog/its-been-year-schools-started-close-due-covid-19.

Ewe, K. 2021, February 16. The wholesome appeal of watching people study on YouTube. Vice. https://www.vice.com/en/article/wx8yb9/study-with-me-gongbang-youtube-video-trend-asmr.

Examsoft BIPA Settlement. 2022. Welcome to the Examsoft BIPA settlement. https://www.esbipasettlement.com/.

Faek, R. 2021, April 18. Self-censorship in Arab higher education: An untold problem. Al-Fanar Media. https://www.al-fanarmedia.org/2021/04/self-censorship-in-arab-higher-education-an-untold-problem/.

Fairphone. https://www.fairphone.com/en/.

Fairplay. 2020, April 16. An open letter to policy makers, data protection authorities, and providers worldwide, regarding rapid edtech adoption. https://fairplayforkids.org/edtech-letter-blog/.

Fakiya, V. 2021, August 10. How South African edtech startup, FoondaMate, is helping students study with WhatsApp. TechPoint Africa. https://techpoint.africa/2021/08/10/south-african-edtech-foondamate-whatsapp/.

Fask, A., Englander, F. & Wang, Z. 2014. Do online exams facilitate cheating? An experiment designed to separate possible cheating from the effect of the online test taking environment. *Journal of Academic Ethics*, 12(2). https://doi.org/10.1007/s10805-014-9207-1.

Fatafta, M., Mnejja, K. & Anthonio, F. 2021, July 7. Internet shutdowns during exams: When MENA governments fail the test. Access Now. https://www.accessnow.org/mena-internet-shutdowns-during-exams/.

Fearn, N. 2021, March 8. Remote learning shows the power of the cloud to transform education. *Financial Times*. https://www.ft.com/content/3596847e-a981-42c0-8a6c-bc1c52d5cf04.

Feathers, T. & Rose, J. 2020, September 24. Students are rebelling against eye-tracking exam surveillance tools. Vice. https://www.vice.com/en/article/n7wxvd/students-are-rebelling-against-eye-tracking-exam-surveillance-tools.

Feathers, T. 2019, August 20. Flawed algorithms are grading millions of students' essays. Vice. https://www.vice.com/en/article/pa7djj9/flawed-algorithms-are-grading-millions-of-students-essays.

Feathers, T. 2020, October 21. An exam surveillance company is trying to silence critics with lawsuits. Vice. https://www.vice.com/en/article/7k9zjy/an-exam-surveillance-company-is-trying-to-silence-critics-with-lawsuits.

Feathers, T. 2021, April 8. Proctorio is using racist algorithms to detect faces. Vice. https://www.vice.com/en/article/g5gxg3/proctorio-is-using-racist-algorithms-to-detect-faces.

Feathers, T. 2021, February 26. Schools are abandoning invasive proctoring software after student backlash. Vice. https://www.vice.com/en/article/7k9ag4/schools-are-abandoning-invasive-proctoring-software-after-student-backlash.

Feathers, T. 2021, March 2. Major universities are using race as a "high impact predictor" of student success. The Markup. https://themarkup.org/machine-learning/2021/03/02/major-universities-are-using-race-as-a-high-impact-predictor-of-student-success.

Fedders, B. 2019. The constant and expanding classroom: Surveillance in K-12 public schools. *North Carolina Law Review*, 97(6). https://scholarship.law.unc.edu/nclr/vol97/iss6/4/.

Federal Communications Commission. 2020, March 15. FCC grants T-Mobile temporary spectrum access during coronavirus. Press release. https://www.fcc.gov/document/fcc-grants-t-mobile-temporary-spectrum-access-during-coronavirus.

Federal Ministry of Education, Nigeria. https://education.gov.ng/.

Ferguson, L. 2021. Vulnerable children's right to education, school exclusion, and pandemic law-making. *Emotional and Behavioural Difficulties*, 26(1): 101–115. https://www.tandfonline.com/doi/full/10.1080/13632752.2021.1913351.

Ferguson, N. et al. 2006, April 26. Strategies for mitigating an influenza pandemic. *Nature*, 442: 448–452. https://www.nature.com/articles/nature04795.

Ferlazzo, L. 2021, March 9. 'There is no playbook' for how to do hybrid teaching. *Education Week*. https://www.edweek.org/teaching-learning/opinion-there-is-no-playbook-for-how-to-do-hybrid-teaching/2021/03.

Field, T. et al. 1996. Massage therapy reduces anxiety and enhances eeg pattern of alertness and math computations. *International Journal of Neuroscience*, 86(3–4): 197–205. https://doi.org/10.3109/00207459608986710.

Fight for the Future. Proctorio and its CEO are worse than a proctology exam. https://www.proctorioisworsethanaproctologyexam.com.

Find Solution Ai. 2023. Product features. https://www.findsolutionai.com.

Finkelhor, D., Turner, H.A., Shattuck, A. & Hamby, S.L. 2013. Violence, crime, and abuse exposure in a national sample of children and youth: An update. *JAMA Pediatrics*, 167(7): 614–621. https://jamanetwork.com/journals/jamapediatrics/fullarticle/1686983.

Fischer, C. et al. 2020. Mining big data in education: Affordances and challenges. *Review of Research in Education*, 44(1): 130–160. https://doi.org/10.3102/0091732X20903304.

Fisher, A. & Margolis, J. 2002. Unlocking the clubhouse: the Carnegie Mellon experience. *Inroads SIGCSE Bulletin*, 34(2): 79–83. https://dl.acm.org/doi/10.1145/543812.543836.

Fitzpatrick, B.R., Berends, M., Ferrare, J.J. & Waddington, R.J. 2020. Virtual illusion: Comparing student achievement and teacher and classroom characteristics in online and brick-and-mortar charter schools. *Educational Researcher*, 49(3): 161–175. https://doi.org/10.3102/0013189X20909814.

Fitzsimmons, C. 2022, January 23. 'Sick of the disruption': Dramatic rise in children registered for home schooling. *Sydney Morning Herald*. https://www.smh.com.au/national/nsw/sick-of-the-disruption-dramatic-rise-in-children-registered-for-home-schooling-20220119-p59pfc.html.

Flaherty, C. 2020, May 11. Big proctor. *Inside Higher Ed*. https://www.insidehighered.com/news/2020/05/11/online-proctoring-surging-during-covid-19.

Flaherty, C. 2021, February 1. No more Proctorio. *Inside Higher Ed*. https://www.insidehighered.com/news/2021/02/01/u-illinois-says-goodbye-proctorio.

Fleming, N. 2021, January 23. After Covid, will digital learning be the new normal? *The Guardian*. https://www.theguardian.com/education/2021/jan/23/after-covid-will-digital-learning-be-the-new-normal.

Fontanet, A., Grant, R., Greve-Isdahl, M. & Sridhar, D. 2021, February 24. Covid-19: Keeping schools as safe as possible. *BMJ*, 372. https://doi.org/10.1136/bmj.n524.

Forbes Kazakhstan. 2020, April 5. Казахстанский стартап предоставил всем желающим бесплатный доступ к онлайн-урокам [Kazakh startup provides everyone with free access to online lessons]. https://forbes.kz/process/kazahstanskiy_startap_predostavil_vsem_besplatnyiy_dostup_k_onlayn-urokam/.

Forbes Kazakhstan. 2021, April 16. Как выходец из аула создал одну из крупнейших образовательных платформ в Казахстане [How a native of the village created one of the largest educational platforms in Kazakhstan]. https://forbes.kz/process/education/millionyi_besplatno_1618536199/.

Ford, K. 2021, October 11. Addressing the gender digital divide is critical to ensure no one is left behind from COVID-19. Young Lives. https://www.younglives.org.uk/news/addressing-gender-digital-divide-critical-ensure-no-one-left-behind-covid-19.

Forrest, K.B. 2021. *When Machines Can Be Judge, Jury, and Executioner: Justice in the Age of Artificial Intelligence*. Hackensack, NJ: World Scientific Publishing Company.

Forti, V., Balde, C., Kuehr, R. & Bel, G. 2020, July. *The Global E-Waste Monitor 2020: Quantities, Flows and the Circular Economy Potential*. United Nations University/United Nations Institute for Training, International Telecommunication Union, and Research and International Solid Waste Association. https://collections.unu.edu/view/UNU:7737.

Fortin, J. 2022, April 20. More pandemic fallout: The chronically absent student. *New York Times*. https://www.nytimes.com/2022/04/20/us/school-absence-attendance-rate-covid.html.

Foster, V., Comini, N. & Srinivasan, S. 2021, May 6. Improving data infrastructure helps ensure equitable access for poor people in poor countries. World Bank Blogs. https://blogs.worldbank.org/opendata/improving-data-infrastructure-helps-ensure-equitable-access-poor-people-poor-countries.

Foucault, M. 1975. *Discipline and Punish: The Birth of the Prison*. New York: Pantheon.

Fowler, G. 2020, August 10. Back-to-school laptop guide: Pandemic survival edition. *Washington Post*. https://www.washingtonpost.com/technology/2020/08/10/laptop-buyers-guide-distance-learning/.

France, P.E. 2020. *Reclaiming Personalized Learning: A Pedagogy for Restoring Equity and Humanity in Our Classrooms*. Thousand Oaks, CA: Corwin.

Franceinfo Afrique. 2020, June 29. Burkina Faso: malgré le coronavirus, les enfants travaillent toujours dans la carrière de Pissy [Burkina Faso: Despite the coronavirus, children are still working in Pissy's quarry]. https://www.francetvinfo.fr/monde/afrique/burkina-faso/burkina-faso-malgre-le-coronavirus-les-enfants-travaillent-toujours-dans-la-carriere-de-pissy_4023037.html.

Frank, R.H. 2020, June 5. Don't kid yourself: Online lectures are here to stay. *New York Times*. https://www.nytimes.com/2020/06/05/business/online-learning-winner-coronavirus.html.

Frankenfield, J. 2022, September 28. What Is EdTech? Definition, example, pros & cons. *Investopedia*. https://www.investopedia.com/terms/e/edtech.asp.

Fredman, S. 2021. A human rights approach: The right to education in the time of COVID-19. *Child Development*, 92(5): e900–e903. https://srcd.onlinelibrary.wiley.com/doi/10.1111/cdev.13654.

Freed, B. 2021, August 6. Texas school district paid $547K ransomware demand. EDSCOOP. https://edscoop.com/texas-school-paid-547k-ransomware-jam/.

Freed, B. 2021, July 23. 44% of education institutions targeted by ransomware in 2020, survey finds. EDSCOOP. https://edscoop.com/ransomware-education-institutions-sophos/.

Frenkel, S., Mac, R. & Isaac, M. 2021, October 16. Instagram struggles with fears of losing its 'pipeline': Young users. *New York Times*. https://www.nytimes.com/2021/10/16/technology/instagram-teens.html.

Frieden, T.R., Duncan, A. & Spellings, M. 2020, July 9. These 8 basic steps will let us reopen schools. *The Atlantic*. https://www.theatlantic.com/ideas/archive/2020/07/eight-steps-reopen-schools/613939/.

Friedman, M. 1962. *Capitalism and Freedom*. Chicago: University of Chicago Press.

Friedman, S.D. 2008, November 25. Do not waste this crisis. *Harvard Business Review*. https://hbr.org/2008/11/dont-waste-this-crisis.

Froehlich, M. 2021, July 27. Helping parents feel more comfortable with tech. Edutopia. https://www.edutopia.org/article/helping-parents-feel-more-comfortable-tech.

Fukumoto, K., McClean, C.T. & Nakagawa, K. 2021. No causal effect of school closures in Japan on the spread of COVID-19 in spring 2020. *Nature Medicine*, 27(12): 2111–2119. https://www.ncbi.nlm.nih.gov/pmc/articles/PMC8674136/.

Gallup Pakistan. 2020. National opinion poll on support and opposition for remote (online) education. https://gallup.com.pk/post/29335.

Gao, N., Lafortune, J. & Hill, L. 2020, October. *Who is Losing Ground with Distance Learning in California?* Public Policy Institute of California. https://www.ppic.org/wp-content/uploads/who-is-losing-ground-with-distance-learning-in-california-october-2020.pdf.

Garlen, J.C. 2021. The end of innocence: Childhood and schooling for a post-pandemic world. *Journal of Teaching and Learning*, 15(2): 21–39. https://jtl.uwindsor.ca/index.php/jtl/article/view/6724.

Gassman-Pines, A., Ananat, E., Fitz-Henley, J. & Leer, J. 2022, January. Effects of daily school and care disruptions during the covid-19 pandemic on child mental health. National Bureau of Economic Research. Working paper 29659. https://www.nber.org/papers/w29659.

Geiger, G. 2021, March 5. Students are easily cheating 'state-of-the-art' test proctoring tech. Vice. https://www.vice.com/en/article/3an98j/students-are-easily-cheating-state-of-the-art-test-proctoring-tech.

Geiger, G. et al. 2023, March 6. Suspicion machines. Lighthouse Reports. https://www.lighthousereports.com/investigation/suspicion-machines/.

Gendron, M., Lindquist, K.A., Barsalou, L. & Barrett, L.F. 2012. Emotion words shape emotion percepts. *Emotion* 12(2). https://psycnet.apa.org/record/2012-03012-001.

Gendron, M., Roberson, D., van der Vyver, J.M. & Barrett, L.F. 2014. Perceptions of emotion from facial expressions are not culturally universal: Evidence from a remote culture. *Emotion* 14(2). https://pubmed.ncbi.nlm.nih.gov/24708506/.

Gershgorn, D. 2021, February 19. The shoddy science behind emotional recognition tech. OneZero. https://onezero.medium.com/the-shoddy-science-behind-emotional-recognition-tech-2e847fc526a0.

GETChina Insights. 2019, September 9. Schools using facial recognition system sparks privacy concerns in China. Medium. https://edtechchina.medium.com/schools-using-facial-recognition-system-sparks-privacy-concerns-in-china-d4f706e5cfd0.

Ghallager, R. 2020, December 17. Best practices for securing your virtual classroom. Zoom. Blog post. https://blog.zoom.us/best-practices-for-securing-your-virtual-classroom/.

Giannini, S. 2020, May 15. Distance learning denied. Global Education Monitoring (GEM) Report. https://gemreportunesco.wordpress.com/2020/05/15/distance-learning-denied/.

Gifford, J. & Pyshkin, K. 2020. *Education Technology. Coronavirus and Beyond*. Credit Suisse. https://www.credit-suisse.com/media/assets/microsite/docs/responsibleinvesting/cs-education-technology-spread.pdf.

Gikandi, H. 2020, October 16. After months of closure, Kenya's schools adjust to sudden reopening. The World. https://theworld.org/stories/2020-10-16/after-months-closure-kenyas-schools-adjust-sudden-reopening.

Gill, V. 2022, October 14. E-waste: Five billion phones to be thrown away in 2022. BBC News. https://www.bbc.com/news/science-environment-63245150.

Gillespie, T. 2014. The relevance of algorithms. In T. Gillespie, P. J. Boczkowski, & K. A. Foot. (eds). *Media technologies: Essays on communication, materiality, and society*. London: MIT Press.

Gilliard, C. 2017. Pedagogy and the logic of platforms. *EDUCAUSE Review*, 52(4): 64–65. https://er.educause.edu/articles/2017/7/pedagogy-and-the-logic-of-platforms.

Gillum, J. & Kao, J. 2019, June 25. Aggression detectors: The unproven, invasive surveillance technology schools are using to monitor students. ProPublica. https://features.propublica.org/aggression-detector/the-unproven-invasive-surveillance-technology-schools-are-using-to-monitor-students/.

Gilmore, N. 2020, August 14. America's school nursing crisis came at the worst time. *Saturday Evening Post*. https://www.saturdayeveningpost.com/2020/08/americas-school-nursing-crisis-came-at-the-worst-time/.

Gilraine, M. 2020. Air filters, pollution and student achievement. EdWorkingPaper 19-188. Retrieved from Annenberg Institute at Brown University. https://doi.org/10.26300/7mcr-8a10.

Ginsburg, K.R., Committee on Communications & Committee on Psychosocial Aspects of Child and Family Health. 2007, January. The importance of play in promoting healthy child development and maintaining strong parent-child bonds. *Pediatrics*, 119(1): 182–191. https://pubmed.ncbi.nlm.nih.gov/17200287/.

Girl Effect & Vodafone Foundation. 2018. *Real Girls, Real Lives, Connected*. https://www.global.girleffect.org/stories/real-girls-real-lives-connected/.

Global Coalition to Protect Education from Attack. 2022. The Safe Schools Declaration. https://ssd.protectingeducation.org/safe-schools-declaration-and-guidelines-on-military-use/.

GlobalData Thematic Research. 2021, August 2. China's edtech companies face an uncertain financial future. Verdict. https://www.verdict.co.uk/chinas-edtech-companies-face-an-uncertain-financial-future/.

Goldhaber, D. et al. 2022, May. *The Consequences of Remote and Hybrid Instruction During the Pandemic*. Center for Education Policy Research, Harvard University. https://cepr.harvard.edu/files/cepr/files/5-4.pdf.

Goldstein, D. & Parlapiano, A. 2021, August 7. The kindergarten exodus. *New York Times*. https://www.nytimes.com/2021/08/07/us/covid-kindergarten-enrollment.html.

Goldstein, D. 2022, January 21. Back to school, but still learning online. *New York Times*. https://www.nytimes.com/2022/01/21/us/online-tutoring-stimulus-funding.html.

Goldstein, J. & Otterman, S. 2022, March 17. What New York got wrong about the pandemic, and what it got right. *New York Times*. https://www.nytimes.com/2022/03/17/nyregion/new-york-pandemic-lessons.html.

Goleman, D. & Norris, G. 2010, April 4. How green is my iPad? *New York Times*. https://archive.nytimes.com/www.nytimes.com/interactive/2010/04/04/opinion/04opchart.html.

Goodman, P.S. & Bradsher, K. 2021, August 30. The world is still short of everything. get used to it. *New York Times*. https://www.nytimes.com/2021/08/30/business/supply-chain-shortages.html.

Goodnough, A. 2020, August 14. Families priced out of 'learning pods' seek alternatives. *New York Times*. https://www.nytimes.com/2020/08/14/us/covid-schools-learning-pods.html.

Google for Education. 2018. *Future of the Classroom: Emerging trends in the K-12 Education*. https://services.google.com/fh/files/misc/future_of_the_classroom_emerging_trends_in_k12_education.pdf.

Google for Education. 2022. Distinguish yourself in your classroom and career with certifications from Google for Education. https://edu.google.com/intl/ALL_us/for-educators/certification-programs/product-expertise/.

Google for Education. 2022. Google Workspace for Education Terms of Service. https://workspace.google.com/terms/education_terms.html.

Google Play. 2022. Google Classroom. https://play.google.com/store/apps/details?id=com.google.android.apps.classroom.

Google. 2020. G Suite for Education (Online) Agreement. https://workspace.google.com/terms/2020/education_terms.html.

Google. 2022. Giving teachers and families the tools and tips they need to help keep students learning. Teach from Anywhere. https://teachfromanywhere.google/intl/en/.

Google. 2022. Teach from Anywhere. https://teachfromanywhere.google/intl/en/.

Goudeau, S., Sanrey, C., Stanczak, A., Manstead, A. & Darnon, C. 2021. Why lockdown and distance learning during the COVID-19 pandemic are likely to increase the social class achievement gap. *Nature Human Behaviour*, 5(10): 1273–1281. https://doi.org/10.1038/s41562-021-01212-7.

Gould, E. 2020, August 18. Remote learning is a bad joke. *The Atlantic*. https://www.theatlantic.com/ideas/archive/2020/08/kindergartener-virtual-education/615316/.

Graham, L.M. & Van Zyl-Chavarro, A.B. 2018. Part III rights to culture: Ch. 13 Indigenous education and the UNDRIP: Article 14. In Hohmann, J. & Weller, M. (eds). *The UN Declaration on the Rights of Indigenous Peoples: A Commentary*. Oxford: Oxford University Press.

Graham, R. 2021, October 19. Christian schools boom in a revolt against curriculum and pandemic rules. *New York Times*. https://www.nytimes.com/2021/10/19/us/christian-schools-growth.html.

Grajek, S. 2020, April 10. EDUCAUSE COVID-19 quickpoll results: Grading and proctoring. *EDUCAUSE Review*. https://er.educause.edu/blogs/2020/4/educause-covid-19-quickpoll-results-grading-and-proctoring.

Grant-Chapman, H., Laird, E. & Venzke, C. 2021, September 21. Student activity monitoring software: Research insights and recommendations. Center for Democracy and Technology. https://cdt.org/insights/student-activity-monitoring-software-research-insights-and-recommendations/.

Grant, H., Hayden, S., Kumar, R. & Taylor, L. 2021, April 5. 'I miss school': 800m children still not fully back in classes. *The Guardian*. https://www.theguardian.com/global-development/2021/apr/05/schools-800-million-children-education-disrupted.

Gray, P. 2011. The decline of play and the rise of psychopathology in children and adolescents. *American Journal of Play*, 3(4): 443–463. https://www.researchgate.net/publication/265449180_The_Decline_of_Play_and_the_Rise_of_Psychopathology_in_Children_and_Adolescents.

Green, F. 2020. *Schoolwork in Lockdown: New Evidence on the Epidemic of Educational Poverty. LLAKES Research Paper 67*. UCL Institute of Education and Centre for Learning and Life Chances in Knowledge Economies and Societies. https://www.llakes.ac.uk/wp-content/uploads/2021/01/67-Francis-Green-Research-Paper-combined-file.pdf.

Greene, D. 2021. *The Promise of Access: Technology, Inequality, and the Political Economy of Hope*. Cambridge, MA: MIT Press.

Greene, P. 2019, July 15. What can we learn from an experimental high tech Wunderschool failure? Forbes. https://www.forbes.com/sites/petergreene/2019/07/15/what-can-we-learn-from-an-experimental-high-tech-charter-wunderschool-failure/.

Grose, J. 2022, September 1. School is for care. *New York Times*. https://www.nytimes.com/2022/09/01/opinion/us-school-care.html.

Gulson, K.N., Sellar, S. & Webb, P.T. 2022. *Algorithms of Education: How Datafication and Artificial Intelligence Shape Policy*. Minneapolis: University of Minnesota Press.

Gunes, H. & Pantic, M. 2010. Automatic, dimensional and continuous emotion recognition. *International Journal of Synthetic Emotions*, 1(1). https://ibug.doc.ic.ac.uk/media/uploads/documents/GunesPantic_IJSE_2010_camera.pdf.

Gupta, R. 2020, May 15. No internet, no electricity: Online education a struggle for rural students. SheThePeople. https://www.shethepeople.tv/home-top-video/online-eduction-rural-students-india.

Haidt, J. & Twenge, J.M. 2021, July 31. This is our chance to pull teenagers out of the smartphone trap. *New York Times*. https://www.nytimes.com/2021/07/31/opinion/smartphone-iphone-social-media-isolation.html.

Haidt, J. 2021, November 21. The dangerous experiment on teen girls. *The Atlantic*. https://www.theatlantic.com/ideas/archive/2021/11/facebooks-dangerous-experiment-teen-girls/620767/.

Haidt, J. 2022, April 11. Why the past 10 years of American life have been uniquely stupid. *The Atlantic*. https://www.theatlantic.com/magazine/archive/2022/05/social-media-democracy-trust-babel/629369/.

Hallett, V. 2021, February 10. How the pandemic is changing children's friendships. *National Geographic*. https://www.nationalgeographic.co.uk/family/2021/02/how-the-pandemic-is-changing-childrens-friendships.

Hamamra, B., Qabaha, A. & Daragmeh, A. 2022. Online education and surveillance during COVID-19 pandemic in Palestinian universities. *International Studies in Sociology of Education*, 31(4): 446–466. https://www.tandfonline.com/doi/full/10.1080/09620214.2021.2016473.

Hancock, B. 2022, April 12. Open Letter to VC: Proctorio risks student privacy, mental health. https://tertangala.net/?p=596.

Hannon, T. 2021, May 19. FCC approves school bus Wi-Fi hotspots under COVID-19 emergency connectivity fund. *School Transportation News*. https://stnonline.com/news/fcc-approves-school-bus-wi-fi-hotspots-under-covid-19-emergency-connectivity-fund/.

Hansen, M. & Komljenovic, J. 2022. Automating Learning Situations in EdTech: Techno-Commercial Logic of Assetisation. *Postdigital Science and Education*, 5. https://doi.org/10.1007/s42438-022-00359-4.

Hao, K. 2020, December 4. We read the paper that forced Timnit Gebru out of Google. Here's what it says. *MIT Technology Review*. https://www.technologyreview.com/2020/12/04/1013294/google-ai-ethics-research-paper-forced-out-timnit-gebru/.

Harkness, T. 2020, August 18. How Ofqual failed the algorithm test. UnHerd. https://unherd.com/2020/08/how-ofqual-failed-the-algorithm-test/.

Harris, A. 2014, May 9. How this startup's "micro-school" network could change the way we educate now. Fast Company. https://www.fastcompany.com/3028073/how-this-startups-micro-school-network-could-change-the-way-we-educate-now.

Harris, B. 2021, April 3. Tears, sleepless nights and small victories: How first-year teachers are weathering the crisis. *Southern Maryland Chronicle*. https://southernmarylandchronicle.com/2021/04/03/tears-sleepless-nights-and-small-victories-how-first-year-teachers-are-weathering-the-crisis/.

Harris, E.A. 2020, April 27. 'It was just too much': How remote learning is breaking parents. *New York Times*. https://www.nytimes.com/2020/04/27/nyregion/coronavirus-homeschooling-parents.html.

Harwell, D. 2020, April 1. Mass school closures in the wake of the coronavirus are driving a new wave of student surveillance. *Washington Post*. https://www.washingtonpost.com/technology/2020/04/01/online-proctoring-college-exams-coronavirus/.

Harwell, D. 2020, November 12. Cheating-detection companies made millions during the pandemic. Now students are fighting back. *Washington Post*. https://www.washingtonpost.com/technology/2020/11/12/test-monitoring-student-revolt/.

Hawkins, S. 2022, March 15. Proctor360 faces class action for collecting student biometrics. Bloomberg Law. https://news.bloomberglaw.com/privacy-and-data-security/proctor360-faces-class-action-for-collecting-student-biometrics.

Head, J.R. et al. 2021, April 14. School closures reduced social mixing of children during COVID-19 with implications for transmission risk and school reopening policies. *Journal of the Royal Society Interface*, 18(177). https://royalsocietypublishing.org/doi/10.1098/rsif.2020.0970.

Hearne, B. & Rodrigues, P. 2021, November. *The International Student Experience: Impact of the Covid-19 Pandemic on International Students in Ireland*. Next Steps for Teaching and Learning. https://www.researchgate.net/publication/356148792_The_International_Student_Experience_Impact_of_the_Covid-19_Pandemic_on_International_Students_in_Ireland.

Heaven, D. 2020, February 26. Why faces don't always tell the truth about feelings. *Nature*. https://www.nature.com/articles/d41586-020-00507-5.

Help Your Teen Now. 2021, March 24. Recognizing if cyberbullying is happening over Zoom classes. Blog post. https://helpyourteennow.com/cyberbullying-in-online-zoom-classes/.

Hendry, J. 2018, January 30. Govts dump NAPLAN robo marking plans. iTnews. https://www.itnews.com.au/news/govts-dump-naplan-robo-marking-plans-482044.

Henriques-Gomes, L. 2020, August 19. Australian children with disabilities excluded from online learning during pandemic, inquiry told. *The Guardian*. https://www.theguardian.com/australia-news/2020/aug/19/australian-children-with-disabilities-excluded-from-online-learning-during-pandemic-inquiry-told.

Hern, A. 2020, August 21. Ofqual's A-level algorithm: Why did it fail to make the grade? *The Guardian*. https://www.theguardian.com/education/2020/aug/21/ofqual-exams-algorithm-why-did-it-fail-make-grade-a-levels.

Hern, A. 2021, September 2. UK children's digital privacy code comes into effect. *The Guardian*. https://www.theguardian.com/technology/2021/sep/02/uk-childrens-digital-privacy-code-comes-into-effect.

Hernandez, M.D., Anthonio, F., Cheng, S. & Skok, A. 2022, April 28. Internet shutdowns in 2021: The return of digital authoritarianism. Access Now. https://www.accessnow.org/internet-shutdowns-2021/.

Herold, B. 2016, January 11. The future of big data and analytics in K-12 education. *Education Week*. https://www.edweek.org/policy-politics/the-future-of-big-data-and-analytics-in-k-12-education/2016/01.

Herold, B. 2020, July 23. Schools handed out millions of digital devices under COVID-19. Now, thousands are missing. *Education Week*. https://www.edweek.org/technology/schools-handed-out-millions-of-digital-devices-under-covid-19-now-thousands-are-missing/2020/07.

Hershberg, E., Flinn-Palcic, A. & Kambhu, C. 2020, June 2. *The COVID-19 Pandemic and Latin American Universities*. Center for Latin American & Latino Studies at American University. https://www.american.edu/centers/latin-american-latino-studies/upload/la-higher-ed-covid-final.pdf.

Hevia, F.J., Vergara-Lope, S., Velásquez-Durán, A. & Calderón, D. 2022. Estimation of the fundamental learning loss and learning poverty related to COVID-19 pandemic in Mexico. *International Journal of Educational Development*, 88. https://doi.org/10.1016/j.ijedudev.2021.102515.

Hew, K.F. & Cheung, W.S. 2014. Students' and instructors' use of massive open online courses (MOOCs): Motivations and challenges. *Educational Research Review*, 12: 45–58. https://doi.org/10.1016/j.edurev.2014.05.001.

High, P. 2018, August 20. How 174-year-old Pearson is developing the Netflix of education. Forbes. https://www.forbes.com/sites/peterhigh/2018/08/20/how-174-year-old-pearson-is-developing-the-netflix-of-education/.

Hill, K. 2022, May 27. Accused of cheating by an algorithm, and a professor she had never met. *New York Times*. https://www.nytimes.com/2022/05/27/technology/college-students-cheating-software-honorlock.html.

Hillis, S.D. et al. 2021, July 20. Global minimum estimates of children affected by COVID-19-associated orphanhood and deaths of caregivers: a modelling study. The Lancet, 398(10298): 391–402. https://doi.org/10.1016/S0140-6736(21)01253-8.

Hillman, V. & Esquivel, M. 2022, May 18. Algorithmic personalization is disrupting a healthy teaching environment. London School of Economics. https://blogs.lse.ac.uk/medialse/2022/05/18/algorithmic-personalization-is-disrupting-a-healthy-teaching-environment/.

Hillman, V., Noula, I. & Wagner, B. 2021, July 14. Big tech firms can't be trusted to decide children's futures. *Jacobin*. https://jacobin.com/2021/07/big-tech-children-future-covid-pandemic-education-privacy-data.

Hirsh-Pasek, K. et al. 2015. Putting education in 'educational' apps: Lessons from the science of learning. *Psychological Science in the Public Interest*, 16(1): 3–34. https://doi.org/10.1177/1529100615569721.

Hobbs, C.N., Kreiner, D.S., Honeycutt, M.W., Hinds, R.M. & Brockman, C.J. 2010. The illusion of control in a virtual reality setting. *North American Journal of Psychology*, 12(3). https://www.proquest.com/docview/821544774.

Hodgson, D. & Papadimoulis, F. 2022, September. *Pulp and Paper*. International Energy Agency. https://www.iea.org/reports/pulp-and-paper.

Hole-in-the-Wall Education Ltd. About HiWEL: Beginnings. https://web.archive.org/web/20071013033113/http://www.hole-in-the-wall.com/Beginnings.html.

HolonIQ. 2020, August 6. Global EdTech market to reach $404B by 2025 – 16.3% CAGR. https://www.holoniq.com/notes/global-education-technology-market-to-reach-404b-by-2025/.

HolonIQ. 2020, May 21. Prototyping global education stock indices. https://www.holoniq.com/notes/prototyping-global-education-stock-indices/.

HolonIQ. 2020, October 15. EdTech unicorn mega-funding evolution. https://www.holoniq.com/notes/edtech-unicorn-mega-funding-evolution.

HolonIQ. 2021. Education technology in 10 charts: Everything you need to know about the global EdTech market in 10 charts. https://www.holoniq.com/edtech-in-10-charts.

HolonIQ. 2022, January 2. Global EdTech venture capital report: Full year 2021. https://www.holoniq.com/notes/global-edtech-venture-capital-report-full-year-2021.

HolonIQ. 2022. Global EdTech unicorns: The complete list of global EdTech unicorns. https://www.holoniq.com/edtech-unicorns.

Hooper, L., Livingstone, S. & Pothong, K. 2022. *Problems with Data Governance in UK Schools: The Cases of Google Classroom and ClassDojo*. Digital Futures Commission & 5Rights Foundation. https://digitalfuturescommission.org.uk/wp-content/uploads/2022/08/Problems-with-data-governance-in-UK-schools.pdf.

Horwitz, S. 2015, June 22. Cooperation over coercion: The importance of unsupervised childhood play for democracy and liberalism. SSRN. http://dx.doi.org/10.2139/ssrn.2621848.

House of Commons Education Committee. 2021, July 21. Strengthening Home Education: Third Report of Session 2021–22. https://committees.parliament.uk/publications/6974/documents/72808/default/.

House of Commons Women and Equalities Committee. 2020. Body Image Survey Results. First Special Report of Session 2019–21. https://committees.parliament.uk/publications/2691/documents/26657/default/.

Hubler, S. 2020, May 10. Keeping online testing honest? Or an Orwellian overreach? *New York Times*. https://www.nytimes.com/2020/05/10/us/online-testing-cheating-universities-coronavirus.html.

Human Rights Watch. 2020, August 26. Impact of Covid-19 on children's education in Africa. 35th ordinary session. https://www.hrw.org/news/2020/08/26/impact-covid-19-childrens-education-africa#_edn6.

Human Rights Watch. 2020, June 19. Myanmar: End world's longest internet shutdown. https://www.hrw.org/news/2020/06/19/myanmar-end-worlds-longest-internet-shutdown.

Human Rights Watch. 2021, May 17. "It feels like maybe I won't ever go to school again": Children, parents, and teachers describe the impact of Covid school closures. https://www.hrw.org/video-photos/interactive/2021/05/17/it-feels-maybe-i-wont-ever-go-school-again.

Human Rights Watch. 2021, May 17. *"Years Don't Wait for Them": Increased Inequalities in Children's Right to Education Due to the Covid-19 Pandemic*. https://www.hrw.org/report/2021/05/17/years-dont-wait-them/increased-inequalities-childrens-right-education-due-covid.

Human Rights Watch. 2022, May 25. *"How Dare They Peep into My Private Life?": Children's Rights Violations by Governments that Endorsed Online Learning During the Covid-19 Pandemic*. https://www.hrw.org/report/2022/05/25/how-dare-they-peep-my-private-life/childrens-rights-violations-governments.

Human Rights Watch. 2022, May 25. Governments harm children's rights in online learning. https://www.hrw.org/news/2022/05/25/governments-harm-childrens-rights-online-learning.

Hume AI. 2023. Expressive language. Hume AI. https://hume.ai/.

Hutton, J.S., Dudley, J., Horowitz-Kraus, T., DeWitt, T. & Holland, S.K. 2020. Associations between screen-based media use and brain white matter integrity in preschool-aged children. *JAMA Pediatrics*, 174(1): e193869. https://pubmed.ncbi.nlm.nih.gov/31682712/.

Ibanez, J. 2022, July 5. Indonesia's Ruangguru acquires two edtech startups. *Tech in Asia*. https://www.techinasia.com/indonesias-ruangguru-acquires-edtech-startups.

Ibarrarán, P. 2012, March 6. And the jury is back: One Laptop per Child is not enough. Inter-American Development Bank. Blog post. https://blogs.iadb.org/efectividad-desarrollo/en/and-the-jury-is-back-one-laptop-per-child-is-not-enough/.

Igo, S.E. 2022, April 6. The price of privacy. *The Atlantic*. https://www.theatlantic.com/magazine/archive/2022/05/privacy-law-technology-california-gajda-seek-and-hide/629373/.

Impey, C. 2020, July 23. Massive online open courses see exponential growth during COVID-19 pandemic. The Conversation. http://theconversation.com/massive-online-open-courses-see-exponential-growth-during-covid-19-pandemic-141859.

India Today. 2021, October 8. Why are students moving from private schools to government schools amidst Covid-19? https://www.indiatoday.in/education-today/news/story/students-moving-from-private-schools-to-government-schools-1858123-2021-10-08.

Information Commissioner's Office. 2023. Introduction to the Children's code. https://ico.org.uk/for-organisations/uk-gdpr-guidance-and-resources/childrens-information/childrens-code-guidance-and-resources/introduction-to-the-childrens-code/.

Inotai, E. 2021, January 19. Learning losses may lead to earning losses. Visegrad / Insight. https://visegradinsight.eu/learning-losses-may-lead-to-earning-losses/.

Insights for Education. 2021, January 25. *One Year of School Disruption*. https://img1.wsimg.com/blobby/go/104fc727-3bad-4ff5-944f-c281d3ceda7f/20210125_One year of school disruption_Insight.pdf.

International Baccalaureate. 2020. IB Assessment for May 2020 examination session during COVID-19 pandemic. https://www.ibo.org/globalassets/new-structure/covid-19/pdfs/assessment-model-letter-may-2020-en.pdf.

International Commission on the Futures of Education. 2021. *Reimagining Our Futures Together: A New Social Contract for Education*. UNESCO. https://unesdoc.unesco.org/ark:/48223/pf0000379707.

International Data Corporation. 2021. Cited in Business Wire. 2021, April 29. Tablet and Chromebook shipments continue to surge during the first quarter, according to IDC. https://www.businesswire.com/news/home/20210429005992/en/Tablet-and-Chromebook-Shipments-Continue-to-Surge-During-the-First-Quarter-According-to-IDC.

International Data Corporation. 2022, January 2022. Tablet and Chromebook shipments slowed in the fourth quarter but saw solid growth for 2021, according to IDC. https://www.idc.com/getdoc.jsp?containerId=prUS48826122.

International Labour Organization & UNICEF. 2021. *Child Labour: Global Estimates 2020, Trends and the Road Forward*. https://www.ilo.org/wcmsp5/groups/public/---ed_norm/---ipec/documents/publication/wcms_797515.pdf.

International Labour Organization. 2020, November 27. Fallout of COVID-19: Working moms are being squeezed out of the labour force. https://ilostat.ilo.org/fallout-of-covid-19-working-moms-are-being-squeezed-out-of-the-labour-force/.

International Labour Organization. 2021, June 12. How COVID-19 has accelerated child labour in the construction sector. https://www.ilo.org/africa/technical-cooperation/accel-africa/WCMS_801839/lang--en/index.htm.

International Labour Organization. 2021, June 2. An update on the youth labour market impact of the COVID-19 crisis. Briefing note. https://www.ilo.org/emppolicy/pubs/WCMS_795479/lang--en/index.htm.

International Labour Organization. 2022, March 8. Over 2 million moms left the labour force in 2020 according to new global estimates. https://ilostat.ilo.org/over-2-million-moms-left-the-labour-force-in-2020-according-to-new-global-estimates/.

International Rights Advocates. 2022. Multinational companies are liable for human rights abuses within their supply chains. https://www.internationalrightsadvocates.org/cases/cobalt.

Ipsos. 2022, January 17. Pharmaceutical and banking companies and governments are now seen as more trustworthy. Ipsos. https://www.ipsos.com/en/global-trustworthiness-monitor-2021.

Iran International. 2020, September 27. Iranian parents say schools pressuring girls to wear hijab in online classes. https://old.iranintl.com/en/iran-in-brief/iranian-parents-say-schools-pressuring-girls-wear-hijab-online-classes.

iReady & Curriculum Associates. 2021. *Academic Achievement at the End of the 2020–2021 School Year*. https://www.curriculumassociates.com/-/media/mainsite/files/i-ready/iready-understanding-student-needs-paper-spring-results-2021.pdf.

Isaac, M. & Frenkel, S. 2021, October 4. Gone in minutes, out for hours: Outage shakes Facebook. *New York Times*. https://www.nytimes.com/2021/10/04/technology/facebook-down.html.

ITU & UNESCO. 2020, September. *The State of Broadband 2020: Tackling Digital Inequalities – A Decade for Action*. https://www.itu.int/hub/publication/s-pol-broadband-21-2020/.

ITU Publications. 2018. *Measuring the Information Society Report: Volume 1, 2008*. International Telecommunication Union. https://www.itu.int/en/ITU-D/Statistics/Documents/publications/misr2018/MISR-2018-Vol-1-E.pdf.

ITU Publications. 2020, August. *Connecting Humanity: Assessing Investment Needs of Connecting Humanity to the Internet by 2030*. https://www.itu.int/dms_pub/itu-d/opb/gen/D-GEN-INVEST.CON-2020-PDF-E.pdf.

ITU Publications. 2020. *Measuring Digital Development: Facts and Figures 2020*. https://www.itu.int/en/ITU-D/Statistics/Documents/facts/FactsFigures2020.pdf.

ITU Publications. 2021, July. Bridging the gender divide. https://www.itu.int/en/mediacentre/backgrounders/Pages/bridging-the-gender-divide.aspx.

ITU Publications. 2021, October. *Connect2Recover: A methodology for identifying Connectivity Gaps and Strengthening Resilience in the New Normal*. https://www.itu.int/dms_pub/itu-d/opb/tnd/D-TND-04-2021-PDF-E.pdf.

ITU Publications. 2021. *Digital Trends in Africa 2021: Information and Communication Technology Trends and Developments in the Africa Region, 2017-2020*. https://www.itu.int/dms_pub/itu-d/opb/ind/D-IND-DIG_TRENDS_AFR.01-2021-PDF-E.pdf.

ITU Publications. 2021. *Measuring Digital Development: Facts and Figures 2021*. https://www.itu.int/en/ITU-D/Statistics/Documents/facts/FactsFigures2021.pdf.

ITU Publications. 2022. November 15. *ITU Facts and Figures 2022*. The gender digital divide. https://www.itu.int/itu-d/reports/statistics/2022/11/24/ff22-the-gender-digital-divide/.

Izard, C.E. 2010. The many meanings/aspects of emotion: Definitions, functions, activation, and regulation. *Emotion Review*, 2(4). https://journals.sagepub.com/doi/10.1177/1754073910374661.

J.S. 2020, August 31. Remove online proctoring methods from Auburn University. Change.org. https://www.change.org/p/auburn-university-remove-online-proctoring-methods-from-auburn-university.

Jabar, M.A. 2010, June 1. How do Japanese schools promote parental involvement? *International Journal of Social Sciences and Humanity Studies*, 2(1). https://dergipark.org.tr/en/pub/ijsshs/issue/26223/276230.

Jack, A. 2020, July 9. Students and teachers hit at International Baccalaureate grading. *Financial Times*. https://www.ft.com/content/ee0f4d97-4e0c-4bc3-8350-19855e70f0cf.

Jack, A. 2021, April 6. Invest now to repair 'huge' learning loss, educators urge. *Financial Times*. https://www.ft.com/content/b3d0cc12-61de-4143-91a6-ab9f98bbc7a9.

Jacobson, L. 2021, March 16. The teens who clean homes during Zoom classes: Juggling work and school in the pandemic. *The Guardian*. https://www.theguardian.com/us-news/2021/mar/16/us-teens-school-work-keep-families-afloat-recession.

Japan Data. 2020, November 17. Suicide rate for minors highest ever in Japan. Nippon.com. https://www.nippon.com/en/japan-data/h00857/.

Japan Times. 2022, March 20. Pandemic-related college dropouts up 40% in Japan. https://www.japantimes.co.jp/news/2022/03/02/national/pandemic-college-dropouts-2021/.

Jargon, J. 2019, June 18. How 13 became the internet's age of adulthood. *Wall Street Journal*. https://www.wsj.com/articles/how-13-became-the-internets-age-of-adulthood-11560850201.

Jarke, J. & Breiter, A. (eds). 2021. *The Datafication of Education*. Abingdon, Oxfordshire: Routledge.

Jazzi Brown. 2020. April 8. Request to ban FIU from forcing students to use Honorlock. Change.org. https://www.change.org/p/mark-b-rosenberg-request-to-ban-fiu-from-forcing-students-to-use-honorlock.

Jerome, J. 2021, April 15. Privacy is key: Holding EdTech accountable. Heinrich-Böll-Stiftung. https://us.boell.org/en/2021/03/31/privacy-key-holding-edtech-accountable.

Jerry Rothwell. 2018, August 30. *The School in the Cloud (2018)*. https://jerryrothwell.com/2018/08/30/theschoolinthecloud/.

Jetha, N. 2022, August 31. New report finds digital classrooms flout data protection law to exploit children's data for commercial gain. Digital Futures Commission. https://digitalfuturescommission.org.uk/blog/new-report-finds-digital-classrooms-flout-data-protection-law-to-exploit-childrens-data-for-commercial-gain/.

Jiang, J. 2018, August 22. How teens and parents navigate screen time and device distractions. Pew Research Center. https://www.pewresearch.org/internet/2018/08/22/how-teens-and-parents-navigate-screen-time-and-device-distractions/.

Johnson, S. 2021, October 5. One in five 15- to 24-year-olds globally 'often feel depressed', finds Unicef. The Guardian. https://www.theguardian.com/global-development/2021/oct/05/one-in-five-15-to-24-year-olds-globally-often-feel-depressed-finds-unicef.

Joung, M. 2020, August 17. Students protest tuition hikes as universities continue online. VOA News. https://www.voanews.com/a/covid-19-pandemic_students-protest-tuition-hikes-universities-continue-online/6194550.html.

Jurgenson, N. & Davis, J.L. 2014. Context collapse: Theorizing context collusions and collisions. Information, Communication & Society, 17(4). https://www.tandfonline.com/doi/abs/10.1080/1369118X.2014.888458.

Kadari-Ovadia, S. 2022, January 26. Israel sees fivefold increase in homeschooling requests over last decade. Haaretz. https://www.haaretz.com/israel-news/2022-01-26/ty-article/.premium/israel-sees-fivefold-increase-in-homeschooling-requests-over-last-decade/0000017f-db62-df9c-a17f-ff7acc870000.

Kakuchi, S. 2021, November 26. Student dropout rate due to COVID-19 is still rising. University World News. https://www.universityworldnews.com/post.php?story=202111261339042.

Kamenetz, A. 2022, September 1. School is for everyone. New York Times. https://www.nytimes.com/2022/09/01/opinion/us-school-history.html.

Kamiya, G. 2020, December 11. The carbon footprint of streaming video: fact-checking the headlines. International Energy Agency. https://www.iea.org/commentaries/the-carbon-footprint-of-streaming-video-fact-checking-the-headlines.

Kane, T. 2022, May 22. Kids are far, far behind in school. The Atlantic. https://www.theatlantic.com/ideas/archive/2022/05/schools-learning-loss-remote-covid-education/629938/.

Kang, C., Alba, D. & Satariano, A. 2020, March 26. Surging traffic is slowing down our internet. New York Times. https://www.nytimes.com/2020/03/26/business/coronavirus-internet-traffic-speed.html.

Karingada, K.T. & Sony, M. 2021. Demonstration of the relationship between MSD and online learning during the COVID-19 pandemic. Journal of Applied Research in Higher Education. https://doi.org/10.1108/JARHE-08-2020-0269.

Katzenbach, C. & Ulbricht, L. 2019. Algorithmic governance. Internet Policy Review, 8(4). https://policyreview.info/concepts/algorithmic-governance.

Kay, S. 2020, October 10. New report calls for dedicated 'Office for Edtech' to drive change. Schools Week. https://schoolsweek.co.uk/new-report-calls-for-dedicated-office-for-edtech-to-drive-change/.

Kayyem, J. 2020, July 6. Reopening schools was just an afterthought. The Atlantic. https://www.theatlantic.com/ideas/archive/2020/07/reopening-bars-easy-schools-are-difficult/613861/.

Kearney, R. 2021. Touch: Recovering Our Most Vital Sense. New York: Columbia University Press.

Kelion, L. 2019, September 24. Google wins landmark right to be forgotten case. BBC News. https://www.bbc.com/news/technology-49808208.

Kelley, J. 2020, December 22. ExamSoft flags one-third of California Bar Exam test takers for cheating. Electronic Frontier Foundation. https://www.eff.org/deeplinks/2020/12/examsoft-flags-one-third-california-bar-exam-test-takers-cheating.

Kelley, J. 2020, September 25. Students are pushing back against proctoring surveillance apps. Electronic Frontier Foundation. https://www.eff.org/deeplinks/2020/09/students-are-pushing-back-against-proctoring-surveillance-apps.

Kelley, J. 2021, June 22. A long overdue reckoning for online proctoring companies may finally be here. Electronic Frontier Foundation. https://www.eff.org/deeplinks/2021/06/long-overdue-reckoning-online-proctoring-companies-may-finally-be-here.

Kelley, J. 2022, August 25. Federal judge: Invasive online proctoring 'room scans' are unconstitutional. Electronic Frontier Foundation. https://www.eff.org/deeplinks/2022/08/federal-judge-invasive-online-proctoring-room-scans-are-also-unconstitutional.

Kelley, J. 2022, March 24. Stop invasive remote proctoring: Pass California's Student Test Taker Privacy Protection Act. Electronic Frontier Foundation. https://www.eff.org/deeplinks/2022/03/stop-invasive-remote-proctoring-pass-californias-student-test-taker-privacy.

Kelley, J., Budington, B. & Cope, S. 2021, April 15. Proctoring tools and dragnet investigations rob students of due process. Electronic Frontier Foundation. https://www.eff.org/deeplinks/2021/04/proctoring-tools-and-dragnet-investigations-rob-students-due-process.

Kelly, A. 2019, December 16. Apple and Google named in US lawsuit over Congolese child cobalt mining deaths. *The Guardian*. https://www.theguardian.com/global-development/2019/dec/16/apple-and-google-named-in-us-lawsuit-over-congolese-child-cobalt-mining-deaths.

Kelly, C. 2021, April 27. Gaming: The next super platform. Accenture. https://www.accenture.com/us-en/insights/software-platforms/gaming-the-next-super-platform.

Kelly, G., Graham, J., Bronfman, J. & Garton, S. 2019. *2019 State of Edtech Privacy Report*. Common Sense. https://privacy.commonsense.org/content/resource/state-of-edtech-2019/cs-2019-state-of-edtech-privacy-report.pdf.

Ken's Tech Tips. 2018, November 3. Download speeds: What do 2G, 3G, 4G & 5G actually mean? https://kenstechtips.com/index.php/download-speeds-2g-3g-and-4g-actual-meaning.

Keniston, K. 2002. Grassroots ICT projects in India: Some preliminary hypotheses. *ASCI Journal of Management*, 31(1&2). http://web.mit.edu/~kken/Public/PAPERS/ASCI_Journal_Intro__ASCI_version_.html.

Kennedy, K. 2019, June 25. UK government launches global Edtech Hub. The Pie News. https://thepienews.com/news/118082/.

Kharbat, F.F. & Abu Daabes, A.S. 2021. E-proctored exams during the COVID-19 pandemic: A close understanding. *Education and Information Technologies*, 26(6). https://doi.org/10.1007/s10639-021-10458-7.

Khullar, D. 2022, September 26. Living with our pandemic trade-offs. *New Yorker*. https://www.newyorker.com/magazine/2022/09/26/living-with-our-pandemic-trade-offs.

Kibbe, K. 2019, July 2. Tech billionaires wasted millions on failed education startup AltSchool. InsideHook. https://www.insidehook.com/daily_brief/news-opinion/tech-billionaires-wasted-millions-on-failed-education-startup-altschool.

Kim, J. 2020, December 29. Remote schooling brings bigger losses for children still learning to speak English. *New York Times*. https://www.nytimes.com/2020/12/29/world/remote-schooling-brings-bigger-losses-for-children-still-learning-to-speak-english.html.

Kimmons, R. & Veletsianos, G. 2021, February 23. Proctoring software in higher ed: Prevalence and patterns. *EDUCAUSE Review*. https://er.educause.edu/articles/2021/2/proctoring-software-in-higher-ed-prevalence-and-patterns.

King, K. 2021, February 14. Remote learning during Covid-19 is causing children to gain weight, doctors warn. *Wall Street Journal*. https://www.wsj.com/articles/remote-learning-during-covid-19-is-causing-children-to-gain-weight-doctors-warn-11613298602.

Kippin, S. & Cairney, P. 2022. The COVID-19 exams fiasco across the UK: Four nations and two windows of opportunity. *British Politics*, 17(1). https://doi.org/10.1057/s41293-021-00162-y.

Kirkpatrick, D. 2016, September 12. Google: 53% of mobile users abandon sites that take over 3 seconds to load. *Marketing Dive*. https://www.marketingdive.com/news/google-53-of-mobile-users-abandon-sites-that-take-over-3-seconds-to-load/426070/.

Kirp, D., Wechsler, M., Gardner, M. & Tinubu Ali, T. 2022. *Disrupting Disruption: The Steady Work of Transforming Schools*. Oxford: Oxford University Press.

Klass, P. 2019, May 20. Is 'digital addiction' a real threat to kids? *New York Times*. https://www.nytimes.com/2019/05/20/well/family/is-digital-addiction-a-real-threat-to-kids.html.

Klass, P. 2020, August 17. How children's sleep habits have changed in the pandemic. *New York Times*. https://www.nytimes.com/2020/08/17/well/family/children-sleep-pandemic.html.

Klass, P. 2020, July 27. The pandemic's toll on children with special needs and their parents. *New York Times*. https://www.nytimes.com/2020/07/27/well/family/children-special-needs-pandemic.html.

Klass, P. 2021, March 16. How children read differently from books vs. screens. *New York Times*. https://www.nytimes.com/2021/03/16/well/family/children-reading-screens-books.html.

Klein, A. 2021, April 20. During COVID-19, schools have made a mad dash to 1-to-1 computing. What happens next? *Education Week*. https://www.edweek.org/technology/during-covid-19-schools-have-made-a-mad-dash-to-1-to-1-computing-what-happens-next/2021/04.

Klein, A. 2022, January 10. Thousands of school websites went down in a cyberattack. It'll happen again, experts say. *Education Week*. https://www.edweek.org/technology/thousands-of-school-websites-went-down-in-a-cyberattack-itll-happen-again-experts-say/2022/01.

Klein, A. 2022, March 8. Tech fatigue is real for teachers and students. Here's how to ease the burden. *Education Week*. https://www.edweek.org/technology/tech-fatigue-is-real-for-teachers-and-students-heres-how-to-ease-the-burden/2022/03.

Klein, E. 2022, August 7. I didn't want it to be true, but the medium really is the message. *New York Times*. https://www.nytimes.com/2022/08/07/opinion/media-message-twitter-instagram.html.

Klein, N. 2008. *The Shock Doctrine: The Rise of Disaster Capitalism*. London: Penguin Books.

Klein, N. 2020, May 13. How big tech plans to profit from the pandemic. *The Guardian*. https://www.theguardian.com/news/2020/may/13/naomi-klein-how-big-tech-plans-to-profit-from-coronavirus-pandemic.

Klemp, N. & Kemp, K. 2022, January 31. Decoding the so-called 'sex recession': How a partnership mindset shift may be the secret to restoring intimacy. Parent Map. https://www.parentmap.com/article/decoding-so-called-sex-recession.

Kneese, T. 2021, January 27. How a dead professor is teaching a university art history class. Slate. https://slate.com/technology/2021/01/dead-professor-teaching-online-class.html.

Koenig, R. 2020, Jun 11. The post-pandemic outlook for edtech. EdSurge. https://www.edsurge.com/news/2020-06-11-the-post-pandemic-outlook-for-edtech.

Konnikova, M. 2014, November 26. Is internet addiction a real thing? *New Yorker*. http://www.newyorker.com/science/maria-konnikova/internet-addiction-real-thing.

Krause, J. 2020, April 8. F*** COVID SCHOOL. Jill Krause. Blog post. https://jillkrause.com/f-covid-school/.

Krauth, O. & Kobin, B. 2021, February 2. New lawsuit seeks to force Kentucky public schools to reopen during the pandemic. *Louisville Courier Journal*. https://www.courier-journal.com/story/news/education/2021/02/02/covid-19-kentucky-lawsuit-seeks-force-reopening-public-schools/4364190001/.

Krishnan, M. 2022, January 8. Covid setback for schoolchildren in India as dropout rate surges. RFI. https://www.rfi.fr/en/international/20220108-covid-setback-for-schoolchildren-in-india-as-dropout-rate-surges.

Kshetri, N. 2021, September 15. Cybercriminals use pandemic to attack schools and colleges. The Conversation. http://theconversation.com/cybercriminals-use-pandemic-to-attack-schools-and-colleges-167619.

Kumar, A. 2019, December 19. Shutting down the Internet to shut up critics. Human Rights Watch. https://www.hrw.org/news/2019/12/19/shutting-down-internet-shut-critics.

Kumar, J.A., Bervell, B. & Osman, S. 2020. Google classroom: Insights from Malaysian higher education students' and instructors' experiences. *Education and Information Technologies*, 25(5): 4175–4195. https://link.springer.com/article/10.1007/s10639-020-10163-x.

Kyodo News. 2021. Suicides among Japanese students hit record high in 2020.https://english.kyodonews.net/news/2021/03/a5e87a264301-suicides-among-japanese-students-hit-record-high-in-2020.html.

LaBarre, S. 2020, September 3. Zoom is failing teachers. Here's how they would redesign it. Fast Company. https://www.fastcompany.com/90542917/zoom-is-failing-teachers-heres-how-they-would-redesign-it.

Ladd, J.M., Tucker, J.A. & Kates, S. 2018. *2018 American Institutional Confidence Poll: The Health of American Democracy in an Era of Hyper Polarization*. Report by the Baker Center for Leadership & Governance, Georgetown University, & the John S. and James L. Knight Foundation. https://www.aicpoll.org/uploads/5/3/6/6/5366295/2018-american-institutional-confidence-poll-1.pdf.

Lamont, T. 2021, February 18. The student and the algorithm: How the exam results fiasco threatened one pupil's future. *The Guardian*. https://www.theguardian.com/education/2021/feb/18/the-student-and-the-algorithm-how-the-exam-results-fiasco-threatened-one-pupils-future.

Langthaler, M. 2021, March. Lessons from COVID 19: Digitalization calls for strong public education systems. NORRAG. https://resources.norrag.org/resource/638/lessons-from-covid-19-digitalization-calls-for-strong-public-education-systems-by-margarita-langthaler.

Lapowsky, I. 2015, May 4. Inside the school Silicon Valley thinks will save education. Wired. https://www.wired.com/2015/05/altschool/.

Lareau, A. 1989. *Home Advantage: Social Class and Parental Intervention in Elementary Education*. Philadelphia, PA: Falmer Press.

Larmer, B. 2018, July 5. E-waste offers an economic opportunity as well as toxicity. *New York Times*. https://www.nytimes.com/2018/07/05/magazine/e-waste-offers-an-economic-opportunity-as-well-as-toxicity.html.

Launder, M. 2021, October 27. Reverse 'devastating' public health cuts, school nurses tell government. *Nursing in Practice*. https://www.nursinginpractice.com/community-nursing/reverse-devastating-public-health-cuts-school-nurses-tell-government/.

Lazare, M. 2021, February 17. A peek at what's next for Google Classroom. Google Education. Blog post. https://blog.google/outreach-initiatives/education/classroom-roadmap/.

Le Nestour, A. & Moscoviz, L. 2020, April 24. Five findings from a new phone survey in Senegal. Center for Global Development. Blog post. https://www.cgdev.org/blog/five-findings-new-phone-survey-senegal.

Le Nestour, A., Mbaye, S. & Moscoviz, L. 2020, *Phone survey on the COVID crisis in Senegal*. Harvard Dataverse. https://doi.org/10.7910/DVN/9XE95F/95RW9C.

Le Parisien. 2021, April 8. Nouveaux bugs du dispositif «Ma classe à la maison», victime de «cyberattaques» [New bugs in the "My class at home" device, victim of "cyberattacks"]. https://www.leparisien.fr/societe/nouveaux-bugs-du-dispositif-ma-classe-a-la-maison-victime-de-cyberattaques-08-04-2021-4YOFIJO5OZDGJG23X6NGGNMIZE.php.

Le, H.M. 2019. Private encroachment through crisis-making: The privatization of education for refugees. *Education Policy Analysis Archives*, 27(26): 126–126. https://doi.org/10.14507/epaa.27.4325.

Learning, Media and Technology. https://www.tandfonline.com/toc/cjem20/current.

Learning Network. 2020, April 9. What students are saying about remote learning. *New York Times*. https://www.nytimes.com/2020/04/09/learning/what-students-are-saying-about-remote-learning.html.

Learning Network. 2020, October 8. What students are saying about socially-distant friendships, school accountability and lessons from animals. *New York Times*. https://www.nytimes.com/2020/10/08/learning/what-students-are-saying-about-socially-distant-friendships-school-accountability-and-lessons-from-animals.html.

Lee, E. & Sheng, W. 2021, July 26. Chinese edtech upended by sweeping regulations. TechNode. http://technode.com/2021/07/26/chinese-edtech-upended-by-sweeping-regulations/.

Lee, E. 2021, January 25. Edtech firm Huohua Siwei valued at $1.5 billion. TechNode. http://technode.com/2021/01/25/edtech-firm-huohua-siwei-valued-at-1-5-billion/.

Legal Cheek. 2020, August 13. Proctoring problems: Bar students urinate in bottles and buckets over fears online exams will be terminated. https://www.legalcheek.com/2020/08/proctoring-problems-bar-students-urinate-in-bottles-and-buckets-over-fears-online-exams-will-be-terminated/.

Legal Services NYC. 2022, January 7. Low-income families sue departments of education to force them to provide working devices, internet, and instruction for periods of remote learning. https://www.legalservicesnyc.org/news-and-events/press-room/1748-low-income-families-sue-departments-of-education-to-force-them-to-provide-working-devices-internet-and-instruction-for-periods-of-remote-learning.

Leprince-Ringuet, D. 2020, January 23. Government wants more tech in schools: Paying for it will be the first challenge. ZDNet. https://www.zdnet.com/article/government-wants-more-tech-in-schools-paying-for-it-will-be-the-first-challenge/.

Letter prepared by ProctorU attorneys. 2020, March 24. Re: Errors and misrepresentations regarding ProctorU on-line proctoring services. https://pubcit.typepad.com/files/demanded-apology-letter.pdf.

Letters. 2020, August 17. Inbuilt biases and the problem of algorithms. *The Guardian*. https://www.theguardian.com/education/2020/aug/17/inbuilt-biases-and-the-problem-of-algorithms.

Levin, D.A. 2021. *The State of K-12 Cybersecurity: 2020 Year in Review*. EdTech Strategies/K-12 Cybersecurity Resource Center & K12 Security Information Exchange. https://static1.squarespace.com/static/5e441b46adfb340b05008fe7/t/620d58f6f14b822a371b8c7b/1645041911977/StateofK12Cybersecurity-2020.pdf.

Levinson, M., Cevik, M. & Lipsitch, M. 2020. Reopening primary schools during the pandemic. *New England Journal of Medicine*, 383(10): 981–985. https://www.nejm.org/doi/10.1056/NEJMms2024920.

Lewis, S. 2022, July 17. Why is tech giant Apple trying to teach our teachers? The Conversation. https://theconversation.com/why-is-tech-giant-apple-trying-to-teach-our-teachers-186752.

Lewis, T. 2021, April 15. Schools can open safely during COVID, the latest evidence shows. *Scientific American*. https://www.scientificamerican.com/article/schools-can-open-safely-during-covid-the-latest-evidence-shows/.

Li, C. & Lalani, F. 2020, April 29. The COVID-19 pandemic has changed education forever. This is how. World Economic Forum. https://www.weforum.org/agenda/2020/04/coronavirus-education-global-covid19-online-digital-learning/.

Li, G. et al. 2020, August. Education and EdTech during COVID-19: Evidence from a large-scale survey during school closures in China. Rural Education Action Program. Working paper. https://fsi-live.s3.us-west-1.amazonaws.com/s3fs-public/education_and_edtech_during_covid-19-final-08032020.pdf.

Li, H., Arnsperger, L. & Cerny, M. 2020, June 30. Censorship fears and vampire hours. The China Project. https://thechinaproject.com/2020/06/30/chinese-international-students-zoom-and-remote-learning/.

Li, J. 2020, March 11. In China, quarantined students can pay $1.40 to cheat an online class. Quartz. https://qz.com/1816351/chinese-students-quarantined-from-coronavirus-can-pay-1-40-to-cheat-an-online-class.

Li, P. & Jourdan, A. 2018, May 17. Sleepy pupils in the picture at high-tech Chinese school. Reuters. https://www.reuters.com/article/us-china-surveillance-education-idUSKCN1II123.

Lichand, G., Dória, C.A., Neto, O.L. & Cossi Fernandes, J.P. 2022, May. The impacts of remote learning in secondary education: evidence from Brazil during the pandemic. *Nature Human Behaviour*, 6: 1079–1086. https://www.nature.com/articles/s41562-022-01350-6.

Lieberman, M. 2020, June 2. Like it or not, K-12 schools are doing a digital leapfrog during COVID-19. *Education Week*. https://www.edweek.org/technology/like-it-or-not-k-12-schools-are-doing-a-digital-leapfrog-during-covid-19/2020/06.

Lightman, A. 2022, January 15. This is no way to be human. *The Atlantic*. https://www.theatlantic.com/technology/archive/2022/01/machine-garden-natureless-world/621268/.

Lin, X. & Gao, L. 2020. Students' sense of community and perspectives of taking synchronous and asynchronous online courses. *Asian Journal of Distance Education*, 15(1): 169–179. https://eric.ed.gov/?id=EJ1289947.

Lindblad, S. 2021, September 28. Only in Sweden primary school remained open. University of Gothenburg. https://www.gu.se/en/news/only-in-sweden-primary-school-remained-open.

Lindquist, K.A., Barrett, L.F., Bliss-Moreau, E. & Russell, J.A. 2006. Language and the perception of emotion. *Emotion* 6(1). https://psycnet.apa.org/record/2006-04603-012.

Linkletter, I. 2022, October 16. Stand against Proctorio's SLAPP. GoFundMe. https://www.gofundme.com/f/stand-against-proctorio.

Linn, S. 2005. *Consuming Kids: Protecting Our Children from the Onslaught of Marketing and Advertising*. New York: Anchor Books.

Literat, I. 2021, February 25. "Teachers act like we're robots": TikTok as a window into youth experiences of online learning during COVID-19. *AERA Open*, 7. https://doi.org/10.1177/2332858421995537.

Liyaghatdar, Z., Pezeshkian, Z., Mohammadi-Dehcheshmeh, M. & Ebrahimie, E. 2021. Fast school closures correspond with a lower rate of COVID-19 incidence and deaths in most countries. *Informatics in Medicine Unlocked*, 27: 100805. https://www.sciencedirect.com/science/article/pii/S2352914821002720.

Lockee, B.B. 2021, January. Online education in the post-COVID era. *Nature Electronics*, 4(1): 5–6. https://www.nature.com/articles/s41928-020-00534-0.

Lockett, H., McMorrow, R. & Yu, S. 2021, August 3. China's Tencent imposes controls to tackle gaming addiction among children. *Financial Times*. https://www.ft.com/content/1ee4f40b-cad8-45f7-b8dd-de25b89736d3.

Lohr, S. 2020, May 26. Remember the MOOCs? After near-death, they're booming. *New York Times*. https://www.nytimes.com/2020/05/26/technology/moocs-online-learning.html.

Loizos, C. 2017, November 22. AltSchool wants to change how kids learn, but fears have surfaced that it's failing students. TechCrunch. https://techcrunch.com/2017/11/22/altschool-wants-to-change-how-kids-learn-but-fears-that-its-failing-students-are-surfacing/.

Lorenz, T. 2020, March 20. 'Zoombombing': When video conferences go wrong. *New York Times*. https://www.nytimes.com/2020/03/20/style/zoombombing-zoom-trolling.html.

Low, J., Dujacquier, D. & Kaur, S. 2021, February. *Bridging the Digital Divide: Improving Digital Inclusion in Southeast Asia*. Roland Berger. https://www.rolandberger.com/en/Insights/Publications/Bridging-the-digital-divide.html.

Loziak, A., Fedakova, D. & Čopková, R. 2020. Work-related stressors of female teachers during Covid-19 school closure. *Journal of Women's Entrepreneurship and Education*, 3–4: 59–78. https://www.library.ien.bg.ac.rs/index.php/jwee/article/view/1304.

Lu, C. & Darragh, E. 2021, November 5. Remote test proctoring apps are a form of mass surveillance. *Teen Vogue*. https://www.teenvogue.com/story/remote-proctoring-apps-tests.

Lu, S. 2021, July 31. China's edtech crackdown isn't what you think. Here's why. Protocol. https://www.protocol.com/china/china-edtech-crackdown-education-inequality.

Lucas, D.V. 2020, March 19. Letter from Bradley law firm to UCSB faculty association. https://pubcit.typepad.com/files/bradley-bullying-letter.pdf.

Ludvigsen, K. 2023, March 1. ChatGPT's electricity consumption. Towards Data Science. https://towardsdatascience.com/chatgpts-electricity-consumption-7873483feac4.

Luijten, M.A.J. et al. 2020. The impact of lockdown during the COVID-19 pandemic on mental and social health of children and adolescents. *Quality of Life Research*, 30: 2795–2804. https://doi.org/10.1007/s11136-021-02861-x.

Luterman, S. 2022, February 1. 'We feel like we lost two years of education': School closings are more complicated for parents of children with disabilities. The 19th. https://19thnews.org/2022/02/covid-school-closures-remote-learning-complicated-students-disabilities/.

Lynch, M. 2019, January 15. Edtech should complement good pedagogy, not attempt to replace it. The Tech Advocate. https://www.thetechedvocate.org/edtech-should-complement-good-pedagogy-not-attempt-to-replace-it/.

Lyngaas, S. 2022, January 7. Ransomware attack affects the websites of 5,000 schools. CNN. https://www.cnn.com/2022/01/07/politics/ransomware-schools-website/index.html.

Mackee, N. 2019, August 19. Screen time in under 2s "breathtaking". *InSight+*. https://insightplus.mja.com.au/2019/32/screen-time-in-under-2s-breathtaking/.

Madda, M.J. 2015, July 15. A peek Into Silicon Valley's newest bet: AltSchool. Medium. https://brightthemag.com/a-peek-into-silicon-valley-s-latest-bet-altschool-abf6c6973ecd.

Madhav, K.C., Sherchand, S.P. & Sherchan, S. 2017. Association between screen time and depression among US adults. *Preventive medicine reports*, 8: 67–71. https://pubmed.ncbi.nlm.nih.gov/28879072.

Madhav, N. et al. 2007. Pandemics: Risks, impacts, and mitigation. In Jameson D.T. et al. (eds). *Disease Control Priorities, Third Edition (Volume 9): Improving Health and Reducing Poverty*. World Bank Publications. Available at http://dcp-3.org/sites/default/files/chapters/DCP3%20Volume%209_Ch%2017.pdf.

Madigan, S., Browne, D., Racine, N., Mori, C. & Tough, S. 2019. Association between screen time and children's performance on a developmental screening test. *JAMA Pediatrics*, 173(3): 244–250. https://pubmed.ncbi.nlm.nih.gov/30688984/.

Majumdar, D. 2021, June 9. Coursera's IPO windfall: the takeaways for Indian ed-tech companies that plan to get listed. *Economic Times*. https://economictimes.indiatimes.com/prime/technology-and-startups/courseras-ipo-windfall-the-takeaways-for-indian-ed-tech-companies-that-plan-to-get-listed/primearticleshow/83346852.cms.

Maldonado, J. & De Witte, K. 2021. The effect of school closures on standardised student test. *British Educational Research Journal*, 48(1): 49–94. https://doi.org/10.1002/berj.3754.

Malhotra, S. 2020, May 15. DU exams 2020: Our survey finds 85% students against online exams, 76% don't have study material in Delhi University. DU EXPRESS. https://duexpress.in/du-exams-2020-our-survey-finds-85-students-against-online-exams-76-dont-have-study-material-in-delhi-university/.

Malik, D. 2020, April 29. Terms of services - A section often ignored because of its length (infographic). Digital Information World. https://www.digitalinformationworld.com/2020/04/the-length-of-the-fine-print-for-popular-apps-facebook-microsoft-tiktok.html.

Malik, K. 2020, August 23. The cruel exams algorithm has laid bare the unfairness at the heart of our schools. *The Observer*. https://www.theguardian.com/commentisfree/2020/aug/23/the-cruel-exams-algorithm-has-laid-bare-the-unfairness-at-the-heart-of-our-schools.

Malkus, N. 2022, July. *Pandemic Enrollment Fallout: School District Enrollment Changes Across COVID-19 Response*. American Enterprise Institute. https://www.aei.org/wp-content/uploads/2022/07/Pandemic-Enrollment-Fallout.pdf.

Mamun, S. 2020, August 7. Covid-19: Over 45% secondary school students may drop out. *Dhaka Tribune*. https://www.dhakatribune.com/bangladesh/2020/08/07/covid-19-over-45-secondary-school-students-may-drop-out.

Markel, H. 2020, July 13. Analysis: Why some schools stayed open during the 1918 flu pandemic. PBS NewsHour. https://www.pbs.org/newshour/health/analysis-why-some-schools-stayed-open-during-the-1918-flu-pandemic.

Markets and Markets. 2022. Emotion detection and recognition (EDR) market. https://www.marketsandmarkets.com/Market-Reports/emotion-detection-recognition-market-23376176.html.

MarketWatch. 2022, December 26. Remote proctoring solutions market size was valued at USD 566.75 Million in 2021 and is expected to expand at a CAGR of 19.54% to 2027. Press release. https://www.marketwatch.com/press-release/remote-proctoring-solutions-market-size-was-valued-at-usd-56675-million-in-2021-and-is-expected-to-expand-at-a-cagr-of-1954-to-2027-2022-12-26.

MarketWatch. 2023, March 29. Remote proctoring solutions market share by 2031. Press release. https://www.marketwatch.com/press-release/remote-proctoring-solutions-market-share-by-2031-2023-03-29.

Markow, W. & Hughes, D. 2018. *The New Foundational Skills of the Digital Economy*. Business-Higher Education Forum & Burning Glass Technologies. https://www.burning-glass.com/wp-content/uploads/New_Foundational_Skills.pdf.

Marte, J. 2021, October 9. Women left U.S. workforce last month, but in fewer numbers than a year ago. Reuters. https://www.reuters.com/business/women-left-us-workforce-last-month-fewer-numbers-than-year-ago-2021-10-08/.

Martins, D. 2021, June 30. Amazon is still the undisputed king of cloud. The Street. https://www.thestreet.com/amazon/aws/amazon-is-still-the-undisputed-king-of-cloud.

Masanet, E., Shehabi, A., Lei, N., Smith, S. & Koomey, J. 2020. Recalibrating global data center energy-use estimates. *Science*, 367(6481): 984–986. https://www.science.org/doi/10.1126/science.aba3758.

Mascarenhas, L. 2021, June 28. Cases of type 2 diabetes among children more than doubled during the coronavirus pandemic, research finds. CNN. https://edition.cnn.com/2021/06/25/health/diabetes-children-pandemic-wellness/index.html.

Mascarenhas, N. 2020, October 22. Chinese live tutoring app Yuanfudao is now worth $15.5 billion. TechCrunch. https://techcrunch.com/2020/10/22/chinese-live-tutoring-app-yuanfudao-is-now-worth-15-5-billion/.

Maslej, N. et al. 2023, April. *The AI Index 2023 Annual Report*. AI Index Steering Committee, Institute for Human-Centered AI, Stanford University. https://aiindex.stanford.edu/wp-content/uploads/2023/04/HAI_AI-Index-Report_2023.pdf.

Mathur, P. 2020, October 22. China's Yuanfudao claims global edtech valuation crown. PitchBook. https://pitchbook.com/news/articles/yuanfudao-edtech-valuation-china.

Mayer, R.E. 2019, January 4. Computer games in education. *Annual Review of Psychology*, 70(1): 531–549. https://doi.org/10.1146/annurev-psych-010418-102744.

Mazar, N., Amir, O. & Ariely, D. 2008. The dishonesty of honest people: A theory of self-concept maintenance. *Journal of Marketing Research*, 45(6). https://doi.org/10.1509/jmkr.45.6.633.

Mbukwa-Ngwira, J. et al. 2021, March 19. Impact of COVID-19 on the education of children with disabilities in Malawi: Results from a survey with parents. Education and Development Forum. https://www.ukfiet.org/2021/impact-of-covid-19-on-the-education-of-children-with-disabilities-in-malawi-results-from-a-survey-with-parents/.

McBride, M. 2021, February 16. Sign on, Zoom in, drop out: Covid-19 sparks fears over early school leaving. *Irish Times*. https://www.irishtimes.com/news/education/sign-on-zoom-in-drop-out-covid-19-sparks-fears-over-early-school-leaving-1.4480245.

McCabe, D.L., Trevino, L.K. & Butterfield, K.D. 2001. Cheating in academic institutions: A decade of research. *Ethics & Behavior*, 11(3). https://doi.org/10.1207/S15327019EB1103_2.

McClain-Nhlapo, C. 2020, May 11. An inclusive response to COVID-19: Education for children with disabilities. Global Partnership for Education. https://www.globalpartnership.org/blog/inclusive-response-covid-19-education-children-disabilities.

McKenzie, L. 2020, October 20. Ed-Tech specialist fights Proctorio lawsuit. *Inside Higher Ed*. https://www.insidehighered.com/quicktakes/2020/10/20/ed-tech-specialist-fights-proctorio-lawsuit.

McKenzie, L. 2021, April 9. Coursera IPO 'seized on the right moment'. *Inside Higher Ed*. https://www.insidehighered.com/news/2021/04/09/coursera-valuation-exceeds-expectations.

McKinsey & Company. 2022, April 4. How COVID-19 caused a global learning crisis. https://www.mckinsey.com/industries/education/our-insights/how-covid-19-caused-a-global-learning-crisis.

McKinsey & Company. 2022. May 2. Educational technology in the age of COVID-19. Podcast. https://www.mckinsey.com/il/podcast/educational-technology-in-the-age-of-covid.

McMahon, S.D. et al. Violence against educators and school personnel: Crisis during COVID. American Psychological Association. https://www.apa.org/education-career/k12/violence-educators-technical-report.pdf.

McMallum, S. & Gerken, T. 2022, September 5. Instagram fined €405m over children's data privacy. BBC News. https://www.bbc.com/news/technology-62800884.

McMorris-Santoro, E. 2021, March 8. Thousands of students have dropped out of school due to Covid-19. These are the educators trying to track them down. CNN. https://www.cnn.com/2021/03/06/us/covid-pandemic-high-school-dropout/index.html.

McNeill, S. 2021, June 30. "They don't understand the fear we have": How China's long reach of repression undermines academic freedom at Australia's universities. Human Rights Watch. https://www.hrw.org/report/2021/06/30/they-dont-understand-fear-we-have/how-chinas-long-reach-repression-undermines.

Mead, R. 2016, February 28. Learn different: Silicon Valley disrupts education. *New Yorker*. https://www.newyorker.com/magazine/2016/03/07/altschools-disrupted-education.

Meazure Learning. 2021, May 24. ProctorU to discontinue exam integrity services that rely exclusively on AI. Press release. https://www.meazurelearning.com/resources/proctoru-to-discontinue-exam-integrity-services-that-rely-exclusively-on-ai.

Meazure Learning. 2023. Privacy Policy. https://www.meazurelearning.com/privacy-policy.

Mehmood, F. 2021. *Covid-19: Bridging the Digital Divide in Education*. Centre for Human Rights. https://cfhr.com.pk/wp-content/uploads/2022/01/Covid-19-Bridging-the-Digital-Divide-in-Education-CFHR-Report-2022.pdf.

Meinck, S., Fraillon, J. & Strietholt, R. 2022. *The Impact of the COVID-19 Pandemic on Education: International Evidence from the Responses to Educational Disruption Survey (REDS)*. UNESCO & International Association for the Evaluation of Educational Achievement. https://unesdoc.unesco.org/ark:/48223/pf0000380398.

Meisenzahl, M. 2020, April 15. Students bored of homeschooling spam Google Classroom app with one-star reviews thanks to a TikTok meme. Business Insider. https://www.businessinsider.com/google-classroom-app-spammed-with-one-star-reviews-by-students-2020-4.

Merikko, J. & Kivimäki, V. 2022, October 13. "Replacing teachers? Doubt it." Practitioners' views on adaptive learning technologies' impact on the teaching profession. *Frontiers in Education*, 7. https://www.frontiersin.org/articles/10.3389/feduc.2022.1010255.

Mervosh, S. & Wu, A. 2022, October 24. Math scores fell in nearly every state, and reading dipped on national exam. *New York Times*. https://www.nytimes.com/2022/10/24/us/math-reading-scores-pandemic.html.

Meyer, J.W., Ramirez, F.O. & Soysal, Y.N. 1992. World Expansion of Mass Education, 1870–1980. *Sociology of Education*, 65(2): 128–149. https://www.jstor.org/stable/2112679.

Miao, F. et al. 2022. *Guidelines for ICT in Education Policies and Masterplans*. UNESCO. https://unesdoc.unesco.org/ark:/48223/pf0000380926.

Miao, F., Holmes, W., Huang, R. & Zhang, H. 2021. *AI and Education: Guidance for Policymakers*. UNESCO. https://unesdoc.unesco.org/ark:/48223/pf0000376709.

Miao, F., Huang, R., Liu, D. & Zhuang, R. 2020. *Ensuring Effective Distance Learning during COVID-19 Disruption: Guidance for Teachers*. UNESCO. https://unesdoc.unesco.org/ark:/48223/pf0000375116.

Miao, T. 2022, January 21. Can EdTech be the path forward for China's education industry? GRC Insights. https://insights.grcglobalgroup.com/can-edtech-be-the-path-forward-for-chinas-education-industry/.

Michele Fabiola Lawson. 2021, September 1. The DRC mining industry: Child labor and formalization of small-scale mining. Wilson Center. https://www.wilsoncenter.org/blog-post/drc-mining-industry-child-labor-and-formalization-small-scale-mining.

Microsoft Security Intelligence. 2022. Cyberthreats, viruses, and malware. https://www.microsoft.com/en-us/wdsi/threats.

Microsoft. 2022. Microsoft Learn Educator Center: Microsoft Educator program. https://learn.microsoft.com/en-us/training/educator-center/programs/microsoft-educator/.

MIET AFRICA. 2021, June. *The Impact of COVID-19 on Adolescents and Young People in the Southern African Development Community Region*. https://mietafrica.org/wp-content/uploads/2021/07/REPORT-Impact_COVID_19_AYP_SADCRegional.pdf.

Miller, C.C. & Sanger-Katz, M. 2022, February 28. School is back in person, but the five-day school week often isn't. *New York Times*. https://www.nytimes.com/2022/02/28/upshot/schools-covid-closings.html.

Miller, V. 2020, November 16. Iowa universities plugging holes in massive transition to online. *The Gazette*. https://www.thegazette.com/education/iowa-universities-plugging-holes-in-massive-transition-to-online/.

Ministry of Ecological Transition and Territorial Cohesion. 2021, December 1. Indice de réparabilité [Reparability index]. Government of France. https://www.ecologie.gouv.fr/indice-reparabilite.

Ministry of Education of the People's Republic of China. 2021, March 31. 教育部办公厅关于进一步加强中小学生睡眠管理工作的通知 [Notice of the general office of the ministry of education on further strengthening the sleep management of primary and middle school students]. http://www.moe.gov.cn/srcsite/A06/s3321/202104/t20210401_523901.html.

Ministry of Education Singapore. 2022. Educational technology plan. http://www.moe.gov.sg/education-in-sg/educational-technology-journey/edtech-plan.

Ministry of Education, Republic of Kenya. 2020, May. *Kenya Basic Education Covid-19 Emergency Response Plan*. https://planipolis.iiep.unesco.org/sites/default/files/ressources/kenya_emergency_response_plan_4_may_2020.pdf.

Ministry of Education. 2021, May 26. Estudiantes de enseñanza media no alcanzaron el 60% de los aprendizajes necesarios en 2020 [High school students did not reach 60% of the necessary learning in 2020]. https://www.mineduc.cl/en-ensenanza-media-no-se-alcanzo-el-60-de-los-aprendizajes-minimos/.

Misk Foundation. 2020. *The Impact of COVID-19 on Saudi Youth*. https://misk.org.sa/wp-content/uploads/2021/12/Misk-covid-report.pdf.

MIT Media Lab 2023. Project Overview - AttentivU. MIT Media Lab. https://www.media.mit.edu/projects/attentivu/overview/.

Mitra, S. & Rana, V. 2001. Children and the Internet: Experiments with minimally invasive education in India. *British Journal of Educational Technology*, 32: 221–232. https://doi.org/10.1111/1467-8535.00192.

Mitra, S. 2000. Minimally invasive education for mass computer literacy. Paper presented as the CRIDALA 2000 conference, Hong Kong, 21–25 June. https://www.researchgate.net/publication/228356449_Minimally_invasive_education_for_mass_computer_literacy.

Mitra, S. 2009. Remote presence: Technologies for 'beaming' teachers where they cannot go. *Journal of Emerging Technologies in Web Intelligence*, 1(1): 55–59. https://www.researchgate.net/publication/42802925_Remote_Presence_Technologies_for_'Beaming'_Teachers_Where_They_Cannot_Go\.

Mitra, S. 2010. The child-driven education. TED Talks. https://www.ted.com/talks/sugata_mitra_the_child_driven_education.

Mitra, S. 2012. *Beyond the Hole in the Wall: Discover the Power of Self-Organized Learning*. Independently published.

Mitra, S. 2013. Build a school in the cloud. TED Talks. https://www.ted.com/talks/sugata_mitra_build_a_school_in_the_cloud.

Mitra, S. 2019. *The School in the Cloud: The Emerging Future of Learning*. London: SAGE Publishing.

Mizunoya, S. et al. 2020. *How Many Children and Young People Have Internet Access at Home? Estimating Digital Connectivity During the COVID-19 Pandemic*. UNICEF & ITU. https://data.unicef.org/resources/children-and-young-people-internet-access-at-home-during-covid19/.

Mlaba, K. 2020, November 25. Over 300,000 South African children may have dropped out of primary school during COVID-19. *Global Citizen*. https://www.globalcitizen.org/en/content/south-africa-children-school-drop-out-covid-19/.

Mlambo-Ngcuka, P. & Albrectsen, A. 2020, May 4. Opinion: We cannot allow COVID-19 to reinforce the digital gender divide. Devex. https://www.devex.com/news/opinion-we-cannot-allow-covid-19-to-reinforce-the-digital-gender-divide-97118.

Mokolé, J. & Toukan, E. 2020, 21 July. Community schools continue teaching and learning during Covid-19 in the Central African Republic. REACH. Harvard Graduate School of Education. https://www.reach.gse.harvard.edu/blogs/covid-19/series/community-schools-continue-teaching-and-learning-during-covid-19-in-the-central-african-republic.

Molitorisz, S. 2020. *Net Privacy: How We Can Be Free in an Age of Surveillance*. Montreal: McGill-Queen's University Press.

Montacute, R. & Cullinane, C. 2021, January 21. *Learning in Lockdown*. The Sutton Trust. https://www.suttontrust.com/our-research/learning-in-lockdown/.

Montacute, R. 2020, April. *Social Mobility and Covid-19: Implications of the Covid-19 Crisis for Educational Inequality*. The Sutton Trust. https://dera.ioe.ac.uk/35323/2/COVID-19-and-Social-Mobility-1.pdf.

Montgomery, M. 2019, September 3. This math EdTech startup says it's found a winning formula with on-demand tutoring. Forbes. https://www.forbes.com/sites/mikemontgomery/2019/09/03/this-math-edtech-says-its-found-a-winning-formula-with-on-demand-tutoring/.

Moon, L. 2018, May 16. Pay attention at the back: School uses facial scans to monitor pupils. *South China Morning Post*. https://www.scmp.com/news/china/society/article/2146387/pay-attention-back-chinese-school-installs-facial-recognition.

Moondore, A., Blades, M., Oates, C. & Blumberg, F. 2009. Young children's ability to recognize advertisements in web page designs. *British Journal of Developmental Psychology*, 27. https://www.researchgate.net/publication/40459548_Young_children%27s_ability_to_recognize_advertisements_in_Web_page_designs.

Morning Consult. 2020. *Special Report: The State of Consumer Trust*. https://morningconsult.com/wp-content/uploads/2020/01/Morning-Consult-The-State-of-Consumer-Trust.pdf.

Morozov, E. 2014. *To Save Everything, Click Here: The Folly of Technological Solutionism*. New York: Public Affairs.

Morris, A. & Anthes, E. 2021, August 23. For some college students, remote learning is a game changer. *New York Times*. https://www.nytimes.com/2021/08/23/health/covid-college-disabilities-students.html.

Moscardino, U., Dicataldo, R., Roch, M., Carbone, M. & Mammarella, I.C. 2021. Parental stress during COVID-19: A brief report on the role of distance education and family resources in an Italian sample. *Current Psychology*, 40(11). https://link.springer.com/article/10.1007/s12144-021-01454-8.

Mosher, R., Hartwell, A. & Brown, B. 2021, May 6. 5 factors that contribute to students finishing high school. The Conversation. https://theconversation.com/5-factors-that-contribute-to-students-finishing-high-school-155282.

Moyer, M.W. 2020, July 22. Pods, microschools and tutors: Can parents solve the education crisis on their own? *New York Times*. https://www.nytimes.com/2020/07/22/parenting/school-pods-coronavirus.html.

Mueed, A. et al. 2022. School closures help reduce the spread of COVID-19: A pre- and post-intervention analysis in Pakistan. *PLOS Global Health*, 2(4): e0000266. https://journals.plos.org/globalpublichealth/article?id=10.1371/journal.pgph.0000266.

Mullan, J. & Taddese, A. 2020. *Edtech in Sierra Leone: A Rapid Scan*. EdTech Hub. https://docs.edtechhub.org/lib/C5MWWQI2/download/SL8ULFEM/Mullan_Taddese_2020_EdTech%20in%20Sierra%20Leone.pdf.

Mullaney, T.S., Peters, B., Hicks, M. & Philip, K. (eds). 2021. *Your Computer is on Fire*. Cambridge, MA: MIT Press.

Munoz-Najar, A. et al. 2021. *Remote Learning During COVID-19: Lessons from Today, Principles for Tomorrow*. World Bank Group. https://documents1.worldbank.org/curated/en/160271637074230077/pdf/Remote-Learning-During-COVID-19-Lessons-from-Today-Principles-for-Tomorrow.pdf.

Murphy, H. 2020, October 13. She was going into labor. But she had a bar exam to finish. *New York Times*. https://www.nytimes.com/2020/10/13/us/bar-exam-labor.html.

Musaddiq, T., Stange, K., Bacher-Hicks, A. & Goodman, J. 2021, September. The pandemic's effect on demand for public schools, homeschooling, and private schools. Working paper. Education Policy Initiative and Wheelock Education Policy Center. https://edpolicy.umich.edu/sites/epi/files/2021-09/Pandemics%20Effect%20Demand%20Public%20Schools%20Working%20Paper%20Final%20%281%29.pdf.

Muster, H. 2017, September 13. Was ist EdTech (Educational Technology) und wie kommt sie zum Einsatz? [What is EdTech (Educational Technology) and how is it used?]. PINKTUM. https://www.pinktum.com/de/blog/edtech-educational-technology-und-was-dahinter-steckt/.

Mweyeri, M. & Gathuru, G. 2021, September 27. The impact of Covid-19 on education in Kenya. IEA Kenya. https://ieakenya.or.ke/blog/the-impact-of-covid-19-on-education-in-kenya/.

Nabi, R.L. & Krcmar, M. 2016. It takes two: The effect of child characteristics on U.S. parents' motivations for allowing electronic media use. *Journal of Children and Media*, 10(3): 285–303. https://www.tandfonline.com/doi/abs/10.1080/17482798.2016.1162185.

Nadaf, A.H. 2021. 'Lockdown within a lockdown': The 'digital redlining' and paralyzed online teaching during COVID-19 in Kashmir, a conflict territory. *Communication, Culture and Critique*, 14(2): 343–346. https://doi.org/10.1093/ccc/tcab019.

Nagata, J.M. et al. 2021. Screen time use among US adolescents during the COVID-19 pandemic: Findings from the Adolescent Brain Cognitive Development (ABCD) study. *JAMA Pediatrics*. https://jamanetwork.com/journals/jamapediatrics/fullarticle/2785686.

Naslund, J.A., Bondre, A., Torous, J. & Aschbrenner, K.A. 2020. Social media and mental health: benefits, risks, and opportunities for research and practice. *Journal of Technology in Behavioral Science*, 5(3): 245–257. https://link.springer.com/article/10.1007/s41347-020-00134-x.

National Assessment of Educational Progress. 2022, November 8. Reading and mathematics scores decline during COVID-19 pandemic. https://www.nationsreportcard.gov/highlights/ltt/2022/.

National Center for Education Statistics. 2022, July 6. More than 80 percent of U.S. Public schools report pandemic has negatively impacted student behavior and socio-emotional development. Press release. https://nces.ed.gov/whatsnew/press_releases/07_06_2022.asp.

National Crime Agency. 2020, April 4. Law enforcement in coronavirus online safety push as National Crime Agency reveals 300,000 in UK pose sexual threat to children. https://www.nationalcrimeagency.gov.uk/news/onlinesafetyathome.

National School Boards Association. 2019, April 1. Data on disabilities. https://www.nsba.org:443/ASBJ/2019/April/Graduation-Rates-Students-Disabilities.

National Student Clearinghouse Research Center. 2021, June 10. Spring 2021: Current term enrollment estimates. https://nscresearchcenter.org/current-term-enrollment-estimates/.

Nayar, V. 2021, February 21. Misplaced celebrations: How edtech changed education from necessity to privilege. *Economic Times*. https://economictimes.indiatimes.com/small-biz/security-tech/technology/misplaced-celebrations-how-edtech-changed-education-from-necessity-to-privilege/articleshow/81121682.cms.

Nelson, C. 2022. Babies need humans, not screens. UNICEF. https://www.unicef.org/parenting/child-development/babies-screen-time.

NetBlocks. 2022, March 4. Widespread internet outage registered in Iran amid reports of fire at datacenter. https://netblocks.org/reports/widespread-internet-outage-registered-in-iran-amid-reports-of-fire-at-datacenter-eBOQzz8Z.

Neuman, S.B. 2007. The knowledge gap: Implications for early education. Dickinson, D.K. & Neuman, S.B. *Handbook of Early Literacy Research*. Vol. 2. New York: Guilford Press.

New York Times. 2020, April 23. Teachers and students describe a remote-learning life. https://www.nytimes.com/2020/04/23/education/learning/coronavirus-teachers-students-remote-learning.html.

Newberry L. 021, October 25. 8 to 3: Why friendship is hard for many teens right now. *Los Angeles Times*. https://www.latimes.com/california/newsletter/2021-10-25/8-to-3-how-to-help-struggling-teens-8-to-3.

Newsmantraa. 2022, January 31. Online exam proctoring software market is going to boom with ProctorU, Pearson Vue, PSI Services, ExamSoft, Verificient. Digital Journal. https://www.digitaljournal.com/pr/online-exam-proctoring-software-market-is-going-to-boom-with-proctoru-pearson-vue-psi-services-examsoft-verificient.

Newton, D. 2021, April 26. From admissions to teaching to grading, AI is infiltrating higher education. The Hechinger Report. http://hechingerreport.org/from-admissions-to-teaching-to-grading-ai-is-infiltrating-higher-education/.

NHS Digital. 2020, October 22. Mental health of children and young people in England, 2020: Wave 1 follow up to the 2017 survey. https://digital.nhs.uk/data-and-information/publications/statistical/mental-health-of-children-and-young-people-in-england/2020-wave-1-follow-up.

Nicandro, V., Khandelwal, A. & Weitzman, A. 2020, June 1. Please, let students turn their videos off in class. *Stanford Daily*. https://www.stanforddaily.com/2020/06/01/please-let-students-turn-their-videos-off-in-class/.

Nicolai, S. 2019, October 9. Introducing the EdTech Hub. EdTech Hub. https://edtechhub.org/2019/10/09/introducing-the-edtech-hub/.

Nietzel, N. 2021, June 10. Latest numbers show largest college enrollment decline in a decade. Forbes. https://www.forbes.com/sites/michaeltnietzel/2021/06/10/updated-numbers-show-largest-college-enrollment-decline-in-a-decade/.

Ninkovic, S. 2021. *Untethered: Overcome Distraction, Build Healthy Digital Habits, and Use Tech to Create a Life You Love*. Independently published.

Noeth, R.J. & Volkov, B.B. 2004. *Evaluating the Effectiveness of Technology in Our Schools: ACT Policy Report*. https://www.act.org/content/dam/act/unsecured/documents/school_tech.pdf.

Norris, S. 2022, December 7. Online proctored exams: Are they here to stay? *The Review*. https://udreview.com/online-proctored-exams-are-they-here-to-stay/.

Norris, T. 2021, March 10. Tax 'pandemic profiteering' by tech companies to help fund public education. The Conversation. https://theconversation.com/tax-pandemic-profiteering-by-tech-companies-to-help-fund-public-education-155705.

Nortajuddin, A. 2020, November 3. More school dropouts in a pandemic? *Asean Post*. https://theaseanpost.com/article/more-school-dropouts-pandemic.

North Star Marketing. 2021. Stories of recruitment success during the pandemic. https://www.northstarmarketing.com/how-to-pivot-your-private-school-marketing-strategy-during-crisis/.

Novak, J. 2021, November 26. We're longing for the one thing the metaverse can't give us. *New York Times*. https://www.nytimes.com/2021/11/26/opinion/touch-starvation-metaverse-virtual-worlds.html.

Nowicki, J. 2020, November 19. *Distance Learning: Challenges Providing Services to K-12 English Learners and Students with Disabilities During COVID-19*. United States Government Accountability Office. https://www.gao.gov/products/gao-21-43.

Nuzzo, J.B. & Sharfstein, J.M. 2020, July 1. We have to focus on opening schools, not bars. *New York Times*. https://www.nytimes.com/2020/07/01/opinion/coronavirus-schools.html.

O'Leary, J. 2022, September 22. Reducing the cost of cyber-attacks in higher education. Global Education News. https://qs-gen.com/reducing-the-cost-of-cyber-attacks-in-higher-education/.

O'Neil, C. 2016. *Weapons of Math Destruction: How Big Data Increases Inequality and Threatens Democracy*. New York: Crown.

O'Sullivan, D., Duffy, C. & Jorgensen, S. 2021, October 4. Instagram promoted pages glorifying eating disorders to teen accounts. CNN. https://edition.cnn.com/2021/10/04/tech/instagram-facebook-eating-disorders/index.html.

Obar, J.A. & Oeldorf-Hirsch, A. 2018, June 1. The biggest lie on the internet: Ignoring the privacy policies and terms of service policies of social networking services. *Information, Communication & Society*. TPRC 44: The 44th Research Conference on Communication, Information and Internet Policy. https://papers.ssrn.com/abstract=2757465.

Office of Educational Technology. 2022. Meet the OET team. https://tech.ed.gov/team/.

Office of Governor Gavin Newsom. 2022, September 15. Governor Newsom signs first-in-nation bill protecting children's online data and privacy. https://www.gov.ca.gov/2022/09/15/governor-newsom-signs-first-in-nation-bill-protecting-childrens-online-data-and-privacy/.

Ofman, D. 2020, November 19. Siberian student scales birch tree for internet access as classes move online. The World. https://theworld.org/stories/2020-11-19/siberian-student-scales-birch-tree-internet-access-classes-move-online.

OneClass. 2020, April 1. 75% of college students unhappy with quality of e-learning during Covid-19. Blog post. https://oneclass.com/blog/featured/177356-7525-of-college-students-unhappy-with-quality-of-elearning-during-covid-19.en.html.

OneClass. 2020, May 1. Will you withdraw if your current school only offers remote / e-learning option for Fall 2020. Blog post. https://oneclass.com/blog/featured/178552-will-you-withdraw-if-your-current-school-only-offers-remote-2F-e-learning-option-for-fall-2020.en.html.

Ontario Universities and Colleges Coalition. 2020, July 2. Letter to the Minister of Colleges and Universities. https://ocufa.on.ca/assets/OUCC-letter-to-MCU-on-ProctorTrack.pdf.

Operation Enduring Clusterfuck Teacher Gift Idea Funny Coffee Ceramic Mug,11 oz and 15 oz. Available on amazon.co.uk. Operation Enduring Clusterfuck Teacher Ceramic Mug. https://www.amazon.co.uk/Operation-Enduring-Clusterfuck-Teacher-Ceramic/dp/B08S6MK3J3.

Orange. 2021, January 19. Orange takes a leading role in the US to Europe route with two new generation submarine cables linking the East Coast to France. https://internationalcarriers.orange.com/en/news/orange-takes-a-leading-role-in-the-us-to-europe-route-with-two-new-generation-submarine-cables-linking-the-east-coast-to-france.html.

Orben, A. & Przybylski, A.K. 2019. The association between adolescent well-being and digital technology use. *Nature Human Behaviour*, 3(2): 173–182. https://doi.org/10.1038/s41562-018-0506-1.

Oremus, W. 2020, September 12. The privatized internet is failing our kids. OneZero. https://onezero.medium.com/the-travesty-of-remote-learning-is-unfolding-in-real-time-6307975560e8.

Organisation for Economic Co-operation and Development. 2015. *Students, Computers and Learning: Making the Connection*. https://www.oecd.org/publications/students-computers-and-learning-9789264239555-en.htm.

Organisation for Economic Co-operation and Development. 2020, December. *Lessons for Education from COVID-19: A Policy Maker's Handbook for More Resilient Systems*. https://www.oecd-ilibrary.org/education/lessons-for-education-from-covid-19_0a530888-en.

Organisation for Economic Co-operation and Development. 2020, May 4. Keeping the internet up and running in times of crisis. https://www.oecd.org/coronavirus/policy-responses/keeping-the-internet-up-and-running-in-times-of-crisis-4017c4c9/.

Organisation for Economic Co-operation and Development. 2020. New OECD PISA report reveals challenge of online learning for many students and schools. https://www.oecd.org/education/new-oecd-pisa-report-reveals-challenge-of-online-learning-for-many-students-and-schools.htm.

Organisation for Economic Co-operation and Development. 2020. *PISA 2018 Results (Volume V): Effective Policies, Successful Schools*. https://www.oecd.org/education/pisa-2018-results-volume-v-ca768d40-en.htm.

Organisation for Economic Co-operation and Development. 2021, June. *What's Next? Lessons on Education Recovery: Findings from a Survey of Ministries of Education amid the COVID-19 Pandemic*. https://www.oecd-ilibrary.org/docserver/697bc36e-en.pdf.

Organisation for Economic Co-operation and Development. 2021. *OECD Digital Education Outlook 2021: Pushing the Frontiers with Artificial Intelligence, Blockchain and Robots*. https://doi.org/10.1787/589b283f-en.

Organisation for Economic Co-operation and Development. 2021. *Using Digital Technologies for Early Education during COVID-19: OECD Report for the G20 2020 Education Working Group*. https://doi.org/10.1787/fe8d68ad-en.

Oriomoni, A. 2022, June 8. Tension between U of T law and disabled students raises a broader policy implication: lawyer. *Law Times*. https://www.lawtimesnews.com/resources/legal-education/tension-between-u-of-t-law-and-disabled-students-raises-a-broader-policy-implication-lawyer/367300.

Orlando, A. 2020, April 13. Kids are growing up wired — and that's changing their brains. *Discover*. https://www.discovermagazine.com/mind/screen-time-is-replacing-playtime-and-thats-changing-kids-brains.

Oster, E. 2020, November 20. Schools are not spreading covid-19. This new data makes the case. *Washington Post*. https://www.washingtonpost.com/opinions/2020/11/20/covid-19-schools-data-reopening-safety/.

Oster, E. 2020, October 9. Schools aren't super-spreaders. *The Atlantic*. https://www.theatlantic.com/ideas/archive/2020/10/schools-arent-superspreaders/616669/.

Oxford University Press. 2021. *Addressing the Deepening Digital Divide*. https://oup.foleon.com/report/digital-divide/cover/.

Padmanabhan, V. & Alexander, S. 2019, March 11. The curious case of electrification in India amid discom blackouts. Mint. https://www.livemint.com/elections/lok-sabha-elections/the-curious-case-of-electrification-in-india-amid-power-discom-blackouts-1552257301715.html.

Palandrani, P. 2020, July 14. Introducing the Global X Education ETF (EDUT). Global X. https://www.globalxetfs.com/introducing-the-global-x-education-etf-edut/.

Palfrey, Q., Good, N., Ghamrawi, L., Monge, W. & Boag, W. 2020, September 1. Privacy considerations as schools and parents expand utilization of ed tech apps during the COVID-19 pandemic. International Digital Accountability Council. https://digitalwatchdog.org/wp-content/uploads/2020/09/IDAC-Ed-Tech-Report-912020.pdf.

Pandya, A. & Lodha, P. 2021. Social connectedness, excessive screen time during COVID-19 and mental health: A review of current evidence. *Frontiers in Human Dynamics*, 3: 45. https://www.frontiersin.org/article/10.3389/fhumd.2021.684137.

Pangrazi, L. & Sefton-Green, J. 2022. *Learning to Live with Datafication: Educational Case Studies and Initiatives from Across the World*. Abingdon, Oxfordshire: Routledge.

Papert, S. 1981. *Mindstorms: Children, Computers and Powerful Ideas*. New York: Basic Books.

Pappano, L. 2012, November 2. The year of the MOOC. *New York Times*. https://www.nytimes.com/2012/11/04/education/edlife/massive-open-online-courses-are-multiplying-at-a-rapid-pace.html.

Pappas, S. 2020, April 1. What do we really know about kids and screens? *Monitor on Psychology*, 51(3). https://www.apa.org/monitor/2020/04/cover-kids-screens.

Paquet, G. 2005. *The New Geo-Governance: A Baroque Approach (Governance Series)*. Ottawa: University of Ottawa Press.

Park, G. 2021, July 1. The 'metaverse' is growing. And now you can directly invest in it. *Washington Post*. https://www.washingtonpost.com/video-games/2021/07/01/metaverse-investments/.

Parks, M.R. 2014. Big data in communication research: Its contents and discontents. *Journal of Communication*, 64(2). http://onlinelibrary.wiley.com/doi/abs/10.1111/jcom.12090.

Parliamentlive.tv. 2020, September 2. The impact of COVID-19 on education and children's services. https://parliamentlive.tv/Event/Index/a3d523ca-09fc-49a5-84e3-d50c3a3bcbe3.

Patil, A. & Bromwich, J.E. 2020, September 29. How it feels when software watches you take tests. *New York Times*. https://www.nytimes.com/2020/09/29/style/testing-schools-proctorio.html.

Patterson, D. 2021, March 11. Schools have become the leading targets of ransomware attacks. CBS News. https://www.cbsnews.com/news/schools-popular-ransomware-targets/.

Paul, K. 2022, August 30. First-of-its-kind legislation will keep California's children safer while online. *The Guardian*. https://www.theguardian.com/technology/2022/aug/30/california-protect-children-online-privacy.

Paulich, K.N., Ross, J., Lessem, J. & Hewitt, J. 2021. Screen time and early adolescent mental health, academic, and social outcomes in 9- and 10-year-old children: Utilizing the Adolescent Brain Cognitive Development (ABCD) study. *PLOS ONE*, 16(9). https://doi.org/10.1371/journal.pone.0256591.

Pearson. 2020. *The Global Learner Survey: August 2020*. https://plc.pearson.com/sites/pearson-corp/files/Pearson_Global-Learners-Survey_2020_FINAL.pdf.

Pellini, A. 2021, February 19. EdTech and Covid-19: Lessons from around the world. EdTech Hub. https://edexec.co.uk/edtech-lessons-from-around-the-world-part-two/.

Pelly, S. 2021, October 1. Whistleblower: Facebook is misleading the public on progress against hate speech, violence, misinformation. 60-minutes. CBS News. https://www.cbsnews.com/news/facebook-whistleblower-frances-haugen-misinformation-public-60-minutes-2021-10-03/.

People for Education. 2022, February 14. Major changes coming to online learning in Ontario. https://peopleforeducation.ca/our-work/major-changes-coming-to-online-learning-in-ontario/.

Pereda, N. & Díaz-Faes, D.A. 2020. Family violence against children in the wake of COVID-19 pandemic: A review of current perspectives and risk factors. *Child and Adolescent Psychiatry and Mental Health*, 14(1): 40. https://capmh.biomedcentral.com/articles/10.1186/s13034-020-00347-1.

Perkowitz, S. 2021. The bias in the machine: Facial recognition technology and racial disparities. *MIT Case Studies in Social and Ethical Responsibilities of Computing* (Winter). https://mit-serc.pubpub.org/pub/bias-in-machine/release/1.

Pesce, N.L. 2020, January 18. Americans trust Amazon and Google more than the police or the government. Market Watch. https://www.marketwatch.com/story/people-trust-amazon-and-google-more-than-the-police-or-the-government-2020-01-14.

Pew Research Center. 2018, April 17. *The Expanded Edition: The Future of Well-Being in a Tech-Saturated World*. https://assets.pewresearch.org/wp-content/uploads/sites/14/2018/04/16140055/PI_2018.04.17_Future-of-Well-Being_EXPANDED.pdf.

Phair, R. 2020, April 3. During the coronavirus crisis, children need books more than ever! *OECD Education and Skills Today*. https://oecdedutoday.com/during-coronavirus-crisis-children-need-books/.

Pier, L., Christian, M., Tymeson, H. & Meyer, R.H. 2021, June. *COVID-19 Impacts on Student Learning: Evidence from Interim Assessments in California*. Policy Analysis for California Education. https://edpolicyinca.org/publications/covid-19-impacts-student-learning.

Pierce, S. 2020, May 15. Touch starvation is a consequence of COVID-19's physical distancing. Texas Medical Center. https://www.tmc.edu/news/2020/05/touch-starvation/.

Piketty, T. 2014. *Capital in the Twenty-First Century*. Cambridge, MA: Belknap Press.

Pikoos, T.D., Buzwell, S., Sharp, G. & Rossell, S.L. 2021, December. The Zoom effect: Exploring the impact of video calling on appearance dissatisfaction and interest in aesthetic treatment during the COVID-19 pandemic. *Aesthetic Surgery Journal*, 41(12). https://doi.org/10.1093/asj/sjab257.

Piper, H., Garratt, D. & Taylor, B. 2013. Child abuse, child protection and defensive 'touch' in PE teaching and sports coaching. *Sport, Education and Society*, 18(5): 583–598. https://doi.org/10.1080/13573322.2012.735653.

Pires, F. 2022, April 18. Intel develops controversial AI to detect emotional states of students. Tom's Hardware. https://www.tomshardware.com/news/intel-students-ai-controversy.

Population Council. 2021. *Promises to Keep: Impact of Covid-19 on Adolescents in Kenya*. https://www.popcouncil.org/uploads/pdfs/2021PGY_ImpactCovidAdolKenya.pdf.

Porter, H. 2014, January 18. The internet revolution versus the House of Lords. *The Observer*. https://www.theguardian.com/commentisfree/2014/jan/18/house-of-lords-debate-world-wide-web.

Portillo, J., Garay, U., Tejada, E. & Bilbao, N. 2020. Self-perception of the digital competence of educators during the COVID-19 Pandemic: A cross-analysis of different educational stages. *Sustainability*, 12(23): 101–128. https://doi.org/10.3390/su122310128.

Portuguese School of Luanda. 2022, January 15. Comunicado – Retoma das aulas na modalidade presencial [Announcement – Resumption of classes in face-to-face modality]. https://www.epluanda.pt/9315-comunicado-retoma-das-aulas-na-modalidade-presencial.

Postman, N. 1993. *Technopoly: The Surrender of Culture to Technology*. New York: Vintage Books.

Postman, N. 2005. *Amusing Ourselves to Death: Public Discourse In The Age Of Show Business*. New York: Penguin Books.

Pota, V. et al. 2021, September. *Turning to Technology: A Global Survey of Teachers' Responses to the Covid-19 Pandemic*. T4 and EdTech Hub. https://t4.education/t4-insights/reports/turning-to-technology.

Pothong, K., Atabey, A., Turner, S. & Livingstone, S. 2022, June 19. The DFC to launch education data reality. Digital Futures Commission. https://digitalfuturescommission.org.uk/blog/the-dfc-to-launch-education-data-reality/.

Precarity Lab. 2020. *Technoprecarious*. London: Goldsmiths Press.

Presidency of the Dominican Republic. 2022, January 7. Gobierno llama al reinicio de clases próximo martes 11 de enero de manera presencial y voluntaria [Government calls for the restart of classes next Tuesday, January 11 in person and voluntarily]. https://presidencia.gob.do/noticias/gobierno-llama-al-reinicio-de-clases-proximo-martes-11-de-enero-de-manera-presencial-y.

Press Association. 2022, February 14. Most 5-year-olds spend too much time online, survey shows. Bloomberg. https://www.bloomberg.com/news/articles/2022-02-14/most-5-year-olds-spend-too-much-time-online-survey-shows.

Price, C. 2018. *How to Break Up with Your Phone: The 30-Day Plan to Take Back Your Life*. Berkeley, CA: Ten Speed Press.

Proctorio. 2020, April 13. Letter to Shea Swauger and *Hybrid Pedagogy*. https://drive.google.com/file/d/1IYD1YIbSL-t8rWy70hyps8cV9IKigV0Y/view.

Proctorio. 2023. Our platform. https://proctorio.com/.

Proctorio. 2023. Proctorio Gradebook in Canvas. http://www.fullerton.edu/it/services/software/proctorio/Canvas%20Proctorio%20Gradebook.pdf.

ProctorU. 2020. ProctorU CCPA privacy policy. https://archive.md/FM8ba.

Prothero, A. & Harwin, A. 2019, April 18. Many online charter schools fail to graduate even half of their students on time. *Education Week*. https://www.edweek.org/teaching-learning/many-online-charter-schools-fail-to-graduate-even-half-of-their-students-on-time/2019/04.

Public Citizen. 2020, March 25. Can ProctorU be trusted with students' personal data? Consumer Law & Policy. Blog post. https://pubcit.typepad.com/clpblog/2020/03/can-proctoru-be-trusted-with-students-personal-data.html.

Qiang, X. 2019. The road to digital unfreedom. *Journal of Democracy*, 30(1). https://muse.jhu.edu/article/713722.

Querolo, N. & Singh, S. 2021, August 9. Schools brace for more cyberattacks after record in 2020. Bloomberg. https://www.bloomberg.com/news/features/2021-08-09/schools-brace-for-more-cyberattacks-after-record-2020.

Quinn, B. & Adams, R. 2020, August 20. England exams row timeline: Was Ofqual warned of algorithm bias? *The Guardian*. https://www.theguardian.com/education/2020/aug/20/england-exams-row-timeline-was-ofqual-warned-of-algorithm-bias.

Quintanilla, D. 2021, July 29. Latinx college enrollment was rising before Covid but the pandemic has taken a toll. CNBC. https://www.cnbc.com/2021/07/29/latinx-college-enrollment-was-rising-before-covid-but-the-pandemic-has-taken-a-toll.html.

Qustodio. 2021, April. *Screen Time All the Time: Apps and Kids, a Year Trapped behind Screens*. https://qweb.cdn.prismic.io/qweb/da3cbc01-68b0-4e50-a18f-a9a3a0c74a72_EN_Kids+and+Apps+annual+report_20210408.pdf.

Racheva, V. 2018, December. Social aspects of synchronous virtual learning environments. *AIP Conference Proceedings*, 2048 (1). https://doi.org/10.1063/1.5082050.

Racine, N. et al. 2021. Global prevalence of depressive and anxiety symptoms in children and adolescents during COVID-19: A meta-analysis. *JAMA Pediatrics*, 175(11): 1142–1150. https://doi.org/10.1001/jamapediatrics.2021.2482.

Radesky, J.S. et al. 2020, July. Young children's use of smartphones and tablets. *Pediatrics*, 146(1). http://pediatrics.aappublications.org/content/146/1/e20193518.abstract.

Rafalow, M.H. 2020. *Digital Divisions: How Schools Create Inequality in the Tech Era*. Chicago: University of Chicago Press.

Rajghatta, C. 2013, February 7. NRI education pioneer, Dr Sugata Mitra, wins $ 1 million TED prize. *Times of India*. https://timesofindia.indiatimes.com/nri/us-canada-news/nri-education-pioneer-dr-sugata-mitra-wins-1-million-ted-prize/articleshow/18705008.cms.

Rakoff, J.S. 2021, June 10. Sentenced by algorithm. *New York Review of Books*. https://www.nybooks.com/articles/2021/06/10/prison-terms-sentenced-by-algorithm/.

Rankin, J. 2023. Exam day: What to expect. ProctorU. https://support.proctoru.com/hc/en-us/articles/360043565051-Exam-Day-What-to-Expect.

Rauf, D. 2020, April 16. Coronavirus squeezes supply of Chromebooks, iPads, and other digital learning devices. *Education Week*. https://www.edweek.org/education-industry/coronavirus-squeezes-supply-of-chromebooks-ipads-and-other-digital-learning-devices/2020/04.

Rauf, D. 2021, July 26. Another education company goes public: Instructure IPO gives ed-tech firm $2.9 billion valuation. EdWeek Market Brief. https://marketbrief.edweek.org/marketplace-k-12/another-education-company-goes-public-instructure-ipo-gives-ed-tech-firm-2-9-billion-valuation/.

Ravi, V. 2020, April 22. Test anxiety and losing internet connection during online exams. Vijay Ravi. https://vijayravi.blog/blog/f/test-anxiety-and-losing-internet-connection-during-online-exams.

Ravitch, D. 2013, May 31. How will inBloom help students and schools? Diane Ravitch's blog. https://dianeravitch.net/2013/05/31/how-will-inbloom-help-students-and-schools/.

Ravitch, D. 2016, February 23. Wendy Lecker: Why "personalized learning" is neither. Diane Ravitch's blog. https://dianeravitch.net/2016/02/23/wendy-lecker-why-personalized-learning-is-neither/.

Ray, B.D. 2021, September 9. How many homeschool students are there in the United States? Pre-Covid-19 and post-Covid-19: New data. National Home Education Research Institute. https://www.nheri.org/how-many-homeschool-students-are-there-in-the-united-states-pre-covid-19-and-post-covid-19/.

Reboot. 2023. The industries with the longest Terms and Conditions. https://www.rebootonline.com/digital-pr/assets/industries-with-longest-terms-and-conditions/.

Reddy, V., Soudien, C. & Winnaar, L. 2020, May 5. Impact of school closures on education outcomes in South Africa. The Conversation. https://theconversation.com/impact-of-school-closures-on-education-outcomes-in-south-africa-136889.

Reich, J. 2020. *Failure to Disrupt: Why Technology Alone Can't Transform Education*. Cambridge, MA: Harvard University Press.

Reich, J. 2021, April 15. Tinkering with tech: How the pandemic exposed the flaws of digital education. Heinrich-Böll-Stiftung. https://us.boell.org/en/2021/03/31/tinkering-tech-how-pandemic-exposed-flaws-digital-education.

Reich, J. 2021. Ed tech's failure during the pandemic, and what comes after. *Phi Delta Kappan*, 102(6): 20–24. https://journals.sagepub.com/doi/10.1177/0031721721998149.

Reich, J. et al. 2020, July. *What's Lost, What's Left, What's Next: Lessons Learned from the Lived Experiences of Teachers during the Pandemic*. Teaching Systems Lab. https://edarxiv.org/8exp9.

Reichman, H. 2020. An egregious case of legal bullying. *Academe*. Blog post. https://academeblog.org/2020/03/27/an-egregious-case-of-legal-bullying/.

Reneau, A. 2020, April 15. School districts are transforming buses into WiFi hotspots for students without internet. Upworthy. https://www.upworthy.com/school-buses-become-wifi-hotspots-for-students.

Restart Project. 2018. Mobiles: the global carbon footprint. https://therestartproject.org/the-global-footprint-of-mobiles/.

Reuters. 2009, February 17. Oscar favorite Slumdog Millionaire inspired by NIIT's 'Hole in the Wall' initiative. https://web.archive.org/web/20090301093437/http://www.reuters.com/article/pressRelease/idUS191330+17-Feb-2009+BW20090217.

Reuters. 2020, April 30. Zoom says it has 300 million daily meeting participants, not users. https://www.reuters.com/article/us-zoom-video-commn-encryption/zoom-says-it-has-300-million-daily-meeting-participants-not-users-idUSKBN22C1T4.

Reuters. 2020, June 28. Chinese online tutor Zuoyebang raises $750 million in fresh round. https://www.reuters.com/article/us-zuoyebang-fundraiisng-idINKBN240093.

Reuters. 2020, September 2. Virtual schooling in pandemic sharpens divide for Bolivia's poor. https://www.reuters.com/article/us-health-coronavirus-bolivia-education-idUSKBN25T20F.

Reynard, M. 2020, November 4. L'éducation en situations de crise: Rapport de la délégation suisse présenté par le conseiller national Mathias Reynard [Education in crisis situations: Report of the Swiss delegation presented by national councillor Mathias Reynard]. Committee on Education, Communication and Cultural Affairs and Network of Young Parliamentarians. http://apf.francophonie.org/IMG/pdf/rapport_sur_l_education_en_situations_de_crise.pdf.

Rezaeipour, M. 2020. COVID-19-related weight gain in school-aged children. Letter to the editor. *International Journal of Endocrinology and Metabolism*, 19(1). https://www.ncbi.nlm.nih.gov/pmc/articles/PMC8010564/.

Ribner, A.D. et al. 2021. Screen time in the Coronavirus 2019 era: International trends of increasing use among 3- to 7-year-old children. *The Journal of Pediatrics*, 239: 59-66.e1. https://doi.org/10.1016/j.jpeds.2021.08.068.

Richard Blumenthal, Senator for Connecticut. 2020, December 3. Blumenthal leads call for virtual exam software companies to improve equity, accessibility & privacy for students amid troubling reports. Press release. https://www.blumenthal.senate.gov/newsroom/press/release/blumenthal-leads-call-for-virtual-exam-software-companies-to-improve-equity-accessibility-and-privacy-for-students-amid-troubling-reports.

Richards, E. 2020, May 24. Coronavirus' online school is hard enough. What if you're still learning to speak English? *USA Today*. https://eu.usatoday.com/in-depth/news/education/2020/05/14/coronavirus-online-classes-school-closures-esl-students-learn-english/5178145002/.

Richardson, T. 2020, April 27. Online learning portal crashes as students return to school. InDaily. https://indaily.com.au/news/2020/04/27/online-learning-portal-crashes-as-students-return-to-school/.

Richler, D. 2004. *Quality Education for Persons with Disabilities*. UNESCO. https://unesdoc.unesco.org/ark:/48223/pf0000146694.

Richtel, M. 2021, January 16. Children's screen time has soared in the pandemic, alarming parents and researchers. *New York Times*. https://www.nytimes.com/2021/01/16/health/covid-kids-tech-use.html.

Rimmer, S., McGuire, K. & Gill, N. 2020, December 16. Stressed out, dropping out: COVID has taken its toll on uni students. The Conversation. https://theconversation.com/stressed-out-dropping-out-covid-has-taken-its-toll-on-uni-students-152004.

Rivers, M., Suarez, K. & Gallón, N. 2020, August 27. Mexico's solution to the Covid-19 educational crisis: Put school on television. CNN. https://edition.cnn.com/2020/08/22/americas/mexico-covid-19-classes-on-tv-intl/index.html.

Rize ETF. 2020, September 3. Specialist thematic ETF pioneer Rize ETF launches sustainable food and education ETFs. Press release. https://rizeetf.com/wp-content/uploads/2020/09/03Sep20_Press_Release_Rize-launches-two-new-ETFs.pdf.

Robb, M.B., Bay, W. & Vennegaard, T. 2017. *The New Normal: Parents, Teens, and Digital Devices in Japan*. USC Annenberg & Common Sense. https://assets.uscannenberg.org/docs/CS_DigitalDevicesJapan_v8_press.pdf.

Robb, M.B., Bay, W. & Vennegaard, T. 2019. *The New Normal: Parents, Teens, and Mobile Devices in Mexico*. USC Annenberg & Common Sense. https://www.commonsensemedia.org/sites/default/files/research/report/2019_thenewnormalmexico-final-release_eng-092519_web.pdf.

Roberto, M. 2020, June 30. 80 Law students sue University of Nairobi over online classes, exams. TUKO. https://www.tuko.co.ke/365407-80-law-students-sue-university-nairobi-online-classes-exams-citing-inequality.html.

Robinson, K. 2006. Do schools kill creativity? TED Talks. https://www.ted.com/talks/sir_ken_robinson_do_schools_kill_creativity.

Robinson, K. 2013. How to escape education's death valley. TED Talks. https://www.ted.com/talks/sir_ken_robinson_how_to_escape_education_s_death_valley.

Robinson, M. 2017, November 21. Tech billionaires spent $170 million on a new kind of school — now classrooms are shrinking and some parents say their kids are 'guinea pigs'. Business Insider. https://www.businessinsider.com/altschool-why-parents-leaving-2017-11.

Robinson, T.N. et al. 2017. Screen media exposure and obesity in children and adolescents. *Pediatrics*, 140(2): 97–101. https://doi.org/10.1542/peds.2016-1758K.

Robles, Y. 2020, April 14. In Aurora online learning, students and parents are missing the teacher connection and support. Chalkbeat. https://co.chalkbeat.org/2020/4/13/21225487/in-aurora-online-learning-students-and-parents-are-missing-the-teacher-connection-and-support.

Rodriguez, A. 2021, November 1. Screen time among teenagers during COVID more than doubled outside of virtual school, study finds. *USA Today*. https://eu.usatoday.com/story/news/health/2021/11/01/covid-screen-time-among-teens-doubles-during-pandemic-study-finds/6230769001/.

Rodriguez, M., Cobo, C., Muñoz-Najar, A. & Ciarrusta, I. 2021. *Remote Learning during the Global School Lockdown: Multi Country Lessons*. World Bank Group. https://documents1.worldbank.org/curated/en/668741627975171644/pdf/Remote-Learning-During-the-Global-School-Lockdown-Multi-Country-Lessons.pdf.

Rohwerder, S. 2020, February 21. Secondary impacts of major disease outbreaks in low- and middle-income countries. K4D Helpdesk Report 756. Institute of Development Studies. https://opendocs.ids.ac.uk/opendocs/bitstream/handle/20.500.12413/15129/756_Secondary_impacts_of_major_disease_outbreak_%20in_low_income_countries.pdf.

Roof, K. & Tse, C. 2021, October 28. Udemy raising $421 million in top-of-range IPO. Bloomberg. https://www.bloomberg.com/news/articles/2021-10-28/udemy-is-said-to-raise-421-million-in-top-of-range-ipo.

Rose, J. 2012, May 9. How to break free of our 19th-century factory-model education system. *The Atlantic*. https://www.theatlantic.com/business/archive/2012/05/how-to-break-free-of-our-19th-century-factory-model-education-system/256881/.

Rose, J. 2022, February 23. Proctorio is going after digital rights groups that bash their proctoring software. Vice. https://www.vice.com/en/article/epxqgw/proctorio-is-going-after-digital-rights-groups-that-bash-their-proctoring-software.

Rosenberg, N.Y. 2017, April 28. 'Green schools' use EdTech to save the environment. EdTechReview. https://edtechreview.in/trends-insights/trends/2762-green-schools-use-tech.

Roy, S. 2022, May 18. How pandemic has brought changes in edtech sector. *Business Standard*. https://www.business-standard.com/podcast/education/how-pandemic-has-brought-changes-in-edtech-sector-120091600700_1.html.

Rozelle, S., Rahimi, H., Wang, H. & Dill, E. 2020, March 30. Lockdowns are protecting China's rural families from COVID-19, but the economic burden is heavy. International Food Policy Research Institute. Blog post. https://www.ifpri.org/blog/lockdowns-are-protecting-chinas-rural-families-covid-19-economic-burden-heavy.

Ruangguru. 2021, April 19. Ruangguru secures USD 55 million new investment led by Tiger Global Management. https://www.ruangguru.com/blog/ruangguru-secures-usd-55-million-new-investment-led-by-tiger-global-management.

Ruehl, M., Jack, A. & Riordan, P. 2020, March 18. Coronavirus proves a bonanza for Asia edtech start-ups. *Financial Times*. https://www.ft.com/content/879ba44b-fa16-4a9d-afa4-f7f4e149edec.

Russell, J.A. & Dols, J.M.F. (eds) 2017. *The Science of Facial Expression*. Oxford: Oxford University Press.

Russell, M. 2019. AltSchool's out: Zuckerberg-backed startup that tried to rethink education calls it quits. *San Francisco Chronicle*. https://www.sfchronicle.com/business/article/AltSchool-s-out-Zuckerberg-backed-startup-that-14058785.php.

Russell, N. 2020, July 27. I can't keep doing this. Please open the schools. *The Atlantic*. https://www.theatlantic.com/ideas/archive/2020/07/please-open-schools/614605/.

Sajn, N. 2022, January 12. Right to repair. Briefing paper. European Parliament. https://www.europarl.europa.eu/thinktank/en/document/EPRS_BRI(2022)698869.

Saltman, K.J. 2007. *Schooling and the Politics of Disaster*. New York: Routledge.

Sandle, T. 2020, January 29. Report finds only 1 percent reads 'Terms & Conditions'. Digital Journal. https://www.digitaljournal.com/business/report-finds-only-1-percent-reads-terms-conditions/article/566127.

Santhakumar, V. 2021, August 22. Will edtech devalue teachers? *University World News*. https://www.universityworldnews.com/post.php?story=202108171255039.

Sarangapani, P., Thirumalai, B., Ramanathan, A., Kumar, R. & Ramchand, M. 2021. *No Teacher, No Class: State of the Education Report for India, 2021*. UNESCO Office in New Delhi. https://unesdoc.unesco.org/ark:/48223/pf0000379115.

Satariano, A. & Mac, R. 2021, September 27. Facebook delays Instagram app for users 13 and younger. *New York Times*. https://www.nytimes.com/2021/09/27/technology/facebook-instagram-for-kids.html.

Satariano, A. & Mozur, P. 2021, October 22. Russia is censoring the internet, with coercion and black boxes. *New York Times*. https://www.nytimes.com/2021/10/22/technology/russia-internet-censorship-putin.html.

Satariano, A. 2015, June 10. What happens when an ex-Google executive creates a school system? Bloomberg. https://www.bloomberg.com/news/features/2015-06-10/what-happens-when-an-ex-google-executive-creates-a-school-system-.

Satariano, A. 2022, April 27. Meta fined $275 million for breaking E.U. data privacy law. *New York Times*. https://www.nytimes.com/2022/11/28/business/meta-fine-eu-privacy.html.

Satariano, A. 2022, March 24. E.U. takes aim at big tech's power with landmark digital act. *New York Times*. https://www.nytimes.com/2022/03/24/technology/eu-regulation-apple-meta-google.html.

Satariano, A. 2022, November 28. Meta fined $275 million for breaking E.U. data privacy law. *New York Times*. https://www.nytimes.com/2022/11/28/business/meta-fine-eu-privacy.html.

Satariano, A. 2022, September 5. Meta fined $400 million for treatment of children's data on Instagram. *New York Times*. https://www.nytimes.com/2022/09/05/business/meta-children-data-protection-europe.html.

Save our Future. 2020. *Averting an Education Catastrophe for the World's Children*. https://saveourfuture.world/white-paper/.

Sawchuck, S. & Sparks, S. 2020, December 2. Kids are behind in math because of COVID-19. Here's what research says could help. *Education Week*. https://www.edweek.org/teaching-learning/kids-are-behind-in-math-because-of-covid-19-heres-what-research-says-could-help/2020/12.

Sawers, P. 2022, July 18. Denmark bans Chromebooks and Google Workspace in schools over data transfer risks. TechCrunch. https://techcrunch.com/2022/07/18/denmark-bans-chromebooks-and-google-workspace-in-schools-over-gdpr/.

Sayadi, E. & Samaro, D. 2020, October 5. Internet shutdowns in Algeria and Sudan: Damaging practices during exceptional circumstances. Access Now. https://www.accessnow.org/internet-shutdowns-in-algeria-and-sudan-damaging-practices-during-exceptional-circumstances/.

Schanzenbach, D. & Pitts, A. 2020, May 13. *Estimates of Food Insecurity during the COVID-19 Crisis: Results from the COVID Impact Survey, Week 1 (April 20-26, 2020)*. Institute for Policy Research Rapid Research Report. https://www.ipr.northwestern.edu/documents/reports/food-insecurity-covid_week1_report-13-may-2020.pdf.

Schleicher, A. 2021, April 19. Repeating the school year not the answer to COVID learning losses: Andreas Schleicher. *OECD Education and Skills Today*. https://oecdedutoday.com/repeating-school-year-not-the-answer-to-covid-learning-losses/.

Schmall, E. & Yasir, S. 2022, January 27. India schools stay closed, and hopes fade for a lost generation. *New York Times*. https://www.nytimes.com/2022/01/27/world/asia/india-schools.html.

Schmidt, S. 2020, August 19. The centers helping child abuse victims have seen 40,000 fewer kids amid the pandemic. *Washington Post*. https://www.washingtonpost.com/dc-md-va/2020/08/19/child-abuse-victims-plunge-pandemic/.

Scholz, S., Hagen, W. & Lee, C. 2021, June 22. The increasing threat of ransomware in higher education. *EDUCAUSE Review*. https://er.educause.edu/articles/2021/6/the-increasing-threat-of-ransomware-in-higher-education.

SchoolHouse Connection & Poverty Solutions at the University of Michigan. 2020. *Lost in the Masked Shuffle & Virtual Void: Children and Youth Experiencing Homelessness amidst the Pandemic*. https://schoolhouseconnection.org/wp-content/uploads/2020/11/Lost-in-the-Masked-Shuffle-and-Virtual-Void.pdf.

Schult, J., Mahler, M., Faut, B. & Lindner, M.A. 2021. Did students learn less during the COVID-19 pandemic? Reading and mathematics competencies before and after the first pandemic wave. *School Effectiveness and School Improvement*, 33(4): 544–563. https://doi.org/10.1080/09243453.2022.2061014.

Schwartz, S. 2018, May 10. Decoding Fortnite: 5 things educators need to know about the hit video game. *Education Week*. https://www.edweek.org/technology/decoding-fortnite-5-things-educators-need-to-know-about-the-hit-video-game/2018/05.

Schwartz, S. 2018, May 31. Fortnite may be addictive, but could also promote learning, say Stanford experts. *Education Week*. https://www.edweek.org/technology/fortnite-may-be-addictive-but-could-also-promote-learning-say-stanford-experts/2018/05.

Scott, M., Cerulus, L. & Overly, S. 2019, May 25. How Silicon Valley gamed the world's toughest privacy rules. *POLITICO*. https://www.politico.com/story/2019/05/25/how-silicon-valley-gamed-the-worlds-toughest-privacy-rules-1466148.

Sean Coughlan, Katherine Sellgren, & Judith Burns. 2020. A-levels: Anger over 'unfair' results this year. BBC News. https://www.bbc.com/news/education-53759832.

Sedmark, T. 2020, October 15. Fall 2020 undergraduate enrollment down 4% compared to same time last year. National Student Clearinghouse. Press release. https://www.studentclearinghouse.org/blog/fall-2020-undergraduate-enrollment-down-4-compared-to-same-time-last-year/.

Seguin, D., Kuenzel, E., Morton, J.B. & Duerden, E.G. 2021. School's out: Parenting stress and screen time use in school-age children during the COVID-19 pandemic. *Journal of Affective Disorders Reports*, 6: 100217. https://www.sciencedirect.com/science/article/pii/S2666915321001438.

Seldon, A. & Abidoye, O. 2018. *The Fourth Education Revolution. Will Artificial Intelligence Liberate or Infantilise Humanity?* Buckingham, UK: University of Buckingham Press.

Selwyn, N. 2018, October 22. EdTech is killing us all: Facing up to the environmental consequences of digital education. EduResearch Matters. https://www.aare.edu.au/blog/?p=3293.

Shaer, M. 2022, November 28. Where does all the cardboard come from? I had to know. *New York Times*. https://www.nytimes.com/2022/11/28/magazine/cardboard-international-paper.html.

Shah, D. 2020, May 2. How different MOOC providers are responding to the pandemic (updated). Class Central. https://www.classcentral.com/report/mooc-providers-response-to-the-pandemic/.

Shah, N. 2020, November 30. It's starting to sink in: Schools before bars. *POLITICO*. https://www.politico.com/news/2020/11/20/its-starting-to-sink-in-schools-before-bars-438555.

Shanahan, M. 2020, December 11. Students stranded after ProctorU crash. *Honi Soit*. https://honisoit.com/2020/12/students-stranded-after-proctoru-crash/.

Sharma, K. 2020, November 12. As online classes drag on, fatigued students 'losing interest, becoming asocial', say parents. The Print. https://theprint.in/india/education/as-online-classes-drag-on-fatigued-students-losing-interest-becoming-asocial-say-parents/542253/.

Sharma, R. 2022, January 3. Apple (AAPL) Becomes world's first $3 trillion company. Investopedia. https://www.investopedia.com/apple-becomes-first-3-trillion-dollar-company-5214650.

Sharma, S. 2022, January 24. Education sector hounded by cyberattacks in 2021. CSO. https://www.csoonline.com/article/3647760/education-sector-hounded-by-cyberattacks-in-2021.html.

Shleifer, E. & Kologrivaya, K. 2021, June 29. Out of lockdown: China's edtech market confronts the post-pandemic world. *South China Morning Post*. https://www.scmp.com/tech/tech-trends/article/3139056/out-lockdown-chinas-edtech-market-confronts-post-pandemic-world.

Shu, C. 2020, December 28. Chinese online education app Zuoyebang raises $1.6 billion from investors including Alibaba. TechCrunch. https://techcrunch.com/2020/12/28/chinese-online-education-app-zuoyebang-raises-1-6-billion-from-investors-including-alibaba/.

Sil, D. 2020, August 14. Online learning platform Adda247 registers 5X revenue growth in vernacular business amid COVID-19 lockdown. *Entrepreneur India*. https://www.entrepreneur.com/article/354777.

Simon, C. 2021, 9 July. How COVID taught America about inequity in education. The Harvard Gazette. https://news.harvard.edu/gazette/story/2021/07/how-covid-taught-america-about-inequity-in-education/.

Simonite, T. 2019, July 22. The best algorithms still struggle to recognize black faces. Wired. https://www.wired.com/story/best-algorithms-struggle-recognize-black-faces-equally/.

Simonite, T. 2020, July 10. Meet the secret algorithm that's keeping students out of college. Wired. https://www.wired.com/story/algorithm-set-students-grades-altered-futures/.

Simpson, D. 2021. Apple, Google, Tesla, Microsoft beat child labor mine suit. Law360. https://www.law360.com/articles/1437141/apple-google-tesla-microsoft-beat-child-labor-mine-suit.

Singer, N. & Krolik, A. 2021, May 9. Online cheating charges upend Dartmouth medical school. *New York Times*. https://www.nytimes.com/2021/05/09/technology/dartmouth-geisel-medical-cheating.html.

Singer, N. 2017, May 13. How Google took over the classroom. *New York Times*. https://www.nytimes.com/2017/05/13/technology/google-education-chromebooks-schools.html.

Singer, N. 2022. A cyberattack illuminates the shaky state of student privacy. *New York Times*. https://www.nytimes.com/2022/07/31/business/student-privacy-illuminate-hack.html.

Singer, S. 2020, September 13. The everyday exhaustion of teaching during a global pandemic. Gad Fly on the Wall. Blog post. https://gadflyonthewallblog.com/2020/09/13/the-everyday-exhaustion-of-teaching-during-a-global-pandemic/.

Singh, R. & Raj, Y. 2020, October 26. India: Ed-tech companies and the consumer protection act. Mondaq. https://www.mondaq.com/india/dodd-frank-consumer-protection-act/998116/ed-tech-companies-and-the-consumer-protection-act.

Singha, M. 2022, December 17. Don't want online classes, say students. *Times of India*. http://timesofindia.indiatimes.com/articleshow/96532448.cms.

Siu, W. 2022, November 26. I make video games. I won't let my daughters play them. *New York Times*. https://www.nytimes.com/2022/10/02/opinion/video-game-addiction.html.

Skolnik, S. 2020, December 30. Ninety percent of suspected cheaters cleared by California Bar. Bloomberg Law. https://news.bloomberglaw.com/business-and-practice/ninety-percent-of-suspected-cheaters-cleared-by-california-bar.

Sky News. 2018, April 18. Emoji leading to 'serious decline' in English skills. https://news.sky.com/story/emoji-leading-to-serious-decline-in-english-skills-11336247.

Smith, F.J. 1913, July 9. The evolution of the motion picture: VI – Looking into the future with Thomas A. Edison. *New York Dramatic Mirror*. New York (Old Fulton). http://www.laviemoderne.net/images/forum_pics/2017/20171116%20New%20York%20NY%20Dramatic%20Mirror%201913%20Mar-Apr%201914%20Grayscale%20-%200690.pdf.

Smith, M. 2020, December 6. A mom's view: online learning isn't working for students, parents or teachers. Here's what's happening in my home. The 74. https://www.the74million.org/article/a-moms-view-online-learning-isnt-working-for-students-parents-or-teachers-heres-whats-happening-in-my-home/.

Solomon, J. 2019, August 9. Survey: Kids quit most sports by age 11. Aspen Institute Project Play. https://www.aspenprojectplay.org/national-youth-sport-survey/kids-quit-most-sports-by-age-11.

Solove, D. 2014. Why did inBloom die? A hard lesson about education privacy. Teach Privacy. https://teachprivacy.com/inbloom-die-hard-lesson-education-privacy/.

Source Forge. 2023. Online proctoring software: Compare the top online proctoring software of 2023. https://sourceforge.net/software/online-proctoring/.

Sovereign. 2021, September 16. China makes sweeping reforms to 'edtech' sector. https://www.sovereigngroup.com/news/news-and-views/china-makes-sweeping-reforms-to-edtech-sector/.

Spataro, J. 2020, March 11. Helping teachers and students make the switch to remote learning. Microsoft 365. https://www.microsoft.com/en-us/microsoft-365/blog/2020/03/11/helping-teachers-students-switch-remote-learning/.

Spilka, D. 2021, April 18. Duolingo's IPO is a roaring success for retail investors. Investing.com. https://uk.investing.com/analysis/duolingos-ipo-is-a-roaring-success-for-retail-investors-200493881.

Spillane, J. 2022, April 6. App ratings and reviews: 2021 benchmarks. Business 2 Community. https://www.business2community.com/mobile-apps/app-ratings-and-reviews-2021-benchmarks-02396808.

St. George, D. 2022, September 1. American students' test scores plunge to levels unseen for decades. *Washington Post*. https://www.washingtonpost.com/education/2022/09/01/student-test-scores-plunged-pandemic/.

Stanford Graduate School of Education. 2022. Learning, design and technology (LDT) MS degree. https://online.stanford.edu/programs/learning-design-and-technology-ldt-ms-degree.

Stanistreet, P., Elfert, M. & Atchoarena, D. 2021, April. Education in the age of COVID-19: Implications for the future. *International Review of Education*, 67(1–2). https://link.springer.com/journal/11159/volumes-and-issues/67-1.

State of California. 2003. Electronic Waste Recycling Act of 2003. *CalRecycle*. https://calrecycle.ca.gov/electronics/act2003/.

Statista. 2022, January. Chromebook unit shipments worldwide from 2019 to 2022. https://www.statista.com/statistics/749890/worldwide-chromebook-unit-shipments/.

Statista. 2022. Number of monthly active Facebook users worldwide as of 4th quarter 2021. https://www.statista.com/statistics/264810/number-of-monthly-active-facebook-users-worldwide/.

Stavridou, A. et al. 2021. Obesity in children and adolescents during COVID-19 pandemic. *Children*, 8(2). https://pubmed.ncbi.nlm.nih.gov/33673078/.

Steiner-Adair, C. & Barker, T. 2014. *The Big Disconnect: Protecting Childhood and Family Relationships in the Digital Age*. New York: Harper.

Stempel, J. 2021, June 21. Harvard defeats students' lawsuit over lack of COVID-19 tuition refunds. Reuters. https://www.reuters.com/legal/government/harvard-defeats-students-lawsuit-over-lack-covid-19-tuition-refunds-2021-06-21/.

Stern, A.M., Reilly, M.B., Cetron, M.S. & Markel, H. 2010, April 1. "Better off in school": School medical inspection as a public health strategy during the 1918–1919 influenza pandemic in the United States. *Public Health Reports*, 125(3): 63–70. https://journals.sagepub.com/doi/10.1177/00333549101250S309.

Stevenson, A. 2021, July 26. China moves against private tutoring companies, causing shares to plunge. *New York Times*. https://www.nytimes.com/2021/07/26/business/china-private-education.html.

Stevenson, A., Chien, A.C. & Li, C. 2021, August 27. China's celebrity culture is raucous. The authorities want to change that. *New York Times*. https://www.nytimes.com/2021/08/27/business/media/china-celebrity-culture.html.

Stewart, H. & Weale, S. 2020, August 17. Exam results: Gavin Williamson poised for algorithm climbdown. *The Guardian*. https://www.theguardian.com/education/2020/aug/17/no-10-hints-ministers-set-ditch-a-level-results-algorithm-england.

Stewart, H. 2020, August 26. Boris Johnson blames 'mutant algorithm' for exams fiasco. *The Guardian*. https://www.theguardian.com/politics/2020/aug/26/boris-johnson-blames-mutant-algorithm-for-exams-fiasco.

Stiglic, N. & Viner, R.M. 2019. Effects of screentime on the health and well-being of children and adolescents: A systematic review of reviews. *BMJ Open*, 9(1). http://bmjopen.bmj.com/content/9/1/e023191.abstract.

Stokel-Walker, C. 2023, February 10. The generative AI race has a dirty secret. Wired. https://www.wired.com/story/the-generative-ai-search-race-has-a-dirty-secret/.

Stommel, J. 2014, November 17. Critical Digital Pedagogy: A definition. *Hybrid Pedagogy*. https://hybridpedagogy.org/critical-digital-pedagogy-definition/.

Stone, A. 2022, March 15. Is dated technology contributing to the great teacher resignation? *EdTech: Focus on Higher Education*. https://edtechmagazine.com/k12/article/2022/03/dated-technology-contributing-great-teacher-resignation.

Strauss, V. 2020, July 20. The huge problem with education 'pandemic pods' suddenly popping up. *Washington Post*. https://www.washingtonpost.com/education/2020/07/22/huge-problem-with-education-pandemic-pods-suddenly-popping-up/.

Strauss, V. 2021. $100 million Gates-funded student data project ends in failure. *Washington Post*. https://www.washingtonpost.com/news/answer-sheet/wp/2014/04/21/100-million-gates-funded-student-data-project-ends-in-failure/.

Subramanian, S. 2021, July 4. The lost year in education. Maclean's. https://www.macleans.ca/longforms/covid-19-pandemic-disrupted-schooling-impact/.

Subramanian, S. 2021. *How to Feel: The Science and Meaning of Touch*. New York: Columbia University Press.

Sullivan, P. 2020, October 9. Private schools hold new attraction for rich parents. *New York Times*. https://www.nytimes.com/2020/10/09/your-money/private-schools-wealthy-parents.html.

Summanen, M. 2021, December 28. Pulp and paper industry trends to watch in 2022. Forest2Market. https://www.forest2market.com/blog/pulp-paper-industry-trends-to-watch-in-2022.

Supreme Court of India Civil Appellate Jurisdiction. 2020. WRIT Petition (Civil) No. 1030 of 2020: Rakesh Kumar Agarwalla vs. National Law School of India University, Bengaluru. https://main.sci.gov.in/

Susilowati, I.H., Nugraha, S., Alimoeso, S. & Hasiholan, B.P. 2021. Screen time for preschool children: Learning from home during the COVID-19 pandemic. *Global Pediatric Health*, 8. https://doi.org/10.1177/2333794X211017836.

Suvarna, A. & Patwardhan, N. 2022, February 2. Edtech companies set to get a boost from government's digitization push. Mint. https://www.livemint.com/budget/edtech-companies-set-to-get-a-boost-from-government-s-digitization-push-11643742423720.html.

Swauger, S. 2020, April 2. Our bodies encoded: Algorithmic test proctoring in higher education. *Hybrid Pedagogy*. https://hybridpedagogy.org/our-bodies-encoded-algorithmic-test-proctoring-in-higher-education/.

Swauger, S. 2021, November 12. The next normal: Algorithms will take over college, from admissions to advising. *Washington Post*. https://www.washingtonpost.com/outlook/next-normal-algorithms-college/2021/11/12/366fe8dc-4264-11ec-a3aa-0255edc02eb7_story.html.

Swiss Fund Data. 2022. Credit Suisse (Lux) Edutainment Equity Fund B USD. https://www.swissfunddata.ch/sfdpub/en/funds/chart/114188#tab-content.

Sydow, L. 2020. Mobile Minute: Global classrooms rely on education apps as remote learning accelerates. App Annie. Blog post. https://www.appannie.com/en/insights/mobile-minute/education-apps-grow-remote-learning-coronavirus/.

Tadayon, A. 2020, November 30. California parents sue state alleging inequity in distance learning. EdSource. https://edsource.org/updates/california-parents-sue-state-alleging-inequity-in-distance-learning.

Tait, A. 2021, September 19. Beeban Kidron v. Silicon Valley: One woman's fight to protect children online. *The Observer*. https://www.theguardian.com/film/2021/sep/19/beeban-kidron-v-silicon-valley-one-womans-fight-to-protect-children-online.

Tally, B. 2007. Digital technology and the end of social studies education. *Theory & Research in Social Education*, 35(2): 305–321. https://doi.org/10.1080/00933104.2007.10473337.

Tamez-Robledo, N. 2021, January 11. Schools are a lifeline for homeless students. COVID-19 is severing the connection. EdSurge. https://www.edsurge.com/news/2021-01-11-schools-are-a-lifeline-for-homeless-students-covid-19-is-severing-the-connection.

Tancredi, H. 2020. *Consulting Students with Disability: A Practice Guide for Educators and Other Professionals*. Queensland University of Technology Centre for Inclusive Education. https://research.qut.edu.au/c4ie/wp-content/uploads/sites/281/2022/02/Practice_Guides_Student_Consultation.pdf.

Tawil, S. & West, M. 2020. February 28. The world has been moving learning to digital portals for decades. The coronavirus just turned it into a sprint. UNESCO. https://en.unesco.org/futuresofeducation/ideas-lab/moving-learning-digital-portals.

Teach For All. 2020, May 12. Radio lessons help keep teachers and students connected during lockdown. https://teachforall.org/news/radio-lessons-help-keep-teachers-and-students-connected-during-lockdown.

TED. 2022. History of TED. https://www.ted.com/about/our-organization/history-of-ted.

TED. 2022. Sugata Mitra: Education researcher. https://www.ted.com/speakers/sugata_mitra.

TED. Search results for 'education'. https://www.ted.com/search?q=education.

Tedeschi, E. 2020, October 29. The mystery of how many mothers have left work because of school closings. *New York Times*. https://www.nytimes.com/2020/10/29/upshot/mothers-leaving-jobs-pandemic.html.

Telecom Regulatory Authority of India. 2020, March 29. Subject: Measures regarding ensuring availability of recharge vouchers and payment options for prepaid services. Letter. https://www.medianama.com/wp-content/uploads/TRAI-Prepaid-Letter.pdf.

Telefonica. 2021, July 7. The value of connectivity and open internet. https://www.telefonica.com/en/communication-room/blog/the-value-of-connectivity-and-open-internet/.

Temkin, M. 2021, November 1. Edtech backers rewarded as IPO pipeline heats up. PitchBook. https://pitchbook.com/news/articles/edtech-online-learning-pandemic-ipos.

TEQSA. 2020. *Foundations for Good Practice: The Student Experience of Online Learning in Australian Higher Education During the COVID-19 Pandemic*. Australian Government. Tertiary Education Quality and Standards Agency. https://www.teqsa.gov.au/sites/default/files/student-experience-of-online-learning-in-australian-he-during-covid-19.pdf.

Teräs, M., Suoranta, J., Teräs, H. & Curcher, M. 2020. Post-Covid-19 education and education technology 'solutionism': A seller's market. *Postdigital Science and Education*, 2(3). https://www.ncbi.nlm.nih.gov/pmc/articles/PMC7355515/.

Terrisse, A. 2020, September 28. How has the pandemic changed the face of edtech? EU-Startups. https://www.eu-startups.com/2020/09/how-has-the-pandemic-changed-the-face-of-edtech/.

Texas A&M International University. 2023. Instructional technology and distance education services: Proctorio. Texas A&M International University. https://www.tamiu.edu/distance/technology/proctorio.shtml.

Thai PBS World. 2021, June 5. School uniform filters created to help students in online class. https://www.thaipbsworld.com/school-uniform-filters-created-to-help-students-in-online-class/.

Thales Group. 2021, April 5. 5G technology and networks (speed, use cases, rollout). https://www.thalesgroup.com/en/markets/digital-identity-and-security/mobile/inspired/5G.

THE Journal. 2021, September 9. Ed tech use continues growth beyond the peak of the pandemic. https://thejournal.com/articles/2021/09/09/ed-tech-use-accelerates-beyond-the-peak-of-the-pandemic.aspx.

TheStrive Studies. 2017, October 15. Study with me (with music) 2.5 hours Pomodoro session! YouTube video. https://www.youtube.com/watch?v=dmDbesougG0.

Thompson, F. 2020, August 12. Lawsuit filed against Washington state for 'denying basic education' to special needs children amid COVID-19. FOX 13. https://www.q13fox.com/news/lawsuit-filed-against-washington-state-for-denying-basic-education-to-special-needs-children-amid-covid-19.

Thompson, N. 2021. Types of remote proctoring: What's the best fit for me? Assessment Systems. https://assess.com/types-of-remote-proctoring/.

Thorsten Benner. 2021, September 8. The 'Zoomification' of academia: Addressing risks to academic freedom. Global Public Policy Institute. https://gppi.net/2021/09/08/the-zoomification-of-academia-addressing-risks-to-academic-freedom.

Three Amigos. 2020, August 3. Eve Project: Excellence in virtual teaching - Results V1. https://amigos-3.com/eve-project.

Thürmann, E., Vollmer, H. & Pieper, I. 2010, November. Language(s) of schooling: Focusing on vulnerable learners. The Linguistic and Educational Integration of Children And Adolescents from Migrant Backgrounds. Language Policy Division, Council of Europe. https://rm.coe.int/16805a1caf.

Tibken, S. 2021, June 28. The broadband gap's dirty secret: Redlining still exists in digital form. CNET. https://www.cnet.com/features/the-broadband-gaps-dirty-secret-redlining-still-exists-in-digital-form/.

Tiffany, G. 2020, August 12. Algorithmic grading is not an answer to the challenges of the pandemic. Algorithm Watch. https://algorithmwatch.org/en/uk-algorithmic-grading-gcse/.

Tiffany, K. 2018, October 25. In Amazon we trust — but why? Vox. https://www.vox.com/the-goods/2018/10/25/18022956/amazon-trust-survey-american-institutions-ranked-georgetown.

Times of India. 2020, November 26. The Times of India & BYJU's kickstart #KeepLearning initiative to empower parents, students and teachers overcome e-learning challenges. https://timesofindia.indiatimes.com/spotlight/toi-byjus-kickstart-keeplearning-initiative-to-empower-parents-students-and-teachers-overcome-e-learning-challenges/articleshow/79367891.cms.

Tobin, L. 2009, March 3. Slumdog professor. *The Guardian*. https://www.theguardian.com/education/2009/mar/03/professor-sugata-mitra.

Tobisch, A. & Dresel, M. 2017. Negatively or positively biased? Dependencies of teachers' judgments and expectations based on students' ethnic and social backgrounds. *Social Psychology of Education*, 20(4): 731–752. https://doi.org/10.1007/s11218-017-9392-z.

Tokatly Latzer, I., Leitner, Y. & Karnieli-Miller, O. 2021. Core experiences of parents of children with autism during the COVID-19 pandemic lockdown. *Autism*, 25(4): 1047–1059. https://journals.sagepub.com/doi/full/10.1177/1362361320984317.

Tooth, L., Moss, K., Hockey, R. & Mishra, G. 2019. Adherence to screen time recommendations for Australian children aged 0–12 years. *Medical Journal of Australia*, 211(4): 181–182. https://www.mja.com.au/journal/2019/211/4/adherence-screen-time-recommendations-australian-children-aged-0-12-years.

Torchia, R. 2022, January 20. New Adobe product simplifies digital design. *EdTech: Focus on Higher Education*. https://edtechmagazine.com/k12/article/2022/01/new-adobe-product-simplifies-digital-design.

Towler, B. 2022, May 31. E-readers vs books: Which are better for the environment? Commercial Waste. https://commercialwaste.trade/e-readers-vs-books-better-environment/.

Transcript of Brookings webinar. 2020, September 14. Beyond reopening: A leapfrog moment to transform education? Available at https://www.brookings.edu/wp-content/uploads/2020/09/global_20200914_reopening_education_transcript.pdf.

Treglia, D. et al. 2021. *Hidden Pain: Children Who Lost a Parent or Caregiver to COVID-19 and What the Nation Can Do to Help Them*. COVID Collaborative and Social Policy Analytics. https://www.covidcollaborative.us/assets/uploads/img/HIDDEN-PAIN-FINAL.pdf.

Tria, E. 2021, May 4. The impact of Covid-19 on child labour in cobalt mines in the DRC. Humanium. https://www.humanium.org/en/the-impact-of-covid-19-on-child-labour-in-cobalt-mines-in-the-drc/.

Tribunal administratif de Montreuil. 2022, December 14. No. 2216570. https://www.laquadrature.net/wp-content/uploads/sites/8/2022/12/1120693769_2216570P_ordo_anon.pdf.

Tribune. 2022, May 3. Give priority to regular classes in Punjab: Democratic Teachers Front. https://www.tribuneindia.com/news/ludhiana/give-priority-to-regular-classes-democratic-teachers-front-391360.

Troseth, G.L., Strouse, G.A., Verdine, B.N. & Saylor, M.M. 2018. Let's chat: On-screen social responsiveness is not sufficient to support toddlers' word learning from video. *Frontiers in Psychology*, 9. https://www.frontiersin.org/article/10.3389/fpsyg.2018.02195.

Trucano, M. 2010, April 30. Worst practice in ICT use in education. World Bank Blogs. https://blogs.worldbank.org/edutech/worst-practice.

Trucano, M. 2012, March 23. Evaluating one laptop per child (OLPC) in Peru. World Bank Blogs. https://blogs.worldbank.org/edutech/olpc-peru2.

Trucano, M. 2020, April 2. How ministries of education work with mobile operators, telecom providers, ISPs and others to increase access to digital resources during COVID19-driven school closures (Coronavirus). World Bank Blogs. https://blogs.worldbank.org/education/how-ministries-education-work-mobile-operators-telecom-providers-isps-and-others-increase.

Tse, C. & Roof, K. 2021, March 30. Coursera prices IPO at top of range to raise $519 million. Bloomberg. https://www.bloomberg.com/news/articles/2021-03-31/online-educator-coursera-s-top-of-range-ipo-raises-519-million.

Tufekci, Z. 2021, September 20. The pandemic is no excuse to surveil students. *The Atlantic*. https://www.theatlantic.com/technology/archive/2020/09/pandemic-no-excuse-colleges-surveil-students/616015/.

Tung, L. 2019, June 25. Amazon, Facebook internet outage: Verizon blamed for 'cascading catastrophic failure'. ZDNet. https://www.zdnet.com/article/amazon-facebook-internet-outage-verizon-blamed-for-cascading-catastrophic-failure/.

Tuohy, W. 2021, November 1. "Like the worst kind of bully": Spike in video calls leads to image problems. *Sydney Morning Herald*. https://www.smh.com.au/national/like-the-worst-kind-of-bully-spike-in-video-calls-leads-image-problems-20211031-p594ok.html.

Turkle, S. 2015. *Reclaiming Conversation: The Power Of Talk in a Digital Age*. New York: Penguin Books.

Turkle, S. 2017. *Alone Together: Why We Expect More from Technology and Less from Each Other*. New York: Basic Books.

Turner, C. 2020, October 7. Homeless families struggle with impossible choices as school closures continue. NPR. https://www.npr.org/2020/10/07/920320592/an-impossible-choice-for-homeless-parents-a-job-or-their-childs-education.

Turner, S., Pothong, K. & Livingstone, S. 2022. *Education Data Reality: The Challenges for Schools in Managing Children's Education Data*. Digital Futures Commission, 5Rights Foundation. https://digitalfuturescommission.org.uk/wp-content/uploads/2022/06/Education-data-reality-report.pdf.

Twenge, J.M. et al. 2021. Worldwide increases in adolescent loneliness. *Journal of Adolescence*, 93: 257–269. https://pubmed.ncbi.nlm.nih.gov/34294429/.

Twenge, J.M., Cooper, A.B., Joiner, T., Duffy, M. & Binau, S. 2019. Age, period, and cohort trends in mood disorder indicators and suicide-related outcomes in a nationally representative dataset, 2005–2017. *Journal of Abnormal Psychology*, 128(3): 185–199. https://doi.org/10.1037/abn0000410.

Twenge, J.M., Joiner, T.E., Rogers, M.L. & Martin, G.N. 2018. Increases in depressive symptoms, suicide-related outcomes, and suicide rates among U.S. adolescents after 2010 and links to increased new media screen time. *Clinical Psychological Science*, 6(1): 3–17. https://doi.org/10.1177/2167702617723376.

Twenge, J.M., Martin, G.N. & Campbell, W.K. 2018, September 18. Decreases in psychological well-being among American adolescents after 2012 and links to screen time during the rise of smartphone technology. *Emotion*, 18(6): 765–780. https://doi.org/10.1037/emo0000403.

Tyack, D.B. & Cuban, Larry. 1995. *Tinkering toward Utopia: A Century of Public School Reform*. Cambridge, MA: Harvard University Press.

Tyers-Chowdhury, A. & Binder, G. 2021. *What We know about the Gender Digital Divide for Girls: A Literature Review*. UNICEF. https://www.unicef.org/eap/media/8311/file/What we know about the gender digital divide for girls: A literature review.pdf.

Tysons Reporter. 2020, August 19. Poll: What do you think of 'learning pods' for kids? https://www.tysonsreporter.com/2020/08/19/poll-what-do-you-think-of-learning-pods-for-kids/.

UCL News. 2021, May 10. Smartphones have led to the 'death of proximity'. https://www.ucl.ac.uk/news/2021/may/smartphones-have-led-death-proximity.

Udemy. 2020. *Online Education Steps Up: What the World Is Learning (From Home)*. Special Report. https://research.udemy.com/wp-content/uploads/2020/04/Online-Education-Steps-Up-2020-2021-Rebrand-v2-gs.pdf.

Uhls, Y.T. & Robb, M.B. 2017. How parents mediate children's media consumption. In Blumberg, F.C. & Brooks, P.J. (eds). *Cognitive Development in Digital Contexts*. Cambridge, MA: Academic Press.

UK Government Department of Education. 2021, 27 April. Catch-up premium. https://www.gov.uk/government/publications/catch-up-premium-coronavirus-covid-19/catch-up-premium.

UK Government. 2021, August 24. [Withdrawn] Coronavirus (COVID-19): guidance for care staff supporting adults with learning disabilities and autistic adults. https://www.gov.uk/government/publications/covid-19-supporting-adults-with-learning-disabilities-and-autistic-adults/coronavirus-covid-19-guidance-for-care-staff-supporting-adults-with-learning-disabilities-and-autistic-adults.

UN General Assembly Human Rights Council. 2016, April 6. Report of the Special Rapporteur on the right to education. https://documents-dds-ny.un.org/doc/UNDOC/GEN/G16/070/33/PDF/G1607033.pdf.

UN General Assembly Human Rights Council. 2020, June 30. Right to education: impact of the coronavirus disease crisis on the right to education—concerns, challenges and opportunities. Report of the Special Rapporteur on the right to education. https://documents-dds-ny.un.org/doc/UNDOC/GEN/G20/158/03/PDF/G2015803.pdf.

UN General Assembly Human Rights Council. 2022, April 19. Impact of the digitalization of education on the right to education. Report of the Special Rapporteur on the right to education. https://documents-dds-ny.un.org/doc/UNDOC/GEN/G22/322/37/PDF/G2232237.pdf.

UNEP. N.d. E-Waste 2.0. https://wedocs.unep.org/bitstream/handle/20.500.11822/7587/e_waste_infog_en.pdf.

UNESCO Institute for Lifelong Learning. 2015, September 16. Pink phone, Cambodia. https://uil.unesco.org/case-study/effective-practices-database-litbase-0/pink-phone-cambodia.

UNESCO Institute for Statistics. 2016. Out-of-school children and youth. http://uis.unesco.org/en/topic/out-school-children-and-youth.

UNESCO, in collaboration with McKinsey & Company. 2020, July. *COVID-19 Response - Remediation: Helping Students Catch Up on Lost Learning, with a Focus on Closing Equity Gaps*. Version 2. https://www.mckinsey.com/~/media/McKinsey/About Us/COVID Response Center/Overview/COVID-19 Education Response Toolkit/202010_UNESCO-McKinsey Response Toolkit_Remediation_VF.pdf.

UNESCO, UNICEF & World Bank. 2020, October. *What Have We Learnt? Overview of Findings from a Survey of Ministries of Education on National Responses to COVID-19*. https://tcg.uis.unesco.org/wp-content/uploads/sites/4/2020/10/National-Education-Responses-to-COVID-19-WEB-final_EN.pdf.

UNESCO, UNICEF, & World Bank. 2022. *Where Are We on Education Recovery?* https://unesdoc.unesco.org/ark:/48223/pf0000381091.

UNESCO, UNICEF, World Bank & World Food Programme. 2020, June. *Framework for Reopening Schools*. https://unesdoc.unesco.org/ark:/48223/pf0000373348.

UNESCO. 2017. *UNESCO-Pearson Initiative for Literacy: Improved Livelihoods in a Digital World*. https://unesdoc.unesco.org/ark:/48223/pf0000247599.

UNESCO. 2018. *A Lifeline to Learning: Leveraging Mobile Technology to Support Education for Refugees*. UNESCO. https://unesdoc.unesco.org/ark:/48223/pf0000261278.

UNESCO. 2018. *Global Education Monitoring Report 2017/8. Accountability in Education: Meeting Our Commitments*. https://en.unesco.org/gem-report/report/2017/accountability-education.

UNESCO. 2018. *UNESCO ICT Competency Framework for Teachers: Version 3*. https://unesdoc.unesco.org/ark:/48223/pf0000265721.

UNESCO. 2019, November 25. Recommendation on Open Educational Resources (OER). https://www.unesco.org/en/legal-affairs/recommendation-open-educational-resources-oer.

UNESCO. 2019. *Right to Education Handbook*. https://unesdoc.unesco.org/ark:/48223/pf0000366556.

UNESCO. 2020, June 23. UNESCO report on inclusion in education shows 40% of poorest countries did not provide specific support to disadvantaged learners during COVID-19 crisis. Press release. https://en.unesco.org/news/unesco-report-inclusion-education-shows-40-poorest-countries-did-not-provide-specific-support.

UNESCO. 2020, May 5. New guidelines provide roadmap for safe reopening of schools. Press release. https://en.unesco.org/news/new-guidelines-provide-roadmap-safe-reopening-schools.

UNESCO. 2020, October 16. Why the world must urgently strengthen learning and protect finance for education. https://en.unesco.org/news/why-world-must-urgently-strengthen-learning-and-protect-finance-education.

UNESCO. 2020. *Education in a Post-COVID World: Nine Ideas for Public Action. International Commission on the Futures of Education*. https://en.unesco.org/news/education-post-covid-world-nine-ideas-public-action.

UNESCO. 2020. *UNESCO COVID-19 Education Response: Education Sector Issue Notes*. Issue note no. 7.1–April 2020. https://unesdoc.unesco.org/ark:/48223/pf0000373275.

UNESCO. 2020. *UNESCO COVID-19 Education Response: Education Sector Issue Notes*. Issue note no. 2.5 - June 2020. https://unesdoc.unesco.org/ark:/48223/pf0000373815.

UNESCO. 2021, February 2022. COVID-19: Two-thirds of poorer countries are cutting their education budgets at a time when they can least afford to. https://en.unesco.org/gem-report/sites/default/files/Education_Finance_Watch_PR_Eng_0.pdf.

UNESCO. 2021, March 19. One year into COVID-19 education disruption: Where do we stand? https://en.unesco.org/news/one-year-covid-19-education-disruption-where-do-we-stand.

UNESCO. 2021. Draft text of the recommendation on the ethics of artificial intelligence. https://unesdoc.unesco.org/ark:/48223/pf0000377897.

UNESCO. 2021. Paris Declaration: A Global Call for Investing in the Futures of Education. https://unesdoc.unesco.org/ark:/48223/pf0000380116.

UNESCO. 2021. UNESCO figures show two thirds of an academic year lost on average worldwide due to COVID-19 school closures. https://en.unesco.org/news/unesco-figures-show-two-thirds-academic-year-lost-average-worldwide-due-covid-19-school.

UNESCO. 2021. *When Schools Shut: Gendered Impacts of COVID-19 School Closures*. https://unesdoc.unesco.org/ark:/48223/pf0000379270.

UNESCO. 2022, July 15. Thematic action track 4 on digital learning and transformation. United Nations Transforming Education Summit. Discussion paper. https://transformingeducationsummit.sdg4education2030.org/system/files/2022-07/Digital%20AT4%20dicussion%20paper%20July%202022.pdf.

UNESCO. 2022, September. International Literacy Day: Transforming literacy learning spaces. https://en.unesco.org/sites/default/files/ild-2022-cn-en.pdf.

UNESCO. 2022. COVID-19 Recovery. Education: From school closure to recovery. Monitoring of school closures https://en.unesco.org/covid19/educationresponse.

UNESCO. 2022. Ethics of artificial intelligence. https://www.unesco.org/en/artificial-intelligence/recommendation-ethics.

UNESCO. 2022. Global Education Coalition. https://globaleducationcoalition.unesco.org/.

UNESCO. 2022. Global monitoring of school closures caused by COVID-19 pandemic. https://covid19.uis.unesco.org/global-monitoring-school-closures-covid19/.

UNESCO. 2022. *Leave No Child Behind: Global Report on Boys' Disengagement from Education*. https://unesdoc.unesco.org/ark:/48223/pf0000381105.

UNESCO. 2022. *National Distance Learning Programmes in Response to the COVID-19 Education Disruption: Case Study of the Kingdom of Saudi Arabia*. https://unesdoc.unesco.org/ark:/48223/pf0000381533.

UNESCO. 2022. *The RewirEd Global Declaration on Connectivity for Education: #ConnectivityDeclaration*. https://unesdoc.unesco.org/ark:/48223/pf0000381482.

UNESCO. 2022. UNESCO Map on School Closures: COVID-19 educational response: Country dashboard. https://covid19.uis.unesco.org/global-monitoring-school-closures-covid19/country-dashboard/.

UNESCO. 2023. *Global Education Monitoring Report 2023. Technology in Education: A Tool on Whose Terms?* https://unesdoc.unesco.org/ark:/48223/pf0000385723.locale=en

UnethicalLifeProTips. 2019, February 22. ULPT: When taking an online proctored exam, write answers on your computer screen in expo marker or put post-it notes on it. https://www.reddit.com/r/UnethicalLifeProTips/comments/f7kly0/ulpt_when_taking_an_online_proctored_exam_write/.

UNICEF et al. 2020, April. *COVID-19 and Its Implications for Protecting Children Online*. https://www.unicef.org/media/67396/file/COVID-19%20and%20Its%20Implications%20for%20Protecting%20Children%20Online.pdf.

UNICEF, WHO & IFRC. 2020, March. COVID-19: IFRC, UNICEF and WHO issue guidance to protect children and support safe school operations. Press release. https://www.unicef.org/pacificislands/press-releases/covid-19-ifrc-unicef-and-who-issue-guidance-protect-children-and-support-safe-school.

UNICEF. 2020, June 4. Unequal access to remote schooling amid COVID-19 threatens to deepen global learning crisis. Press release. https://www.unicef.org/pressreleases/ unequal-access-remote-schooling-amid-covid- 19-threatens-deepen-global-learning.

UNICEF. 2020, December 3. UNICEF calls for inclusion of children and young persons with disabilities. Press release. https://uzbekistan.un.org/en/104300-unicef-calls-inclusion-children-and-young-persons-disabilities.

UNICEF. 2020, December 8. COVID-19: UNICEF warns of continued damage to learning and well-being as number of children affected by school closures soars again. Press release. https://www.unicef.org/turkey/en/press-releases/covid-19-unicef-warns-continued-damage-learning-and-well-being-number-children.

UNICEF. 2020, December. *Children with Disabilities: Ensuring Their Inclusion in COVID-19 Response Strategies and Evidence Generation*. https://data.unicef.org/resources/children-with-disabilities-ensuring-inclusion-in-covid-19-response/.

UNICEF. 2020, November 17. Nine million children in Ghana to benefit from learning programmes supported by UNICEF and Mastercard Foundation partnership. Press release. https://www.unicef.org/ghana/press-releases/nine-million-children-ghana-benefit-learning-programmes-supported-unicef-and.

UNICEF. 2020. COVID-19: Are children able to continue learning during school closures? Factsheet. https://data.unicef.org/resources/remote-learning-reachability-factsheet/.

UNICEF. 2021, December 9. COVID-19 'biggest global crisis for children in our 75-year history' – UNICEF. Press release. https://www.unicef.org/yemen/press-releases/covid-19-biggest-global-crisis-children-our-75-year-history-unicef.

UNICEF. 2021, January 27. Nutrition crisis looms as more than 39 billion in-school meals missed since start of pandemic – UNICEF & World Food Programme. Press release. https://www.unicef.org/press-releases/nutrition-crisis-looms-more-39-billion-school-meals-missed-start-pandemic-unicef-and.

UNICEF. 2021, July 15. COVID-19 pandemic leads to major backsliding on childhood vaccinations, new WHO, UNICEF data shows. Press release. https://www.unicef.org/press-releases/covid-19-pandemic-leads-major-backsliding-childhood-vaccinations-new-who-unicef-data.

UNICEF. 2021, June 9. Child labour rises to 160 million – first increase in two decades. Press release. https://www.unicef.org/press-releases/child-labour-rises-160-million-first-increase-two-decades.

UNICEF. 2021, September 16. Around 2 in 3 children are still out of the classroom in Latin America and the Caribbean. Press release. https://www.unicef.org/press-releases/around-2-3-children-are-still-out-classroom-latin-america-and-caribbean.

UNICEF. 2021. *Reopening with Resilience: Lessons from Remote Learning during COVID-19*. https://www.unicef-irc.org/publications/1220-reopening-with-resilience-lessons-from-remote-learning-during-covid19.html.

UNICEF. 2021. *The State of the World's Children 2021: On My Mind – Promoting, Protecting and Caring for Children's Mental Health*. https://www.unicef.org/media/114636/file/SOWC-2021-full-report-English.pdf.

UNICEF. 2021. *What We Know about the Gender Digital Divide for Girls: A Literature Review*. https://www.unicef.org/eap/media/8311/file/What we know about the gender digital divide for girls: A literature review.pdf.

UNICEF. 2022, December 12. 1 in 3 digital learning platforms developed during COVID-19 no longer functional. Press release. https://www.unicef.org/press-releases/1-3-digital-learning-platforms-developed-during-covid-19-no-longer-functional.

UNICEF. 2022, January 23. COVID:19 Scale of education loss 'nearly insurmountable', warns UNICEF. Press release. https://www.unicef.org/press-releases/covid19-scale-education-loss-nearly-insurmountable-warns-unicef.

UNICEF. 2022, March 1. UNICEF and Extreme Tech Challenge announce strategic partnership to advance the future of learning. Press release. https://www.unicef.org/innovation/press-releases/unicef-and-extreme-tech-challenge-announce-strategic-partnership-advance-future.

United Nations University. 2020, July 2. Global e-waste surging: Up 21% in 5 years. https://unu.edu/media-relations/releases/global-e-waste-surging-up-21-in-5-years.html.

United Nations. 1948. Article 26. Universal Declaration of Human Rights. https://www.un.org/en/about-us/universal-declaration-of-human-rights.

United Nations. 1989. Convention on the Rights of the Child. https://www.ohchr.org/en/instruments-mechanisms/instruments/convention-rights-child.

United Nations. 2007. Article 14. United Nations Declaration on the Rights of Indigenous Peoples. https://www.un.org/development/desa/indigenouspeoples/wp-content/uploads/sites/19/2018/11/UNDRIP_E_web.pdf.

United Nations. 2020, August. Policy Brief: Education during COVID-19 and beyond. https://www.un.org/development/desa/dspd/wp-content/uploads/sites/22/2020/08/sg_policy_brief_covid-19_and_education_august_2020.pdf.

United Nations. 2020, May 29. Road map for digital cooperation: Implementation of the recommendations of the High-level Panel on Digital Cooperation. Report of the Secretary-General. https://documents-dds-ny.un.org/doc/UNDOC/GEN/N20/102/51/PDF/N2010251.pdf.

United Nations. 2020, May. *Policy Brief: A Disability-Inclusive Response to COVID-19*. https://unsdg.un.org/sites/default/files/2020-05/Policy-Brief-A-Disability-Inclusive-Response-to-COVID-19.pdf.

United Nations. 2021, March 4. Mental health alert for 332 million children linked to COVID-19 lockdown policies: UNICEF. https://news.un.org/en/story/2021/03/1086372.

United Nations. 2022, September 19. Gateways to public digital learning: A multi-partner initiative to create and strengthen inclusive digital learning platforms and content. United Nations Transforming Education Summit. Spotlight session. https://www.un.org/sites/un2.un.org/files/2022/09/gateways_to_public_digital_learning_long.pdf.

United Nations. 2022. Assuring and improving quality public digital learning for all. United Nations Transforming Education Summit. https://www.un.org/en/transforming-education-summit/digital-learning-all.

United Nations. 2022. Factsheet on persons with disabilities. Department of Economic and Social Affairs. https://www.un.org/development/desa/disabilities/resources/factsheet-on-persons-with-disabilities.html.

United States District Court Northern District of Ohio Eastern Division. Case No. 1:21-cv-00500. Aaron M. Ogletree v. Cleveland State University. https://bbgohio.com/wp-content/uploads/2022/08/MSJ-decision.pdf.

University of California San Francisco. 2020, June 26. Update on IT security incident at UCSF. https://www.ucsf.edu/news/2020/06/417911/update-it-security-incident-ucsf.

University of California Santa Barbara Faculty Association. 2020, March 13. Letter to the chancellor and executive vice chancellor. https://pubcit.typepad.com/files/proctoru_2020-copy.pdf.

USA Facts. 2020, June 4. 4.4 million households with children don't have consistent access to computers for online learning during the pandemic. https://usafacts.org/articles/internet-access-students-at-home/#.

User review. 2022, September 28. Unusable app. Google Classroom. Ratings and Reviews. https://apps.apple.com/us/app/google-classroom/id924620788.

Uwezo. 2020. *Are Our Children Learning? The Status of Remote-Learning among School-Going Children in Kenya During the Covid-19 Crisis*. Usawa Agenda. https://www.humanitarianresponse.info/sites/www.humanitarianresponse.info/files/documents/files/are_our_children_learning_-_remote_learning_-_uwezo_usawa-agenda-2020-report_1.pdf.

Valencia, J. 2020, October 8. Mexico City tortilla shop provides free Wi-Fi for kids to access virtual school. The World. https://theworld.org/stories/2020-10-08/mexico-city-tortilla-shop-provides-free-wi-fi-kids-access-virtual-school.

Vall-Roqué, H., Andrés, A. & Saldaña, C. 2021. The impact of COVID-19 lockdown on social network sites use, body image disturbances and self-esteem among adolescent and young women. *Progress in Neuro-Psychopharmacology and Biological Psychiatry*, 110: 110293. https://www.sciencedirect.com/science/article/pii/S027858462100052X.

Vallee, H.Q. la & Duarte, N. 2019, August 12. Algorithmic systems in education: Incorporating equity and fairness when using student data. Center for Democracy and Technology. https://cdt.org/insights/algorithmic-systems-in-education-incorporating-equity-and-fairness-when-using-student-data/.

van Cappelle, F. & Evers, V. 2005, January. Investigating the effects of unsupervised computer use on educationally disadvantaged children's knowledge and understanding of computers. *IEEE Transactions on Pattern Analysis and Machine Intelligence (PAMI)*. https://www.researchgate.net/publication/237134201_Investigating_the_effects_of_unsupervised_computer_use_on_educationally_disadvantaged_children's_knowledge_and_understanding_of_computers.

van Cappelle, F. 2003. The darker side of the digital divide – Inequalities of opportunities in public computer usage in rural India. Master's thesis. University of Amsterdam. https://www.academia.edu/s/af9b1d15c8.

Varea, V. & González-Calvo, G. 2020. Touchless classes and absent bodies: Reaching physical education in times of Covid-19. *Sport, Education and Society*, 26(8): 831–845. https://doi.org/10.1080/13573322.2020.1791814.

Vartabedian, M. 2020, March 19. Ed-tech startups and investors shift into overdrive amid coronavirus crisis. *Wall Street Journal*. https://www.wsj.com/articles/ed-tech-startups-and-investors-shift-into-overdrive-amid-coronavirus-crisis-11584615601.

Vegas, E. 2020, April 14. School closures, government responses, and learning inequality around the world during COVID-19. Brookings. https://www.brookings.edu/research/school-closures-government-responses-and-learning-inequality-around-the-world-during-covid-19/.

Vegas, E. 2022, April. *COVID-19's Impact on Learning Losses and Learning Inequality in Colombia*. Center for Universal Education at Brookings. https://www.brookings.edu/wp-content/uploads/2022/04/COVID-19s-impact-on-learning-losses_Final.pdf.

Venkataramakrishnan, S. 2021, January 10. Algorithms and the coronavirus pandemic. *Financial Times*. https://www.ft.com/content/16f4ded0-e86b-4f77-8b05-67d555838941.

Vera, K. & Ellis, B. 2020, October 15. Virtual learning: A teacher's perspective. *The Lion's Roar*. https://mhslionsroar.com/15991/features/virtual-learning-a-teachers-perspective/.

Verdoodt, V., Fordyce, R., Archbold, L., Gordon, F. & Clifford, D. 2021. Esports and the platforming of child's play during covid-19. *International Journal of Children's Rights*, 29(2): 496–520. https://brill.com/view/journals/chil/29/2/article-p496_496.xml.

Verger, A., Fontdevila, C. & Zancajo, A. 2016. *The Privatization of Education: A Political Economy of Global Education Reform*. New York: Teachers College Press.

Verger, A., Fontdevila, C. & Zancajo, A. 2017. Multiple paths towards education privatization in a globalizing world: A cultural political economy review. *Journal of Education Policy*, 32(6): 757–787. https://doi.org/10.1080/02680939.2017.1318453.

Vernekar, N., Pandey, P., Rai, A.N., Pichhili, A.R. & Singhal, K. 2021, September. *Starting from Scratch: The Role of Parents, Teachers, and Tech in Early Childhood Education during COVID-19*. Vidhi Centre for Legal Policy. https://vidhilegalpolicy.in/research/starting-from-scratch-the-role-of-parents-teachers-and-tech-in-early-childhood-education-during-covid-19/.

Vieyra Molina, A., Belden, M., de la Calle, J.R. & Martinezparente, A. 2020, July. *The Impact of the COVID-19 Pandemic on Higher Education in Mexico, Colombia and Peru*. EY-Parthenon Education. https://assets.ey.com/content/dam/ey-sites/ey-com/es_mx/topics/covid-19/ey-parthenon-educacion.pdf.

Villamil, S. et al. 2021, June 26. 1+1=4? Latin America confronts a pandemic education crisis. *New York Times*. https://www.nytimes.com/2021/06/26/world/americas/latin-america-pandemic-education.html.

Villegas, L. & Garcia, A. 2022, April. Educating English learners during the pandemic: Insights from experts, advocates, and practitioners. New America. https://files.eric.ed.gov/fulltext/ED619505.pdf.

Vincent, J. 2019, July 25. AI 'emotion recognition' can't be trusted. The Verge. https://www.theverge.com/2019/7/25/8929793/emotion-recognition-analysis-ai-machine-learning-facial-expression-review.

Vlachos, J., Hertegård, E. & B. Svaleryd, H. 2021, February 11. The effects of school closures on SARS-CoV-2 among parents and teachers. *Proceedings of the National Academy of Sciences*, 118(9). https://www.pnas.org/doi/full/10.1073/pnas.2020834118.

VOA News. 2021, July 29. World leaders pledge $4 billion to public education affected by pandemic. https://www.voanews.com/a/europe_world-leaders-pledge-4-billion-public-education-affected-pandemic/6208915.html.

BIBLIOGRAPHY

Vogels, E., Gelles-Watnick, R. & Massarat, N. 2022, August 10. *Teens, Social Media and Technology 2022*. Pew Research Center. https://www.pewresearch.org/internet/wp-content/uploads/sites/9/2022/08/PI_2022.08.10_Teens-and-Tech_FINAL.pdf.

von Lautz-Cauzanet, E. 2022. EdTech: Why the project-based approach must change in order to contribute to system resilience. *PROSPECTS*, 51: 573–581. https://doi.org/10.1007/s11125-021-09580-8.

Vosloo, S. 2018. *Guidelines: Designing Inclusive Digital Solutions and Developing Digital Skills*. UNESCO Education Sector. https://unesdoc.unesco.org/ark:/48223/pf0000265537.

Vu, B.T. & Savonitto, I.O. 2020, July 21. *Building Back Better: Education Systems for Resilience, Equity and Quality in the Age of COVID-19*. World Bank. http://documents1.worldbank.org/curated/en/497341595425543327/Building-Back-Better-Education-Systems-for-Resilience-Equity-and-Quality-in-the-Age-of-COVID-19.pdf.

Waldrop, T. 2020, August 19. Here's what happened when students went to school during the 1918 pandemic. CNN. https://www.cnn.com/2020/08/19/us/schools-flu-pandemic-1918-trnd/index.html.

Walker, T. 2023, February 3. Cell phone bans in school are back. How far will they go? National Education Association. https://www.nea.org/advocating-for-change/new-from-nea/cellphone-bans-school-are-back-how-far-will-they-go.

Walsh, J.J. et al. 2018. Associations between 24 hour movement behaviours and global cognition in US children: A cross-sectional observational study. *Lancet Child & Adolescent Health*, 2(11): 783–791. https://pubmed.ncbi.nlm.nih.gov/30268792/.

Wan, T. 2019, June 28. AltSchool gets an alt-name and new leadership. EdSurge. https://www.edsurge.com/news/2019-06-28-altschool-gets-an-alt-name-and-new-leadership.

Wan, T. 2020, March 23. A lockdown abroad disrupts testing at home. EdSurge. https://www.edsurge.com/news/2020-03-23-a-lockdown-abroad-disrupts-a-major-online-education-service-proctoring.

Wan, T. 2021, January 15. The edtech company formerly known as AltSchool sold its tech. So what's left? EdSurge. https://www.edsurge.com/news/2021-01-15-the-edtech-company-formerly-known-as-altschool-sold-its-tech-so-what-s-left.

Wan, T. 2021, July 1. U.S Edtech roars with over $3.2 billion invested in first half of 2021. Medium. https://medium.com/reach-capital/u-s-edtech-roars-with-over-3-2-billion-invested-in-first-half-of-2021-d69049dbce30.

Wang, J. et al. 2021. Progression of myopia in school-aged children after COVID-19 home confinement. *JAMA Ophthalmic* 139(3):293-300. https://jamanetwork.com/journals/jamaophthalmology/fullarticle/2774808.

Wang, X. 2020, March 5. The word from Wuhan. *London Review of Books*, 42(5). https://www.lrb.co.uk/the-paper/v42/n05/wang-xiuying/the-word-from-wuhan.

Wang, X. 2021, January 20. After a Covid-led boom in 2020, what next for China's K-12 edtech? CompassList. https://www.compasslist.com/research-analysis/after-a-covid-led-boom-in-2020-what-next-for-chinas-k-12-edtech.

Wanqing, Z. 2022, February 21. Chinese school faces backlash over use of facial recognition scanners. SixthTone. https://www.sixthtone.com/news/1009712.

Warren, T.H. 2022, January 30. Why churches should drop their online services. *New York Times*. https://www.nytimes.com/2022/01/30/opinion/church-online-services-covid.html.

Warschauer, M. 2002. Reconceptualizing the digital divide. *First Monday*, 7(7). https://journals.uic.edu/ojs/index.php/fm/article/download/967/888.

Wasserman, D., Iosue, M., Wuestefeld, A. & Carli V. 2020, October. Adaptation of evidence-based suicide prevention strategies during and after the COVID-19 pandemic. *World Psychiatry*, 19(3). https://onlinelibrary.wiley.com/doi/10.1002/wps.20801.

Watermeyer, R., Crick, T., Knight, C. & Goodall, J. 2020, April 9. Forced shift to online teaching in pandemic unleashes educators' deepest job fears. Nature Index. https://www.nature.com/nature-index/news-blog/forceshift-to-online-teaching-in-coronavirus-pandemic-unleashes-educators-deepest-job-fears-.

Waters, A. & Miikkulainen, R. 2013. GRADE: Machine learning support for graduate admissions. *AI Magazine*, 35(1). https://doi.org/10.1609/aimag.v35i1.2504.

Watson, G.R. & Sottile, J. 2010. Cheating in the digital age: Do students cheat more in online courses? *Online Journal of Distance Learning Administration*, 13(1). https://eric.ed.gov/?id=EJ877536.

Watters, A. 2021. *Teaching Machines: The History of Personalized Learning*. Cambridge, MA: MIT Press.

Webb, D., Barringer, K., Torrance, R. & Mitchell, J. 2020. *Girls' Education and EdTech: A Rapid Evidence Review*. EdTech Hub. https://docs.edtechhub.org/lib/CZBRW85R.

Webster, N. 1787, December. On the education of youth in America. *American Magazine*. Available at https://americainclass.org/sources/makingrevolution/independence/text3/websteramericanidentity.pdf.

WEEE Forum. 2022, October 14. International E-waste Day: Of ~16 billion mobile phones possessed worldwide, ~5.3 billion will become waste in 2022. https://weee-forum.org/ws_news/of-16-billion-mobile-phones-possessed-worldwide-5-3-billion-will-become-waste-in-2022/.

Weller, M. 2018, July 2. Twenty years of Edtech. *EDUCAUSE Review*. https://er.educause.edu/articles/2018/7/twenty-years-of-edtech.

Weller, M. 2020. *25 Years of Ed Tech*. Alberta: Athabasca University Press.

Welsh Government (Hwb). 2020, April 3. Online safety at home - Support and resources for parents and carers. https://hwb.gov.wales/zones/keeping-safe-online/news/articles/b8862e72-5d6a-4022-938d-8f37977dc34c.

Wen, L.S. 2021, February 24. Both sides of the school reopening debate have it wrong. *Washington Post*. https://www.washingtonpost.com/opinions/2021/02/24/both-sides-school-reopening-debate-have-it-wrong/.

Werber, C. 2015, November 6. How Ebola led to more teenage pregnancy in West Africa. Quartz. https://qz.com/africa/543354/how-ebola-led-to-more-teenage-pregnancy-in-west-africa.

West, M. & Chew, H.E. 2014. *Reading in the Mobile Era: A Study of Mobile Reading in Developing Countries*. UNESCO. https://unesdoc.unesco.org/ark:/48223/pf0000227436.

West, M., Kraut, R. & Chew, H.E. 2019. *I'd Blush if I Could: Closing Gender Divides in Digital Skills through Education*. EQUALS Skills Coalition & UNESCO. https://unesdoc.unesco.org/ark:/48223/pf0000367416.

Whalen, A. 2020, March 19. Students are targeting Zoom and Classroom with bad reviews to end homework during coronavirus outbreak. *Newsweek*. https://www.newsweek.com/google-zoom-classroom-students-schools-closed-coronavirus-china-1493309.

White House Briefing Room. 2021, October 8. Statement of President Joe Biden on signing the K-12 Cybersecurity Act into law. https://www.whitehouse.gov/briefing-room/statements-releases/2021/10/08/statement-of-president-joe-biden-on-signing-the-k-12-cybersecurity-act-into-law/.

WHO, UNICEF, & UNESCO. 2020, September 14. Considerations for school-related public health measures in the context of COVID-19. Annex to Considerations in adjusting public health and social measures in the context of COVID-19. https://www.who.int/publications/i/item/considerations-for-school-related-public-health-measures-in-the-context-of-covid-19.

Wiggins, C. & Jones, M. 2023. *How Data Happened: A History from the Age of Reason to the Age of Algorithms*. New York: W. W. Norton & Company.

Wightwick, A. 2022, October 31. Students launch legal action against Cardiff and other universities for worse experience during Covid and staff strikes. Wales Online. https://www.walesonline.co.uk/news/education/students-launch-legal-action-against-25390845.

Wiley Network. 2020, September 21. How today's culture encourages student cheating (and what to do about it). https://www.wiley.com/en-us/network/education/instructors/teaching-strategies/how-todays-culture-encourages-student-cheating-and-what-to-do-about-it.

Will, M. 2020, October 20. Most educators require kids to turn cameras on in virtual class, despite equity concerns. *Education Week*. https://www.edweek.org/teaching-learning/most-educators-require-kids-to-turn-cameras-on-in-virtual-class-despite-equity-concerns/2020/10.

Willadsen, H. & Hornstrup Jespersen, M. 2021, April 6. Blogpost on student attention in the online school. Copenhagen Center for Social Data Science. https://sodas.ku.dk/projects/distract/distract-news/blogpost-on-student-attention-in-the-online-school/.

Williams, A. 2015, September 19. Meet Alpha: The next 'next generation'. *New York Times*. https://www.nytimes.com/2015/09/19/fashion/meet-alpha-the-next-next-generation.html.

Williams, J.W. & White, A. 2021. *Digital Minimalism in Everyday Life: Overcome Technology Addiction, Declutter Your Mind, and Reclaim Your Freedom*. Orlando, FL: Alakai Publishing.

Williams, S. 2020, September 30. Edtech case study: Using technology to enhance the teaching of Arabic. *New Statesman*. https://www.newstatesman.com/edtech-startup-focus/2020/09/edtech-case-study-using-technology-enhance-teaching-arabic-0.

Williamson, B. & Hogan, A. 2021, February 10. Pandemic privatization and digitalization in higher education. *Code Acts in Education*. https://codeactsineducation.wordpress.com/2021/02/10/pandemic-privatization-digitalization-higher-education/.

Williamson, B. 2019. Datafication of education. In Beetham, H. & Sharpe, R. (eds) *Rethinking Pedagogy for a Digital Age*. London: Routledge. Available at https://www.researchgate.net/publication/334008102_Datafication_of_Education.

Williamson, B. 2020, December 15. New financial actors and valuation platforms in education technology markets. *Code Acts in Education*. https://codeactsineducation.wordpress.com/2020/12/15/new-financial-platforms-education/.

Williamson, B. 2020, July 10. "The edtech pandemic shock", by Ben Williamson & Anna Hogan. *Education International*. https://www.ei-ie.org/en/item/23423:the-edtech-pandemic-shock-by-ben-williamson-anna-hogan.

Williamson, B. 2020, March 17. Emergency edtech. *Code Acts in Education*. https://codeactsineducation.wordpress.com/2020/03/17/emergency-edtech/.

Williamson, B. 2020, September 15. Edtech index investing. *Code Acts in Education*. https://codeactsineducation.wordpress.com/2020/09/15/edtech-index-investing/.

Williamson, B. 2021, May 28. Google's plans to bring AI to education make its dominance in classrooms more alarming. Fast Company. https://www.fastcompany.com/90641049/google-education-classroom-ai.

Williamson, B. 2021, September 8. New biological data and knowledge in education. *Code Acts in Education*. https://codeactsineducation.wordpress.com/2021/09/08/new-biological-data-knowledge-education/.

Williamson, B. 2021. Meta-edtech. *Learning, Media and Technology*, 46(1). https://doi.org/10.1080/17439884.2021.1876089.

Williamson, B. 2022, March 17. Google magic. *Code Acts in Education*. https://codeactsineducation.wordpress.com/2022/03/17/google-magic/.

Williamson, B., Gulson, K.N., Perrotta, C. & Witzenberger, K. 2022, July 11. Amazon and the new global connective architectures of education governance. *Harvard Educational Review*, 92(2): 231–256. https://doi.org/10.17763/1943-5045-92.2.231.

Williamson, B., Gulson, K.N., Perrotta, C. & Witzenberger, K. 2022, July 12. How Amazon operates in education. *Code Acts in Education*. https://codeactsineducation.wordpress.com/2022/07/12/how-amazon-operates-in-education/.

Wilson, J. 2013, June 11. Filmmaker to make documentary about TED Prize winner Sugata Mitra. TED. Blog post. https://blog.ted.com/filmmaker-to-make-documentary-about-ted-prize-winner-sugata-mitra/.

Winters, M. 2017, May 8. The hard truths and false starts about edtech efficacy research. EdSurge. https://www.edsurge.com/news/2017-05-08-the-hard-truths-and-false-starts-about-edtech-efficacy-research.

Winther, D. 2017. *How Does the Time Children Spend Using Digital Technology Impact Their Mental Well-being, Social Relationships and Physical Activity? An Evidence-focused Literature Review*. UNICEF Office of Research. https://www.unicef-irc.org/publications/925-how-does-the-time-children-spend-using-digital-technology-impact-their-mental-well.html.

Winthrop, R. & McGivney, E. 2015, June 10. Why wait 100 years? Bridging the gap in global education. Brookings. https://www.brookings.edu/research/why-wait-100-years-bridging-the-gap-in-global-education/.

Wohlheiter, K. 2020, November 11. Online school and bullying – Know the signs and how to prevent it. Nemours Children's Health. Blog post. https://blog.nemours.org/2020/11/online-school-and-bullying-know-the-signs-and-how-to-prevent-it/.

Woldeab, D. & Brothen, T. 2019. 21st Century assessment: Online proctoring, test anxiety, and student performance. *International Journal of E-Learning & Distance Education*, 34(1). https://www.ijede.ca/index.php/jde/article/view/1106.

Wolf, M. 2018. *Reader, Come Home: The Reading Brain in a Digital World*. New York: Harper.

Wolf. N. 1991. *The Beauty Myth: How Images of Female Beauty Are Used Against Women*. New York: William Morrow & Co.

Wong, B. 2020, September 17. How remote learning has changed the nature of school bullying. HuffPost. https://www.huffpost.com/entry/bullying-problem-remote-learning_l_5f61214fc5b68d1b09c8dc16.

Woo, J. 2020, July 1. Students file suit for tuition cuts as pandemic disrupts learning. Yonhap News Agency. https://en.yna.co.kr/view/AEN20200701008900315.

Woodland, L. et al. 2021. Why did some parents not send their children back to school following school closures during the COVID-19 pandemic: a cross-sectional survey. *BMJ Paediatrics Open*, 5(1): e001014. https://pubmed.ncbi.nlm.nih.gov/34611551/.

World Bank, UNESCO, UNICEF, USAID, FCDO, & Bill & Melinda Gates Foundation. 2022. *The State of Global Learning Poverty*. https://www.unicef.org/media/122921/file/State%20of%20Learning%20Poverty%202022.pdf.

World Bank. 2017. Education: Children with disabilities are being left behind, says World Bank/GPE report. Press release. https://www.worldbank.org/en/news/press-release/2017/12/01/children-with-disabilities-are-being-left-behind.

World Bank. 2020, December 2. COVID-19 prompts urgency of bridging digital divide in Central Asia. Press release. https://www.worldbank.org/en/news/press-release/2020/12/02/urgency-of-bridging-digital-divide-in-central-asia-increases-as-a-result-of-the-covid-19-pandemic.

World Bank. 2020, December 6. Learning losses from COVID-19 could cost this generation of students close to $17 trillion in lifetime earnings. Press release. https://www.worldbank.org/en/news/press-release/2021/12/06/learning-losses-from-covid-19-could-cost-this-generation-of-students-close-to-17-trillion-in-lifetime-earnings.

World Bank. 2020, November 10. Ask why: Reimagining human connections technology and innovation in education at the World Bank. https://www.worldbank.org/en/topic/edutech/brief/ask-why-reimagining-human-connections-technology-and-innovation-in-education-at-the-world-bank.

World Bank. 2020. Access to electricity (% of population) - Sub-Saharan Africa (excluding high income). https://data.worldbank.org/indicator/EG.ELC.ACCS.ZS?view=map&locations=ZF.

World Bank. 2021, February 22. *Education Finance Watch 2021*. World Bank Group. https://www.worldbank.org/en/topic/education/publication/education-finance-watch-2021.

World Bank. 2021, May 19. Thinking inside the 'box': Pakistan turns to education TV during COVID-19. https://www.worldbank.org/en/news/feature/2021/05/19/pakistan-turns-to-education-tv.

World Bank. 2021. *Acting Now to Protect the Human Capital of Our Children: The Costs of and Response to COVID-19 Pandemic's Impact on the Education Sector in Latin America and the Caribbean*. https://openknowledge.worldbank.org/handle/10986/35276.

World Bank. 2021. *World Development Report 2021: Data for Better Lives*. https://elibrary.worldbank.org/doi/epdf/10.1596/978-1-4648-1600-0.

World Bank. 2022, June 23. *The State of Global Learning Poverty: 2022 Update*. Conference edition. https://thedocs.worldbank.org/en/doc/e52f55322528903b27f1b7e61238e416-0200022022/original/Learning-poverty-report-2022-06-21-final-V7-0-conferenceEdition.pdf.

World Bank. 2022. Data: Population, total – Low income. https://data.worldbank.org/indicator/SP.POP.TOTL?locations=XM.

World Bank. 2022. Data: World Bank country and lending groups. https://datahelpdesk.worldbank.org/knowledgebase/articles/906519-world-bank-country-and-lending-groups.

World Bank. 2022. GDP (current US$). https://data.worldbank.org/indicator/NY.GDP.MKTP.CD.

World Economic Forum. 2016, January 20. *Digital Media and Society: Implications in a Hyperconnected Era*. https://www.weforum.org/reports/digital-media-and-society-implications-in-a-hyperconnected-era/.

World Health Organization 2021, November 24. Disability and health. Press release. https://www.who.int/news-room/fact-sheets/detail/disability-and-health.

World Health Organization. 2011. *World Report on Disability*. https://www.who.int/publications/i/item/9789241564182.

World Health Organization. 2019, September 9. Suicide: One person dies every 40 seconds. Press release. https://www.who.int/news/item/09-09-2019-suicide-one-person-dies-every-40-seconds.

World Health Organization. 2019. *Guidelines on Physical Activity, Sedentary Behaviour and Sleep for Children under 5 Years of Age*. https://apps.who.int/iris/bitstream/handle/10665/311664/9789241550536-eng.pdf.

World Health Organization. 2020, December 8. Schooling in the time of COVID-19: Opening statement at high-level meeting on keeping schools open and protecting all children amid surging COVID-19 cases. https://www.who.int/europe/news/item/08-12-2020-schooling-in-the-time-of-covid-19-opening-statement-at-high-level-meeting-on-keeping-schools-open-and-protecting-all-children-amid-surging-covid-19-cases.

World Health Organization. 2020, October 22. Addictive behaviours: Gaming disorder. https://www.who.int/news-room/questions-and-answers/item/addictive-behaviours-gaming-disorder.

World Health Organization. 2020, October 23. Update 39 – What we know about COVID-19 transmission in schools. https://www.who.int/publications/m/item/update-39-what-we-know-about-covid-19-transmission-in-schools.

World Health Organization. 2020, October 5. COVID-19 disrupting mental health services in most countries, WHO survey. Press release. https://www.who.int/news/item/05-10-2020-covid-19-disrupting-mental-health-services-in-most-countries-who-survey.

World Health Organization. 2020, September 15. WHO Director-General's introductory remarks at the press briefing with UNESCO and UNICEF. https://www.who.int/director-general/speeches/detail/who-director-general-s-introductory-remarks-at-the-press-briefing-with-unesco-and-unicef.

World Health Organization. 2021, June 10. School reopening can't wait. https://www.who.int/westernpacific/news-room/commentaries/detail-hq/school-reopening-can-t-wait.

World Health Organization. 2021, June 15. Facts in pictures: E-waste and child health. https://www.who.int/news-room/facts-in-pictures/detail/e-waste-and-child-health.

World Health Organization. 2021, June. *Children and Digital Dumpsites: E-Waste Exposure and Child Health*. https://www.who.int/publications/i/item/9789240023901.

World Health Organization. 2022, July 23. WHO Director-General declares the ongoing monkeypox outbreak a Public Health Emergency of International Concern. Press release. https://www.who.int/europe/news/item/23-07-2022-who-director-general-declares-the-ongoing-monkeypox-outbreak-a-public-health-event-of-international-concern.

World Health Organization. 2030, May 5. WHO Director-General's opening remarks at the media briefing – 5 May 2023. https://www.who.int/news-room/speeches/item/who-director-general-s-opening-remarks-at-the-media-briefing---5-may-2023.

World Wide Web Foundation. 2015. *Women's Rights Online: Translating Access into Empowerment*. https://webfoundation.org/research/womens-rights-online-2015/.

Wößmann, L. et al. 2020. Education in the coronavirus crisis: How did schoolchildren spend their time when schools were closed, and what educational measures do the Germans advocate? *ifo Schnelldienst*, 73(9): 25–39. https://www.ifo.de/en/publikationen/2020/article-journal/education-coronavirus-crisis-how-did-schoolchildren-spend-their.

Wright, A. 2022, March 3. Home schooling: A growing trend. School Governance. https://www.schoolgovernance.net.au/news/home-schooling-a-growing-trend.

Wu, J.T. et al. 2021, November 22. A global assessment of the impact of school closure in reducing COVID-19 spread. *Philosophical Transactions of the Royal Society A: Mathematical, Physical and Engineering Sciences*, 380(2214): https://doi.org/10.1098/rsta.2021.0124.

Yang, M. & Beardsley, E. 2023, May 22. European watchdog fines Meta $1.3 billion over privacy violations. NPR. https://www.npr.org/2023/05/22/1177472768/eu-europe-meta-facebook-instagram-record-fine-data-privacy.

Yard, E. et al. 2021, June 11. Emergency department visits for suspected suicide attempts among persons aged 12–25 years before and during the COVID-19 pandemic — United States, January 2019–May 2021. *Morbidity and Mortality Weekly Report*, 70(24). https://stacks.cdc.gov/view/cdc/107051.

Yasar, K. 2021, March 26. Does Zoom notify me if someone takes a screenshot? MUO. https://www.makeuseof.com/does-zoom-notify-screenshot/.

Yglesias, M. 2020, January 8. Installing air filters in classrooms has surprisingly large educational benefits. Vox. https://www.vox.com/2020/1/8/21051869/indoor-air-pollution-student-achievement.

Yoo-Brannon, J. 2021, September 30. We need to make schools human again. That means treating teachers with respect. EdSurge. https://www.edsurge.com/news/2021-09-30-we-need-to-make-schools-human-again-that-means-treating-teachers-with-respect.

Yorke, L., Rose, P., Bayley, S., Meshesha, D.W. & Ramchandani, P. 2021. *The Importance of Students' Socio-Emotional Learning, Mental Health, and Wellbeing in the Time of COVID-19*. RISE. https://doi.org/10.35489/BSG-RISE-RI_2021/025.

Young, J. 2021, July 28. Early edtech giant PowerSchool goes public. EdSurge. https://www.edsurge.com/news/2021-07-28-early-edtech-giant-powerschool-goes-public.

Young, J.R. 2021, November 29. Automated proctoring swept in during pandemic. It's likely to stick around, despite concerns. EdSurge. https://www.edsurge.com/news/2021-11-19-automated-proctoring-swept-in-during-pandemic-it-s-likely-to-stick-around-despite-concerns.

Yuan, E.S. 2020, April 1. A message to our users. Zoom. Blog post. https://blog.zoom.us/a-message-to-our-users/.

Yuhas, A. 2020, August 24. Partial Zoom outage is fixed after school disruptions. *New York Times*. https://www.nytimes.com/2020/08/24/business/zoom-down.html.

Yusuf, M. 2021, January 4. Kenyan schools reopen despite coronavirus concerns. VOA News. https://www.voanews.com/a/africa_kenyan-schools-reopen-despite-coronavirus-concerns/6200298.html.

Zagmout, A. 2020. Justice for May 2020 IB Graduates - Build a Better Future! #IBSCANDAL. Change.org. https://www.change.org/p/international-baccalaureate-organisation-ibo-justice-for-may-2020-ib-graduates-build-a-better-future.

Zahariades, D. 2017. *Digital Detox: Unplug to Reclaim Your Life*. Independently published.

Zahra-Malik, M. 2020, May 14. The coronavirus effect on Pakistan's digital divide. BBC. https://www.bbc.com/worklife/article/20200713-the-coronavirus-effect-on-pakistans-digital-divide.

Zavala, F. et al. 2020, July 24. *Impactos de la crisis del COVID-19 en la educación y respuesta de política en Colombia [Impacts of the COVID-19 crisis on education and policy response in Colombia]*. World Bank. http://documents1.worldbank.org/curated/en/461641598291954248/pdf/Impactos-de-la-Crisis-del-Covid-19-en-la-Educacion-y-Respuestas-de-Politica-en-Colombia.pdf.

Zăvoianu, E.A. & Pânişoară, I.-O. 2021. Teachers' perception of the phenomenon of cyberbullying during the Covid-19 pandemic. *LUMEN Proceedings*, 17. https://proceedings.lumenpublishing.com/ojs/index.php/lumenproceedings/article/view/752.

Zhou, N. 2020, December 2. Up to 50% of university students unhappy with online learning, regulator finds. *The Guardian*. https://www.theguardian.com/australia-news/2020/dec/02/up-to-50-of-university-students-unhappy-with-online-learning-regulator-finds.

Zimmerman, A. & Veiga, C. 2020, May 7. NYC allows Zoom (once again) for remote learning. Chalkbeat. https://ny.chalkbeat.org/2020/5/6/21249689/nyc-schools-education-zoom-ban-reversed.

Zoom. 2021, September. Primary and Secondary Schools Privacy Statement. https://explore.zoom.us/en/schools-privacy-statement/.

Zoom. 2021. Annual Report: Fiscal 2021. https://investors.zoom.us/static-files/a17fd391-13ae-429b-8cb3-bfd95b61b007.

Zuboff, S. 2021, November 12. You are the object of a secret extraction operation. *New York Times*. https://www.nytimes.com/2021/11/12/opinion/facebook-privacy.html.

Zweig, D. 2020, July 30. $25,000 pod schools: How well-to-do children will weather the pandemic. *New York Times*. https://www.nytimes.com/2020/07/30/nyregion/pod-schools-hastings-on-hudson.html.

9781041123668